D0436289

PLAY THERAPY WITH CHILDREN IN CRISIS
Second Edition

Play Therapy
with Children in Crisis

Second Edition

INDIVIDUAL, GROUP, AND FAMILY TREATMENT

Edited by

NANCY BOYD WEBB

Foreword by Lenore Terr

THE GUILFORD PRESS
New York   London

© 1999 The Guilford Press
A Division of Guilford Publications, Inc.
72 Spring Street, New York, NY 10012
http://www.guilford.com

Printed in the United States of America

This book is printed on acid-free paper.

Last digit is print number: 9   8   7   6   5   4   3   2

Library of Congress Cataloging-in-Publication Data

Play therapy with children in crisis : individual group, and family
  treatment / edited by Nancy Boyd Webb : foreword by Lenora Terr.—
  2nd ed.
        p.   cm.
    includes bibliographical references and Index.
    ISBN 1-57230-485-5 (hc)
    1. Play therapy Case studies.   2. Crisis intervention (Mental
health services) Case studies.   I. Webb, Nancy Boyd, 1932–   .
    [DNLM: 1. Crisis Intervention—Child Case Report   2. Crisis
Intervention—Infant Case Report.   3. Play Therapy—Child Case
Report.   4. Play Therapy—Infant Case Report.   WS 350.2 P7227   1999]
RJ505.P6P56   1999
618.92'89165—dc21
DNLM/DLC
for Library of Congress   99-35764
                                                                    CIP

To Mary Ann Quaranta,

Dean, Fordham University Graduate School of Social Service

Mentor, role model, friend, and inspiration over the past twenty years, whose special appreciation of childhood and of the importance of child and family therapy has stimulated my teaching, writing, and practice.

—N. B. W.

About the Editor

Nancy Boyd Webb, DSW, BCD, RPT-S, is a leading authority on play therapy with children who have experienced trauma and loss. Her best-selling books, *Play Therapy with Children in Crisis: A Casebook for Practitioners* (1991), *Helping Bereaved Children: A Handbook for Practitioners* (1993), and *Social Work Practice with Children* (1996), are considered essential references for university courses and for agencies and mental health practitioners who work with children. Her videotape, *Techniques of Play Therapy: A Clinical Demonstration* (1994), won a bronze medal at the New York Festivals International Non-Broadcast Media Competition, and the Chinese translation of *Play Therapy with Children in Crisis* was published in Taipei in 1998. She is the editor of the series Social Work Practice with Children and Families (The Guilford Press).

Dr. Webb, a board-certified diplomate in clinical social work and a registered play therapy supervisor, presents frequently at play therapy, social work, and mental health conferences in the United States and abroad. She has been a professor on the faculty of the Fordham University Graduate School of Social Service since 1979, and was appointed in fall 1997 to the rank of University Distinguished Professor of Social Work. She established the Post-Master's Certificate Program in Child and Adolescent Therapy in 1985 at Fordham to meet the need in the metropolitan New York area for training in play therapy. In addition to teaching and writing, Dr. Webb maintains a clinical practice and supervises and consults with schools and agencies. She lectures and conducts workshops throughout the United States, Canada, Australia, Europe, and the Far East.

Contributors

Teresa Bevin, MA, Professor, Department of Mental Health, Montgomery College, Takoma Park, Maryland

Joyce Bluestone, MSW, Adjunct Instructor, Graduate School of Social Service, Fordham University, Tarrytown, New York

Nelly F. de Ridder, MSW, ACSW/R, doctoral candidate, School of Social Work, New York University, New York, New York; Social Worker, Westchester Jewish Community Services, Mt. Vernon, New York; Adjunct Instructor, Graduate School of Social Service, Fordham University, Tarrytown, New York

Joan S. Doyle, ACSW, LISW, BCD, Assistant Executive Director of Out-of-Home Services, Berea Children's Home and Family Services, Berea, Ohio

Roey C. Ficaro, MSW, Drug and Alcohol Prevention Counselor, Westchester County Schools, New York; private clinical practice, Mt. Kisco, New York

Victor Fornari, MD, Associate Chairman for Education and Training, Department of Psychiatry, North Shore University Hospital, Manhasset, New York; Associate Professor of Clinical Psychiatry, New York University School of Medicine, New York, New York

Robin F. Goodman, PhD, ATR, Clinical Assistant Professor, Department of Psychiatry, and first Behavioral Health Team Leader, Pediatric Hematology and Oncology, New York University Medical Center, New York, New York; private practice, New York, New York

Carol P. Kaplan, PhD, Associate Professor, Graduate School of Social Service, Fordham University, New York, New York

Maxine Lynn, MSW, Director of Field Instruction, Graduate School of Social Service, Fordham University, New York, New York

Danielle Nisivoccia, DSW, Clinical Associate Professor, Graduate School of Social Service, Fordham University, New York, New York

Jane Price Osuna, MSW, ACSW, Social Worker, Inpatient Adolescent Unit, Bronx Children's Psychiatric Center, Bronx, New York

David Pelcovitz, PhD, Chief Child and Adolescent Psychologist, Division of Child and Adolescent Psychiatry, North Shore University Hospital, Manhasset, New York

Howard Robinson, MA, MSW, DSW, Assistant Professor, Graduate School of Social Service, and Assistant Director, Post-Master's Certificate Program in Child and Adolescent Therapy, Graduate School of Social Service, Fordham University, Tarrytown, New York

Katherine Ryan, PhD, LCSW, private practice, Richmond, Virginia; Adjunct Faculty, School of Social Work, Virginia Commonwealth University, Richmond, Virginia

David Stoop, LISW(SC), CCSW(NC), owner, Peripatetic Seminars, Inman, South Carolina; Assessment Coordinator, Hampton Center, Greenville, South Carolina; private practice, St. Luke's Hospital, Columbus, North Carolina

Virginia C. Strand, DSW, BCD, Associate Professor and Director, Child and Families Institute for Research, Support and Training, and Graduate School of Social Service, Fordham University, Tarrytown, New York

Louise M. Tonning, MS, LCSW, private practice, Greenwich, Connecticut; Certified School Social Worker, New Canaan Public Schools, New Canaan, Connecticut; Clinical Social Worker, Family Centers, Inc., New Canaan, Connecticut; Staff Therapist, Child Guidance Center of Greater Bridgeport, Bridgeport, Connecticut

Nancy Boyd Webb, DSW, BCD, RPT-S, Director, Post-Master's Certificate Program in Child and Adolescent Therapy, and University Distinguished Professor of Social Work, Graduate School of Social Service, Fordham University, Tarrytown, New York

Brenda Williams-Gray, CSW, Unit Director, Children's Village, Dobbs Ferry, New York

Leslie H. Wind, MSW, ACSW, LMSW-ACP, doctoral candidate, Department of Social Work, University of Southern California, Los Angeles, California

Foreword

Play is activity aimed primarily at having fun. Yet play often carries victories far beyond simple recreation. It stimulates leaps of learning, flexibility, and creativity. For those young people who have experienced frightening life events—family disruption, illness, or trauma—play offers a second chance, an opportunity for reworking and rebuilding. Play can even bring about a cure for those individuals lucky enough to be able to play with a mental health professional.

Nancy Boyd Webb has devoted a lifetime to play theory and practice: to observing, working with, and reporting on the play of troubled children. In this book, as in the first edition of *Play Therapy with Children in Crisis*, she has brought together a stellar group of experts who write about a range of fascinating youngsters and their experiences in therapy. She has pulled together these chapters with grace, ensuring their readability and scholarship.

A few particularly impressive—perhaps even playful—qualities of this book might especially be noted. A number of these true tales of therapy have been given second acts in this new edition. Because follow-up contacts were made 7–9 years later, a fuller, more rewarding account could be presented this time around. This makes for unique and particularly interesting case material.

The "stage directions" printed in italics in the case examples help us to imagine at any given moment just how a certain child looked, reacted, and moved. They engage the reader directly. Now the reader is playing, too. A column with the therapist's observations, reactions, theoretical underpinnings, and treatment plans guides the reader through each of the case studies. Again, this built-in and playful revelation of the therapist's mind enables the reader to learn in a creative and flexible fashion.

The joy of play counters in the reader's mind the vicarious miseries imparted from the horrible crises that some of these children have had to endure. Play itself corrects some of the unhappiness projected by extreme external events. Everywhere in this book, the writers give us conceptual and curative aspects of the play experience. And this balm is imparted directly to the reader.

So I invite my fellow readers to enjoy this book as I have. Savor the sad, terrifying, but always interesting stories. And watch the pictures of pretend and gamesmanship that are described in words and in black and white illustrations. Put yourself into the scenarios, and play. Nancy Boyd Webb and her coauthors will see to it that you have a little fun and learn a great deal.

LENORE TERR, MD
University of California, San Francisco

Preface

In the eight years since I wrote the Preface to the first edition of this book, some things have changed with regard to therapy with children in crisis, while other things have remained the same. The changes have evolved from our fuller understanding of the impact of crises on children, and from our greater experience in helping children who have been exposed to crises of various kinds. In addition, managed care has emerged as a controlling factor in treatment planning for children, as for all clients. We have learned to utilize short-term, intermittent, and group therapy to help children recover from their exposure to crisis. Although traditional one-on-one intervention continues to be appropriate, particularly for those children who have experienced severe circumstances such as a suicide in the family or extensive and multiple trauma, many children can benefit from briefer methods. The group approaches described here move as quickly as possible from exploration of the children's anxiety associated with the crisis events to an acknowledgment of their strengths and resilience as survivors. This positive emphasis promotes mastery over their past crisis experience and refocuses the children on their present interactions and future opportunities.

This edition includes eight completely new chapters, four of which present group treatment for children who have experienced crises and for whom group therapy is the "treatment of choice." These crises include experiences of sexual abuse, having a relative affected by HIV/AIDS, living in a substance-disordered family, or witnessing violence at home and in the community. For children who have experienced these crises, a support or therapy group crosses the isolation barrier many children feel when they incorrectly assume that their experience is unique. Individual or family therapy cannot provide this critical peer support. Therefore, some chapters in this edition present a combination of individual, group, and family treatment.

As I approached the task of revising the first edition, I hoped it would be possible to obtain some updates on the cases that had already been described in such detail. Although many years had passed, I suspected that some authors/clinicians would be able to contact their former clients. (Note that all the cases in both editions have been disguised to protect the confidentiality of the children and the families.) This exciting prospect proved a reality in six cases. In teaching and in staff training since the first edition appeared in 1991, I have invited my university students and agency practitioners to speculate about the adolescent status of the children in the book. Now readers can learn what happened to Michael, who was first seen in therapy at age 4 (Chapter 3), and to Randy, seen at age 10 (Chapter 6), and the two young girls who each had a parent die suddenly (Chapter 10). Other cases discussed in the first edition and appearing with follow-up contacts here include Sergio, who became mute after witnessing his mother's rape (Chapter 7), Tim, who had childhood cancer (Chapter 17), and Mary, whose mother and brother were killed in a plane crash (Chapter 18). Now we can learn about these children as adolescents and, in the process, consider the extent to which early intervention may have helped some of them. In other cases we see the extent to which multiple intervening variables may limit the effectiveness of treatment.

Factors that remain constant in regard to therapy with children over the past decade include the basic methods of helping children, beginning with the therapeutic relationship as the foundation on which all treatment approaches rest. Play therapy continues to provide the key to understanding the child's inner world. Numerous examples in both editions demonstrate the power of play as symbolic communication. Child therapists must learn to communicate in the child's play language. I am deeply grateful to the clinicians who have written so explicitly about their work and to the clients and families who granted them permission to do so. We need these detailed examples of actual practice in order to study different approaches to helping. It is my hope that future children and families will benefit from these contributions.

NANCY BOYD WEBB
Fordham University

Acknowledgments

This book, which contains chapters by 18 different authors, reflects the knowledge, skills, and collaboration of many people. First, I am deeply grateful to the authors for their willingness to share the detailed processes of their work, including the revelation and analysis of their thoughts during the ongoing treatment process. All the authors completed the necessary rewriting in a professional manner; their commitment to the book was commendable from the first-draft stage.

The Guilford Press also merits my thanks. Seymour Weingarten, Editor-in-Chief, and Rochelle Serwator, Editor, provided the encouragement that motivated me to stick with the tedium of editing, reminding me of the importance of the finished product for educators and practitioners. Other Guilford personnel who assisted at various stages include Anna Brackett, Senior Production Editor; Paul Gordon, Art Director; and Christine Luberto, Marketing Associate. Over the past ten years of my association with The Guilford Press, I have been impressed and pleased with the staff's ability to move smoothly from the proposal phase of a book (its germination) to its eventual birth.

I also want to thank the support staff and student assistants at Fordham's Graduate School of Social Service who have helped in various ways. These include (in alphabetical order) DeVonne Allen, Roxie Bullock, Matthew DiCarlo, Marla Mendillo, Emy O'Connell, Stephanie Sheehan, and our reference librarian, Chris Campbell. Each of them has made a contribution to this book, and I am very grateful to them.

My husband, Kempton Webb, has offered both moral and tangible support in numerous ways that attest to his good nature and to the strength of our marital bond. Although I have often been at the computer instead of sailing with him, we both take great pleasure in the final product (and then we sail together).

Finally, none of these efforts would have been possible without the children and families who gave us permission to write about our work with them, so that it could benefit future children and families.

NANCY BOYD WEBB
Fordham University

Contents

PART III. VARIOUS FAMILY CRISES

PART V. THE CRISES OF CATASTROPHIC EVENTS AND WAR

PART VI. SUPPORT FOR THERAPISTS

PART I

Introduction

CHAPTER 1

Assessment of the Child in Crisis

NANCY BOYD WEBB

Children, like adults, experience crises in the natural course of their lives. Contrary to the myth of the magic years of childhood as a period of guileless innocence and carefree play, the reality of the preteen years, like that of later life, includes stressful experiences that provoke anger, jealousy, fear, and grief as well as joy and pleasure. The parent who protests, when confronted with a child's problems, "But these are supposed to be the best years of his life!" has forgotten that negative fallout from stress affects the young as well as the old.

Although stress in itself is not harmful (Selye, 1978), it may precipitate a crisis if the anxiety accompanying it exceeds the individual's ability to adapt. Anxiety that paralyzes or seriously interferes with usual functioning propels an individual (child or adult) into a state of crisis.

People have different levels of stress tolerance, however, as well as different modes of responding to stress. The formation of psychological defenses and symptoms typically occurs as a result of attempts to "fight" the anxiety or flee from it (the "fight-or-flight" responses; Selye, 1978). Young children are particularly vulnerable to stress because of their youth, immature defenses, and lack of life experience. They often require assistance to obtain relief from their anxiety and to learn new coping methods.

This book recognizes the vast range of stressful events that may impair everyday functioning and cause emotional pain to young children. The focus of this chapter is on making an assessment of the child in crisis. This assessment includes an evaluation of individual, family, and contextual factors as these interact with the particular crisis situation.

DEFINITION OF CRISIS

An underlying principle of crisis intervention theory maintains that crises can and do happen to everyone (Gilliland & James, 1997; Golan, 1978). No previous pathology should be assumed when, for example, a rescue worker discovers a child in a mute, stunned condition following an earthquake that has destroyed the child's home. Although individual differences influence personal vulnerability to breakdown and the form and timing of the disturbance, no one is immune from the possibility of such an occurrence in the aftermath of a crisis. Situations of extreme stress cause overload and create malfunctioning in the system.

Gilliland and James (1997, p. 3) define "crisis" as "a perception of an event or situation as an intolerable difficulty that exceeds the resources and coping mechanisms of the person. Unless the person obtains relief, the crisis has the potential to cause severe affective, cognitive, and behavioral malfunctioning." This emphasis on the *perception* of the event, rather than on the event itself, appropriately draws attention to the unique underlying meaning of the situation to each individual. Different people experience the same situation differently, and idiosyncratic factors determine their separate perceptions of the crisis.

For example, following the news of the sudden death of their classmate in an automobile accident, a group of third-grade children exhibited anxiety reactions ranging from mild to severe. All the children in the victim's class displayed some degree of shock, concern, and curiosity about the death, but individual reactions varied greatly. One child told his teacher the next day (falsely) that his father had died suddenly the previous evening. Another child complained of headaches and stomachaches for a week with no physical cause, and a third child had frightening nightmares for several weeks about being chased by a monster. However, most of the children in the class did not develop symptoms and did not appear to be traumatized by the death, in the opinions of the teachers and the school social worker. The child with the nightmares had been a close friend of the dead child; their favorite shared activity had been playing war games that involved chasing and killing. This child benefited from brief therapy in which the dynamics of winning and losing, and acceptance of the unpredictable, were played out symbolically. The child's symptoms disappeared after six play therapy sessions. See Webb (1993) for a full discussion of this case.

Anna Freud (1965, p. 139) states that "traumatic events should not be taken at their face value, but should be translated into their specific meaning for the given child." Green, Wilson, and Lindy (1985, p. 59) point out that "different people who are present at the same event will have different outcomes because, not only will their experiences differ, but the individual characteristics they bring to bear upon the psychological processing are different, and this processing may take place in differing recovery environments."

For a child in crisis, the "recovery environment" holds particular significance because of the child's dependence on family members and other adults to provide support and guidance. Thus the assessment of the child in crisis includes an analysis of individual factors interacting with the resources of the family and the social support network, in the face of a particular crisis situation.

TRIPARTITE CRISIS ASSESSMENT

Three different sets of interacting variables must be assessed for each unique crisis event:

1. The nature of the crisis situation.
2. The idiosyncratic characteristics of the individual.
3. The strengths and weaknesses of the individual's support system.

Figure 1.1 illustrates the components of this tripartite crisis assessment and suggests how the impact of a specific crisis situation depends on the balancing of the interacting influences among the three sets of variables.

Other authors have posited four factors or groups of factors as affecting the individual's response to exposure to traumatic stress. These are (1) the circumstances of the trauma, (2) reactivation of trauma from earlier developmental periods, (3) the phase of development at which trauma occurs, and (4) the social context during and after the trauma (Marmar, Foy, Kagan, & Pynoos, 1994). This conceptualization is actually very similar to the tripartite model. The second factor in the four-part model,

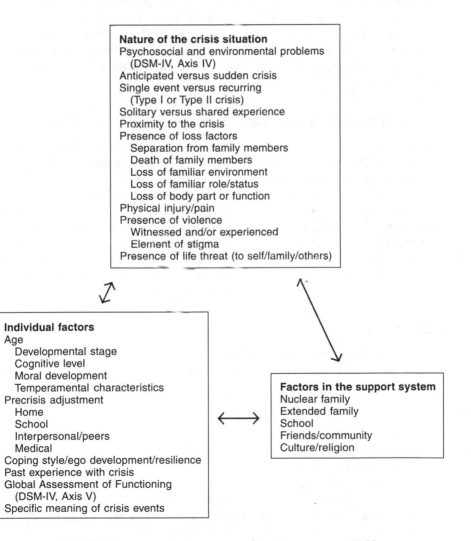

FIGURE 1.1. Interactive components of a crisis assessment: Webb.

the reactivation of trauma from earlier developmental periods, is considered in the tripartite model when one is analyzing individual factors and the individual's past experience with crisis.

THE NATURE OF THE CRISIS SITUATION

Although the individual's *perception* of a crisis takes precedence over the objective circumstances of the event or situation, analysis of the specific components of the crisis situation adds to an understanding of its impact. For example, a child who was subjected to harsh and repeated beatings by a drug-abusing father did not become dysfunctional until the father threatened to kill himself and the entire family. It is important to learn as many details as possible about both the precipitating event and the background of the crisis situation. In this example, the father's threat was the precipitating event for a child who was already vulnerable as a result of the chronic abuse.

Psychosocial and Environmental Problems (DSM-IV, Axis IV)

The fourth edition of the *Diagnostic and Statistical Manual of Mental Disorders* (DSM-IV; American Psychiatric Association, 1994) lists nine categories of problems that can be reported on Axis IV (see Table 1.1). Many of the listed problems can actually constitute crisis situations, although the intent of the DSM classification is to present these psychosocial and environmental problems as indicative of the *context* in which the individual's difficulties developed. Although most psychosocial and environmental problems are indicated in Axis IV, when the problems constitute the *primary* focus of attention, these should also be recorded on Axis I (American Psychiatric Association, 1994, p. 29). This will be true of many cases like the ones presented in this book.

Other Factors

Other factors that contribute to the analysis of the nature of the crisis situation should also be considered in making a crisis assessment. These, as listed in Figure 1.1, are as follows:

- Anticipated versus sudden crisis
- Single versus recurring crisis events
- Solitary versus shared crisis experience
- Proximity to the crisis
- Presence of loss factors
- Physical injury or pain
- Presence of violence (witnessed or experienced; clement of stigma)
- Degree of life threat (to self/family/others)

TABLE 1.1. Psychosocial and Environmental Problems (DSM-IV, Axis IV)

- **Problems with primary support group**—e.g., death of a family member; health problems in family; disruption of family by separation, divorce, or estrangement; removal from the home; remarriage of parent; sexual or physical abuse; parental overprotection; neglect of child; inadequate discipline; discord with siblings; birth of a sibling
- **Problems related to the social environment**—e.g., death or loss of friend; inadequate social support; living alone; difficulty with acculturation; discrimination; adjustment to life-cycle transition (such as retirement)
- **Educational problems**—e.g., illiteracy; academic problems; discord with teachers or classmates; inadequate school environment
- **Occupational problems**—e.g., unemployment; threat of job loss; stressful work schedule; difficult work conditions; job dissatisfaction; job change; discord with boss or co-workers
- **Housing problems**—e.g., homelessness; inadequate housing; unsafe neighborhood; discord with neighbors or landlord
- **Economic problems**—e.g., extreme poverty; inadequate finances; insufficient welfare support
- **Problems with access to health care services**—e.g., inadequate health care services; transportation to health care facilities unavailable; inadequate health insurance
- **Problems related to interaction with the legal system/crime**—e.g., arrest; incarceration; litigation; victim of crime
- **Other psychosocial and environmental problems**—e.g., exposure to disasters, war, other hostilities; discord with nonfamily caregivers such as counselor, social worker, or physician; unavailability of social service agencies

Note. From American Psychiatric Association (1994, pp. 29–30). Copyright 1994 by the American Psychiatric Association. Reprinted by permission.

Anticipated versus Sudden Crisis

The Scout motto, "Be prepared," implies by contrast the undesirability of unpreparedness. Arkin (1974, p. 11) notes in referring to sudden death that "what human beings dread most is being taken by surprise, which they feel unprepared [for] and unable to master."

Some events that lead to crisis are by their nature unpredictable. Examples include natural disasters with no preliminary warning, the sudden death of a parent who was previously well, and the killing and injury of innocent bystanders in a wanton shooting episode. These contrast with other situations that gradually build up to a crisis. Examples of anticipated crises include a family's move to another community, the departure of the father from the home as the beginning of a marital separation, and the terminal illness of a family member. Stressful events that develop toward a predictable outcome present the opportunity for gradual comprehension and assimilation of the impending transition or loss. The ego does not have to absorb abruptly the painful reality of an irrevocable event.

Janis (1977), in studying the reactions of preoperative surgical patients, found that a moderate amount of anticipatory fear about an impending operation permitted patients to develop effective inner defenses. In contrast, situations in which the patients did not worry beforehand made them less able to cope with the pain and discomfort following surgery. Janis postulated the concept of the "work of worry-ing" and concluded that "a person will be better able to tolerate suffering and dys-function if he worries about it beforehand, rather than maintaining expectations of personal invulnerability" (1977, p. 284). Similarly, studies of Vietnam veterans (Chemtob et al., 1990) showed that adequate preparation for a stressful event pro-tects individuals from the effects of stress.

We do not know how applicable these studies are to children. Many well-meaning adults deliberately try to shield children from worry, and they avoid ex-posing them until the last minute to situations they believe will prove upsetting. This prevents children from "getting ready" psychologically and bracing themselves for the upcoming stressful encounter.

There is a growing body of children's literature (Fassler, 1987; see also various books published by the Magination Press, a division of Brunner/Mazel) dedicated to helping children, through the medium of stories, to master stressful life events such as a grandfather's death, hospitalization, parental divorce, and moving. The crisis techniques of "role rehearsal" and "anticipatory guidance" (Parad & Parad, 1990) help clients prepare in advance for future stressful situations. For example, a child who has advance knowledge, through pictures and explanations, about surgical masks and medical procedures shows less anxiety when confronted with these in the hospi-tal. According to Kliman's (1968) concept of "psychological immunization," "mas-tery in advance" through reflection or fantasy provides enhanced coping in future stressful situations. A folk saying claims that "a job well dreaded is more than half done." Even though the dreading is unpleasant, it permits anticipatory problem solving and psychological preparation. Since individuals confronted with sudden crises lack this opportunity, they experience more debilitating stress than do indi-viduals facing crises that have been anticipated.

Single versus Recurring Crisis Events: Type I or Type II Crisis

The notion of the "straw that breaks the camel's back" suggests that accumulated stress weighs so heavily that not even minor additional stressors can be tolerated. Thus the precipitating factor in a crisis may not be as significant as the events that have preceded it and created a "vulnerable state" for the individual (Golan, 1978). In the earlier example of the child who suffered repeated physical abuse, a relatively minor occurrence such as a scolding from a teacher could have precipitated a crisis because of the child's vulnerable state.

Individuals have different levels of stress tolerance. However, multiple crisis events exact demands for adaptation that eventually deplete emotional reserves, even in individuals with high tolerance levels. Although successful resolution of a crisis may result in greater personal strength and more versatile coping, psychic assaults from repeated, multiple crisis events will ultimately result in disorganization and fragmentation of even adequate coping abilities.

Terr (1991) presented the concepts of Type I trauma, which occurs following *one* sudden shock, and of Type II trauma, which is "precipitated by a *series* of external blows" (p. 19; emphasis added). Responses to Type I traumas include detailed memories and misperceptions, whereas reactions to Type II traumas involve denial, numbing, dissociation, and rage. Sometimes the two types of traumas coexist; when untreated, they can lead to serious disorders in both childhood and in adulthood.

Solitary versus Shared Crisis Experience

If "misery loves company," then we would expect the sharing of crisis experiences to afford a degree of comfort and support that is absent when an individual undergoes a stressful crisis alone. Certainly the dynamic of guilt ("Why me?") and issues of personal responsibility ("How could this crisis have been avoided?") are irrelevant or greatly reduced in situations of shared crisis. Although every crisis is experienced ultimately on a personal level, the knowledge that others are enduring similar turmoil may reduce the stigma of victimization. For example, a child victim of incest may gain extraordinary benefits from participation in a group of similarly victimized children.

However, the commonality of a shared crisis event does not automatically lead to bonding among the individuals involved. Terr (1979), reporting on the aftermath of the kidnapping of a school bus of summer school students, found that the traumatized youngsters avoided contact with one another after the horrible experience was over. As if to escape the memories of their ordeal, these children tried to blend into the community and to stay away from their fellow students, who reminded them of the frightening experience. It may be relevant that avoidance of reminders of the traumatic event is one of the main characteristics of posttraumatic stress disorder (PTSD), as discussed later in this chapter.

When a crisis situation conveys stigma, an individual understandably avoids identification with it. Violent deaths by murder or suicide often burden the survivors with the shame of stigma, added to the stress of tragic loss (see "Presence of Violence/Degree of Life Threat," below). In such situations, the positive effects of the sharing of crisis seem to be lessened.

The extent to which sharing of the crisis situation helps children probably depends on their age, since peers exert more influence during the latency years. Thus the impact of the shared versus solitary crisis experience seems valid mainly from latency onward, with the possible exception of stigmatized crises.

Proximity to the Crisis

A research study in California following a sniper attack in a school playground (Pynoos & Nader, 1989) found that children who were in closer physical proximity to the shooting developed more symptoms of PTSD than children who were on the periphery or not on the playground when the attack occurred. Proximity to the shooting resulted in more severe responses, both soon after the event and 14 months later (Nader, Pynoos, Fairbanks, & Frederick, 1990).

These findings, which seem intuitively valid, confirm that proximity to a crisis results in intense sensory responses together with a heightened sense of life threat, all of which can contribute to symptom formation. Treatment planning should therefore take into consideration the individual's proximity to the crisis, with those closest to the frightening situation being targeted for timely preventive intervention.

Presence of Loss Factors/Physical Injury or Pain

Loss plays a major role in many crisis situations, and the attendant reactions of confusion, anger, and desperation may be understood as mourning responses associated with the loss. When losses include death of or separation from a family member, grief and mourning are appropriate. Less obvious losses occur in such situations as moving or school promotion. These require giving up a familiar location or status and developing new relationships. Teachers attest to the high level of anxiety in September until children become comfortable with the expectations and people in their new grade. This anxiety usually does not cause a state of crisis for most children, but it can put them into a vulnerable state in which their ability to cope is reduced temporarily.

The converse of loss is attachment. If no positive bonding existed, no mourning would be necessary. Bowlby's (1969) seminal work on attachment highlighted the biological source of the need for proximity in human relationships, with the prototype of attachment being the mother–infant relationship. Although object constancy permits the mental retention of loved persons in the memory, nonetheless a child whose parents separate is no longer in daily contact with one of his or her attachment figures, and thus suffers the loss both of this figure and of the intact nuclear family. Other losses often include a change of residence, school, and lifestyle. But it is the loss of contact with an attachment object (the nonresident parent) that results in the most serious deprivation. Multiple losses cause multiple stressors, adding to the potential for crisis.

Illness, although a common occurrence for children, introduces a number of temporary or permanent restrictions on a child's life, which the child experiences as losses. The child with a terminal illness, for example, must adapt to bodily changes, environmental restrictions, changed expectations for the future, and changed relationships based on others' altered perceptions of him or her. These all constitute losses, which also prevail to a minor degree for the child who remains home from school for a week with chickenpox. Physical injury or pain constitutes a serious threat to the child's basic sense of body integrity, compounding the other stresses associated with medical treatment. The family has an important role in helping the child cope with a serious medical crisis. (See Kaplan, Chapter 16, and Goodman, Chapter 17, this volume, for further discussion of this.)

Losses constitute a central part of any crisis assessment. Both losses that are "vague," such as the loss of a sense of predictability about the environment (e.g., following a flood or earthquake), and more evident losses, such as the death of a pet, should be identified. A crisis assessment must include past as well as present losses, since memories of past experiences of loss and bereavement are typically reawakened in current loss situations. This is discussed further in the section on assessment of individual factors.

Presence of Violence/Degree of Life Threat

We live in a violent world that does not shield children from graphic exposure to conflict in all forms and locales, including the family, school, and community. Star (1980) states that American society maintains a high baseline tolerance for violence, and that within the family this takes the form of child abuse, spouse or partner abuse, incest, and other assaultive episodes. Pynoos and Eth (1985, p. 19) believe that "children who witness extreme acts of violence represent a population at significant risk of developing anxiety, depressive, phobic, conduct, and posttraumatic stress disorders." Indeed, the presence of severe life threat in which the individual's response involves intense fear, helplessness, and horror constitutes the precondition for the diagnosis of PTSD in DSM-IV, as discussed later in this chapter. The child witness may experience traumatic helplessness and cognitive confusion when confronted with human-induced acts of violence. The child witness who, in addition to *observing* violence, also suffers personal injury may develop subsequent dissociative symptoms and multiple personality disorder, according to Putnam and colleagues (Putnam, Post, & Guroff, 1984; Putnam, 1997). (Although multiple personality disorder has been renamed dissociative identity disorder in DSM-IV, it is still widely known by its former name.)

When violence results in death, and the community and newspapers sensationalize the surrounding events, the people involved may feel overwhelmed by an emotional battery of reactions, including shame, hatred, and guilt (Shneidman, 1981, p. 350). The family can either help or hinder the child in these circumstances, which all too often cause the family members to close ranks and create a barrier of silence around the traumatic events (Eth & Pynoos, 1985, p. 177).

Summary

The 10-item Crisis Situation Rating Form (Table 1.2) facilitates a review of the components of the crisis situation as discussed above. This rating form can assist intake workers and other involved professionals in formulating a comprehensive overview of the crisis situation within a compact format. The rating of the crisis situation must be combined with an assessment of individual and support system factors, in order to obtain a full understanding of the crisis in all its complexity.

ASSESSMENT OF THE INDIVIDUAL CHILD IN CRISIS

"The susceptibility of any child to psychic trauma is a function of several parameters, including genetic, constitutional, and personality makeup; past life experiences; the state of mind and phase of development; the content and intensity of the event; and the family circumstances" (Eth & Pynoos, 1980, p. 286). Having focused first on the nature of the crisis situation, we turn now to a review of the individual factors that constitute the second part of the tripartite crisis assessment.

TABLE 1.2. Crisis Situation Rating Form: Webb

1. Psychosocial and environmental problems (DSM-IV, Axis IV)
   List problems _____

2. Anticipated _____ or sudden _____ crisis (check where appropriate)
   Amount of preparation _____

3. Single _____ or recurring _____ crisis events
   (List discrete crisis events)
   a. _____ c. _____
   b. _____ d. _____

4. Solitary _____ or shared _____ crisis experience
   Number of other individuals involved _____

5. Proximity to the crisis
   Near _____ or far _____ or _____ (describe)

6. Presence of loss factor
   a. Separation from family members (list relationship and length of separation) _____
      _____
      _____

   b. Death of family members (list relationship and cause of death) _____
      _____
      _____

   c. Loss of familiar environment (describe) _____
      _____
      _____

   d. Loss of familiar role/status (describe, temporary or permanent?) _____
      _____
      _____

   e. Loss of body part or function (describe, with prognosis) _____
      _____
      _____

7. Physical injury or pain (describe, with prognosis) _____
   _____
   _____

8. Presence of violence: verbal and/or physical
   a. Witnessed _____ Verbal _____ Physical _____
   b. Experienced _____ Verbal _____ Physical _____

9. Degree of life threat
   a. Personal (describe) _____
      _____
      _____

   b. To family members (describe, identifying relationship) _____
      _____
      _____

   c. To others (describe) _____
      _____
      _____

10. Other components of the crisis situation _____
    _____
    _____

Note. This form is one part of a three-part crisis assessment, which also includes an assessment of individual and support system factors.

The standard diagnostic assessment of a child calls for a knowledge of normal child development, child psychopathology, and a diagnostic classification system such as DSM-IV. According to Chethik (1989, p. 37), "the purpose of the assessment is to shed light on specific problematic areas and explicate the underlying forces that have created the difficulties." Mishne (1983, p. 25) clarifies further that "the objectives in an assessment are to determine how, and in what areas, the child differs from others of the same age; to assess the chronicity of the child's problems; to appraise areas of strength in the child and the child's family; and to aid in conceptualizing some hypothesis about possible contaminating factors—be they past, present, constitutional, or family induced."

In a situation in which a family seeks help for a child about a troublesome problem, the traditional assessment process typically consists of several interviews with the child and the parents (separately and in different combinations), in order to gather historical and observational data on which to base a dynamic assessment and treatment plan. Information from such sources as school psychologists, pediatricians, teachers, and child psychiatrists can also contribute to the assessment, depending on the particular circumstances of each case. The completion of a thorough assessment of a child is a time-consuming process that frequently takes several weeks (Greenspan & Greenspan, 1991). Unfortunately, in the present climate of managed care, the "ideal" assessment process may have to be abbreviated.

The Nature of the Crisis Assessment

In actual practice, crisis situations almost *never* lend themselves to a methodical, thorough data collection process, because "the crisis worker generally does not have time to either gather or analyze all the background and other assessment data that might normally be available under less stressful conditions. . . . [Therefore,] the ability to make a quick evaluation of the degree of client disequilibrium and immobility—and to be flexible enough to change one's evaluation as changing conditions warrant—is a priority skill" (Gilliland & James, 1997, p. 38).

The pressure on the crisis therapist is intense. If a family and/or child is disorganized and in panic, the therapist must not join with these feelings. The challenge to formulate an assessment in crisis permits some abbreviation of the assessment process, but the crisis therapist still must strive to understand the meaning of the crisis to the client. This usually requires a thorough exploration of both the precipitating event and any similar past events.

In some instances this review process, which may take several hours, has a calming influence on the family members, especially when they begin to connect their feelings about past losses and the present crisis. For example, a 5-year-old boy began bedwetting when his stepfather of 6 months was hospitalized suddenly for an appendectomy. In the assessment interview with the child, the play therapist set up a doll play situation in which the father doll had to have an operation. The child played out a fantasy scene in which the stepfather was going to die and in which the little boy doll was "bad" and had to be punished. It seemed probable that this child's unresolved feelings about the death of his biological father (2 years prior) were being evoked in the current situation because of the stepfather's medical emergency. The child's mother readily understood this connection during the evaluation interview, and she was able to reassure her son later that the stepfather's operation would be minor and not fatal. This reassurance clarified the difference between the current, relatively minor medical procedure and the serious heart attack of the child's father, thus helping the child to understand more about his father's death.

The crisis assessment differs from the standard assessment in that the therapist's judgment must determine the specific type and timing of information to be obtained. This judgment assumes a knowledge base that views the present crisis situation from the perspective of child development and of typical individual and family responses to stress. The crisis therapist works from the same knowledge base as other child therapists, but, because of time constraints, applies this knowledge selectively.

For example, in a situation of a 6-year-old's refusal to separate from the mother following the brutal murder of a favorite babysitter, the crisis therapist focused the assessment inquiry on the child's caretaking history, past reactions to separations, and previous experiences with death. The parents' reactions to this horrible event also required exploration. The process of obtaining school and medical reports, on the other hand, was postponed in favor of dealing with the parents' urgent concerns about how much to tell the child about the murder and whether to take the child to the funeral.

Individual Factors in the Assessment of the Child in Crisis

Six groups of factors are considered in making an assessment of the child. These are itemized in Figure 1.1 and may be recorded on the form Individual Factors in the Assessment of the Child in Crisis (Table 1.3), which affords a compact overview of the child's development, level of functioning, and past experience with crisis. The specific groups of individual factors pertaining to the child are as follows:

- Age/developmental factors
- Precrisis adjustment
- Coping style/ego development/resilience
- Past experience with crisis
- Global Assessment of Functioning (DSM-IV, Axis V)
- Specific meaning of crisis to the child

Age/Developmental Factors

The child's age at intake automatically places him or her into a specific developmental stage, with corresponding expectations about the child's probable level of cognitive and moral development. For example, a 6-year-old boy whose 2-year-old sibling drowned in the family well was already struggling with the tasks of Erikson's (1963) stage of initiative versus guilt, while cognitively explaining most occurrences in concrete egocentric terms (Piaget, 1969) and operating on the principle of immi-nent justice, according to Kohlberg's (1964) view of moral development. The crisis

TABLE 1.3. Individual Factors in the Assessment of the Child in Crisis: Webb

1. Age _____ years _____ months
   Date of birth _____
   Date of assessment _____
   a. Developmental stage
      A. Freud _____
      Erikson _____
   b. Cognitive level
      Piaget _____
   c. Moral development
      Kohlberg _____
   d. Temperamental characteristics
      Thomas and Chess _____
2. Precrisis adjustment
   a. Home (as reported by parents)   Good _____ Fair _____ Poor _____
   b. School (as reported by parents and teachers)   Good _____ Fair _____ Poor _____
   c. Interpersonal/peers   Good _____ Fair _____ Poor _____
   d. Medical (as reported by parents and pediatrician)—describe serious illnesses, operations, and injuries since birth, with dates and outcome _____

      Past or current use of medications _____

3. Coping style/ego development (as reported by parents and observed in interviews with child)
   a. Degree of anxiety   High _____ Moderate _____ Low _____
   b. Ability to separate from parent   High anxiety _____ Some anxiety _____ No anxiety _____
   c. Child's ability to discuss the problem/crisis situation   Good _____ Fair _____ None _____
   d. Presence of symptoms (describe, including the extent to which these bind the anxiety)

   e. Defenses (list, indicating appropriateness) _____

   f. Degree of resilience   High _____ Moderate _____ Low _____
4. Child's past experience with crises
   a. Previous losses (list, giving age) _____

   b. Major life transitions/adjustments (list, giving age) _____

   c. Past experience with violence _____

   d. Other (describe) _____

5. Global assessment of functioning (DSM-IV, Axis V)
   Current _____ Past year _____
6. Specific meaning of crisis to the child: Why is this crisis situation so difficult for this child at this time? (describe) _____

Note. This form is one part of a three-part crisis assessment, which also includes an assessment of the nature of the crisis situation and support system factors.

of the sibling's death was superimposed on the child's normal developmental process. Mowbray (1988, p. 198) warns that "combined with young children's egocentrism, their primitive sense of moral development may have some serious consequences for how they react to traumatic events. . . . [They may believe that] if something bad happens, then they must have deserved it." In the crisis situation just described, an intake therapist with a solid knowledge of child development connected the child's presenting symptoms of nightmares to the child's anxiety related to his distorted thoughts about blame and causality. Of course, this had to be explored and confirmed in a play interview with the child. Although the child needed help in alleviating his feelings of guilt, the presenting symptoms "made sense" in the context of the child's age and developmental stage. The treatment of this case is discussed by Kaplan and Joslin (1993).

Anna Freud (1962, pp. 149–150) stated that "the diagnostician's task is to ascertain where a given child stands on the developmental scale, whether his position is age-adequate, retarded, or precocious . . . and to what extent the observable internal and external circumstances and existent symptoms are interfering with the possibilities of future growth." In the example above, the danger existed that the stress from "external circumstances" (the death of a sibling) would interfere with the child's developmental progress; therefore, therapy was indicated.

A therapist who understands Anna Freud's concept of "developmental lines" (Freud, 1963) can use this framework for viewing childhood disturbances. Erikson's (1963) concept of development as consisting of discrete tasks to be mastered during specific stages offers another useful tool for the diagnostician, as does a knowledge of Piaget's (1969) stages of cognitive development and Kohlberg's (1964) stages of moral development.

A child's temperament also has an impact on his or her response to stress and therefore merits assessment. In several decades of research, Thomas and Chess (1981) isolated nine dimensions of temperament, which Wertlieb, Weigel, Springer, and Feldstein (1987) analyzed for the relationship between stress and behavior. They concluded that temperament may moderate a person's reaction to stress and that it interacts with contextual factors such as social supports.

It seems logical that a child who is jumpy, distractible, and an intense reactor prior to a crisis will respond with an exaggeration of these behaviors when confronted with the stress of a crisis. Three distinct profiles of child temperament synthesize Thomas and Chess's nine dimensions of temperament (Chess & Thomas, 1986); these are the "difficult child," the "easy child," and the "slow-to-warm child." These general categories of temperamental style are identified from parental reports during the assessment process. More information regarding the interview scoring procedure for the assessment of temperament may be obtained from Chess and Thomas (1986) and Thomas and Chess (1981).

Precrisis Adjustment

Information about how a child was getting along at home and at school and with peers prior to the crisis helps a therapist to gauge the impact of the stress on the child. For example, a child who was unhappy, withdrawn, and performing poorly in school prior to a serious fire that destroyed the family home may become seriously depressed in response to this crisis. However, another child with a history of successful functioning both at home and in school may respond in a similar situation with mild irritability toward family members and some decreased concentration in school, but nonetheless without major problematic symptoms.

Because stress is viewed as an onslaught that depletes emotional reserves, some estimate regarding the level of the child's precrisis functioning is necessary. Parents, and sometimes the child himself or herself, can truthfully answer the question "How was your child [or were you] getting along at home [or in school or with friends] before this terrible thing happened? Would you rate it as good, fair, or poor?" This can be indicated on the recording form in Table 1.3, together with a record of any serious illnesses, operations, or injuries, and the year of occurrence and the outcome of each. Use of medications should also be recorded.

Coping Style/Ego Development/Resilience

The next category also refers to the child's *precrisis* adjustment and temperamental style. In tandem with the DSM-IV's Global Assessment of Functioning (discussed below), it indicates the child's resilience and use of defenses. However, the ego development of any child is in a state of flux, and a complete assessment of such development requires more information than is generally available to the crisis therapist. Therefore, a complete assessment of object relations, drive regulation and control, and autonomous and synthetic functions of the ego is neither possible nor appropriate when a child and family present themselves in a crisis situation. Furthermore, since "crisis" by definition typically implies disorganization, only a tentative evaluation can be made based on the child's history of previous functioning.

The child's *current* level of adjustment (and anxiety) may be reflected in his or her ability to separate from the parent(s), his or her ability to acknowledge the problem/crisis situation, and the presence of symptoms. It is of great interest to note how completely the child's symptoms bind the anxiety and what strengths and defenses are evident. Some typical defenses of children in situations of severe psychological trauma are reported by Pruett (1984) as denial through fantasy, projection, passive aggression (turning against the self), hypochrondriasis, somatization, and acting out. For example, when a 9-year-old depressed boy denied that he still felt troubled by his mother's suicide 2 years previously, it was difficult for the crisis therapist to challenge this defense until she began to understand his school underachievement as "self-destructive" behavior. Usually when individuals come for help in the midst of a crisis situation, they feel overwhelmed by stress and are open to help. However, with the passage of time their defenses rigidify, and it becomes more difficult to challenge the denial effectively. In this case, the boy's denial of his feelings interfered with his school and social adjustment. Whereas denial may help bereaved children *in the short term,* it is counterproductive when it becomes extended over a long period of time.

The term "resilient" has been used to describe children who demonstrate successful adaptation despite high-risk status, chronic stress, or prolonged or severe trauma

(Egeland, Carlson, & Stroufe, 1993; Garmezy, 1993; Masten, Best, & Garmezy, 1990). "Resilience" is defined as "the ability to recover readily from illness, depression, adversity, or the like" (*Webster's College Dictionary*, 1968, p. 1146),

If we consider resilience to be an *internal* capacity, we must also acknowledge that this ability inevitably interacts with *external* factors, which may be either nurturing and supportive or difficult and depriving (or some combination of the two). Thus, resilience is a transactional *process* that "develops over time in the context of environmental support" (Egeland et al., 1993, p. 518). However, the existence of risk factors such as poverty, parental divorce, parental alcoholism, and parental mental illness by no means sentences a child to negative life outcomes, according to Rak and Patterson (1996). These authors optimistically report that protective factors, such as individual temperament and unexpected sources of support in the family and community, can buffer a child who is at high risk and help such a child succeed in life. This contrasts with a statement by Egeland et al. (1993, p. 519) that "the negative effects of poverty seem to be cumulative and increase as the child gets older."

Clearly, there are multiple factors affecting each child in each situation—factors that the tripartite assessment presented here and illustrated in the many cases in this book summarizes. This approach to assessment provides an essential tool for identifying and evaluating the various contributing elements that help or hinder a child's unique adaptation in different crisis situations.

Child's Past Experience with Crisis

The experts differ about whether past experiences with crisis strengthen or weaken an individual's capacity to cope with subsequent crises. Parad and Parad (1990) and Kliman (1968) believe that success in coping with crises has an ego-strengthening effect, insofar as new coping strategies have been learned, which build up the individual's "immunity" to future breakdown. On the other hand, Anthony (1986, p. 304) states that "we do not know whether a hard life steels the child . . . or sensitizes him to adversity." Referring to Terr's (1979, 1981) work following the kidnapping and burial alive in a school bus of 26 school children aged 5–14, Anthony (1986, p. 304) notes that "an experience of overwhelming anxiety is not a potentially toughening experience but rather poses a significant and persistent burden on the child's personality development." Garmezy (1986, p. 386) comments that "we are very much in an early and less sophisticated stage of research on children's responsiveness to severe stress." This is so because of the multiplicity of influencing variables, the difficulty of following children longitudinally, and the problems in attempting to utilize longitudinal experimental designs.

As a guide to understanding a child's possible vulnerability to present and future crises, the assessment form identifying individual factors (Table 1.3) provides space for recording the child's past experience with loss, with violence, and with major life transitions. Allan and Anderson (1986, p. 144), reviewing a major study by Sandler and Ramsay (1980), state that "loss events (e.g., death of a parent, sibling, or friend; divorce and separation) were the main eliciters of crisis reactions in children, followed by family troubles (e.g., abuse, neglect, loss of job). Lower on the scale were primary environmental changes (e.g., moving, attending a new school, or when mother begins work), sibling difficulties, physical harm (e.g., illness, accidents, and violence), and disasters (e.g., fire, flood, and earthquakes)." A review of the child's history helps the crisis therapist understand and evaluate the child's current level of anxiety.

Global Assessment of Functioning (DSM-IV, Axis V)

The therapist can use the Global Assessment of Functioning Scale (Axis V of DSM-IV) to rate a child's overall psychological, social, and occupational functioning. The rating scale assumes a continuum of mental health–illness from a rank of 100, indicating excellent functioning in many different activities, to 1, representing very poor functioning (i.e., severe danger of harm to self or others or of suicide), or 0, representing inadequate information. See DSM-IV (American Psychiatric Association, 1994, pp. 30–32) for a description of the scale and how to use it.

The Global Assessment of Functioning rating is usually intended to be for the current period, in contrast to the previous version of this scale in DSM-III-R (American Psychiatric Association, 1987), which permitted two ratings—one current, and the other indicating the highest level of functioning during the past year. Because individuals typically become disorganized due to the anxiety generated in a crisis, a rating of the highest level of functioning in the past year gives an important indication of their precrisis adjustment. This information is especially significant to the therapist, since it suggests an individual's potential for recovery. Therefore, I recommend that two Global Assessment of Functioning ratings be made for children in crisis, in order to facilitate the assessment of prognosis.

Specific Meaning of Crisis to the Child

Just as an intake worker often questions, "Why is the client coming for help now, rather than a month or a year ago?", the crisis therapist must try to understand what it is about this particular crisis situation that makes it intolerable for this particular child at this particular time. Obviously, some crisis events are so horrendous that an extreme reaction is appropriate. Nonetheless, every individual will attach personal meaning to a horrible event, and this requires exploration in order for treatment efforts to be focused appropriately.

In one shared disaster experience, the destruction of an apartment complex by fire, one child was consumed by guilt because he escaped unharmed while his brother suffered a broken leg and smoke inhalation. An important component of the child's guilt was the fact that the boys had been fighting just before the fire alarm went off and the injured boy had accused his brother of being selfish. After the fire, the uninjured 7-year-old felt convinced that his brother was right and that if he had done "the right thing," he might have saved his brother from injury.

Questions that help uncover the hidden meaning of a crisis for an individual child are the following:

- "Do you remember what you were doing just before [the crisis event] happened?"
- "Do you think there is anything that you could have done to have avoided [the crisis event]?"
- "What have you been thinking about most since [the crisis event] happened?"

Sometimes the child can clarify the personal meaning of the crisis. In the example of the brothers in the fire, the intake worker says to the uninjured boy, "I wonder if maybe you're worrying about not having saved your brother, and about why he was hurt and you were not." In a case like this, when the conflict is close enough to the surface, the child may acknowledge it openly. Other times, it is not possible or desirable to seek confirmation, since this might be too threatening. Whether openly acknowledged by the child or not, the underlying meaning of the crisis must be understood by the crisis therapist, so that treatment goals can be appropriately established.

FACTORS IN THE SUPPORT SYSTEM

A crisis happens to a specific individual in the context of his or her social and physical environment. We now consider some of the features of the surrounding environment that either help or hinder the individual in crisis. Assessment of the support system is particularly important for children in crisis, because their youth and dependence make them especially reliant on others to assist them.

Nuclear and Extended Family

A genogram is the starting point for identifying all family members who potentially can provide support to a child in crisis. In the process of creating a three-generation genogram with the family at the time of intake, the crisis therapist learns not only the names of family members but also their geographic location, their frequency of contact with one another, and something about the quality of their various relationships. It is helpful to ask in completing the genogram, "Of all these various family members, which ones do you consider most important to the child?" The response sometimes reveals the influence of an aunt or uncle in the child's life, which might not otherwise be known. The family's demographic characteristics (e.g., age, social class, level of education) and their cultural characteristics often affect the particular way the family members respond in crisis. For example, Gleser, Green, and Winget (1981) have found that better-educated people seem to adjust more successfully following a disaster, and Lindy, Grace, and Green (1981) have pointed out that the cultural backgrounds of different groups influence the way a crisis event is perceived and the nature of the response.

These variables are complex and difficult to evaluate. For example, bettereducated people may have more financial resources that may contribute to their improved response. Anthropologists and family therapists have been attempting for several decades to identify specific values typical of distinct cultural groups and the impact of these values on the family system (Kluckhohn, 1958; Spiegel, 1982; McGoldrick, 1982; McGoldrick, Gordano, & Pearce, 1996). McGoldrick states categorically that "the language and customs of a culture will influence whether or not a symptom is labeled a problem . . . [and that] problems (whether physical or mental) can be neither diagnosed nor treated without understanding the frame of reference of the person seeking help as well as that of the helper" (1982, p. 6). Thus an assessment must identify and weigh the significance of cultural factors related to the family's reaction to the crisis situation.

Freud and Burlingham (1943) commented on the relevance of the parents' reactions in a shared traumatic situation to the nature of the child's response. Benedek (1985), however, recognizes that this places a great burden on parents who themselves may be traumatized. Even in a noncrisis situation, "financial constraints, absorption in professional development, moves, or deaths of significant relatives can significantly encroach on the adult's available energy to parent effectively" (Chethik, 1989, p. 33). Thus the intake therapist must identify available resources and difficulties within the support system of the child in crisis.

School, Friends, and Community Supports

The Eco-Map (Hartman, 1978) provides a diagrammatic tool for illustrating the available types of support surrounding a family or household (see Figure 1.2). This is an excellent means of analyzing potential resources in a child's network of friends, church, school, health care, and other institutions. The Beatles sang about getting by with a little help from their friends; Benedek (1985) stresses the importance of significant, caring human relationships in situations where the child and parents have been traumatized together. It is not surprising that more supportive environments tend to be associated with a better adjustment to stress (Green et al., 1985). However, individual characteristics ultimately determine how well available supports are utilized. For example, an individual who is in a vulnerable state as a result of an "overdose" of past crises may be unable to cope even when excellent supports are available.

We must also recognize that children growing up in poverty frequently lack the supportive resources available to other children. Huston (1995) states that parents living in poverty often experience more financial stress and suffer more depression and psychological distress than more affluent parents do. Therefore, parental support may be absent for those children who most need adult protection, due to their dangerous inner-city neighborhoods with very high levels of interpersonal violence (Fick, Osofsky, & Lewis, 1994). The ideal of a safe, nurturing, supportive environment is far from the reality of many children of poverty.

Psychosocial and Environmental Problems (DSM-IV, Axis IV)

Details about the *context* in which an individual's difficulties have developed, as well as the nature of the crisis situation (discussed previously), should be recorded on Axis

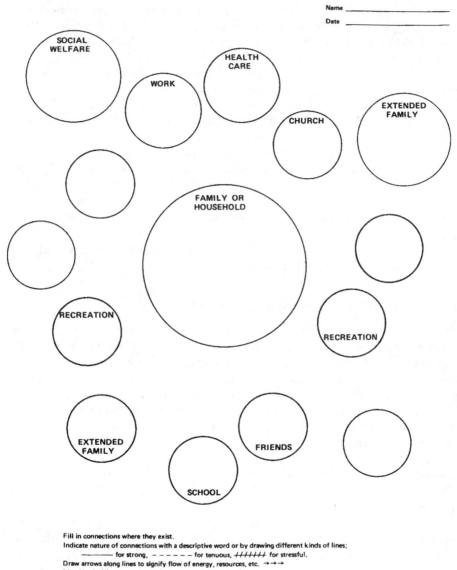

FIGURE 1.2. Eco-Map. From Hartman (1978). Copyright 1978 by Family Service Association of America. Reprinted by permission.

IV of DSM-IV (American Psychiatric Association, 1994; see Table 1.1). Because psychosocial and environmental problems often play a key role in the development and continuation of a mental disorder, these should be listed in order to take them into account in the overall treatment plan. Family and community problems will affect children to varying degrees, depending on their scope and intensity. For example, a child living in a run-down tenement building surrounded by gang warfare will probably react more strongly if he or she witnesses a shooting than would a child the same age who lived in a safe neighborhood.

Summary

A tripartite crisis assessment analyzes the interaction among the three components of the tripartite model: the nature of the crisis situation, individual factors, and factors in the support system. The assessment tools useful for this purpose are the Crisis Situation Rating Form (Table 1.2), the Individual Factors in the Assessment of the Child in Crisis form (Table 1.3), a genogram, and the Eco-Map (Figure 1.2). A complete crisis assessment includes an abundance of data that these four assessment tools organize and summarize in a compact, useful format.

TERMINOLOGY CLARIFICATION: DISTINCTIONS BETWEEN "CRISIS" AND "POSTTRAUMATIC STRESS RESPONSE"

The title of this book, *Play Therapy with Children in Crisis* (rather than . . . *in Trauma*), reflects my deliberate intent to focus on crisis situations that may or may not result in subsequent traumatization and symptom formation. At the beginning of this chapter, I have presented Gilliland and James's (1997, p. 3) definition of crisis in terms of "an intolerable difficulty" with "the *potential* [my emphasis] to cause severe affective, cognitive, and behavioral malfunctioning." Timely crisis intervention can avert later symptom formation by helping the individual express his or her feelings and begin to deal with the crisis situation *before* anxiety mounts and conflicts escalate to disabling proportions.

Crisis intervention services are usually short-term, because most crises by their very nature are time-limited. "A minimum of therapeutic intervention during the brief crisis period can often produce a maximum therapeutic effect through the use of supportive social resources and focused treatment techniques" (Parad & Parad, 1990, p. 9).

In discussing crisis, we often refer to "stress overload." This overload causes distress to the individual, which, if not relieved, may lead to a psychiatric disorder such as PTSD. McFarlane (1990, p. 70) states that "the degree of distress caused by an event is the major factor determining the probability of the onset of psychiatric disorder. Therefore, a crisis intervention approach that aims to lessen the distress of traumatized people and bolsters their coping strategies is likely to be useful for the primary prevention of PTSD."

The concept of PTSD was first included in DSM-III in 1980 to describe symptoms following an unusually traumatic event. The resulting symptoms include re-experiencing the traumatic event, becoming numb, and being less involved with the external world, as well as other autonomic, dysphoric, and cognitive symptoms (American Psychiatric Association, 1980). According to DSM-III, the disorder can occur during childhood, or at any age (American Psychiatric Association, 1980).

Table 1.4 lists the diagnostic criteria for PTSD as these have been more fully elaborated in DSM-IV (American Psychiatric Association, 1994). This symptom list does not differ radically from that in DSM-III-R (American Psychiatric Association, 1987), which was considered "ground-breaking" because it presented a cluster of four symptom criteria that were related to the intensity and duration of the exposure to the stressor (Fletcher, 1996). In the 1987 version, PTSD was considered a normal reaction to abnormal circumstances, but removal of the stressor was no guarantee that the symptoms would diminish.

DSM-IV notes that younger children may experience distressing dreams, although these may be dreams about monsters and other threats rather than about the traumatic event itself. Furthermore, young children may relive the trauma in action through repetitive play, without the sense that they are reliving the past, and they may also experience assorted physical symptoms (e.g., headaches and stomachaches) as part of their response to trauma (American Psychiatric Association, 1994).

Critics of the PTSD diagnosis point out that "the distinctions between persons with the normal stress response and those with PTSD are blurred, particularly soon after the event" (McFarlane, 1990, p. 71). With regard to the applicability of the concept to children, Garmezy (1986, p. 391) cautions against "assigning to children popular diagnostic labels used with adults. Posttraumatic stress disorder may not be a wholly appropriate diagnosis for children's anxiety reactions to stress." However, other researchers emphasize that "children [do] experience the full range of posttraumatic stress symptoms" (Pynoos, Steinberg, & Goenjian, 1996, p. 333; see also Fletcher, 1996). Estimates show that approximately 36% of children exposed to traumatic events are later diagnosed with PTSD (Fletcher, 1996).

This makes me wonder about the factors that protect the considerable number of children exposed to traumatic events (approximately 64%) who do *not* develop PTSD. Numerous factors affect the eventual development of symptoms. Because of this, I prefer the term "crisis," rather than "trauma," in dealing with children under extreme stress. Ideally, the use of timely crisis intervention to relieve children's distress will remove the current distress and prevent the later development of symptoms.

REFERENCES

Allan, J., & Anderson, E. (1986). Children and crises: A classroom guidance approach. *Elementary School Guidance and Counseling, 21*(2), 143–149.

American Psychiatric Association. (1980). *Diagnostic and statistical manual of mental disorders* (3rd ed.). Washington, DC: Author.

TABLE 1.4. DSM-IV Diagnostic Criteria for Posttraumatic Stress Disorder (PTSD)

A. The person has been exposed to a traumatic event in which both of the following were present:

   (1) the person experienced, witnessed, or was confronted with an event or events that involved actual or threatened death or serious injury, or a threat the physical integrity of self or others
   (2) the person's response involved intense fear, helplessness, or horror, **Note:** In children, this may be expressed instead by disorganized or agitated behavior

B. The traumatic event is persistently reexperienced in one (or more) of the following ways:

   (1) recurrent and intrusive distressing recollection of the event, including images, thoughts, or perceptions. **Note:** In young children, repetitive play may occur in which themes or aspects of the trauma are expressed.
   (2) recurrent distressing dreams of the event. **Note:** In children, there may be frightening dreams without recognizable content.
   (3) acting or feeling as if the traumatic event were recurring (includes a sense of reliving the experience, illusions, hallucinations, and dissociative flashback episodes, including those that occur on awakening or when intoxicated). **Note:** In young children, trauma-specific reenactment may occur.
   (4) intense psychological distress at exposure to internal or external cues that symbolize or resemble an aspect of the traumatic event
   (5) physiological reactivity on exposure to internal or external cues that symbolize or resemble an aspect of the traumatic event

C. Persistent avoidance of stimuli associated with the trauma and numbing of general responsiveness (not present before the trauma), as indicated by three (or more) of the following:

   (1) efforts to avoid thoughts, feelings, or conversations associated with the trauma
   (2) efforts to avoid activities, places, or people that arouse recollections of the trauma
   (3) inability to recall an important aspect of the trauma
   (4) markedly diminished interest or participation in significant activities
   (5) feeling of detachment or estrangement from others
   (6) restricted range of affect (e.g., unable to have loving feelings)
   (7) sense of a foreshortened future (e.g., does not expect to have a career, marriage, children, or a normal life span)

D. Persistent symptoms of increased arousal (not present before the trauma), as indicated by two (or more) of the following:

   (1) difficulty falling or staying asleep
   (2) irritability or outbursts of anger
   (3) difficulty concentrating
   (4) hypervigilance
   (5) exaggerated startle response

E. Duration of the disturbance (symptoms in Criteria B, C, and D) is more than 1 month.

F. The disturbance causes clinically significant distress or impairment in social, occupational, or other important areas of functioning.

Specify if:
   Acute: if duration of symptoms is less than 3 months
   Chronic: if duration of symptoms is 3 months or more

Specify if:
   With Delayed Onset: if onset of symptoms is at least 6 months after the stressor

Note. From American Psychiatric Association (1994, pp. 250–251). Copyright 1994 by the American Psychiatric Association. Reprinted by permission.

American Psychiatric Association. (1987). *Diagnostic and statistical manual of mental disorders* (3rd ed., rev.). Washington, DC: Author.

American Psychiatric Association. (1994). *Diagnostic and statistical manual of mental disorders* (4th ed.). Washington, DC: Author.

Anthony, E. J. (1986). Children's reactions to severe stress. *Journal of the American Academy of Child Psychiatry, 25,* 299–305.

Arkin, A. M. (1974). Notes on anticipatory grief. In B. Schoenberg, A. C. Carr, A. H. Kutscher, D. Peretz, & I. K. Goldberg (Eds.), *Anticipatory grief* (pp. 10–13). New York: Columbia University Press.

Benedek, E. P. (1985). Children and psychic trauma: A brief review of contemporary thinking. In S. Eth & R. S. Pynoos (Eds.), *Post-traumatic stress disorder in children* (pp. 3–16). Washington, DC: American Psychiatric Press.

Bowlby, J. (1969). *Attachment and loss: Vol. 1. Attachment.* London: Hogarth Press.

Chemtob, C. M., Bauer, G. B., Neller, G., Hamada, R., Glisson, C., & Stevens, V. (1990). Posttraumatic stress disorder among Special Forces Vietnam veterans. *Military Medicine, 155,* 16–20.

Chess, S., & Thomas, A. (1986). *Temperament in clinical practice.* New York: Guilford Press.

Chethik, M. (1989). *Techniques of child therapy: Psychodynamic strategies.* New York: Guilford Press.

Egeland, B., Carlson, E., & Sroufe, L.A. (1993). Resilience as process. *Development and Psychopathology, 5,* 517–528.

Erikson, E. H. (1963). *Childhood and society* (rev. ed.). New York: Norton.

Eth, S., & Pynoos, R. S. (1980). Psychiatric interventions with children traumatized by violence. In D. H. Schetky & E. P. Benedek (Eds.), *Emerging issues in child psychiatry and the law* (pp. 285–309). New York: Brunner/Mazel.

Eth, S., & Pynoos, R. S. (1985). Interaction of trauma and grief in childhood. In S. Eth & R. S. Pynoos (Eds.), *Post-traumatic stress disorder in children* (pp. 171–186). Washington, DC: American Psychiatric Press.

Fassler, J. (1987). *Helping children cope: Mastering stress through books and stories.* New York: Free Press.

Fick, A. C., Osofsky, J. D., & Lewis, M. L. (1994). Perceptions of violence: Children, parents, and police officers. In R. S. Pynoos (Ed.), *Posttraumatic stress disorder: A clinical review* (pp. 261–276). Lutherville, MD: Sidram Press.

Fletcher, K. E. (1996). Childhood posttraumatic stress disorder. In E. J. Mash & R. A. Barkley (Eds.), *Child psychopathology* (pp. 242–276). New York: Guilford Press.

Freud, A. (1962). Assessment of childhood disturbances. *Psychoanalytic Study of the Child, 17,* 149–158.

Freud, A. (1963). The concept of developmental lines. *Psychoanalytic Study of the Child, 18,* 245–265.

Freud, A. (1965). *Normality and pathology in childhood.* New York: International Universities Press.

Freud, A., & Burlingham, D. T. (1943). *War and children.* London: Medical War Books.

Garmezy, N. (1986). Children under severe stress: Critique and commentary. *Journal of the Academy of Child Psychiatry, 25,* 384–392.

Garmezy, N. (1993). Stress-resistant children: The search for protective factors. In J. E. Stevenson (Ed.), *Recent research in developmental psychopathology* (pp. 213–233). Oxford: Pergamon Press.

Gilliland, B. E., & James, R. K. (1997). *Crisis intervention strategies* (3rd ed.). Pacific Grove, CA: Brooks/Cole.

Gleser, G. C., Green, B. L., & Winget, C. N. (1981). *Prolonged psychosocial effects of disaster: A study of Buffalo Creek.* New York: Academic Press.

Golan, N. (1978). *Treatment in crisis situations.* New York: Free Press.

Green, B. L., Wilson, J. P., & Lindy, J. D. (1985). Conceptualizing post-traumatic stress disorder: A psychosocial framework. In C. R. Figley (Ed.), *Trauma and its wake: The study and treatment of post-traumatic stress disorder* (pp. 53–69). New York: Brunner/Mazel.

Greenspan, S. T., & Greenspan, N. T. (1991). *The clinical interview of the child* (2nd ed.). Washington, DC: American Psychiatric Press.

Hartman, A. (1978). Diagrammatic assessment of family relationships. *Social Casework, 59,* 465–476.

Huston, A. C. (1995, August). *Children in poverty and public policy.* Presidential address presented at the meeting of Division 7 (Developmental Psychology) of the American Psychological Association, New York.

Janis, I. L. (1977). Adaptive personality changes. In A. Monat & R. S. Lazarus (Eds.), *Stress and coping* (pp. 272–284). New York: Columbia University Press.

Kaplan, C. P., & Joslin, H. (1993). Accidental sibling death: Case of Peter, age 6. In N. B. Webb (Ed.), *Helping bereaved children: A handbook for practitioners* (pp. 118–136). New York: Guilford Press.

Kliman, G. (1968). *Psychological emergencies of childhood.* New York: Grune & Stratton.

Kluckhohn, F. R. (1958). Variations in basic values of family systems. In N. W. Bell & E. F. Vogel (Eds.), *A modern introduction to the family* (pp. 319 330). New York: Free Press.

Kohlberg, L. (1964). Development of moral character and moral ideology. In M. L. Hoffman & L. W. Hoffman (Eds.), *Review of child development* (Vol. 1, pp. 383–431). New York: Russell Sage Foundation.

Lindy, J. D., Grace, M. C., & Green, B. L. (1981). Survivors: Outreach to a reluctant population. *American Journal of Orthopsychiatry, 51,* 468–478.

Marmar, C. R., Foy, D., Kagan, B., & Pynoos, R. S. (1994). An integrated approach for treating posttraumatic stress. In R. S. Pynoos (Ed.), *Posttraumatic stress disorder: A clinical review* (pp. 825 888). Lutherville, MD: Sidram Press.

Masten, A. S., Best, K. M., & Garmezy, N. (1990). Resilience and development: Contributions from the study of children who overcome adversity. *Development and Psychopathology, 2,* 425–444.

McFarlane, A. C. (1990). Post-traumatic stress syndrome revisited. In H. J. Parad & L. G. Parad (Eds.), *Crisis intervention book 2: The practitioner's sourcebook for brief therapy* (pp. 69–92). Milwaukee, WI: Family Service America.

McGoldrick, M. (1982). Ethnicity and family therapy: An overview. In M. McGoldrick, J. K. Pearce, & J. Giordano (Eds.), *Ethnicity and family therapy* (pp. 3–30). New York: Guilford Press.

McGoldrick, M., Giordano, J., & Pearce, J. K. (1996). *Ethnicity and family therapy* (2nd ed.). New York: Guilford Press.

Mishne, J. M. (1983). *Clinical work with children.* New York: Free Press.

Mowbray, C. T. (1988). Post-traumatic therapy for children who are victims of violence. In F. M. Ochberg (Ed.), *Post-traumatic therapy and victims of violence* (pp. 196–212). New York: Brunner/Mazel.

Nader, K., Pynoos, R. S., Fairbanks, L., & Frederick, C. (1990). Children's PTSD reactions one year after a sniper attack at their school. *American Journal of Psychiatry, 147,* 1526–1530.

Parad, H. J., & Parad, L. G. (Eds.). (1990). *Crisis intervention book 2: The practitioner's sourcebook for brief therapy.* Milwaukee, WI: Family Service America.

Piaget, J. (1969). *The psychology of the child.* New York: Basic Books.

Pruett, K. D. (1984). A chronology of defensive adaptations to severe psychological trauma. *Psychoanalytic Study of the Child, 39,* 591–612.

Putnam, F. W. (1997). *Dissociation in children and adolescents.* New York: Guilford Press.

Putnam, F. W., Post, R. M., & Guroff, J. J. (1984). *One hundred cases of multiple personality disorder.* Paper presented at the annual meeting of the American Psychiatric Association, Los Angeles.

Pynoos, R. S., & Eth, S. (1985). Children traumatized by witnessing acts of personal violence. In S. Eth & R. S. Pynoos (Eds.), *Post-traumatic stress disorder in children* (pp. 19–43). Washington, DC: American Psychiatric Press.

Pynoos, R. S. , & Nader, K. (1989). Children's memory and proximity to violence. *Journal of the American Academy of Child and Adolescent Psychiatry, 28,* 236–241.

Pynoos, R. S., Steinberg, A. M., & Goenjian, A. (1996). Traumatic stress in childhood and adolescence. In B. A. van der Kolk, A. C. McFarlane, & L. Weisaeth (Eds.), *Traumatic stress: The effects of overwhelming experience on mind, body, and society* (pp. 331–358). New York: Guilford Press.

Rak, C. F., & Patterson, L. E. (1996). Promoting resilience in at-risk children. *Journal of Counseling and Development, 74,* 368–373.

Sandler, I. R., & Ramsay, T. B. (1980). Dimensional analysis of children's stressful life events. *American Journal of Community Psychology, 8,* 285–302.

Selye, H. (1978). *The stress of life.* New York: McGraw-Hill.

Shneidman, E. S. (1981). *Postvention:* The care of the bereaved. *Suicide and Life-Threatening Behavior, 11,* 349–359.

Spiegel, J. (1982). An ecological model of ethnic families. In M. McGoldrick, J. K. Pearce, & J. Giordano (Eds.), *Ethnicity and family therapy* (pp. 32–51). New York: Guilford Press.

Star, B. (1980). Patterns in family violence. *Social Casework, 61*(6), 339–343.

Terr, L. C. (1979). Children of Chowchilla. *Psychoanalytic Study of the Child, 34,* 547–623.

Terr, L. C. (1981). Forbidden games: Post-traumatic child's play. *Journal of the American Academy of Child Psychiatry, 20,* 741–759.

Terr, L. C. (1991). Childhood traumas: An outline and overview. *American Journal of Psychiatry, 148*(1), 10–20.

Thomas, A., & Chess, S. (1981). The role of temperament in the contributions of individuals to their development. In R. M. Lerner & N. A. Busch-Rossnagel (Eds.), *Individuals as producers of their development* (pp. 231–254). New York: Academic Press.

Webb, N. B. (1993). Traumatic death of friend/peer: Case of Susan, Age 9. In N. B. Webb (Ed.), *Helping bereaved children: A handbook for practitioners* (pp. 189–211). New York: Guilford Press.

Webster's College Dictionary. (1968). New York: Random House.

Wertlieb, D., Weigel, C., Springer, T., & Feldstein, M. (1987). Temperament as a moderator of children's stressful experiences. *American Journal of Orthopsychiatry, 57*(2), 234–245.

CHAPTER 2

Play Therapy Crisis Intervention with Children

NANCY BOYD WEBB

Play therapy ingeniously undertakes the hard work of child psychotherapy in the appealing guise of play. Since children behave and think differently from adults, the approach to working with them must reflect this difference. Play therapy has adapted its methods to accommodate to the world of childhood, using the medium of play as the means for communicating symbolically with the child.

Few children willingly admit that they have "problems," even when their parents are at their wits' ends because of the children's nightmares, shyness, or aggressive behavior. These children come for therapy only because they have no other recourse in the face of their parents' or teachers' complaints about their behavior. Once in the therapist's office, moreover, these children cannot endure a discussion about their "problem" with a strange adult. The well-meaning but inexperienced therapist who asks a youngster the typical open-ended question appropriate for adults—"So tell me about what brings you here today"—had better be prepared for a blank stare, a shrug of the shoulders, or (at best) "My mother said you wanted to talk to me." If it is hard for adults to seek help and discuss their emotional distress in therapy, how much more so is it for children! Fortunately, play therapy techniques come to the rescue, providing initial enticement for engaging a child, and ongoing appeal during the process of treatment.

Play has been used in child therapy since the 1920s, when Anna Freud (1926/ 1946) employed games and toys as a way to build a relationship with her child patients. Another child analyst, Melanie Klein (1932), used children's play as the basis for interpretations to the children. Other play therapy pioneers include David Levy (1938), who helped children reenact traumatic events through a structured play format, and Frederick Allen (1942), Claude Moustakas (1959), and Virginia Axline (1947), all of whom emphasized the power of the therapeutic relationship in conjunction with children's natural growth processes as key to helping the children individuate and develop basic self-esteem (positive regard). Achievement of these goals in nondirective play therapy occurs through recognition of a child's feelings as expressed in the play, and through the therapist's belief in the child's strengths and potential for growth and change.

The considerable differences between the theoretical perspectives and working procedures of these early play therapists and their current followers have been reviewed elsewhere (James, 1977; Mishne, 1983; Schaefer & O'Connor, 1983; Wolt-mann, 1955/1964) and are not repeated here. It is remarkable that despite their differences, these therapists and their current followers all recognized the unique meaning of play to children and the importance of understanding the symbolism of children's play language. The operating assumption is that "through play the child will reveal meaningful information regarding his or her emotional problems" (Johnson, Rasbury, & Siegel, 1986, p. 8). Bettelheim (1987, p. 35) comments that "the child's play is motivated by inner processes, desires, problems, and anxieties. . . . play is the royal road to the child's conscious and unconscious inner world; if we want to understand his inner world and help him with it, we must learn to walk this road."

DEFINITION AND PURPOSES OF PLAY THERAPY

What Is Play Therapy?

Definition

"Play therapy" is a helping interaction between a trained adult and a child that seeks to relieve the child's emotional distress through the symbolic communication of play. "The assumption is that children will express and work through [their] emotional conflicts . . . within the metaphor of play" (Reid, 1986, p. 261). The play therapist not only helps bring about relief of clinical symptoms (important as this may be to parents and child), but also works toward removal of impediments to the child's continuing development, so that the prospects for the child's future growth are en-hanced (Enzer, 1988).

These dual play therapy goals (i.e., symptom relief and removing obstacles to the child's growth) are illustrated in the case of a 10-year-old child with a sleep distur-bance. The therapist helped the child identify a number of self-soothing activities that she could employ other than going into her parents' bedroom when she woke up in the middle of the night. The successful outcome in this case (which also employed a series of planned rewards from the parents when the child did not disturb them) re-sulted not only in cessation of the nighttime waking, but also in an increase in the child's confidence about her ability to deal successfully with her internal distress. The case illustrates both symptom alleviation and enhancement of coping abilities. The play therapy with this girl utilized art techniques to help her externalize her fears on paper and portray her anticipated positive mood at a future time when she would no longer feel afraid. (A full discussion of this case appears in Webb, 1996.)

In ways that will become clear in the various detailed case examples in this book, the "therapy" of play therapy involves far more than merely playing with a child. Through the interpersonal interactions with the therapist, the child experiences acceptance, catharsis, reduction of troublesome affects, redirection of impulses, and a corrective emotional experience (Enzer, 1988). In the safety of the "holding envi-ronment" of the playroom, the child can express his or her feelings in fantasy; this permits eventual working through and mastery (Reid, 1986), which then may carry over to the child's everyday life. However, "play, in itself, will not ordinarily produce changes in the therapist's office any more than it will in the schoolyard. [It is] the therapist's interventions and utilizations of the play [that] are critical" (Chethik, 1989, pp. 48–49).

Balance between Verbal and Play Interactions

Many of the therapist's interactions in play therapy are verbal as well as behavioral. Indeed, Enzer (1988) believes that assisting a child toward greater verbalization is one of the primary goals of play therapy. A child's ability to verbalize depends on his or her age and level of cognitive development. According to Erikson (quoted by Woltmann, 1955/1964, p. 31), "the child uses play to make up for defeats, sufferings, and frustrations, *especially resulting from . . . limited use of language*" (my emphasis). Winnicott (1971, p. 39) reminds us that "the child does not usually possess the command of language that can convey the infinite subtleties that are to be found in play." Play, however, must never become an end unto itself in play therapy. I repeatedly instruct child therapy interns and beginning child therapists that *when a child can talk about his or her anxieties, we should listen and encourage more verbalization.* However, playing serves as a safe refuge when anxiety mounts and the child needs to retreat from verbalized connections to his or her own life. Play also frequently serves as the means for establishing the therapeutic relationship. My usual procedure in the initial session with a child is to say that I am a doctor who helps children and families with their troubles and their worries, and that "sometimes we talk and sometimes we play." This gives the child permission to use verbalization or play according to his or her own ability and level of comfort.

Bettelheim (1977) warns about direct interpretation from the symbolism of fairy tales (which are a form of play) to a child's own life, since he believes that making the child aware of the meaning behind a tale will create confusion and deprive the child of a needed symbolic (fantasy) outlet. It has been my own experience, as illustrated in the case of Michael (see Webb, Chapter 3, this volume), that work in a displaced fashion (e.g., through family dolls) can bring symptom relief without any interpretation from the play to the child's life. This is especially true in work with preschool-age children.

By late latency, the child's verbal communication skills have usually increased, and there is less reliance on symbolic play (Sarnoff, 1987). Kaplan (Chapter 16, this volume) demonstrates the shifting balance among verbalization, large-muscle play activity (Nerf ball and skateboarding), and doodling in the case of an 11-year-old boy whose anxiety in discussions about his illness propelled him away from verbalization and toward physical activities that permitted him to deny the possible serious implications of his blood disorder.

Up to What Age Is Play Therapy Appropriate?

As the preceding discussion suggests, play therapy is an appropriate treatment modality through late latency, with the likelihood that the balance between verbal and play interactions will shift gradually as a child gets older. Play usually dominates over verbalization in the preschool years, whereas the opposite situation will probably prevail as the child approaches puberty.

There is no hard and fast rule about this. Art techniques, for example, may be used as a medium for therapy throughout the lifespan, as can some board games and visualization techniques. On the other hand, some play therapy materials such as dolls may be spurned by latency-age boys who consider them "girls' toys," whereas these same boys will engage in play with animal puppets and in drawing activities such as cartooning (see Doyle & Stoop's case [Chapter 6, this volume] of 10-year-old Randy, who constructed an elaborate cartoon lifeline and used it in play involving animal puppets).

Terr (1989, p. 15) notes that "traumatized youngsters appear to indulge in play at much older ages than do nontraumatized youngsters." Therefore, the opportunity to play must be available to facilitate the symbolic expression of experiences that are too horrible to verbalize. This may have been an operating factor in the case of Randy (see Doyle & Stoop, Chapter 6). The sensitive therapist observes the child for clues as to his or her play preferences, while always seeking to help the child toward the maximum level of articulation that he or she is capable of.

Purposes of Play Therapy

The primary purpose of play therapy is to help troubled children express their conflicts and anxieties through the medium of play in the context of a therapeutic relationship. The therapist's conscious direction of the child's play activity gives it purpose, meaning, and value in treatment, according to Amster (1943). Amster outlines the following six purposes served by play therapy:

- Aids diagnostic understanding
- Helps establish the treatment relationship
- Provides a medium for working through defenses and handling anxieties
- Assists in the verbalization of feelings
- Helps the child act out unconscious material and relieve the accompanying tensions
- Enlarges the child's play interests for eventual use outside of therapy

Each child's situation is unique; therefore, the work with individual children will have different emphases, depending on the specific assessment of the child's problem situation. Since the focus of this book is on play therapy with children in crisis, the discussion that follows focuses on the special play therapy approaches that deal with children in situations of crisis and trauma.

PLAY THERAPY IN CRISIS SITUATIONS

Erikson (1950/1964) viewed play as a child's means of achieving mastery over traumatic experiences. The make-believe element, according to Woltmann (1955/1964,

p. 24), "eliminates guilt feelings which would appear if action could result in real harm and damage and enables the child to be victorious over forces otherwise above his reach and capacity." Thus, for example, a child who has been subjected to painful medical procedures may earnestly play out giving injections and other treatments to a doll in doll play. In crisis situations, the child has felt helpless and afraid. Through replay of the crisis experience, the child transforms the passivity and impotence he or she experienced into activity and power. Instead of being the hurting patient, the child becomes the administrator of pain in his or her fantasy. Mishne (1983, p. 272) comments that "traumatic experiences are repeated to achieve belated mastery. . . . the painful tension of the original trauma is relived, under somewhat more favorable conditions (e.g., in play) . . . that is under the control of the child." Quoting Walder (1933), Mishne (1983, p. 273) elaborates that "when an event is too difficult or large to assimilate immediately, it must be chewed again and again; in this way, a passively experienced event is converted into an actively experienced one." Just as a mourning adult needs to review over and over the details surrounding the death of a loved one, a traumatized child may repeatedly seek to reconstruct a crisis experience symbolically through play.

However, when posttraumatic play takes the form of secretive, monotonous, ritualized play, it may fail to relieve the child. Terr (1983) describes this type of play in 26 children in Chowchilla, California, who were overwhelmed with anxiety following the sudden and intense traumatic experience of being kidnapped and buried alive for 16 hours in a school bus. Based on her work with these children, and on a review of the literature, Terr (1983) believes that a severely traumatized child needs to verbalize as well as to play. She recommends a form of child psychotherapy using preset or prearranged play, in which the therapist deliberately encourages the child to reenact the trauma by providing the child with play materials suggestive of the traumatic experience. This psychotherapeutic reconstruction includes a verbal review of the traumatic experience, in which the therapist helps the child obtain relief from the guilt and fear associated with the trauma. Examples of preset or prearranged play in this book are Strand's work with a victim of sexual abuse (Chapter 5) and Bevin's work with a 9-year-old refugee (Chapter 7).

David Levy's (1938, 1939) early work with traumatized children, which he termed "release therapy," "abreaction therapy," and "control play," represents landmark treatment using preset or prearranged play. Unlike Terr (1983), Levy did not use verbalization, nor did he interpret a child's feelings during the play. "In release therapy the interpretive function of the therapist is reduced to a minimum and may be absent, especially in children age 2, 3, and 4" (Levy, 1939, p. 716). Terr believes that Levy's abreactive treatment remains currently applicable and valid in situations containing a "stressful, if not 'traumatic' effect" (Terr, 1983, p. 314). This may characterize my case of the 4-year-old child witness of parental violence (see Webb, Chapter 3), who needed to abreact repeated replay of his experience through family doll play reenactment but who resisted "corrective denouement" play (Terr, 1983), which would have allowed me to change his violent story ending to a less violent outcome. The child's symptom relief in this case occurred primarily through abreaction and gradual mastery of the associated anxiety.

RANGE OF PLAY THERAPY METHODS

Whether the treatment philosophy of the therapist results in a nondirective or a prearranged play therapy approach, the well-trained play therapist employs a variety of play therapy materials and techniques in working with children in crisis. Although few playrooms are equipped with all of the play therapy materials listed below and described in case examples in the book, it is important that a range of choices be available to each child. The therapist must be sufficiently familiar with the materials to maintain focus on the child and his or her play communication.

The discussion that follows reviews some of the major play therapy methods, with suggestions about necessary materials. (For a video demonstration of different play therapy techniques, see Webb, 1994.)

Art Techniques

The graphic and plastic arts have broad application and appeal to children and adults of all ages. According to Rubin (1984, pp. 269, 273), "it is the peculiar power of art to be able to symbolize not only intrapsychic events, but interpersonal ones as well, and to collapse multileveled or sequential happenings into a single visual statement. . . . the art therapist combines both an intuitive, inspired approach with a rational analytic one, alternating and integrating them in tune with the needs of the situation."

There are numerous examples in this book of play therapy using art techniques. Both the immature "circular scribbles" drawing of a preschooler (Tonning, Chapter 9) and the elaborate cartoon lifeline of a 10-year-old boy (Doyle & Stoop, Chapter 6) were visual portrayals of feelings that neither child could adequately express verbally. Talking about such drawings, when a child is able and willing to do so, permits the associated feelings to enter conscious awareness gradually; this relieves the child of the pressure to continue to repress them.

In the Draw-a-Person and Draw-Your-Family exercises (DiLeo, 1973; Malchiodi, 1998), the play therapist learns about the child's perceptions of his or her own body, as well as of family relationships. When the child has a physical illness, he or she may convey this through a self-portrait even while verbally denying the significance of the diagnosis (see the case example in Goodman, Chapter 17). Robinson's analysis of a 10-year-old's family drawing (Chapter 12), in which no family members were portrayed by the child in a protective role, provided important diagnostic clues regarding the boy's sense of impending disaster.

Winnicott's (1971) "squiggle technique" is an excellent icebreaker with children who claim they cannot draw. In this situation, the therapist tells the child that no drawing ability is necessary, since the game involves the players' taking turns making pictures out of each other's scribbles. When this is employed as a projective technique, the child subsequently can be asked to select his or her favorite squiggle drawing in a series and then to make up a story about it. A chapter in the first edition of this book demonstrated the use of group squiggles with children in the setting of a shelter following an earthquake in Santa Cruz, California (Hofmann & Rogers, 1991).

Modeling clay provides a safe outlet for aggressive feelings, since the clay often requires pounding, poking, squeezing, and cutting to achieve the form a child desires. This modality lends itself to family and group play as well as individual therapy, since each member may create an individual project or the group may work on a joint product (Oaklander, 1988).

Soft Play-Doh is easier for younger children to handle than is modeling clay, and its greater malleability lends it to being squished between the fingers, thus offering an additional sensory experience. Hurley (1991) illustrates a young girl's anxious use of Plasticine (a material similar to Play-Doh) following her father's suicide by gunshot. The child created several heads that corresponded to the members of her family; she mutilated one head, and then anxiously turned to other play activities. She was not ready to talk about her father's death, but her play conveyed her anxious feelings related to her father's violent death.

Suggested Art Supplies

- Colored markers; crayons; Cray-Pas
- Paper of different colors; construction paper (full color range)
- Scissors; glue; paste; Scotch tape; stapler
- Water colors; finger paints
- Paper doilies; magazines for cutting out pictures for collages
- Modeling clay (assorted colors); Play-Doh (Kenner); rolling pins, cookie cutters, and assorted modeling tools

Doll Play

Doll play has particular appeal to preschool children of both sexes and to latency-age girls. Latency-age boys frequently choose to play with army men or soldiers, together with trucks and assorted army equipment (see Robinson's case example in Chapter 12).

Miniature bendable family dolls lend themselves to reenactment of exchanges a child has witnessed in his or her own family. The therapist can learn a great deal from watching and listening to the child's play with the family dolls. Often a preschool child unabashedly names the family dolls to correspond with his or her own family members, and/or selects their hair color and size to match those in his or her own family. In situations like these, as in my work with Michael (Chapter 3), the child's identification with the family doll play seems indisputable.

Anatomically correct dolls are now routinely used in the assessment of sexual abuse, along with a carefully sequenced line of questioning that encourages the child to demonstrate with the dolls experiences that happened to him or her (Shamroy, 1987). Strand's work with a 6-year-old girl (Chapter 5) illustrates the use of anatomically correct dolls in the assessment of family sexual abuse.

Stuffed animals sometimes take the place of human figures in a child's representational play. The child displaces onto the toy the feelings and conflicts that he or she may previously have repressed. In one example of this type of play therapy, toy mother and baby stuffed panda bears were employed in treatment with a 6-year-old child whose mother had died when he was 18 months old (Masur, 1991).

Suggested Supplies for Doll Play

- Bendable 6-inch family doll set (including mother, father, girl, boy, baby, grandmother, grandfather, teenager, woman, and man); these doll sets are available with skin and hair color to correspond to various racial groups
- Set of doll furniture including kitchen, bedroom, and bathroom, or complete playhouse (Fisher-Price)
- Life-size infant doll with bottle
- Stuffed animals: monkey, bears, "monster," and so forth
- Army men (miniatures) and assorted war equipment
- "Trouble" dolls (miniature set of seven dolls in a tiny box); therapist's explanation suggests that one doll each day of the week will "magically" work on resolving child's problems during sleep
- Medical kit, including complete equipment (stethoscope, reflex hammer, pill box, tongue depressors, thermometer, injection "needles," bandages)
- Rescue personnel (police officers, firefighters, nurses, and doctors); it is helpful to have some toy police cars and ambulances as well
- Fantasy figures: fairy godmother, Aladdin and his lamp, a witch, a mermaid, angels, and devils

The principle is to provide the child with an array of figures that will permit the widest possible expression of feelings, conflicts, and reenactments of traumatic events.

Puppet Play

The use of puppets in play therapy, like the use of dolls, rests on the assumption that the child (1) identifies with a doll or puppet, (2) projects his or her own feelings onto the play figure, and (3) displaces his or her conflicts onto the doll or puppet. Both doll and puppet play allow the child and therapist to talk about feelings and thoughts that "belong" to the doll or puppet, and that the child therefore does not have to acknowledge as his or her own. According to Woltmann (1951/1964, p. 398) "puppets are capable of representing specific personalities, either directly or indirectly, or specific sides or aspects of personalities." However, fantasy also prevails when puppets are used; a puppet that is beaten does not feel real pain, and simulated aggression and killing allow puppet play to go far beyond the limits of human endurance. Another very important feature of puppet (and doll) play is the opportunity to repeat over and over a traumatic experience and its various outcomes. Use of puppet play is described in this book by Bluestone in Chapter 10 (involving two dramatized play sessions of latency-age girls who each had a parent who died suddenly) and by Doyle and Stoop in Chapter 6 (demonstrating how puppetry can facilitate a life review process).

Puppet play has been used extensively in hospitals to help children anticipate and recover from surgery and other medical procedures (Linn, 1977, 1978; Alger, Linn, & Beardslee, 1985). Because of the distancing implicit in puppet play, a child can create a separate person that expresses thoughts and feelings the child cannot express directly. The play therapist encourages such expression through symbolic play, while also helping the child (through the puppet) find constructive ways to cope (Alger et al., 1985).

Suggested Supplies for Puppet Play

- Family hand puppets (mother, father, boy, girl, etc.)
- Animal hand puppets (an assortment that will permit the expression of a range of emotions—e.g., "neutral" characters such as rabbits or squirrels, and more "aggressive" characters such as lions or alligators)
- Finger puppets (animal or insect)
- Various fantasy or "rescue" puppet figures

Although the use of any puppet will vary in the hands of different children, the provision of a wide variety of puppets gives the child choices and permits a range of emotional expressions. I have found that it is helpful to have several puppets of one type of animal or insect, so that children can enact typical family scenes. The combined use of hand and finger puppets of the same category of animal or insect naturally connotes adult and child characters. I used these in play therapy with a 4-year-old child who had severe separation anxiety, pretending that the "mother" bee was going out to get honey to bring back to her "child" bees, who remained home with an "adult" ladybug sitter (Webb, 1996). Insect hand puppets (e.g., ladybugs, spiders, bees, dragonflies, and grasshoppers) provide useful opportunities for children to master through play their fear of insects, and to express in fantasy their "superiority" over the "small" creatures that stimulate fear in many of their peers.

Storytelling

From the time of the Bible, stories have captured the human imagination through creative use of fantasy. Stories may be told, read, or watched, depending on the circumstances of the historical moment. All methods involve distancing, identification, and projection. Children, in listening to stories, learn to exercise the power of their imaginations as they envision animal or human characters coping with situations similar in some respect to those in their own everyday lives. Children who watch television may similarly identify with the characters portrayed.

Richard Gardner's (1971) mutual storytelling technique combines the appeal and distancing component of storytelling in a play therapy approach that helps a child consider alternative solutions to problem situations. In Gardner's method, the child tells a story to which the therapist responds with an adaptation using "healthier conflict resolution," involving the same story characters and themes as in the child's story. As an additional enticement to the child's participation, Gardner uses audiotape and videotape recordings, which allow the child subsequently to hear or see himself or herself telling the stories.

Storytelling Adaptations

Although Gardner's approach is highly structured, it lends itself to various adaptations (as demonstrated in Chapter 3 of this book by my work with Michael, in which storytelling was combined with family doll play). The therapist sets a scene in a kitchen, for example, using family dolls and miniature dollhouse furniture; after introducing the doll family, the therapist invites the child to act out a family interaction by asking the child to demonstrate "what happens next."

Other adaptations of storytelling involve writing down the child's stories and putting them into a "book," with a cover drawn by the child on construction paper and the pages stapled together. Sometimes this technique is used to record a child's experiences in a crisis situation, such as an earthquake (Hofmann & Rogers, 1991); in other cases this method has been used to record the life history of children in foster care (Aust, 1981; Backhaus, 1984).

The therapist can, when appropriate, encourage the child's written fantasy by suggesting that the child write down his or her stories at home. I often give "blank books" to latency-age children as birthday gifts, in order to provide them with an outlet for their written story creations, which they can later bring to the therapy session and share.

Responding to the Child's Story

As with other creative media (i.e., art), the therapist's use of the child's story productions depends on the assessment and treatment goals in each situation. An analysis of the repeated themes in stories or art provides the therapist with diagnostic or added information related to the child's conflicts and feelings. The extent to which the therapist uses the information gained from these indirect techniques depends on the unique factors of each situation. Play therapy is both an art and a science, dependent on the skills and judgment of the therapist. Sometimes the therapist will use the fantasy material with the child in a displaced manner, keeping the disguise; at other times the therapist may question whether the child notices some resemblance between the fantasy he or she has created and the child's own life. The therapist's training and beliefs about working in a displaced manner versus making interpretations to the child's life inevitably guides the treatment approach.

Although the techniques for uncovering the child's inner world through art and stories may seem deceptively simple, the therapeutic management of and response to the child's revelations depend on a thorough understanding of child development, children's typical responses to stress, and the nature of symbolic communication. As Rubin (1984, p. 300) cautions, the therapist should "proceed with open eyes, and with respect for the value of the child, as well as the power of art." Regular supervision is essential for beginning therapists.

Board Games

Fantasy play naturally and gradually recedes in middle childhood as a child becomes more reality-oriented, and organized games begin to take precedence over imaginative play. Interest in games with rules comes to the fore between 7 and 11 years of age, when the child has achieved the level of cognitive development characterized by logical and objective thinking (Piaget, 1962). Game playing requires observance of self-discipline (waiting for one's turn), cooperation, and obeying rules (Schaefer & Reid, 1986). These ego control functions are beyond the capabilities of most preschool children.

Schaefer and Reid (1986) comment that "few clinicians are aware of the therapeutic potential of games for school-age children and teenagers. . . . most therapists associate play therapy with the clinical use of sensory–motor and pretend play with young children" (p. ix). The value of using board games with latency-age children has been cited in the professional literature (Schaefer & Reid, 1986; Nickerson & O'Laughlin, 1983). Knowledgeable child therapists view game play as a means to refine diagnosis (by observing how a child plays a game), as an opportunity to enhance ego functions (by helping the child master frustration tolerance and self-control), and as a natural route to improving the child's socialization skills (Schaefer & Reid, 1986).

Board games that hold special appeal for latency-age children include both standard commercial games and games that have been designed specifically for therapy purposes. Examples of the former are Life, Clue, and Connect Four; examples of therapeutic games are The Talking, Feeling, and Doing Game and The Ungame. These and others are listed below, with names of manufacturers. In Chapter 11 of this book, Osuna and I describe the use of an original board game to help an 8-year-old child identify and talk about his feelings.

The concept of winning and losing is implicit in most board games, through accumulation of token "chips" or through progression around a track based on the chance roll of the dice. Children's reactions to winning and losing, and their occasional attempts to change the rules and even to cheat, all become matters for therapeutic discussion. Although most games do not elicit extensive fantasy material from a child, their utility in providing an interactional experience that can be simultaneously enjoyed and analyzed ultimately proves ego-enhancing to the child.

Suggested Board Games

Standard

• Battleship (Milton Bradley)	Ages 8 to adult
• Clue (Parker Brothers)	No ages specified (probably best for 9 to adult)
• Connect Four (Milton Bradley)	Ages 7 and up
• Life (Milton Bradley)	Ages 9 to adult
• Sorry (Parker Brothers)	Ages 6 to adult
• Operation (Milton Bradley)	Ages 6 to adult

Therapeutic
- Stress Strategies (Stress Education   Ages 8 to 14
  Center, Libertyville, IL 60048)
- The Talking, Feeling, and Doing   Ages 6 to adult
  Game (Creative Therapeutics,
  155 County Road,
  Cresskill, NJ 07026)
- The Ungame (P.O. Box 6382,   Five versions: "kids" (ages 5–12),
  Anaheim, CA 92816)   teens, family, couples, all ages
- The Storytelling Card Game   Ages 4–12
  (Creative Therapeutics, as above)
- The Goodbye Game   Ages 6 to adult
  (Childswork/Childsplay,
  Secaucus, NJ 07094)

Other Assorted Play Therapy Techniques

The possibilities for using play therapeutically are limited only by the imagination and creativity of the child and therapist. Insofar as any object may be used symbolically and/or idiosyncratically, it would be impossible to discuss comprehensively or demonstrate, even in a book devoted in its entirety to play therapy, an exhaustive inventory of play therapy techniques. In more than 30 years as a play therapist, I continue to "discover" new activities to use creatively and therapeutically with children. Some of my more recent discoveries include (1) the use of sand play (the Erica method, which originated in Sweden in the 1940s but is not widely practiced in the United States; see Lowenfeld, 1967, and Dundas, 1978); (2) the use of photographs in therapy (see Krauss & Fryrear, 1983; Sedgwick, 1980; Weiser, 1988); and (3) the use of seeds, plants, and gardening. These methods have been very effective with physically ill children as a way of counteracting their own frustrations about their illness (see Wojtasik & Sanborn, 1991).

Other, less "novel" play therapy materials include the use of construction toys, such as building blocks and Lego sets; toy telephones; miniature farm animals; and miniature "villages."

A Cautionary Note

No therapy office can or should resemble a toy store! This would be overstimulating to most children and countertherapeutic. Many years ago, when renting office space on an hourly basis, I learned that it is possible to carry "the basics" for play therapy in a large satchel. These included paper, markers, scissors, tape, stapler, a few puppets, family dolls, one board game, and a small tape recorder. The selection of materials varied with the ages and interests of the particular child clients who had appointments on a particular day. Children will use their imaginations when allowed to do so, and sometimes simplicity brings benefits that diversity may confuse and obscure.

ROLE OF THE PLAY THERAPIST

In play therapy, as in every form of psychotherapy, the therapist tailors his or her interventions to the needs of each client and the specific treatment goals of each case. Ross (1959/1964, p. 121) states that "depending on the manifest needs of the child, the therapist should either take a passive observing role or an active, participating one."

Following thoughtful consideration about the implications of his or her attitude and actions on the child, the therapist chooses among the following alternative roles:

1. *Participating.* The therapist plays along with the child, being careful to follow the child's lead and not to jump ahead of the child.

2. *Limiting.* The therapist serves as auxiliary ego, attempting to strengthen the child's own ego functioning by emphasizing rules, encouraging frustration tolerance, and setting limits.

3. *Interpreting.* The therapist gently makes connections between the child's symbolic play and the child's own life. This approach should be used cautiously and only after a positive treatment relationship has been established. As previously discussed, some therapists do not interpret children's play.

Enzer (1988) enumerates the following functions of the play therapist, which also apply to other forms of psychotherapy:

- Develop a therapeutic alliance
- Help the client with understanding
- Link understanding with feelings
- Reduce troublesome feelings
- Work through defenses
- Find more acceptable modes of expressing affect

In carrying out these role functions, the play therapist may engage in the following activities sequentially, simultaneously, or selectively, according to Enzer (1988):

- Observe the child's play
- Ask the child to describe the play activity
- Suggest motivations or feelings in the context and metaphor of the play
- Focus on the child's affect or behavior
- Become part of the play itself
- Set limits when the need arises

It is clear from this, and from the many case examples in this book, that the role of the play therapist is complex. In addition to playing with the child, the therapist is simultaneously trying to understand the themes and underlying meaning of the child's play, in order to provide communication that validates the child's feelings while also sharing a new vision to help the child through his or her struggles.

TRAINING IN CHILD THERAPY

Just as a child psychiatrist must first demonstrate competence in treating adults before undertaking the board examinations for child psychiatry, I believe that mental health practitioners seeking to become child therapists should also do so only after some solid experience in working with adults. Because of their youthful dependence, work with children inevitably includes work with adults, and a family focus is often essential. Child therapists must be able to relate helpfully to parents and other caretakers as well as to children; all too often, treatment failure results from failure to engage parents or caretakers adequately as allies in children's treatment.

Many schools of social work offer elective courses in treatment of children and adolescents, and the internships of such programs on both the undergraduate and graduate levels often involve work with children and families. Fortunately, close supervision is a hallmark of these internships, since the challenges and pitfalls of working with child clients, parents, and families demand the careful attention of seasoned practitioners. Mishne (1983) views child therapy as a specialty requiring lengthy ongoing training, experience, and supervision; these help the therapist to "acquire a therapeutic objective empathic response . . . that controls against regression and acting out through and/or with patients" (p. 13).

Some child therapy training programs in different areas of the United States are listed at the end of this book. A supervised internship is an integral part of these programs, regardless of the number of years of experience or educational background of the trainees. Because of the complexity and special demands of child therapy, supervision is essential for identifying and monitoring countertransference (Webb, 1989).

GROUP AND FAMILY PLAY THERAPY

Many of the same techniques and materials appropriate to play therapy with an individual child can also be used effectively with the child and his or her family and in play therapy groups. Several chapters in this book demonstrate play therapy with children in groups: Nisivoccia and Lynn (Chapter 4) discuss the important role of group support in helping children who had witnessed violence in the home and community; Pelcovitz (Chapter 8) describes sensitive group work with children who had been sexually abused by a school employee; de Ridder (Chapter 15) details the power of a mutual support group for children affected by HIV; and Ficaro (Chapter 13) describes a combination of individual, family, and group approaches in her work with an 11-year-old girl in a substance-disordered family.

In a review of techniques for treating psychic trauma in children, Terr (1989, p. 3) states that "no generally accepted research study has established one certain technique as standard. . . . Among the individual treatment modalities available, play therapy, psychodynamic psychotherapy, cognitive and behavioral therapies, and medication hold the most promise. *A combination of several of these treatments would, in most cases, be the best program available today*" (my emphasis).

By far the majority of chapters in this book describe parent counseling, family therapy, and/or children's group therapy in addition to individual play therapy with the child. When an entire family has experienced a crisis, it is logical to treat the family members together to implement mutual support and enhance their coping skills, in addition to offering individual therapy as indicated. Since children live in a family system, a crisis experienced by one member necessarily reverberates to others.

The fact that this book focuses on play therapy as a method for treating individual children in crisis by no means denies the validity and necessity of utilizing family therapy and group therapy approaches in conjunction with individual play therapy. Readers who want more information regarding family play therapy may consult Griff (1983), Irwin and Malloy (1975), Schaefer and Carey (1994), and Ziegler (1980). Overviews of children's group therapy can be found in Schiffer (1984) and Slavson and Schiffer (1975).

PARENT COUNSELING

When a child client lives with one or both parents, the therapist must include them in the treatment plan as a vital component of the child's treatment. Lieberman (1979, p. 225) maintains that "unless parents collaborate in treatment, little can be done to help the child." Arnold (1978, p. 12) clarifies that "it is the parent's relationship with the child that is essential for the child's mental health, not the professional's relationship with the child," and states elsewhere that "An effective parent is the child's most important therapist" (p. 6). Conveying to a parent that he or she will serve as an essential ally of the therapist forms the basis for the parent–therapist alliance. Many child therapists keep this alliance vital by meeting with parents once a month to discuss their children's behavior and reactions, and by establishing a telephone policy inviting parents to notify them of any matters of concern about the children. A therapist respects the confidentiality of the child client by refraining from reporting verbatim comments made by the child in treatment, and by discussing with the parent only general issues related to the child's treatment.

Sometimes it is appropriate for a child's therapist to meet with the parent(s) in the child's presence. This should occur following advanced planning and involvement of the child with regard to the purpose of the meeting. An example of planned parent–child–therapist meetings occurred in the case of the 10-year-old girl with the nightly sleep disturbance. The treatment approach in this case involved individual play therapy with the child, in addition to child–parent–therapist sessions to implement a behavior modification approach as a supplement to the play therapy.

The ultimate method of parental involvement in a child's treatment is filial therapy (Furman, 1979; van Fleet, 1994). This method includes a diagnostic study and interviews with the child, and subsequent work with the parent(s) alone to help the parent(s) interact more effectively with the child. This is a therapy with limited goals; the parent(s) work with the therapist to help the child, who does not receive individual professional treatment.

VERSATILE APPLICATION OF PLAY THERAPY

The play therapy approaches described in this book are generally applicable to children up to 12 or 13 years of age. They can be used in a variety of health, child welfare, educational, and mental health settings by a wide range of play therapists, such as school social workers, child life specialists, early childhood educators, disaster workers, pastoral counselors, pediatric nurses, and child welfare workers, in addition to child therapists from the mental health professions of psychology, clinical social work, and psychiatry. Many of these professionals do not have formal training in play therapy, although they may have knowledge about normal and pathological child development. Our hope is that this volume will spark the interest of these professionals in delving into the world of childhood and becoming more knowledgeable and comfortable communicating with children through the symbolic language of play, as a means of helping the children overcome the effects of crises and achieve optimal growth.

REFERENCES

Alger, I., Linn, S., & Beardslee, W (1985). Puppetry as a therapeutic tool for hospitalized children. *Hospital and Community Psychiatry, 36*(2), 129–130.

Allen, F. (1942). *Psychotherapy with children.* New York: Norton.

Amster, F. (1943). Differential uses of play in treatment of young children. *American Journal of Orthopsychiatry, 13*, 62–68.

Arnold, L. E. (1978). *Helping parents help their children.* New York: Brunner/Mazel.

Aust, P. H. (1981). Using the life story book to treat children in placement. *Child Welfare, 60*, 535–560.

Axline, V. (1947). *Play therapy.* Boston: Houghton Mifflin.

Backhaus, K. (1984). Life books: Tool for working with children in placement. *Social Work, 29*(6), 551–554.

Bettelheim, B. (1977). *The uses of enchantment: The meaning and importance of fairy tales.* New York: Vintage Books.

Bettelheim, B. (1987). The importance of play. *The Atlantic Monthly,* March, pp. 35–46.

Chethik, M. (1989). *Techniques of child therapy: Psychodynamic strategies.* New York: Guilford Press.

DiLeo, J. H. (1973). *Children's drawings as diagnostic aids.* New York: Brunner/Mazel.

Dundas, E. (1978). *Symbols come alive in the sand.* Aptos, CA: Aptos Press.

Enzer, N. B. (1988). *Overview of play therapy.* Paper presented at the annual meeting of the American Academy of Child and Adolescent Psychiatry, Seattle, WA.

Erikson, E. (1964). Toys and reasons. In M. R. Haworth (Ed.), *Child psychotherapy* (pp. 3–11). New York: Basic Books. (Original work published 1950)

Freud, A. (1946). *The psychoanalytic treatment of children.* London: Imago Press. (Original work published 1926)

Furman, E. (1979). Filial therapy. In J. Noshpitz (Ed.), *Basic handbook of child psychiatry* (Vol. 3, pp. 149–158). New York: Basic Books.

Gardner, R. A. (1971). *Therapeutic communication with children: The mutual storytelling technique.* New York: Jason Aronson.

Griff, M. D. (1983). Family play therapy. In C. E. Schaefer & K. J. O'Connor (Eds.), *Handbook of play therapy* (pp. 65–75). New York: Wiley.

Hofmann, J., & Rogers, P. (1991). A crisis play group in a shelter following the Santa Cruz earthquake. In N. B. Webb (Ed.), *Play therapy with children in crisis: A casebook for practitioners* (pp. 379–395). New York: Guilford Press.

Hurley, D. (1991). The crisis of paternal suicide: Case of Cathy, age 4½. In N. B. Webb (Ed.), *Play therapy with children in crisis: A casebook for practitioners* (pp. 237–253). New York: Guilford Press.

Irwin, E. C., & Malloy, E. S. (1975). Family puppet interview. *Family Process, 14*, 179–191.

James, D. O. (1977). *Play therapy.* New York: Dabor Science.

Johnson, J. H., Rasbury, W. C., & Siegel, L. J. (1986). *Approaches to child treatment.* New York: Pergamon Press.

Klein, M. (1932). *The psychoanalysis of children.* London: Hogarth Press.

Krauss, D. A., & Fryrear, J. L. (1983). *Phototherapy in mental health.* Springfield, IL: Charles C Thomas.

Levy, D. (1938). Release therapy in young children. *Psychiatry, 1*, 387–389.

Levy, D. (1939). Release therapy. *American Journal of Orthopsychiatry, 9*, 713–736.

Lieberman, F. (1979). *Social work with children.* New York: Human Sciences Press.

Linn, S. (1977). Puppets and hospitalized children: Talking about feelings. *Journal for the Association of the Care of Children in Hospitals, 5*, 5–11.

Linn, S. (1978). Puppet therapy in hospitals: Helping children cope. *Journal of the American Medical Women's Association, 33*, 61–65.

Lowenfeld, M. (1967). *Play in childhood* . New York: Wiley.

Malchiodi, C. A. (1998). *Understanding children's drawings.* New York: Guilford Press.

Masur, C. (1991). The crisis of early maternal loss: Unresolved grief of 6-year-old Chris in foster care. In N. B. Webb (Ed.), *Play therapy with children in crisis: A casebook for practitioners* (pp. 164–176). New York: Guilford Press.

Mishne, J. M. (1983). *Clinical work with children.* New York: Free Press.

Moustakas, C. (1959). *Psychotherapy with children.* New York: Harper & Row.

Nickerson, E. T., & O'Laughlin, K. S. (1983). The therapeutic use of games. In C. E. Schaefer & K. J. O'Connor (Eds.), *Handbook of play therapy* (pp. 174–187). New York: Wiley.

Oaklander, V. (1988). *Windows to our children.* Highland, NY: Center for Gestalt Development.

Piaget, J. (1962). *Play, dreams, and imitation in childhood.* New York: Norton.

Reid, S. E. (1986). Therapeutic use of card games with learning-disabled children. In C. E. Schaefer & S. E. Reid (Eds.), *Game play* (pp. 257–276). New York: Wiley.

Ross, A. O. (1964). The practice of clinical child psychology. In M. R. Haworth (Ed.), *Child psychotherapy* (pp. 121–125). New York: Basic Books. (Original work published 1959)

Rubin, J. A. (1984). *Child art therapy* (2nd ed.). New York: Van Nostrand Reinhold.

Sarnoff, C. A. (1987). *Psychotherapeutic strategies in late latency through early adolescence.* Northvale, NJ: Jason Aronson.

Schaefer, C. E., & Carey, L. (Eds.). (1994). *Family play therapy.* Northvale, NJ: Jason Aronson.

Schaefer, C. E., & O'Connor, K. J. (Eds.). (1983). *Handbook of play therapy.* New York: Wiley.

Schaefer, C. E., & Reid, S. E. (Eds.). (1986). *Game play.* New York: Wiley.

Schiffer, M. (1984). *Children's group therapy: Methods and case histories.* New York: Free Press.

Sedgwick, R. (1980). The use of photoanalysis and family memorabilia in the study of family interaction. *Corrective and Social Psychiatry Journal, 25*(4), 137–141

Shamroy, J. A. (1987). Interviewing the sexually abused child with anatomically correct dolls. *Social Work, 32*, 165–166.

Slavson, S. R., & Schiffer, M. (1975). *Group psychotherapies for children: A textbook*. New York: International Universities Press.

Terr, L. C. (1983). Play therapy and psychic trauma: A preliminary report. In C. E. Schaefer & K. J. O'Connor (Eds.), *Handbook of play therapy* (pp. 308–319). New York: Wiley.

Terr, L. C. (1989). Treating psychic trauma in children: A preliminary discussion. *Journal of Traumatic Stress*, 2, 3–20.

van Fleet, R. (1994). *Filial therapy: Strengthening parent–child relationships through play*. Sarasota, FL: Professional Resource Press.

Walder, R. (1933). The psychoanalytic theory of play. *Psychoanalytic Quarterly*, 2, 208–224.

Webb, N. B. (1989). Supervision of child therapy: Analyzing therapeutic impasses and monitoring counter-transference. *The Clinical Supervisor*, 7(4), 61–76.

Webb, N. B. (1994). *Play therapy techniques: A clinical demonstration* [Videotape]. New York: Guilford Press.

Webb, N. B. (1996). *Social work practice with children*. New York: Guilford Press.

Weiser, J. (1988). Phototherapy using snapshots and photointeractions in therapy with youth. In C. E. Schaefer (Ed.), *Innovative interventions in child and adolescent therapy* (pp. 339–376). New York: Wiley.

Winnicott, D. W. (1971). *Playing and reality*. New York: Basic Books.

Wojtasik, S., & Sanborn, S. (1991). The crisis of acute hospitalization: Case of Seth, age 7. In N. B. Webb (Ed.), *Play therapy with children in crisis: A casebook for practitioners* (pp. 295–309). New York: Guilford Press.

Woltmann, A. G. (1964). The use of puppetry as a projective method in therapy. In M. R. Haworth (Ed.), *Child psychotherapy* (pp. 395–399). New York: Basic Books. (Original work published 1951)

Woltmann, A. G. (1964). Varieties of play techniques. In M. R. Haworth (Ed.), *Child psychotherapy* (pp. 20–32). New York: Basic Books. (Original work published 1955)

Ziegler, R. G. (1980). Task-focused therapy with children and families. *American Journal of Psychotherapy*, 34, 107–118.

PART II

The Crises of Violence and Abuse

CHAPTER 3

The Child Witness of Parental Violence

Case of Michael, Age 4, and Follow-Up at Age 16

NANCY BOYD WEBB

Parental fighting, divorce, and remarriage occur with great frequency in American homes, despite the pain and disruption that accompany these events. Such familial upheavals seriously threaten children's sense of security. Factors such as a child's age, his or her previous level of adjustment and coping ability, and the level of environmental support all shape the specific response of the child to stressful events. A preschool child, whose developmental stage is characterized by narcissism, often believes that his or her behavior caused the parents' fighting. Furthermore, when one parent leaves the home, the young child fears similar abandonment by the other parent. This anxiety can overwhelm an immature ego and precipitate a crisis state.

The case presented in this chapter depicts such a crisis in the life of a 4-year-old boy whose brief life history resonated with family turmoil, causing him to experience emotional and behavioral breakdown. The child's inability to adapt to an unraveling sequence of crisis events seriously compromised his development and interfered with his ability to relate to peers. Play therapy with the child utilized art, family dolls, and tape-recorded storytelling to encourage ventilation and verbalization of the child's anger in the playroom. This resulted in an eventual reduction of his aggressive outbursts, and in improvement in his ability to cope with his anger.

Often crises occur as multiple rather than singular events. The term "crisis" in this chapter refers to an upset of a steady state in which the individual's usual coping is inadequate to meet the perceived demands of the situation (Parad, 1977). In the case of Michael, age 4, a number of crises were identified during the initial evaluation. (Michael's age at the time of each crisis is given in parentheses.)

1. Witnessing of parental violence: Michael's mother reported being beaten by his father five times in the child's presence (Michael, between 18 and 30 months of age)
2. Father's leaving the family home (Michael, age 2½ years)
3. Parental divorce (Michael, age 4 years)
4. Mother and child's move to home of mother's fiancé (Michael, age 4 years)
5. Mother's impending remarriage (when Michael would be 4½ years)
6. Threat of child's exclusion from day care program because of his aggressive behavior (Michael, age 4¼ years)

Any one of these crises could precipitate emotional turmoil in a preschool child. Their combined impact caused Michael to feel tremendous anger, which he turned against himself and others. Without therapeutic intervention, he seemed headed for a future of acting-out behavior, as suggested by his unpredictable, uncontrollable outbursts and aggression toward other children in his day care program.

The literature on the intergenerational transmission of family violence warns that a male child who witnesses paternal abuse of the mother is at high risk for modeling similar behavior when he becomes a husband (Rosenbaum & O'Leary, 1981; Hershorn & Rosenbaum, 1985). Data from a nationally representative sample showed that "observing hitting between one's parents is more strongly related to involvement in severe marital aggression than is being hit as a teenager by one's parent" (Kalmuss, 1984, p. 11).

In addition to potential *future* repercussions stemming from witnessing parental violence, more immediate aftereffects for the child witness take the form of adjustment difficulties similar to the behaviors and reactions found in a group of children who were physically abused by their parents (Jaffee, Wolfe, Wilson, & Zak, 1986). Problems reported on the Child Behavior Checklist (Achenbach & Edelbrock, 1981) included destroying things belonging to self or others, fighting, disobedience at home or school, and feelings of being unloved and lonely. Jacobson (1978) reports that the parental behavior most closely associated with a child's poor adjustment or dysfunction is physical violence. Furthermore, preschool children who witness conjugal violence exhibit delay or absence in the development of empathy and of other prosocial behaviors (Fantuzzo et al., 1991). These authors emphasize that the impact on preschool children of witnessing interparental violence is greater than the impact on older children.

Even very early trauma was remembered in behavior and was reenacted in play in a study (Terr, 1988) of 20 children who were under the age of 5 at the time of documented traumatic events. Terr (1988, p. 103) concluded that "traumatic events create lasting visual images" that later may be verbalized or reenacted in play, which often "converts passive into active experiences." This appeared to be the operating dynamic in the case of Michael, who surely felt helpless in witnessing his parents' fighting and whose play in therapy enabled him to identify with powerful, destructive fantasy figures.

In addition to the traumatic experience of witnessing parental aggression, Michael had to endure the loss of his father—initially in his father's departure from the home, and subsequently in the father's frequent failures to appear for scheduled visits. The attachment literature documents the significance of a child's attachment to the father as well as to the mother from the age of 8½ months onward (Kotelchuck, 1972; Lamb, 1976). It is probable that Michael was attached to his father and that he experienced a sense of loss when his father left the home when Michael was 2½, since his father had been his regular caretaker while his mother was working. Bowlby's (1960, 1961) research demonstrated that children as young as 6 months of age displayed sadness and grief following the loss of loved objects. Kelly and Wallerstein (1975) found that 44% of children aged 2½ to 6 years old in their study were designated as in "significantly deteriorated psychological condition(s)" 1 year following parental divorce. Michael came for therapy a few months after his parents' divorce was final. Although he could not cognitively comprehend the true meaning of the divorce because of his young age, he nonetheless had experienced the loss of his father. His aggressive behavior conveyed his confusion, helplessness, and fury.

Following the death of a parent, a child may attempt to compensate for the loss through identification with the interests, mannerisms, traits, and behavior of the dead parent (Gardner, 1983). In Michael's case, his father was not dead, but was absent because of divorce. Michael, however, still loved his father and wanted to be strong like him. Through identification he could keep his absent father with him, and by assuming the ferocious, powerful role he had witnessed and admired in his father, he could banish the helpless and powerless feelings of a 4-year-old.

The treatment of a child such as Michael must respect the child's feelings of grief and encourage appropriate expression of the loss, both symbolically through play and verbally. In Michael's case, his therapy also needed to provide a safe place for expressing the confusion, helplessness, and anger related to his witnessing of violent behavior between his parents. Terr (1989), referring to David Levy's (1939) "abreactive therapy," states that Levy's approach—which involves no interpretations by the therapist of the child's spontaneous play—works well with very young, externally stressed children. When the therapist enunciates the accompanying feelings being played out by the child, abreaction can occur, according to Terr (1989, p. 14), and "an entire treatment through play may be engineered without stepping far beyond the metaphor of the 'game.'" Much of the early therapy with Michael involved such abreaction, with statements by the therapist (myself) naming the feelings he was expressing, without making the connections to his own life. Michael's pressured need to "play out" his experiences dominated the first phase of therapy, conveying his need to discharge his tensions in a safe place where he was accepted. Eth and Pynoos (1980), referring to the impact of violence on a child's emerging pattern of identification, suggest that long-term psychodynamic therapy may be necessary to free a child from the disabling legacy of violence. Michael's therapy, which lasted a year and a half, not only resulted in symptom reduction, which facilitated a healthier adjustment for him in his present life; it also strengthened his coping ability by permitting alternative methods for expressing his anger.

THE CASE: MICHAEL SPIVAK, AGE 4

Presenting Problem

Michael's mother, at the insistence of his day care teacher, consulted me about her 4-year-old son. The teacher was concerned because Michael bullied other children, had frequent tantrums, and was verbally abusive to his teachers. Mrs. Spivak, who had been recently divorced from Michael's father after an 18-month separation, shared the teacher's concern about Michael. She was also worried about his bad temper and tendency to cry a lot at home.

Family Information

Mrs. Spivak and Michael had recently moved in with her fiancé. The mother's re-marriage was to occur in 4 months. Michael's father (who was living with another woman and her teenage daughter) visited Michael erratically, according to Mrs. Spivak, and had been physically abusive to her in front of Michael on several occasions prior to the separation. We know that the traumatic impact of witnessing violence is heightened when the victim is the child's primary caretaker (Fick, Osofsky, & Lewis, 1994).

The family composition at the time of the initial evaluation was as follows:

Michael	Age 4 years, 3 months
Mrs. Spivak	Age 32; divorced; employed as a bank teller; engaged to Mr. Carbone
Mr. Carbone ("Bill")	Age 62; divorced; father of three adult sons with whom he ran a restaurant business; had several grandchildren Michael's age
Mr. Spivak	Age 35; divorced; employed by telephone company; visited Michael erratically; living with girlfriend and her teenage daughter

First Interview (Parents)

When a problem involves a child under 10 years of age, I usually see the relevant adult(s) alone prior to seeing the child in one or more subsequent evaluation interviews. The purpose of the initial interview is to obtain a detailed history of the problem and a developmental history of the child. It is also important to discuss with the parent(s) how to prepare the child for the upcoming evaluation. The parents can be instructed to state clearly and nonpunitively to the child that they are concerned about how best to help him or her, and that they have already spoken with someone who helps children and families.

In this case I wanted a fuller description of the range and intensity of the presenting problem, including the response of the school personnel and the parents to Michael's outbursts. In addition, I wanted to know more about the extent of the parental fighting that Michael had witnessed, as well as what Michael had been told about the reason for the separation and divorce. Another important factor to be evaluated was the quality of the child's relationship with both his father and his future stepfather.

Mrs. Spivak and Mr. Carbone came together for the intake interview. Mrs. Spivak presented as an attractive woman, whose eyes teared up frequently as she spoke of her concern for her son. Mr. Carbone, a kindly, grandfatherly man, conveyed his affection for Michael, whom he had known for over a year and whom he described as "spunky," "strong-willed," and "very bright."

Michael's developmental history was unremarkable except for speech, which occurred early (6 months) and was "advanced," according to the mother. Mrs. Spivak had worked until the day of Michael's birth, and she returned to work when he was 4 months old. Michael was cared for sometimes by his father (who worked nights) and sometimes by a sitter in the sitter's home. He entered day care at age 3½.

According to Mrs. Spivak, when Michael was a toddler, his father had lost his job several times; Mr. Spivak alternated between working 7 days a week and being at home unemployed during this period. He also drank excessively and physically abused Mrs. Spivak five times in front of Michael. One fight occurred in the kitchen and resulted in both parents' falling on the floor on top of Michael, who was then 18 months old. Mrs. Spivak's injuries on that occasion caused facial bleeding and necessitated a trip to the emergency room. The mother believed that Michael's present fear of the sight of blood originated from witnessing this fight.

Currently, Mr. Spivak had visitation privileges every other weekend. However, he frequently disappointed Michael by not appearing for a scheduled visit. The mother had told Michael that the reason she and his father were divorced was that they didn't love each other any more. Michael knew that his mother and Mr. Carbone, whom he called "Bill," planned to be married, and he said, "Then I'll have two daddies." Mr. Carbone stated that he liked to read to Michael at night, and that they spent time together taking care of several dogs Mr. Carbone was raising to enter in dog shows.

Mrs. Spivak said that she disciplined Michael either verbally or by withholding privileges (TV watching). Mr. Spivak had never hit Michael. Sometimes when Michael was angry, he scratched his face and pulled his eyelids down on his cheek, or poked himself in the eye with his finger. Bedtime was frequently a problem, and the teacher had told the mother that she thought Michael was overtired. The mother believed that Michael "resisted" falling asleep, and at night he often cried out and moaned in his sleep. His favorite play activities included toy spaceships, robots, and army men. He did not have friends in their neighborhood and usually played alone.

The day care teacher elaborated on the presenting problem in a telephone conference. She described a child who seemed "angry all the time"—who either ignored his peers or yelled at them, shaking his fist menacingly. When he was frustrated, he paced up and down or stamped his feet and cried. He was also destructive and had threatened to cut his sneakers or the tablecloth with scissors. The day care director viewed Michael as a very bright but immature and explosive child who lost control easily.

First Interview (Child)

The mother had prepared Michael for his first interview according to my suggestions. A cute boy with excellent speech, Michael brought a Mickey Mouse doll with him and showed no separation anxiety about leaving his mother to come with me into the playroom. I told Michael, "I am a doctor who helps children and families with their troubles and their worries." Michael responded that he had "lots of worries," and elaborated by mentioning headaches and stomachaches. I clarified that I was not a medical doctor, saying, "I help children sometimes by talking with them and sometimes by playing."

Michael displayed age-appropriate knowledge of numbers and colors, and he spoke clearly with an excellent vocabulary. He conveyed a sense of bravado in the session, flexing his muscles, inviting me to feel his biceps, and referring to himself as "big and strong." He denied any fears or feelings of sadness and denied that he fought with other children, although he remembered that his parents used to fight, and he admitted to trying to fight his daddy one time.

Preliminary Assessment and Treatment Plan

This case involved a 4-year-old in crisis—a child who had repeatedly witnessed his parents' violent relationship during the first 2½ years of his life and who, chrono- logically in the Oedipal stage, now faced the task of affirming his male identity with a father who had physically hurt his mother and frequently disappointed him by erratic visits. Michael's show of bravado in flexing his muscles and referring to him- self as "big and strong" suggested that he viewed muscular strength as very desir- able. Indeed, this is the fantasy of many 4-year-old boys. However, in Michael's case, achieving this identity implied hurting others, and this put him into conflict with the adults he most wanted to please—his mother and his teachers. In a paradoxical, no-win situation, he vented his anger at himself in self-destructive behavior (pok- ing at his eyes) or in futile foot-stomping rages at day care.

Michael had witnessed the physical abuse of his mother between the ages of 18 and 30 months. This age spans the separation–individuation phase of development (Mahler, Pine, & Bergman, 1975), when a young child is developing object constancy and learning that "good" and "bad" qualities can be fused in the same person. In Michael's case, his father was sometimes the "good" parent (when he took care of him) and at other times was aggressive and "bad" toward his mother. The father eventually left the home and frequently failed to visit when Michael expected him. The undependability of the attachment object (father) created intense anxiety and feelings of insecurity in the child, which in turn provoked rage. Michael had no suitable outlet for his anger. He admitted that he tried to fight his father, but his father was seldom present now, and so his aggression was turned toward either him- self or others.

Recently, a new and different father figure had entered Michael's life. This cir- cumstance promised another view of masculinity—one that included kindness to ani- mals and people. When Michael said proudly, "Then I'll have two daddies," I realized the danger of the child's splitting his perceptions into the "good daddy" and the "bad daddy." The mother's obvious pleasure at her upcoming marriage and choice of hus- band seemed to bode well for Michael's future well-being. However, the uncertain role of Michael's father in the child's future required further exploration.

Reflecting on Michael's presenting symptoms several years after I described them in the first edition of this book, I now see many reasons for considering a diagnosis of posttraumatic stress disorder. These included Michael's sleep disturbance (diffi- culty falling asleep and nightmares); his irritability and outbursts of anger; and his aggressive play reenactments of brutal fight scenes (to be described below). Taken together, these symptoms strongly suggested that Michael had been traumatized by witnessing his parents' violent physical battles.

The treatment plan included weekly play therapy sessions for Michael and once-a-month parent counseling sessions with the mother and future stepfather. In addition, an observational visit to the day care center was planned, and I offered to be available for telephone consultation to the day care director and Michael's teacher. Finally, I planned to contact Michael's father and offer him the opportunity to meet with me, to obtain his views about his child's development and to help me assess and encourage his plans for future involvement with Michael.

Specific treatment goals in working with Michael included the following:

1. Helping the child realize that the divorce was not his fault
2. Reassuring the child that his mother would not abandon him
→ 3. Helping the child express his anger verbally and symbolically through play
4. Helping the child toward a masculine identity that included both strength and kindness

Recommendations for Michael's mother and future stepfather were that they should convey these ideas to Michael:

1. Reassurance about their love for him and their wish to have him in their *new* family
2. The understanding that hitting was *not* permitted, but that verbal expression of anger was encouraged
3. Support for his desire to see his father, with no negative verbalization from them about the father

Play Therapy Sessions

First Eight Sessions: Summary

The early work with Michael involved developing the treatment relationship and obtaining a fuller understanding of his conflicts. I usually began the sessions by asking routinely about day care, about visits with his father, and about how he was sleeping. Michael knew that these issues were connected with coming to therapy, and he sometimes would admit to being involved in a fight at "school" (day care) or to having trouble sleeping because of ghosts, the existence of which he never doubted because of the *Ghostbusters* movies and toy replicas.

Michael's ability to discuss his "problems" and "worries" was understandably quite limited because of his age. Therefore, after 5 or 10 minutes of conversation and snacks (which usually began the session), Michael would ask to draw or play, and the therapy moved to the level of symbolic communication.

Michael's most frequently chosen activity during the first eight sessions was drawing, accompanied by a steady stream of commentary, which he liked to have me write on each drawing as he worked. The subjects of Michael's art included space capsules, robots, whales, sharks, and space invaders. War and violent destruction were constant themes, as good and bad "Voltrons" with long swords attacked one another and became obliterated in blood and whirlpools. (See sketch on book jacket.) Often it was difficult for me to keep up with the fast-paced violent action, with body parts being chopped off and the "bad" fantasy figure almost always defeating the "good."

Michael's absorption in the imaginary violent world he created on paper was impressive. The robots were vividly real to him, and he would become exasperated with me when I occasionally interrupted to ask for clarification or repetition of details. After finishing a drawing that, following a 20-minute battle scene, consisted of a mass of red and black scribbles, Michael would ask me to read the story connected to the drawing. As I began to read, Michael would correct my version by adding details with an annoyed voice, suggesting that I was not fully capturing the richness of the violence as he conceived it.

This was true. It was literally impossible to keep up with the pressured portrayal of this child's primitive rage fantasies. He seemed to feel driven to produce violent scenes, and he resisted vehemently any of my attempts to offer a different ending with the "good" hero winning.

I wondered at times whether Michael's steady outpouring of blood and gore provided beneficial relief to him. Was this a "playing out" of his conflicts, just as an adult in therapy "talks out" his or her pain? How much of this violent play would be necessary before he moved toward more "constructive" solutions? Was Michael "stuck"? And was there a danger that playing destructively in sessions would fan the fires of Michael's aggression and cause it to spread uncontrolled into his real world?

I also analyzed my own feelings about the child's destructive play. Was I trying to move Michael away from the violence because it made me uncomfortable, or because I doubted the validity of his cathartic expression? It certainly was true that sessions with Michael were intense and often left me feeling that a whirlwind had blown through my office, despite the fact that Michael was *not* hyperactive (and in fact had an excellent attention span for his age). He really *worked* in therapy. I realized that Michael's play stimulated in me some of the confusion he felt about his own life, in a parallel process. He made me feel overwhelmed.

As a means of exploring the tenacity of Michael's need to express violent themes, I decided to introduce some new play materials into the next session. I planned to offer Michael a set of eight bendable family dolls and some dollhouse kitchen furniture. I also decided to audiotape the session as a means of analyzing Michael's verbalizations. Michael had been introduced to the family dolls in the evaluation session but had not played with them subsequently.

Ninth Session

The ninth session began with the usual snack and review of Michael's week. Michael did not report on any matters that seemed to require exploration. I then told Michael that I had something different today: the doll family Michael had already seen, plus some kitchen furniture and a tape recorder. If Michael wanted to make up some stories about the family, I would record them, and then we could play them back and he could hear his own voice. This appealed to Michael, and he spent about 5 minutes experimenting with the use of the tape recorder. (The doll family consisted of a mother, father, little boy, little girl, grandfather, grandmother, teenage girl, and adult woman [teacher/babysitter]). A small rocking horse and a set of kitchen furniture were on the play table.

Content of Session	Rationale/Analysis
THERAPIST (*speaking into tape recorder*): This is Michael, and he's going to make up a story.	
CHILD (*in falsetto voice*): The little boy is going to ride on the rocking horse. Ohhhhh! (*Puts boy doll on miniature rocking horse and rocks it vigorously. The doll falls off. Imitates crying sound and then puts little girl on rocking horse and repeats.*) Now I'm going on the rocking horse (*crying noises*).	
T: They're *both* crying. Now the mommy's coming in (*holds mother doll*). What's she going to say? (*Moving mother doll toward child dolls.*)	
C: (*Continues to make crying sounds.*)	
T: Oh, you children! You're crying, you're crying!	
C: We fell off the rocking chair.	
T: Oh (*comforting tone*), that's too bad! You just come and sit on my lap and you'll feel better.	I am trying to see how Michael will respond to comforting.
C (*in normal voice*): I feel better (*laughs*).	
T (*commenting on child's play actions*): Now they're getting on the horse again. Two together.	
C: Rock, rock, rock, rock (*sing-song*). (*The child dolls fall off again and start crying again; then child himself abruptly falls off the chair in which he is seated and looks at therapist with a very surprised expression.*)	Does Michael want to sit on my lap?
T: Whoops! You just fell, too! Are you all right? I'm sorry. You fell down.	
C: I'm all right. (*Sings cheerfully and briefly, no words; resumes playing, making the two child dolls fight.*)	He seems reassured but moves to more aggressive play.
C: This is the new karate. Boop!	
T: Are the kids playing karate?	I'm checking to see that I under-
C: Yeah! Bop! Ugh (*Grunting noises.*)	stand correctly.
T: One kicked the other one. In comes the daddy (*holding father doll*), and he says, "What are you kids doing, kicking each other?"	
C: We're doing karate!	
T (*in father's voice*): I don't want you to hurt each other!	

C: We're not (*then crying sounds as doll play fight continues*).

T: The little girl is crying because the little boy kicked her! Now what's going to happen?

C (*crying sounds continue*): The father's going to come and pick her up and spank the little boy.

I let Michael control the play, according to the usual practice in play therapy.

T (*taking part of father*): You shouldn't have kicked her. You're a bad boy. You shouldn't have kicked your sister. I'm going to spank you. Bam. Bam. Bam. (*Father doll spanks boy doll.*)

C: (*Cries; says in an aside, "This will be my room."*)

I'm wondering if it's helpful for me do this because of the parental violence in the house. But this is what Michael has directed.

T (*in father's voice*): You go to your room, and you stay there. (*To child*) What's the daddy going to do to the little girl?

I am again asking Michael to direct play.

C: Pick her up.

T (*in father's comforting voice*): You poor sweetie! Do you feel better now?

C (*in normal voice*): When I get a baby sister, I'm going to give her a hug, and I'm not going to hit her. We're going to play with my "pewter."

T: "Pewter"?

C: It plays games [i.e., "computer"].

T: You're going to let your baby sister play with it?

C: Yeah! Only when she's 4.

T: And then how old will you be?

C: Same age as her.

Michael departs from play and identifies girl doll as his future baby sister. (His mother and Bill do indeed have a baby girl 9 months after their wedding. However, this was a fantasy at this point, possibly stimulated by his mother's intention/wish. I don't know this for a fact.)

Preoperational thinking.

T: Really? I thought you might be older because you have a head start on her. How can you be 4 and she be 4 when she's not born yet?

C: She's not born yet! When we get the house, I'm going to have her.

T: Later on.

I know he can't answer this, but I wonder how he will respond. Sounds as if there has been some planning for the future.

C: Today I'm not getting the new house. (*Returns to doll play; picks up girl child doll and says in falsetto*): I feel better, Daddy.

I'm intrigued that he wants to continue the play.

T: The little girl feels all better. What about the little boy? He's still up in his room.

C: He doesn't like his room (*motions to therapist to resume playing with the father doll*).

I wonder if he's talking about himself here.

T: What's the daddy going to say to the little boy?

C: He's [the little boy] going to say (*falsetto*) I'm sorry, Daddy. I won't do that again.

T: And what does the daddy say to him?

C (*in strong, "male" voice*): If I see you do that again, you're going to get a *real* spanking. (*In falsetto voice*) I'm sorry, baby sister. (*Then makes little girl doll kick little boy doll, and little boy begins to cry.*) Wa-a-a-a!

Michael's mother says that neither parent had used corporal punishment, so this must be a reflection of Michael's own fear of aggression from his father.

T: Now he's crying! And now what's the daddy saying? What's going on here?

C (*falsetto*): First he kicked me, now I kicked him.

T (*in father's voice*): Oh, you children are impossible! I don't know what to do with you!

C (*aside*): Put me in my bedroom.

Michael identifies male doll as himself. He is directing the play.

T (*in father's voice*): You have to go upstairs and go to your room at once.

C (*crying sounds*): She kicked me!

T (*in father's voice*): See, that's what happens when you kick people. It hurts, and you get hurt yourself.

C (*normal voice*): Guess how many [times] I got lost from my mom?

Sudden transition.

T: How many?

C: Twice.

T: You got lost!

C: Yup.

T: Where were you? In a store?

C: (*No response; silence.*)

T (*repeats question*): Where were you when you got lost?

C: I got lost twice. And I don't want to tell you.

T: You don't want to tell me! Were you afraid? It's not fun to get lost!

I wonder what Michael is defending against.

C: Yeah. I couldn't find my mom.

T: What did you do? Did you speak to someone? Did you say to someone, "I'm lost"?

C: Yeah.

T: Did they help you find your mother?

C: No.

T: They didn't?!

C: No.

T: Did your mommy find you?

C: (*Nods yes.*)

T: And what did she say to you?

C: She said (*funny voice*) Oh! Why did this boy get lost?

T (*repeats*): Why *did* you get lost?

> Will he tell now? I sense that this is "loaded."

C: 'Cause I *love* to get lost!

T: You do (*surprised voice*)? Why?

C: 'Cause I like to.

T: You like to!

C: 'Cause I like to find my daddy.

> Now I get it! This is so sad!

T: You go to find your daddy.

C: Yeah. But he's not there. (*His voice is full of disappointment.*)

T (*repeats sadly*): But he's not there.

C (*quickly and almost unintelligibly*): So I trade him for a new Bill.

T: You're looking for a new Bill?

C: No. The same Bill that I have before.

> I am confused here.

T: You were looking for Bill and you went the wrong way?

(*Pause.*)

T: You thought you were looking for your daddy?

(*Interruption: sound of loud fire whistle interrupting session.*) [*Note:* Office is located next to a firehouse.]

> I have to think quickly about the significance of this sequence. It seems that since Michael could not find his "real" daddy, he will settle for the father figure who is current in his life.

T: That's that fire whistle again.

C: What happened?

T: There must be a fire someplace. The fire engine's going to go and put out the fire.

> Interruption in the flow of very significant material. Will we be able to stay with the topic, or will Michael be distracted? I am worried and annoyed.

C: Why?

T: Because people don't want to leave the fire burning. I don't know where it is.

C: Maybe it's coming from *my* house.

T: I don't think so.

C: Why?

T: Because you live too far away. This fire must be someplace close by.

> Michael lives 45 minutes from the office.

C: No. It's at *my* house.

T: I don't think so. Is Bill home at your house today?

He is egocentric and also "expects the worst."

C: Yes. Mommy dropped him off first. I was sleeping.

T: You were sleeping in the car?

I'm trying to offer reassurance that the "protector" is at home.

C (*returning to doll play; in falsetto; picks up child doll*): Daddy, Daddy.

Michael returns to play with father doll. I am relieved.

T (*repeats, trying to encourage child to continue*): Daddy, please wake up. I want to talk to you.

C (*in Daddy's voice*): What child?

T: What does the little boy want to say to the daddy?

I want Michael to select the father's words.

C: Daddy, I love you! Daddy, I'm sorry, I'm sorry! (*Father doll hugs the little boy doll.*) I love you, too.

Which "Daddy" is he talking to? His own father or Bill?

T (*commenting on child's play; he is grasping all the dolls in his two fists*): Everyone's all hugging each other. The daddy and the little boy and the little girl and the mommy and the gramma and grampy are all hugging each other, and the teacher [adult female]. And they're all happy and no one's fighting any more. No one is kicking and no one is fighting.

A very moving scene. The tension level has diminished. Is this forgiveness for misdeeds?

C: We're all the family. Can I hear my voice now?

T: Yes. (*Therapist rewinds tape and child listens intently to the entire replay, smiling broadly at the end.*)

This is a natural stopping point. I am very moved by Michael's wish to have his family together.

It was time to conclude the session after the replay, so Michael and I put the dolls away, and I gave him his appointment card for next week to give to his mother in the waiting room.

In this session Michael initiated punishment for aggression, apology, and finally forgiveness. Michael was no longer stuck in repetition of violence; he was envisioning through his play how he would be forgiven after apology, and loved despite his angry acting-out behavior. The change in play material from art to family dolls and tape-recorded storytelling stimulated reenactment of the child's life situation.

The child's mourning search for the lost father followed his early aggressive play with child dolls. It suggested that the two events were connected in the child's thinking. Did Michael think he had driven his father away because he was bad? ("Daddy, I'm sorry, I'm sorry!"). This would bear watching in future sessions, as would the rapid replacement of the lost father. It was impossible to determine which "Daddy" was intended in the concluding reunion scene, but my hope was that Michael was beginning to merge the two male father figures.

My role was not to interpret any of Michael's play, but to participate in the play at his direction. I did provide the new play materials, but the script of the play was

Michael's, and in my demeanor I attempted to convey acceptance of him and a wish to understand all of his feelings and his conflicts.

Tenth Session

Prior to the next session, Mrs. Spivak had telephoned me to report that Michael's behavior had deteriorated in day care following a weekend visit with his father. Michael had tried to strangle a child, had bitten another child (drawing blood), and had thrown rocks when he was on the playground. His teacher was threatening to exclude him from an upcoming school outing. The mother was very concerned about Michael—not only because the day care staff was upset, but because the wedding was to take place in 2 weeks and Mrs. Spivak hoped that Michael would not behave aggressively with Bill's grandchildren at the reception.

When I went to the waiting room to greet Michael, he was sitting with his head on his mother's lap. His mother told me that he did not want to come today. I said, "Maybe Michael has had a tough week, and I'd like to help him with that." With this mild encouragement, Michael stood up and accompanied me, carrying with him two plastic toys he had brought from home, which he called the Land Shark and the Bashasaurus.

Michael put his toys on the floor, and then immediately asked for the doll family and began playing with the boy and girl dolls and the rocking horse, as in the beginning of the previous session. Usually when a child brings items from home, I initiate discussion about them; however, Michael seemed very purposeful in his intentions to play with the doll family, and I decided to let the play evolve naturally. After a brief segment consisting of the child dolls' falling off the horse and crying, the following exchange occurred:

Content of Session	Rationale/Analysis
THERAPIST: What's the little boy going to say to the little girl?	
CHILD: I hate you!	
T: Why do you hate her!	
C: Bop! Oh! Oh! Oh!	
T: They're fighting. What are they fighting about?	
C: Bop. Bop.	
T: They're fighting. Do you know what's going to happen? This is the teacher, and she's gong to say, "Why are you children fighting?"	I am trying to tie it in events at day care this past week.
C: 'Cause we like to fight all day.	
T: Why?	I know that "why" questions are often impossible for children to answer, but I'm reaching for sources of guilt or anxiety.
C: Bop. Whop.	
T: You're going to hurt each other. One of you may start to bleed.	

C: Bleed! Bop. Whop.

T: And then what's going to happen?

C: Oh! Oh!

T: And then what's the teacher going to do?

C: I don't know.

T: Does the little girl want the teacher to pick her up? And sit in her lap?

Will the child doll accept a comforting adult?

C (*sing-song voice*): The little girl fell down off the cliff (*knocks child doll on floor*).

Michael ignores my attempt to guide.

T: She fell off the cliff! That's pretty serious!

C: The little boy pushed her off the cliff.

T: So now what's going to happen?

I am pursuing the concept from last session that aggression has consequences.

C: He's going to be punished (*sad voice*).

T: How's he going to be punished?

C: He has to stay away.

T: He can't play any more (*sad voice*). How does he feel?

I'm simulating day care events.

C: Bad (*sad voice*).

T: He feels very bad, doesn't he?

C: Can I hear my voice now?

Michael elects to distance himself from bad/sad feelings by asking for tape replay.

T: Yes (*rewinds and replays tape*).

(*Pause.*)

T: This is the little boy, and he's living with his mommy, and he's going to go to visit his daddy in his house over here. It's the weekend. This is the daddy's house over here.

I attempt to explore Michael's weekend with his father. I set up the beginning of a play scene.

C: Why did the daddy move?

Michael may be asking about his real-life situation.

T: Because the mommy and the daddy don't love each other any more, and they don't live together any more. But the daddy still loves the little boy, so the little boy's going to go and visit him for the weekend, and you tell me what they are going to do.

C: She's going on the bridge. Oh! (*Makes child doll fall again, as in previous story.*)

T: She's going to fall down.

C: She fell down on the cliff. Oh! (*More—unintelligible.*)

Same theme as in earlier story.

T: Did you go out for a hike over the weekend? Did you go out on a cliff!

I'm trying to understand the derivation of the "cliff" play.

C: Goo, goo, goo (*shakes head no*). The grampa is sleeping. This little girl wants to sit down and eat. She's eating her lunch.

T: This is the daddy's house! And is he going to give the little boy lunch, too?

C: No! It's the *mommy's* house (*emphasis*).

T: So here's the mommy (*holding mother doll*).

C: She's going to open something. (*Little girl doll begins to cry.*) Oh, oh, oh, Mommy.

T: What's Mommy going to do?

C: She slammed the lunch apart. She's kicking it off the table.

T: Why would she do that?

C: 'Cause she has to do it. She likes to throw it on the table. Ah, oh, oh!

T: Is Mommy upset?

C: No. Mommy's fine. She's happy. Ah! Bop! Bop! Ugh! (*Struggling noises.*)

T: The mommy and daddy are fighting.

C: (*Knocks down kitchen chairs and table and continues to make fighting noises.*)

T: Everyone's falling down, and the kitchen is falling apart.

C: (*Noises/struggling and grunting noises; continues for 2 minutes with fight scene and noises.*)

T: And what's the little girl doing?

C: You mean the big girl, the mommy?

T: No, the little one. Is she still on the floor?

C: She's tired. 'Cause the daddy . . . She punched him on the tush and fell down. Can I hear my voice now?

T: Yes you can (*rewinds and plays the tape*). (*After replay, child resumes fight.*)

T: The little boy and little girl are back in the kitchen fighting.

C: (*Fighting noises.*)

T: See if you can help them make up and be friends.

C: No! They want to be fighting. Oh! Bam!

T: They already finished their fight. Now they want to be friends.

Again, I am trying to reconstruct the weekend visit with his father.

This is confusing! He may be mixing up his mom's current status with a past memory.

Is this a reconstruction of one of the fights Michael witnessed?

I'm trying to help Michael verbalize the feelings of the child witness to the fight.
Michael moves away from memory of trying to fight his father. I recall that in the first session with me, Michael had spoken about hitting his daddy once.

I am trying to initiate self-control.

I am unsuccessful in my attempt to direct his play.

C: (*Continues the fight.*)

T: How can they be friends?

C: They knock their brains out.

T: That's not very friendly! Imagine this is the babysitter (*introduces new doll*). I'm going to come over and say, "You chidren are fighting too much. I want you to come and sit on my lap."

Michael really *needs* to play out his aggression.

C: No! We like to fight all day (*continues fighting*). We knock your brains out all day.

T: Come on! Let's have some snacks. Let's go to the refrigerator and get some ice cream. Here's some ice cream for the little girl (*smacks lips*), and here's some for the little boy. The little boy and the little girl are going to sit down at the table. Let's sit down and enjoy our snack.

I am deliberately trying to interrupt the fight scene and change the pace.

C: Put all the ice cream on the table.

T: Now we're going to have a little party. What kind of ice cream do you want?

C: Vanilla and chocolate.

He joins me for fantasy food.

T: Yummy. What's the little girl's name?

C: Jessica.

This is the name of Bill's grand-daughter.

T: And what's the little boy's name?

C: Michael.

He identifies with boy doll.

T: They like to have a snack.

C: How about she (*referring to sister doll*)?

T: Is she going to have some, too?

C: (*Nods yes.*) And soon, who comes in (*holding mother and father dolls*)?

T: There's the mommy and the daddy.

C: (*Begins having Mother and Daddy fight.*) Do you want a bash in the mouth? (*Loud screams.*) (*Michael now begins playing with the Land Shark toy he brought to the session, putting the child doll into the Land Shark's mouth and speaking with a very angry voice.*)

Michael cannot accept oral nurturing for long before moving to oral aggression.

C: Yeow!!

The violence is escalating.

T: You've got the little girl in the Land Shark's mouth. Poor little girl!

C (*making chewing noises and groans*): Mmmmmm!

T: What's the mommy going to say when she sees her little girl in such trouble?

C (*high-pitched voice, unintelligible*): Grampa.

He identifies a relative as a helper.

T: Where's my little girl? Help! Help me, Grampa! We've got to rescue her.

C: And you saw the big Land Shark coming. Then the Bashasaurus came to bash his head off, like that (*manipulating a cannonball on a string and swinging it to hit any objects in its way*). Ah, ha ha ha (*menacingly*).

T: Well, she's awfully frightened, but I think she's going to be all right.

I'm trying to name the feelings and give reassurance. Michael seems to ignore me.

C (*speaking as Bashasaurus*): With the Land Shark in my way, watch out.

T: Now what are this daddy and this grampy going to do?

I'm aware of trying to end the violence.

C (*speaking as father/grandfather*): They say, "Get that girl out or I'm going to hurt you."

T (*speaking to Land Shark*): Yes. You've got to give us back our child. Open your mouth and let her come out.

C: Hey! Let *me* do this problem. Bash in the mouth. Bimbo! (*Bashasaurus attacks Land Shark.*) Bash!

Is Michael identifying with Bashasaurus?

T: He's [Bashasaurus] going to rescue the little girl.

C: (*Continues battle, with Bashasaurus attacking the Land Shark; extended fight scene.*)

T: That must be all the Land Shark can take.

C: And this little boy's getting up. (*Child doll punches Land Shark.*)

I'm also feeling that this has gone too far!

T: He's going to hit him too. And I think that's the end of the Land Shark. He couldn't still do that after everyone's hitting him like that. That must be the end of him. He must be opening his mouth up, and the little girl is going to say, "Let me out of here. I want to get out of this Shark's mouth."

The doll punches the Land Shark just as Michael hit his father. I am attempting to conclude this violent scene.

C: (*Says something menacing and continues to fight, putting boy doll in Land Shark's mouth.*)

T: Isn't someone going to rescue those poor children? Now he has two in his mouth. Isn't someone going to rescue them?

It's starting up again!

Clearly, he is not going to let *me* change this drama!

An extended fight scene followed, in which the Bashasaurus and the Land Shark continued to fight. All of the family dolls were helpless in the battle, and all of them ended up again in the mouth of the Land Shark. Michael then resumed his attacking play, with the doll family sitting in the cab of the Bashasaurus and trying to attack the Land Shark. Michael's voice was angry as he repeatedly had the cannonball hit the Land Shark with noisy sound effects.

Content of Session	Rationale/Analysis
CHILD: Do you want a bash in the mouth? Or a bash everywhere? Oh! Oh! He's gonna bash me blank over. Bash. Bang. Now look what you've done! (*Makes music sound.*) Da-da-da-dum. Press the button. Bash! (*Singing between bouts of hitting Land Shark with cannonball.*) Press the button.	He shifts quickly from anger to singing. Very labile.
THERAPIST: We have to finish soon, because our time is almost up.	
C (*alarmed*): Our time is almost up? Turn on the flashlight.	
T: We see the light shining on the Land Shark.	
C (*dramatic*): It makes me sick! My mouth! My mouth is getting lightning. I hate lightning! I'm getting sick!	
T: That's the end of the Land Shark. He fell down on the ground. That's the end of that one.	
C: Oh. You idiot! Look what you did again! (*Moving Land Shark along rug.*) See how his mouth moves!	Some of this verbalization sounds like "adult" talk. (Maybe words he heard when his parents fought?)
T: I see how his mouth moves when you drive him on the rug. I'm going to start packing up the furniture, Michael.	
C: Oh. Why are you going to start packing up the furniture?	He sounds almost panicky.
T: Because it's time to get ready to go. That's what we do when it's time to go. We get packed up and get ready to go.	
C: I want to stay for a little more.	
T: A little more. Until I finish packing up.	
C: (*Sings, then starts playing with flashlight. Tries to engage therapist in "ghost" play, with shadow on wall.*) Get him! Get him! Hyena.	
T (*hits shadow*): I got him.	
C (*continues*): Get him again.	
T: I can't reach it any more.	
C: (*Laughing, moves shadow down.*)	
T: I got it. Do you have a flashlight in your room?	I'm changing the pace back to reality.

C: A big one. I can't carry it.

T: Can you turn it on at night if you wake up?

C: No. Can I play with the furniture? The family stuff?

T: We're all finished for today.

C (*whines*): Oh. Can I make a picture?

T: No time today. It's 10 to 6, and it's time to stop for today.

C: Why?

T: Next time, if you want to draw, you can. You did a lot of things today.

C: I want to play with the furniture some more.

T: Next time when you come, we'll decide right away what you want to do. OK?

C: Guess what? I'm going to bring these two again (*leaving with the Land Shark and the Bashasaurus*).

I'm remembering his bad dreams, and make a note to discuss the flashlight with his mom.

I should have commented on how hard it is for Michael to leave today.

He's not finished yet!

This was a difficult session for several reasons. First, the mother's phone call had aroused some pressure on me to "calm Michael down," so that the day care situation would not get out of hand and so that Michael would "behave himself" for the wedding. Although I knew intellectually that it was not within my power (or anyone else's) to magically diffuse this child's anger, nonetheless I sincerely hoped to help Michael feel less at the mercy of his rage. Trying to replay some of the frustrating events in Michael's life during the past week, I made several attempts early in the session to tie Michael's play to day care events (introducing the teacher doll) and to the weekend visit with his father (setting up the family doll play situation with the child doll visiting the father). The second attempt resulted in the major battle scene in the kitchen, which seemed to recapitulate the traumatic fights Michael had witnessed between his parents. I realized how tremendously significant this reenactment was, including the reference to the child doll's hitting the daddy. In retrospect, I wish I had said something about the child's wanting to stop the fight, but being too little to do so. Michael did not speak any words during this fight scene; he only made grunts and groans, suggesting that he was reenacting a preverbal, visually imprinted memory.

In the second half of the session, Michael would not allow me to intervene in situations of repeated violence in which brute force dominated and the family was helplessly victimized by the barrage of primitive oral aggression. Because of its vehemence and relentlessness, this aggression (which has only been summarized here) was difficult to witness. Michael made me helpless by refusing to allow me to intervene and alter the course of events in his fantasy world, just as he had been helpless when he witnessed the fights between his parents and feebly tried to stop them. This was a true parallel process.

A long-term goal for Michael was that he would learn to tolerate his own anger and talk about it, but not blindly act it out. It was far too early in his therapy for him to be able to tolerate alternatives to the immediate drive discharge. Just as an adult who is enraged by the betrayal of a loved one needs to go over and over his or her feelings of despair and fury before beginning to reconstruct his or her life, so also would Michael need to reexperience the scenes of powerlessness and violence he had witnessed before he could be motivated to behave in a more mature way. In a case like this, it is the therapist's role at this early stage to stand by the child, recognizing feelings, offering support, and giving occasional hints that things can work out differently.

Because of the degree of violence expressed in this session, I decided to telephone Michael's father after this session, to ask him whether any particularly upsetting events had occurred during Michael's weekend visit. I had had one previous meeting with Mr. Spivak, in which I had emphasized the importance of Mr. Spivak's regular contact with Michael.

In relation to the weekend visit with Michael, Mr. Spivak initially said that things were "OK." However, he noticed a "change" in Michael's behavior toward the end of the visit, when he went to play by himself and seemed "distant." At the very end of the conversation, Mr. Spivak asked me, "Do you think an argument between me and my girlfriend could have triggered this [Michael's behavior during the past week]?"

I explained to Mr. Spivak that Michael was indeed very sensitive about arguments, because of the fighting he had witnessed between him and his mother. I suggested that in the future, it would be advisable to avoid (insofar as possible) arguments or fights while Michael was visiting.

COMMENTS

The two detailed sessions presented here represent a preliminary exploration of a child's feelings associated with (1) the crisis of repeated witnessing of physical violence between his parents and the subsequent loss of his father through the separation and divorce; and (2) the reawakening of fears and helplessness associated with this memory, precipitated by witnessing an argument between his father and the father's girlfriend.

The concept of a crisis as a single upsetting event is clearly not applicable in this case. This preschool child had been so traumatized by witnessing repeated violence between his parents, and by the subsequent loss of his father, that his energies were not available for developing peer relationships even when his present situation was relatively stable. The child remained vulnerable to floods of primitive rage whenever his current life stirred up memories of the extreme helplessness he had experienced as a very young child.

The early treatment of this child required permitting him to reenact and play out his experience of aggression and helplessness. Without making a direct connection to his *own* life, I validated many of the child's feelings symbolically through play (at a point in the session not reported here, I said, "The poor little boy; he didn't do anything to deserve this; he must be very angry and sad!"). Audiotaping Michael's stories permitted him to listen to himself, and thereby to get some distance from the gruesome aggression of his stories. His drawings had been another means for externalizing his fears: Putting them on paper with all of his accompanying graphic sensory detail gave Michael a sense of cathartic relief, while also relocating the frightening images outside of his body. According to Gaensbauer (1996, p. 20), "the crucial factor in the development of a therapeutic process is the extent to which the traumatic affects can be identified and brought to the surface in a managed way."

Much of the work during the first year of treatment focused on Michael's loss of his father ("He's too sick in his feelings to come and see you now. Maybe you'll see him again when you are much bigger") and on his adjustment to his sister's birth and his new school. The later treatment included some behavior modification techniques, rewarding Michael for demonstrating increased ability to control his angry outbursts at home and at school. This segment of work coincided with a very happy period in the mother's life; because of her own improved circumstances, the mother was able to follow through with various suggestions for supporting Michael.

This case demonstrates a child's reaction to multiple family crises. It also demonstrates the stabilizing effect of therapy with a preschool child who was already evidencing disturbed behavior and who, without intervention, probably would have been identified in the future as an antisocial, acting-out, destructive youngster.

His teacher's report at the end of Michael's kindergarten year stated, "Michael likes 'writing' books. His books are very interesting. He shows excellent creative and expressive abilities. He has shown tremendous growth in his social and emotional development."

FOLLOW-UP: MICHAEL, AGE 16

The prospect of contacting a former client after the passage of many years stirred up many conflicting feelings in me. Of course I had thought about Michael and his family many times over the years, and I frequently invited my students who read the case (as described in the first edition of this book) to speculate about Michael's future, especially about his adolescent years. Although his family situation was stable at the time I closed the case, when he was about 6 years old, I also knew that there were many points of vulnerabilities, and that many factors could intervene to throw Michael and his family off track. Among factors that could have a strong impact was the future role of Michael's father in his life, as well as the health and emotional stamina of his stepfather, who would be in the position of parenting a teenager during his own advancing years. I also wondered whether this new marriage would withstand the pressures associated with Bill's extensive family, and whether Michael would feel like an "outsider" after the birth of his sister, who was the biological child of his mother and Bill.

Michael's mother had informed me soon after her remarriage that Michael's father not only had discontinued child support, but had agreed to Bill's court petition to adopt Michael. So Michael had begun elementary school using his new name and feeling happy (according to his mother) that he was a part of a new family. His father was not planning to have ongoing contact with Michael.

I wrote a letter to the family, stating that I would like to see Michael for a single session to follow up on how he was doing currently (this proved to be 10 years after I closed the case). After a month with no response, I attempted to reach the family through the last telephone number in my file, but the person who answered my call told me that she had had the number for 4 years. I knew the telephone number of Bill's business, but I hesitated to use it. What if Michael's mother and Bill had divorced, or what if Bill had died and the mother had moved away? Another few weeks passed as I waited for contact. The post office could not help. In desperation, I called the business and heard the mother's voice! Again my mind raced, and I wondered whether Bill had died and she had inherited the business.

The suspense was soon over. Michael's mother reported that all was going very well in the family. Michael was planning to go to college; according to his mother, he "could do better," but he wanted to be a writer and had a specific university in mind. Bill, now age 74, still went to work every day. He had had some health "scares," but so far he was doing well. I was very relieved. However, I really wanted to see Michael, and I wondered whether he would agree. Could he remember coming to see me every week and "playing"? Would he want to distance himself from the torments of his childhood, or have a negative view of therapists (as is common with many adolescents?). Again my desire to see him left me with mixed feelings, although everything his mom told me about him seemed positive. The mother promised to speak to Michael and let me know. She expressed some doubts about "opening up all that again," and as I explored this with her, she meant Michael's relationship with his biological father. She stated that Michael had never expressed a desire to see his father, even when his dad occasionally sent him a birthday card. Michael's mother kept track of her former husband through her contacts with her former sister-in-law. However, she had not said anything to Michael about his father, preferring to wait until he asked.

The mother did not call me back about Michael's reaction to the prospect of seeing me. When I called her again, she admitted that she had had some second thoughts about talking to him about this. She seemed to think that it might be upsetting for Michael to recall the unhappy events of his preschool years. She said that it seemed better to her "to let sleeping dogs lie." I said that I had not wanted to pressure her or Michael in any way, and that, as Michael's mother, she certainly knew what was best for him. She had in fact given me a detailed report on Michael's current situation, with permission to write about it in this edition. I thanked her, and ended the conversation by stating that it made me very happy to know that Michael was doing so well. I acknowledged her good judgment for getting Michael the help he had so desperately needed as a preschooler. Expressing my best wishes for her own and Michael's future, I said goodbye.

Although I felt personally disappointed about not seeing Michael as a young man, at the same time I felt that his mother had made the right decision in not even telling him about my request. She was undoubtedly correct that even one session with me would stir up some of those old memories of rage and pain. It really would not be fair to him to expect that we could talk once and then say goodbye again. Much as I wanted to see Michael to gratify my own curiosity and genuine interest in him, I knew that most adolescents probably would not welcome the opportunity to meet a former therapist. If he did not want to see his father, why would he want to see the therapist who knew about all the fighting between his parents that had ended in their divorce? As an adolescent, Michael was able to push aside or even totally repress these memories. I think that Michael's mother's instincts were correct for Michael's developmental stage. Certainly he will need to revisit the scenes buried in his memory at some time in his adulthood. This logically will occur when he contemplates marriage himself, or when he becomes a father. At that time, perhaps his mother will tell Michael about how she needed to find help for him when he was a very little boy because he was so severely affected by his parents' fighting. I wonder if she will tell him that his therapist wrote about how troubled and how brave he was in trying to deal with his feelings. I really wonder what he would say if he saw the "Voltron" drawings again, and if some of our work together remains in his memories.

STUDY QUESTIONS

1. This case demonstrates a mixture of "directive" and "nondirective" play therapy. Discuss when you think it is appropriate to use either approach, giving reasons.

2. Is it appropriate for a therapist to attempt to reduce, interrupt, or provide a "happy ending" to a child's repeated, insistent enactments of violence? How can the therapist help the child make the transition to reality after such violent play?

3. Discuss the effect on a therapist of working with a child who is consumed with rage. What particular pitfalls must the therapist avoid in working with such a child?

4. How can a therapist most effectively consult with a child's day care center and/or school when the presenting and ongoing problem involves the child's aggressive acting-out behavior toward other children in the group setting?

5. What do you think about Michael's mother's decision not to tell him about his therapist's invitation to see him for one follow-up session? Discuss the possible pros and cons for Michael in the event that such a meeting had occurred.

6. What do you consider the prognosis in this case as Michael enters late adolescence and young adulthood? Can you envision any particular vulnerabilities for him?

REFERENCES

Achenbach, T., & Edelbrock, C. (1981). Behavioral problems and competencies reported by parents of normal and disturbed children aged 4 through 16. *Monographs of the Society for Research in Child Development*, 46(1, Serial No. 188).

Bowlby, J. (1960). Grief and mourning in infancy and early childhood. *Psychoanalytic Study of the Child*, 15, 9–52.

Bowlby, J. (1961). Childhood mourning and its implications for psychiatry. *American Journal of Psychiatry*, 118, 481–498.

Eth, S., & Pynoos, R. S. (1980). Psychiatric interventions with children traumatized by violence. In D. H. Schetky & E. P. Benedek (Eds.), *Emerging issues in child psychiatry and the law* (pp. 285–309). New York: Brunner/Mazel.

Fantuzzo, J. W., DePaola, L. M., Lambert, L., Martino, T., Anderson, G., & Sutton, S. (1991). Effects of interparental violence on the psychological adjustment and competencies of young children. *Journal of Consulting and Clinical Psychology*, 59(2), 258–265.

Fick, A. C., Osofsky, J. D., & Lewis, M. L. (1994). Perceptions of violence: Children, parents, and police officers. In R. S. Pynoos (Ed.), *Posttraumatic stress disorder: A clinical review* (pp. 261–276). Lutherville, MD: Sidram Press.

Gaensbauer, T. (1996). Developmental and therapeutic aspects of treating infants and toddlers who have witnessed violence. In J. D. Osofsky & E. Fenichel (Eds.), *Islands of safety: Assessing and treating young victims of violence* (pp. 15–20). Washington, DC: Zero to Three.

Gardner, R. A. (1983). Children's reactions to parental death. In J. E. Schowalter, P. R. Patterson, M. Tallmer, A. H. Kutscher, S. V. Gullo, & D. Peretz (Eds.), *The child and death* (pp. 104–124). New York: Columbia University Press.

Hershorn, M., & Rosenbaum, A. (1985). Children of marital violence: A close look at the unintended victims. *American Journal of Orthopsychiatry*, 55(2), 260–266.

Jacobson, D. S. (1978). The impact of marital separation/divorce on children: Interpersonal hostility and child adjustment. *Journal of Divorce*, 2, 3–19.

Jaffe, P., Wolfe, D., Wilson, S., & Zak, L. (1986). Similarities in behavioral and social maladjustment among child victims and witnesses to family violence. *American Journal of Orthopsychiatry*, 56(1), 142–146.

Kalmuss, D. (1984). The intergenerational transmission of marital aggression. *Journal of Marriage and the Family*, 46, 11–19.

Kelly, J., & Wallerstein, J. (1975). The effects of parental divorce: Experience of the preschool child. *Journal of the American Academy of Child Psychiatry*, 14(4), 600–616.

Kotelchuck, M. (1972). *The nature of the child's tie to his father*. Unpublished doctoral dissertation, Harvard University.

Lamb, M. E. (1976). *The role of the father in child development*. New York: Wiley.

Levy, D. (1939). Release therapy. *American Journal of Orthopsychiatry*, 9, 713–736.

Mahler, M. S., Pine, E., & Bergman, A. (1975). *The psychological birth of the human infant*. New York: Basic Books.

Parad, H. J. (1977). Crisis intervention. In J. Turner (Ed.), *Encyclopedia of social work* (18th ed., pp. 228–237). Washington, DC: National Association of Social Workers.

Rosenbaum, A., & O'Leary, K. (1981). Children: The unintended victims of marital violence. *American Journal of Orthopsychiatry*, 51(4), 692–699.

Terr, L. (1988). What happens to early memories of trauma?: A study of twenty children under age five at the time of documented traumatic events. *Journal of the American Academy of Child and Adolescent Psychiatry*, 27(1), 96–104.

Terr, L. (1989). Treating psychic trauma in childhood in children: A preliminary discussion. *Journal of Traumatic Stress*, 2, 3–20.

CHAPTER 4

Helping Forgotten Victims

Using Activity Groups
with Children Who Witness Violence

DANIELLE NISIVOCCIA
MAXINE LYNN

A child is having lunch with her parents in an outdoor cafe when suddenly a man is knifed in front of them. She makes a comment about its being like TV and finishes her french fries. It is only later that night that the child awakens from a nightmare. Seven other children witness a drive-by shooting in which one of their friends is killed in the crossfire. In a third incident, a child watches her dad become violent with her mom, but realizes that if she tells anyone "they" may take her away. Another child witnesses his mom being raped, but is sworn to secrecy by her. Children who enter our country as immigrants have often witnessed the violence of war and/or terrorists, but they fear reprisals if they tell anyone. Although the mass media are filled with violence, the witnessing of violent acts has varying effects on different individuals.

CHILDREN AND VIOLENCE

The United States is the most violent country in the industrialized world, and violence is becoming a defining characteristic of U.S. culture (Emde, 1993; Osofsky, 1997; Richters, 1993). As many as 80–90% of young children (Guterman & Cameron, 1997), and three out of four elementary and high school students of color in urban areas, have witnessed at least one violent act in the home or community (Garbarino, Dubrow, Kostelny, & Pardo, 1992; Lorion & Saltzman, 1993). The recent epidemic of violence in white middle-class schools in Alaska, Arkansas, Colorado, Kentucky, Mississippi, and Oregon (Egan, 1998, p. A1) demonstrates the fact that no child is protected from the possibility of witnessing violence.

Children who witness violence in their home and community can be profoundly traumatized by it. The youth who are indirectly affected become forgotten victims. Adults either are unaware of the impact of such acts on children or try to minimize it, fearing that talking about the violence will upset the children. They are rarely given the opportunity to express and identify emotions related to violent events. Young children are especially vulnerable because of their limited life experiences and immature cognitive, emotional, and social development (Garbarino et al., 1992). This chapter focuses on the use of activity groups for latency-age children who witness violence; such groups give them opportunities to move beyond the experiences they have witnessed. The chapter also illustrates, through a discussion of the stages of group development, activities that are best suited to group members' age, gender, and type of experience.

DEVELOPMENTAL ISSUES AND VIOLENCE

Latency-age children (those aged between 7 and 12 years) are developing their cognitive, sensorimotor, moral, affective, and social learning skills. Their world has begun to shift from the family to the outside world of school, neighborhood, peer groups, and nonparental adult role models. They are increasingly able to tolerate frustration, to derive satisfaction from activities, to think operationally, to solve problems, to understand right and wrong, and to empathize with others. They are working on their emerging sense of competence, mastery, and autonomy (Garbarino et al., 1992; Germain, 1991). Therefore, latency-age children who witness the disturbing effects of violence may experience feelings of anxiety, fear, and helplessness (Osofsky, 1997).

Children who have witnessed violence often develop a range of physical, affective, cognitive, and behavioral difficulties (Whitlock, 1997) characterized by the giving up of play, avoidance of closeness, lack of trust, fear of adults, shame, and isolation. Their behavioral symptoms may include somatization, gaps in language development, poor impulse control, difficulty handling separation, poor peer relationships, and avoidance of closeness. Sometimes they regress to earlier modes of relating (Osofsky, 1997). These adjustment difficulties may not be directly noticed, except among boys who externalize with aggressive acts, and girls who somatize and develop depression. When the symptoms are ignored, children's sense of basic trust, autonomy, and initiative may be compromised (Lorion & Saltzman, 1993), and their risk for psychiatric problems increases (Garbarino et al., 1992). Delinquent behavior or substance abuse during adolescence can result.

THE USE OF GROUPS WITH CHILDREN

Group work and programmed activities can provide a nurturing environment for these children while giving them opportunities to have corrective emotional experiences and to increase their interpersonal skills. The use of groups builds on the strengths of the children and helps move them beyond the experiences they have witnessed. Interventions include helping the children learn mutual aid processes, thereby increasing their social networks.

When children witness violent acts in their home or communities, they often have confused generational boundaries, and role reversal can occur (Roseby & Johnston, 1995). A group is an arena for children to redefine their boundaries through activities. Major content areas that can be worked with through various group activities include the following (Grusznski, Brink, & Edleson, 1988; Peled & Davis, 1995):

- Expressions of feelings
- Issues of isolation and shame
- Establishing responsibility for the violence
- Conflict resolution

The group becomes an ideal modality because it breaks isolation, deals with shame, raises self-esteem, helps children recognize effective limits, and enhances relatedness. The curative elements of peer interaction, universalization, therapeutic leadership of adults, and the "group as a benign mother" highlight the importance of this model (Connors, Schamess, & Strieder, 1997).

The group work approach that is most useful is developed from the mainstream model of social group work. This allows the development of a "natural helping network" that takes into account each child in his or her environment. The worker intervenes to develop support and mutual aid (Haran, 1988; Papell & Rothman, 1980). The goals of the group include learning to trust, to share, to make friends, to recognize feelings, and to deal with conflicts.

Children often reenact family scenes in the group, or use it to get negative attention because this is how they get their needs met at home. The group permits the youngsters to develop new patterns of interaction in ways other than through abusive interaction. The group also provides an arena to define violence and offers effective ways to cope with the feelings that are generated. Moreover, it allows members to experience cohesiveness and mutual aid.

Activity Programming in Groups

The use of structured group activities has a rich history in social group work (Henry, 1992; Kurland & Salmon, 1998; Malekoff, 1997). Activity is the "vehicle through which relationships are made and the interests of the group and its members are fulfilled" (Middleman, 1968, p. 67). The values and purposes of program activities with children's groups include opportunities to create something imaginative and expressive. This approach allows the group leader to directly observe each member's interactions, to encourage less articulate members to express thoughts and feelings through the activities, to encourage a sense of mutual aid and mastery, and to improve members' self-esteem (Kurland & Salmon, 1998). The activity must relate to the group's needs and abilities, based on its stage of development (Lynn & Nisivoccia, 1995; Vinter, 1985).

Children symbolize and express their conscious and unconscious worlds through play and action. Activity itself is viewed as therapeutic (Henry, 1992; Middleman, 1968). Erikson (1963) viewed play as a child's means of achieving mastery over traumatic experiences, and it can be viewed as the most natural method of self-healing. Children use play to reconstruct traumatic experiences and to reenact these repetitively (Garbarino et al., 1992; Webb, 1996; Whitlock, 1997). Group leaders need to demonstrate concern and protection, and to keep in mind that the process is more important than completing the activity.

Before using an activity, a group leader should consider the following: (1) the purpose that the activity will achieve; (2) the relationship demand (i.e., the degree of intimacy vs. distance, sharing vs. competition, cooperation vs. conflict); (3) the focus (i.e., individual, group, or both); (4) required skills; (5) decision-making opportunities for the individual and the group; (6) appropriateness to members' life situations; (7) cultural sensitivity; (8) impact on behavioral expression; (9) timing within the session and the stage of development of the group; and (10) availability of resources (Northen, 1988). The leader must interpret the way that the activity is being used as a metaphor for behavior (Wilson & Ryland, 1949), as well as assume responsibility for directing the activity.

Roles of the Group Leader

In order to create a safe enough environment for traumatized children, the many roles of the group leader/therapist/social group worker need to include those of supporter, protector, director, and mediator. Schwartz (1976) emphasizes that the worker has the function of mediating the transaction in which the individual and group reach out to each other. Since traumatized children often have poor peer relationships and little trust in adults, the group activity can help bridge the gap by assuming the qualities of a holding environment and "a benign mother" (Lee & Nisivoccia-Park, 1983, p. 204; see also Scheidlinger, 1974; Slavson & Schieffer, 1975; Winnicott, 1965). The leader needs to plan each activity carefully to fit in with the group's goals, the dynamics of the particular group, the group's stage of development, and the individual needs of the children, as well as to establish clear limits and help group members deal with reality.

Planning: Specifics in Getting Started

In planning a group, one needs to decide on the membership criteria. Ideally, the size should be six to eight children. The children should be of similar gender and age, as there are major dynamics to deal with in latency when gender is mixed, and there are vast differences in children's cognitive and developmental levels when the age span is too broad. Therefore, we recommend no more than a 3-year difference in age among members. The goal is to plan a group in which individual members will feel comfortable, and in which the group as a whole can develop cohesion. Some children may be too psychotic and retreat into total fantasy, may act extremely aggressively, and/or may have no social skills. They will not benefit from the group. Occasionally, the horrific details of the violence may have so traumatized a child that he or she cannot function, and therefore cannot be in a group. Also, this child's experiences may frighten other children. Such children may require a period of individual treatment before they can benefit from a group experience.

Stages of Group Development

Groups in general follow discrete and dynamic stages of development (Garland, Jones, & Kolodny, 1967; Henry, 1992). The particular group being described in this chapter is time-limited to 12 sessions and develops within a sequence of four stages. Table 4.1

TABLE 4.1. Content and Process Goals of Group Sessions, and Agenda of Activities

Session	Content goals	Process goals	Activities
1	Defining purpose and contract Establishing confidentiality Setting norms Getting acquainted	Seeking commonalities Creating nurturing environment	Name tags Pass the Squeeze
2	Sharing information and feelings Recontracting Further exploration	Building group cohesion and trust Reinforcing norms	Drawing family picture Defining violence Rumor Clinic Giving group a name
3	Defining violence Dealing with violence	Defining power and control issues Setting boundaries	Good Hand, Bad Hand Rumor Clinic
4	Exploring meaning of violence and how it affects each person	Defining power and control issues Recontracting	Good Hand, Bad Hand Role play
5	Working through issues of violence Teaching problem solving	Enhancing coping and adaptation Building cohesion, intimacy	Enactment of a story
6	Exploring violent words Self-disclosure Working through issues of isolation	Building trust and mutual aid	Using code words to make a poster
7	Connecting the external violent words Separating the members from the violent acts	Feeling vulnerable Risking Dealing with ambivalence	Tic-Tac-Toe Wish List Role play
8	Establishing responsibility Separating the members from the violent acts	Conflict resolution Testing group norms Differentiation	Creating a song Identifying feelings with ball game
9	Developing protection Understanding members' feelings	Increasing coping, adaptation, and conflict resolution skills to enhance cohesion	Role play Putting on a play Taping a list of feelings on one's back and having others respond
10	Understanding the differences among feelings, needs, and thoughts Defining what is important	Recognizing and accepting each other as distinct individuals	Drawing a person/member and filling in head (thoughts), heart (feelings), and stomach (needs)
11	Raising termination issues Creating rituals for endings	Helping members begin to separate from the group Dealing with regression	Composing a group letter or poem Planning a party
12	Talking about gains Sharing feelings about lossers and leaving	Allowing the boundaries to dissipate Helping members cope with sadness	Writing and exchanging goodbye cards Writing one thing each member did not get from the group Party

Note. Session 1 corresponds to the first stage of the four-stage model described in text; sessions 2–3 correspond to the second stage; sessions 4–10 correspond to the middle stage; and sessions 11–12 correspond to the final stage.

describes the goals and activities for each session, and indicates in a footnote how the sessions are linked to the four-stage model described below. The table is a guide and should not lock the leader into the pressure of having to complete or even initiate any one activity. The goals are separated into process and content objectives. Process goals are characterized by the relationships between members, the relationships between members and the leader, and the dynamics of the group as a whole. The content goals are the actualizations of the tasks (Toseland & Rivas, 1998).

The first stage constitutes the beginning of the group. This stage is critical, because it sets the context for work and responds to the need to create a safe environment. The children are wondering what is going to happen and who will take care of them. They worry about whether the leader and other members will like them, whether they will be expected to share any secrets, and what dangers may exist in the group. Their behavior is generally characterized by approach and avoidance. A clear contract must be developed. Sharing personal experiences is encouraged. Although abuse between members is not acceptable, all feelings are acceptable. Attacking someone in the group is not a good thing. All of these issues need to be developed as group norms. Through activities, ground rules are set, cohesion is built, and a safe environment is created.

The second stage involves more sharing of content related to personal issues and self-disclosure (Garland et al., 1973). Activities are introduced that build empathy. Power and control issues are also heightened in this stage, and setting clear, firm limits is important. The leader needs to reduce obstacles so that the middle stage can develop.

The middle stage consists of the essential work of the group. Members deal openly with how their experiences of violence have affected them. Their abilities to hear each other, express feelings, and self-disclose increase. Problem solving and mutual aid skills are utilized. The leader can be less active as members help each other to work on their tasks.

The final stage deals with the meaning of separation and a review of the gains made by each member. The children focus on the meaning of endings and on how they can approach other adults or peers with their concerns and feelings about violence.

CASE EXAMPLE: A GROUP FOR CHILD WITNESSES OF VIOLENCE

Group Formation

The site for this group was an urban public school. The school is often the first major institution that all families deal with and the first place where children's difficulties surface. It is a natural environment and provides many opportunities for social work and mental health intervention on behalf of children (Congress & Lynn, 1994; Meyer, 1976).

The referral sources included guidance counselors and teachers. Each child was seen individually to hear her concerns and tell her about the group. Parents were sent a permission slip home and encouraged to call with questions. Reasons for referral included prior knowledge of what a child had experienced, a drop in grades and/or in attendance, or interpersonal difficulties with peers or teachers.

The group was held in a small classroom. Each session was 45 minutes long and corresponded to a music period in the school. The group was composed of nine girls between 9 and 11 years of age. Twelve girls were chosen initially, but two girls' parents refused to sign permission slips, and one girl did not want to be in the group.

The children in the group were in regular classes and had not yet demonstrated symptoms severe enough to require an intervention from a mental health clinic. This group model could be utilized in other settings (e.g., a shelter, an after-school program, or a clinic). The crises for children such as these are often unnoticed in comparison with those for individuals who are directly affected by the violence. One may only notice such children when they hide after a loud noise, when their grades go down, when they fear a class trip, when they create disturbing drawings, when they make frequent trips to the nurse or bathroom, when they become withdrawn during play periods, or when they suddenly become involved in aggressive acts.

Membership of the Group

• Josie was 10 years old and had recently come from a South American country. She had witnessed her mother being raped in her country of origin. Teachers reported that she got upset if any boy brushed by her.

• Rosemarie was 9½ years old and of Puerto Rican background. She had witnessed a knife fight in school and had told her parent that she did not want to return to school. The guidance counselor noted that the child was restless and reported having nightmares.

• Kenyetta was 9 years old and African American. She had also witnessed the knife fight and had told everyone in graphic detail about the incident. She was aggressive, was often involved in fights herself, and frequently argued with the teachers and staff.

• Alexandra, 11 years old, was of Croatian background and a recent immigrant. Her family reported that she had witnessed terrorists murdering her neighbors. She was quiet and daydreamed a lot, and was enrolled in an English-as-a-second-language class. Her teachers reported that she often complained of stomachaches and that she did not eat much.

• Laura, 10½ years old, was African American. She had told her teacher that her parents were always fighting. The teacher reported that she was often late for school, was sleepy in class, had disheveled clothes, and refused to participate in school activities. Her grades were also dropping.

• Kay (Kahital), 10 years old, was from India. She was terrified to come to school after witnessing a bike being taken from another child. The teacher reported that her parents were overly concerned and came to school over the incident.

- Maria, 11 years old, was of Dominican background. A bullet from a drive-by shooting had come through her bedroom window. She was shy and reticent. Her teacher reported that she asked to have her seat in class moved away from the window.
- Rosa, 10 years old, was of Puerto Rican background. She lived with her mother and two siblings in a shelter for victims of domestic violence. The teacher reported that she stole crayons, trinkets, and pennies.
- Evelina, 10 years old, was a tall, light-skinned interracial child who was ungainly and awkward. She also lived in the shelter for victims of domestic violence with her mother. The teacher reported that the child was isolated and was the victim of bullying and teasing.

Session 1

The room was arranged with chairs around a table. Everyone was there except Evelina, who was absent. The girls looked around, but didn't say much at first. They were greeted by Beth, the social worker who was the leader of this group (and who is the "I" in what follows).

Content of Session

ROSEMARIE: I'm missing music.

KENYETTA: Why are we here?

LAURA: Are we in trouble?

LEADER: Let me remind you who I am. I'm Beth, a social worker who works at this school 2 days a week. And no, you're not in trouble. You were invited to the group because it has come to our attention that each of you has seen something terrible and may have some feelings about it. When I met with each of you alone, some of you shared that you wanted to make friends and had some concerns about school. We will be meeting every week for 12 weeks for one class period. I guess we should start off getting to know one another.

KENYETTA: I already know Rosemarie.

LAURA: What if I don't want to stay?

(*Maria arrives late and explains that she had to go to the bathroom.*)

ROSA: Can we have the cookies now?

(*In unison, the rest of them either nod their heads yes or say, "Yes, cookies, cookies."*)

Analysis and Feelings

Approach–avoidance behavior. The girls want to know why they are here and why they were put in the group. They are anxious that they may be in trouble and need clarification about why they have been invited. I quickly reintroduce myself and reflect their concerns about being in trouble by letting them know that they are *not* in trouble. The purpose and brief contract are shared, along with the fact that "they are all in the same boat" because of having "seen something terrible." By making the unknown known and letting them know what they have in common, I have taken a risk by "saying the taboo" in an attempt to lessen the beginning anxiety.

Again, approach–avoidance behavior. I decide not to address it as an individual issue.

Food is both nurturing and fills a void. It also gives the group something "safer" to focus on and affords a worker an opportunity to

LEADER: Let me share how I think we might do things together, and then I'd like to hear from you if this is OK. Each meeting we will have an activity where we will do something together. Then we will have a snack, and we'll talk about the activity. No one has to come to the group, but when we met alone you all seemed to like the idea. You also don't have to participate in the activity. What happens between all of you and myself is not to be shared outside of the room; it's sort of like our secret. However, if there are times that secrets have to be shared with the school or your parents, I will talk to you privately about it.

LAURA: Well, what secret would you tell?

LEADER: Things about someone hurting you.

be giving. Usually I give it at the end as gratification and a reward.

I "lend my vision" about the structure and expectation of the group members and what they will be doing, thus beginning to establish the norms of the group. At this point I remind them that I have spoken with each one of them previously alone, and that they do not have to come to the group or participate in the activity if they don't want to. The issue of confidentiality is presented in a child's language.

The group is getting a better understanding about what secrets stay in the group and what I may have to share.

KENYETTA: I think that we should have the cookies first.

KAY: Well, I can wait a little while.

LEADER: Let's find out who wants the cookies now.

(They all yell, "Me, me, me.")

LEADER: (Goes over to get the snacks and places them on the table.)

KENYETTA: There are 24 cookies. We each get 3.

Kenyetta is a fairly aggressive, needy child. I will have to do some limit setting.

I am trying to assess each individual's needs.

I decide to serve the snacks now to create a more nurturing environment and to continue to engage the group members in getting to know one another.

LEADER: That's really good. Would you like to help pass out the cookies?

I recognize this child's abilities at math and try to channel her behavior.

KENYETTA: Can I have your other two?

ROSA: Can I have an extra one?

LEADER: Do you want to pour the milk, Kay?

(Food is distributed.)

The children are both needy and assertive. They are beginning to test me and the norms of the group. I attempt to get others involved.

LEADER: I'm kind of concerned that not everyone knows who everybody is in here yet. I have some name tags, stickers, and crayons on the table; each of you can write the name that you'd like to be called in the group, and decorate your tag any way that you'd like.

(The girls begin decorating their name tags while eating the cookies.)

The girls' anxieties have lessened with the snack, and I begin the activity of decorating a name tag as a way of getting acquainted and talking about themselves.

LEADER: I see that you are finished. Before you put them on, I'd like for each of you to introduce yourself and tell us how you decorated your name tag. I'm going to show you: My name is Beth and I've drawn a cookie, because we've started the group off with cookies today.

> I participate in the activity and use my name tag as a model.

ROSEMARIE: Can I be first?

LEADER: Yes.

ROSEMARIE: I am Rosemarie and I drew a sun, 'cause I like the color yellow on sunny days.

> This child makes a positive beginning.

KENYETTA: I am Kenyetta and I used red, black, and green, 'cause those are the colors of my flag.

ALEXANDRA: I thought that our flag was red, white, and blue?

> The activity is helping individuals to begin disclosing safe information about themselves and to get a sense of one another.

KENYETTA: That is the American flag. I am talking about Africa.

KAY: I'm from Bombay. . . .

LEADER: Who hasn't gone yet?

(The other girls introduce themselves in turn.)

Now I'd like to introduce a game that deals with signals we send each other. These will be signals through your hands. It starts off with my squeezing one person's hand a certain number of times, and that person passes it on to the next person, and so on. The last person has to tell us how many squeezes it was.

> I make sure that everyone gets an opportunity to participate. I want to help them get acquainted through another (more intimate/ physical) activity, the game of Pass the Squeeze.

ROSA: This is like Telephone.

> Rosa's remark makes the unknown known, as Telephone is a game that some of them know.

JOSIE *(nervously)*: Do we really have to squeeze hands?

> I wonder whether this is "too much, too fast" for this child.

KENYETTA: How else are you going to play the game?

LEADER: Remember, you don't have to play if you don't want to. Does anyone else have any feelings about it?

KAY: It is OK to squeeze hands, 'cause we're all girls here.

LEADER: Who wants to start?

ROSA: I'll start. (*Reaches for leader's hand, giving it three firm squeezes.*)

> I again reinforce the contract and recognize that they do not have to participate in an activity if they don't want to. By doing so, I continue to make a safe environment and allow each person to proceed at her own pace. One member verbalizes what might be an issue for some of the other girls.

(The girls play the game, and the last person whose hand got squeezed calls out the number of squeezes she received, only to find out that it is different from Rosa's three squeezes. The group does this several times, laughing and determined to "get it right.")

Everyone is participating. It appears to be a nonthreatening intervention and a way to begin to establish a sense of trust and getting acquainted. It also gives the girls an opportunity to move around the room.

LEADER: We only have a little time left today. How did you think the meeting went?

I am letting the group know that time is about up and asking for feedback.

KENYETTA: I liked the cookies. Could we name the group?

(Two other members chime in, "Yes, let's name the group.")

A sign that the members are beginning to get invested and want to take some ownership of the group.

LEADER: OK, next week bring in your ideas for names. I'm still curious to know what the rest of you thought about today.

I am impressed that they want to take ownership of the group by naming it. I ask for feedback so that the group can be tailored to the girls' needs.

ROSEMARIE: Can we meet at a different time? I don't like to miss music.

She is not convinced that she wants to remain in the group.

MARIA: I had a good time.

Session 2

The group arrived. The snacks were not yet out. I (Beth) welcomed and recognized Evelina, who was not at the first meeting, and asked her to introduce herself.

Content of Session

Analysis and Feelings

LEADER: Would someone tell Evelina what the group is about and what we did last week?

I want to make sure that the new member knows what the group is about. I use the opportunity to reinforce the purpose, renegoiate the contract of the group, and get a sense of the girls' perception of it.

KENYETTA: We ate cookies and played a game! Are we having cookies now?

LEADER: Does anyone else want to share why we are meeting?

(The members have blank looks on their faces.)

LEADER: *(Repeats the group's purpose from the first meeting and asks each member to introduce herself to the new member, which they proceed to do. She then reminds them that the last week they decided to name the group,*

It is apparent that they are not ready to talk about the purpose of the group, as they do not feel safe with the members, me, or the process. I do not push them, but continue the activities of getting acquainted and naming the group, which will help to establish initial cohesion.

and asks if they have any ideas. The group members seem to like this idea. They call out the names of their favorite singing groups, such as the Spice Girls, and begin to sing some of the songs.)

KENYETTA: What about the Dream Girls?

ALEXANDRA: Who are they? *(Kenyetta gets out of her seat and begins to imitate them.)*

ROSA: Let's call it Selena's Sisters.

ALEXANDRA: Why not Beth's Girls?

KENYETTA: I think Dream Girls is the best.

KAY: Why is that?

KENYETTA: Because the Dream Girls always sing happy songs, and Selina was murdered.

> I know that some of the members have nightmares. Is this a way to approach this topic in disguise?

ALEXANDRA: Who is Selina? How did she get murdered?

> This is the first spontaneous reference to violence in the group.

JOSIE: Some crazy friend of hers shot her.

ROSEMARIE: Yeah, that was sad.

JOSIE: That is why you got to be careful about making friends.

> She is revealing her defenses.

LEADER: I wonder—what about making friends in the group?

(The group members chime in and say, "Not in here," "We are not going to kill each other here.")

KAY: I'm not so sure that we're going to make friends.

KENYETTA: So are we going to name the group?

> There are several group dynamics going on: early power and control issues; decision making; issues of ethnic diversity; and information about violence and murder. Because the group needs to become a safe place, I address possible concerns that they may have in the group. Again, I am "saying the taboo."

LEADER: It seems like we've got several things to deal with today, all of them important. One is naming the group. The other is your concerns about being a member of the group, and if you remember, one of the purposes of our group is to deal with some of the bad things that you have seen.

> I point out that there are several important issues going on, and I focus on what it is like to be a member of a group and the group's purpose. Thus I am building and reinforcing group norms.
> I wonder if they all are ready to admit this.

ROSA: I think that the group name should be about all of us, and I don't know anything about the Dream Girls.

(At this point Kenyetta gets up and does a quite animated imitation of the Dream Girls. Laura gets up and joins her.)

KAY: We can call ourselves Daisies.

> This child is trying to avoid the violent connection.

ROSEMARIE: What about the Sunflowers?

LEADER: We have several good names that have been suggested. What do you want to do about it?

KENYETTA (*shouting*): I want the Dream Girls, and so do Laura and Evelina!

ROSEMARIE: Evelina didn't say that, or any other name.

LEADER: I think that this might be a good time to talk about how you make a decision as a group.

KAY: In our class we vote.

MARIA: Yeah, but at my house my mother always decides.

LEADER: In this group everyone needs to be involved in making a decision.

(*After a brief period of deliberating, the group decides to take a vote, and the Dream Girls win. The leader notes that Kenyetta bullies Evelina and Alexandra into voting for the Dream Girls. The leader asks the group members whether they are all satisfied with the results, and some say yes more enthusiastically than others.*)

LEADER: The next thing that will help us get to know each other is for you to draw a picture of your family or who you live with.

(*Several members remark, "I can't draw."*)

LEADER: I can't draw much either.

(*Rosa reaches over and takes a whole bunch of crayons. Evelina breaks hers in half and hides them.*)

KENYETTA (*yelling*): I don't have the colors I need.

ROSEMARIE (*in exasperation*): I just can't do this.

(*The leader gets up and moves to help Rosemarie. Kenyetta jumps up and loudly demands that Rosa give her some of the crayons. The rest of the members are engaged in the drawing.*)

LEADER: I think we need to take a moment to stop and look at what is going on.

KENYETTA: I'll tell you what is going on. Rosa took all the crayons.

MARIA: That's not true. I have some crayons.

KAY: Me, too.

ALEXANDRA: I've finished. Kenyetta can have my crayons.

The deliberating process has given the members a greater opportunity to share their preferences. It also offers them an early opportunity to make a decision together about the group, thereby increasing their sense of ownership and cohesion.

I intervene to establish boundaries and group norms.

Two of the members self-disclose.

This activity will help the members get acquainted and continue to share information and feelings.

I share/self-disclose that I too am not good at drawing.

Initially, I ignore the group's behavior and focus on Rosemarie. Realizing quickly that the four of them (Rosemarie, Rosa, Evelina, and Kenyetta) cannot share, I intervene to look at the process or what is going on, thus making a demand for work.

ROSA: (*Says some profanity in Spanish.*)

ROSEMARIE (*looking at the leader*): I hope you don't know what she said.

LEADER: Maybe we'd better talk about what being a member of a group is about.

KAY: I think that you should give us five crayons each. That way we'd all have the same.

Again, I am trying to build and reinforce group norms, educating them about the rules of behavior and expectations of being a group member. I am trying to be accepting and nonjudgmental about the members' behavior, and I do not comment on the cursing. I note that there are four very strong members in this group, who happen to be split along racial lines.

LEADER: That's a good idea, Kay. But I wonder if what we need to talk about is sharing.

MARIA: I think that Kenyetta and Rosa are mad at each other.

ROSEMARIE: Kenyetta always wants everything her way.

KENYETTA: No, I don't!

KAY: I saw you take extra milk at lunch.

Kay is becoming the superego and indigenous leader. I praise her efforts at coming up with a solution and move the group discussion to "sharing," a critical characteristic for being a good group member.

ALEXANDRA: Are we going to have a snack today?

LEADER: Yes, it's about that time, and over the snack we can continue talking about this and your family drawings.

(*The leader asks Alexandra and Josie to give out the snacks. Then the group talks about setting rules. The members discuss cursing in the group and what to do when they are angry at each other. They share their drawings. The leader notices that there is some embarrassment. She asks the group members whether perhaps they did not want to do the activity and were afraid to tell her. She reinforces that they do not have to participate in every activity.*)

The conflict among some of the members appears to have raised anxiety in other group members, who are uncomfortable and want to do something safer. I recognize that time is almost up and encourage them to continue the discussion over the snacks, as well as to share their family drawings.

Session 3

From the first two sessions, I identified the following themes: (1) learning to be in the group and (2) the setting of boundaries. There was an emerging scapegoat, Kenyetta. The members were fearful of sharing information about themselves, and there was concern about getting their needs met. Conflicts were developing that were characteristic of power and control. I was also aware that there were only 10 more sessions and that the group members needed to accomplish the purpose of defining and dealing with their experiences of violence. The power and control issues were some of the obstacles that could prevent the group members from accomplishing these tasks. The following critical incidents from session 3 illustrate the themes noted above.

Rosemarie and Josie arrived together. Rosemarie announced that she was glad that Kenyetta wasn't there. She added, "If Kenyetta stays, I'm leaving."

Content of Session	Analysis and Feelings
LEADER: It sounds like you are pretty angry.	I am reaching for the feeling.
(The group members continue to arrive. Kenyetta is brought down by a teacher's aide, who tells me that she must accompany the child back to class.)	
LEADER: What's going on?	Many things happen in a school setting. I wonder what I am about to hear.
(A couple of the members challengingly ask, "You don't know?")	
ROSA: I heard that Kenyetta hit Ms. Lee [the lunchroom aide].	
LAURA: Kenyetta was in a big fight.	
KENYETTA (angrily): You don't know. It wasn't my fault.	Will this anger frighten the girls?
ROSEMARIE: I really don't want to stay if she's in the room.	
KENYETTA: So leave.	
LEADER: I hear a lot of anger here, and maybe you're even angry at me, but I think we need to hear from Kenyetta, if she wants to tell us, since some of us were not there and didn't know what happened.	This meeting is going to require a lot of work. I don't really know much about their personal issues, so I do need to hear Kenyetta's version of this.
KAY: Yeah, I don't know what happened. Let's find out. Tell us Kenyetta.	Great support!
KENYETTA: While I was eating lunch, Linda came over and knocked my tray and the milk spilled all over me. She didn't even say nothing, so I kicked her. Then the bitch pulled my braids. So I had to defend myself.	
MARIA (quietly): I don't like this.	I am aware of heightened anxiety and fear in the group and in myself. It seems as if violence is erupting in the group. Several members are becoming anxious.
LAURA: Enough already.	
KENYETTA: I'm not finished. Ms. Lee came over and broke up the fight and attacked me. So I had to protect myself, so I picked up the juice and threw it in her face, and that's why I missed 3 days of school.	I am shocked at this girl's open aggression against an adult!

EVELINA: You're crazy! The teachers are not allowed to attack anyone.

ROSEMARIE: Linda is my friend, and she has got a big black and blue mark, and she's not a bitch; you are!

LEADER: It seems to me what is being talked about here is what this group is about, which is how to deal with violence all around you.

LAURA: It makes me feel really awful when my friends fight, because my parents fight all the time.

ROSEMARIE: Well, then, we'll all feel a lot better if Kenyetta is out of the group.

KENYETTA: Well, maybe you should leave.

LEADER: Actually, the decision who stays and leaves is *my* decision. Maybe you are angry at the way I'm leading the group, or that I can't stop bad things from happening.

EVELINA: Well, it is a bad world out there, and we got to protect ourselves.

KAY: Can you protect yourself without hurting someone?

ALEXANDRA: It is really awful for friends to fight with friends.

ROSA: Well, we don't have to be friends in here.

JOSIE: Bad things happen from fighting.

LEADER: It seems as if all of you share having seen bad things happen or having had bad things happen to you, or someone was either seriously hurt or killed.

(*There is a momentary silence. The leader then introduces the Good Hand, Bad Hand activity by suggesting that the group do an activity that looks at these issues. She distributes pieces of paper and asks the members first to trace both their hands, and then to fill in one hand with all the good things that a hand can do and the other with all the bad things. During the activity, the members ask the leader how to spell various words. After the members complete the activity, the leader begins to process what they did.*)

LEADER: You all have some very creative hands. Would anyone like to tell us about the good hand?

KAY: A good hand can draw pretty pictures, can pet a cat, and hug you.

Some of the members feel safe enough to express aggressive feelings. They are also questioning the role of authority.

I try to connect the outside world with what is going on in the group and the purpose.

She is making a good connection.

I am trying to tackle the scapegoating phenomenon and assume responsibility. This is an important power and control issue.

Again, I reintroduce the purpose of the group and make a demand for work.

The activity provides a structure to raise the issues in a less threatening manner. The polarization of Kenyetta and Rosemarie is extreme, and there needs to be some deflection. This is characteristic of the second stage of group development. I hope that the activity will accomplish this purpose.

MARIA: Yeah. It can put makeup and fingernail polish on.

JOSIE: It can make you feel better.

(*Some of the other members continue to share what a good hand can do.*)

LEADER: Now let's talk about what a bad hand can do.

KENYETTA (*quickly, shouting*): Pulls hair, punches, pinches.

LEADER: Thanks, Kenyetta, now let's give someone else a turn.

EVELINA: Yeah, slaps.

ROSA: Steals, fights with other people.

MARIA: Shoots.

JOSIE (*quietly*): Do you mean a gun?

KENYETTA: Cutting someone with a knife.

LAURA: That's terrible.

LEADER: It seems as if you girls have a lot of similar ideas, and that we can find ways to work on this stuff together.

(*The leader asks the members to cut out their individual hands and put them together on a large piece of poster board to make a group picture. While this is going on, Rosemarie and Kenyetta keep an appreciable distance. The snack is served. During this time, the leader asks the group members how they thought the meeting went today.*)

ROSEMARIE: Well, I still think that Kenyetta shouldn't be in the group, because she's the reason I sometimes don't want to come to school.

LEADER: I'm confused. Could you tell me more?

ROSEMARIE: When people go to school, they can get hurt.

ALEXANDRA: Yes, but people can get hurt outside of school also.

(*Josie and Maria nod their heads in agreement.*)

LEADER: It seems that each of you have seen some bad things, and perhaps we should spend some time telling each other about it. Would someone like to start?

LAURA: You're not supposed to tell your business to strangers.

Throughout the activity, the members often have the same thing written down. This demonstrates the commonality the members have with each other.

I am struggling to build cohesion. The group has become a parallel process, and a microcosm of their life and what they have experienced.

I want the members to process this session.

Actualization of group's purpose.

KAY: I don't want to talk about it, either.

LEADER: I know that these kinds of things are hard to talk about, but I bet that you are really worrying about them.

(The girls sheepishly nod.)

LEADER: I know that it is getting near the end of the meeting, and I'm still concerned about Kenyetta and Rosemarie.

ROSEMARIE: I don't like this group.

LAURA: Me, either.

EVELINA: I like the snacks.

ROSA: I like the games.

ALEXANDRA: And I like meeting new people.

LEADER: Well, I hear that some of you like coming here, and some of you don't like some of what is going on in the group. So next week we can discuss this. Rosemarie, I'd like you to come next week, and if you still feel that you don't want to be a member of the group, you don't have to come back any more.

ROSEMARIE: I'll stay in this group if Kenyetta goes.

KENYETTA: I'll go when I damn well feel like it.

(Some of the members begin to leave.)

LEADER: Seems like Kenyetta and Rosemarie want to stay, so I think next week we need to talk about how to be in the group together.

I am aware of their resistance and difficulty trusting; still, I am attempting to help them get the feelings into words.

I am making a demand for work. It is early in the group life for this, but the opportunity is there. There is some general group resistance, and some members were testing me.

I try to bring the conflict out in the open, as well as to provide options.

I am caught among needing to deal with what is going on, the time frame, and the need to find closure.

Session 3 was characterized by the intensity of power and control issues and by testing of me as the leader. These were enacted, with two major themes emerging; Kenyetta and Rosemarie represented the polarization of these themes. The issues of a group member's exhibiting violence and another member's witnessing the violence paralleled the reason for the group's being. This led to members' heightened anxiety, which precipitated scapegoating and the group's resistance. The girls were uncomfortable being in the group and were looking for protection from me.

Session 4

I realized that I must deal with the powerful content generated in session 3, exemplified in the struggle between Kenyetta and Rosemarie. These were obstacles that could prevent the work from occurring. The group needed to develop cohesion and work on issues of trust, which would lead to recontracting. Therefore, the activity would have to be a powerful intervention to help the group move into this challenge.

Upon arrival, I thankfully noted that the group members were not as angry as when they left the previous week. I then initiated a series of activities.

As I was using a blackboard to brainstorm a list of all the things the members would like to have happen in the group and another list of things that they would not like to have happen in the group, I noted a heightening of the struggle between Kenyetta and Rosemarie. The two girls did not seem to want to deal with this directly, so I suggested that two other members of the group do a role play of Kenyetta and Rosemarie together in the group. Kay and Laura volunteered. At one point I asked Kay (as Kenyetta) to think about what Rosemarie might be feeling, and asked Laura (as Rosemarie) to think about what Kenyetta might be feeling. Kenyetta shouted out, "This is stupid! I want to stop!" Kay pointed out that Kenyetta sounded scared. Kenyetta replied with bravado, "I'm not scared of anything." I used this incident to explore different experiences that had scared the group members. Several of the girls shared experiences. However, Josie's experience (in which she described in detail how a man attacked her mother) was the most profound.

Upon hearing Josie's story, the group became silent. Several girls started to cry, and others asked Josie what she did when this was happening. Josie described how she hid and afterwards helped her mother. I reinforced the importance of expressing the full range of feelings, including sadness and anger. The girls elaborated about how mean and violent men and boys can be. This sharing created a common feeling, which increased cohesiveness.

The final activity was having the members draw a picture of something that would make them feel better. I asked them to share their pictures with the other members. It is important to note that I did not come into this session with prescribed activities, but chose to let the activities emerge from the content and process of the group.

Sessions 5 and 6

During session 5 the group worked through some of the early power and control issues, which were characterized by "storming" and conflict (Garland et al., 1973). Although tensions between Kenyetta and Rosemarie had not totally dissipated, some conflict resolution had taken place. The members had also begun to take risks by sharing some of their experiences and feelings about violence; thus the work of the group had begun. I now needed to use the activities to increase the feeling of cohesion, sharing, belonging, and mutual aid.

In session 6 I introduced the activity of making a collective poster containing code words that would generalize the members' feelings about the group and violence. It would also give them an opportunity to work and play together. I decided to have them work as one large group to enhance cohesion. A summary of highlights of the session follows.

I began the activity by giving each member an index card, colored markers, and glue. I told them that I was going to call out a word, and that on the card they were to write another word that it reminded them of, or that they associated with it. I then said, "The word that I am thinking of is 'group.'" The girls looked around, and someone said, "What does 'group' remind me of?" When they had finished, I gave them another index card. I told them that the second word I was thinking of was "violence," and that they were to do the same as they did for the first word. The group members were pensive, but continued the activity by writing on the second index card. I continued by giving them a large piece of poster board and telling them that they were to place and glue all their individual cards into some kind of meaningful whole-group picture or design. As they did this, there was a lot of discussion as to how it would be laid out and what their design should look like. Although there was some debate regarding what it would look like, the members were able to work together with minimal intervention from me. After they glued the cards on, I told the members to use the markers to draw connections between the cards. Again, there was a lot of process regarding the connections and meaning attached to them. Finally, I told them to draw or write anything they would like to have on the poster that was missing. I asked them to talk among themselves about the poster and explain it to me. (The poster is depicted in Figure 4.1.)

Kay began by saying that the cards in the top left corner in a circle were the words representing "group." They had written the name "Dream Girls" around these words to represent their group's name. The various words on the associated index cards were "school," "snacks," "fun," "talking," and so forth. Rosemarie jumped in and took over, explaining that the words representing "violence" (e.g., "scared," "mean," "hate," "hide"), which were running like railroad tracks off the poster board with arrows, were "stuff" they were trying to get rid of and that made them feel bad. They all took turns explaining the various connections that they made, with some making reference to the "scary stuff" that they had experienced, and wishing and dreaming that it would go away.

Clearly, the group was learning how to work together, as the members began to share more of their feelings about violence during this session. Although the tensions and cliques had not totally dissolved, the group was feeling safer for the members, and mutual aid was developing.

Session 7

I believed that the girls might now be able to risk more about themselves and their experiences with violence, and I introduced the game of Tic-Tac-Toe Wish List to facilitate this. Each member was asked to make a tic-tac-toe grid. Alexandra declared that she did not know how to play the game. While expressing surprise, several of the girls explained it to her. I then instructed them to write in each space something that they wished was different in their home or neighborhood. Rosa said that she couldn't think of so many things. I explained that even though there were nine spaces, they could put the same thing in all the spaces if they wanted to. The group spent some time filling in the spaces, and several of the members helped each other and asked me how to spell various words. I then explained that they were to take turns stating one of the wishes that they put in their grids; other members were to cross off that box on their grids if they had a similar item. When tic-tac-toe was achieved, the winning members would be given a prize. I had brought in special candies to distribute to the winners. An excerpt of the group's process follows:

FIGURE 4.1. A collective poster with code words indicating the members' feelings about the group (at top left) and violence (at right).

Content of Session	Analysis and Feelings
LEADER: Seems like everyone is ready; who would like to begin?	I am wondering whether the group will be able to trust and share in more depth.
KENYETTA: I'll be first. I wish people were not so mean to me. (*Some of the girls look at her in surprise.*)	I note other members' nonverbal behaviors and feel pleased that Kenyetta is able to express caring about how others treat her.
LEADER: Does anyone else have something like that? Like you wish people like your brother, sister, teacher, or parents would not pick on you, or do mean things to other people?	I am making a demand for work.
(*Several of the girls raise their hands and quietly state who the person is that is mean. I tell them that they can cross those off the grid, and then ask who wants to be next.*)	
MARIA: I wish I lived somewhere that did not have guns!	
LEADER: Does anyone else have something like that? That they wish they didn't live in a neighborhood that did not have such terrible things as guns? If so, cross it off.	
ALEXANDRA: Where I used to live, you could hear guns a lot at night. It's scary. You have to be really careful. We don't go out at night.	These kids have really had to cope with fear.
LEADER: Yes, gunfire and guns are scary. You do have to be careful. OK, who would like to be next?	I am validating their feelings.
ROSEMARIE: I wished that kids at school were nicer and wouldn't fight.	
KENYETTA: Yeah, me too. Those boys on the playground had knives. My mother said that I've got to protect myself.	
ROSEMARIE: Yeah, but not from us. We wouldn't hurt you.	
LEADER: Well, I guess it is sometimes hard to know who you can trust. All right, does anyone have tic-tac-toe yet? (*No response.*) Well, let's see who is next.	
ROSA: I wish that my family had a nice apartment.	
LEADER: OK, does anyone else have something like that—like a better or different place to live?	
EVELINA: OK, I do. Tic-tac-toe.	
LEADER: OK, we have a winner. Here is your prize.	

I continued to let the members go around telling what they had in their grids. I had to draw Josie out, as she was shy because of her limited language skills. As they went around, the girls continued to risk and self-disclose more. I continued to validate their feelings while allowing the process to unfold naturally as the group continued to play and work. At the end of the game, I told the members they were all "winners," and distributed the prizes evenly among them.

Sessions 8, 9, and 10

Sessions 8, 9, and 10 were representative of the late middle phase of group development. The group was cohesive. Issues of individuation and differentiation occurred. The girls were more in touch with their feelings. In session 8, they wrote a song around the theme "Let's make the world safe." This activity brought Kenyetta and Rosemarie together, since both had lovely voices. Alexandra and Kay were wonderful writers. The other girls provided rhythm and instrumentation.

The critical incident from these three sessions that is described here involved an activity dealing with separating thoughts, feelings, and needs. I placed a large piece of brown paper with a rough sketch of a human being (see Figure 4.2) on the floor. I then asked the group to think about what should go into each part, defining the head as thoughts, the heart as feelings, and the stomach as needs.

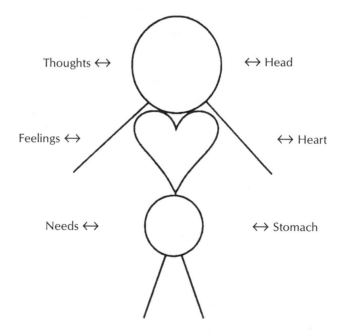

FIGURE 4.2. Outline of a human being, allowing space for thoughts (in the head), feelings (in the heart), and needs (in the stomach).

Content of Session

Analysis and Feelings

LEADER: Before we do this activity, you may want to decorate the outline so it looks more like a person.

(One member calls out, "That's right, you can't draw," to the leader.)

Signs of intimacy.

KENYETTA *(getting down on the floor)*: The outline is me. It's my size and brown.

KAY: You're thinner than the outline.

ALEXANDRA: I'm taller than it.

(The girls decide to put hair on the head. This leads to a discussion of what kind and style.)

KENYETTA: It should be curly or with braids.

JOSIE: Why not blond like Alexandra?

ROSEMARIE: Kenyetta, your hair isn't curly like Laura's.

LEADER: It seems that all of you have differences, and perhaps you can share what these are.

I feel that it is time to raise the issue of their different racial and ethnic backgrounds.

ROSA: Kay's hair is so beautiful and long.

EVELINA: I hate my hair. It always has snags, and it hurts to brush it out.

KENYETTA: I could fix your hair like my mom does.

MARIA: My mother is really good with hair. She works at a beauty parlor and has this cream which takes out knots.

LAURA: You mean conditioner.

I note that mutual aid and general concern have developed.

ALEXANDRA: One time we didn't have water for 10 days, and my hair had all these bugs.

(Several girls say, "Ugh.")

EVELINA: Do you mean lice?

ALEXANDRA: I'm not sure. My mother had to cut my hair real short and use this horrible stuff.

ROSA: Your hair is real pretty now. Someday I'm going to make my hair blond like yours.

KAY: Alexandra, is that why you came to this country?

ALEXANDRA: We had to come here because everyone was killing everyone where I lived. It really is much better here.

EVELINA: Well, not always. Where I live, people hurt and kill each other. There are lots of bugs and sometimes worse than that. Rosa, did you see the rats?

ROSA: (*Ignores Evelina.*) What kind of hair should we put on this figure?

JOSIE: Rosa, do you live in the same building with Evelina?

EVELINA: We live in this shelter. It's gross.

ROSA: Evelina, it's none of their business.

KAY: When I first came here, we lived with 10 relatives in two rooms until we could find a place to live. It was hard.

ROSA: Beth, let's do the activity.

LEADER: Rosa, yes, we will finish the activity, but I was curious and interested in all of your different experiences in how you are living at home.

EVELINA: I don't have a real home.

ROSA: There's nothing to talk about.

ROSEMARIE: We are different not only because of where we live. I feel closer to Josie and Rosa because they are Spanish and they aren't mean like some of the members can be.

KAY: I'm not Spanish.

KENYETTA: I'm not mean. I'm just protecting myself.

The group is focused on exploring differences, and I deliberately make minimal interventions. The members are experiencing some intimate moments, and there is increased sharing. However, Rosa wants to remain secretive about her living conditions. The members want to know more, but also are protective of Rosa's need to remain silent.

What an important insight!

Session 11

The focus of the final two sessions was on termination and endings. This was difficult, since the group had now developed into a cohesive unit where differences were verbalized and a sense of belonging was established. The members had learned how to establish mutual aid, how to make decisions, and how to solve problems. Many of the girls had found ways to use the group to fulfill their needs beyond the original purpose. For some of the members, it had become an opportunity to develop successful peer relationships.

Activities in sessions 11 and 12 included planning and having a party, writing a group poem, making goodbye cards, and taking and distributing a group photo. The process reflected a review of the life of the group.

In session 11, the critical incident (as described below) was the response to endings.

Content of Session

LEADER: We only have two more sessions, and I'd like for you to think about how the group can end its work together.

Analysis and Feelings

Termination issues are raised. Due to the neediness of the members, endings are going to be a difficult process.

KENYETTA: So why does it have to end? We're in school to the end of June.

EVELINA: Yeah, that's not fair. We can stay to the end of June.

KAY: Well, when we started, you said that it was only going to be 12 sessions.

ROSEMARIE: I only just began liking the group.

LAURA: Why do we have to end?

ALEXANDRA: Maybe we don't have to end. | The members reflect ambivalence.

LEADER: Endings are really hard when you've worked so hard to make friends. | Recognition of feelings.

ROSA: Well, we are still here. What are we doing today?

LEADER: There are a couple of things that we can do today. I would like for you to plan a party for next week. | I am setting the structure for a successful ending.

KENYETTA: Are you going to bring us presents? | This member reflects the group's neediness.

LEADER: Perhaps you can make each other cards for presents, or maybe you want to write a group poem and I can make copies for next week.

The group members initially decided to make cards. I told them to write their names on a piece of paper. They put these in a bag, and each drew the name of a person she would make a card for. The members also planned a party. The girls refused to talk directly about the ending, but their feelings about one another and the group came out in the messages in the cards that they made and exchanged with one another. In fact, the messages became the group poem. At the end of the meeting, Rosa grabbed the leftover snacks as she left the room. Josie announced that she might not be able to come next week.

Session 12

The purpose of the last session of any group is to review the gains of the group, help members separate from each other, and provide them with a successful termination experience. The girls entered the room in a somewhat "hyper" state. One of the members brought a "boom box," announcing, "It's party time."

Content of Session

Analysis and Feelings

LEADER: Seems like everyone is in a good mood, and we are going to have a lot of time to party. However, I think that we need to cut the music for a few minutes to talk. Has anyone seen Josie? | The group's mood is regressive, and I need to set limits. The group's boundaries are beginning to disperse, and cohesion is breaking apart.

KENYETTA: We've done enough talking in this group.

Intimacy should not be encouraged in the final stage of group development.

LAURA: Josie's not here today.

I'm sorry to hear this.

KAY: Gee, I thought everyone would come today. It's special.

LEADER: Yes, the group has been special, and it has been all of your hard work that has made it that way.

I reaffirm the positive experience.

(*The pizza arrives, and the girls get distracted from the talking. They want to eat and return to the discussion.*)

LEADER: I wonder if each of you would mention one thing that you got from the group, and one thing that you did not get but would have liked to have gotten from the group.

I am making a demand for work.

ROSA: I don't see why the group has to end.

LEADER: Rosa, it seems like you really like the group. Maybe you can share why you don't want the group to end.

I am reaching for the positives.

ROSA: I like the snacks and making stuff. And some of the girls are my friends now.

ALEXANDRA: I liked meeting new girls. I never knew that people did violent things in America. I thought everything would be good here.

ROSEMARIE: Yeah, mean things can happen anywhere.

MARIA: Even in your own room.

KAY: I didn't think that you had to be so careful here.

KENYETTA: That's why you got to protect yourself.

She continues to feel vulnerable.

(*The members continue to discuss actualization of the group's purpose.*)

LEADER: I think that we've found in the group that everyone protects themselves differently. One of the important things that happened here was that you were able to begin to talk about the bad things that you have seen.

KENYETTA: Enough talk. Let's party.

Kenyetta continues to demonstrate her leadership abilities and oppositional behavior.

(*During the party period, the members talk about how sometimes they don't like each other. They also discuss the friendships they have made in the group, and ask the leader whether she likes them.*)

CONCLUSION

This chapter has provided an example of a time-limited latency-age children's group, formed to deal with the issues and concerns affecting children who witness violence. It is our belief that this type of intervention can help such children learn new ways of coping, provide a socialization experience, and reduce some of their overt symptoms. It is a mechanism that can prevent more serious behavioral difficulties in the future.

Children such as the girls described here are all struggling with aggressive feelings, issues about their racial and ethnic identities, insufficient nurturance and stability at home, and feelings of inadequacy and sadness. A group leader needs to choose the points of intervention carefully. This group intervention alone cannot change a child's parental or neighborhood environment, or result in a total change in behavior. However, it can help such children feel less alone through the provision of successful peer relationships, a trusting relationship with an adult, and a safe place to begin to share their anxieties and feelings in relation to the violence they have witnessed. It helps the children learn how to be safe while fulfilling important needs in a violent world (Malekoff, 1997).

The chapter also demonstrates the use of activity as a means of facilitating the work of the group. One can see the interweaving of process and content, as well as the stages of group development. Ultimately, it is our hope that time-limited, purposeful group interventions such as this will be more frequently utilized in various practice settings.

STUDY QUESTIONS

1. Name several interventions that were critical to maintaining the group's purpose. How can a leader ensure that a group stays on track?

2. Discuss the issues of setting limits. How can a leader respond if members are openly defiant?

3. Discuss an issue that emerged that was not dealt with in the group described here. How would you have handled it?

4. Outline an activity that is not mentioned. In what stage of group development would you use it?

5. Using this model of intervention, what other purposes or issues could a group like this deal with?

6. Discuss the pressures on a group leader of working with children who have witnessed violence. How can leaders deal with their own anxieties about this?

REFERENCES

Congress, E., & Lynn, M. (1994). Group work programs in public schools: Ethical dilemmas and cultural diversity. *Social Work in Education, 16*(2), 107–114.

Connors, K., Schamess, G., & Strieder, F. (1997). Children's treatment groups: General principles and their application to group treatment with cumulatively traumatized children. In J. Brandell (Ed.), *Theory and practice in clinical social work* (pp. 288–314). New York: Free Press.

Egan, T. (1998, June 14). From adolescent angst to shooting up schools. *The New York Times*, pp. A1, A22

Emde, R. (1993). The horror! The horror!: Reflections on our culture of violence and its implications for early development and morality. In D. Reiss, J. Richters, M. Radke-Yarrow, & D. Scharff (Eds.), *Children and violence* (pp. 119–123). New York: Guilford Press.

Erikson, E. (1963). *Childhood and society* (rev. ed.). New York: Norton.

Garbarino, J., Dubrow, N., Kostelny, K., & Pardo, C. (1992). *Children in danger: Coping with the consequences of community violence*. San Francisco: Jossey-Bass.

Garland, J., Jones, H., & Kolodny, R. (1973). A model for stages of development in social work groups. In S. Bernstein (Ed.), *Explorations in group work* (pp. 17–71). Boston: Milford House.

Germain, C. (1991). *Human behavior in the social environment: An ecological view*. New York: Columbia University Press.

Grusznski, R., Brink, J., & Edleson, J. (1988). Support and education groups for children of battered women. *Child Welfare, 67*(5), 431–444.

Guterman, N., & Cameron, M. (1997) Assessing the impact of community violence on children and youths. *Social Work, 42*(5), 495–505.

Haran, J. (1988). The use of group work to help children cope with the violent death of a class mate. *Social Work with Groups, 11*(3), 79–92.

Henry, S. (1992). *Group skills in social work: A four-dimensional approach* (2nd ed.). Pacific Grove, CA: Brooks/Cole.

Kurland, R., & Salmon, R. (1998). *Teaching a methods course in social work with groups*. Alexandria, VA: Council on Social Work Education.

Lee, J., & Nisivoccia-Park, D. (1983). A group approach to the depressed adolescent girl in foster care. In E. Buchholz & J. Mishne (Eds.), *Ego and self psychology* (pp. 185–207). New York: Jason Aronson.

Lorion, R., & Saltzman, W. (1993). Children's exposure to community violence: Following a path from concern to research to action. In D. Reiss, J. Richters, M. Radke-Yarrow, & D. Scharff (Eds.), *Children and violence* (pp. 55–65). New York: Guilford Press.

Lynn, M., & Nisivoccia, D. (1995). Activity-oriented group work with the mentally ill: Enhancing socialization. *Social Work with Groups, 18*(2–3), 95–106.

Malekoff, A. (1997). *Group work with adolescents: Principles and practice*. New York: Guilford Press.

Meyer, C. (1976). *Social work practice*. New York: Free Press.

Middleman, R. (1968). *The non-verbal method in working with groups*. New York: Association Press.

Northen, H. (1988). *Social work with groups*. New York: Columbia University Press.

Osofsky, J. (Ed.). (1997). *Children in a violent society*. New York: Guilford Press.

Papell, C., & Rothman, B. (1980). Relating the mainstream model of social work with groups to group psychotherapy and the structured group approach. *Social Work with Groups, 3*(2), 5–23.

Peled, E., & Davis, D. (1995). *Groupwork with children of battered women: A practitioner's manual*. Thousand Oaks, CA: Sage.

Richters, J. (1993). Community violence and children's development: Toward a research agenda for the 1990's. In D. Reiss, J. Richters, M. Radke-Yarrow, & D. Scharff (Eds.), *Children and violence* (pp. 55–65). New York: Guilford Press.

Roseby, V., & Johnston, J. (1995). Clinical interventions with latency-age children of high conflict and violence. *American Journal of Orthopsychiatry*, 65(1), 48–59.

Scheidlinger, S. (1974). On the concept of the "mother group." *International Journal of Group Psychotherapy*, 24(4), 417–428.

Schwartz, W. (1976). Between client and system: The mediating function. In R. Roberts & H. Northen (Eds.), *Theories of social work with groups* (pp. 171–197). New York: Columbia University Press.

Slavson, S., & Schieffer, M. (1975). *Group psychotherapy for children*. New York: International Universities Press.

Toseland, R., & Rivas, R. (1998). *An introduction to group work practice* (3rd ed.). Needham Heights, MA: Allyn & Bacon.

Vinter, R. (1985). Program activities: An analysis of their effects on participants behavior. In M. Sundel, P. Glasser, R. Sarri, & R. Vinter (Eds.), *Individual change through small groups* (2nd ed., pp. 237–250). New York: Free Press.

Webb, N. (1996). *Social work practice with children*. New York: Guilford Press.

Whitlock, J. (1997). National hospital for kids in crisis: Continuing education seminar examines how violence and trauma affect our children. *Healing Magazine*, 2(1), 4–7.

Wilson, G., & Ryland, G. (1949). *Social group work practice*. Cambridge, MA: Riverside Press.

Winnicott, D. (1965). *The maturational process and the facilitating environment*. New York: International Universities Press.

CHAPTER 5

The Assessment and Treatment of Family Sexual Abuse

Case of Rosa, Age 6

VIRGINIA C. STRAND

This chapter describes assessment and brief treatment with a child about whom there were suspicions of family sexual abuse. The term "family sexual abuse" is used here to denote sexual abuse of a child by a parent or parent substitute (stepfather, live-in paramour); it is used in lieu of the term "incest," since it is more consistent with recent conceptualizations about sexual molestation by adults of children with whom they have a familiar bond.

In such a case, the focus in the initial sessions is on establishing whether the child has indeed been sexually abused. If (as in the case described here) it appears to be so, the next steps involve assessing the impact of the abuse and developing long-term treatment goals, including protection from future risk. The protective concerns that arise in cases of child sexual abuse in general and family sexual abuse in particular often complicate therapeutic intervention; they usually call for collaboration between mental health services and child protective services (CPS) and/or the family court system. The chapter details strategies for exploration of possible sexual abuse with a 6-year-old child, outlines the protective steps taken in the case, and briefly describes the design of long-term treatment intervention. Issues confronting a 14-year-old adolescent with a history of family sexual abuse at age 6 are then discussed in the form of prognostic implications.

THEORETICAL FRAMEWORK

Since the publication of the first edition of this book (Webb, 1991), there has been an explosion in the literature on child sexual abuse (Friedrich, 1990, 1995; Gil,1991, 1996; Gil & Cavanaugh Johnson, 1993). Similarly, there has been an enormous increase in both the clinical and research literature about the impact of trauma in general on childhood development (Armsworth & Holaday, 1993; van der Kolk & Fisler, 1994). The contributions from these authors have shed new light on our understanding of the psychological ramifications in childhood, as well as suggesting therapeutic remedies. These authors come primarily from clinical practice backgrounds. During the same time period, academic researchers (primarily from the fields of developmental and social psychology) have published extensive studies of children's memory and suggestibility (Ceci, Ross, & Toglia, 1987; Goodman & Bottoms, 1993; Loftus & Christian, 1989). The latter have highlighted the need to be attentive to developmental considerations in evaluating children who present with a history of possible sexual abuse.

As I have noted elsewhere (Strand, 1994), the need for thorough and comprehensive evaluations in cases of suspected child sexual abuse, and the frequent need for the evaluator to report the findings to a family court, argue for separating assessment from treatment and in having different professionals undertake the two tasks. Although this was not the process in the case reported here, it is one that the reader is encouraged to consider, despite the fact that in current practice the option of separating evaluation from treatment may not be routinely available. The case description presented here suggests an approach that tries to safeguard the integrity of the therapeutic process with the child and family, while at the same time relating to the protective concerns that require interaction between the therapist and the authorities responsible for the protection of the child.

Armsworth and Holaday (1993), Gil (1996), and van der Kolk and Fisler (1994) have all added to Burgess's (1987) concept of "trauma encapsulation," introduced in my chapter in the first edition of this book. As described by Burgess, trauma encapsulation is a child's tendency to hold memories of a traumatic event, as well as overwhelming feelings associated with these memories, in an unprocessed state in short-term memory. Whereas Burgess contributed to an understanding of the mechanism by which many children cope with trauma, van der Kolk and Fisler (1994) have given us a better understanding of the manner in which traumatic experiences of abuse and neglect in childhood disturb a child's ability to regulate affect, control impulses, and damage the development of basic trust (a prerequisite to sustaining interpersonal relationships). Armsworth and Holaday (1993), in their summary of the literature on the impact of childhood abuse and neglect, underscore the impact on the child's cognitive development as well. Key to earlier concepts, and reinforced by the work of Gil (1996) and van der Kolk and Fisler (1994), is the notion that the defensive structure that evolves to cope with the impact of the acute or chronic traumatic events often consumes the psychic energy needed to accomplish normal developmental tasks, resulting in the emotional and behavioral symptoms widely cited in the literature (Briere & Runtz, 1988a, 1988b; Gelinas, 1983). Typical symptoms of sexually abused children include age-inappropriate sexual knowledge or sexual behavior; sleeping and eating disturbances; aggressive and antisocial behaviors; feelings of guilt, blame, and other depressive symptoms; self-deprecating or self-destructive behaviors; hyperarousal; inability to concentrate; and other anxiety symptoms seen in children with posttraumatic stress disorder.

In order to resolve the trauma of sexual abuse that has resulted in serious emotional and behavioral disturbance, the therapist must focus directly on this experience. The trauma can be reexperienced and reworked—either directly through the verbalization of details, emotions, and memories surrounding the abuse, or indirectly, symbolically, through play therapy. Gil (1996) describes this as the "structured processing of trauma." The emphasis on addressing the trauma is similar to the process detailed by Hartman and Burgess (1988), who identify six phases of treatment; their model includes an emphasis on shoring up defenses before encouraging the surfacing of traumatic material.

The six phases described below parallel but are not identical to those put forth by Hartman and Burgess (1988), and incorporate some of the concepts identified by Gil (1996). These are designed to provide guidelines for intervention. The first two phases focus on identification and assessment of the impact of sexual abuse. The latter four outline strategies for ongoing intervention and treatment once the fact of abuse has been established. The six phases are (1) developmental assessment and exploration for sexual abuse, (2) obtaining a sexual abuse history, (3) enhancing ego strengths, (4) surfacing traumatic material, (5) working through, and (6) resolution.

Developmental Assessment and Exploration for Sexual Abuse

One of the first tasks upon referral of a child in a case where a suspicion of child sexual abuse exists is to complete a developmental assessment. This is necessary in order to correctly interpret statements or disclosures that the child may make regarding incidents of sexual abuse. This assessment can be achieved through the combination of a clinical interview with the child and the taking of a developmental history. In addition to evaluating the child's social, emotional, and cognitive development, it is important to ascertain whether the child knows the difference between the truth and a lie, and whether there is any reason (e.g., limited cognitive abilities, serious mental illness) to believe that the child cannot distinguish between fact and fantasy. The ability to make these distinctions may have significant legal as well as clinical implications. The accuracy of the child's memory is an additionally significant factor. Although young children may be more susceptible than adults to misleading statements, this does not seem to be the case when it comes to central detail— that is, the description of the sexual activity itself (Friedrich, 1990).

A developmental history augments the clinical interview with the child. The child's parent(s) and other caretakers are the primary source of information for this history. The history should include information about the child's knowledge of sexuality, including, for a younger child, the child's exposure to sexual activity between parents or other adults and to sexually explicit magazines or videos. Behaviors found to be unusual in children who have not been sexually abused include attempting or simulating intercourse, inserting objects in the vagina or rectum, and touching the breasts of an adult (Friedrich, 1990). In some instances, particularly those in which questions about severe developmental delay or possible neurological impairment are concerns, psychological testing and/or psychiatric evaluation may be an important tool in the assessment.

Although an important goal is to establish the level of appropriate communication in the interview with the child, the results of the developmental assessment may also provide essential information about whether the child's presentation is or is not consistent with that of a sexually abused child. In terms of investigative interviewing techniques, it is critical to proceed using open-ended questions initially. As outlined by Myers (1992), questions can be conceptualized as proceeding from less suggestive questions, such as open-ended and then focused questions, to those that are clearly coercive. The reader may consult his work on this subject for a more detailed review of specific questioning techniques.

Obtaining a Sexual Abuse History

If it is established that the child has experienced incidents of sexual abuse, an exploration of the history is in order. This step involves the assessment of the impact of the sexual abuse itself. I have found it helpful to use the conceptual framework developed by Suzanne Sgroi (1984) as a guide. The phases she originally described are discussed below, augmented by research carried out and clinical understandings developed since the first edition of this book was published.

Engagement

Most children are abused by adults they know (Russell, 1986). Therefore, it is within the framework of a preexisting relationship that an adult engages a child in sexual activity. This phase is nonsexual. Typically, the adult uses his or her authority as a parent, teacher, or other person in a position of power relative to the child to manipulate the child. A child's willingness to please important or feared adults is easily exploited. Although threats may be employed, corruption of the child's trust, attachment, and/or affection is more usual. Those who do therapy with sex offenders have come to call this process "grooming the child," to describe the course in which the adult prepares a child for sexual interaction (Salter, 1995).

An adult may actively seek to strengthen the relationship with a child, engaging the child in games, assuming the role of teacher or educator, or becoming involved in daily child care routines. The use of pornographic magazines and videotapes to normalize the sexual activity is becoming an increasingly common ploy. All of these approaches are geared toward having the child accept the sexual contact as "normal" and thereby decreasing the child's tendency to disclose the activity.

Sexual Interaction

The second phase captures the range of sexual activity that an adult may engage in with a child. There may be a progression of activities, particularly if the adult has access to the same child over time. Sexual interaction in this scenario may begin with less intrusive sexual acts (such as fondling or sexual kissing) and progress to more intrusive acts (such as oral–genital contact and penetration, either anal or vaginal) over time. Another pattern is for the adult to engage the child repeatedly in the same kind of activity from the beginning. When the offender has access and opportunity because of an ongoing relationship with a child, the molestation usually recurs. Adults who are motivated to be sexual with children may also become involved with numerous children over time.

Secrecy

One of the most difficult aspects of child sexual abuse, both for the child and for the adults who are attempting to protect a child, is the shroud of secrecy surrounding the abuse. An adult who molests a child wants to minimize the chance of disclosure. Therefore, in addition to almost always choosing situations where he or she is alone with the child, the adult will communicate to the child that the sexual behavior is to be kept a secret. This communication may be covert (through the adult's secretive, furtive behavior) or more overt (through direct statements that the sexual activity is to be kept a secret). Verbal manipulations that rely on the child's attachment to other significant figures (e.g., "Don't tell your mother about this; she couldn't handle it") to outright threats to the child ("If you tell anyone, you will be sorry") may be employed by the adult.

Children who know that the abusing adults are violent or physically abusive persons may be coerced into keeping the secret if, for example, they are threatened with being hit or beaten. Adults sometimes resort to physical abuse to manipulate the children into not telling. Children depend on the adults around them for support and survival, and they almost always understand the message about secrecy and do not reveal the sexual activity.

Disclosure

The disclosure of sexual abuse, when it occurs, may be delayed or unconvincing. Often the disclosure is accidental, as when a child is discovered to have gonorrhea, or when another victim or friend of the victim discloses against the wishes of the child who has been sexually abused. Other times the disclosure is purposeful. Many times the disclosure will occur in response to specific questions asked by a concerned significant other who begins to suspect that something is amiss. It is not unusual for the child to initially disclose only one incident or one activity, even when many have occurred. It is important to understand that disclosure is often a process and not an event. Additional incidents, if they have occurred, may only emerge over time.

Suppression

The tendency for a child to retract, recant, or minimize an initial report of sexual abuse is common. It must be remembered that the child or adolescent has actively tried to keep the memories out of awareness because of the overwhelming feelings that are associated with those memories. Therefore, discussing the incidents even in the presence of a supportive adult is painful, as it brings those feelings to the surface. The pressure on the child to minimize or recant is therefore immense. Many children feel they are to blame for the abuse, and talking about it may stir up feelings of guilt, despair, fear, and/or embarrassment. The range and intensity of feelings depend not only on the child's relationship with the offender, but also on the child's age. Children may fear rejection by the offender or by members of the family.

Sometimes these fears are real, such as in cases where family members pressure the child to withhold or retract allegations.

Obtaining information about these five phases will provide information not only about the duration and nature of the sexual abuse, but also about the context of the relationship with the offender and the family dynamics. The next step in treatment is to prepare the child for surfacing the trauma and working it through.

Enhancing Ego Strengths

Critical to the healing process is the step of enhancing ego strengths prior to focused efforts to surface memories of the sexual abuse. Although details about some incidents and accompanying memories may have been elicited during the first two steps as described above, the treatment emphasis on surfacing the traumatic material will focus on reworking the emotional and cognitive responses to the fact of the abuse. For this to be effective, it is important that the child feel safe and protected from further abuse. Protecting the child may entail a range of interventions—removing the child from the abusive home, orders of protection restraining the alleged offender from contact, supervised contact, or some combination of these.

Increasing the child's self-soothing and self-comforting abilities are two of the major goals of strengthening ego capacities. One way to accomplish this is to help the child identify activities that make him or her feel good, reduce anxiety, or channel aggression. Examples of such activities include searching out people to whom the child can talk, listening to music, writing, learning relaxation exercises, or finding active outlets for aggressive play. The therapist can be optimally effective if he or she works with the parent as well as the child in identifying and using these activities.

Surfacing the Trauma

When the child has been prepared in a developmentally appropriate fashion for the uncomfortable feelings that may accompany the reexperiencing, retelling, or reliving of the abusive incidents, the work of surfacing the trauma can begin. (In practice, of course, the demarcations between the phases of treatment are not always so clear.) Tools now available to assist with surfacing the trauma include anatomical dolls or drawings, special workbooks, and board games. I use workbooks (e.g., Stowell & Dietzel, 1982) not only to trigger memories, but also to enhance self-esteem. The board game Play It Safe with SASA (Speak out About Sexual Abuse) serves a similar function for children aged 4–11 (it is available from SASA & Company, 2008 LaBrea Terrace, Los Angeles, CA 90046). The use of anatomically correct dolls is illustrated below in my description of the work with Rosa. Traditional play materials—art supplies, dolls, dollhouses, action figures, and so forth—continue to be the foundation of play therapy with children and can be used creatively.

How can one think about the impact of sexual abuse and the effects that are likely to occur? The work of David Finkelhor and Angela Browne (1985) provides a useful conceptualization for understanding the impact. Others have suggested different organizing frameworks for thinking about the impact of trauma. Friedrich (1995), for example, suggests that trauma affects three areas of the self: attachment, self-regulation, and self-esteem. These concepts are integrated into the discussion below.

Finkelhor and Browne (1985) state that four dynamics are manifested in victims of sexual trauma: (1) sexual traumatization, (2) stigmatization, (3) betrayal, and (4) powerlessness. All four are likely to be experienced, although the mix will vary depending on a child's age, the nature of the abuse, and the relationship between the child and the offender.

"Sexual traumatization" refers to the impairment of healthy sexual functioning because of the sexual nature of the trauma. The varying degree of impairment includes confusion between sexuality and affection, confusion about sexual norms, age-inappropriate sexual knowledge and sexual behavior, negative associations to sexual feelings, a tendency to form erotic attachments, sexual dysfunction, confusion about sexual identity, and in some instances reenactment through the sexual abuse of others. Any given child will experience one or more of these, and in surfacing the traumatic material, these distortions become the focus of treatment.

"Stigmatization" refers to the tendency of victims to blame themselves for the abuse, and to feel shame, guilt, and self-hate. Depression, low self-esteem, and poor self-image are often consequences. Self-deprecating behaviors (inability to assert one's rights or needs), self-mutilating behaviors (self-inflicted injuries, anorexia nervosa, bulimia nervosa, and/or self-destructive behaviors (suicidal ideation or gestures, substance abuse) are common presentations of this dynamic. All children who have been sexually abused are likely to manifest one or more of these attitudes toward themselves, and the therapist should be alert for the specific manifestations in a given child.

"Betrayal" refers to the betrayal of trust experienced by the victim of sexual abuse. This leads to difficulty in interpersonal relationships, as evidenced by difficulty in forming relationships, guardedness, suspiciousness, ambivalence, and choosing relationships in which one is exploited. Antisocial attitudes and behaviors may evolve in response to the rage and anger associated with the betrayal. Though all children may have some difficulties in this area because of the sexual abuse, the degree to which this is a problematic area usually relates not only to the nature of the relationship with the offender, but also to the response of other significant adults once the child has disclosed the abuse.

The fourth dynamic, "powerlessness," relates to the sense of helplessness and vulnerability engendered in the child victim of sexual abuse. Anxiety symptoms and disorders (including phobias), dissociative disorders, and regressive behaviors are appropriately clustered with this characteristic and are among those that need to be addressed in this phase of treatment.

Working Through

It is difficult to separate the surfacing of traumatic memories from the stage of working through. In practice, it is not unusual for there to be a period where events are surfaced and worked through, followed by the need to return to the phase of enhancing ego strengths before additional traumatic material can be surfaced. However, treatment priorities can be set in terms of the traumagenic dynamics discussed above. For example, the betrayal dynamic is often a useful place for the therapist to begin. As the therapist builds an alliance with the child, the child's ability to trust and the extent to which this capacity may have been compromised become evident. In the work of developing the relationship, issues centering around betrayal are likely to evolve, presenting the opportunity to rework the ability to trust within the framework of the therapeutic relationship.

The child's symptom presentation may provide clues to the most salient dynamics. For example, the child who is extremely anxious and avoidant, or who qualifies for a formal diagnosis of posttraumatic stress disorder, may be reacting primarily with feeling of helplessness to the trauma of the abuse. On the other hand, the child who is withdrawn, depressed, and withholding may be feeling more guilt and self-blame than helplessness, and this may be the focus of treatment initially. Ultimately, the goal in treatment is to rework the emotional reactions and cognitive distortions so that the child has the psychic energy to pursue normal developmental tasks (Gil, 1996; Jehu, Klassen, & Gasen, 1985–1986).

Resolution

The notion of "resolution" may not have the same meaning as it once did. Although the goal is to free the child from the debilitating effects of emotional preoccupation with traumatic material and to reduce cognitive distortions, in practice this may be difficult to do in one course of treatment. Beverly James (1989) has introduced a useful analysis in presenting the notion of sequential treatment experiences. Her suggestion is that some of the impact may be resolved in one treatment experience, and that other life experiences may trigger the need for additional therapy at a later time. These experiences may be either developmental or extraordinary in nature. In the present climate of short-term therapy, the restrictions brought about by managed care, and other dynamics that make long-term treatment infeasible, serial or sequential episodes of treatment may be a more realistic framework for therapy with sexually abused children.

THE CASE: ROSA TORRES, AGE 6

Family Information

Rosa Torres, age 6, was referred by CPS for evaluation and short-term treatment after allegations of child sexual abuse had been reported. The family included Rosa; her mother, Lisa, 34; her father, Roberto, 39; an older half-brother, Jorge, 17; and a 2-year-old sister, Sabrina. Rosa, her mother, Jorge, and Sabrina were currently living with Mrs. Torres's mother and father in the maternal grandparents' home. Mr. Torres was living with his mother and had visitation with Rosa and Sabrina one night during the week and every weekend.

Mrs. Torres was born in Puerto Rico and came to New York City as a young child with her mother and older brother. This brother was killed as a teenager in a gang fight. Mrs. Torres became a nurse and married Roberto Torres at age 26. She had never been married to Jorge's father.

Roberto was also Puerto Rican, but was born in New York City. After he graduated from high school, he worked his way up in a mail-order business to the position of salesman. He had been married twice before and had two children (both boys) from his earlier marriages. He had no contact with either son.

Rosa's parents had been separated for approximately 6 months at the time of the first interview. According to the CPS worker who referred the child, both parents wanted physical custody of Rosa. Three weeks prior to the first interview, Mrs. Torres had called in a report of alleged sexual abuse against Mr. Torres, reportedly on the basis of a disclosure by Rosa that "Daddy was touching my private parts." Mrs. Torres had also asked the court to suspend visitation with the father until the CPS investigation was complete. The judge did not suspend visitation, but ruled that visits between the father and child would be supervised by a CPS worker until CPS had completed its investigation.

Presenting Problem

At the point of intake, the CPS worker had had two interviews with Rosa and had met individually with the mother, the father, and the maternal grandmother. Rosa had not disclosed any details to the worker regarding the alleged sexual abuse beyond saying that "Daddy touched me in my private."

The CPS worker had had the child examined by a physician experienced in child sexual abuse. The examination was inconclusive, and no specific findings were consistent with child sexual abuse.

The purposes of the referral to me were as follows: to evaluate the possibility of sexual abuse, to prepare for testimony in court if this possibility could be substantiated, and to assess and document the ongoing treatment needs of Rosa and/or family members. Since the court views "blind" evaluations as more objective, the developmental history normally gathered from a parent at the beginning of treatment was delayed until after the first interview with the child.

First Interview

Rosa was brought to the first interview by her mother and grandmother. I met them in the waiting room and introduced myself to all three. I then asked Rosa whether she wanted to come with me to see the toys in the playroom. Rosa was initially reluctant, standing with her body turned sideways to me and avoiding eye contact. With a little coaxing from her mother and my offer of something to drink, she was induced into going into the playroom. I stopped in the kitchen along the way to the playroom to get Rosa some juice.

Content of Session	Therapist's Rationale
THERAPIST: Rosa, do you remember my name?	
ROSA: (*Shakes head no.*)	
T: Well, it's Dr. Strand. Do you think that you can say that?	
R: Dr. Strand (*very clearly*).	
T: Do you know why your mother brought you to see me today?	I am setting the context for our meeting.
R: (*Avoids eye contact, nods head yes, moves toward the shelves that hold toys.*) It's about my daddy.	I'm glad to learn that she has been prepared.
T: Yes, your mother has told me that she is worried that you may have been upset by some things that your father did. I will want to talk with you about that later after we know each other a little better, but first we are just going to spend some time getting to know each other. (*Helps Rosa bring out toy dishes, and invites her to set up whatever she wants.*) So, I wonder, could you tell me a little bit about yourself? I know that you are 6 . . .	I'm moving to nonthreatening subjects to engage her.
R: My birthday is March 13th.	
T: I see you know your birthday. Where do you live?	
R: Yonkers.	
T: And do you have a best friend?	
R: Maria; she lives on my street (*busily playing with toy dishes*).	
T: (*Still playing with dishes—Rosa has asked therapist to play house with her.*) Do you live in a house or in an apartment building?	I am taking advantage of the play theme to get potentially significant information.
R: We live with my grandmother, and she lives on the first floor of a house. My aunt and my cousins live upstairs.	
T: And where did you live before that?	
R: We lived in a big building on the third floor.	
T: And where you live now, does everyone have their own bedroom?	I'm getting information about sleeping arrangements that may be useful later.
R: Well, Sabrina and I sleep with my mommy, and Grandma and Grandpa have their own bedroom. And Jorge sleeps on the couch in the living room.	
T: What about when your father lived with you? Where did you sleep then?	

R: I had my own room then.

T: Did your mommy and daddy always sleep together?

R: No, sometimes Daddy slept on the couch, and sometimes he slept with me.

T: Where was the couch?

R: In the living room.

I continued to play with Rosa and to pursue information about her daily life, especially about who took care of her on a regular basis. Through this line of inquiry, I learned that Rosa used to go to a babysitter named Diane when her mother worked. Rosa's grandmother took care of her now after school when her mother was working. Rosa reported that her father used to put her to bed at night. Some of the details of the bedtime routine emerged. It appeared that her father would often read Rosa a story and give her juice. He would also get her up in the morning and get her ready for school.

During this conversation, using the play materials at hand, I interwove questions aimed at establishing developmental information. I also attempted to establish the nature of the child's relationships with family members, especially with her father and mother.

Content of Session	Therapist's Rationale
THERAPIST: Who would you say that you like the best in your family?	I am trying to understand how Rosa feels about her father.
ROSA: My father, but my mother, too.	
T: Can you tell me why?	
R: He plays games with me and takes me places. My mother used to hit me more, but now she's nice.	
T: I know that you do not see your father as much now as before. Do you remember what kinds of things you used to do with him?	
R: Well, before, Daddy would pick me up and take me to Mimi's [the father's mother's] house. It's fun there.	She has positive feelings about her paternal grandmother's house
T: And what about now?	
R: I miss him sometimes. I only get to see him now in Miss Ramos's [the CPS worker's] office.	

I went on to discuss Rosa's feelings about each member of her family. Jorge was "OK," but he "won't play with me much." Sabrina "takes too much of Mommy's time," and "Mimi," her father's mother, was favored over "Grandma," with whom she was currently living. From this interchange, it appeared that Rosa was quite attached to her father, and that her mother appeared as a more distant and possibly punitive figure than her father.

Before the end of the session—since Rosa appeared to be engaged, was playing readily, and was more open in answering my questions—I made the decision to broach the issue of sexual abuse. Before doing this, however, I wanted to know the child's words for the genitals and secondary sexual characteristics. A set of anatomically correct dolls (available from Teach-A-Bodies, 2544 Boyd, Fort Worth, TX 76109) served this purpose.

Content of Session	Therapist's Rationale
THERAPIST: I'd like to talk with you now about something that may be a little more difficult to talk about. I have some special dolls that I would like to show you. (*Points to the breasts on the female child doll.*) What do you call these?	I acknowledge that this may be difficult.
ROSA: Titties.	
T: And this (*pointing to the vagina*)?	
R: Vagina.	I will need to explore whether she has learned the term from the CPS investigation or whether there is another explanation for this.
T: Do you have another word for it too?	
R: I forget.	

I asked Rosa whether she could identify the buttocks and anus on a male and female doll, as well as the penis on the male doll. She used the words "butt," "butt-hole," and "penis" for these parts. When I next asked whether she knew what the "private parts" of the body were, and whether she could point to them on the dolls, she correctly pointed to the nipples, vagina, buttocks, and anus of the female dolls and the penis, anus, and buttocks of the male dolls.

Content of Session	Therapist's Rationale
THERAPIST: Now, Rosa, I have to ask you a question that may be a little harder for you to answer. Did anyone ever want you to touch their private parts?	
ROSA: No (*moving away from therapist, avoiding eye contact*).	She is uncomfortable.
T: Did anyone ever want to touch your private parts?	
R: I would not let them.	
T: Who wanted to?	Note that this is an open-ended question; the father is not introduced. Although Rosa is not denying contact, she's not ready to talk. It is clear that raising this material has generated a great deal of anxiety.
R: I forget. (*At this point Rosa has moved almost as far away from the therapist as she can get in the room.*)	

T: It looks like this is hard for you to talk about,   I try to acknowledge and accept her
and I can see that you maybe don't know me well   feelings.
enough yet to want to talk about it any more.
Would you like to get back to playing for a little
while before we stop for today?

The rest of the session was devoted to play with the dollhouse and discussion of nonthreatening material. The session ended about 10 minutes after the interchange centering around the anatomically correct dolls.

Developmental History

Mrs. Torres was seen separately at the end of the session with Rosa, for the purpose of obtaining a developmental history. She reported that Rosa had been 3 weeks overdue and that she had been delivered by cesarean section. Mrs. Torres had been very anxious during the pregnancy, as she had had three miscarriages before Rosa's birth. However, Rosa was a healthy baby who walked, talked, and was toilet-trained all before schedule. At age 2 Rosa fell and broke some of her front teeth. Aside from that and an accident when she fell and bruised herself badly at 3½, Rosa had had no major accidents, injuries, or illnesses. Rosa entered kindergarten at age 5 and was now in first grade, where she was having problems: distractibility, poor attention span, difficulties forming age-appropriate peer relationships, cognitive delays interfering with language acquisition, and overall immaturity.

In terms of education about sexuality, Mrs. Torres reported that since Rosa had started talking to her about what her father had done, she had taught her the correct words for the vagina and penis. Before that, Rosa had used the terms "cookie" and "birdie." Mrs. Torres stated that Rosa had had many questions about where babies come from when she was pregnant with Sabrina. Mrs. Torres reported telling Rosa that when "God was ready for you to have a baby, he helped mommies grow a baby in their stomach." Mrs. Torres stated that she had always taught Rosa not to touch herself "down there," and that Rosa's preoccupation with masturbation over the last few months was very upsetting to her. In terms of exposure to sexual acts between herself and her husband, Mrs. Torres reported that Rosa, at age 4, had once come into their bedroom when they were engaged in intercourse. Since that time, she had been very careful not to expose Rosa to their sex life. She also discussed the fact that her husband sometimes watched sexually explicit videotapes, but she did not want him to have them in the house, and she did not think that Rosa had ever seen these.

Mrs. Torres said that her husband had begun to share Rosa's caretaking when she was 2 and continued to do so until the parents separated. He got her up in the morning and insisted on putting her to bed at night, even when Mrs. Torres was home. He would also take her to his mother's for breakfast several times a week, and they had used his mother more than hers for babysitting while they were living together. Rosa had been in a day care program since she was 2. Mrs. Torres's mother now took care of her after school.

Mrs. Torres reported that she had separated from Mr. Torres about 6 months ago and moved back in with her parents. Visitation with Rosa by Mr. Torres was irregular until 4 months ago, when he began to pick her up every Saturday and to keep her overnight at his mother's home.

In terms of age-inappropriate sexual behavior, Mrs. Torres reported that Rosa had begun to masturbate excessively about a year ago. It was so noticeable that the teacher referred to it as "provocative"; the teacher also reported incidents in which Rosa would pull her pants down in front of boys and try to touch their penises. Mrs. Torres also reported that in the last 4 months, Rosa had been pulling at her underpants. She said that this behavior was especially noticeable on Sundays, after Rosa had been with her father. It was so noticeable that Mrs. Torres tried different detergents and bought a different type of underpants for Rosa, thinking that these might be causing the irritation.

Mrs. Torres stated that starting about a year ago, Rosa had begun waking up with nightmares. Rosa had also become extremely oppositional in the last year. She would stomp her feet and run out of the room when her mother attempted to discipline her. Inattentiveness and difficulty concentrating at school had affected her performance in school this year.

Mrs. Torres reported that Rosa was increasingly reluctant to go on visitations with her father, coming up with such excuses as "I'm sick" or "I don't want to go." She would not get dressed sometimes, and then would want to wear lots of clothes, including pants over shorts. Rosa was also evidencing some fear of men. She was reluctant to approach her maternal grandfather, with whom she had previously been close, and seemed anxious about being around men.

Preliminary Assessment

In the initial session, Rosa presented as a child of average intelligence, with verbal skills appropriate to a first-grader. She was slight of build, with thin, shoulder-length brown hair and large, dark brown eyes. Her fine motor skills and memory capability appeared within normal limits. Emotionally, there was evidence of depression and heavy reliance on avoidance when confronted with anxiety-provoking material. Behavioral symptoms reported by the mother included regression, fearful responses to men, and oppositional behavior. School records substantiated a decline in performance, difficulty concentrating, and behavioral problems with peers.

Although the nature of the child's reaction to the parents' separation and pending divorce had not been explored in detail in the first session, there were some clues to the family dynamics and her attachment to her parents. Her father emerged as possibly the more nurturing figure, in that he was remembered by Rosa as the one who used to put her to bed every night and the one who took her places and did fun things with her. This dynamic was consistent with the mother's report about the amount of time and attention Mr. Torres had devoted to his daughter.

In Rosa's eyes, Mrs. Torres emerged as the more emotionally distant parent. One of the first things that Rosa mentioned about her mother was that her mother spanked her. However, Rosa also disclosed that she now slept with her mother and, by implication, felt safer now that she was with her at night. The interaction that I observed between Rosa and her mother in the waiting room illustrated Rosa's dependence on her mother.

In terms of the sexual abuse allegations, her answers to the questions asked about touching of private parts of the body were striking. Also remarkable was the fact that she did not answer "No" to the question "Did anyone ever want to touch your private parts?", but said, "I would not let them." She also did not deny that someone touched her, but said that "I forget" the name of that person.

Children who have been sexually victimized often feel that they are to blame for the victimization, and in order to avoid the anxiety associated with guilt, they deny the victimization. Although reluctance to talk about the father and ambivalent feelings about him would be normal for any child caught in the middle of a conflicted parental relationship, the responses noted above raised a red flag in my mind. However, in the interest of maintaining the therapeutic relationship that had begun to develop, but that was clearly threatened by my introduction of this sensitive topic, it seemed wiser to defer pursuit of this issue to a later session.

Second and Third Sessions

In the second and third sessions, Rosa remained very resistant to talking about any of the sexual abuse allegations, continuing to say that she "forgot" whether anyone had touched her. I conceptualized my task in these first three sessions as building a therapeutic relationship and beginning to make an assessment of ego strengths. As a result, by the end of the third session, Rosa was responding more fully and becoming engaged with me. Rosa perceived her mother as a protective, helping figure some of the time, and Rosa was mature enough in her cognitive and motor development to know how to take care of and comfort herself. Therefore, it was possible to introduce the idea that Rosa could help herself to feel better when she got upset. I clarified that she might become upset when she was asked to talk about things that she did not want to talk about. The concept of using the therapy sessions for both "work" and "play" was introduced. The "work" was talking about the upsetting things that Daddy and/or Mommy did, and the "play" was playing with anything she wanted in the playroom.

It is important to note that the interviewer in a case such as this one asks the child nonleading, open-ended questions, in which there is choice, or questions are restated to obtain clarification. However, it is not always possible to avoid asking leading questions; indeed, depending on the context of a line of questions and/or the developmental age of the child, they may be appropriate.

Fourth Session

At the beginning of the fourth session, I asked Rosa whether she understood why she was here. She responded, "To work and to play." When asked what the "work" was, she stated that it was "talking about Daddy." Fifteen minutes into this session, after playing with toys of Rosa's choice, I introduced the issue of the sexual abuse allegations.

Content of Session	Therapist's Rationale
THERAPIST: I am worried that maybe your father did some things that you are afraid to talk about. I wonder if you could just show me with the dolls what happened, since it is hard to talk about it.	I am testing the hypothesis that abuse may have occurred with an invitation to play it out.
ROSA: (*Throws female child doll and adult male doll to therapist.*) Daddy would be in my room a lot.	
T: Do you know why he would come in?	
R: When Daddy was nervous, he would sleep with me.	
T: How was Daddy nervous?	It is important to get details about Rosa's meaning.
R: (*Stands with her hands at her sides, holds her body straight and shakes all over.*)	This could conceivably be an imitation of a person having an orgasm.
T: What would happen next?	
R: The bed would get all wet.	
T: After Daddy got nervous and shook all over, the bed got wet?	This is a clarifying question.
R: Yes.	
T: Would you get wet?	
R: No.	
T: What would happen next?	
R: He would go to the bathroom to clean up.	
T: And then what would happen.	
R: I'm tired of talking.	Rosa's anxiety is building.
T: OK. You know that I said that we would not have to work the whole time, but I have one more question. Would this happen a lot or a little?	
R: A lot of times (*moving away, fidgeting, avoiding eye contact*).	
T: You have done a good job talking about something that seems to make you upset. (*Rosa nods.*) What would help you feel better now?	I am acknowledging Rosa's feelings.
R: I want to play Chutes and Ladders.	

The rest of the session was devoted to playing a board game, without any further attempts on my part to reintroduce the subject of her father. By the end of the session, Rosa appeared to have reestablished her equilibrium; she enjoyed her snack and was not anxious to leave when the time was up.

Fifth Session

Rosa started the session by saying that she wanted to play a board game. After playing two games, I made an effort to engage her in conversation about her father, which she avoided strenuously.

Content of Session

Therapist's Rationale

THERAPIST: Are you scared?

ROSA: (*Sitting and looking at floor; no answer.*)

T: Can you tell me, are you scared or mad?

R: Scared.

Rosa's feelings about breaking the secret may be a major obstacle to discussing the details of the abuse.

T: Are you afraid that something bad will happen to you if you talk more about Daddy?

R: Yes (*in a low voice*).

T: Can you tell me what you are afraid of?

R: (*Shakes head no.*)

It is important to pursue the reasons she feels uncomfortable talking about the abuse.

T: Are you afraid that something will happen to Mommy?

R: (*Nods yes.*)

T: Can you tell me what you are afraid of?

R: No.

T: Are you afraid that something will happen to Daddy?

R: (*No answer.*)

T: Would you like to stop for today and go see your mother?

Rosa appears to be immobilized by the feelings that have been aroused.

R: Yes.

T: OK. Let's stop for today.

When we got to the waiting room, Rosa stood silently by her mother's side, holding her hand. Her mother gave her a hug, and in response to her mother's gentle questioning, she said that she was scared and upset and wanted to go home.

Mrs. Torres then reported that Rosa had said to her after the last visit with her father that Mr. Torres had told Rosa he would shoot her mother if Rosa talked about what she and Daddy did. Mrs. Torres said that she had told Rosa that Daddy was saying that to scare her and would not really do that. She said to me that although Mr. Torres did have a gun, she did not believe that he would hurt either one of them, although he was capable of saying this kind of thing to scare Rosa.

Prior to the next session with Rosa, which was 2 weeks away because of an intervening holiday, another supervised visit was planned with Rosa's father. I telephoned the CPS worker to discuss what Mrs. Torres had said happened on the last visit. The CPS worker said that Mrs. Torres had told her this also, and that rather than watching the visit between Mr. Torres and Rosa through a glass partition, she would stay in the room with them on the next visit.

After the supervised visit, and before the next therapy session with me, the CPS worker called me to discuss how the visit had gone. She said that she had terminated the visit early because she felt that Mr. Torres was acting inappropriately with Rosa, crying and saying that he loved her and would never do anything to hurt her. The CPS worker said that she explained to Mr. Torres that he would have to "get himself together" so that Rosa did not feel burdened emotionally.

This was important for planning for the next session. The information from the CPS worker validated the mother's perception that the father was capable of being inappropriate with Rosa. It also indicated that the CPS worker could be an ally in the treatment process.

Sixth Session

Rosa again started the session by wanting to play a board game. She appeared relaxed and talked relatively easily. She said that she had had fun over the weekend with her mother and grandmother, who had taken her to a movie. She also said that she had seen her father and that she had been glad to see him.

Content of Session	Therapist's Rationale
THERAPIST: You know, Rosa, your mom has told me a little more about exactly what she is worried about that your dad has done.	I am trying to reduce the child's burden to keep a secret.
ROSA (*combing a large, stuffed toy dog*): This is a nice dog.	
T: Are you still scared to talk about what happened?	I'm exploring to see how Rosa may have been intimidated into keeping a secret.
R: (*Moves to the floor of the playroom, picks at toys on the shelves.*) Yes.	
T: Are you afraid of Daddy?	
R (*not looking at therapist*): Yes.	
T: Will Daddy hurt you if you tell?	
R: Yes.	
T: How?	
R: He will kill me.	It is very hard for a child to have to deal with a threat like this!
T: How?	
R: Shoot me.	
T: (*Takes adult male anatomically correct doll, places it on one side of the room, and begins to surround it with toy soldiers, all with guns pointing at the adult male doll.*)	I decide to try to see whether symbolically, through play, Rosa can be helped to feel safe.

You know what? We are going to pretend that this
is Daddy, and we are going to put all these soldiers
around him to protect you from him. (*Puts down
nine soldiers as she counts.*) Do you want to put more?

R: Yes. (*Takes over, putting every toy soldier in the
collection—30 in all—around the figure of "Daddy."*)

T: Oh, and let's put this police car between you and
Daddy as well, to make sure that you are really safe.
(*Places toy police car between soldiers and Rosa, so that
both soldiers and police car are now in between.*) You
know, Rosa, not only are you safe here, but in real
life, your daddy can only see you when Miss Ramos
is there with you. Do you feel safe with Miss Ramos?

R: Yes, and do you know she made my daddy leave
when he was worrying me?

T: Yes, she did tell me that, and I am glad that she
did that. . . . Do you remember how you told me
that Daddy gets into bed with you and how he gets
nervous?

R: Yes.

T: Does he touch himself?

R: (*Stands up as she begins to talk, looking directly at
therapist, gesturing with hands.*) He touches his
private parts.

T: With his elbow?

An effort to get detail without
asking leading questions.

R: Nooooo, with his hands. He did it in the living
room, too.

T: Was he standing or sitting?

Focused questions.

R: Sitting, like this. (*Squats down and puts her hands
between her legs.*)

T: What was he doing?

R: Touching his birdie with his hands.

T: This is a birdie (*pointing to the penis on the adult
male doll*)?

R: Yes, and that's a cookie (*points to the vagina on the
female child doll*).

T: What happened then?

R: Stuff came out of the end (*makes a face*), and it
got all over the couch.

T: Did he do this in your bedroom, too?

Although this is a leading question, note that Rosa's answer is not
confined to naming the bedroom;
she elaborates.

R (*animated*): Yes, all over the house, all over the
house, in his bedroom, too.

T: Did he ever want you to touch his birdie?

R: Yes, he wanted me to, but I didn't.

T: Did he ever want to touch your cookie?

R: Yes, he wanted to, but I didn't let him. (*At this point Rosa is getting very excited. She takes the adult male doll and pulls the pants off, pulling and twisting the penis.*)

T: Why don't we pretend that he [the father doll] is dead?

R: Yes, yes, we'll bury him. (*Puts him under the throw rug on the floor and steps hard on the doll.*)

T: I talk to a lot of children whose daddies have done these things. Sometimes children don't want to let their daddy touch them, but daddies are bigger and stronger and sometimes they make the children touch them, or put their birdie against their cookie.

R: He wanted to put his birdie against me, but I wouldn't let him do it.

T: You would try not to let him do it, but would he do it anyway?

R: Yes, but sometimes I would run away.

T: Where would you go?

R: To my secret place and hide. (*Gets up and goes and stomps on the doll under the rug again.*)

T: When your daddy would put his birdie against your cookie, was it hard or soft?

R: Hard.

T: Would it move or stay still?

R: Move.

T: And would stuff come out of the end?

R: (*Nods yes.*)

T: And would it get on you?

R: Sometimes, and sometimes it got on the furniture, too. Once it got on the couch in the living room, and we had to spray to take the smell away.

T: Did he ever want you to put your mouth on his birdie?

R: I didn't want to, but he wanted me to.

I am using her terms.

Although, again, these are leading questions, Rosa continues to respond and add detail.

I am trying to help her feel safe and reduce her tension.

I'm normalizing Rosa's experience and reassuring her.

T: Did he ever put anything on his birdie to make it taste better?

R: (*Looks up at therapist, surprised.*) Yes, peanut butter, honey, lotion, all kinds of things.

T: Did that make it taste good?

R (*adamant*): No! No! No!

T: How did it taste?

R: It tasted yucky.

T: Did your daddy put his finger in your cookie?

R: Yes.

T: Which finger?

R: (*Shows therapist the middle finger of her hand.*)

T: Did it move or stay still?

R: Moved. (*Illustrates by taking her finger, squatting down, and rubbing her finger on her vaginal area over her tights.*)

T: How did it feel when Daddy did that?

R: It hurt.

T: Have you told your mom everything that you told me?

R: No, not the part about his putting his birdie in my mouth and against my cookie . . . only that he touched my cookie.

T: Can I tell your mom?

R: (*Nods yes readily.*)

This question reflects a knowledge of one way adult males attempt to entice children.

She confirms the oral–genital contact.

I need to know how safe Rosa feels with her mother.

During the rest of the session, I reviewed what Rosa had disclosed, putting this review in the context of being sure that I had heard Rosa correctly. This allowed Rosa to reaffirm what she had already said and to add or correct details that I might have missed or misunderstood. I also brought up again the issue of Rosa's being afraid of her father. Rosa was able to explain that she had seen her father's gun, and that she thought that he would shoot her and her mother just as she had seen him shoot a dog once. Despite this fear, she appeared to have been reassured by her developing confidence in her mother's ability to protect her and the increasing closeness of their relationship. The reality of supervised contact with her father, which reinforced her feelings of safety without her having to "lose" her father, was also reassuring. The evolution of a trusting relationship with me, coupled with these external factors, enabled Rosa to make a fuller disclosure than had been possible before.

Based on the information presented by Rosa during the first six sessions, it was possible to determine that her presentation was consistent with a child who has been sexually abused. Engagement was achieved through the nature of the parent–child relationship in general and the special relationship with Rosa that the father had fostered through his caretaking activities. He had clearly attempted to normalize the sexual contact by introducing it originally under the guise of a normal bedtime routine. The sexual interaction consisted of genital fondling, oral–genital contact, and penis-to-vagina contact. The sensory detail (i.e., the penis felt hard, the finger hurt, there was a smell when "stuff" came out of the end of the penis) and peripheral detail (e.g., he was sitting, it happened all over the house) provided contextual grounding for the sexual acts. Secrecy was obtained through manipulation of the child's trust and dependence, as well as through overt threats. Disclosure was delayed (as is often the case), and suppression was evident in the process of the disclosure over the course of the sessions, as well as by the fear response in the sessions.

This opinion was communicated to CPS following the sixth session.

Seventh through Ninth Sessions

In the seventh session, I reviewed with Rosa what I had told her mother and the CPS worker. This discussion stimulated Rosa to act out the "killing" of her father again.

Content of Session	Therapist's Rationale
THERAPIST: You are pretty angry at your father for the things that he did to you, aren't you?	
ROSA: Yes! (*Hits at father doll.*)	
T: Well, it is OK to be angry and feel like you would want to kill him.	
R: I know. Mommy said she is mad too, and that there is something wrong with him.	
T: Well, I don't know if there is something wrong with him. . . . I do know that he made a big mistake in touching you. Do you know what happens when someone makes a mistake?	I attempt to reframe the "bad" or "sick" parent as one who has made a mistake.
R: They get punished.	
T: Do you think that your dad should get punished?	
R: Yes, but I don't want him to go to jail. Mommy says she wants him to go to jail.	
T: Well, I don't know about jail, but I do think he needs to learn how to be a better daddy before he takes care of you by himself again. There are places that he can go to get help to learn how to be a better daddy, and that is what I will help him do if he wants to. In the meantime, he can only see you with Miss Ramos.	
R: Yes, I know. Would you like to play Chutes and Ladders?	

Rosa was clearly more comfortable with her angry feelings now that she had been given permission to express them and nothing bad had happened. It is important to note that she continued to see her father in supervised visits, which contributed to her sense that she had not "lost" her father through her "betrayal" of the secret.

The mother, by contrast, was enraged when she learned that the details of sexual abuse were more intrusive than she had first realized. She was consequently very unhappy about the continued visits. One of my roles in talking with Mrs. Torres was to clarify the strong attachment between Rosa and her father, and to emphasize the importance for Rosa of a continuing relationship with him.

The material that emerged in the next two sessions made it possible to assess the impact of the sexual victimization on Rosa, according to the model of traumagenic dynamics outlined earlier in this chapter. The presence of sexual traumatization was profound. The nature and duration of the abuse had left Rosa with distorted images of sexuality and had generated a tendency to eroticize relationships inappropriately. The threat of the use of force had created a sense of powerlessness, which was manifested in dissociative responses and regressive behavior. Rosa felt betrayed by both parents, which resulted in a damaged self-image. Rosa's self-esteem had been further damaged by the shame and guilt associated with the stigmatization dynamic.

In Rosa's case, the regressive behaviors and fear response engendered by the father's threats suggested that the powerlessness dynamic, along with that of traumatic sexualization, was the most salient for her. Thus therapeutic interventions aimed at decreasing feelings of helplessness and increasing feelings of success and competence were recommended. Rosa had already begun to incorporate the age-inappropriate sexual contact into her gender identity; the tendency to eroticize relationships and her impulsive, sexualized play suggested the need for therapeutic interventions that would allow for the expression of these feelings in the therapy hour, with the aim of gradually reducing the need for this. At the same time, Mrs. Torres and Rosa's other caretakers needed help in setting appropriate limits and helping Rosa to restrain such behavior in her social settings, since this would impair her ability to develop appropriate family and peer relationships. Consequently, strategies aimed at helping Rosa in these areas were the first priority.

Summary of Treatment with Rosa at Age 6

The goals in intervention in child sexual abuse are (1) to protect the child; (2) to restrain the offender; and (3) to rehabilitate all family members, if possible. In the instance of emerging and unclear disclosure of sexual abuse, the focus in the intervention must be on surfacing the trauma in order to help establish the fact of the sexual abuse.

In this case, as in most cases of family sexual abuse, it was necessary to establish the fact of abuse in the family court. This would then establish the need for limited and/or supervised contact between the offending parent and the child, as a means of protecting the child from further abuse. As a result of my initial assessment, I was asked to testify about my findings in family court. The law in New York State, as in other states, makes it impossible to make a determination of the fact of child sexual abuse if the child does not testify, without some evidence that corroborates the child's out-of-court statements. Without any medical evidence, the most powerful corroboration is the testimony of a mental health expert in child sexual abuse as to the consistency and validity of the child's presentation. I testified that Rosa's presentation was consistent with that of other sexually abused children, and the court adjudicated Rosa as a sexually abused child.

The supervised visitation arrangement was continued, and all family members were ordered to seek treatment. In this manner, the court was in effect restraining the father from harming Rosa, at the same time that it was demonstrating an understanding of the need for therapeutic intervention with Mr. Torres. Although the family court in New York State cannot force a father to *attend* treatment, it can make changes in visitation contingent on the recommendation of the treating therapist. This is what the court did in the Torres case. Mr. Torres continued to deny the allegations and did not accept the recommendation to seek treatment. However, Rosa was protected from further unsupervised contact. Mrs. Torres continued Rosa in treatment, which proceeded according to the priorities outlined above. Mrs. Torres also started therapy for herself and Jorge. This began the process of rehabilitation for the child and her immediate family.

EIGHT YEARS LATER: HYPOTHETICAL ISSUES AND OUTCOMES FOR ROSA

What follows are some predictions based on my brief contact with Rosa and her mother. This was a case referred by CPS, and I had no role with the family beyond the evaluation and short-term intervention. Therefore, I have not seen the family since the initial consultation.

A number of issues could be salient, depending, of course, on what ensued in the intervening years. It is impossible to know with any certainty what Rosa's issues might be at age 14. Since her father contested the sexual abuse allegations, one suspects that there might have been ongoing disputes over visitation and/or custody. These kinds of cases are extremely problematic, and an ideal approach would have been for the court to establish therapeutic management of Rosa's case. This would have established a team of therapists, including a separate therapist for Mr. Torres and possibly a separate one for Mrs. Torres as well. It would have been important for Rosa to have her own therapist. Had this occurred, I would perhaps have continued with Rosa, depending on an assessment of Mr. Torres's willingness to cooperate with me as the continuing therapist.

If Mr. Torres continued to deny the allegations, refused referral to a therapist specializing in work with sex offenders, and yet pressed for unsupervised visitation, at some point a number of questions would need to be addressed:

- How connected was Mr. Torres to his children?
- Were there clinical reasons to try to continue Rosa's relationship with Mr. Torres, even if he continued to deny the allegations?

- How long should supervised visitation be continued?
- How long could it be continued? (If CPS workers had been providing supervised visitation, this would have been discontinued after the family court decision, leaving the family to make arrangements for private supervision.)
- Would Mrs. Torres divorce her husband?
- Would CPS press for termination of parental rights? If Mr. Torres won the right to unsupervised visitation through a court proceeding, this would make court-ordered therapeutic management all the more necessary.

These are the types of questions that create ongoing stress for children who have been sexually abused by a family member.

Another factor is the role that ethnicity would play for Rosa and her family. In Hispanic families, commitment to the family is important. This might have affected (and might continue to affect) Mrs. Torres's choices. It might have been difficult for her to accept the idea of divorce. Her family of origin's response to the separation would be important. Would her relatives urge her to look for a way to reconcile, or would they support continued separation and a possible divorce? What would their attitude be toward continued contact between Mr. Torres and his children? The ethnic group's priorities might also affect Mrs. Torres's view of herself. Would the emphasis in the Hispanic family on the woman's role as mother contribute to a heightened sense of guilt and self-blame for allowing the abusive situation to occur? Or would this fuel her commitment to being a better mother to Rosa?

Clearly, the manner in which these issues evolved would have an enormous impact on Rosa. If her mother became involved in continual legal battles with Mr. Torres, this would undoubtedly cause emotional as well as financial strain, and could affect how psychologically available the mother was to Rosa. Jorge's connection to his stepfather, and the role he would play if a contested scenario arose, would also be an important factor. Rosa's relationship with the paternal grandmother would merit consideration as well: Rosa liked going to visit this grandmother, and termination of this contact because of her father's behavior might constitute a real loss for this child. All of this would make it important for a team of therapists to continue to be involved.

Even in the best-case scenario—in which Mr. Torres accepted responsibility for his actions and went into treatment—there would be many issues for Rosa at age 14. If these had been addressed as fully as possible in an early intervention, there would be new concerns with the onset of adolescence. Primary among these would be those triggered by Rosa's emerging sexuality. Given Rosa's primary reaction in childhood (feelings of helplessness and powerlessness, and the tendency to eroticize relationships), she might experience difficulty integrating her sense of sexuality into her social relationships. One issue that could arise might be her ability to negotiate a mutual relationship in the course of dating and experimentation with her sexuality.

Values from her Hispanic background might interact with Rosa's view of herself. There is a high value placed on being a virgin in her culture; to what extent would her earlier experiences heighten her sense of herself as "damaged goods"? This would have a different salience at age 14 than at age 6. If this were to increase Rosa's sense of being different from others, it could affect her peer relationships. If she were to feel different from other girls her age because of her early sexual abuse experience, this could emerge as a barrier to close interpersonal relationships.

Another ongoing issue for Rosa would be telling about her experience. If her developmental stage were to trigger conflicting feelings, in whom could she confide? Especially in new relationships with peers and/or other people unaware of her background, how would she learn whom to tell and how much to tell? Teenagers typically assume "instant intimacy" with both female and male friends. They may "tell all" only to regret it later. Negotiations centering around these questions can be an important focus of therapy at this age.

Any or all of these problematic issues might be mitigated by individual and family strengths. Rosa's temperament, her emotional resilience, and the extent of her family and peer support would all play a role. All would need to be considered in determining treatment goals for Rosa as a young adolescent, if she were to involve herself in therapy. At age 6, she had the experience of a short-term contact with a therapist who respected her feelings. Ideally, this memory would enable her to reach out to a school social worker or other counselor as an adolescent, and would enable her to continue her process of understanding what happened to her.

STUDY QUESTIONS

1. How can the therapist help a custodial parent understand an abused child's need to continue contact with the abusive parent?

2. If Rosa had not wanted the therapist to discuss her disclosure of abuse with the mother, how could this have been handled with the child?

3. The therapist testified in an adversarial proceeding against the father. If the mother had not wanted to terminate her relationship with the father, what might the implications have been for the therapist's alliance with the mother?

4. What issues could arise for the mother if, at age 14, Rosa became symptomatic because of the earlier history of abuse?

REFERENCES

Armsworth, M., & Holaday, M. (1993). The effects of psychological trauma on children and adolescents. *Journal of Counseling and Development, 72,* 49–56.

Briere, J., & Runtz, M. (1988a). Symptomatology associated with childhood sexual victimization in a non-clinical sample. *Child Abuse and Neglect, 12,* 51–59.

Briere, J., & Runtz, M. (1988b). Post sexual abuse trauma. In G. E. Wyatt & G. J. Powell (Eds.), *Lasting effect of child sexual abuse* (pp. 85–99). Beverly Hills, CA: Sage.

Burgess, A. (1987). Child molesting: Assessing impact in multiple victims (Part I). *Archives of Psychiatric Nursing, 1,* 33–39.

Ceci, S.J., Ross, D. & Toglia, M. (1987). Suggestibility of children's memory: Psycholegal implications. *Journal of Experimental Psychology: General, 116,* 38–49.

Finkelhor, D., & Browne, A. (1985). The traumatic impact of child sexual abuse: A conceptualization. *American Journal of Orthopsychiatry, 55,* 530–541.

Friedrich, W. N. (1990). *Psychotherapy of sexually abused children and adolescents.* New York: Norton.

Friedrich, W. N. (1995). *Psychotherapy with sexually abused boys: An integrated approach.* Newbury Park, CA: Sage.

Gelinas, D. (1983). The persisting negative effects of incest. *Psychiatry, 46,* 312–332.

Gil, E. (1991). *The healing power of play.* New York: Guilford Press.

Gil, E. (1996). *Treating abused adolescents.* New York: Guilford Press.

Gil, E., & Cavanaugh Johnson, T. (1993). *Sexualized children.* Rockville, MD: Launch Press.

Goodman, G. S., & Bottoms, B. L. (Eds.). (1993). *Child victims, child witnesses.* New York: Guilford Press.

Hartman, C. R., & Burgess, A. W. (1988). Information processing of trauma. *Journal of Interpersonal Violence, 3,* 443–457.

James, B. (1989). *Treating traumatized children: New insights and creative Interventions.* Lexington, MA: Lexington Books.

Jehu, D., Klassen, C., & Gazen, M. (1985–1986). Cognitive restructuring of distorted beliefs associated with childhood sexual abuse. *Journal of Social Work and Human Sexuality, 4,* 49–69.

Loftus, E. F., & Christian, S. A. (1989). Malleability of memory for emotional events. In T. Archer & L. Nilsson (Eds.), *Aversion, avoidance, and anxiety: Perspectives on aversively motivated behavior* (pp. 311–322). Hillsdale, NJ: Erlbaum.

Myers, J. (1992). *Legal issues in child abuse and neglect.* Newbury Park, CA: Sage.

Russell, D. (1986). *The secret trauma.* New York: Basic Books.

Salter, A. C. (1995). *Transforming trauma.* Newbury Park, CA: Sage.

Sgroi, S. (1984). *Clinical handbook of intervention in child sexual abuse.* Lexington, MA: Lexington Books.

Stowell, J., & Dietzel, M. (1982). *My very own book about me.* (Available from Super Kids, Lutheran Social Service, 1226 N. Howard, Spokane, WA 99201; ages 3–7)

Strand, V. (1994). Clinical social work and the family court: A new role in child sexual abuse cases. *Child and Adolescent Social Work Journal, 11,* 107–122.

van der Kolk, B., & Fisler, R. (1994). Childhood abuse and neglect and loss of self-regulation. *Bulletin of the Menninger Clinic, 58,* 145–168.

Webb, N. B. (Ed.). (1991). *Play therapy with children in crisis: A casebook for practitioners.* New York: Guilford Press.

CHAPTER 6

Witness and Victim of Multiple Abuses

Case of Randy, Age 10, in a Residential Treatment Center, and Follow-Up at Age 19 in Prison

JOAN S. DOYLE
DAVID STOOP

This chapter is about Randy, a black boy of 10, whose childhood slipped away without his ever having known about bedtime stories, teddy bears, ducks in the bathtub, a comforting good-night kiss, or what it was like to be a gleam in his mother's eyes.

Randy was diagnosed as having posttraumatic stress disorder (PTSD) resulting from chronic, severe abuse and torture. Not even this diagnosis can adequately describe those years of horror when, according to Randy, "nobody helped." What happened to Randy can more accurately be described as "soul murder"—the deliberate attempt to eradicate or compromise the separate identity of another person (Shengold, 1989, p. 2).

Born to a heroin-addicted mother, Randy endured from that precarious beginning extreme physical, sexual, and emotional abuse and neglect. The mother, a prostitute, sold Randy at ages 3 and 4 into prostitution in order to support her drug habit. During his early years, Randy frequently witnessed his mother having sexual intercourse with her clients—and, on one occasion, her fatal shooting of a "john" who was abusing her. This act resulted in a 10- to 20-year prison sentence for Randy's mother. Randy was also present when his beloved great-aunt had a heart attack and died. At age 7, Randy was kidnapped by members of a satanic cult for ritualistic purposes, sexually abused, and tortured with lighted matches.

Compounding all of these traumatic events were numerous out-of-home placements for Randy. In his last placement with a maternal aunt, he set fire to her house after receiving a brutal beating from her for misbehaving in church. The fire caused her death and the deaths of her husband and two of Randy's cousins, a 16-year-old boy and a 6-month-old baby girl. Randy escaped injury by running outside the house to safety. This act of arson resulted in Randy's placement in a children's psychiatric hospital for a mental health evaluation.

During the entire length of his 6-week stay in the hospital, Randy refused to talk to his therapist, or any other member of the treatment team, about either the fire or any of the other traumatic events earlier in his life. The discharge recommendation was for intensive psychotherapeutic intervention in a secure residential setting, in order for Randy to deal with his increasingly dangerous and dysfunctional trauma-related symptoms and behaviors. These included two other incidents of fire setting, school problems (he could not read), stealing, high-risk behaviors (e.g., playing on train tracks with a train coming), enuresis, nightmares, suicide attempts, repeatedly running away, drug and alcohol abuse, sexual provocativeness, extreme aggressiveness, and an inability to identify or express his feelings verbally (only his eyes occasionally mirrored the unbearable pain he had endured).

In accepting this case in a secure residential treatment facility for children, we knew that the treatment process for Randy would be long, arduous, and of a serial nature. Randy's experiences as both victim and witness of trauma, and his diagnosis of PTSD (American Psychiatric Association, 1994), necessitated a variety of collaborative treatment approaches. Terr (1989b) lists the following range of possible approaches to treatment of PTSD in children: family, group, and individual treatments; play therapy; psychodynamic psychotherapy; cognitive and behavioral therapies; and medication.

A sophisticated residential treatment setting, such as the one in which Randy was placed, is able to provide all of these intervention modalities, plus a holistic therapeutic environment that includes the following: a cottage milieu; special education in the form of on-grounds classrooms for children with severe behavior handicap/learning disabilities; recreational therapy; physical development; music therapy; woods therapy; garden therapy; and nursing, psychological, psychiatric, medical, dental, and other specialized services. In setting up an effective treatment plan for traumatized children referred to our residential program, we have found that exposure to all of these treatment team resources is necessary in order for the healing process to occur. For the purposes of this chapter, however, we focus on the work of the play therapist (who in this case was David Stoop) with Randy.

Because Randy had been extremely treatment-resistant in the hospital, where he was provided the conventional treatment modalities, it was decided to attempt to engage him in the treatment process through use of some innovative, play therapy/ creative arts approaches. These included puppets, masks, a cartoon lifeline, guided imagery (Dunne, 1988), and warm-up exercises (Sternberg & Garcia, 1989).

Therapists who feel uncomfortable about taking a creative approach in therapy may persist in using the more traditional modes of therapy (i.e., talking) even when the results are unproductive. These professionals may erroneously assume that creative expression in therapy requires artistic talent on the therapist's part. However, it is the creative process itself that is therapeutic, not the product (Naitove, 1981).

Puppetry has almost unlimited potential as a therapeutic medium, because it represents an integration of sculpture, design, movement, expression, and other elements of the arts (Renfro, 1984). A puppet helps a child to feel at ease, since it redirects the focus of attention away from the child, and serves as a protective shield behind which the child may temporarily take refuge and assume a new persona. The puppet helps the shy or inhibited child to focus on the puppet's rather than his or her own actions or statements. By encouraging emotional release, puppets offer a wide variety of socially acceptable outlets for discharge of stress-related emotions. In addition, the child experiences alternative emotions and actions through puppet play (Renfro, 1984).

In reexperiencing traumatic events, the child may use the puppet to explore hidden fears by instructing the puppet to overcome these fears. By depersonalizing the situation and exploring the same fears through the persona of the puppet, the child becomes less fearful, because the terrible things that have happened to him or her are now happening to the puppet rather than the child.

For children like Randy—who come from low-socioeconomic-status backgrounds, have been damaged by the ravages of racism, and are isolated from the outside world by the invisible confinements of ghetto life—play in its purest sense is an unfamiliar activity. Puppets can be used with such children to help them experience some of the childhood they have missed (Pazzanese & Wise, 1984).

Some of the most important benefits to be realized from use of puppets with traumatized children include the following (Renfro, 1984):

- Role and situation exploration
- Improved responsiveness and spontaneity
- Development of communication skills
- Opportunity for depersonalization or sublimation of problems through projection
- Self-esteem enhancement
- Provision of needed and appropriate physical contact
- Relief of the child's sense of isolation
- Increase in the child's ability to concentrate
- Improved motor coordination

Through the use of a mask, a child in treatment can learn more about himself or herself and can reveal feelings and emotions not expressed previously. Historically, the mask was used in healing; in today's work in play/creative arts therapy, the mask can help a child express repressed or hidden emotions, depict dilemma or conflict situations, release personal creativity, assume various forms of identity in a group, explore dreams and imagery, and demonstrate and model various social roles (Dunne, 1988).

Another method for sustaining Randy's interest was the use of a cartoon lifeline, which also resulted in drawings of psychodynamic significance. Like puppetry, cartooning distances the participant from the material and provides a creative tool for activating the imagination. In working with cartooning, the therapist uses existing cartoon characters, strips, or single frames, or encourages participants to create their own (Dunne, 1988b). Use of a cartoon lifeline with Randy stimulated his willingness to talk (through puppetry) about the cartoons he had drawn.

In guided imagery, the therapist suggests an imaginary scene and asks whether the child would like to go there, encouraging him or her to relax, close his or her eyes, and focus on what he or she is doing. Through the use of guided imagery, with the child in a relaxed state, the therapist helps him or her to reexperience past traumas in a less threatening manner. Guided imagery may be used in several ways: as a warm-up activity; as an introduction to sensory awareness; in core activities, to demonstrate the variety of individual responses to the same stimuli; and in closure, to restore clients to a calmer state after having dealt with very difficult issues (Naitove, 1981).

The *warm-up exercise* we used with Randy was a basic relaxation technique involving focus and deep breathing: The client is instructed to close his or her eyes and focus on a pleasant scene. The client then controls his or her respiratory system by taking slow, deep breaths. The exercise lasts 5–10 minutes. Its purpose is to reduce distraction, anxiety and overdefensiveness.

Most of us are familiar with children's stories, adult novels, plays, and films that contain characters who are extremes of very, very good and very, very evil. This may be because many of the authors and directors of these works were or are traumatized individuals who, through their storytelling, have tried to rework their own traumatic past. Such was or is the case with Charles Dickens, Rudyard Kipling, and Anton Chekhov (Shengold, 1989); Edgar Allan Poe, Alfred Hitchcock, and Ingmar Bergman (Terr, 1987); and Stephen King (Terr, 1989a). Kipling, in his book *The Light That Failed*, wrote a dedication poem about his mother, portraying her as a loving parent. In reality, his mother cruelly abandoned him when he was only 6 years old. The dedication may have been Kipling's creative attempt to defend against his feelings of rage and sadness centering around his early abandonment and betrayal/loss.

Randy probably did not possess the genius of these renowned authors and directors to enlist in his attempts at trauma integration and resolution. Nonetheless, we believed that he could be helped to find acceptable ways to process and deal with the events in his painful past through involvement in play/creative arts therapy, as well as through more conventional treatment approaches. We hoped that, with much hard work in these areas, Randy would be able over time to "write" a happy ending to his story.

THE CASE: RANDY, AGE 10

Family Information

Randy, 10 years old, was a black youth whose troubled life had begun in the housing projects of a large Northeastern American city. His mother was a 17-year-old prostitute when she gave birth to him; Randy never knew his biological father.

Randy was raised in and among the homeless. During his early years he moved from mission to shelter and from condemned building to junk car lot. As noted earlier, during this time he was sold into prostitution by his mother to support her drug habit. When he was 4 years old, his mother was imprisoned for shooting a client to death, and he was placed in the temporary custody of a children's services board.

For the next 6 years, Randy shuttled back and forth among a variety of relatives. He developed a strong bond with a great-aunt, with whom he lived after being taken from his mother until he was 5 years old, when she died of a heart attack in his presence.

After the great-aunt's death, Randy was placed with a maternal aunt. Unbeknownst to county officials, she was a crack peddler in a part of the city known as "Devil's End." She took Randy with her on her travels into this area. On one occasion he was kidnapped by satanic cult members, who first bound and gagged him and then sodomized him as an act of religion. They concluded this ritual by throwing lighted matches at Randy's genitals. The immediate aftereffects of this horrific experience on Randy, according to the record, included nightmares, enuresis, hypervigilance, exaggerated startle response, verbal and physical aggressiveness, and localized psychogenic amnesia. His aunt was later arrested in a drug raid, and Randy, then age 8, was removed from her custody.

Randy was then placed with another aunt in a small town 100 miles from his city of birth. This aunt and her husband were in their mid-30s and had two children of their own, a teenage son and a 6-month-old daughter. They had been able to rise above their own background of poverty into the black middle class.

Randy was illiterate, despite being in the third grade. When he began fighting in the learning-disabled class, he was placed in a class for the behaviorally handicapped. His aunt and uncle, steeped in the Baptist tradition, were strict disciplinarians. When Randy began to use obscene language, they would confine him to his room, but this form of punishment worked for only a short while. Randy, at age 9, would simply climb out of his first-floor window and run away. The couple felt forced to use more drastic measures to control Randy's behavior, and they resorted to corporal punishment (strapping him with a belt). Following a strapping after his caretakers learned of a stealing incident at school, Randy set a stuffed bear on fire in his room. The fire was discovered and extinguished.

A few weeks later Randy misbehaved while attending church. His aunt and uncle were mortified and furious with him for such sacrilegious behavior, and on returning home gave Randy a severe beating and banished him to the basement for the night. Randy had a secret stash of matches and a cigarette lighter in the basement. In the early morning hours, he allegedly ascended the basement stairs and poured a trail of lighter fluid up the stairway to the base of the bedroom doors. Then Randy set the path of accelerant on fire with a match and escaped through the back door. The entire family perished in the blaze.

Randy was hospitalized in this town after he was discovered by neighbors and firefighters in the back yard. He was screaming hysterically and was naked. He was then moved back to the town of his birth and placed in a psychiatric hospital for children. After 6 weeks, Randy was discharged from the hospital to a secure residential treatment setting.

Presenting Problems

Randy's life of ever-spiraling trauma—including nomadic unsettledness during his preschool years, the witnessing of violence and death to loved ones, and cult sexual abuse—resulted in a fierce struggle to master his anxiety, which was rooted in chronic powerlessness. Randy's frenzied attempts to control his anxiety took the form of aggression in school, flight from punishment, increasingly sexualized acting out, suicide attempts, and homicidal fire setting. Once he was the powerless object or bystander witnessing hostile and incomprehensible acts; now, armed with the experiences of his past, he was waging war with the whole world.

First Interview (Summary)

Randy entered my office. (As noted earlier, David Stroop was the play therapist in this case, and he is the "I" in what follows.) As he walked to the chair, he appeared to be moving within the rhythm of a rap song. Sunglasses masked his eyes; his T-shirt read "Run DMC." The bottom half of his head was shaved in a semicircle around the back, and the word "bad" was carved as a signature at the nape of the neck.

As I asked basic questions related to the record, Randy increasingly teetered on the back legs of his chair. When I asked him why he wore sunglasses inside, he remarked in the typical voice of a 10-year-old, "You want to know about the fire, don't you? I didn't do it. What time is it, anyway? How long do I have to stay in here?"

I calmly stated, "We're going to get along just fine." "Huh," he replied. "White people give up on black people." "I'll be back tomorrow," I said. "Can I go?" he asked anxiously. I nodded.

The tone in the initial interview in my office was rife with tension. Randy adorned himself in "street" garb and immediately introduced the racial roadblock. As a white male, I felt painfully conscious of the racial issue and concerned about whether I would be able to bridge our two worlds. I was a bit nervous, thinking that Randy might act out in order to fulfill the prophecy of "white rejection." I wanted to avoid verbal and physical confrontation at all costs. I retreated by reassuring him I would be seeing him tomorrow. I admit I was relieved when Randy exited the office.

Of note, my office is located within the 12-resident secure treatment unit. Therapy is regularly scheduled once per week with each of the 12 residents.

Preliminary Assessment and Treatment Plan

Control and power appeared to be the primary dynamics displayed by Randy. The opposite feelings of powerlessness—triggered when Randy became anxious or felt he was not in control—were buried, albeit not far from the surface; they were covered by Randy's aggressive style. The traumatic events of abuse, loss through death, and being an innocent, helpless witness to violence fueled Randy's ever-recurrent compulsion to repeat and replay the drama of power over powerlessness.

Randy's aggressive behavior, like his other behaviors originating in the severe traumas of his past, met his need for survival and helped him gain mastery of his victimization. In Randy's case, setting fires might have originally met his need to express the rage related to having been sexually abused and then tortured by fire. According to James (1989), an individual who experiences a great deal of power and relief of tension after the act of fire setting may become addicted to these same feelings, which then leads to dangerous repetition of this behavior. It was possible that Randy, if untreated, could assume such a profile.

The goal of treatment for Randy was to bring his self-destructive, aggressive behaviors under control. Using the concept of traumagenic states (James, 1989), the clinical team identified the following issues that would have to be addressed in Randy's treatment, either in the present or at some future developmental stage:

powerlessness, destructiveness, eroticization, self-blame, stigmatization, fragmentation of bodily experience, betrayal, and loss, as well as a possible dissociative state.

The treatment intervention to be described in this chapter consisted of four therapy sessions that addressed the issues centering around the traumagenic state of powerlessness—the pivotal event of ritual abuse in a satanic cult. In order to master the trauma, bridge-building exercises were introduced to link fragmented past events and to empower Randy through the experience of self-expression in a safe venue. The actual fire-setting incident would be dealt with at a later state in treatment, when Randy's ego strength had been enhanced.

In addition to once-per-week individual therapy sessions, Randy participated in twice-weekly group therapy. In our treatment setting, these groups focus on development of the following skills: anger management techniques, including the quieting reflex and breathing/relaxation exercises; success imagery skill exercises; and social skills learned through role play and public practice.

Although family therapy is also an active part of the treatment plan for many residents, this unfortunately was not possible for Randy because of his mother's confinement in prison.

The following description of four individual therapy sessions demonstrates the use of a cartoon lifeline of Randy's own making, and the stories he created about the characters in the lifeline. The lifeline was formulated in the first session. The second session featured a bridge-building exercise between two characters from the lifeline, enlarged on masks. The third session included a puppetry exercise based on characters in the lifeline. The fourth session introduced a handmade fire puppet, to permit the issue of fire to be broached in a nonthreatening space.

Play Therapy Sessions

It took a month and a half to attain the trust necessary to attempt the exercises and activities presented here. I often had to seek Randy out and persuade him to come to therapy. He almost always resisted, but ultimately agreed to come. In fact, he did not miss a session. These early weeks were rough going, since Randy was frequently verbally assaultive. I believed the only way I could win his trust was to refrain from using my authority to countermand his assaults. In addition, I was always available on a daily basis. I frequently saw Randy on the unit and would often speak to him, using my knowledge of music and sports to engage him in conversation. I used humor whenever possible, and always reacted to his humor when it was appropriate to do so. In a sense, I outlasted his attempts to drive me away.

First Session

The materials needed for this session included the following: a table; large sheets of white paper divided into equal blocks prior to the session; crayons, markers, and pencils; and a bagful of magic stick-ons, to be added to the lifeline. I prepared most of the magic stick-ons ahead of time, but some could also be created by Randy himself.

The first session included two activities: Tell a Story, a warm-up exercise enabling the client to enter a state of suspended disbelief; and the cartoon lifeline, a fun, nonthreatening story creation in which fragmented parts could later be brought together.

Tell a Story. Randy entered my office in casual attire, as was his custom, and slouched in the chair at the table. I sat at the table opposite him. His head was down and resting on his hand.

Content of Session	Rationale/Analysis
THERAPIST: I'd like to try something different today. Let's you and me tell a story. This is how you do it. I say a line and stop. You pick up where I left off, and we go back and forth.	I'm introducing the sentence completion format for the exercise.
RANDY: (*Sits up straight in his chair.*)	
T: I was walking through the woods and . . .	
R: I fell into a hole . . .	The hole may represent birth–death cycle or painful event or remorse (a moral event).
T: And there was a shadow above the hole . . .	
R: And the shadow was a man . . .	
T: But then the sun came out . . .	Sun = fire = power.
R: And burned down all the trees . . . (*Smiles sheepishly.*)	
T: And the shadow called out . . .	
R: And the man in the hole yelled back . . .	
T: There's a gun . . .	Power of the word.
R: And the man died . . .	
T: But the man rose up from the dead . . .	
R: And died again . . .	Randy never says that the gun was fired. Also, Randy keeps open whether it was death of shadow-man or of man in hole.
T: Dirt fell from the sky into the hole . . .	
R: A flower grew up out of the dirt. (*Takes off his sunglasses.*)	
T: And it started to rain . . .	
R: The flower grew . . .	Resurrection metaphor—suggests hopeful prognosis.
T: And became . . .	
R: A man. The end.	

Cartoon Lifeline (see Appendix A). I laid the white sheets of paper out on the table in front of Randy. For filling in the lifeline blocks, Randy had the choice of crayons, markers, or pencils. The magic stick-ons, in a paper bag, were to be placed on the lifeline later when it was complete.

Content of Session

Rationale/Analysis

THERAPIST: You did very well with that story. Now we're going to do another story in a new and different way. You like the comics in the paper? (*Randy's face lights up.*) This will be our very own comic strip . . . a kind of cartoon. (*Points to each block on the paper.*) Each block is a year in a life. (*Proceeds to write 0 through 11 above the blocks in chronological order.*) Sound like fun? (*Randy nods. His eyes are intent and expressive.*) You have a choice of crayons, Magic Markers, or pencils. Ready?

Choice = power.

RANDY: I was born ready.

I'm glad he appears interested.

T: OK, great. Draw two characters in each block for each year in the story. After you draw the characters, have them say something to each other like they do in the funny papers. Put your words in a caption or bubble. Got it?

R: Got it, dude.

T: The first block is before birth, when a baby is in its mother's tummy.

Randy has had numerous confrontations with a pregnant child care worker named Maggie. Safe displacement of rage: Staff member white/mother black.

Outline of pregnant woman in orange. Half of baby's head is orange. Rest of baby is brown. Brown strands connect mother's and baby's heads. Randy identifies self with fetus.

R: (*Chooses crayon for the first block. Teeters on the back legs of his chair and smiles defiantly.*) I hate her [referring to Maggie, the pregnant child care worker].

Randy's negative feelings about his mother are displaced onto Maggie.

T: OK. Next block. Year 1.

The child has a large open hand ready to receive, but the large figure has a rectangular, closed-off hand, which is apparently unable to give.

Both figures are smiling and are in a greeting mode, possibly symbolizing hope and openness toward future.

R: (*Switches to pencil.*)

T: Who are these two characters?

R: Stick people.

T: Do they have names?

R: No names.

Stick figure—bereft of power.

Names in ancient world are magical keys that unlock the mystery of a person. Namelessness represents powerlessness and meaninglessness.

The large figure is frowning. "No" appears to be unspoken thought, not spoken words. The large figure recognizes inability to provide for the future.

Hands are unable to clasp.

Box-like hand is suspended in midair, connected to neither figure.

T: Keep on. You're doing great.

R: (*Head down, he intently continues.*)

I want to encourage him.

Appearance of a large full figure. No hands—unable to give or defend self. Eyes covered. Mouthless, yet able to speak. Phallic or gun-like hat.

Child figure is armless and sad/mad. Armless = powerless = abused.

Child stick figure is now sole focus. Smile may represent "happy" period with favorite great-aunt.

Ego is intact—Randy is still able to declare "I am . . ."

R: I don't want to draw two [characters] any more. (*Remains intent but appears to weary.*)

T: You're in charge.

Year 5 is the year he witnesses death of great-aunt.

Handless = powerless.

Frown covers erased smile—great expectations in beginning of year change to disappointment (now chronic).

T: Why so mad?

R: (*Continues drawing, without conversation.*)

The reappearance of the full-figured adult signals an attempt by Randy to empower himself as an adult.

Year 6 represents the end of the spoken word. The future is a question mark.

In contrast to year 3, here the eyes are uncovered, there is a mouth (smile), but there are no feet (unable to move). Power at this age is both enlightening and immobilizing.

T: Ah, he's back.

R: (*Teeters on back legs of chair after drawing year 6. His left arm circles the back of his head, and his left hand covers his mouth from the right.*)

T: Why the question mark?

R: He's a dummy.

Only figure with motion. Motion = power. Power symbolized further in large hands and feet.

Year 7—kidnapping and ritual abuse via sodomy and fire torture.

T: You're doing very well.

R: (*Does not look up or speak.*)

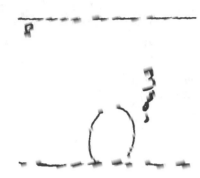

The egg man is ... in the womb ... (progression 3).

Randy's suicidal i... age 8, as detailed in ...

R: I should have started with this one but that's OK.

I: Why the number 3?

R: It's my lucky number.

The egg is hatching. Hope or despair? Is the egg cracked open from the inside or the outside? Does the ego of this world onto t... hatch?

If Randy is dissociative as a result of trauma/abuse, alter ego may be hatching—cracked from inside.

R: (Randy's head is resting on the table as he draws.)

If cracked from outside — moral interpretation? Remorse over death of innocent infant in fire? Is Randy attempting to raise the dead?

Current state of mind:

Fingerprinted as a fire setter, yet troubled at its consequences. Mouth is hidden in the egg— unable to speak.

Still handless and footless despite devouring power of the fire. Revenge always chains one to the past.

R: (Raises his head during the drawing of year 10.)

The possibility of return to the egg or ego-empowered suicide is erased. It's as if life carries one in its current.

The prospects look bleak for the man-child, who is again handless and footless (without motion) and sad. There is sight, however, and the figure appears to be looking back at the split shell.

R: (*Drops his pencil.*) Is it over?

T: Not quite. I've got a bag of magic stickers. I want you to pull the stickers from the bag and place them wherever you want on your comic strip.

R: (*Places the "Invisible Shield" on year 10, current year.*)

T: Why there?

R: To make me safe from getting hit.

R: (*Next places the "Magic Trunk" in crucial year 8.*)

T: What's in the magic trunk?

R: The egg.

The shield could have prevented the fire. Randy uses "me" identification.

Life itself contains a magical seed of hope, which no amount of suffering can destroy.

Key symbol—egg empowered by magic trunk.

Egg = prefire identification with aggressor (transferred from abuse).

Egg = postfire grief.

The ship is a rocket-like ship whose flames have power similar to the sun's. The rocket has the power to exit the earth (split the egg). Randy has really drawn the interior world of the egg in year 2.

Why year 2? Could it be that this is the world created by the mother, who could be the figure in year 2?

R: (*Picks the blank sticker. He looks puzzled.*)

T: This one's for you to draw "your world" on.

R: (*Returns to crayons as in the fetal drawing. The world is egg-shaped and pink. Next he draws a box at the base of the world with an arrow in pink. He then draws the sun with rays in yellow. Finally, he draws yellow rays off the base of the arrow.*)

T: What is that in your world?

R: A ship. (*Places the "Ray Gun" in the fetal picture.*)

T: Why there?

R: I need the gun as I get bigger.

R: (*Places "A Safe Place to Hide" under the year 9.*)

T: Why is it safe?

R: It's in the egg. (*Randy looks at therapist as if this is a stupid question.*)

In year 7, the year of cult abuse, the magic potion ensures safety via flight.

R: (*Places "The Three Bottles" in year 7.*)

T: What's in the bottles?

R: A potion.

T: To drink?

R: No. To make me grow.

The armless child figure and the large figure are wish and fulfillment of the same mind.

R: (*Places "The Road to Where I'm Going" in year 3.*)

T: Where does the road lead?

R: Power.

R: (*Places the final magic sticker, "Hidden Door to Anywhere," in the future—year 11.*)

T: Where do you think the door leads to?

R: Back to the egg.

T: Thank you, Randy. You've done an excellent job. Next time we'll do more neat stuff with our cartoon.

R: (*Exits the office in a hurry.*)

Second Session

The second session 7 days later included two activities: a warm-up exercise, Pass the Prop, and a bridge-building exercise between 2 years in the cartoon lifeline.

Pass the Prop is a game that enables a client to enter a suspended frame of mind and to ease the anxiety that may be generated in a subsequent exercise. The material in Pass the Prop can be any object and is handed back and forth between therapist and client. When the object is received and before it can be passed back, the person must define the object as something other than what it really is. In other words, a pencil can be anything other than a pencil.

The second exercise I did with Randy was a bridge-building game. Materials needed were the following: a table; the cartoon lifeline from the first therapy session; crayons, pencils, and markers; and paper plates (held up to the face and functioning as masks) to facilitate connection between the disparate lifeline characters and years. My hope was that this would enhance cognitive and emotional integrity within Randy's self-story.

Pass the Prop

Content of Session	Rationale/Analysis
(*Therapist, along with several child care workers, watches as Randy lies down and rolls the length of the hallway*	Randy is feeling anxious.

between the classroom and therapist's office. There is a curious mix of raucous laughter and belligerent obscenities emanating from Randy. Therapist coaxes him up off the carpet and into the office.)

THERAPIST: Good to see you, Randy. How was your week?

RANDY: Cool, dude.

T: Great. Now let's try something a little different. You see this triangular-shaped game piece in my hand. When I hand it to you, I want you to tell me what you've got in your hand. Now the fun part is it can be anything you want it to be except a triangle. OK, ready?

R: You start.

T: I'm holding half of a baseball diamond.

R: (*Smiles.*) I'm holding half of a pair of shades [sunglasses].

T: I'm holding in my hand a three-cornered hat.

R: I'm holding in my hand a ship.

T: I'm holding in my hand a woman's dress.

R: I'm holding in my hand the power.

T: Good job.

Cartoon Lifeline Bridge Building—Masks

Content of Session	Rationale/Analysis
THERAPIST: (*Spreads the entire lifeline from first session on the table.*) Remember the comic strip you made last week? Today we're going to bring your comic strip alive. I want you to take a good look at the story you've drawn. Then I want you to pick two characters from the story.	I am offering Randy a choice.
RANDY: (*Scans the lifeline carefully, then closes his eyes and leans back in his chair with an anguished look on his face. He opens his eyes slowly and points toward the large figure in year 3.*)	
T: OK, good. Now on this paper plate, I want you to draw your character and fill your plate with him.	

R: (*Jiggles his legs anxiously as he draws on the plate.*)

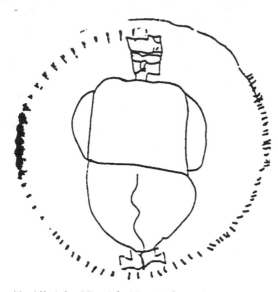

T: All right. Nice job. Now pick another character.

Again, I'm offering him a choice.

R: (*Scans the lifeline again and then points to the figure in the adjacent year, 4.*)

T: OK. Now do the same with this character on this paper plate.

R: (*Proceeds to draw without the anxiety and anguish evidenced in the other mask.*)

T: Abracadabra! Our paper plates have just become masks. Which mask do you want to wear?

R: (*Picks up the large figure from year 3.*)

T: (*Holds up the mask of the child from year 4.*)

R: (*Holds up the mask from year 3.*)

T: (*Talks in the voice of a child.*) What's your name?

R: (*Talks in a deep voice.*) The Rapper. What's your's?

T: Slim.

R: (*Smiles.*)

T: How old are you, Mr. Rapper?

R: I'm 18.

T: I am only 4. I live in a house with lots of people. Where do you live?

R: On the streets, dude.

T: Where are you going?

R: Through the magic door.

T: What's on the other side?

R: The power.

T: What kind of power?

R: Just power.

T: Is your mama over there?

R: No, man, power. I said power.

T: Is there a gun?

R: You're starting to bother me.

T: Will you take me?

R: No. (*Teeters on the back legs of his chair.*)

T: I would also like some of your magic power.

R: Look, Slim. There's only enough for me.

T: Will you come back?

R: No. (*The Rapper mask walks off.*)

T: Goodbye.

R: Are we done?

T: We're done. Excellent job.

The power behind the magic door = survival/mastery over the traumas. The power is magical, like the power of adults through a child's eye. Yet there is the implication that it is greater than raw human violence. There is also anxiety over the power's limited supply, which cannot be shared. Randy must leave childhood behind in order to survive.

Third Session

The third therapy session built on the first two and included two activities: Pass the Prop (the warm-up exercise used during the second session), and bridge building utilizing the Cartoon Lifeline and a variety of puppets.

Pass the Prop

Content of Session	Rationale/Analysis
RANDY: (*Enters therapy in good mood.*)	
THERAPIST: (*Holds up a plastic egg.*) Let's play Pass the Egg. Remember, it has to be something other than an egg. (*Hands Randy the plastic egg.*)	I deliberately choose the egg in order to explore the powerful symbol from the lifeline.
R: (*Takes the plastic egg.*) I have a bomb.	
T: (*Randy passes therapist the plastic egg.*) I have a football in my hand.	
R: A ship.	A ship (part of Randy's design for the blank magic sticker) occurs in the cartoon lifeline at year 2.
T: I have a rock in my hand.	
R: A book.	Power of words—sign of hope.
T: A racetrack.	
R: A baby.	
T: A house.	
R: A gun.	

Puppetry/Cartoon Lifeline. Five puppets were set out on the table: a long, yellow, furry monster (three times the size of the others); a brown, snaggle-toothed walrus; a white monkey; a brown and white bunny; and a rat.

In this bridge-building exercise, Randy was given his choice of two puppets and four blocks/years on the lifeline. These puppets would tell a story about the years on the lifeline. The purpose of this exercise was to engage Randy in an inner-directed dialogue in which Randy expressed feeling and thoughts about the life story. The puppets would remove the need to utilize "old" defense mechanisms.

Content of Session	Rationale/Analysis
THERAPIST: I want you to pick two of the puppets.	
RANDY: (*Picks the long, snake-like monster and the snaggle-toothed walrus.*)	
T: Which puppet would you like to be?	
R: (*Places the snake-like monster puppet on his hand.*)	
T: (*Places the walrus on his hand and changes his voice.*) Hi, I'm Wally, what's your name?	
R: (*Places his dark sunglasses over the snake's eyes and uses a changed, high-pitched voice.*) My name's Cool.	
T: Cool, are you a boy snake or a girl snake?	
R: A boy, dummy.	
T: How old are you?	

R: Not as old as you, old walrus man.

T: Hey, Cool, where would you like to start in the comic strip?

(*Cartoon lifeline is on table in front of Randy.*)

R: Here. (*Randy points first to year 8 and then to year 9 on lifeline.*)

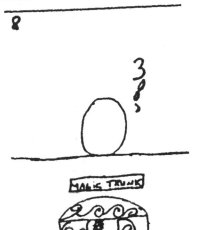

There is hostility in Randy's voice.

On cartoon lifeline, year 7 represents death in many facets, since it is the year of cult abuse. Hence egg drawing in year 8 represents need to return to the safety of the womb. In year 9, the year of the fire setting, the egg is cracking.

T: Cool, what do you think is going on in this picture (*pointing to year 9*)?

R: It's a safe place to hide.

T: What's inside?

R: I'll never tell.

T: Do you need to hide, Cool, because you're scared?

R: The world is scary.

T: Cool, why is the egg cracking?

R: A secret is coming out.

T: Can you tell me the secret?

R: The secret is cracked.

T: How can that be, Cool?

R: Let's go on.

Secret:
  1. Abuse.
  2. Fire-setting confession.

Cracked secret:
  1. Remorse.
  2. Fragmented ego.

T: Tell me about the boy in the egg (*pointing to year 10*).

R: He needs the shield.

T: For protection?

R: From them.

T: Them?

R: They hit me.

T: Why?

R: I'm bad.

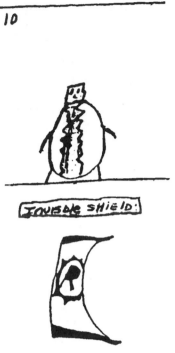

T: Is that why you're frowning (*pointing to year 11*)?

R: I don't like the world. I want to go back in the egg.

T: Why don't you?

R: I can't.

Fourth Session

In the fourth session, puppetry was combined with the cartoon lifeline to enable Randy to proceed safely through his entire lifeline. Materials needed were the following: a table, the cartoon lifeline, and puppets. One of the puppets was a "fire" puppet, a specially handmade red hand puppet with matches glued to the face (see Appendix B). On one side of the fire puppet, the face was smiling. On the other side, the face was frowning.

Warm-Up Exercise. A warm-up exercise was utilized to create a state of suspended disbelief, in order to set the stage for the lifeline with its powerful story.

Cartoon Lifeline. Ten puppets were used: a brown monkey, a white monkey, a bunny, a female child, a male child, the snake-like monster, the walrus, a seal, a frog, a rat, and the fire puppet. They were arranged in a row on the desk on the side of the office. The entire cartoon lifeline was then spread out on the table.

Content of Session	Rationale/Analysis
THERAPIST: I would like you to choose a puppet for each year in the comic strip.	
RANDY: (*Places a puppet on each block: the brown monkey on block 0, the frog on 1, the seal on 2, the walrus on 3, the white monkey on 4, the bunny on 5, the rat on 6, the fire puppet on 7, the snake-like monster on 8, the female child on 9, and the male child on 10. Chooses a nonpuppet red-haired doll lying in a box in therapy office and places it on block 11.*)	
T: Now here's how it works. You will play the puppet character in year 0, and I will play the one in year 1. We will talk and ask questions to get to know each other better. Then you will take the puppet in year 1 and me the one in year 2, and so on down the line.	
R: (*Picks up brown monkey on 0. Therapist picks up frog on 1.*)	Brown in puppet = racial identification.
T: Tell me about yourself.	
R: I was born.	Frog = leaping ability.
T: What was it like in there.	Randy's mother was an injection drug abuser during her pregnancy.
R: Sticky.	
T: What's the gun for?	
R: Protect myself. (*Takes frog from therapist, who picks up seal on 2.*)	Seal relates to ship drawing in the magic sticker for year 2.
T (*as seal*): Can I shake your hand?	

R: (*Makes frog shake hands with seal.*)

T: I'm sad.

R: Why are you sad?

T: Because I'm leaving you soon. (*Hands seal to Randy and picks up walrus on 3.*)

Randy has numerous abandonment issues (mother, great-aunt, family members lost in the fire).

R: (*Makes seal shake head no.*)

T: Mr. Seal, why are you saying "No"?

R: Say "No" to drugs.

Walrus = adult = empowerment over separation anxiety in loss of mother?

T: Have you seen drugs?

R: Yes, Mr. Walrus. (*Takes walrus from therapist, who picks up white monkey on 4.*)

Randy has witnessed world of drugs/prostitution.

R (*as walrus*): I want your toys.

Toys = childhood.

T (*as white monkey*): Which of you is asking?

R: Both.

T: Both of you are in the puppet?

R: Yes. (*Takes white monkey from therapist, who picks up bunny on 5.*)

R (*as white monkey*): I am happy.

T (*as bunny*): Why?

R: I have toys.

T: I don't have any toys. I want your toys.

R: Here, you may play with some of them. (*Takes bunny from therapist, who picks up rat on 6.*)

The happy bunny is the antithesis of angry child in year 5.

T (*as rat*): Are you happy now?

R (*as bunny*): Yes. (*Takes rat from therapist, who picks up fire puppet on 7.*)

R (*as rat*): Why are you smiling?

T: (*Shows smiling face of fire puppet.*) Because you're happy now.

Smiling fire face = warmth, comfort, beauty.

R: Are you a lighter?

T: No, a fireman. That's why I'm running.

R: I'm a dummy.

T: Why do you say that?

R: Because my friend died?

Randy looks at the fire puppet without emotion. He wonders whether puppet is a lighter. (A lighter was allegedly used in the fire-setting incident.)

T: Your friend from year 3? (*Points back to year 3.*)

Death of friend may be death of aunt, death of infant in fire, or death of part of self.

R: Yes. (*Takes fire puppet from therapist, who picks up snake-like monster on 8.*)

Friend in 3 now missing is small boy.

R: (*Places angry/sad "fire" puppet face toward therapist.*)

Snake-like monster is associated with year 8, as in third session.

T (*as snake-like monster*): Mr. Fire, are you mad or sad?

Identification with anger/sadness matches cult abuse trauma at age 7.

R: Sad.

T: Why?

R: The fire.

T: What fire?

R: The fire that spreads.

T: Where is the fire?

R: (*Gets quiet.*)

Maybe he is immobilized by his conflicting emotions.

T: Do the magic bottles put the fire out?

R: No. They help me run faster. (*Takes snake-like monster from therapist, who picks up female child on 9.*)

T (*as female child*): What's it like in the egg, Sammy the snake?

R (*as snake-like monster*): It's cold in here.

T: Do you need a fire to keep warm?

R: No. I need toys. (*Takes female child from therapist, who picks up male child on 10.*)

T (*as male child*): I want out.

R (*as female child*): But it's not safe out there.

Female child may be related to female infant who died in fire. Remorse at innocent death?

T: But I have to see the world. (*Hands male child to Randy and picks up the nonpuppet red-haired doll on 11.*)

T (*as red-haired doll*): What is the dark part in the middle of the eggs?

R (*as male child*): Toys.

Numerous references to toys/childhood.

T: How can you and your toys get out?

R: The power.

May have assumed falsely that power must come from inside.

T: What power.

R: He-Man.

He-Man = TV cartoon character.

T: Now you can pick any year and go back.

R: (*Replaces fire puppet at 7 with male child puppet. Holds on to red-haired doll.*)

T (*as male child*): Why are you sad?

Reference to frown in panel 11.

R (*as doll*): The world's not as great as I thought it
would be.

T: Do you want back in?

R: Sometimes. (*Pause.*) Are we done?

T: We're done. You've done a great job. Thank you.

COMMENTS

I was surprised that Randy went as far as he did with the exercise just described. In
retrospect, I might have probed more into Randy's degree of responsibility for the
actual fire-setting scenario. He may have been readier for it in displaced play than I
expected from his earlier resistance. (Also, the session might have benefited from a
better selection of puppets with a wider range of emotions, particularly angry/scary
puppets.) The cartoon lifeline, the fire puppet, and the other puppets were reintro-
duced at later stages of therapy.

Anniversary dates presented opportunities for engaging Randy in "heavy" issues: the fire-setting date; the various death dates, moving dates, and abuse dates;
and his own birth date.

Guided imagery and other relaxation techniques were utilized to balance the
"hard work" of therapy when trauma was reexperienced.

From Randy's play, I believed that his prognosis was fair. There were hopeful
features in the Tell a Story, Pass the Prop, and cartoon lifeline responses. There was
also much unresolved anger and much sadness.

FOLLOW-UP: RANDY, AGE 19

As Randy improved, he was stepped down in treatment from our secure unit to our
open residential unit and finally to our group home setting. During his first 6 months
at the community-based group home, he attended the highly structured, on-grounds
classroom for severely behavior-disordered children at the residential treatment center.
After this, however, he was mainstreamed into the local high school's severe behavior handicapped unit. This was approximately 22 months after the early sessions
reported here. In all, Randy resided in the residential treatment center and the group
home for 3 years and 3 months. He had difficulty in his peer relationships, especially with females. He was eventually suspended from school for hitting a girl he
had been dating. He alleged she hit him first, but witnesses said otherwise.

While on suspension, Randy, age 13, ran away from the group home. After 14
days had elapsed, his referral county requested he be discharged for policy reasons.
Rumors suggested that he was living on the streets and pimping.

The interpersonal problems of behaviorally troubled children like Randy have
been repeatedly documented in children with histories of avoidant attachment. "These

children are more likely to behave aggressively toward peers, to misread environmental and interpersonal cues and to engage in bullying and other hostile behaviors" (Penzerro & Lein, 1995, p. 354). van der Kolk and Greenberg (1987, p. 64) have found that "children exposed to disruptions of attachment to their primary caregivers through separation, abuse, or neglect, often develop extreme reactivity to internal and external stimulation: that is, they overreact to subsequent situations and have trouble modulating anxiety and aggression."

In the fall of 1997, I was finally able to learn Randy's whereabouts. He, then age 19, was in a medium-security prison serving a 2- to 10-year sentence for attempted robbery. He would be eligible for a parole hearing in July 2000. Early predictors of delinquency and violence were, of course, rampant in Randy's case history: prenatal and perinatal complications, antisocial behavioral problems, maternal rejection, child abuse/neglect, maternal absence (incarceration), lack of parental involvement, and a learning disability (Buka & Earls, 1994). The lack of a secure attachment bond was also relevant in Randy's case. Negative outcomes for someone as vulnerable as Randy can include "unemployment, school drop out, relationship troubles, teen parenthood and incarceration in young adulthood" (Penzerro & Lein, 1995, p. 352). Gil (1991) in her clinical observations of how abused children outwardly express their emotions, includes fire setting, cruelty to animals, aggression, destructiveness, and hostility.

I contacted Randy by phone at the prison. He told me that he had earlier been placed on probation for the attempted robbery. He said that he had "been around a dude who robbed a store while I was with him, but the dude didn't tell it was only him [i.e., not Randy] responsible." Following this, he had violated probation by not keeping appointments with his probation officer. This led to his being put in prison.

He proudly revealed that he was the father of two girls, and stated, "I love them very much." He did add, however, that he really hated both of their mothers! "Intimacy is commonly avoided by child trauma survivors because emotional closeness to others leads to feelings of vulnerability and feelings of loss of control. Intimacy represents a threat, not safety" (James, 1994, p. 15). Randy's love–hate extremes with females were not surprising, in view of his own mother's failure to provide him with the protection or love for which he so desperately longed.

Randy went on to say that his mother was still incarcerated. We had always conjectured that he might get himself sent to prison in order to join symbolically with her. He had once visited his mother while living with us in the treatment center. Since then, as far as we know, their only communication was by letters and phone calls.

I noted with interest Randy's occasional display of real tenderness when speaking of his children, or when recounting news about several friends he had made while in treatment with us. He evidently was capable of forming some relationships that were meaningful to him.

I asked Randy what services had been most helpful and least helpful to him while he was in our treatment center. He said he was thankful for everything; he recognized that we had given him every opportunity and that he alone had "blown it." He went on to say that everything he had learned while in the center had been helpful to him, and that he just wished he could do it all over. In particular, he wished he had not run away from our group home.

He proudly shared with me that he had improved his reading ability through one-to-one tutoring while in prison, and that he planned to get his general equivalency diploma (GED) before leaving prison. (As mentioned earlier, Randy was illiterate at age 9. At our center, he was found to qualify for a formal diagnosis of reading disorder [American Psychiatric Association, 1994].)

Until recently, many researchers believed that trauma behaviors were psychological, with no basis in the physiology of the brain. Now there is research indicating that stress responses that release moderate amounts of adrenaline (and save lives in the short run) can have a long-term negative impact on the brain, causing confusion and impaired learning and memory (Butler, 1997). van der Kolk and Greenberg (1987) make the point that attachment-related trauma—the kind of trauma Randy experienced in his early life with his mother, and again with the sudden loss of his beloved great-aunt—can be particularly damaging:

> Disruptions of attachment during infancy can lead to lasting neurobiological changes. Lack of parental response to separation typically results in a biphasic protest/despair response that may be correlated with hyperactivity or underactivity of neurotransmitter systems. Norephinephrine, dopamine, serotonin and the endogenous opioid and endocrine systems are all involved in the protest/despair response. The developmental stage at which the disruption occurs as well as its severity and duration probably all affect the degree and reversibility of the resulting psychobiological damage. (p. 51)

The part of the brain that appears to be most affected by trauma is the older, emotional part of the brain, including the brain stem and the limbic system. We call these parts "older" because humans share them with animals. Reactions from this part of the brain govern emotions, especially the immediate reactions not mediated by the rational, thinking neocortex. These responses are powerful and have the ability to short-circuit the rest of the brain and body (Schaeffer, 1997).

In Randy's case, one might well ask whether there is any hope for a person who has been traumatized so severely. It is possible that he may be one of the unfortunate minority described by Butler (1997): "For most people the symptoms of PTSD fade in a week, a month, or a year. For an unlucky few individuals the symptoms become hard wired, intractable and unresponsive to therapy" (p. 106). However, positive notes in Randy's case included the absence of repetitious fire themes and child rape themes in his behavior. These issues were addressed in his therapy.

At the end of the 1990s, there is still controversy as to whether the brain changes associated with PTSD are permanent or can be reversed with therapy. Books proving to be useful in helping people recover from trauma include *EMDR: The Breakthrough Therapy for Overcoming Anxiety, Stress and Trauma* (Shapiro, 1997), and *Trauma and Recovery* (Herman, 1992).

CONCLUDING COMMENTS

Our concluding reflections on Randy's life course and prognosis include the following points:

1. Six years passed from Randy's first traumatic experience (being sold into prostitution by his mother at age 3) to the arson/murder at the age of 9 that led to Randy's first treatment intervention at a state psychiatric hospital. It is unrealistic to believe that these crucial years of untreated psychopathological development could be countered by any brief modalities of treatment. Even Randy's several years of intensive residential treatment proved to be too little. For each year that passed, the requirement for intervention rose geometrically. In other words, had Randy been treated at the age of 3 or 4, 6 months to a year of treatment might have sufficed. But as time went on, treatment would have needed to double or triple with each ensuing year. The long interval without intervention and the series of catastrophic events caused severe, possibly irreversible damage.

2. The robbery Randy allegedly committed may have been symbolic of the "robbery" of his childhood.

3. A sign of favorable prognosis is that at this writing, Randy has not set a fire since the arson/murder; nor has he chosen homicide as his crime. In other words, the repetitiveness of Randy's acting-out behaviors has not been literal (e.g., arson upon arson), but symbolic: assaulting a female (the mother theme) and robbery (the taking of things he perceived as unjustly denied to him).

4. Randy's imprisonment recalls the "reproduction" art in the cartoon lifeline (the "egg" in blocks 8 through 11). Randy's symbolic union with his incarcerated mother was probably the unconscious motivating factor. A hopeful sign in this is that the egg in the cartoon lifeline does not stay an egg, but breaks open, producing life. This is perhaps testimony that he will not be permanently "engulfed" into the mother in a symbiotic manner, but may eventually develop some means of protecting himself from himself.

5. Randy apparently became a father with women he did not love, although he has described himself as fond of his children. This is a good sign, because it suggests that he is fond of something in himself. Indeed, Randy was and is likeable; he had, and still has, a genuineness uncharacteristic of sociopaths. We believe that this will prevent Randy from committing suicide.

6. Suicide will not be Randy's coup de grace. Nor will malicious homicide. Randy may end up killing someone, but it will be secondary to a smaller crime or to a domestic dispute. In that meager sense, treatment at our center partially succeeded.

7. Left to his own devices, Randy, lacking a repertoire of inner resources, is likely upon his release from prison to relapse into small-time criminal activity and disputes/violence with women. His loyalty to his mother ironically symbolizes his enduring disappointment at her early inability to protect him.

8. Randy's antipathy toward women and his need to control and dominate them leads us to the following conjecture: His fear of his possible homosexuality may have resulted in attempts to force women to prove he is a man.

9. Prison will not be able to provide Randy with the type of therapeutic environment that might salvage his life. It is more likely to reproduce various aspects of his childhood.

10. With long-term therapeutic interventions of the "holding environment" type and others, such as the creative newer methods used for treatment of PTSD, Randy might have had a better chance.

STUDY QUESTIONS

1. What trauma-related issues would have been relevant for Randy when he entered adolescence? Which will be relevant as he enters adulthood?

2. Discuss the implications of a white therapist treating a black preadolescent boy. How should this be addressed, and what reactions related to racial issues might the therapist anticipate?

3. What spiritual issues are relevant to Randy's case? Do you feel that the strict fundamentalist religious disciplinary practices of his aunt and uncle contributed to Randy's overall traumatization? If so, in what way?

4. Do you agree that Randy may have become involved in robbery as symbolic of the "early robbery" of his childhood? If so, how could a therapist approach this if Randy were in treatment?

5. Is it possible that Randy has absented himself from his two children as males absented themselves from him? Do you think that Randy protected his children/world from himself by becoming incarcerated—returning to the egg (prison)? If so, what suggestions would you have for dealing with this?

6. Do you think that Randy may still be accessible to treatment as a young man? Discuss the pros and cons of a female therapist. Will Randy commit suicide when his mother dies?

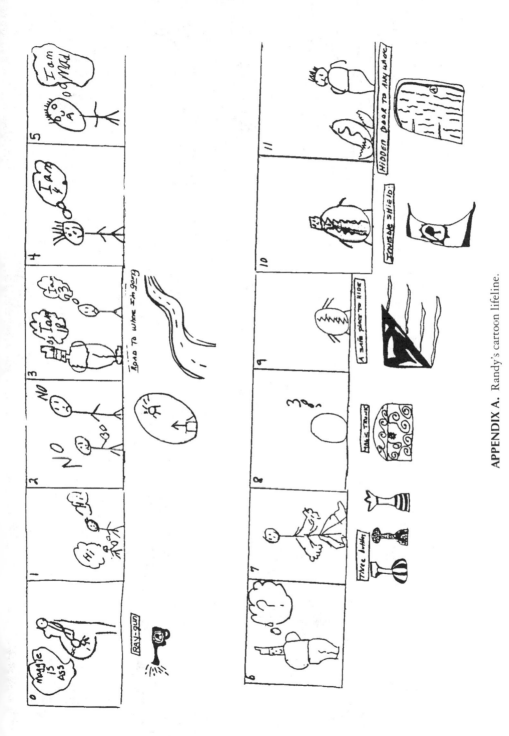

APPENDIX A. Randy's cartoon lifeline.

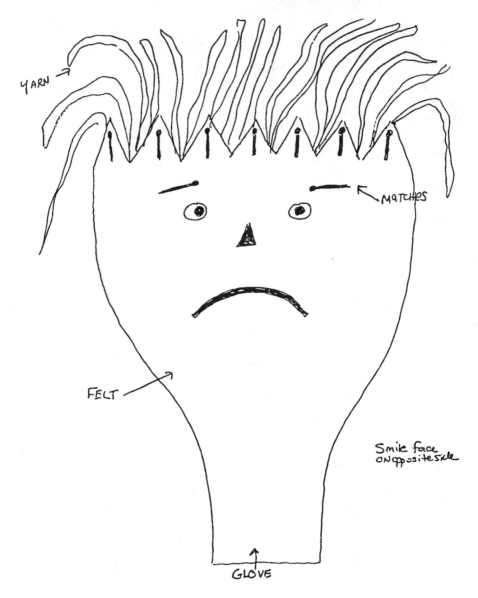

APPENDIX B. Fire puppet (angry/sad face).

REFERENCES

American Psychiatric Association. (1994). *Diagnostic and statistical manual of mental disorders* (4th ed.). Washington, DC: Author.

Buka, S., & Earls, F. (1994). Practical matters: Early predictors of violence can guide public policy. *Child and Adolescent Behavior Letter, 10*(1), 2.

Butler, K. (1997, October). After shock. *Health*, pp. 106–108.

Dunne, P. (1988). Drama therapy techniques in one-to-one treatment with disturbed children and adolescents. *The Arts in Psychotherapy, 15*, 139–149.

Gil, E. (1991). *The healing power of play: Working with abused children.* New York: Guilford Press.

Herman, J. (1992). *Trauma and recovery.* New York: Basic Books.

James, B. (1989). *Treating traumatized children.* Lexington, MA: Lexington Books.

James, B. (1994). *Handbook for treatment of attachment–trauma problems in children.* New York: Free Press.

Naitove, C. (1981). A multi-arts approach to drama therapy with adolescents and young adults. In G. Schattnery & R. Courtney (Eds.), *Drama in therapy for adolescents* (pp. 243–259). New York: Drama Book Specialists.

Pazzanese, E., & Wise, D. (1984). Building self-esteem through puppetry. In N. Renfro (Ed.), *Puppetry, language and the special child* (p. 140). Austin, TX: Nancy Renfro Studio.

Penzerro, R. M., & Lein, L. (1995). Burning their bridges: Disordered attachment and foster care discharge. *Child Welfare, 74*(2), 352–354.

Renfro, N. (1984). A personal perspective. In N. Renfro (Ed.), *Puppetry, language and the special child* (pp. 16–24). Austin, TX: Nancy Renfro Studio.

Schaeffer, M. (1997, Winter).Trauma and brain changes. In *Tell the truth* (p. 1). Cleveland, OH: Joining Together to Stop Sexual Abuse.

Scott, J., Sr. (1996). *The handbook of brief psychotherapy by hypnoanalysis.* Winfield, IL: Relaxed Books.

Shapiro, F. (1997). *EMDR: The breakthrough therapy for overcoming anxiety, stress and trauma.* New York: Basic Books.

Shengold, L. (1989). *Soul murder.* New Haven, CT: Yale University Press.

Sternberg, P., & Garcia, A. (1989). *Sociodrama: Who's in your shoes?* New York: Praeger.

Terr, L. (1987). Psychic trauma and the creative product: A look at the early lives and later work of Poe, Magritte, Hitchcock, and Bergman. *Psychoanalytic Study of the Child, 42*, 545–572.

Terr, L. (1989a). Terror writing by the formerly terrified: A look at Stephen King. *Psychoanalytic Study of the Child, 44*, 369–390.

Terr, L. (1989b). Treating psychic trauma in children: A preliminary discussion. *Journal of Traumatic Stress, 2*(1), 3–20.

van der Kolk, B., & Greenberg, M. T. (1987). The psychobiology of the trauma response: Hyperarousal, constriction, and addiction to traumatic reexposure. In B. van der Kolk (Ed.), *Psychological trauma* (pp. 63–87). Washington, DC: American Psychiatric Press.

CHAPTER 7

Multiple Traumas of Refugees— Near Drowning and Witnessing of Maternal Rape

Case of Sergio, Age 9, and Follow-Up at Age 16

TERESA BEVIN

Sergio was a 9-year-old boy from Nicaragua who was referred to the Multicultural School Based Mental Health Program of Children's Hospital National Medical Center in Washington, DC. The reason for referral, as described by his teacher, was a "panic-like reaction" to new situations. After a psychological evaluation and several interviews with the child and his parents, it was determined that Sergio was suffering from symptoms consistent with posttraumatic stress disorder (PTSD, a disorder frequently associated with war veterans) and dysthymic disorder. Under the heading of "Anxiety Disorders," the fourth edition of the *Diagnostic and Statistical Manual of Mental Disorders* (DSM-IV) describes some of the main criteria for PTSD as follows:

> The essential feature of [PTSD] is the development of characteristic symptoms following exposure to an extreme traumatic stressor involving direct personal experience of an event that involves actual or threatened death or serious injury, or other threat to one's physical integrity; or witnessing an event that involves death, injury, or a threat to the physical integrity of another person. . . . The person's response to the event must involve intense fear, helplessness, or horror (or in children, the response must involve disorganized or agitated behavior). . . . The characteristic symptoms resulting from the exposure to the extreme trauma include persistent reexperiencing of the traumatic event . . . , persistent avoidance of stimuli associated with the trauma and numbing of general responsiveness . . . , and persistent symptoms of increased arousal. . . . (American Psychiatric Association, 1994, p. 424)

The DSM-IV includes the following under the subheading "Specific Culture and Age Features":

> In younger children, distressing dreams of the event may, within several weeks change into generalized nightmares of monsters . . . or of threats to self or others. . . . the reliving of the trauma may occur through repetitive play. (p. 426)

Dysthymic disorder, on the other hand, is described as a "depressed mood . . . for most of the day more days than not" (American Psychiatric Association, 1994, p. 345).

The focus in this chapter is on the key aspects of play therapy used to help this traumatized child process and understand the traumatic events he survived during his migration to the United States from Nicaragua. Sergio's posttraumatic play is described as it occurred spontaneously, as well as in situations prearranged by the therapist (myself) to elicit the reenactment of traumatic events. The case history of Sergio is of special interest to professionals concerned with the impact of violence and war on survivors—both children and other family members who endured or witnessed terror, pain, and humiliation.

Play therapy has been utilized successfully with children who have been traumatized, either in combination with other methods of treatment or as the sole method of treatment to help children work through the emotions associated with the trauma (Gil, 1991; James, 1989). According to Terr (1983, p. 318), "Those cases in which play therapy alone can be expected to succeed are those in which the trauma is limited and without extensive intrusion past the child's coping and defense mechanisms." In Sergio's case, as in most cases of psychic trauma, it was difficult to judge the degree of damage to his coping mechanisms inflicted by the trauma. Only time and a trial of therapy would reveal whether play therapy would relieve his symptoms.

There are different directions a therapist may take to explore the meaning of a child's posttraumatic play. Terr (1983) outlines two different approaches: (1) therapeutic reconstruction of the event or events, and (2) therapeutic interpretation based upon observation of the child's spontaneous play. Sergio's treatment was based on both of these methods.

Pynoos and Eth (1985, p. 23) refer to the psychic trauma suffered "when an individual is exposed to an overwhelming event and is rendered helpless in the face of intolerable danger, anxiety, or instinctual arousal." Sergio had witnessed life-threatening violence to his mother during their immigration. The aftereffects on a child witness, according to Pynoos and Eth, often include intrusive imagery that interferes with learning and posttraumatic guilt connected to the child's imagined failure to intervene. Therapeutic intervention with the child witness attempts to recapture the worst moment of the trauma and gives the child the opportunity to reconstruct the event in play according to his or her wish about how the outcome might have been different (Pynoos & Eth, 1985). This form of reconstructive play not only facilitates the undoing of a horrible memory, but converts the child's role from passivity and helplessness to one of activity and control.

THE CASE: SERGIO MORA, AGE 9

Family Information

Father	Manuel Mora, mid-30s, heavy machinery operator
Mother	Nita Mora, early 30s, cook and part-time babysitter
Son	Sergio, 9, fourth grade
Daughter	Raquel, 3

Presenting Problem

A few months after arriving from Nicaragua via Mexico with his mother and sister, Sergio, then 7 years old, was placed in the second grade at a public school. (This was 2 years prior to beginning treatment.) Even though his teacher spoke Spanish and was sensitive to the normal confusion and shock of recent immigrants, she could not engage Sergio in most class activities. Whenever she called his name or requested his participation, he would become rigid, shake, and occasionally cover his face with his hands. He appeared completely unable to cope with the simplest challenges of everyday school life.

In addition to his difficulties with his teacher, Sergio would not play with other children. Instead, he would place himself in a corner of the playground as if he were avoiding the touch or even the approach of another child. When one of his class-mates confronted him or attempted to engage him in a game, he would sit on the floor and sob uncontrollably, hiding his face. van der Kolk (1996, p. 188) states that PTSD sufferers' repeated revisiting of the past, due to their inability to integrate traumatic memories, is "mirrored physiologically in the continuing misinterpreta-tions of innocuous stimuli as potential threats." Sergio's teacher reported that dur-ing a field trip to a zoo, Sergio refused to walk over a wooden bridge and had to be left with a teacher's aide on one side of the creek. The aide said that he seemed ter-rified of the rushing water, pulling away from it, and even telling her to go on and let him stay by himself. Pynoos, Steinberg, and Goenjian (1996, p. 340) address the issue of traumatic reminders, and state that "unanticipated reminders can evoke a sense of unpreparedness that exacerbates fears."

Obviously, Sergio needed evaluation and treatment in order to function ade-quately in his new environment. The disturbance significantly interfered with his academic achievement, his social development, and most activities of daily life that required his interaction with others.

First Interviews

Sergio's Parents

During the first interview with Sergio's parents, the reasons for his panic and inse-curities became clear. In Nicaragua, the parents owned a small plot of land, which they cultivated; however, it was located in an area where gunfights frequently dis-rupted their life, making it risky for Sergio to walk to school. When Sergio turned 7, his father came by himself to the United States to find employment. Nita and the children were to join Manuel as soon as he could send them enough money to pay someone who would help them to cross the Mexican border illegally. Legal immi-gration was out of the question for a simple family of few means. A "coyote" (usu-ally a Mexican with legal papers to enter and exit the United States) was eventually located to assist them on the trip across the border.

According to his mother, at age 7 Sergio was a normal, fun-loving child who missed his father and wished very much to join him. Manuel had written several letters telling them of the apartment he had rented for them, of how he had learned to work with heavy machines used to construct tall buildings, and of how much happier they would be in their new home. He always had a special message for Sergio, which the child asked to have read to him over and over.

The crossing of the Rio Grande was the first truly traumatic event Sergio was to survive. Nita was carrying clothes and food in a basket on her head, while she carried little Raquel, then 1, in her arms. Sergio was to cross by gripping her skirts. Because it was dark, Nita couldn't find the rope that the "coyote" was supposed to have left for her to guide her through a shallow part of the river. The water was much deeper and the current much stronger than she expected. She stumbled and fell to her knees, and Sergio, who fell with her, was dragged away by the current. Nita had the lucidity to cross, put the baby on firm ground, place her in the clothes basket, and dive after Sergio, who had managed to hang on to some entangled driftwood not far from the shore. He was terrified and shivering but alive. As soon as Nita pulled him to shore, they changed their clothes, and the "coyote" appeared to take them the rest of the way. However, instead of taking them to safety, he threatened Nita at gunpoint; there was a struggle, and Nita was raped while Sergio watched in terror. As reported by his mother, Sergio did not speak again until he was in the arms of his father 2 days later. Pynoos and Nader (1989, p. 570) report that some of the children in their study "attempted to mute their awareness of what was happening." Sergio may have felt doubly vulnerable in the company of his mother and could only bring himself to speak when he felt safer, with his father.

Sergio's entrance into school 2 months after this incident left him ill prepared to face any more strangers. His parents were immediately concerned that he was unable to make friends, to speak up, or to involve himself with any aspect of life outside the home. He would talk with his parents and play with his sister at home, but he would not venture outside by himself or with anyone besides his parents. They were often aware of his walking around in his room during the night. Pynoos and Nader (1989) report that the children in their study were "hypervigilant about personal safety and all became conscious about the security of their homes" (p. 570). Manuel spoke with tears in his eyes about Sergio's fearful, reclusive attitude; he remembered his son as formerly gregarious and full of mischief. Nita, having ignored her own trauma and distress, wanted nothing more than to have her child's cheerful temperament back. She prepared Sergio for our first interview by telling him that someone who "understood children's fears" was going to talk to him in Spanish and help him sleep better and have a better time in school.

Sergio

Sergio had difficulty responding verbally to my questions, and used mostly gestures and head movements to agree or disagree. Slightly overweight, he seemed to slump into the chair, and only occasionally did he look directly at me. His voice trembled as he answered in single words, such as "yes," "no," "sometimes," and "maybe." However, he was oriented to time, place, person, and situation, resisting distraction while paying attention to my questions. His intelligence, memory, and ability for abstraction appeared to be within normal limits. As far as I could determine, his thinking revealed no evidence of hallucinations or other perceptual anomalies, and no distortions of body image or disturbances of his sense of self. Although he chose not to describe any of the events reported by his parents, he admitted to having intrusive thoughts and nightmares revolving around the trauma.

My questions were mostly geared toward Sergio's everyday life until I asked him about "bad dreams" and later about "bad thoughts." With his head low, he spoke softly in Spanish, since his English was not yet fluent. He spoke of bad dreams that "came to him" almost every night. When I asked for details, he kept silent. He stated that "bad thoughts" came to him while at school sometimes, and that he was afraid someone would hurt his little sister while he was at school. I asked him to draw his family, which he did without hesitation—concentrating on every detail, sticking out the tip of his tongue, and pressing hard on the paper (see Figure 7.1). In the drawing, his father, wearing a hard hat, was standing firmly on the ground while his mother, his sister, and he had no ground to stand on, and he appeared as small as his little sister. As stated by Pynoos and Nader (1989), "Witnessing these violent sexual assaults increased the sense of vulnerability in these children. . . . After seeing that a grown woman, especially a parent, can be violated, the child may feel much more vulnerable" (p. 572). But the fact that he had no trouble drawing gave me hope for this young survivor, who could not bring himself to talk about his experiences but could express himself through pictures. Drawing aspects of the trauma was an indirect communication, whereas "speaking" the stories was too direct a confrontation with his own terror. Through drawings, Sergio could release pent-up emotions without fear of hurting others or being ridiculed for having certain feelings.

FIGURE 7.1. Sergio's drawing of his family done during the initial interview.

Drawing helps children uncover attitudes and feelings buried in the unconscious. Ironically, children at different stages of development often express their belief that they "can't draw," which is a learned attitude caused by criticism of early attempts at self-expression. Fortunately for Sergio, his own creative capacity was still intact.

Preliminary Assessment and Treatment Plan

With the information from the family interviews, from Sergio's interviews and drawings, and from his teacher and teacher's aide, our team (composed of two psychiatrists, a clinical psychologist, a child development specialist, and two social workers) concluded that this child was suffering from PTSD. Consequently, I knew that a simple challenge or new experience could trigger at any moment the feelings associated with the original trauma. Furthermore, Sergio's generally depressed and withdrawn mood pointed to dysrhymic disorder as well. The combination of PTSD and dysthymia resulted in a total collapse of his sense of security. He could no longer rely on appropriate emotional responses to otherwise normal, everyday events.

Given the severity of Sergio's symptoms, it was agreed that I, a child development specialist, would see him for 1 hour of individual treatment twice a week at school. In addition, I would visit his home one evening a week, to allow his parents to participate in family sessions as cosurvivors of the trauma.

The main goals set for Sergio were to increase his speech production and social interaction and to improve his mood, while decreasing his panic-like reactions, passivity, and tendency to worry excessively. The treatment methods would include a combination of drawing, playing, some journal writing, and some guided imagery. Whatever appeared to engage and interest Sergio would become the predominant method of treatment.

The first task was to establish a rapport with him and to gain his trust, so that he could begin (however slowly) to share his deepest fears and perceptions, distorted by the horror of his experiences. The fact that his parents were going to be closely involved made me feel confident that Sergio's prognosis was favorable. I had the impression that Sergio customarily refrained from expressing his feelings to his parents, for fear of causing them additional suffering. Furthermore, Sergio expressed some perplexity at the fact that he could not control his emotional responses to simple events that he knew cognitively were not meant to hurt him. He knew he had a problem and seemed to welcome the prospect of working with someone who wanted to help him.

Play Therapy Sessions

After several initial sessions that included talking, storytelling, drawing, and playing guessing games, the more directive play therapy sessions began.

Fourth Session

During the first half of our fourth play therapy session, I attempted to engage Sergio in play with a dollhouse and family figures. He categorically considered a dollhouse a girl's toy and believed this sort of play to be too "sissy" for him, as he had been raised in a Hispanic, fundamentally "macho" culture. He watched with interest, however, while I placed the little people in different rooms; he removed the roof and put it back on, then sat on the floor next to me to watch me "play." I asked him whether he had ever seen a grownup sitting on the floor, playing. He shook his head, smiling. I then showed him some cowboys and Indians, which he seemed to find more to his liking. He manipulated the little men without saying a word; he stood them up side by side, and later one behind the other, while checking at intervals to see if I was watching him.

I deliberately refrained from presenting Sergio with toys that related to his experiences or guiding his play in the early sessions. One of the most significant ways in which PTSD manifests itself in children is repetitive play in which themes or aspects of the trauma are expressed (Terr, 1983). Sergio's spontaneous play did not reflect a repetitive quality, but rather seemed focused on motives other than reenacting the traumatic events. As it turned out, the initial sessions helped him feel more comfortable with me, which was the purpose. He was obviously pleased to find out that I would be bringing him out of his classroom twice a week to "play." He seemed to understand that the sessions were in part aimed toward relieving the stress that being in class represented for him.

Fifth Session

I brought a baby bathtub, which I half filled with water. Little Playskool figures were laid outside the tub. I added a flat piece of wood, about 5" × 5", which I left floating in the water. It should be kept in mind that all the verbal exchanges between myself (as the therapist) and Sergio have been translated from Spanish. The most significant exchanges in this fifth session were as follows:

Content of Session	Therapist's Rationale/Analysis
THERAPIST: (*Sits on the floor by the tub. Begins to manipulate the Playskool dolls.*)	This is a silent invitation to play.
CHILD: (*Sits next to the therapist. Observes quietly, with interest. After a few minutes, begins to use the piece of wood as a boat, making it "sail" through the water He pushes the "boat" with one finger, carefully avoiding a "crash" against the sides of the tub. This goes on for at least 1 minute, alternating slow and fast movements of the boat. He begins to produce "sound effects" with his mouth, imitating a motor, like a hum.*)	I am encouraged by his participation in some water play. I expect him to be somewhat afraid of water after his near-drowning experience, and I am pleasantly surprised that his anxiety does not block his ability to play as a typical 9-year-old boy.
T: (*Puts one of the dolls in the water and speaks in a falsetto.*) Ooh . . . I love swimming. (*Holds the doll; makes the doll go under the water as well.*)	
C: (*Stops the "boat" to observe.*) I think the water is too deep for him, and people don't like that.	Sergio is relating to his fear of deep water, as "experienced" by the doll.

T: What is it that people don't like?

C: Going under water. Only the guys who work under water like it.

T: How come they like it?

C: They work there, and they have all the air tanks and stuff.

T: So you think that the water is too deep for someone without special equipment?

C: Yes.

I am probing for his associations.

Clearly, this was his experience. I debate whether to begin relating the play to his trauma, but decide to wait instead, raising his level of anxiety.

T: Should we drain some water out?

C: Yes.

I am trying to meet Sergio halfway, hoping he will feel more comfortable.

T: (*Takes the tub to a sink and drains half the water out. Sets it down.*)

C: (*Observes quietly, while holding the wet doll in his hand.*)

T: Do you think it will be OK now?

C: (*Places the doll in the water. Still covers its head.*) It's still a little too deep for him, but I think it'll be OK. (*Places the wooden square back in the water, puts the doll on it, and "sails" from one end of the tub to the other. The sailing is slower and more deliberate, as the "boat" drags a little on the bottom in shallower water.*)

I am hoping he will be able to participate in some reenactment.

Maybe it is time to begin to approach the river-crossing experience.

T: (*Places two more dolls in the water, making them "dive," "swim," "squeal," and "jump," and then letting them float.*)

I am hoping for a reaction.

C: (*Does not seem to pay any attention at first. Then begins to observe carefully. Pushes the boat in my direction and places one of the floating dolls on the boat.*)

T: What is he doing?

C: Taking him on the boat.

T: Why?

C: So he doesn't get tired.

T: Tired of what?

C: Swimming.

I'm trying to encourage him to expand.

T: Has he been swimming for a long time?

C: Not very long, but he's tired.

T: Was he drowning?

C: No, he was crampy.

T: From swimming?

C: Yeah.

Cramping is often the precursor of, and almost as traumatic as, drowning.

T: Who is the sailor?

C: He's not a sailor.

T: Who is he?

C: The daddy.

T: Hmm.

C: (*Sails slowly while looking at the other dolls.*) Oh
. . . (*talking for the sailor*) I have to get them too!
. . . Turn around, turn around. (*Turns the boat
around and picks the other dolls up and puts them on
the boat.*)

T: Who are they?

C: The daddy's kids.

T: Where's the mommy?

C: Right here (*picking one doll*).

T: Where are they going?

C: They're going fishing first, then they go home.

Perhaps Sergio is expressing his wish
that his father had been with them.
I'm not ready with a response that
will help him. Maybe I should say,
"It feels safer with the daddy there."

Sergio is focusing on negative
aspects of water, eased by the
presence of someone who can save
those in danger. The daddy is really
taking charge.

Sergio speaks as if describing his
own former family life back home.
He obviously seeks to substitute a
happy memory for the trauma he
experienced.

It was obvious that Sergio was beginning to relax. His speech production increased remarkably during this session, and his body language was more spontaneous. At times he seemed lost in play, unaware of whether or not I was watching him.

Sixth Session

Sergio appeared cheerful. The same materials were laid out: the tub, the piece of wood,
and the Playskool dolls. He sat down without being told and began to place the dolls
on the piece of wood. I allowed him to play freely for several minutes. I had plans for
him, however, and wanted to "guide" the play session a little more than in previous
sessions. Terr (1983) states that "preset or prearranged play therapy allows the child
to 'find' toys which the therapist believes are applicable to the terrifying events"
(p. 315). Sometimes, however, providing significant material is not enough to elicit
reenactment, and the situation has to be manipulated as well. I suggested that we
would pretend that the "people" needed to get from one side of the tub to the other
without a boat, because they didn't have one. He resisted at first my wanting to dominate the game; I gave in some if he would give in some. He finally agreed to follow
my lead for a while. The most relevant exchanges were as follows:

Content of Session   Therapist's Rationale/Analysis

THERAPIST: What should the water be . . . the
ocean, or a river?

CHILD: A swimming pool.

Sergio may be resisting an anxiety-producing scenario.

T: OK, we can pretend it is a swimming pool first, and then a river.

I believe th at he needs to approach his anxiety, and I feel confident that I will not allow him to become overwhelmed.

C: Back in Nicaragua, my dad caught a real big fish in the river.

Sergio begins to make positive associations.

T: Great! . . . What kind of fish was it?

C: A silver fish.

T: I bet it was tasty.

Although his play is related to water (the topic of the trauma), his thinking has some positive associations.

C: Yeah. We baked it.

T: Mmmmmmm.

C: Mmmmmmm. (*Rubs his stomach.*)

T: Now, what about our game?

I need to help him confront his fears (even though he would rather remain with his positive associations).

C: OK.

T: How are they going to cross?

C: The water is too deep.

T: Do you want to help me drain some of it?

C: I'll do it!

T: Fine, but I will have to help you, because the tub is very heavy now.

Sergio is eager to take an active part in the preparations. I want him to assume some control in the reenactment, even though I know he felt helpless in reality.

C: OK. (*The tub is drained.*)

T: Is this better?

C: Yes.

T: I'll watch.

C: OK. (*Talking and doing.*) The father is bigger, and he's not scared. He is going to help this one first, then come back fast, take the other, then come back fast, then take the mother. Now they are all on the other side.

Again, the anxiety is relieved by the presence of a benevolent, powerful character. If only it had happened this way! Could I say something about this? (But I don't want him to resent his father for "allowing" this to happen.)

T: Good. You did that very well. Why don't we try it as a river now?

C: (*Pauses for a moment in thought. Scratches his ear for several minutes.*)

T: Well?

C: OK, it's a river. But it doesn't look like a river at all. It looks more like a swimming pool.

He is resisting the scenario.

T: I know. But when you are playing you can make believe anything, even if it doesn't look like it. . . . Right?

C: Right.

T: So let's keep playing.   He seems to need my encourage-
                                              ment at this point.
C: OK.

T: Can you make them cross the river?

C: Yeah, that's easy.

T: Can you try not to do it so fast this time, so I   Sergio may want to "rush" through
can really see?   the scene. I want to slow him
                                                       down.
C: OK.

T: Let's go, then.

C: They need a rope!   He may want a delay or seek a way
                                              to relieve his anxiety.
T: A rope?

C: So they can hold it, and nobody can drown.   He is relating to the original plan
                                                for his family's crossing.
T: I'll find one. Wait for me.

C: OK.

T: (*Goes to find a piece of string. On returning, finds*   Sergio is anticipating a "difficult"
child clutching all dolls, away from the tub.) Here's the   situation and is trying to move the
rope.   family away from danger.

C: We need to tie it over there (*points to a chair*),
and I'll hold it over here. (*Sets dolls on the floor in
order to tie the string.*)

T: You are doing a good job.

C: (*Ties one end to a chair close by, holds the other end, and*   He performs these actions as if
"*walks*" *each doll along the string to the other side, slowly.*)   involved in a well-rehearsed ritual.
                                                       Perhaps this is the way he "thought"
T: I guess they made it.   it was going to be, and wishes it had
                                                       been.
C: Yeah. They made it.

T: What happens if they try to do it without the
rope?

C: It's dangerous.

T: You know about that, right?   I am moving to recollections of the
                                              trauma, and wondering whether he
C: Yeah!   will tolerate a more accurate
                                              reenactment.
T: You didn't have a rope to cross the river, right?

C: Right.

T: What did that feel like?

C: Scary.   He is responding with one or two
                                              words only, as he did during his
T: What did you think could happen to you?   first interview. I know it is hard for
                                              him, and I don't like to be the
C: I could drown.   person who urges him to recall the
                                              painful memories.
T: Do you still think about that?

C: Yeah.

T: But you made it.

C: Yeah, I made it.

T: Do you want to show me how it happened, with the little man?

C: OK. (*Talking and doing.*) The water is deep. Help! . . . The current is pushing, pushing, pushing. I'm drowning, help, help! Mom! (*Gulps.*) I'm tired! . . . I can't touch the bottom! Help! . . . The water is dirty and it tastes bad! . . . Yuk! . . . Help me! Mom! (*Pauses.*)

T: And then what happened?

C: Mom got me out.

T: She's strong.

C: Yeah, she's strong.

T: What did you feel when you were drowning?

C: I had to cough and cough, and I swallowed a lot of black water.

T: You have to be very strong to endure that.

C: Yeah . . . I'm strong (*puffing his chest*).

T: What would you like to do next?

C: Play with something else. I think you have Play-Doh in your bag.

T: Yes, I do. You must have seen it.

C: No. I smelled it!

T: It does smell funny.

C: Yeah.

T: I would like you to show me how your mom got you out of the water.

C: Later. OK?

T: OK.

I am focusing on reality of outcome. I want him to have a positive association with this.

Now he is really talking!

Sergio avoids talking about his terror and gives basic information about the events, separate from his feelings.

I provide reassurance.

He seeks to move away from painful memories. I don't blame him.

Sergio focuses on his resourcefulness.

I guess he can't tolerate dealing with the trauma any more today. He may have been feeling positive and may not want to be brought back to negative memories.

Some of Sergio's actions were performed as if he had done the same thing many times before. He knew exactly how to tie the rope, and the movements of his hands were almost mechanical. This might indicate that Sergio had repeated the play privately, even though there was no rope for them during the real events. It might also suggest that he had mentally rehearsed his expectations.

Seventh Session

During the seventh session, I used guided imagery for the first half hour. Sergio and I pretended we were back where it all happened. I began with some relaxation exercises. Later I suggested to him that he close his eyes and imagine the place so well that he could almost touch it. I reassured him that I would be with him. I explained to him that it would be like a game—like walking into a storybook, only this story was not one of his favorites. We had discussed that there are good stories and bad stories, and that we all have both kinds in our lives. In order for me to really share his "bad" story, he had to tell me how everything happened really slowly, because I might get scared and I wanted him to hold my hand, as I might not be as brave as he. I did this because I wanted to offer support to the child. This session was a very important one for Sergio. He let down his guard and gave in to some of the deepest emotions associated with the episode. He took the job of giving me a tour of the horror scene very seriously. He held onto my hand very tightly and cried softly as he talked for much of the period of the guided imagery. However, he did not want to continue when he reached the part in which he, his mother, and his little sister encountered the "coyote" again, because he was "very tired." That had to be reserved for another session.

During the second half hour, I convinced Sergio to play with the dollhouse and pretend the "family" figures were his own family. He showed me what the family would do on the weekends. He indicated that he liked to spend time playing with his little sister, reenacting some of their games. At some point he introduced his cousin, who, according to Sergio, was a bully. There was not a fifth doll, so he took a rectangular eraser out of his pocket and used it to impersonate this character. He expressed his distrust for his cousin, from whom he felt he had to defend his sister, because he was "never, ever going to let anybody push her around."

Eighth Session

I brought three handmade rag dolls, two males and one female, to the eighth session. I started by comparing a rag doll's body to our bodies when we are relaxed. He quickly grasped the idea and related well to the concept of relaxation, which he understood but had not been able to achieve completely until that moment. After he had some time to play freely and to throw the dolls around as if they were performing great acrobatic feats, I decided to attempt a "role play" of his mother's rape. By now, I felt that Sergio and I had established a good enough rapport to try together to reach the part of his experience that had clearly caused him the most pain. He did not completely understand what had happened, biologically, but he had seen his mother in mortal danger, attacked, pushed to the ground, pinned down, and humiliated. This memory was dreadful and had become almost unreal to him. Sergio could not completely understand the aggressor's motives, but he knew it was an ugly, violent act. The threat of losing his mother, and perhaps of being killed himself, was outside his grasp. The key aspects of this play therapy session were as follows:

Content of Session

THERAPIST: Sergio, I would like you to show me what happened after you crossed the river and found the "coyote."

CHILD: (*Grimaces as if faced with an insurmountable task.*)

T: I know this is difficult for you.

C: It's boring.

T: C'mon, you see it as boring because it is something you don't want to remember. You know that you are safe now, and your mom is safe. Show me with the dolls. What do you say?

C: Aw . . . OK. (*Sits motionless for a few moments as if gathering strength. He has a male doll at one side and a female doll at the other. Talking and doing.*) He came out of the bushes to talk to my mom. (*Pause.*)

T: What did he say?

C: I don't know. (*Pause.*)

T: Then what?

C: He had a gun and he put it on my mom, right here. (*Points to the throat; pause.*)

T: On her throat? . . . That's terrible!

C: Like this (*more graphically*).

T: Go on, honey, you're doing great.

C: He pushed my mom to the ground.

T: Show me with the doll.

C: Then he talked real ugly to my mom; he said bad words.

T: What did he say?

C: He said, "You bitch, I know what you want." (*Holds the male doll menacingly over the female doll.*) . . . But I don't know what else he said.

T: That's OK; go on.

C: My mom told him that she didn't want me to see, but he told her to shut up or she would be sorry.

T: You are so brave, and you are doing so well. Show me what happened. (*Points at the dolls.*)

Therapist's Rationale/Analysis

I am moving to recollections about the second part of his trauma.

I know this is his defense against anxiety.

I provide gentle confrontation plus reality reassurance.

It pains me that he has to reexperience this terrible scene. But I know that it will have a healing effect on him, so I encourage more details.

I am normalizing his fear.

Sergio seems encouraged by my reaction.

I want him to know that he doesn't have to be afraid of shocking me.

It is important to get as many specific details as possible.

Sergio appears to block his memory of the obscenities, or doesn't want to repeat them.

This was a horrible experience for both mother and child.

I provide more encouragement.

C: (*Puts the male doll over the female doll. Shows struggle, fighting. Pushes the male onto the female. Presses down as if to crush her. Stops.*)

T: What were you doing when all this was happening?

C: I was crying, with my sister. (*Indicates by gesturers that he had held his sister during the incident.*)

I'm touched by the way he tried to protect his sister while seeking some comfort himself in holding her.

T: What did you think?

C: He was going to hurt my mom.

T: What was that like for you, inside? (*Indicates the heart.*)

C: Scary. (*Pause.*)

I understand how terrified he must have been.

T: Was it dark?

C: Yeah. It was dark.

The darkness made the scene even more terrifying for him.

T: What happened next?

C: He pushed us into a truck and drove to a woman's house.

T: And then what?

C: My mom called my father, and he came the day after.

Sergio seems relieved at this point.

T: How was your mom after all that?

C: She cried a little bit after he did that to her, but he told her to shut up or he would hurt us. (*Pause.*)

T: Then . . .

C: He opened the door on my mom's side and yelled that if she wanted to be left right there for the Migra [U.S. Immigration and Naturalization Service] to find us, he would push us out on the road. (*Pause.*). He was mean.

Both mother and child must have been overwhelmed by the idea that something even worse could happen.

T: Yes, he was. . . . What happened when your father arrived?

C: We went home.

T: Did you tell your dad?

C: No, because my mom said we couldn't until we were at home. She didn't want my dad to kill the man, because the Migra could send us all back to Nicaragua.

The order to "shut up" had many ramifications. Could this be the source of his mutism?

T: I see. . . . What happened when he found out?

C: My mom told him, and he was mad, and he cried, and he squeezed us together. Because we have to stay together.

How very reassuring that the father did not explode!

T: And it's all over now.	I am focusing on reality of outcome.
C: Yeah. It's all over (*sighs in relief*).	
T: And your mom is OK.	
C: She's OK.	And both Sergio and his sister are OK.

There was a great sense of satisfaction for me after this session. It was obvious that Sergio had released some of the negative emotions and fears associated with the traumatic event by reenacting it and talking about it for the first time. His mother reported that after this session, he told her that he was beginning to forget about it all and wished she could forget as well. This indicated that he was beginning to feel relief and was attempting to share it with his mother, who he knew wanted him to forget.

Ninth Session

Pynoos and Nader (1989, p. 570) found that "boys, especially, reported feeling guilty for not successfully intervening during the assault of their mothers." Therefore I decided to devote this session to exploring what would have happened if Sergio had been a lot bigger when the "coyote" attacked his mother. Sergio really put himself into this. The same rag dolls were used. Some of the most important exchanges were as follows:

Content of Session	Therapist's Rationale/Analysis
THERAPIST: Let's pretend that you could have become anything you wanted when the man came out of the bushes.	
CHILD: OK.	
T: What would you have wanted to be?	I am hoping to empower Sergio in his fantasy.
C: A big, big guy. Real big, like my father.	
T: Fine. You can be as big as your father now.	
C: (*Picks up the male doll he has assigned as the "bad guy" and holds the "good guy" doll facing it.*) You are not going to hurt her, you hear me? (*Overpowers the "bad guy" while he talks.*) And this is for being ugly, and this is for being mean, and this is for having a big gun. (*Grabs the doll by the feet and hits the floor with its head, repeatedly, until he seems tired. Finally, he throws the "bad guy" doll into a corner of the room with a big tumble.*) There, that'll show him.	Sergio ventilates his anger. I am glad that he can do this. His anger is justified. I hope it will never get out of control in his everyday life.
T: You did great! (*Applauds.*)	I want to validate his feelings.
C: I finished him, didn't I? (*Grins triumphantly.*)	

Tenth Session

The following session, and several others, were devoted to Sergio's feelings toward the "coyote" as well as his nightmares. His fear had been transformed into anger by now. He thrashed the "bad guy" rag doll on several occasions. He pretended to be a giant, crushing the man and transforming his previously awesome strength into the powerlessness of a child. The reversal of roles seemed to give Sergio the strength to cope with the traumatic events of the past in his new, "safe" environment. After he reduced the enemy to a more manageable size, all the other threats in his life began to diminish in importance; this gave him a new outlook, renewed self-esteem, and finally a place among his peers. Furthermore, his new control over his emotions helped him continue to learn about the world around him and about his own strength. Sergio understood that he alone had dispelled the clouds and had begun the process of burying the beast.

COMMENTS

Sergio's case is typical of the experiences of many children from war-torn countries who enter the United States. As previously stated, PTSD is not a disorder that afflicts war veterans and other adults only. Those of us who work with war survivors usually refer to entire families as "survivors and cosurvivors." They must learn to use their own self-healing powers while maintaining family cohesion. The very nature of their trauma has forced these children and their families to go beyond ordinary efforts to survive, to function, and to master tasks (Flies-Moffat & Moffat, 1984).

In Sergio's case, every therapy session started with a period of relaxation—one of the most important skills that survivors must learn, to counteract the everyday stressors that create a domino-effect reaction going back to the original trauma. Sergio was taught to relax a group of muscles at a time, first contracting them and then letting go. This way he could feel what it was like for a muscle to be relaxed as opposed to contracted. He understood the principle of relaxation almost immediately, but had trouble achieving the effect at the beginning. In time, however, he would start his relaxation exercises by himself, without prompting. He learned the process well enough to use it in order to help himself fall asleep.

The acting out of traumatic events with nonthreatening objects such as toys can help place the events in the perspective of the past, where they belong. This approach accelerates the process of adapting to life after trauma. Through the manipulation of dolls, Sergio subconsciously identified his own maladaptive coping techniques (such as panicking and crying in order to be left alone); this helped him to conceptualize the aftereffects of his trauma at some level, and to recognize his posttrauma behaviors and feelings.

The involvement of his parents in therapy, their willingness to work with their child, and their courage to face their own humiliation and anger were of primary importance to Sergio's recovery. He and his mother recalled the events together, and then his father joined in and cried with them. The whole process was difficult for Sergio's father. It was puzzling for him, a Hispanic male raised in a "macho" culture, to see his son incapable of "shaking himself up" from his distress. An uneducated man, he felt very threatened by this and even thought of himself as less of a man for not being able to be tougher with his son, so he would "stop whining." His understanding was of great importance to Sergio, who revered his father.

Sergio belonged with his family; his parents and sister were his foundation to continue growing and developing normally. He was fortunate, considering all he had endured, to have parents who loved and respected him, and who (in spite of their lack of education) were willing to participate in his treatment.

When I was faced with Sergio's initial state—that of a pitiful child who could not cope with the slightest stress—it was difficult to determine how far or how fast he could be encouraged to confront his pain. He was difficult to engage at first, but perhaps he could have been pushed harder, sooner. The speed of his recovery and his quick grasp of concepts and ideas, as well as his cooperative nature, indicated that his regenerative powers were in far better shape than I had initially believed.

After more than a year of individual treatment, Sergio began to participate once a week in group therapy with children who were all survivors. Sergio still had work to do to improve his ability to interact with his peers. He was not assertive and lacked confidence in his own intelligence at times. However, he was attending a special class for children who were interested in space and aerodynamics. He continued to make conscious efforts to extend himself, to reach out. I felt confident that Sergio was on his way and would succeed.

It would be impossible to identify the one factor that was critical in the management of this case. I attribute most of the credit for the positive outcome to a combination of treatment approaches and methods. By sharing his fear and his humiliation with me in a displaced manner through play, Sergio began to share what he thought was his alone to endure. The play reenactment helped him turn passivity into activity and provided an outlet for his frustration and anger. I was there with him, appreciating his honesty, praising his efforts, and treating him and his experience with complete respect. Sergio, as a survivor, found the courage to persist and face the monster.

UPDATE: SERGIO, AGE 16

After 2 years of group therapy, Sergio dropped out against his parents' wishes, stating that he didn't need it any more. At school, he consistently appeared well adjusted at that time, but his parents were concerned about his remaining hypervigilance and his temper outbursts (which had increased). During his second year at middle school, Sergio began to show signs of trouble at school as well. He became aggressive toward certain classmates; at home, be refused to obey his parents and locked himself in his bedroom for hours at a time. His parents reported that at times he expressed a wish to die. As stated by Pynoos and Nader (1989), children who witness the sexual assault of their mothers often face "challenges to their self-esteem, stress in intrafamilial and peer relationships, and changes in future orientation" (p. 572). The school counselor referred him to a well-regarded male therapist who specializes in treating adolescents with discipline problems who have been victims of abuse or trauma. Sergio, now age 16, is still attending sessions every 2 weeks, and his mother reports remarkable progress. Sergio is now attending high school and says that he wants to go to college and be a teacher. He and his father spend a great deal of time together and enjoy fishing trips, which suggests that the water no longer holds frightening memories for Sergio.

STUDY QUESTIONS

1. Would you have handled this case differently in regard to sequence, orienting questions, or the materials used?

2. At the end of the sixth session, would you have asked such an open question as "What would you like to do next?", or would you have continued in the same direction? Explain.

3. In your view, can play therapy benefit children of any culture, and how much knowledge does a therapist need to have about a child's culture?

4. How can the therapist explain to the parents the need for reenactment of events and emotional release through play, when their wish is for their child to forget the trauma?

5. Do you think the therapist should have explored Sergio's understanding about the sexual nature of the assault on his mother? If so, at what point and how could this have been addressed?

REFERENCES

American Psychiatric Association. (1994). *Diagnostic and statistical manual of mental disorders* (4th ed.) Washington, DC: Author.

Flies-Moffat, L., & Moffat, J. G. (1984). Families after trauma: An education and human services resources. In *MidPoint: Survivors and Families* (pp. 38–39). Minneapolis: State Board of Vocational Education.

Gil, E. (1991). *The healing power of play*. New York: Guilford Press.

James, B. (1989). *Treating traumatized children: New insights and creative innovations*. Lexington, MA: Lexington Books.

Pynoos, R. S., & Eth, S. (1985). *Witnessing acts of personal violence*. In S. Eth & R. S. Pynoos, *Post-traumatic stress disorder in children* (pp. 19–43). Washingron, DC: American Psychiatric Press.

Pynoos, R. S., & Nader, K. (1989). Children who witness the sexual assaults of their mothers. *Journal of the American Academy of Child and Adolescent Psychiatry, 27*, 567–572.

Pynoos, R. S., Steinberg, A. M., & Goenjian, A. (1996). Traumatic stress in childhood and adolescence: Recent developments and current controversies. In B. A. van der Kolk, A. C. McFarlane, & L. Weisaeth (Eds.), *Traumatic stress* (pp. 331–358). New York: Guilford Press.

Terr, L. C. (1983). Play therapy and psychic trauma: A preliminary report. In C. E. Schaefer & K. J. O'Connor (Eds.), *Handbook of play therapy* (pp. 308–319). New York: Wiley.

van der Kolk, B. A. (1996). The complexity of adaptation to trauma. In B. A. van der Kolk, A. C. McFarlane, & L. Weisaeth (Eds.), *Traumatic stress* (pp. 182–188). New York: Guilford Press.

CHAPTER 8

Betrayed by a Trusted Adult

Structured Time-Limited Group Therapy with Elementary
School Children Abused by a School Employee

DAVID PELCOVITZ

This chapter describes a short-term structured group psychotherapy intervention for
a group of girls sexually abused by an employee of their school district. The presentation details an 18-session intervention for six girls, all of whom were abused by
the same man. After a brief review of the literature on structured group treatment
for sexual abuse, the content of the group sessions with the girls is presented, with
an emphasis on techniques employed to help them deal with the cognitive, emotional, and behavioral effects of the abuse.

RATIONALE FOR GROUP THERAPY
WITH SEXUALLY ABUSED CHILDREN

Structured group psychotherapy for sexually abused children has been singled out
as a particularly effective short-term treatment for this population (e.g., De Luca,
Hazen, & Cutler, 1993; Larzelere, Collins, & Collins, 1993; Finkelhor & Berliner,
1995). In a survey of incest treatment, experts Forseth and Brown (1981) reported
that group therapy was cited most often as the treatment of choice for victims of
intrafamilial sexual abuse. Group therapy is particularly well suited for helping children organize and express their memories and feelings regarding the trauma. In the
case of children who were victimized by the same perpetrator (e.g., victims of abuse
in a day care setting or a Scout troop), sharing and verbalizing abuse-related material in a supportive context with survivors of the same trauma can be a powerful vehicle
for lessening the feelings of stigmatization and damage that so frequently accompany this form of victimization.

A number of studies have systematically evaluated the effectiveness of different treatments for child victims of sexual abuse (Finkelhor & Berliner, 1995). There
is a growing consensus that the most effective therapeutic approaches in dealing with
victims of abuse are trauma-specific—that is, structured and direct approaches aimed
at helping the children integrate memories and feelings related to the abuse (Finkelhor
& Berliner, 1995; Friedrich, 1994; James, 1994). After an extensive review of the
empirical literature on treatment of sexually abused children, Finkelhor and Berliner (1995) have concluded that research lends support for the effectiveness of abuse-
focused, directive therapies.

The objectives of group therapy for sexually abused children are informed by our knowledge about the aftermath of such abuse. Research has shown that sexual abuse often interferes with self-regulatory processes (Cole & Putnam, 1992), the ability to trust others (e.g., Roth, Newman, Pelcovitz, van der Kolk, & Mandel, 1997), and the capacity for intimacy (e.g., Finkelhor, Hotaling, Lewis, & Smith, 1989). In a comprehensive review of empirical studies investigating the effects of sexual abuse on children, Kendall-Tackett, Williams, and Finkelhor (1993) found that although no one symptom characterized a majority of sexually abused children, victims were at particular risk for posttraumatic stress disorder, behavior problems, sexualized behaviors, poor self-esteem, and abuse-specific fears. Penetration, duration, frequency of the abuse, use of force, the perpetrator's relationship to the child, and level of maternal support all were found to affect the degree of symptomatology.

In the case of a child abused by someone outside the family, many of the effects and dynamics are similar to those seen in survivors of incest. However, when a child's family is supportive and the abuser is not of particular emotional importance to the child, then long-term effects may be less severe. The differences between the dynamics and prognosis of abuse perpetrated by relatives versus nonrelatives highlight the potential value of groups designed specifically for survivors of extrafamilial sexual abuse.

The ultimate purpose of group therapy for young victims of sexual abuse is to help them view their victimization as something bad that happened to them, rather than an indication that they are living in an unsafe world where they are inevitably destined to repeat their victimization. Virtually all structured groups for this population also focus on the following (Berliner & MacQuivey, 1983; De Luca et al., 1993; Larzelere et al., 1993; Mandell et al., 1989; Nelki & Watter, 1989; Sturkie, 1994):

- The validation and expression of feelings surrounding the abuse
- Reduction of feelings of responsibility and guilt
- Educating the children about the use of abuse prevention strategies
- Assisting the children in the integration of conflicted feelings toward the perpetrator(s)

Although there is a rich literature describing both structured and nonstructured approaches to work with victims of intrafamilial sexual abuse, there are virtually no descriptions of groups made up only of extrafamilially abused children. Yet, as suggested above, there is evidence that the dynamics and treatment of extrafamilial sexual abuse differ in some ways from those of victims of incest. For example, a recent study found that in victims of extrafamilial sexual assault, the children's perceptions of self-blame and guilt for the abuse were particularly salient dynamics that were predictive of depression, fear, and feelings of powerlessness (Ligezinska, Firestone, Manion, & McIntyre, 1996). One can speculate that in contrast to incest, where the blame is obviously borne by the adult family member who violates his or her role as the child's protector, "allowing" sexual contact with somebody outside of the family is more likely to be perceived by the child as his or her own fault.

CASE EXAMPLE: GROUP FOR CHILD VICTIMS OF EXTRAFAMILIAL SEXUAL ABUSE

Group Composition

The group was made up of six girls who were victimized by the same sexual abuser. The girls attended two elementary schools in the same school district in a predominantly white, middle-class community. They ranged in age from 9 to 11 years, and were enrolled in fourth through sixth grades. The group members were as follows:

- Lisa, age 10
- Melissa, age 11
- Sharon, age 9
- Kristin, age 11
- Kathy, age 9
- Maria, age 11

Background and Abuse Circumstances

The sexual abuse took place during a period that began 2 years before the group was formed, and ended just before the beginning of the academic year in which the group took place. The offender was Greg, a music teacher in his early 40s, who was looked up to by many of the children and their parents as a friendly and warm member of their community. The sexual abuse included fondling of the children's genitals, oral sex, and sodomy. The children also at times witnessed the victimization of their peers. The offender used many of the methods common to perpetrators of sexual abuse, including gaining the children's trust by giving them candy and small gifts, and playing various nonsexual games that "groomed" them for increasing levels of sexual activity. Secrecy was ensured via threats to harm family members if the children disclosed the abuse. Disclosure of the abuse was accidental and was not initiated by any of the victims. The group began approximately 6 months after the disclosure of the abuse, and shortly after Greg pled guilty and received a lengthy prison sentence. The children and parents were told that to help other therapists help other children, I might, at some point, write about the group. The parents and children agreed after they were assured that their names and some minor circumstances surrounding details of the abuse would be changed to protect their confidentiality.

Planning the Group

Gender of Group Participants

The literature on group therapy for victims of sexual abuse addresses a number of general issues, which are relevant in the planning of a group. There is a consensus that same-sex and same-developmental-stage groups are preferable to groups that mix boys and girls, or that include children whose ages differ by more than 2–4 years

(Sturkie, 1994). The advantages of same-sex groups include more common interests, less stimulation and distraction, and greater comfort in discussing sexual issues (Mandell et al., 1989). The group described here consisted only of females. Males victimized by this offender were seen in a different group.

Cotherapists

The literature on group therapy for victims of sexual abuse addresses a number of general issues that are relevant in the planning of a group. After reviewing the clinical literature on the use of cotherapists in groups for sexually abused children, Haugaard and Reppucci (1988) conclude that having both a male and a female therapist lead a group has the advantage of eliciting the children's feelings about men and women in a manner that would be more difficult with a single therapist. For example, when a male cotherapist is working with children who have been victimized by a male abuser, displaced feelings of anger and/or fear directed toward the male cotherapist can be used to help the children identify and deal with unresolved feelings regarding the abuse. Consequently, the group described here had a male and a female therapist as coleaders. (I was the male cotherapist.)

Parallel Treatment of Parents

Experts in the field of abuse have advocated parallel treatment of the parents of victims of extrafamilial sexual abuse. There is a growing literature documenting the profound effects on parental functioning of having a child who is a victim of extrafamilial sexual abuse (Manion, McIntyre, Firestone, & Ligezinska, 1996). In a study of children sexually abused in day care centers, Hartman, Burgess, Burgess, and Kelley (1992) found a strong correlation between the symptoms of parents and those of their children. Parents who continue to experience posttraumatic symptoms secondary to their children's abuse may complicate the children's ability to recover fully from the impact of their victimization. Consequently, having a therapist (or cotherapists) lead sessions with parents at the same time that their children are being seen can serve the important purpose of helping them deal with the effects of their children's abuse on themselves. The focus of these sessions is to inform the parents about the issues being discussed in the children's group, and to help them understand and deal with the feelings these topics engender in them. In addition, the groups serve to educate the parents regarding the effects of the abuse, as well as to provide specific assistance to parents in dealing with their children's abuse-related emotional and behavioral difficulties.

During the children's sessions described in this chapter, the parents met in another room with another therapist. After every session, we (the children's cotherapists) met with the parents and their therapist to give them an update on the girls' progress. To ensure confidentiality, we reviewed with the girls the content of what was shared with parents. Only issues that they agreed in advance could be discussed were raised in the parent group.

Timing of Group Therapy

The issue of timing of group therapy when a group of children have been abused together is one of great complexity. On the one hand, the clinical literature suggests that the sooner therapy begins, the better the prognosis (Terr, 1990). On the other hand, group therapy can, from a legal standpoint, seriously complicate the ability of prosecutors to bring an abuser to justice. By definition, the nature of such groups includes group discussion of events experienced jointly by children, which defense attorneys can use to claim that children's memories were irrevocably contaminated (Reed, 1996). As a result of these concerns, the group described here did not start until the abuser had pled guilty and it was clear that the group would not hamper the district attorney's ability to adjudicate the case. It should be noted, however, that civil suits were still pending against the abuser. We handled this by explaining to the parents that our beliefs about what might be best for the children from an *emotional* standpoint did not necessarily conform to what was best from a *legal* standpoint. Parents were encouraged to consult with their attorneys. However, we made it clear that we believed the children's mental health needs would be best met by as early a therapeutic intervention as possible.

Goals of the Group

There is a general consensus in the literature regarding the goals of groups in the treatment of sexual abuse (e.g., Mandell et al., 1989; Sturkie, 1994). Specifically, at some point in the course of the group meetings, the following themes were directly addressed:

- The need for the children to share memories of the abuse
- Feelings of guilt and responsibility for the abuse
- Anger at the abuser and/or other adults for failing to protect the children
- Powerlessness
- Prevention strategies, should an adult attempt to abuse the children in the future
- Sex education, with an emphasis on giving the children a common language with their parents for the discussion of sexual issues

Session Content

The group sessions were structured in two stages. The first 8 sessions had as their main aim the provision of a setting where the children were able to share their memories and feelings regarding the abuse. The remaining 10 sessions attempted to help the children deal directly with the effects of the abuse. In this second phase of the group, our efforts to address the sequelae of abuse were guided by the theoretical framework described by Finkelhor and Browne (1985). These authors identify four traumagenic dynamics, which are seen as the core of the psychological injury inflicted by abuse: betrayal, powerlessness, stigmatization, and traumatic sexualization. A structured interview designed to assess posttraumatic symptoms in children (Nader & Pynoos, 1984) was administered to group members and their parents, and more than half of the children revealed the following trauma-induced difficulties:

Symptoms related to traumatic sexualization: Sexual interest and knowledge inappropriate to their age

Symptoms related to betrayal: Preoccupation with anger at the abuser and parents for failing to protect them; clinginess to parents to regain lost trust and security

Symptoms related to stigmatization: Feeling guilty for not protecting peers; shame for "allowing" themselves to be abused

Symptoms related to powerlessness: Free-floating feelings of fear and anxiety; disturbed sleep and dreams; a more passive approach to life than was previously seen by parents

Stage 1: Sharing Memories and Feelings (Sessions 1–8)

Establishing Group Rules and Context (Sessions 1 and 2)

In the first two sessions, rules of the group were discussed. The emphasis of the discussion was on privacy and confidentiality, particularly in relation to the parallel group with parents. The guideline was that although we would discuss the general goals of the group with the parents, no specific information given by the children would be shared without the children's specific permission. The specific goal of the group—providing the children with a forum for discussion of their memories, thoughts, and feelings about the abuse—was emphasized.

Group therapy can, in some ways, recreate a context reminiscent of the abuse. In a group such as this one, therapists speak about "sex" (the abuse and sex education); discussions take place under conditions of "secrecy" (confidentiality); and snacks such as candy are served at the end of each session, which may remind some children of how an abuser bribed them with candy or other treats. It is important for the feelings that these similarities may engender to be addressed early in the group process. In this group, the children were asked to discuss how group therapy was different from abuse. A lively discussion ensued, in which they were able to see that whereas the abuser had enforced secrecy, the decision about whether to talk about the group with parents was theirs and not the therapists'.

Sharing the Secret (Sessions 3–5)

A number of art activities were introduced, in order to help the children share their memories of the abuse. Asked to pretend that they were peering into the window of their music room and draw a picture of what they saw inside, some of the children drew a picture suggesting that they were outside looking in, with the children in the room barely visible. This suggested possible use of dissociation as a coping mechanism for dealing with the traumatic memories, as well as a need to maintain distance.

During the fifth session, for the first time, the children were asked to draw a picture of what they remembered happening to them while they were in the music room. They were then asked to present to the rest of the group what they remembered about their own experiences and the experiences of other group members. Some children drew graphic pictures recreating the abuse, while others demonstrated more avoidant strategies. For example, one child portrayed herself sitting in the back of the room, where there was reported to be less abuse.

Expressing and Labeling Feelings about the Abuse (Sessions 6–8)

When the children were asked to focus on their feelings related to the abuse, intensely angry feelings toward the abuser emerged. As these sessions progressed, some ambivalent feelings were tentatively expressed. For example, the children's drawings at times portrayed Greg in a friendly pose, which led to a discussion of how he was viewed by many in the district as a particularly "nice" and "friendly" man. The issue of ambivalence is a particularly problematic one for latency-age children, who, because of their developmentally based tendency toward concrete thinking, may be likely to revert to more primitive splitting (such as all good or all bad) in response to such a stress-filled issue.

Other feelings discussed by the children during these sessions included fear of abuse by other people in their school and feelings of shame. One child described frequently feeling like hiding from people to avoid having to talk about the abuse.

Stage 2: Coping with the Traumagenic Impact of Abuse (Sessions 9–18)

Traumatic Sexualization: Dealing with the Impact of Abuse on Sexuality (Sessions 9 and 10)

The children initially had considerable difficulty discussing sexual issues. This reluctance seemed to stem from the effects of the abuse, their developmental stage (latency), and the fact that their parents rarely (if ever) openly discussed sexuality with them. Discussions of the children's knowledge of sexual matters revealed many misconceptions about sex, as well a high level of anxiety about the impact that the abuse might have on their future sexual functioning.

At the beginning of the ninth session, one of the children spontaneously brought in a book about sex education, which she had found in her house. This led to an anxiety-laden discussion about sex and its place in the children's lives in light of the abuse. Group members were asked to draw pictures of themselves and of members of the opposite sex. Three of the girls initially drew figures without clothing, laughing in an anxiously regressed manner as they added clothes. One child drew a picture of a figure with both male and female genitalia, and another child steadfastly refused to draw any human figures. Asked to draw a picture of what happened in the music room, she drew a box instead of a human figure, explaining that "Somebody is trapped inside trying to get out."

Sessions 9 and 10 seemed to be characterized by the highest level of overt anxiety and regression. Most of the group members tried to achieve some distance from the content of these sessions by taking frequent bathroom breaks.

At the outset of session 10, the child who had brought in the book expressed feeling sorry that she did, since it led to what she perceived as an embarrassing discussion. By the end of this session, however, there appeared to be a greater level of ease in discussing sexual issues. The children were given the opportunity to ask anonymous questions about sex by writing questions on slips of paper, which were then picked from a "grab bag." The children had numerous questions, the most poignant of which was "Does real sex hurt?" After this and other questions about sex were discussed, the following concerns about their sexuality were aired. (Note that in this and subsequent dialogues, I am "Therapist 1" and my female colleague is "Therapist 2.")

Content of Session

KRISTIN: I heard some kids in school yesterday saying that every girl who Greg touched is a slut.

THERAPIST 1: What Greg did has nothing to do with anybody being a slut. It had to do with *his* need to control children.

MARIA: Greg was a sick dog. That doesn't mean that we're sluts. He was a faggot loser. I hope he drops dead in jail.

SHARON: I heard that "doing it" only means you're a slut if you enjoy it.

THERAPIST 2: It's only natural to feel pleasure when somebody touches you. That has nothing to do with whether somebody is a slut.

KATHY: My mother told my older sister that if she fools around with her boyfriend too much, people will think that she's a tramp.

LISA: I can't stand it when I hear parents talking about sex stuff.

SHARON: How can you talk to them about stuff like this? No way. If I told them everything that happened with Greg, they'd think I was some kind of pervert!

THERAPIST 1: In the parents' group, the therapist has been talking about how important it is to figure out how to talk comfortably about sex with children. This can turn into a topic that is OK to talk with your parents about.

Rationale/Analysis

This child is saddened and angered by the cruelty of other children.

I am trying to help the girls not to perceive what happened with Greg as what "real sex" is about.

She is angry and seems comfortable expressing her feelings.

My colleague is trying to lessen the children's guilt by normalizing the feelings they had during abuse.

The girls raise some negative associations/feelings related to sex. The "damaged goods" reaction seems quite evident.

KATHY: I don't think I'll ever be able to talk to them about the stuff we talk about in here.

At least she has experienced support and openness in the group. But I feel worried about the children's risk for future abuse, unless parents and children can talk more openly with each other about sexual topics.

Betrayal: Dealing with Anger (Sessions 11–13)

Anger at the abuser often dominated the sessions. The girls' verbalizations and art related vivid fantasies of torturing the perpetrator of the abuse. Anger was also expressed at peers whom they had seen being abused, but who did not remember details of the abuse and/or refused to participate in the police investigation. The children felt it wasn't fair that *they* had to go for special help when their fellow victims' denial of the abuse had the short-term benefit of sparing them. Another recurring theme throughout the sessions was the girls' difficulty trusting adults outside their families, particularly adults associated with the school system. The children also expressed difficulty dealing with their anger at their parents for not "protecting" them from the abuse. Even though many of them rationally understood that their parents had no way of knowing about the abuse, on an emotional level they reported anger at them for not being there to stop the abuse from happening.

In an attempt to channel the diffuse anger displayed by the children from the outset of the group, various techniques were used. During session 11, videotapes of various news reports of allegations against Greg and his arrest were shown. This served to focus the children, in a concrete manner, on their feelings toward Greg. The videos seemed to help the children rely less on primitive coping mechanisms such as dissociation. The quality of the ensuing discussion demonstrated more targeted and effective expressions of anger. Interestingly, during this session the children shared their most detailed memories of what happened. The children were asked to fill out a series of sentence completions (Mandell et al., 1989) which required them to share their feelings toward Greg. Some examples of the ways the girls completed the stem "I think this happened to me because . . ." included the following:

- "He was a very sick man and didn't know better."
- "He used to call kids sick puppies, but he was one himself."
- "He must have had something wrong in his mind."

The next two sessions provided a powerful vehicle for helping the children express their anger toward the abuser in a therapeutic manner. A mock trial was held, in which the children assumed different roles in trying Greg for the abuse. First, all of the children were asked to be "court artists" and to draw pictures of Greg at the trial. For most of these two sessions, the girls then took turns as witnesses, prosecutors, and judge, while one of us therapists "gently" played the role of defense attorney. The trial ended with Greg's being found guilty and sentenced to life in prison.

An indication of the powerful impact these sessions had on the children was that when asked at the end of session 13 to draw a picture of Greg, he was portrayed as much more weak and ineffectual, in comparison to the more menacing portraits they had drawn in earlier sessions.

After the children had "sentenced" Greg to life in prison, they discussed how they felt about him.

Content of Session	Rationale/Analysis
MARIA: I hope that Greg gets raped in jail. I hear that in jail that happens to a lot of people.	She is full of rage.
THERAPIST 2: I can understand your feeling angry at Greg and wishing that he has done to him the same things he did to you.	My colleague wants to empathize with the children and validate their anger, but she is saddened at how the abuse has made them vengeful.
MELISSA: Do you remember how Greg was nice to us at the beginning and gave us candy, and asked us to bring in pictures of our families?	Now that anger has been expressed and validated, some children feel ready to share some of their ambivalence—including their more positive memories of Greg.
MARIA: Yeah, we didn't know what an idiot he was then.	
THERAPIST 1: You had no way of knowing. Most of the times when adults are nice, they stay nice and don't end up trying to use children. Do you find it hard to trust other adults now?	
MELISSA: I don't really trust the grownups at school. I don't like being alone with teachers or any other grownup there—you never know.	I wonder how she is feeling about *me*!
LISA: Plenty of the teachers are nice. I'm not afraid to be alone with them.	We therapists are hopeful that, with time, they will all regain appropriate levels of trust with adults.

Stigmatization: Dealing with Shame and Scapegoating (Sessions 14–16)

Sessions 14–16 focused on how the children felt they were viewed as different by peers and family members as a result of the abuse. The sense of stigmatization, which is present in many victims of trauma, is particularly strong in well-publicized cases of sexual abuse. Group members were the subjects of extensive news coverage, and were known to many of their classmates as victims of the abuse. In a number of cases, the initial sympathy that was accorded the victims by the community gave way to scapegoating by peers.

The girls spoke of feeling different and "set apart" from their peers as a result of the abuse. One girl reported being teased by classmates, who "jokingly" warned each other to avoid her because she might have caught AIDS from the abuser. The feelings of damage expressed in earlier sessions gradually gave way to less obvious feelings of shame. Even in later sessions, an intense wish was expressed that the abuse continue to be kept secret from peers and extended family members who did not know of it.

Despite repeated assurance by family members that they were not to blame, some group members persisted in blaming themselves for not stopping the abuse. This was consistent with the clinical and research literature, which finds that many victims of trauma prefer guilt to shame (Janoff-Bulman, 1992); that is, they often find it easier to hold on to some feelings of responsibility as a mechanism for feeling less helpless. Some children blamed themselves for not protecting their friends, or for being forced to take part in sexual games with their peers. Another major source of guilt stemmed from the children's not having told their parents about the abuse. Usually their failure to disclose was related to their believing the perpetrator's threats. The power of these threats was so great that for months after Greg was imprisoned, the children continued to fear that the threats would be carried out.

Gradually, the children began to feel comfortable enough to discuss their fears related to feeling set apart and stigmatized by the abuse. The following discussion took place in session 15, after the girls shared the feeling that most of their close friends were supportive and understanding.

Content of Session

KRISTIN: What will my husband think if he finds out?

THERAPIST 2: This was something bad that happened to you that wasn't your fault. What are you concerned he will think about you?

KRISTIN: I'm afraid that he'll think that I'm a loser, because I let Greg touch me.

LISA: I don't want anybody to know, because I don't want anybody to think that I am a coward for not doing anything to protect my friends.

THERAPIST 1: The threats Greg made were scary; that's why nobody told. It makes sense to decide carefully who you can trust with the information about what happened, but this is different from blaming yourself about something that only Greg can take responsibility for.

MARIA: You know, if we all got together, we probably could have beat him up.

LISA: I'd rather see myself as stupid for not having told than a coward for believing the threats.

THERAPIST 1: Most kids I see who are molested by adults tell me that it's really scary when they're threatened. It's not easy to say no to an adult, especially with somebody like Greg, who most

Rationale/Analysis

We are surprised and upset that after 14 sessions, her feelings of damage are still so evident. But we are touched that she feels safe enough to share this sense of vulnerability, not shared until now.

I am trying to find a balance between encouraging sharing of feelings and recognizing that children need to be discriminating about the people they tell.

I am moved by their quandary, which reflects the near impossibilities that helpless children have to deal with in the face of overwhelm-

parents and kids liked. What would you do if
something like this ever happened again?

MARIA: I'd kick him in the balls and call the cops.

KATHY: I'd tell my parents.

ing threat. I try to empower the
children by discussing prevention
of future abuse.

We are relieved that they choose
active, not passive, options.

Powerlessness: Dealing with Prevention of Future Abuse (Sessions 17 and 18)

The final two sessions approached termination by attempting to redirect the children from an exclusive focus on the abuse to discussion of the future. A videotape
about prevention of sexual abuse was shown (Disney Home Video, 1985), and the
girls were asked to play a "what if" game, which entailed their role-playing various scenarios of how they would deal with abuse should it be attempted in the
future.

   The theme of helplessness was most apparent in the dreams reported by group
participants. One child reported having a recurring dream of being trapped and
unable to get help, stating, "I tried to scream for help but nothing came out." This
issue was also evident in the children's distortion of memories in a manner suggesting that they had been more active in fighting off the abuser than the objective facts
indicated. For example, one girl remembered defending one of her friends, when in
fact the other girls in the group denied that this ever happened. After the discussion
of various prevention strategies, a similar exchange occurred in session 17:

Content of Session

MARIA: Remember when I kicked Greg real hard in
his nuts, and he went crazy because it hurt him so
much?

(*Several other group members say in unison, "You don't
know what you're talking about! That never happened!"*)

MARIA: It did so! You're all a bunch of liars. I really
gave it to him.

THERAPIST 1: I can understand wanting to really
hurt Greg. It must have been very hard to have
somebody make you feel so bad, and to feel that
there was little you could do to defend yourselves.

SHARON: Lots of times I tried to get away from
Greg. He'd get real angry with me.

KATHY: I was afraid to fight him much. I just tried
to pretend that it wasn't happening.

Rationale/Analysis

This girl is among the most
symptomatic in the group, and
seems to have the greatest need to
remember herself as more in
control.

I am upset with the other group
members for the harsh tone they are
taking with Maria. I want to
validate the helplessness underlying
her claims and not get caught up in
fruitless discussion about what
really happened.

We therapists are both heartened
that children are sharing feelings of
helplessness that they were too
defended to share in earlier sessions.

MELISSA: All I know is that if he or anybody ever tries to do it again, I am going to tell my parents and the police.

KRISTIN: Yeah, I'm never going to go through that kind of thing again.

> We are moved and gratified that the girls appear to be integrating the message of protection as an antidote to helplessness.

Summary of Parent Sessions

The parallel parent group was an essential component of the treatment process. This group met multiple needs for the parents:

- Helping the parents go from a passive to an active mode in response to their daughters' victimization
- Dealing with the feeling that they were to blame for their daughters' abuse
- Providing a forum for familiarizing parents with what was being addressed in the children's group, as well as what typical responses they might expect from the girls
- Addressing some parents' discomfort with directly discussing the abuse, in the mistaken belief that "forgetting" would be more beneficial than exploring and integrating the experience

The first eight sessions of the parent group paralleled the process taking place in the girls' group. Rules regarding confidentiality were discussed, and the parents were told that we (the children's cotherapists) would only share details regarding their daughters' sessions that had been preapproved by the girls. Parents were also cautioned that there might be an increase in the girls' level of clinginess and anger, in response to the strong feelings evoked in the sessions where the girls shared the "secret" of the abuse and labeled their feelings about what happened. During the fifth session, one of the mothers disclosed that she herself had been sexually abused as a child. This led to a poignant discussion of how this parent, and perhaps others, felt powerless and ineffectual as a result of their inability to shield their daughters from going through some of the painful events they had experienced in their own childhoods.

The last 10 sessions focused on helping the parents recognize that the abuse did not irrevocably damage their daughters' future. Although feelings of anger and shame at the loss of the girls' "innocence" were validated, the group leader emphasized the remarkable resilience of the girls, as well as the hope that they would incorporate the group's message that the abuse had less to do with the children's own developing sexuality than with Greg's pathological needs. The importance of making discussion of sex an open topic between parents and children was emphasized in several sessions, which reviewed sex education material and included role plays of how to discuss sex with children. Open discussion of sexual issues was framed in the broader context of sexual abuse prevention. One session reviewed a number of prevention techniques that could be utilized by parents. Parents were taught how to

play "what if" games with their children, consisting of role-playing the most pru-
dent responses should any future abuse be attempted. Similarly, parents were encouraged not to avoid discussing the abuse with their daughters, in the mistaken
belief that open discussion would be too upsetting. It was emphasized that one of
the best antidotes to feelings of shame, stigma, and anger on the part of the girls
was providing them with an atmosphere at home that was receptive to direct communication regarding their fears, concerns, and feelings about the abuse.

CONCLUDING COMMENTS

At the termination of the children's group, the major problem areas described by
the children and their parents at the beginning of the group were no longer evident.
The children were not preoccupied with their anger or thoughts about the abuse,
nor were they showing difficulties with sleeping, depression, or somatization. Although this improvement can also be attributed to the passage of time and to the
punishment of the perpetrator, the subjective reports of both the parents and the
children indicated that they found the group very helpful. The group appeared to
be particularly efficacious in lessening feelings of stigmatization and damage, as well
as feelings of isolation and powerlessness.

Two drawings demonstrated the more adaptive way in which the children were
dealing with anger by the end of treatment. The first one, drawn during session 6 in
response to an assignment to draw what would happen if a child saw Greg again,
depicted Greg verbally attacking the girl, who responded by pushing him "down a
hill, and he died." The second picture, drawn during session 17 by the same child in
response to the same assignment, showed the girl being threatened by Greg and
responding by calling the police.

The relatively short-term nature of this group conforms to James's (1994) view
that therapy of traumatized children requires an "open-door" approach. Often after
the termination of a group, it may be necessary to have a child return to therapy at
a later developmental stage, to "work through" the meaning of the trauma in light
of the new stage of development. For example, in some cases, traumatic sexualization of a child may not become fully apparent until the abused child becomes sexually active as an adolescent. In keeping with this philosophy, 6 months after the group
terminated, we had a reunion for the children and their parents. At that time, we
readministered the structured interview designed to assess posttraumatic symptoms
in children (Nader & Pynoos, 1984), which had been given to the children and their
parents before the group began. According to both child and parent responses to
this interview, the lessening of symptoms that was evident at the end of the group
continued to be apparent. Interestingly, however, there was a discrepancy between
child and parent reports. The children reported a virtual disappearance of the vast
majority of symptoms that they had reported at the beginning of the group. None
of the children reported continuing fears, sleep difficulties, or difficulty with anger
related to the abuse. The only exception was that one of the girls stated that she
occasionally continued to feel guilty that she hadn't reported the abuse. The same

girl also indicated occasionally experiencing intrusive abuse-related thoughts. In contrast, although most of the parents felt that there was substantial improvement in their daughters' levels of clinginess, fearfulness, and anger, two-thirds of them noted that their daughters continued to experience difficulty talking with their parents about the abuse. Moreover, the parents believed that at some level, the girls continued to feel responsible for what happened. This finding was surprising, since at the time of the group's termination these reactions did not appear to be present. The fact that the symptoms the parents saw in their children were not reported by the girls when they were asked suggests the interesting possibility that the parents were projecting their own continuing concerns about the effects of the abuse onto the children. Although the children were not willing to discuss the abuse with their parents, they were able to discuss abuse-related concerns appropriately in the group and with selected peers. The continuing feelings of guilt and responsibility were not surprising, in that, as noted earlier, many trauma survivors prefer feelings of responsibility related to the abuse to feelings of shame and helplessness.

It was also interesting that despite the continued difficulties noted by the parents in the follow-up meeting, none of the parents or children wanted to resume psychotherapy. The parents felt that the symptoms they reported were mild and not in need of formal intervention. We therapists agreed with this decision; our rationale was that continued sessions with abused children after the major goals of treatment have been met pose the danger that they and their families may internalize a permanent view of themselves as "victims." It was evident that the girls had gone back in a relatively short period of time to a normal life, bearing very few visible scars of their ordeal. Their ability to return to normal functioning after such a traumatic experience was a testament to their strength and resilience.

STUDY QUESTIONS

1. Discuss how you would feel if you were a male cotherapist in a group of elementary-school-age girls who had been abused by a male. What reactions would you anticipate from the girls, and what responses would be most appropriate and therapeutic for them?

2. How do you explain the children's difficulties talking with their parents—either during the abuse, or later, after the perpetrator was in jail? Do you agree with the author that children may be more vulnerable to future abuse if they cannot speak freely with their parents? Why or why not?

3. What is your reaction to having the children's group leaders meet with the parents and their group leader following the children's group sessions? Discuss the potential pitfalls of this procedure and suggest an alternative strategy. Would you consider *joint* parent–child sessions as feasible at some point? If so, when, and what guidelines should be observed?

4. Suppose that a mother and father of a potential group member disagree about whether their daughter should participate in the group. The father wants to follow his lawyer's advice that participation in a group will contaminate their child's ability to testify in

their civil case against the abuser; the mother wants their child in therapy immediately, regardless of the impact on the lawsuit. How would you approach this conflict? What would you recommend?

5. In light of the author's view that traumatized children may need to be followed as they enter adolescence, how would you follow such children without being intrusive? Would you schedule regular follow-up sessions, or only meet on an "as-needed" basis?

REFERENCES

Berliner, L., & MacQuivey, K. (1983). A therapy group for female adolescent victims of sexual abuse. In R. Rosenbaum (Ed.), *Varieties of short-term therapy groups* (pp. 110–116). New York: McGraw-Hill.

Cole, P., & Putnam, F. W. (1992). Effect of incest on self and social functioning: A developmental psychopathology perspective. *Journal of Consulting and Clinical Psychology, 60,* 174–184.

De Luca, R., Hazen, A., & Cutler, J. (1993), Evaluation of a group counseling program for preadolescent female victims of incest. *Elementary School Guidance and Counseling, 28,* 104–114.

Disney Studios (Producer). (1985). *Too smart for strangers* [Videotape]. Los Angeles: Disney Home Video.

Finkelhor, D., & Berliner, L. (1995). Research on the treatment of sexually abused children: A review and recommendations. *Journal of the American Academy of Child and Adolescent Psychiatry, 34,* 1408–1423.

Finkelhor, D., & Browne, A. (1985). The traumatic impact of child sexual abuse: A conceptualization. *American Journal of Orthopsychiatry, 55,* 530–541.

Finkelhor, D., Hotaling, G., Lewis, I. A., & Smith, C. (1989). Sexual abuse and its relationship to later sexual satisfaction, marital status, religion, and attitudes. *Journal of Interpersonal Violence, 4,* 279–399.

Forseth, L. B., & Brown, A. (1981). A survey of intrafamilial sexual abuse treatment centers: Implications for intervention. *Child Abuse and Neglect, 5,* 177–186.

Friedrich, W. N. (1994). Individual psychotherapy for child abuse victims. *Child Psychiatric Clinics of North America, 3,* 797–812.

Hartman, C. R., Burgess, A. G., Burgess, A. W., & Kelley, S. J. (1992). Extrafamilial child sexual abuse: Family-focused intervention. In A. W. Burgess (Ed.), *Child trauma: Issues and research* (pp. 307–333). New York: Garland Press.

Haugaard, J. J., & Reppucci, N. D. (1988). *The sexual abuse of children: A comprehensive guide to current knowledge and intervention strategies.* San Francisco: Jossey-Bass.

James, B. (1994). *Handbook for treatment of attachment–trauma problems in children.* New York: Free Press.

Janoff-Bulman, R. (1992). *Shattered assumptions: Towards a new psychology of trauma.* New York: Free Press.

Kendall-Tackett, K. A., Williams, L. M., & Finkelhor, D. (1993). Impact of sexual abuse on children: A review and synthesis of recent empirical studies. *Psychological Bulletin, 113,* 164–180.

Larzelere, R. E., Collins, L., & Collins, R. A. (1993). *During and post-treatment effects of group therapy for sexual victimization.* Paper presented at the Conference on Responding to Child Maltreatment, San Diego, CA.

Ligezinska, M., Firestone, P., Manion, I. G., & McIntyre, J. (1996). Children's emotional and behavioral reactions following the disclosure of extrafamilial sexual abuse: Initial effects. *Child Abuse and Neglect, 20*, 111–125.

Mandell, J. G., & Damon, L., with Castaldo, P. C., Tauber, E. S., Monise, L., & Larsen, N. F. (1989). *Group treatment for sexually abused children*. New York: Guilford Press.

Manion, I. G., McIntyre, J., Firestone, P., & Ligezinska, M. (1996). Secondary traumatization in parents following the disclosure of extrafamilial child sexual abuse: Initial effects. *Child Abuse and Neglect, 20*, 1095–1109.

Nader, K., & Pynoos, R. S. (1984). *Childhood post-traumatic stress disorder: Parents' questionnaire/ checklist*. Unpublished manuscript.

Nelki, J., & Watter, J. (1989). A group of sexually abused young children. *Child Abuse and Neglect, 13*, 369–377.

Reed, L. D. (1996). Findings from research on children's suggestibility and implications for conducting child interviews. *Child Maltreatment, 1*, 105–120.

Roth, S., Newman, E., Pelcovitz, D., van der Kolk, B., & Mandel, F. S. (1997). Complex PTSD in victims exposed to sexual and physical abuse: Results from the DSM-IV field trial for post-traumatic stress disorder. *Journal of Traumatic Stress, 10*, 539–555.

Sturkie, K. (1994). Group treatment for sexually abused children: Clinical wisdom and empirical findings. *Child Psychiatric Clinics of North America, 3*, 813–830.

Terr, L. (1990). *Too scared to cry: Psychic trauma in childhood*. New York: Harper & Row.

PART III

Various Family Crises

Persistent and Chronic Neglect in the Context of Poverty— When Parents Can't Parent

Case of Ricky, Age 3

LOUISE M. TONNING

THE CHANGING ROLE OF GRANDPARENTS

The epidemic in the use of crack cocaine and other drugs has been accompanied by an increase in the number of grandparents raising grandchildren, particularly, but not exclusively, among African Americans (Burton, 1992; Minkler, Roe, & Price, 1992; Minkler, Roe, & Robertson-Beckley, 1994). Although there is a long cultural and historical tradition of surrogate parenting by African American grandmothers, the need to do so because of illicit drug use is fairly recent. In the past, grandmothers acted as surrogate parents while their teenage or adult daughters remained in the household either to attend school or work. In contrast, these parents are now absent or in need of care themselves, leaving grandparents resentful of their predicament, even though relieved to be able to keep their grandchildren out of foster care by caring for them themselves. Children of drug-addicted mothers may have special needs due to their prenatal exposure to drugs and/or abuse and neglect (Minkler et al., 1994); they may require a more intense level of care than children not prenatally exposed to drugs.

Frequently, African American grandmothers are forced by economic and/or racial barriers to live in an environment of chronic poverty and community violence. Simple activities, such as grocery shopping or letting a child go outside to play, must be timed to avoid drug trafficking (Burton, 1991). Dealing with their own grief in response to recurring traumatic events within this environment makes it more difficult for these grandparents to manage their grandchildren's reactive symptomatic behaviors (Osofsky, Wewers, Hann, & Fick, 1993). As a result of these multiple stressors, African American grandparents parenting grandchildren suffer an increased risk of physical illnesses, alcoholism, smoking, depression, and anxiety (Burton, 1992). Therefore, support from friends, family members, and community resources is vital (McLoyd, 1990; Burton, 1992).

CAREGIVER–CHILD ATTACHMENT

Regardless of the environmental context, however, the course of child development proceeds. The first fundamental task in human social-emotional development is the formation of an attachment bond with a primary caregiver (usually, but not always, the mother). Attachment theory proposes that the quality of care an infant receives determines the quality of the attachment formed (Ainsworth, Blehar, Waters, & Wall, 1978; Bowlby, 1969). Quality of care may be influenced by any number of factors: the caregiver's life situation, her personality and socialization experiences, and/or the infant's temperament and endowment. Stressors that have an impact on the emotional well-being of the infant's caregiver, and on the caregiver's responsiveness and availability to the infant, are expected to affect the quality of the attachment bond (Egeland & Sroufe, 1981).

The quality of the attachment relationship is a critical factor in child development. According to Davies, "the growing body of evidence of empirical studies points to quality of attachment as a fundamental mediator of development" (p. 27). Attachment theory states that an infant develops internal representational models of the self and the attachment figure, based on his or her experience of need satisfaction or frustration. These models include beliefs about the self (self-image), expectations about the behavior of the other, and expectations about the emotional tone of the relationship (Ainsworth et al., 1978; Bowlby, 1969, 1973, 1980; Main, Kaplan, & Cassidy, 1985).

Attachment serves four principal functions (Davies, 1999): First, attachment provides the infant with a sense of security. This is accomplished when the mother or other primary caregiver consistently responds to the infant's cries of distress in order to calm him or her down (Bowlby, 1969). Second, attachment regulates the infant's affective states. Over time, as the caregiver consistently acts to soothe or stimulate the infant, the infant begins to develop the ability to self-regulate. Third, attachment, as a transactional relationship, provides the infant with opportunities to express and share feelings and to learn to communicate and play. Finally, attachment provides the base for exploration. A child who has confidence in his or her attachment relationship will be able to explore his or her environment with confidence (Bowlby, 1969; Stern, 1974, 1985; Lieberman, 1993; Davies, 1999).

Attachment may be described as secure, insecure–avoidant, insecure–ambivalent/resistant (Ainsworth et al., 1978) and insecure–disorganized/disoriented (Main et al., 1985; Main & Solomon, 1990; Davies, 1999). A child whose attachment relationship is secure explores the environment in the presence of the caregiver and after separation responds strongly to his or her return, seeking contact. After the child is comforted, he or she returns to exploration (Ainsworth et al., 1978; Sroufe & Waters, 1977). The child's feelings, both positive and negative, are freely expressed with the confidence that they will be accepted and that help in regulating them will be given (Main & Hesse, 1990).

A child whose attachment relationship is characterized by avoidance explores the environment but has minimal contact with the caregiver. Separation produces no obvious distress. Upon reunion the child avoids contact with the caregiver and ignores any attempts at interaction. Having learned that expressions of distress produce rejection rather than help, the child suppresses feelings, turns away from the caregiver and attends to the outside world (Ainsworth et al., 1978; Sroufe & Waters, 1977; Main et al., 1985; Spangler & Grossman, 1993).

A child whose attachment relationship is characterized by ambivalence/resistance will display an impoverished exploration of the environment (Ainsworth et al., 1978; Sroufe & Waters, 1977). Separation evokes an intense reaction. Upon reunion, the child is caught between the need for close bodily contact with the caregiver and the need to express anger over her absence. So he or she resists contact and fails to be comforted. The child expects to be frustrated rather than comforted, having learned that needs for contact and comfort will be inconsistently met (Ainsworth, 1982). Because attachment needs remain unmet, they become a preoccupation, and the child is unable to explore the environment with abandon (Main et al., 1985; Lieberman, 1993).

A child whose attachment relationship is characterized as disorganized/disoriented has no clear strategy for interacting with the caregiver. When reunited after separation, the child gives contradictory signals such as smiling and averting his or her gaze simultaneously or seeking comfort and then turning away. Without a consistent strategy for getting his or her needs met, the child remains distressed. As a result of contradictory and unpredictable caregiver responses, the child is conflicted between approaching and avoiding, and has no way to know how to negotiate the attachment relationship (Main et al., 1985; Main & Hesse, 1990; Main & Solomon, 1990).

The experience of this first relationship influences the formation of future relationships because it affects what is perceived, how a situation is construed, and which people and situations are sought out or avoided (Ainsworth et al., 1978; Bowlby, 1969, 1973, 1980). Similarly the caregiver's own previously formed cognitive models affect the way the caregiver interacts with the infant, and this tends to create an intergenerational transmission of secure, avoidant, or resistant attachment bonds (Crittenden, 1985) or disorganized/disoriented attachment bonds.

A caregiver's response to an infant—that is, the quality of care—is also affected by the environmental context. Chronic poverty produces psychological distress, which in turn affects a caregiver's responsiveness to a child. Although this distress can be lessened by a system of social supports, there is "a growing body of evidence directly linking parents' emotional states to their parenting behavior" (McLoyd, 1990, p. 322). More psychological reserves are required to negotiate with a child than to spank a child.

In addition, poverty is reported to have an impact on brain development during the critical early years (Shore, 1997), through multiple pathways (Aber & Palmer, 1997): inadequate nutrition (Brown & Pollitt, 1996), substance abuse (Mayes 1996), maternal depression (Belle, 1990), exposure to environmental toxins (National Health/Education Consortium, 1991), and trauma and abuse (Brooks-Gunn, Klebanov, Liaw, & Duncan, 1995). Abused and neglected children are more likely to exhibit behaviors indicating insecure attachment, usually the avoidant type (Crittenden, 1992).

The relevance of the above concepts becomes evident in the detailed case example that follows.

THE CASE: RICKY, AGE 3

The case presented in this chapter is that of an African American male child born into chronic poverty who suffered abuse and neglect from birth, who witnessed the violent beatings of his half-brother, and whose mother was addicted to crack cocaine. Placed with his grandmother at 20 months of age, Ricky responded to the inconsistency of his attachment figures with resistance to contact (Ainsworth et al., 1978). Treatment required the creation of a safe environment in which Ricky could use play to work through his reactions to the violence he had witnessed (Terr, 1989) and risk engaging in a new relationship, thereby developing a more versatile self (Perls, Hefferline, & Goodman, 1969). The modality used was child-centered play therapy (Landreth, 1991).

Presenting Problem

Ricky's grandmother, Mrs. Johnson, contacted the mental health agency at the suggestion of his clinic pediatrician. Ricky, a 3-year-old African American boy, was described by his grandmother as a chronically unhappy child, who cried, whined, had temper tantrums, and bit and fought with other children. He refused to eat unless fed, cried in his sleep, and sat on the floor banging his head "for no reason." He could not concentrate, even on TV programs. Any obvious, direct limit setting, such as saying "no" to Ricky, set off uncontrollable tantrums. Although he was toilet-trained by this time, he continued to wet the bed regularly every night.

Family Information

Mrs. Johnson lived in a run-down public housing project on the outskirts of a large city. The project consisted of clusters of small two-story apartment buildings, arranged around courtyards along winding streets where drug trafficking was evident. Each building housed three or four families. Trash and discarded belongings were piled up at curbsides waiting for collection. Stunted trees and beaten-down crabgrass only seemed to underscore the poverty of the residents. This was Ricky's neighborhood. The composition of his household at intake was as follows:

Ricky	Age 3 years, 3 months
Mrs. Johnson	Age 45; Ricky's paternal grandmother; unemployed, receiving public assistance for Ricky's support
Mr. Johnson	Age 48; Ricky's paternal grandfather; part-time security guard and very active in his church; rarely at home
Evon	Age 23; the Johnsons' younger son; employed part-time at the local youth center
Taisha	Age 2 years, 11 months; daughter of Evon; her mother died of complications after her birth

In addition to these family members living with Ricky, the following significant family members played pivotal roles in Ricky's life:

Sondra	Age 27; Ricky's mother; history of crack addiction; recently released from prison and living alone in

	another city 35 miles away; visitation was sporadic; current drug use was denied; no history of rehabilitation other than while in jail
Vonte	Age 29; Ricky's father; employed in unsteady work; lived alone, but saw Sondra periodically; visited Ricky every week; engaged in conflict with his mother (Mrs. Johnson) over her guardianship of Ricky and his parental visitation
Jon	Age 9; Ricky's half-brother; in third grade; living with his paternal grandparents
Mr. and Mrs. Moore	Jon's paternal grandparents

First Interview (Child's Primary Caregiver)

Mrs. Johnson was asked to come in for the first interview without Ricky, because it was important to be able to speak with her frankly and without distractions. Ricky was too young to be left alone in the waiting room. Not only did he need someone to look after him, but he might become anxious if left in a strange place without his caregiver. Clearly, he should not be present when I spoke with Mrs. Johnson: Children brought for "treatment" already think of themselves as "bad," and listening to a list of complaints from a caregiver only confirms this identity and compromises a positive beginning of the treatment relationship.

In a case such as Ricky's, the goals of the first interview with the child's primary caregiver are to obtain a developmental history of the child, to establish a working relationship with the caregiver, to determine the caregiver's concerns (Webb, 1996), to mutually set preliminary goals for treatment, and to inform the caregiver of the agency expectations (e.g., a 24-hour cancellation notice).

Mrs. Johnson was a well-groomed, heavy-set woman with a solemn look. In her role as grandmother, she had been Ricky's primary caregiver and legal guardian since he was 20 months old. Mrs. Johnson reported that Ricky and his half-brother, Jon, were removed from their mother for chronic abuse and neglect after the children had been left alone at home for 3 days. Jon, then 6, had gone to a neighbor asking for food and diapers. Jon begged the neighbor not to tell he had asked for help because his mom would beat him. Each child was placed with his paternal grandmother. (When Jon was three, his father had disappeared and was presumed dead.) It was assumed that Ricky, like Jon, had been physically abused by his mother; no one knew for sure, however, since Ricky had been at a preverbal age when placed with his grandmother. Even if he had not been beaten himself (which was unlikely), he had certainly witnessed the beatings of his half-brother. Since preverbal children retain memories of abuse or witnessed violence and react to these memories behaviorally (Terr, 1988), Ricky's problematic behavior seemed to confirm these suspicions. Sondra was incarcerated for a year for the abuse and neglect of her children. Ricky's father was not given custody of Ricky because of his ongoing relationship with Sondra.

Developmental History

Mrs. Johnson had had little contact with Sondra or Ricky until he was placed with her, and she had little information concerning Ricky's gestation and birth. As far as she knew, the pregnancy and delivery were normal. The timing of his early developmental milestones was essentially unknown, but presumed to be normal. As noted above, he was toilet-trained at the time of intake, but remained enuretic at night. He had a history of ear infections, but these had subsided by this time. He had been hospitalized for several days for a bout of bronchitis when he was 2½. Ricky had problems with eating, usually refusing what was offered. He was not on any medications.

Although his motor development appeared to be satisfactory, Ricky's language was delayed. Mrs. Johnson reported that she did not believe that Ricky's acquisition of speech and language abilities matched that of her granddaughter, Taisha. She was also worried about his memory: Ricky could remember what happened a month ago, but not what happened today. He would say that he had eaten lunch and give a detailed description of all the foods he had eaten, when in fact he had not had lunch at all. She felt that he could not tell the difference between now and 5 minutes ago.

Extended Family Contacts

Ricky's father, Vonte, visited each week, often taking him for weekends. During these weekend visits his father sometimes left Ricky alone with his mother, Sondra. Following these visits, Ricky's behavior regressed. Any gains Mrs. Johnson had made with Ricky in terms of controlling his behavior were lost. Ricky also occasionally visited his half-brother, Jon, at his grandparents' apartment. Mrs. Johnson reported that Jon had been diagnosed as having attention-deficit/hyperactivity disorder and had been placed on Ritalin. She was concerned that something "chemical" was wrong with Ricky too.

Taisha and her father lived with Ricky and Mr. and Mrs. Johnson, and were an integral part of the household. The children were close in age, and Ricky called Taisha his sister. Ricky, a boisterous and angry youngster, bullied Taisha, who was quiet and nonaggressive. Ricky would often enter a room where Taisha was playing, walk up to her, and hit her for no apparent reason. Although Ricky wanted to be with Taisha constantly, he played parallel to her, not *with* her. This is not unusual for 3-year-olds, who are just beginning to play cooperatively.

Mrs. Johnson described Ricky as a boy with "a lot of anger in him." She said he was "not a happy child." He cried most of the time and was angry and pouty. In the morning, he would refuse to go upstairs and wash up; at meals, as noted earlier, he would not eat what was offered. Even giving Ricky gifts or toys seemed to have no purpose, since he got no joy out of things given him. Agonized by the misery of her grandson, she asked, "How do I make this boy have a happy childhood?"

First Interview (Child)

I approached Ricky in the waiting room where he sat with his grandmother. He was an adorable boy, neatly dressed, with an angelic face and large brown eyes. I introduced myself to him and invited him to come upstairs to play. He separated easily from his grandmother and came upstairs with an air of confidence. Ricky engaged in very little exploration of the playroom. He sat down at the low table and began to draw with a purple crayon.

Content of Session	Analysis/Rationale
THERAPIST: You've decided to draw.	It is important to validate the decisions and choices of a child. In this early assessment phase, we are getting to know each other. Ricky needs to experience the playroom and me as safe.
CHILD: Yes.	
T: You're using a purple crayon.	
C: Yes.	
T: You're drawing all over the paper.	
C: (*Silent; continues to draw.*)	
T: You've got something in mind and you're going to do it the way you want.	Validating observations enable him to continue self-expression.
C: It's a boy.	
T: Oh, a boy. How old is he?	
C: Six.	
T: Six years old. What does he like to do?	
C: He hits, and he's a liar.	Is this his own self-appraisal or a description of someone he knows?
T: Oh. He hits and he lies.	

At this point, Ricky began playing with small plastic dinosaurs, making them fight and fall off the table to the floor. All the while he talked. He appeared to have a very active imagination, but it was very difficult to follow any train of thought. In addition, his articulation was very poor, so that much of what he said was unintelligible. He said something about being hit, but it was not clear by whom or under what circumstances.

Second Play Therapy Session

One week later, Ricky entered the playroom stating that Vonte (his father) had hit him and that Taisha had hit him. He played with the dollhouse, moving the dolls and furniture upstairs, downstairs, and in and out of the house with no apparent order or reason. It seemed as if his play reflected the family chaos that he experienced in his own life. Ricky's uncle, Evon, had brought him for this session, giving me the opportunity to obtain the perspective of another person in Ricky's life. Evon (interviewed with Ricky in the room) stated that he had no trouble handling Ricky. He felt that Ricky's problems were due to the lack of stimulating experiences that had been available to his own daughter, Taisha. He felt that this was the reason why Ricky's development was slower than Taisha's. There was nothing "wrong" with Ricky, in his view.

Session with Ricky's Parents

The following week, Ricky's parents came requesting a meeting. It was apparent that there was considerable conflict and animosity between them and Ricky's grandmother. They felt that Ricky's problematic behavior was due to Mrs. Johnson's favoring Taisha. They expressed the desire to regain custody of Ricky. Their statements that Ricky needed more attention were validated, and I offered to include them in Ricky's treatment.

Preliminary Assessment

Ricky was a 3-year-old whose development had been affected by adverse environmental factors from his infancy. The first task for an infant is to develop trust—that is, a secure attachment to a primary caregiver. It is important for the mother or some other primary caregiver to develop a symbiosis with the infant and to meet the infant's needs predictably and consistently. In this way, the infant comes to experience the world and the people in it as safe and trustworthy. This is the bedrock of attachment formation and, later, of a person's ability to engage in satisfying human relationships (Bowlby, 1969; Erikson, 1950; Mahler, Pine, & Bergman, 1975). Although very little was known about Ricky's care before 20 months of age, the stress of caring for a dependent and therefore totally demanding toddler was probably a difficult task for Ricky's mother to negotiate at the time when she was also caring for a 6-year-old. She might also have been using crack and/or other drugs at the time. Given the fact of his mother's incarceration for abuse and neglect of her children, it is doubtful that the mother and child formed a secure attachment relationship. Therefore, Ricky could be expected to be insecure in his relationships with others. During our initial meetings, he exhibited much bravado and seemed to swagger his way to the playroom. His manner was brusque, and his affect was serious or angry. In this way he was able to keep his emotional distance and attempt to maintain some control over the situation with a strange adult in a new place.

At 18 months, a toddler typically begins developing a sense of independence and separateness from the caregiver. This "separation–individuation" phase is difficult for the child, and is complicated if it is launched from a base of insecure attachment (Mahler et al., 1975). At a time when Ricky needed to be able to return to his mother after his "independent" forays around the kitchen or other living areas, secure in the knowledge that she would be there for him, he found himself with a new caregiver in a new home. He had not had much contact with his grandmother prior to being placed with her. Independence and separateness, so necessary for personality development, held frightening consequences for Ricky.

The development of language also begins during toddlerhood. It is through language that we state who we are—what we like and do not like—and in so doing establish the terms of our relationships with others. Ricky's command of language was poor, and this was of considerable concern to Ricky's grandmother.

At the time of intake, Ricky was entering the Oedipal stage of development and beginning to establish his identity as a male (Freud, 1920/1943). This task was complicated by the fact that his father was inconsistent in his visitation—often leaving Ricky with his mother, Sondra, or with his half-brother, Jon, and Jon's paternal grandparents. These visits were hard on Ricky. They continued the pattern of unpredictability from caregivers and resulted in Ricky's feeling anxious and insecure. Furthermore, because Vonte used hitting as a form of discipline, Ricky feared his father. At the same time, Ricky wanted to spend time with his dad and to be like his dad. Ricky also observed the consistency of the father–child relationship Taisha enjoyed, wanted the same for himself, and was confused and angered by the fact that he did not have the same consistent father–child relationship. His grandfather, a distant figure, was rarely at home, leaving early and coming home late. However, his relationship with his uncle, Evon, did enable him to experience a more consistent male role model.

The Treatment Plan

The treatment plan was for weekly play therapy sessions with Ricky. Given his language difficulties and the trauma he had suffered during his preverbal period, Ricky needed an opportunity to express his confusion, anger, fears, and feelings of helplessness through play. In addition, regular contact with Ricky's custodial grandmother via telephone calls or scheduled meetings was planned, in order to stay in tune with her ongoing concerns, to be available to her as a support and parenting resource, and to educate her concerning Ricky's issues and needs. Referral to the city board of education for a full evaluation of Ricky's educational needs was planned as well.

The overall goal of treatment was to bring Ricky to the normal developmental level (verbal and behavioral) for a 3-year-old. Specific goals for Ricky were as follows:

- Help him to reduce his aggressive behaviors
- Enable him to develop reciprocal peer relationships
- Enable him to express a full range of feelings
- Enable him to experience and express joy, in particular

Although improved language skills would not be a specific treatment goal for a play therapist, all professionals working with children must make every effort through referral and follow-up to ensure that necessary educational services are obtained.

Goals for Mrs. Johnson were as follows:

- Enable her to understand the meaning behind Ricky's behavior
- Assist her to develop ways to restrict overnight visitation
- Develop her sense of entitlement to make decisions concerning Ricky, in spite of challenges to her authority from her son

Goals for Ricky's parents included enabling them to understand Ricky's need for a consistent, reliable relationship with them, and to develop the capacity to understand and acknowledge Ricky's feelings and point of view.

Third Play Therapy Session

Ricky began the next session by going to the child-sized table to draw. As he drew, he stated that his grandmother had beaten him with a belt that morning. He continued to draw, creating a picture of what appeared to be circular scribbles; when asked about his picture, he stated that it showed "parts of Ricky" (see Figure 9.1). Ricky then moved to the dollhouse and again moved the dolls and furniture upstairs, downstairs, and in and out of the house, in the same apparently random fashion as he had done in earlier sessions.

At the end of the session, I questioned Mrs. Johnson about Ricky's statement that she had beaten him that morning. Mrs. Johnson, with some distress, stated that Ricky often described things that had never happened, and added that she was very worried about this. She described the "time-out" method that she used with Ricky; she noted that there was no point in hitting Ricky, since he couldn't tell the difference between right and wrong. I encouraged her to continue to use time out consistently, for 3 minutes each time. I also advised her to call the board of education to request a full evaluation for Ricky, because of his apparent delays in cognitive, social, fine motor, and language development.

Issues of possible abuse are always difficult for a therapist. It is important to take all allegations of abuse seriously, while at the same time not rushing to judgment. Maintaining a relationship with a child's caregiver and providing education in various methods of noncorporal yet firm limit setting can go a long way toward protecting a child. In my own experience and that of my colleagues, reporting of suspected abuse frequently results in abrupt termination of therapy.

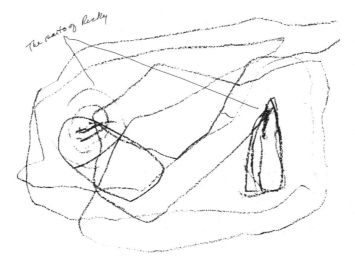

FIGURE 9.1. The parts of Ricky.

Summary of Fourth through Ninth Sessions

Before the fourth session, a young man living in Ricky's neighborhood was gunned down in broad daylight. Both Ricky and his cousin, Taisha, saw the young man lying dead in the street. Because of this tragedy, I decided to see Mrs. Johnson alone in the following session. Grief-stricken, angry, and overwhelmed by the horror of the crisis and her plight of having to live in a violence-filled neighborhood, she cried, "How am I going to raise these children?" I could only sit with her in her grief and anguish.

Subsequent play therapy sessions with Ricky included much doll play with violent themes—fighting, shooting, killing, bleeding, monsters coming into the bedroom and being killed, and so forth. During some of these sessions, Ricky would announce, "I'm finished talking," and insist that Taisha come up to play. (His grandmother usually brought both children to sessions and would wait with Taisha in the waiting room.) Taisha would join him and engage in building with blocks, while Ricky would hit, push, grab toys from, and otherwise bully Taisha.

Play therapy for Ricky was apparently a stressful, anxiety-provoking time. During each session, Ricky asked to go to the bathroom. He wanted me to go with him, and I stood outside the door calling to him to assure him I had not left him on his own. There were several reasons for this anxiety. First, Ricky had to leave his grandmother and Taisha downstairs while he came to the playroom, and he was afraid they would not be there when he returned. He could not tolerate separation from Taisha for more than 20 minutes, after which he would insist that she come upstairs and join him in the session. Second, he was dealing with upsetting family and other issues over which he had little control. Ricky used bossiness and a feigned anger to give himself the feeling that *he* was in control. Finally, he was faced with establishing a relationship with a new person, his therapist (myself). Relationships were difficult for Ricky. He continued his air of arrogance, scowling, ordering me about, and telling me, "Be quiet. I'm not talking to you!" I accepted this attitude from a pint-sized 3-year-old; however, I knew that as Ricky grew older, such behavior would not be easily overlooked by the adults in his life. He would begin to be seen as "bad" and "having an attitude."

Because Ricky's play in these sessions was so aggressive, ample opportunity was provided for me to introduce the idea that people were not for hitting, that Taisha was not for hitting, and that he was not for hitting. This was clearly a novel idea for him; the first time he heard it, he was so shocked that he stepped back, straightened up, and looked at me in utter amazement!

Collateral Sessions with Caregiver

The collateral sessions with Mrs. Johnson during this period focused on discussions of how to use "time outs" and the need for Ricky to understand clearly where he belonged (i.e., with his grandmother) and who was in charge of him (again, his grandmother). Although I emphasized to Mrs. Johnson the connection between Ricky's regressed behavior and his overnight visits with other family members, she was tremendously conflicted over her desire to protect her grandson and her need to maintain an amicable relationship with her son, Ricky's father. Nevertheless, in time she began to set limits on these visits by insisting that they not be overnight. In turn, Ricky began responding to her consistency. When he began to get out of control, Ricky would put himself on "time out" by announcing to her in his usual angry, brusque manner, "I'm going to my room." Ricky was beginning to internalize structure from his grandmother and gain self-control.

Tenth Play Therapy Session

Children's play is the vehicle through which they express issues of concern to them. They play because they do not have the words to express themselves. Occasionally, however, they surprise us and talk to us directly about their worries. As they struggle with words, it is important not to fill in the blanks for them, but to provide them with choices.

Content of Session

CHILD: (*Comes in and sits down in an adult-sized chair.*) Grandma and Vonte were yelling.

THERAPIST: Oh, they were yelling. Who were they yelling at?

C: Grandma was yelling at Vonte, and Vonte was yelling at Grandma.

T: Where were they yelling?

C: In the house.

T: Where were you?

C: In the house.

T: What did you do?

C: I went to my room. Water came out of my eyes.

T: You felt sad.

C: (*No reply. He sits in the chair with his feet on the cushion and his arms at his sides, looking like a crumpled rag doll.*)

T: Look at this piece of paper. I'm going to draw you some pictures. (*Draws some circles to represent different feeling states: sad, with tears; angry, with brows arched; scared, with wide eyes; and happy, with a smile. Shows child each face and labels the feeling.*)

C: That's not my hair!

T: No, that's not like your hair. Your hair is like this (*adding curls*). You were sad when Grandma and

Analysis/Rationale

I am wondering what he has witnessed and how he has understood what he saw and heard.

He evidently doesn't know the word "tears."

An opportunity to teach Ricky about feelings has presented itself.

It is interesting that he readily identifies with the faces. I feel compassion for him. How much he has to absorb at such a young age!

Vonte were yelling (*pointing to the face with tears*). How else did you feel (*showing him the other faces*)?

C: (*Points to the angry face.*)

T: Oh, you were angry too.

C: (*Gets alligator and wolf puppets.*) You take this one. (*Gives therapist the wolf.*) Raah! Graah! (*Takes alligator puppet and pinches therapist hard.*)

Confronted with his anger, Ricky immediately needs to find a way to express it. He is learning a new skill and testing limits at the same time.

T: Remember how I said there were some things you couldn't do here? One of those things is to hurt me. You would like to pinch me, and you can pretend this soft bat is me. You can pinch that. I'm not for pinching.

C: Graah! (*Takes alligator puppet and pinches therapist again.*)

Giving him choices within clear limits allows him to be safely in control and experience himself as a competent decision maker.

T: Ow. If you decide to pinch me again, that means you also decide our playtime is over. I'm not for hurting. Taisha is not for hurting. Grandma is not for hurting.

C: *I'm* not for hurting either!

I'm surprised and pleased he has learned that!

T: No, you're not for hurting or hitting or anything like that.

Eleventh Play Therapy Session

In the session that followed the exchange described above, Ricky spent a good deal of time trying very hard to draw a square. He was clearly frustrated with this effort, but continued nonetheless. I was impressed by his concentrated effort. Such a dramatic change in play generally signifies a change in a child. Ricky had acquired a very important concept with regard to himself and his relationship to others—neither he nor they were for hitting. Mrs. Johnson also reported changes in Ricky. He reportedly had better concentration, had less need to be in control, had fewer tantrums and improved language skills.

At this point, unfortunately, Mrs. Johnson canceled several sessions in succession. Frequently, when children's symptoms begin to subside, caregivers will stop bringing them for therapy. This series of cancellations was followed by my vacation. Consequently, 2 months elapsed between sessions. When he returned, Ricky was angry, and he communicated this to me in a variety of ways over the next several sessions.

Fourteenth Play Therapy Session

Content of Session   Analysis/Rationale

CHILD: I have to go to the bathroom.

THERAPIST: All right, you can go by yourself. You know where the bathroom is.

C: (*Goes, returns, and continues to play with dolls and the dollhouse. He seems preoccupied and is frowning.*)

C: I have to go to the bathroom.

T: You remember, Ricky, that one of the rules is that you can go to the bathroom only once during our playtime.

C: I want to go to the bathroom!

T: You *really* want to go to the bathroom! Remember, I said that you can go to the bathroom only once during our playtime. If you decide to go to the bathroom, you also decide to end our playtime for today.

C: (*Scowls and continues to play with the dolls and dollhouse, now crashing cars into the dollhouse. Looks at therapist deliberately, takes the tray of dolls and dollhouse furniture, and dumps the lot onto the floor. Therapist watches quietly as he repeats this routine until every toy in the office is in a heap in the middle of the floor.*)

C: I'm leaving!

T: OK, Ricky.

C: (*Gets up and walks to the door. As he passes through the door, he turns.*) AND I'M NOT PICKING THEM UP!

Ricky seems both angry and ambivalent. He values our time together, but is angry because I have "disappeared" on him. He may also be testing to see whether I can be trusted to stick to my own rules. He may be trying to leave me the way he perceives I left him.

Here Ricky shows that he can follow the limits set for him and is aware of making a conscious choice.

In this session, Ricky's method of communicating his anger changed from hitting or pinching to dumping toys. This was growth and needed to be supported. Ricky knew from our many previous sessions that he would not be required to pick up after himself. Ricky's expression of anger needed no apology (since no one was hurt and nothing was broken) and was accepted as it was given. In hindsight, Ricky might have been better served if I had commented that he was very angry with me and that he was leaving me the way I had left him. This would have been a model for Ricky to use words, rather than actions, to express his feelings.

Fifteenth Play Therapy Session

When Ricky returned the following week, I greeted him in the usual welcoming manner. It was important to let him know that a show of anger does not end a relationship. He was a bit subdued at first, but quickly realized that he was accepted. Ricky then began to test the limits of his acceptance as well as my consistency. Using the fox puppet, he began pinching me hard. I said that he must be mad at me, and reminded him that I was not for hurting. Ricky continued his pinching, but rather than choosing to break the stated limit for the third and final time (which would cause me to end the session), he announced that he was leaving. He returned shortly thereafter, but I said, "Our time is up for today, Ricky. See you next week." I felt it was important for Ricky to be held accountable for his decisions and the consequences of his decisions. In this way he learned that I respected him and his choices. When Ricky ended the session, I held him to it.

Despite Ricky's angry feelings and limit testing, I sensed that the tone and quality of our relationship had changed. I felt accepted by Ricky, and believed that we had finally achieved a therapeutic alliance.

Sixteenth Play Therapy Session

Ricky came into the office cheerfully and sat down at the small table. He made good eye contact with me while he chatted about how the school bus had broken down, and he showed me how he had learned to use scissors in school. He then went to the dollhouse and played at having people fall and die.

Content of Session	Analysis/Rationale
CHILD: I was angry at you last week.	Relationships are conflicted for Ricky. He does not know when the people he counts on will "disappear." For a young child, death and separation are the same. Ricky seems angry not only at me, but at all those whose presence has been inconsistent. This is a safe place for him to express his anger, but he has not yet learned that he can express his anger and *stay*.
THERAPIST: Yes, I know you were very angry at me.	
C: (*Goes to the puppets, selects fox and alligator, and proceeds to "attack" therapist by pinching.*)	
T: Looks like you're still angry at me, Ricky. I know you'd like to pinch me, but I'm not for pinching. You may pinch the chair or the soft bat and pretend that's me.	
C: (*Continues to pinch therapist with the puppets.*)	
T: Remember, Ricky, I'm not for pinching. I know you're angry and you would like to pinch me. You can pretend the soft bat or the chair is me and pinch one of them. If you choose to pinch me again, you also choose to end our playtime together.	
C: I'm angry! (*Throws down the puppets and walks out the door.*)	I now regret not asking him the reason for his anger with me (even though that is a hard question for most children to answer).

Eighteenth Play Therapy Session

A crisis soon occurred that again changed our relationship. After a session in which Ricky had been able to remain the entire time, I walked him to the waiting room, only to find that Ricky's grandmother was not there waiting for him as she had been all the sessions before. Ricky was thunderstruck. We were informed by the receptionist that she had gone to run an errand. As we walked back to my office, I assured Ricky that his grandmother would be back. Nevertheless, I could see his confidence melt away and his anxiety mount with every step. When we reached my office, Ricky climbed into a chair dejectedly.

Content of Session	Analysis/Rationale
THERAPIST: Would you like me to wrap you in a blanket?	The unexpected absence (i.e., loss) of his grandmother seems to awaken strong needs for nurturance and security, central to an earlier developmental period. Snacks are now appropriate, since nurturance issues are present.
CHILD: (*Nods his head yes.*)	
T: (*Wraps him tightly.*) Would you like some applesauce?	
C: (*Nods his head yes.*)	
T: (*Takes out a small sealed cup of applesauce and begins to feed Ricky as if he were a baby. He eats half a cup in baby-like fashion.*)	
C: I'm a big boy. I'll feed myself.	The need to be competent reasserts itself quickly.
T: OK.	

Over the next five sessions, Ricky's play echoed all the conflicts of his young life. He wanted to be babied, and he wanted to be masterful; he wanted to trust, and yet he feared abandonment. At times his confusion and his anxiety were so great that any small denial or limit sent him into rageful tantrums and head banging.

Caregiver Counseling

Throughout a child's treatment, as noted earlier, it is necessary to meet with the primary caregiver. These meetings should be held on a regular basis—either briefly at the end of a session (if the child can wait alone in the waiting room), separate from the child's sessions, or via the telephone. With Mrs. Johnson, the content of these meetings included behavior management and parenting skills, child development issues as they related to Ricky, and (most frequently) the strife between her and her son over where Ricky belonged. Although Mrs. Johnson had been appointed as Ricky's permanent legal guardian, she had difficulty exercising her authority. Conflict over whether Ricky belonged with her or with her son and Ricky's mother, over visitation with his father, and over what occurred during those visits seemed unending. Invariably Ricky's behavior deteriorated after a visit with his father. I discussed many visitation alternatives with Mrs. Johnson—for instance, having visitors come to see Ricky rather than having him leave to visit others, going with Ricky to visit others, never permitting overnight visits, and so forth. Mrs. Johnson was unable to implement a consistent visitation plan that benefited Ricky. When she allowed Ricky to stay with his father for 10 days during a holiday period, he was left with his mother; after he returned to his grandmother, Ricky reported that his mother had beaten him. In an effort to protect Ricky and give his grandmother additional incentive to set limits with her son, I notified child abuse authorities with a complaint directed against Mrs. Johnson for failing to protect Ricky from potential harm.

When Ricky resumed treatment following his holiday break, he was anxious and regressed in his behavior. He asked for help he did not need. He tearfully insisted that I accompany him to the bathroom, although previously he had been able to go and come back by himself. He insisted on washing his hands for an extended period of time after seeing a small dot of paint on one finger. His artwork (Figure 9.2, done in bright red) and play suggested his attempts to contain the anger and confusion in his life. This anxiety continued through the next week. He began to insist on sleeping with his grandmother and refused to go to his own bed. The conflict between Mrs. Johnson and Ricky's parents continued.

Twenty-Fourth Play Therapy Session

Ricky came into the office with a scowl on his face. He announced that he was angry with Grandma because she had had a fight with his mother. Since Ricky was able to put his feelings and the reason for them into words, I suggested he tell Grandma directly and invited her to come into my office. She did, and Ricky, now 4 years of age, was able to tell his grandmother how he felt and why. Grandma listened, but she also complained about Ricky's throwing toys and refusing to obey her. We talked about how to help Ricky tell her what was upsetting him, and, if necessary, how to help him act out his angry feelings by hitting and kicking an inflatable bop bag or pillow. At this point, I knew that I needed to talk to Mrs. Johnson alone about Ricky's

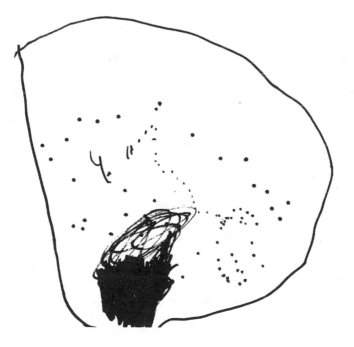

FIGURE 9.2. Contained explosion.

symptoms and the reasons for them, and to advise her to prohibit any more visits with his parents unless she accompanied Ricky.

Content of Session	Analysis/Rationale
THERAPIST: Ricky, go to the waiting room and wait for Grandma. I want to talk to her for a little while. It won't be long.	I am counting on the independence and self-confidence Ricky has displayed in earlier sessions.
CHILD: No! I don't want to. I want to stay.	
T: (*Takes a small teddy bear from her desk and hands it to Ricky.*) Take Teddy with you, and take care of him for me until Grandma and I come to the waiting room. It will be a very short time.	I appeal to Ricky's need to be cared for when I ask him to take care of Teddy for me.
C: Can I keep him?	Ricky takes me by surprise when he asks to keep Teddy. I know I can't refuse him, since Teddy has instantly become a transitional object and therapeutic tool.
T: Yes, you can keep him.	

Subsequent Sessions

In subsequent sessions I asked Ricky to bring Teddy with him when he came for his playtime, but Teddy never came. Ricky was afraid that Teddy would have to stay, even though I explained that Teddy lived with him now and would come only for a visit. I had hoped to use Teddy in the sessions, but he had to be used in absentia. I told Ricky that Teddy was a special bear, because he was in charge of Ricky's worries. For example, if Ricky had a worry that kept him up at night, he could tell Teddy. Teddy would be in charge of the worry all night so that Ricky could go to sleep. The same was true in the day when Ricky went to school. Ricky's job was to learn in school and have fun. Teddy's job was to worry for Ricky, to keep Ricky company when he needed company, and to be his teddy. Teddy was reported (by Grandma) to be good at his job. Ricky was able to sleep in his own bed again. Teddy went everywhere with Ricky, even into the bathtub.

Ricky's anxiety continued, in various degrees of intensity, over the next few weeks of treatment. During this time, there was much family conflict over Ricky, where he should live, and who should be in charge of him. It is difficult for any child to witness conflict among family members; this is especially painful for the child when he is the source of the disagreement. Ricky's attachment to his mother and father had been compromised due to their abuse and inconsistency, and his attachment to his grandmother was fraught with anxiety because of her own uncertainty about keeping him. Since his parents wanted him back, it is likely that they told Ricky this; they probably said negative things about his grandmother as well. I never knew *what* Ricky was told about why he lived with his grandmother. Certainly Mrs. Johnson's ambivalence, coupled with the parents' strong wish to have him back (in spite of their inability to care for him adequately), combined to put Ricky squarely in the middle of a "no-win" situation.

Final Session

In what turned out to be our final session together, Ricky reverted to the gruff manner he had exhibited during our first encounter. There was much scowling, and many times Ricky shouted, "Leave me alone!" I spoke with Mrs. Johnson briefly on the telephone following this session. She informed me that Ricky's mother had petitioned to have unsupervised visits with and custody of Ricky. I suggested to Mrs. Johnson that she consider filing for adoption of Ricky—a subject we had spoken of several times before. Ricky missed his next two appointments. A follow-up call revealed that Mrs. Johnson's telephone had been disconnected. A letter was sent inviting her to call for another appointment. She never did.

CONCLUDING COMMENTS

Ricky was attached to his grandmother, but his attachment was insecure at best. The first developmental task that an infant must accomplish—developing a sense of trust in at least one person—had not been successfully completed before Ricky was forced to move on to the next task. Ricky needed to know that he belonged with his grandmother and that she was his trustworthy refuge and protector. Ricky's fundamental difficulty lay in the fact that his grandmother did not feel entitled to be his primary caregiver. She felt committed to Ricky, but believed she had no right to stand between a father and his son; perhaps she feared that to do so would mean jeopardizing her relationship with her own son, Ricky's father. She may also have felt the need to support her son's male role as father, given the difficulty so many African American men face in maintaining the traditional male roles of provider and head of the household (McLoyd, 1990). Embracing her authority as Ricky's guardian against her son was no doubt more difficult for her, given that her only support for this came from a middle-class white woman. Other family members (Mrs. Johnson's husband, Mr. Johnson, and her second son, Evon) maintained a distant neutrality.

The intergenerational conflict over where Ricky belonged and who was his rightful caregiver proved to be impossible to resolve. Despite the fact that Mrs. Johnson was Ricky's legal guardian, parental rights had not been terminated. Ricky's parents could petition the court for his return, and I was told by child welfare authorities that it was quite probable that Ricky would be returned to his parents. Ricky had no attorney of his own to speak for his "best interests"; even if he did have an attorney, a court could find that his "best interests" lay in his return to his parents.

Ricky's sudden withdrawal from treatment was difficult for me. We never had a chance to say goodbye, and so we had unfinished business. Given a second chance, I would have made a greater effort to engage Ricky's father in treatment. This would have affirmed Mrs. Johnson's desire to support her son in his role as father, and perhaps would have made possible a more positive outcome for Ricky. My focus, however, was on enabling Mrs. Johnson to set clear boundaries and embrace her authority as Ricky's guardian. I was concerned with Ricky's immediate need for consistency and predictability.

I still think about Ricky from time to time. I miss him and hope that Teddy is still doing a good job.

STUDY QUESTIONS

1. Consider the pros and cons of Ricky's remaining with his grandmother and of moving to live with his parents. What conditions would have needed to be addressed in either alternative in order to assure the "best interests" of the child?

2. Discuss the implications for very young children of seeing the dead body of a young man in the street. Critique the therapist's handling of this with the children and grandmother in this case. What would be the ideal management of a situation like this in a therapeutic context?

3. To what extent do you think that issues of race and socioeconomic status affected the treatment of this case? Give some specific strategies that might have helped bridge these differences.

4. Do you think that family sessions might have been helpful in resolving the conflicts between Ricky's parents and his grandmother? If so, what role should the therapist have assumed to prevent escalation of the conflict during sessions?

5. What effect might the unplanned termination have on Ricky? How can the therapist deal with her present feelings about this?

REFERENCES

Aber, L., & Palmer, J. (1997, April). *Poverty and brain development in early childhood.* New York: National Center for Children in Poverty, Columbia School of Public Health.

Ainsworth, M. D. S. (1982). Attachment: Retrospect and prospect. In C. M. Parkes & J. Stevenson-Hinde (Eds.), *The place of attachment in human behavior* (pp. 3–30). New York: Basic Books.

Ainsworth, M. D. S., Blehar, M. C., Waters, E., & Wall, S. (1978). *Patterns of attachment: A psychological study of the Strange Situation.* Hillsdale, NJ: Erlbaum.

Belle, D. (1990). Poverty and women's mental health. *American Psychologist, 45*(3), 385–389.

Bowlby, J.(1969). *Attachment and loss: Vol. 1. Attachment.* New York: Basic Books.

Bowlby, J. (1973). *Attachment and loss: Vol. 2. Separation.* New York: Basic Books.

Bowlby, J. (1980). *Attachment and loss: Vol. 3. Loss.* New York: Basic Books.

Brooks-Gunn, J., Klebanov, P., Liaw, F., & Duncan, G. (1995). Toward an understanding of the effects of poverty upon children. In H. E. Fitzgerald, B. M. Lester, & B. Zuckerman (Eds.), *Children of poverty: Research, health, and policy issues.* New York: Garland Press.

Brown, L., & Pollitt, E. (1996). Malnutrition, poverty and intellectual development. *Scientific American, 274*(2), 38–43.

Burton, L. M. (1991). Drug trafficking schedules and child-care strategies in a high risk neighborhood. *American Enterprise, 2*(3), 34–37.

Burton, L. M. (1992). Black grandparents rearing children of drug-addicted parents: Stressors, outcomes, and social service needs. *The Gerontologist, 32*(6), 744–751.

Crittenden, P. M. (1985). Social networks, quality of child rearing, and child development. *Child Development, 56*, 1299–1313.

Crittenden, P. M. (1992). Children's strategies for coping with adverse home environments: An interpretation using attachment theory. *Child Abuse and Neglect, 16*, 329–343.

Davies, D. (1999). *Child development: A practitioner's guide.* New York: Guilford Press.

Egeland, B., & Sroufe, L. A. (1981). Attachment and early maltreatment. *Child Development, 52*, 44–52.

Erikson, E. (1950). *Childhood and society.* New York: Norton.

Freud, S. (1943). *A general introduction to psychoanalysis* (Trans. J. Riviere). Garden City, NY: Garden City. (Originial work published 1920)

Landreth, G. L. (1991). *Play therapy: The art of the relationship.* Muncie, IN: Accelerated Development.

Lieberman, A. F. (1993). *The emotional life of the toddler.* New York: Free Press.

Mahler, M. S., Pine, F., & Bergman, A. (1975). *The psychological birth of the human infant.* New York: Basic Books.

Main, M., & Hesse, E. (1990). Parents' unresolved traumatic experiences are related to infant disorganized attachment status: Is frightened and/or frightening parental behavior the linking mechanism? In M. T. Greenberg, D. Cicchetti, & E. M. Cummings (Eds.), *Attachment in the preschool years: Theory, research and intervention* (pp. 161–184). Chicago: University of Chicago Press.

Main, M., Kaplan, N., & Cassidy, J. (1985). Security in infancy, childhood and adulthood. A move to the level of representation. In I. Bretherton & E. Waters (Eds.), Growing points of attachment theory and research. *Monographs of the Society for Research in Child Development, 50*(1–2, Serial No. 209), 66–106.

Main, M., & Solomon, J. (1990). Procedures for identifying infants as disorganized/disoriented during the Ainsworth Strange Situation. In M. T. Greenberg, D. Cicchetti, & E. M. Cummings (Eds.), *Attachment in the preschool years: Theory, research and intervention* (pp. 121–160). Chicago: University of Chicago Press.

Mayes, L. (1996, June). *Early experience and the developing brain: The model of prenatal cocaine exposure.* Paper presented at the invitational conference "Brain Development in Young Children: New Frontiers for Research, Policy and Practice," University of Chicago.

McLoyd, V. C. (1990). The impact of economic hardship on black families and children: Psychological distress, parenting, and socioemotional development. *Child Development, 61*, 311–346.

Minkler, M., Roe, K. M., & Price, M. (1992). The physical and emotional health of grandmothers raising grandchildren in the crack cocaine epidemic. *The Gerontologist, 32*(6), 752–761.

Minkler, M., Roe, K. M., & Robertson-Beckley, R. J. (1994). Raising grandchildren from crack-cocaine households: Effects of family and friendship ties of African-American women. *American Journal of Orthopsychiatry, 64*(1), 20–29.

National Health/Education Consortium. (1991, January). Healthy brain development. *National Health/Education Consortium Report*, pp. 4–5.

Osofsky, J. D., Wewers, S., Hann, D. M., & Fick, A. C. (1993). Chronic community violence: What is happening to our children? *Psychiatry, 56*, 36–45.

Perls, F. S., Hefferline, R. F., & Goodman, P. (1969). *Gestalt therapy: Excitement and growth in the human personality.* New York: Julian Press.

Shore, R. (1997). *Rethinking the brain: New insights into early development.* New York: Families and Work Institute.

Spangler, G., & Grossman, K. E. (1993). Biobehavioral organization in securely and insecurely attached infants. *Child Development, 64*, 1439–1450.

Sroufe, L. A., & Waters, E. (1977). Attachment as an organizational construct. *Child Development*, *48*, 1184–1199.

Stern, D. N. (1974). The goal and structure of mother-infant play. *Journal of the American Academy of Child Psychiatry*, *13*, 402–421.

Stern, D. N. (1985). *The interpersonal world of the infant*. New York: Basic Books.

Terr, L. (1988). What happens to early memories of trauma? A study of twenty children under age five at the time of documented traumatic events. *Journal of the American Academy of Child Psychiatry*, *27*(1), 96–104.

Terr, L. (1989). Treating psychic trauma in children: A preliminary discussion. *Journal of Traumatic Stress*, *2*(1), 3–20.

Webb, N. B. (1996). *Social work practice with children*. New York: Guilford Press.

CHAPTER 10

School-Based Peer Therapy to Facilitate Mourning in Latency-Age Children Following Sudden Parental Death

Cases of Joan, Age 10½, and Roberta Age 9½, with Follow-Up 8 Years Later

JOYCE BLUESTONE

The death of a parent is a tragic and excruciating experience for a child. Children often perceive parents as fountains of love and stability, protecting them from an ever-shifting and sometimes hostile world. Therefore, the death of such a loved one leaves a bereft child with a world that may never again be as secure and safe a place as it was before. Sandra Sutherland Fox (1985, p. 16) states that "children who experience the death of a parent or sibling have been reported to be at risk for emotional disorders in adult life." Unresolved grief can potentially interfere with a child's emotional and intellectual development.

The cases described in this chapter involved two middle-latency-age children (9½ and 10½ years old). Most latency-age children understand the finality of death, and they know that people die and do not return. They realize that death will happen to everybody, but "for these children death is far off in the future and remains in the domain of the aged" (Lonetto, 1980, p. 157). Fox (1985, p. 11), referring to Nagy's (1948) pivotal work, states that

> latency children see death in a personified way—as a ghost or angel or space creature, for example—as something that can come and get you. They believe that death can happen to others, particularly the elderly and handicapped, because they cannot run fast and therefore cannot escape when death comes for them. Most children, therefore, don't die because they can run very fast.

Preadolescent children begin to recognize that death is inevitable and that one day it will happen to them. Although such a child cognitively reaches this mature understanding of death, she* is still struggling psychologically with the concept of finality.

---

*I use female pronouns in this chapter to designate all children. I hope that the disadvantages of this convention will be outweighed by the advantages of easier and clearer reading.

GRIEVING IN LATENCY

Can Children Mourn?

Experts disagree about the age at which a child develops the capacity to mourn a parent's death. Bowlby (1963, 1980) contends that infants as young as 6 months of age experience grief reactions resembling those seen in adults. Others (Wolfenstein, 1966; Nagera, 1970) believe that a child's capacity to mourn develops as her ego functions mature, as evidenced by an ability to control impulses, to conduct reality testing, and to comprehend the finality of death.

Bowlby (1960, p. 11) defines grief as "the sequence of subjective states that follow loss and accompany mourning." Grossberg and Crandall (1978) define mourning as encompassing not only the initial grief reaction to the loss, but also the future resolution of that grief. Webb (1993) uses this distinction to clarify that although children grieve (express feelings of loss) at an early developmental stage, they cannot mourn (resolve the loss) until they acquire a mature understanding of the finality and meaning of that loss. Wolfelt (1983) reminds us that grief does not focus on one's ability to understand, but instead upon one's ability to feel. "Therefore, any child mature enough to love is mature enough to grieve" (Wolfelt, 1983, p. 20).

Tasks of Mourning for Children

The current literature (Worden, 1996; Klass, Silverman, & Nickman, 1996), building on the work of Kübler-Ross (1969) and Bowlby (1960, 1963), reports that there are four stages in the grieving process experienced by children: (1) accepting the reality of the loss; (2) experiencing the pain; (3) adjusting to an environment in which the deceased is missing; and (4) relocating the dead person within one's life and finding ways to memorialize the person (Worden, 1996).

In the first phase, the typical reactions are shock, protest, anger, and disbelief. The bereaved child cannot believe that the parent is dead. These feelings of denial are heightened when the death occurs suddenly, as in the case studies of Roberta and Joan presented in this chapter. Children can remain in this stage of denial for a long time by continuing to protest and feel angry at the separation, and by refusing to face the finality of the loss. Such a child must understand that the parent is indeed dead before she can begin to feel the pain of this horrific loss.

The second stage is one of intense emotions in which the bereaved must face and endure a range of painful feelings. A child experiences these feelings as she realizes her permanent loss. If the child's pain and despair is not worked through, it "will manifest in other ways, perhaps somatically or in aberrant behavior patterns" (Worden, 1996, p. 14). During this phase, the child may experience feelings of ambivalence toward the deceased and of responsibility for the death. The ambivalence may stem from the nature of the relationship prior to the death or may arise directly from the actual death experience. "The child's anger at the deceased for abandoning her, and guilt over having driven the dead person away are feelings that are particularly difficult to resolve" (Baker, Sedney, & Gross, 1992, p. 109). The child's task is to acknowledge her feelings of anger and responsibility, while also maintaining her loving and positive memories of the deceased parent.

In the third stage, the child adjusts to her environment without the deceased parent. "The nature of this adjustment is determined by the roles and relationships that the dead parent played in the child's life as well as in the life of the family" (Worden, 1996, p. 15). The bereaved child begins to organize her life without the dead parent. In Roberta's case, she was faced with many daily disruptions upon the death of her mother, who was her primary caretaker. A child's adjustment to death occurs over time, and painful feelings often resurface at different developmental milestones, such as graduation and marriage.

The fourth stage of the grieving process involves finding a place for the dead parent in the child's emotional life. This phase has evolved from Freud's (1917/1957) theory that the primary goal of mourning is to cut the bond (decathect) so that new attachments can be formed. In their discussion of how the bereaved cope with a significant death, Klass et al. (1996) state that "an irreconcilable tension exists, a paradox of letting go and remaining involved" (p. 351). The child needs to try to preserve an ongoing, transforming bond to the deceased, while simultaneously living in the present and forging new relationships. This understanding of the grief process is based on an appreciation of the beauty, complexity, and depth of life, death, and the human condition. According to Klass et al. (1996, p. 351), "it is possible to be bereft and not bereft simultaneously, to have a sense of continuity and yet to know that nothing will ever be the same." Worden (1996, p. 27) notes, "The Harvard Child Bereavement Study has extended our knowledge of the way in which children maintain an ongoing connection to the dead parent. Through a process called 'construction', the child develops an inner representation of the dead parent that changes as the child matures and the intensity of grief lessens." Strategies for maintaining a connection to the deceased parent include the following: "(1) locating the deceased, (2) experiencing the deceased, (3) reaching out to the deceased, (4) remembering (waking memories), and (5) keeping something that belonged to the deceased (linking objects)" (Klass et al., 1996, p. 77).

How Children Grieve

Children require reassurance that, above all else, they will "be taken care of" before they can address the tasks of mourning described here. A bereaved child often feels anxious about the safety of the surviving parent, and these concerns need to be directly addressed with the child. The child also needs to be given honest and age-appropriate information about the deceased parent's death. She needs to be told the facts of the death repeatedly, over a period of time. The child's participation in rituals of mourning (such as the funeral) can help her acknowledge the reality of the loss.

Children, especially through the latency years, use magical thinking to fill in gaps in their understanding (Fox, 1985, p. 14). Since death is such an incomprehensible phenomenon, even older children and adults often resort to magical thinking to understand it. Generally, children of any age employ magical thinking by believing that "what they said, did, wished, feared, or thought caused a person to die" (Fox, 1985, p. 14). Given that children typically assume responsibility for what goes on in their world, adults need to reassure them that they are not responsible for the death of a parent.

A child needs the presence of a consistent and emotionally available adult to support her in her grief. The ability of the surviving parent, or parent surrogate, to function in this role is critical to the child's adjustment. Yet the challenge the surviving parent faces is a daunting one. The caretaker must adjust to the new role of single parent, adapt to being widowed, and support the child in her grief. It is extremely understandable that the parent may feel too upset to help the child cope. Asking for help from a professional, a close friend, and/or a relative can be very helpful for the parent and child, and instrumental in facilitating the child's grief.

Worden (1996, p. 17) emphasizes that "family influences such as size, solvency, structure, style of coping, support, and communication, as well as family stressors, and changes and disruptions in the child's daily life" contribute to the grief reactions of a given child.

The grieving process for children is often gradual and agonizing. It may take several years to mourn and integrate a loss, because children can tolerate only small doses of painful feelings. Often children avoid talking about their feelings with both adults and their peers. Webb (1993, p. 12) states that latency-age children are often averse to "discussing the parent's death with peers, because of the fear of being pitied." Grieving children frequently express their feelings in indirect, delayed, and disguised ways. Children may be mischievous, aggressive, rebellious, or withdrawn, or may displace their feelings onto undeserving adults. Another indirect expression of grief, cited by Worden (1996) from the Harvard Child Bereavement Study, is the tendency for girls to somaticize their loss by experiencing frequent headaches and health problems during the first year after death. Children need adults to "provide an environment where it's safe to grieve—to be sad, mad or bad" (Fox, 1985, p. 36). In a safe environment, adults can begin to identify, normalize, and respect a child's feelings, and to help her find appropriate ways to express her grief.

Children experience a range of strong feelings that can overwhelm them when a parent dies, such as anger, sadness, fear, helplessness, and guilt. They may also idealize the deceased, feel cheated, and/or feel regretful. For most people, anger is a difficult emotion to express, and it feels incongruent to connect grief with anger. Even though it is a universal experience to feel abandoned and angry when someone we care about dies, that feeling makes most of us feel guilty (Fox, 1985, p. 36). Feelings of anger, guilt, and sadness are often undifferentiated and confused. Because these painful emotions tend to be expressed in anger, the grief process becomes exaggerated and prolonged. A child may continue to hope for the parent's return and may have thoughts or fantasies of reuniting with the deceased.

A child's timetable for grieving differs from that of adults. For example, a child may experience shock or denial for a longer duration than adults, unconsciously protecting herself from the emotional pain. Sometimes the child's denial is strong, and she will carry on as if nothing has happened. At other times, the child may feel her pain intensely. This ebb and flow of grieving is typical of the way children cope.

Part of the grieving process requires a child to figure out a way to connect with the deceased parent. This connection goes through various transformations over the child's lifetime. "A retrospective study of college-age women who had lost a parent to death found that as these women got older, they were constantly renegotiating their relationship to their dead parent" (Silverman, 1987). To maintain this continuing bond with the deceased, a child needs to remember the parent and their relationship together: activities shared, happy times, unhappy moments, intimate talks, ways the child was comforted and disciplined, and so forth. All these memories contribute to the grieving process. The child needs to keep her parent's memories alive and conscious. However, the tendency is to bury the memories because they feel intensely painful.

To summarize, adults who are dealing with a latency-age child grieving for the death of a parent must try to create an atmosphere in which the bereaved child can express emotions freely, unhindered by the typical (and usually detrimental) social taboos against such expression. The school social worker should approach the child's crisis as an opportunity for growth, while bearing in mind the intense pain the child is experiencing. Confining expectations to age-appropriate levels, the social worker should understand the following special needs of the bereaved child: (1) the need for security; (2) the child's low tolerance for psychological pain; (3) the need for adult role models; (4) the possibility for suppression and confusion of feelings because of a lack of vocabulary and conceptual development; (5) the need to preserve and foster memories of the deceased; and (6) sensitivity about being "different" from peers (Webb, 1993).

In the cases described in this chapter, Joan was a fifth-grader (10½ years old) whose father had died suddenly and unexpectedly from a heart attack 2 years earlier. Roberta was a fourth-grader (9½ years old) whose mother had committed suicide by shooting herself. The death of their parents was a traumatic experience for Joan and Roberta. Both girls had to deal with the extra burden of their parents' unexpected deaths. Their feelings of shock, denial, and disbelief were extremely intense and contributed to their sense that the respective deaths were wrong and unfair.

DEVELOPMENTAL TASKS OF LATENCY

An overview of the normal developmental tasks for a latency-age child helps in understanding the value of peer pairing as an effective therapeutic technique for such a child. Cameron (1963, p. 79) states that

> latency occurs when the small child emerges from his home into the wider community, specifically, upon entrance into school. The major social change in latency is that, while still a member of his family group, the child goes forth along into the world outside his family, expands his physical and social horizons, and supplements membership in his own family with membership in groups outside it.

Lieberman (1979, p. 98) states that "cooperation, loyalty, gangs, cliques and organized games are the stuff of middle latency—the age of socialization outside the family." The immediate society of the neighborhood and school exert a major influential force in the developing self-concept of latency-age children. They learn to see themselves as others see them, and often according to rather harsh standards.

Simultaneously, the best-friend or special-chum phenomenon becomes an intense and important experience. This relationship usually constitutes a child's first attachment outside the family (Sarnoff, 1978). Cognitive growth is reflected in the child's play and socialization skills. The latency-age child's play is realistic, constructive, logical, objective, and organized. When socializing with others, the middle-latency-age child can differentiate between different views and needs; she can also consider several viewpoints simultaneously. Socialization is a critical task for the 9- and 10-year-old child. Good socialization skills and positive peer experience encourage strong self-image, solid identity, and intact character formation.

THE ROLE OF THE SCHOOL SOCIAL WORKER

The general functions of the school social worker include identification, assessment, and resolution of social and emotional difficulties that may interfere with a child's adjustment and achievement in school. These responsibilities include counseling services—either individual therapy, peer play therapy, or group therapy. In addition, the social worker assists parents to understand and cope with the needs of their children. The social worker advises them about school and community programs and service; collaborates and communicates with school staff members to help them work more effectively with the children; and plays a distinctive role in the school as the centerpiece of a coordinated system responsive to the needs of troubled students (Johnson & Maile, 1987).

In the two cases discussed here, the task of the school social worker (myself) consisted of aiding each latency-age child's transition into preadolescence, while also helping her deal with the psychological trauma concerning the death of a parent.

PLAY THERAPY IN THE SCHOOL

In my role as a school social worker, I use play therapy to help children express and understand their feelings. Play is a child's natural way of expressing herself. Play therapy allows a child to communicate in her own symbolic language. Since children do not easily express their emotions, play helps a child master a conflictual, traumatic, or anxious situation in her life through the act of repetition. Freud (1914/1958) termed this the phenomenon of "repetition compulsion," which is the need to relive, again and again, a painful memory. Freud maintained that an individual unconsciously recreates situations using the conflicted theme as an attempt to gain mastery over the original overwhelming situation. The frequency of the reenactment coincides with the intensity of the trauma.

A child acts out a trauma over and over again in her play, and this reenactment relieves tension and leads to catharsis. When this occurs symbolically in a displaced fashion, the child does not have to claim responsibility for her actions or feelings ("It's only make-believe"). The potential for catharsis is especially evident in fantasy play, particularly in play involving puppetry. Through the use of puppets, a child can begin to grapple with unresolved conflicts and issues; it is the puppet that is acting out different roles, strategies, and outcomes, and "not" the child. Puppetry is safe and fun, and the puppets themselves are intriguing and inviting.

The role of the school social worker in puppet play sometimes takes the form of audience/observer while the child puts on a show with the puppets. The worker may assume a nondirective yet supportive role as the child plays out a scene exploring conflictual material. A catharsis may occur as the youngster/puppeteer acts out conflictual material. At other times, the social worker participates in the show, taking a turn with the puppets and using this opportunity to play out the conflicts presented by the child in a more "therapeutic" form. Both Roberta and Joan were able to express their emotions related to their grieving process through the use of puppetry, as well as through drawings and the trusting friendship they developed with each other.

In summary, play therapy within the framework of peer pairing can meet the needs of grieving latency-age children. It creates a safe environment of peer support/friendship for each child and validates the "normality" of the other's experience. Play therapy is a subtle therapeutic modality that can help a child untangle confused and suppressed emotions. A child gains an element of control through the play activity. It also provides an ideal and safe setting to foster a child's memory of the deceased.

THE CASES: JOAN, AGE 10½, AND ROBERTA, AGE 9½

Joan

Family Information

Joan, age 10½, was in fifth grade. Mrs. Vespa, her mother, 54 years old, was a full-time homemaker and child care provider for neighborhood children. Two older brothers, aged 25 and 26, lived outside the home.

Presenting Problem

Joan's father had died 2 years earlier of a heart attack. Mr. Vespa did not have a history of illness, and his death was very sudden and unanticipated. A couple of months after her father's death, Joan's oldest brother's wife had a miscarriage, and a friend of the family died as well.

Joan had a history in her school career of being extremely shy in the classroom setting. Also, since second grade, her teachers had expressed concern about Joan's weaknesses in reading comprehension and difficulty in following directions. The crisis of her father's death compounded Joan's withdrawn behavior in the classroom setting and her academic difficulties.

Background

In my role as school social worker, I counseled Joan individually once a week following her father's death, throughout her fourth-grade year. In conjunction with working with Joan, I also counseled and collaborated with Mrs. Vespa and Joan's teacher. The major treatment issues were developing a therapeutic alliance with Joan, encouraging her to grieve openly, fostering assertive behavior, and working with Joan and Mrs. Vespa to help them separate more appropriately.

The school psychologist tested Joan because of her academic difficulties. The results suggested impaired intellectual functioning and significant psychological tension related to her feelings of anger and sadness. Joan often expressed anger and had a need to be in control during the counseling sessions. I validated, normalized, and empathized with her feelings, and at times connected her anger directly to her father's death. I also used play to support and explain her emotions. For example, Joan enjoyed playing the game Battleship. In this game, one does not know where the opponent's ships are placed, and the object of the game is to seek out and "bomb" the opponent's ships. Throughout, I emphasized the unpredictability of life, which was metaphorically played out in the game. My purpose was to symbolically validate the experience of her father's untimely and unexpected death. I also wanted to reassure her that she was a survivor and could live a full and active life.

Joan had become sensitized to loss and feared her mother's death or disappearance. As noted earlier, children who have lost one parent through death frequently fear the loss of the other parent. Both Joan and her mother had significant separation problems, which became accentuated following the father's death. I encouraged them to participate in separate age-appropriate activities: Mrs. Vespa would play cards weekly with her neighborhood friends, and Joan would participate in a weekly Girl Scouts program. This would help alleviate Mrs. Vespa's guilt and reassure Joan about her own fears. I also addressed Joan's tendencies to withdraw in the classroom setting. I encouraged and coached her to practice being assertive with her teacher by asking for help and participating in classroom discussions.

The following school year, I continued individual counseling with Joan. During the summer, Joan's maternal grandmother died after a long illness, and one of Joan's brothers disappeared, telling no one his whereabouts. Joan and I had two sessions together, and then Joan told her mother that she did not want to continue counseling. Mrs. Vespa contacted me to let me know that Joan did not want to continue, but it was unclear why Joan was withdrawing at this point. Recalling our last session together, I concluded that Joan felt threatened by my discussing family concerns too directly and too soon. At the time, I was unaware of the effect of speaking about a "family secret" (her brother's plight).

I subsequently spoke with Joan in a nonthreatening manner about what I labeled a "misunderstanding." I reassured her, "It's OK to be angry at me; let's try to work it out," but she was not responsive. For several weeks, I continued to reach out to Joan through casual contact in the school hallway and through notes, but her resistance did not soften.

Roberta

Family Information

Roberta, age 9½, was in the fourth grade. After her mother's suicide, Roberta had moved in with Mr. Trujillo, her father, 36 years old, a gardener. The parents had been separated for 1 year prior to the suicide. Roberta was picked up from school by, and spent weekday afternoons until dinner hour with, Grandma and Grandpa (her mother's parents). The grandparents had moved to the community to help take care of Roberta after her mother's death.

Presenting Problem

Roberta's mother had committed suicide by shooting herself at the beginning of the school year. Roberta's school history included problems with peers, feeling isolated, and at times being scapegoated. The family members were in shock following Mrs. Trujillo's suicide, and they decided to tell Roberta her mother died from an overdose of pills. Mrs. Trujillo had been psychiatrically hospitalized prior to her suicide and had expressed suicidal thoughts daily, indicating that she would take sleeping pills to kill herself. The school was located in a small community. The adage "Bad news travels fast" applied here, and some children cruelly taunted Roberta by saying, "Your mother shot herself." When Roberta questioned her father, he maintained the distorted explanation.

Background

I began seeing Roberta individually, and also met with her father. I advised him to tell Roberta the truth, because this would help instill trust between Roberta and her family and prevent future repercussions when Roberta eventually learned how her mother died. The father followed my recommendations, which led to more open communication about his own feelings, fears, and worries about the suicide and loss. After Roberta and I had a month of individual contact, she expressed interest in talking to other children who had a parent who died.

Considerations Related to Parental Suicide

The suicide uniquely affected Roberta's ability to grieve. "Suicide is the most difficult bereavement crisis for any family to face and resolve in an effective manner" (Cain, 1972, p. 11). The burden of a parental loss is exacerbated when the cause of death is suicide. Added to the already enormous tasks of grieving, suicide survivors feel humiliation, shame, and often a lack of social and emotional support. The social stigma of a suicide contributes to the survivor's denial, distortion, and "conspiracy of silence" about the circumstances of the death (Cain & Fast, 1972).

Eth and Pynoos (1985) argue for early treatment that initially focuses on the circumstances of the trauma, in order to pave the way for more open expressions of grief. A child (or adult) needs to express and deal with feelings of horror connected to the manner of the death, before she can deal with grief reactions of sadness and guilt.

Following a suicide, survivors generally feel engulfed by relentless guilt. They may feel they should have prevented the suicide. A child survivor also imagines, through magical thinking, that she is responsible for the suicide through her thoughts, wishes, or fantasies. The child can be plagued by heightened feelings of abandonment and rejection related to voluntary nature of the suicidal death. It may be too dangerous emotionally for the child to be angry at the deceased. Consequently, the child internalizes and/or inappropriately externalizes her anger. As the child struggles to make sense of intense and often conflicting emotions, it is important to be respectful of the child's own pace and ability to process these intense feelings.

Formation of Peer Therapy Dyad

Both Joan and Roberta had long-standing problems with relationships. Both girls felt socially isolated—a situation that was exaggerated by their parents' deaths. Joan's and Roberta's painful tasks of grieving were complicated by their poor socialization skills. Thus the chosen therapeutic modality was peer pairing, which in a supportive environment encourages increased social skills, self-esteem, and fosters friendship. This approach is beneficial when group or individual therapy proves to be too overwhelming or threatening. Mervis (1985, p. 125) states that

> pairing is also effective in working with children who feel they are very different from others or who have severe family problems. These children need the opportunity to share feelings and experiences, but it can be too risky to expose them to a group setting in which they might be vulnerable to ridicule or rejection. Through peer-pairing, the children gradually can learn to trust others and to share some of their feelings and experiences in a more controlled and accepting environment. When the sharing becomes mutual, the sense of shame and isolation these children feel can be greatly reduced.

The substantial difference in the manner in which each parent died, however (one of natural causes, the other by suicide) created a potential problem for each child. Joan might be overwhelmed and frightened by Roberta's mother's suicide, increasing her own anxieties. Roberta, in turn, might feel more stigmatized and isolated by Joan's reaction to the suicide. This difference could potentially interfere with the mutual aid process.

Nevertheless, the potential benefits of peer therapy outweighed the risks. The children needed support, and their families were too overwhelmed and steeped in crisis to follow through with treatment outside the school context. The peer therapy modality could meet the needs of Roberta, who was feeling isolated and stigmatized, and offered Joan an alternative to individual counseling. I spoke with each child individually to discuss the proposed therapy, its purpose, and its possible value, and to assess their willingness to participate. Each child appeared interested. Joan was more reluctant and ambivalent than Roberta, but both agreed to try it. The following is a summary of the initial session.

Initial Session

As an introduction, we played a game about our names to break the ice and to become familiar with each other in a nonthreatening, fun way. We then discussed the purpose of peer therapy: to talk about worries and troubles, to share concerns about having a parent who died, to make new friends, and to have fun together. I suggested that each girl share some information with the other about the parent who died—for example, which parent died and when. I also suggested that each child say one thing about herself—something she did well. Each made at least one comment about her deceased parent and herself. Toward the end of the session, the girls seemed to be more comfortable with each other.

I then raised the issues of rules and confidentiality. They decided to keep their activities and discussions private, except when one of them wanted to share her experiences with her parent. I described my role with the girls and my involvement with their parents. I explained I would speak occasionally with their parents about some of the general themes they raised, but never give a word-for-word account. The meeting ended on an upbeat note.

I hoped that the peer-pairing modality would provide a supportive atmosphere for Joan and Roberta to share their feelings and experiences about their grieving process. In addition, the process might encourage friendship between the girls, and ultimately improve their socialization skills and self-confidence.

Preliminary Assessment and Treatment Plan

A psychosocial assessment of Roberta revealed a history of low self-esteem and long-standing peer and relationship problems. Her social problems were magnified by her mother's suicide, which increased her feelings of isolation and stigmatization.

Joan had a history of shy and withdrawn behavior and academic weaknesses in the school setting. Within her home environment, she tended to be more social. Several deaths in Joan's family, in addition to current family crises, increased her feelings of inadequacy, vulnerability, and isolation.

The treatment plan for both Joan and Roberta was for them to receive play therapy according to the peer-pairing model. The specific goals for Joan and Roberta were (1) to enable each girl to grieve for the dead parent; (2) to provide opportunities to develop increased socialization and friendship skills; and (3) to develop improved ways to resolve problems.

Contact with Roberta's and Joan's families was maintained. In Joan's case, the goals with Mrs. Vespa were (1) to educate her about Joan's style and pace of grieving, and to clarify how a child's grieving differs from an adult's; (2) to encourage separation between Joan and herself; and (3) to support her to be a more powerful and effective parent. In Roberta's case, the goals were to help the family understand her grieving process and, peripherally, to provide support for the family's mourning process.

Play Therapy Sessions

Session 4: Excerpt

Content of Session

JOAN: I really miss my dad.

THERAPIST: It must be hard.

ROBERTA: There's some kids in my class who are always bothering me. I hate them.

J: That's not very nice; they shouldn't do that. I feel bad for you!

R: Yeah. Charles, the boy I sit next to, he's always picking on me, calling me names, and I get yelled at by Mrs. Barton.

J: I'd hate that too!

T: It must be hard. Do you want us to help you figure out other ways to handle it?

R: OK.

T: Good! What do you do when they call you names? Oh, before I forget, I just wanted to say that one thing that's really great is that you two really support each other. Joan, you have a real nice way of supporting Roberta—that's a good friend. So what do you do when they call you names?

R: I try to ignore it, but then I sometimes call Charles names back.

T: I could understand; it's hard to ignore. It's also really difficult and hurtful to be picked on. It's not an easy problem. Joan, what do you think Roberta should do?

J: I don't know . . . mm . . . maybe switch seats. Yeah, ask the teacher if you can sit next to someone else because Charles keeps bothering you.

T: That's a good idea. What do you think, Roberta?

R: I can try it.

T: Let us know what the teacher says and if it works.

J: I really miss my daddy, but I never cry. I haven't cried once.

T: It sounds like you feel really sad. Do you want to cry?

J: No, I just miss him.

Rationale/Analysis

I am empathizing with Joan, but I now regret not identifying her sadness and longing for her father.

I am reassured by Joan's ability to support Roberta. I am somewhat concerned about using this treatment modality because of the heightened emotions centering around Roberta's mother's suicide.

I am trying to get their permission to heighten their motivation to be involved.

I am acknowledging their strength as friends.

I am empathizing by reflecting the feeling and the content. I am also encouraging shared problem solving.

Following through is important.

Joan wants and needs to express her sadness and grief. I am sad for Joan and feel confused about why she hasn't cried yet. In retrospect, Joan may be attempting to make it easier for her mother by giving her the impression that she is adequately coping with her father's death; or perhaps Joan hasn't felt safe enough to express her sadness.

R: I miss my mommy, and I cry when I'm trying to go to sleep.

Roberta, in this instance, is a role model for Joan.

T: It's really, really hard when a mommy or daddy dies. Naturally, you'd miss them. Roberta, does it help to cry?

R: I don't know. I just cry only in bed—that's when I think about her.

I feel so sad for Roberta. It is hard to think about these children's losses at such young ages.

T: It's OK to cry, to feel sad—that's what people feel when someone really close to them dies. It's really hard. It's good both of you can share your feelings with us.

I am normalizing their sadness. I am also acknowledging their ability to express their pain.

Session 8: Excerpt

Roberta and Joan were each completing a family tree picture. The following interaction occurred while they were coloring their pictures.

Content of Session	Rationale/Analysis
JOAN: I miss my daddy so much!	Joan is in the throes of grieving. She is experiencing intense emotion—pain, despair, loneliness. It is near Father's Day. I miss an opportunity to educate them that important holidays and anniversaries are triggers for their grief.
THERAPIST: It's so hard.	
ROBERTA: Sometimes I can't believe my mom is dead.	
T: I can imagine it must be difficult to think she's dead.	
J: Why did your mom kill herself?	I feel very protective toward Roberta when the suicide question is raised.
R: She had problems, was lonely, and kept her problems inside.	I am proud of the way Roberta is able to respond.
T: It's terrible that she could not find another way to deal with her problems.	It's important to give Roberta the message that there are other ways to deal with serious problems.
R: You're lucky your parents are not dead.	Maybe they think I don't understand.
T: You're right.	
R: It's really hard! Harder for a child than an adult!	Roberta is angry.
J: My daddy can't see me graduate and won't be able to walk me down the aisle when I get married.	Joan is angry too! She raises the theme that grief is an ongoing, lifelong process and is revisited at

T: It must hurt so much not to be able to share important things with your daddy.

important developmental milestones. I feel very touched by her examples.

R: How would you know? Your parents aren't dead.

Roberta is directing her anger at me.

T: I don't blame you for being angry. Sometimes it must look like I don't realize how lucky I am to have both my parents. I just take it for granted.

It is important to validate their anger. Anger is a natural emotion one feels when a parent dies.

J: How do *you* know what it's like?

T: I'm struggling with this. I need you to help me understand what it's like for *you*. Actually, I think you're letting me know how hard it is, how much it hurts, and how angry you feel.

I am trying to acknowledge and empathize with their pain.

R: Why do you want to talk about this?

T: That's a good question. I believe it helps children and adults deal with the loss better to share their feelings with others. I am trying to understand. I need your help.

This is an important message to repeat to Roberta—about how people cope with problems and difficult emotions.

J: I love my daddy so much!

T: Um-hm.

J: I wish I could die and be with my daddy. I miss him so much.

T: It must hurt to miss him so much and not be able to see him.

J: I wish I could be with him. (*Then on the family tree picture she writes, "I love my Dad so much I wish I could die and be with him." She shows Roberta and the therapist her picture, and then rips it up and throws it in the garbage.*)

I feel scared and overwhelmed by Joan's death wish. My own feelings make it hard for me to figure out how to respond to Joan in the session. In retrospect, Joan's wish may also be a clue that she has unfinished business. Another concern I have is how Roberta is interpreting Joan's death wish.

T: I'm sorry it's so painful.

R: Sometimes I can't believe that my mom is dead.

T: That's understandable. It is hard to believe that someone so close to you is dead.

I am trying to normalize her denial.

    I was very concerned that Joan's fantasy about joining her father was not just a wish, but possibly something she might try. I asked Joan to remain in my office following this session. I proceeded to evaluate whether she was a serious suicidal risk. Research by Rosenthal and Rosenthal (1984) reports that even preschoolers can have suicidal thoughts and are capable of suicidal behavior. Fox (1985, p. 16) states that "each bereaved child must be considered potentially at risk for suicide and any kind of communication that suggests such a possibility should be promptly and fully evaluated."

I stated to Joan that I could understand why she would wish to die and be with her daddy. I wondered what ideas she had about dying, due to her profound hurt, sadness, and loneliness. Had she thought about a way to die? If so, how often did she think about this? Had she told anyone about these thoughts? Joan's responses were all negative, and I felt reassured that she was not going to act on her feelings. I let her know that it was very healthy to share her thoughts and feelings with Roberta and me. I also stated to Joan, "It's important to let people you trust know how you feel."

I spoke with her mother and teachers, not directly about Joan's fantasy, but to learn whether Joan's speech or actions indicated that she might be more morose, angry, guilty, or confused. It was critical to know whether Joan had demonstrated any noticeable change in her behavior. Neither her teachers nor her mother had observed any such change, and none of them expressed any concern about Joan. I immediately discussed Joan's suicidal ideation and ongoing therapeutic work with a private clinical supervisor in a formal consultation meeting.

Session 15: Summary

Joan and Roberta decided to put on a puppet show. Their joint decision was prefaced by "We don't want to talk." Both girls felt that I had been pressuring them to express themselves through "talk." Roberta was experiencing denial, disbelief, and shock; Joan was experiencing intense feelings of anger and sadness. Both girls preferred and felt more comfortable with play, expressing themselves symbolically rather than directly.

The puppet play was about drugs, and the moral of their story was "Don't take illegal drugs." There were several puppet characters in the play, and all of them either died after taking drugs or were killed by a character who was a drug dealer. It is ironic that children often state that they do not want to talk about difficult feelings and thoughts, but then proceed to express their emotions symbolically through play. They cannot avoid their feelings of loss, which are "in their hearts, but seldom on their lips" (Weizman & Kamm, 1985, p. 180).

Session 16

Content of Session	Rationale/Analysis
THERAPIST (*excitedly and enthusiastically*): I was thinking about the play you put on last week. Maybe the two of you would like to do a sequel to the first play—you know how there's a *Rocky I*, then *Rocky II*. Well, I thought it was a great and creative play, and maybe you would like to put on another one.	My plan is to try to find a way through the play to help them deal with the death theme.
JOAN AND ROBERTA: (*responding simultaneously and enthusiastically*): Yeah!	
T: I was even thinking about an idea for your next play. How about pretending some of the	

characters who died or were killed could come back to life?

J (*with strong emotion, to Roberta*): Wouldn't you like it if your mom could come back?

R: Yeah.

J: This play is about people who died and come back for one day, but their families can't see them. But the dead people were ghosts, and they can see their families. The characters are John and Jane who died. [John and Jane are children.] Mr. and Mrs. Miller are their parents. [Miller is the name of Joan's teacher, whom she adores.] Hello and welcome to our show. This is the continuation of *Drug Part II*, written by Joan and Roberta.

R (*as parent*): Don't you wish our kids were back? I miss them a lot. (*Sobs aloud.*)

J (*as ghost*): I have a good idea. I could ask God to send their children back. Hello, God. How are you? Could you send John and Jane Miller to their parents? (*Switches to God's voice.*) Maybe I could. Well, probably yes. (*Switches back to ghost's voice.*) Because their parents really miss them. (*Speaks as God again.*) I'll send them. OK. (*Speaks as ghost again.*) Hey, I'm your children's ghost. Do you want to see your children?

R (*angrily*): Yes, how are you going to get them back to life?

J: Go get your wife, OK? God said they could come back for one more day. You want to see them. (*Switches to daughter's voice.*) Hey, Daddy (*very excitedly and lovingly*).

R (*as father, with disbelief and bewilderment*): Jane! John! I'm dreaming!

J: No, you're not. You want me to pinch you?

R: Yeah—Ouch! Honey, do you want to see the children?

J (*as child, full of joy and love*): Mommy! (*The puppets hug each other tightly.*)

R: Lord, thank you! Lord, thank you! (*Screams in horror, then relief.*)

I am pleased at how Joan and Roberta embrace the idea. When parents die suddenly, the bereaved need to create opportunities to say goodbye and work through any unfinished business. This play will give them the chance to meet these needs.

I am wondering whether this is how Joan connects with her father, as a ghost who is watching over her.

I am impressed by Roberta's ability to express her sadness.

She is really getting involved in this. It's exciting.

For Joan, it is as if she were seeing her own father.

I feel deeply moved by the girls' emotional intensity. It feels as if they were really seeing their dead parents again.

J: We can only come back for one day.

R: Thank you, Lord. (*Puppets hug each other tightly.*) Well, what do you want to do? Want to see your friends?

J: Missy! Sandy! [These characters are friends of Jane and John.] Remember us?

R: You're dead!

J: No, we're not, we're alive for one day. Let's go to the sweet shop. (*The scene changes to the sweet shop.*)

J (*as drug dealer*): You want some sugar? It's in this little bottle.

R: I don't know. My mom won't let me have sugar.

J: Just take it.

R: She gets so furious when she sees candy in my room.

J: Take it. It's really good.

R: OK.

J: Here's some more.

R: Mmm . . . It's good.

J: Ha, ha, ha, ha. I sold them drugs and they didn't even know it.

R (*gagging and throwing up*): What kind of sugar is this? This is rotten sugar.

J: Ha! Ha! We fooled you. It's drugs.

I suspect that one of Joan's siblings has a drug problem and that she is struggling with this problem. I do not follow up on this with Joan or her mother, because in the past it has been too threatening for them to talk to me about family problems (brother's plight). I now regret not exploring my suspicions with Joan indirectly through play therapy.

R (*sobbing and screaming aloud*): And their whole family cried. Did you hear what happened to Sandy and Missy?

J: Yeah, we killed them. And we'll kill you, too. Bang, bang—bang, bang!

R: What are you doing?

J: I'm doing what I was taught to do, Dad (*with strong anger*).

R: God is going to send you back.

J: God, we don't want to hear any more. Send us back.

T: Is it the end?

R: No! It's not the end. So eat your popcorn.

Throughout the play, Roberta expresses feelings of sadness. This is symbolic of her feelings toward her mother.

J (*killing the parents and saying to Roberta*): I hate you, I really do, I hate your guts. Go away from me.

R: Is it the end?

J: God, I'm sorry that I asked you to send them down to see their parents, because they killed their parents too.

R: Is it the end now?

J: No! (*Starts singing.*) I wish I was dead, I can't forget. I really wish I was dead because someone is bothering me about the end of the story. I wish I was dead, dead, dead! That pig is such a jerk.

R (*as a pig puppet*): I'm not a jerk!

J: I wish I was dead, dead, dead!

R: So do I, because you are a pain in the neck.

J: Well, I'm going to kill myself right now.

R (*with pained expression*): Oh, don't do that, don't do that, don't do that!

J: (*Falls down and dies.*)

R (*forcefully*): You know something? This is boring. The end!

T: That was a very strong play. I'm concerned about this last piece when Joan said she wanted to kill herself and Roberta responded very forcefully. I wonder if it reminded you of your mother?

R: Yes.

J: I'm sorry, I didn't mean that.

R: I want the next play to be in heaven. OK, Joan?

J: Yeah.

T: This was a very difficult ending, and of course Joan didn't mean anything about Roberta's mother. Are you OK, Roberta?

R: Yeah. Next week the play is in heaven.

I know it's helpful for Joan to express her rage, but it's really hard for me to take in this level of pain.

I think Roberta is having trouble hearing Joan's rage, too. I should have intervened by supporting and validating Joan's rage and acknowledging Roberta's difficulty in listening to her pain.

The death theme is all-pervasive. I believe that it is difficult for Joan to tolerate her feelings of rage and loss, and her death wish surfaces. The only thing that will ease her pain is to rejoin her dad.

Instinctively, Roberta tries to save Joan. Roberta plays out her wish to stop her mother from killing herself. I regret not tuning in to her feelings of anger and powerlessness.

Children often use "boredom" to avoid feelings.

Roberta creates closure by taking control.

I wonder, in retrospect, whether I could have said something about when people *really* want to kill themselves, nobody can stop them (to relieve Roberta of her guilt about her mother).

Session 17

Content of Session

THERAPIST: At the end of the last session, Roberta suggested we put on another play about being in

Rationale/Analysis

After stating, "I listened to the last play," I should ask (but do not) for heaven. I listened to the last play [it was taped], and it was a *very* powerful play with lots of action, feelings, and surprises. I realized that Joan really directed the last play and both of you acted in it. Since Joan was the director for the last play, it would be a good idea to let Roberta be the director this time. OK?

JOAN: All right.

ROBERTA: Yeah. This play is about someone that goes up to heaven.

T: Roberta, you need to give directions to Joan.

R: Joan, why don't you be the rabbit and bunny? The first scene is in heaven.

J: The rabbit and bunny are eating carrots.

R: I don't know what the next scene should be.

T: What do you want to happen next? You want to describe what heaven's like?

R: Yeah. Heaven's like—it's a beautiful day, everything is all white. It's never nighttime. We can go to sleep when we want to.

J: (*Hums in background.*)

R: Do you hear something? Who's that? I don't know what to do.

T: Do you want me to help you?

R: Yeah.

T: Why don't you talk more about heaven, and I'll be the person who comes to visit heaven?

J: It's nice up here.

R: What do you want to do today?

J: I don't know.

R: I have no idea.

J: I'll do what you want to do.

R: I'll do what you want to do.

J: It's your play.

T: Joan's being cooperative about letting you be the director. I know it's awkward for you, Roberta, but you can do it! Take charge and be the director.

---

any feelings and thoughts they have about the last play. I do strongly suggest Roberta as the director, in part for therapeutic reasons—to help her deal with her feelings of powerlessness and helplessness, which relate to her mother's suicide. She wants to create a play in heaven, perhaps to confront her unfinished business with her mother and her need to understand why her death occurred. My other motive is to encourage the girls to take turns and share more equally in their play.

I am encouraging Roberta to be in charge.

She needs some help.

I ask for permission.

They both really seem blocked. It must be frightening to them.

Roberta usually follows Joan's lead, and I purposely encourage her to take the initiative and assert herself more.

R: OK. Let's go play on the swings.

T (*as person visiting heaven*): Hi, there!

R (*fearful*): Who's that?

T: Don't be afraid. My name is Judy. This is my first visit to heaven.

R: How did you get up here?

She is asking about how I died.

T: I walked up those imaginary steps to heaven. Can I tell you a little story about myself? I had these really good friends. They both died, and I've been missing them a lot, and every night I pray to God, and I cry myself to sleep, and I think about these friends a lot. I've been really missing my friends so much. I just wanted one more chance to see them. I think God answered my prayers, and He said I could come up and see them one more time. I'm looking for John and Jane. (*John and Jane appear.*) Hi, John! Hi, Jane! I'm so happy to see you guys! I couldn't believe you guys had died!

I'm incorporating Roberta's own words about how she expresses her sadness into the play. I want them to know that being sad and crying are normal and necessary.

J: Thank you, God, for letting our friend Judy up here.

R: Yeah, for one day.

J: Are you sure this isn't a dream?

R: Yeah.

T: I've been thinking a lot about you. I've been so lonely and sad without you. I've been feeling terrible.

J: How is it on earth?

T: It is spring on earth. It's beautiful right now. I can't wait for summer—swimming, no school, bicycle riding, playing with my friends!

R: But, Judy, we can do whatever we want here.

Roberta and Joan really take me by surprise as they suggest that heaven is the ultimate place to live. I really have to think fast! They raise the question that often arises in the bereaved's mind: Is life worth living after someone you love dies? Children need an affirmation of the priority of life over death!

J: We don't have to go to sleep. You have to go to school, and we don't.

T: Heaven seems like a wonderful place, and I'm relieved because it seems like you're happy and I was worried about you. But I'm really looking forward to earth things—playing with my friends, swimming—I can't wait!

J: Now you are happy without us! You have more friends!

Perhaps I have missed the opportunity to address and identify Joan's anger toward her father. Joan feels deserted and abandoned.

T: You think I don't miss you? Even though I think being alive is wonderful, it doesn't feel the same without you.

J: Then why don't you die and come up here and live with us?

R: Up here, if you want it to be spring, you just wish it, and it comes true.

J: We can wish your birthday.

T: I see what you mean. And, believe me, part of me wants to be with you. I think it's not the best for me. I really, really wish you didn't die.

J: You can't die up here.

R: Yeah, let's wish for candy.

J: Candy, candy, candy.

I realize that Joan's fantasy of reunion with her father is resurfacing.

T: It's hard, what you're talking about. It's not that I don't want to be with you. I miss you so much it hurts. But one thing I figured out since you died is that my memories, my wonderful memories of you, help me. They really help me when I feel sad. Remember when we went to Great Adventures? Wasn't it great?

R: No.

J: It was boring.

R: Up here you can see all these neat things. You should see the rides up here!

T: Yeah, tell me about heaven! What's wonderful about heaven?

R: You can do whatever you want.

J: You can stay up 'til whenever you want.

R: You don't get grounded.

T: Those are pretty good things.

R: Everyone is nice up here.

T: Aha.

R: No one bosses us around.

T: It makes me feel good to hear that you are so happy.

R: What do you want to do next?

My discussion about realistic memories is intended to guide Joan, who is having trouble tolerating them through her grief. One needs to remember in order to negotiate and renegotiate the meaning of the loss over time.

Joan and Roberta still need to talk about heaven. I need to slow down and "be where my clients are."

They are struggling with key questions about death: What happens to people when they die? Where do they go, and what is it like? What does it feel like to be dead?

T: I'm really glad to see that you're both OK. I also wanted to tell you a few things I didn't get a chance to say. I really like both of you. You mean the world to me. It really tears me . . .

I am saying my final goodbye.

J (interrupting): Ah, you're just saying that (in disbelief).

Joan is having trouble tolerating the sadness of the pain of the final goodbye.

T: Let me tell you something. I wouldn't walk all the way up heaven's staircase if I didn't mean it. Every night I think about you guys . . .

R (interrupting, with bored and annoyed expression): OK, OK, let's have fun together, enough talking. (Everyone starts dancing and singing.) Wait a second. I just figured out something. You never have to go down there again, because you see . . .

J (interrupting, with excitement): I have a good idea. Let's ask God if she can stay up here forever!

T: Wait, wait, I don't think I want to.

R: You don't?

J AND R (in unison, both moaning and sighing): Oh! Oh!

R: Why not?

J: Because she wants to be with her other friends and family.

T: Even though I love you guys so much, and I feel so terrible that you guys are dead, and I'm glad you're happy up here, I want to go back home.

J (with excitement): Wait a second! Let's take a picture of all of us!

T: That's a great idea! (Therapist and girls pretend to be taking pictures, and then give each other copies.) This is a very, very special picture to me. I just want to clear something up. Jane, we had a fight 2 days before you died, and I was just feeling terrible about it. I just wanted to make sure you weren't angry at me.

R: I thought we cleared it up the next day.

T: I was feeling guilty.

R: Don't worry. Let's have a fun time!

J: Let's sing a song. (Therapist and girls sing some songs together that the girls learned in the school chorus. Then Joan writes a song and sings it to the therapist.) Oh, Judy, you're my friend. / And I wish you could stay, / But it's too far away. / And so I think you're so funny, / And my friend wants to be your honey.

R: Bye, Judy (crying).

J: Bye (crying).

T: Just remember I'll never, never forget you! The end.

It's too painful for Roberta as well. I regret not acknowledging how saying goodbye is very painful and so deeply sad, and how "normal" it is not to want to feel this level of pain.

Joan is expressing acceptance about the choice of life—a reason to want to live. I am helping them choose life over death, precariously creating a balance between the beauty of heaven and the even better deal on earth.

I am recognizing any guilty feelings either of them might be feeling.

Throughout this play, Joan in particular is dealing with saying goodbye.

I am so touched by their ability to say goodbye with real feeling.

I am moved to tears!

As a follow-up to the plays, I stated to Joan and Roberta: "The wonderful thing about making plays is that we can create all kinds of fantasies. We can pretend anything, as we just did—going to heaven and speaking to someone who died. Sometimes pretending and imagining make us feel better. That is what movies and books are also all about. It is important to remember that it is 'pretend,' not real life."

Review of the Peer Play Therapy Sessions

The therapy sessions were instrumental in encouraging Roberta and Joan to express their feelings gradually, on a weekly basis, and to begin to work slowly through their loss. One of the key ingredients in helping the children grieve was creating a safe environment that would allow the girls to symbolically express their emotions. I helped create a safe milieu by conveying my unconditional belief in the children's worth and value, by listening carefully to them, and by trusting the therapeutic process. Through the use of play therapy, Roberta and Joan were able to express a range of emotions; I was able to identify the painful emotions, and to normalize and validate their feelings and anxieties.

The treatment modality of peer pairing encouraged a budding friendship that increased each girl's feelings of self-worth and improved her social skills. Joan and Roberta shared feelings and experiences that allowed them to feel less lonely in their suffering. Also in the sessions, they struggled with new ways to resolve peer and family problems. It was particularly important for Roberta to understand that there are alternatives to suicide for dealing with serious personal problems.

As stated earlier, the surviving parent or guardian is critical in a latency-age child's ability to work through her grief. As Mishne (1983, p. 206) states, "given the child's complete dependency on home and family, the supports or obstacles within the family must be regarded as most significant." Although I worked with each child's surviving parent, I did not work with the entire family. The optimal treatment plan should include family therapy, so that the therapist can help all family members work through the stress related to sudden death or suicide. When the family is helped to grieve, the latency-age child benefits.

However, in a school setting, the focus is on the child. The school social worker is greatly limited in opportunities to conduct ongoing family therapy. Nevertheless, as a school social worker, I provide referrals to families for family treatment with the appropriate mental health agency or community resource.

FOLLOW-UP: JOAN AND ROBERTA, 8 YEARS LATER

According to her school guidance counselor, Joan graduated from high school with a B average. She was accepted into a reputable out-of-state college and was awarded a scholarship. Socially, Joan participated in a variety of school and community activities. She had a circle of friends with whom she felt respected and liked.

Interestingly, Joan continued to be excessively shy with adults and quiet in the classroom setting. Her mother reported to the counselor that Joan was expressive and open at home, in contrast to the way she related in the school setting.

Clearly Joan was able to overcome her academic difficulties, although the school psychologist had reported that Joan's grief was affecting her intellectual functioning in fourth grade. Joan also continued to work through her separation issues with her mother, enabling her to attend a college away from home. Despite her shyness, Joan was able to function quite well in the school setting, participating in activities and maintaining a solid group of friendships.

Although Joan had been guarded and easily threatened in the individual counseling sessions with me, she felt safe enough in the peer therapy dyad to express her pain and despair. Joan was often assertive in the peer therapy and provided direction for her treatment. In the safety of the peer therapy dyad, Joan was expressive, open, and direct. She demonstrated insight, empathy, and positive problem-solving skills. Her comfort and confidence with peers were exemplified in her relationship with Roberta. This therapy experience was a positive and healing one for Joan. Joan's mother and siblings seemed to be a strong support for her, despite their own grief and crises. I imagine that they provided enough stability, support, and love to help Joan through her adolescent years and with her ongoing grief reactions.

I remember that when Joan was in fifth grade, she expressed how her father's death would have an impact on important milestones in her life. I can only imagine that she thought of her father often as she graduated. I am sure it was a moment in her life filled with much happiness, pride, and hope, yet at the same time mixed with sadness, anger, and longing. This attests to the notion that a child's relationship with a dead parent is ongoing and renegotiated over one's lifetime.

Eight years after the peer therapy sessions, Roberta was a high school senior, and her guidance counselor described her as a "high-risk" student. She had recently been diagnosed with major depression and prescribed antidepressant medication, which she did not take consistently. Although Roberta had the ability to perform academically, she was in danger of not graduating due to her poor attendance. She was extremely lonely and didn't have any close friends. Roberta had a bad temper and could not be trusted to keep confidences. She was sexually promiscuous and had unprotected sex. She also drove her car recklessly.

The school counselor reported that Roberta identified strongly with her mother. She was extremely angry at her father and blamed him for her mother's suicide. When Roberta felt overwhelmed and emotionally low, she would say she understood why her mother resorted to suicide. According to the counselor, Roberta's academic work and social functioning were both uneven. A year earlier, by contrast, Roberta had been attending school regularly, achieving fair grades, and connecting more with her peers.

An interplay among several factors apparently contributed to Roberta's high-risk status. These factors included the family system, the social/cultural context, ongoing death-related issues, and Roberta's personal characteristics.

Historically, the level of stress in Roberta's family was high. Prior to her mother's suicide, Roberta had been coping with her parents' marital separation and her mother's psychiatric hospitalization with suicidal ideation. Roberta had also had her own continuing problems with peers and suffered from low self-esteem. Although my contact with Roberta's family after the suicide was minimal, my impression was that her family had trouble providing a stable and secure home for Roberta. According to Worden (1996, p. 95), "The functioning level of the surviving parent is the most powerful predictor of a child's adjustment to the death. Children with a less well-functioning parent will show more anxiety and depression, and sleep and health problems." In Roberta's case, her father was intellectually limited and emotionally wrought with grief and guilt. Her maternal grandmother was an important female role model, but she was also emotionally devastated by her own sense of loss and guilt. There were guilt-fueled tensions and conflict between Roberta's father and grandmother; each blamed the other for the suicide.

Given that Roberta's mother's death was a suicide, Roberta was (and remains) "at greater risk for suicide and depression" in her future (Hurley, 1991, p. 238). Webb (1993) believes that the way in which a parent dies contributes to the risk level of the bereaved child. These death-related factors include whether the death is sudden; whether it is untimely; whether there is a perception that it might have been prevented; whether it was accompanied by trauma, pain, and violence; and whether there is a stigma. Because all of these factors were present in Roberta's mother's suicide, Roberta's denial and anxiety levels could be high. These factors could also "complicate the grief process and compound reactions of guilt and anger in all of the survivors" (Webb, 1993, p. 36).

It would thus seem that Roberta's limited family support, her mother's suicide, her long-standing peer and relationship difficulties, and her low self-esteem inhibited her ability to work through her grief. All these factors contributed to Roberta's problems as a high school senior facing the challenges of adolescence. Adolescence is a stormy period, raging with turbulence and fraught with physical, social, and psychological upheavals. Under the best of conditions in a stable home environment, the adolescent experiences life with heightened intensity. For the adolescent whose life has been complicated by instability, the struggles can be desperate and literally a question of life and death.

Psychologically separating from parental ties and establishing a self-identity are the most agonizing parts of the adolescent struggle. Roberta's ability to separate was severely compromised. Her inability to resolve conflicts with her father, as well as her struggles in understanding her mother's suicide and reevaluating their relationship, hampered her separation process. She was very angry at her father and overidentified with her mother. Her anger, acting out, and self-destructive behavior were Roberta's ways of breaking away from her dependent ties. Underlying her behavior, depression, and anger, Roberta was suffering from disabling grief.

The peer group is a powerful force in a teenager's life. Roberta's inability to maintain friendships only heightened her rejected, abandoned, and unloved feelings. At a time when being accepted and liked by peers is of the utmost importance, Roberta felt intense loneliness and stigmatization. These emotions reverberated throughout Roberta's adolescence and continually reminded her that her mother had committed suicide.

Roberta was failing at school, failing at relationships outside her family, and failing at preparing for her future. Her upcoming graduation and the demands of adolescence were overwhelming her coping abilities. Roberta's grief was interfering in her social, emotional, and intellectual development. She was in crisis and at risk for suicide. "A number of causal factors are associated with adolescent suicide: depression, stress associated with education and achievement, family problems and peer problems" (Longres, 1995, p. 500). Unfortunately, each of these factors applied to Roberta's situation.

Fortunately, however, Roberta was receiving support from the school system and utilizing all of its resources. When I spoke with her guidance counselor, she was in therapy with the school psychologist and had regular contact with the social worker and other school professionals. I hope that despite her depression and self-destructive behaviors, Roberta can continue to reach out for the help she needs as she matures.

STUDY QUESTIONS

1. Discuss the appropriate procedure to follow when a child expresses suicide ideation. Comment on the response of the school social worker with regard to Joan's verbalized death wish.

2. Compare and contrast the therapist's role in the 16th and 17th play therapy sessions. Describe the therapeutic value for Joan and Roberta when the social worker was more direct in her approach during the 17th session.

3. How did the play therapy techniques encourage the children to grieve? Describe the function of symbolic communication in the therapeutic process, using specific illustrations from the case.

4. If you were the school social worker, how would you have referred Joan's family for family therapy?

5. How can a social worker best deal with personal feelings and reactions when working with a child whose parent killed herself?

6. Do you think that other therapeutic interventions could have been implemented by the school social worker to help Roberta? If you were Roberta's high school social worker, how would you intervene with a treatment plan and/or a referral for Roberta's high-risk profile?

REFERENCES

Baker, J. E., Sedney, M. A., & Gross, E. (1992). Psychological tasks for bereaved children. *American Journal of Orthopsychiatry, 62*(1), 105–116.

Bowlby, J. (1960). Grief and mourning in infancy and early childhood. *Psychoanalytic Study of the Child, 15,* 9–52.

Bowlby, J. (1963). Pathological mourning and childhood mourning. *Journal of the American Psychoanalytical Association, 11,* 500–541.

Bowlby, J. (1980). *Attachment and loss: Vol. 3. Loss*. New York: Basic Books.

Cain, A. C. (Ed.). (1972). *Survivors of suicide*. Springfield, IL: Charles C Thomas.

Cain, A. C., & Fast, I. (1972). Children's disturbed reactions to parent suicide: Distortion and guilt, communication and identification. In A. C. Cain (Ed.), *Survivors of suicide* (pp. 93–111). Springfield, IL: Charles C Thomas.

Cameron, N. (1963). *Personality development and psychopathology*. Boston: Houghton Mifflin.

Eth, S., & Pynoos, R. S. (1985). *Post-traumatic stress disorder in children*. Washington, DC: American Psychiatric Press.

Fox, S. S. (1985). *Good grief: Helping groups of children when a friend dies*. Boston: New England Association for the Education of Young Children.

Freud, S. (1957). Mourning and melancholia. In J. Strachey (Ed. and Trans.), *The standard edition of the complete psychological works of Sigmund Freud* (Vol. 14, pp. 237–260). London: Hogarth Press. (Original work published 1917)

Freud, S. (1958). Remembering, repeating and working through. In J. Strachey (Ed. and Trans.), *The standard edition of the complete psychological works of Sigmund Freud* (Vol. 12, pp. 147–156). London: Hogarth Press. (Original work published 1914)

Grossberg, S. H., & Crandall, L. (1978). Father loss and father absence in preschool children. *Clinical Social Work Journal*, 6(2), 123–134.

Hurley, D. J. (1991). The crisis of parental suicide: Case of Cathy, age 4½. In N. B. Webb (Ed.), *Play therapy with children in crisis: A casebook for practitioners* (pp. 237–253). New York: Guilford Press.

Johnson, S. W., & Maile, L. J. (1987). *Suicide and the schools: A handbook for prevention, intervention and rehabilitation*. Springfield, IL: Charles C Thomas.

Klass, D., Silverman, P. R., & Nickman, S. L. (1996). *Continuing bonds*. Washington, DC: Taylor & Francis.

Kübler-Ross, E. (1969). *On death and dying*. New York: Macmillan.

Lieberman, F. (1979). *Social work with children*. New York: Free Press.

Lonetto, R. (1980). *Children's conceptions of death*. New York: Springer.

Longres, J. F. (1995). *Human behavior in the social environment*. Itasca, IL: F. E. Peacock.

Mervis, B. A. (1985). The use of peer-pairing in child psychotherapy. *Social Work*, 30(2), 124–128.

Mishne, J. (1983). Clinical work with children. *American Journal of Psychiatry*, 141, 520–525.

Nagera, H. (1970). Children's reactions to the death of important objects: A developmental approach. *Psychoanalytic Study of the Child*, 25, 360–400.

Nagy, M. (1948). The child's theories concerning death. *Journal of Genetic Psychology*, 73, 3–7.

Rosenthal, P., & Rosenthal, S. (1984). Suicidal behavior by preschool children. *American Journal of Psychiatry*, 141, 520–525.

Sarnoff, C. (1978). *On latency*. New York: Jason Aronson.

Silverman, P. R. (1987). The impact of parental death on college-age women. *Psychiatric Clinics of North America*, 10, 387–404.

Webb, N. B. (Ed.). (1993). *Helping bereaved children: A handbook for practitioners*. New York: Guilford Press.

Weizman, S. G., & Kamm, P. (1985). *About mourning: Support and guidance for the bereaved*. New York: Human Sciences Press.

Wolfelt, A. (1983). *Helping children cope with grief*. Muncie, IN: Accelerated Development.

Wolfenstein, M. (1966). How is mourning possible? *Psychoanalytic Study of the Child*, 21, 93–123.

Worden, J. W. (1996). *Children and grief*. New York: Guilford Press.

CHAPTER 11

A Suicide Threat Uncovers Multiple Family Problems

Case of Philip, Age 8, Evaluated in a Psychiatric
Emergency Room

JANE PRICE OSUNA
NANCY BOYD WEBB

The impact of divorce on a child is as variable as the circumstances before, during, and after the dissolution of the parents' marriage. Even in the best of circumstances, divorce causes stress to all family members. The response of individual children will depend on their general level of adjustment, plus the specific factors surrounding the marital breakdown. The rupture of family structure and relationships accompanying divorce usually precipitates major changes in a child's life, frequently involving reduced contact with one parent, possibly a change of residence, and sometimes a change of school. Although the adults may view divorce as a necessary and positive solution to an unsatisfying and untenable relationship, young children experience this changed status as a crisis that seriously threatens their stability and well-being.

The case discussed in this chapter is that of Philip, an 8-year-old African American male whose parents had been separated for 4 years and divorced for 2 years, resulting in a 6-year absence of reliable and consistent parenting by two biological parents. He resided with his maternal grandmother, his mother, and his half-sister in a one-bedroom inner-city apartment. Philip was referred to the psychiatric emergency room by his school for an evaluation by the child and adolescent crisis intervention team of a large municipal hospital. The school reported that Philip had expressed a wish to kill himself, and that he actually had begun to carry out the threat by opening a window and preparing to jump.

PSYCHIATRIC EMERGENCIES

A child and adolescent crisis intervention team (such as the one of which Jane Price Osuna was a member at the time Philip was seen) is generally composed of two child psychiatrists and four social workers. Cases are referred to the team from a variety of sources, such as schools, courts, police, other hospital emergency rooms, and ambulance personnel. Initial referrals occur either as "walk-ins" or by telephone.

When a child is referred by telephone, the team determines whether the case is an emergency requiring immediate evaluation or whether an appointment can be scheduled within the next several days. If a child is actively suicidal, homicidal, or psychotic, an evaluation is arranged as soon as possible, since the child is at risk of harming self or others and may need psychiatric hospitalization. Usually the team does not have the luxury of *scheduling* appointments, since the majority of children and adolescents are brought directly into the psychiatric emergency room, without any prior notification to the team.

As part of the evaluation process, team members interview all family members who accompany the child to the emergency room. The child is interviewed both with his or her family members and alone, since this provides the opportunity to observe the child's behavior in both constellations. In addition to family members, team members interview any other adults who bring the child to the emergency room (such as school personnel, group home staff members, and foster parents).

The actual face-to-face interview is supplemented with additional information from any relevant source, since it is important to ascertain how the child functions in his or her varying environments and whether there have been any noticeable variations in behavior, mood, and/or interactions with others (and, if so, the timing of these changes).

An important factor to be assessed throughout the entire initial interview with the child and his or her family and support systems is whether the child needs hospitalization or whether outpatient crisis intervention will be sufficient. If the determination is for crisis intervention as the mode of treatment, a major disruption to the child's life is avoided, since this does not separate the child from his or her familiar home and school environment.

Coming to this determination involves a careful assessment of the child's psychological disturbance and his or her potential for harm to self or others. Even when a child is experiencing a significant amount of psychological stress and may actually be psychotic or suicidal, the child will be allowed to remain at home if the family support system is strong and willing to engage in crisis intervention treatment. In such a case, it is assumed that the family is reasonably capable of following through with therapeutic recommendations.

Separating a child from the family is an undesirable option, since the separation is frequently traumatizing. An example of a situation in which the separation from the family is therapeutically indicated is the overly enmeshed family, in which boundaries are so poorly distinguished that removal of the child from the parent(s) would facilitate treatment. Another instance is a family that lacks an adequate support system (e.g., the family that is burdened by a myriad of problems, and is therefore unable or unwilling to provide the commitment to the child that is essential during this crisis period).

CRISIS INTERVENTION

Treatment actually begins during the intake/evaluation process. Once a determination has been made that crisis intervention is the treatment of choice, the length of the initial contact varies from 1 to approximately 4–5 hours. As Golan (1978, p. 81) states,

> Crisis intervention does not lend itself to neat marking off into the study, diagnosis, treatment planning, treatment, and termination/evaluation steps of the casework process. Instead we speak simply of beginning, middle, and ending phases. They may all take place within a single three hour interview or may be spaced out over several months.

The intent of the crisis intervention is to restore the child to his or her precrisis level of functioning; however, during crisis periods individuals and their families often accomplish more than this circumscribed intent. The high level of discomfort during a crisis not only motivates resolution of the presenting problem, but also permits exploration of underlying factors contributing to the crisis. Treatment may last from two to eight sessions. These are briefer than the initial interview, yet usually longer in duration than the traditional 45-minute psychotherapy session. The initial contact/interview on a team is usually conducted by a social worker, who consults with a child psychiatrist and/or other team members while the interview is in progress and during daily clinical rounds. The team and/or psychiatrist may also offer diagnostic impressions and may participate directly in the ongoing interview once it resumes. Crisis intervention in the hospital emergency room is interdisciplinary and collaborative in nature.

Appointments for follow-up sessions are scheduled at the conclusion of the initial interview. Occasionally a parent may object either to the particular appointment time or to the frequency of the appointments; this may indicate resistance on the family's part and denial of the seriousness of the crisis. Each appointment is made in close proximity to the preceding appointment. The philosophy of crisis intervention dictates a brief amount of time, with an intensive effort to resolve the immediate crisis and return the child and his or her family to their prior level of functioning.

Having briefly described the crisis intervention approach and its application within a psychiatric setting, we now return to the case of Philip. This case highlights three important issues: (1) the effects of divorce on latency-age children, (2) the effects of physical maltreatment on children's development, and (3) the management of suicidal behavior in latency-age children.

Philip was 2 years old and in the Oedipal stage of development when his father left the family. During this phase of development, a child senses that the mother's attention and her warm, soothing touch are not exclusively devoted to him or her. The mother must be shared with the father, and therefore the child is jealous and resentful. He or she would like to be rid of the father. What wish fulfillment young Philip must have experienced when his father actually left the family at this point in his life, giving him much to ponder in later years! Did his jealous wishes cause his father to leave the family? Although Philip, at age 2, was not cognitively aware of the separation or of its significance to his sense of family identity, the foundation for conflict was laid at this time.

Contradictory feelings of love and anger need to be reconciled during the Oedipal period of development. In Philip's case, it is probable that reconciliation was not achieved because of his father's departure. Thus his feelings of hostility toward his father were not adequately resolved during the Oedipal stage, further complicating his sense of identity as a male.

EFFECTS OF DIVORCE ON LATENCY-AGE CHILDREN

It is common for latency-age children to blame themselves for their parents' divorce (Wallerstein & Kelly, 1980; Wallerstein & Blakeslee, 1989). However, in Philip's case this seed of blame had been implanted at an early stage of his life, intertwined with a young child's normal narcissistic wish to have the mother all to himself or herself. This was complicated further by Philip's later wish in latency for his parents' reconciliation. Instead, however, Philip's mother was dating other men and expecting him to accompany her on these excursions. What a psychological dilemma for a young child, as evidenced by Philip's suicidal ideation and gesture!

Weiss (1979) refers to the negative effects of divorce on young children, who learn to suppress their need for their parents' nurturance while becoming prematurely aware of adult concerns. Emery (1988) emphasizes the dynamic of loss and perceived loyalty conflicts when such a child lives in a single-parent family. The precipitants of Philip's gesture and expressed ideation appeared to be connected with actual events in his family life that had occurred prior to the incident. These details are discussed later in the chapter.

EFFECTS OF PHYSICAL MALTREATMENT ON CHILDREN'S DEVELOPMENT

The circumstances that lead up to a divorce may have considerable influence on a child's later adjustment. In some cases children have witnessed and/or experienced extensive parental conflict, including physical and emotional abuse. This unfortunately was true in Philip's case. Camara and Resnick (1988) state that "the methods for resolving conflict in families, rather than the presence or absence of conflict, may be predictive of child health and adjustment" (p.171). As we shall see, there were repeated and serious cases of physical fighting between Philip's parents, and both the father and mother had also abused Philip. In situations such as these, children learn from their parents that physical force is a method for dealing with frustration and disagreement.

Exposure to parental conflict can lead to long-term difficulties, including impaired social adjustment (Camara & Resnick, 1988), lowered self-esteem (Camara & Resnick, 1988), withdrawn behavior (Cicchetti, Rogosch, Lynch, & Holt, 1993), and scapegoating by peers (Cicchetti et al., 1993). Boys in single-parent, mother-headed homes are particularly at risk for lowered self-esteem (Camara & Resnick, 1988), which might well have been a factor in Philip's case. Certainly Philip's situation combined the stressful components of loss (typical in all divorce situations) with the depressing and demoralizing effects of witnessing and experiencing physical abuse by both of his parents.

Several studies point to the insidious effects of maltreatment on children's social adjustment (Cicchetti et al., 1993; Dodge, Pettit, & Bates, 1994). Maltreated children were reported in one study to evidence more withdrawn and maladaptive ("internalizing") behavior than their nonmaltreated agemates (Cicchetti et al., 1993). In a different study, Dodge et al. (1994) found that maltreated children were more likely to experience social failure and ostracism in their peer groups. They explained this as related to a probable disruption in the children's attachment relationships caused by the maltreatment, with future impact on the children's ability to trust in future relationships, including those with peers. Again, we note that the immediate precipitant of Philip's suicidal gesture was an insult from one of his peers, which might have stirred up anxious feelings associated with his lowered self-esteem and his past abuse experiences.

SUICIDE THREATS IN LATENCY-AGE CHILDREN

A suicide threat is always a matter of grave concern, and when it occurs in a latency-age child it merits very careful assessment. Pfeffer (1986) indicates that although suicide rates for latency-age children have gradually increased over time, the actual number of suicides in this age group remains low. An explanation for the lower rate of completed suicide among young children includes Schaffer's (1974) view that the association between affective illness and suicide is less prevalent in children than in adults. Another possible theory is that children are basically less isolated than adults and therefore receive greater emotional support, thus reducing their chances of completing suicide. A third hypothesis is that children are not psychologically mature enough to experience hopelessness and despair, since these feeling states develop with abstract thinking in adolescence.

Although suicide in children under the age of 12 is infrequent, suicidal ideas, threats, and attempts nonetheless deserve attention. Children who have attempted or completed suicide do so often in response to what Pfeffer (1986) labels a "disciplinary crisis." A child's suicide threat is often perceived as a desperate attempt to change a frightening situation. This was confirmed and dramatized in Philip's suicide threat and gesture.

A careful assessment of suicidal risk must follow a child's expressed ideation or gesture. The evaluation/interview should consider the degree of risk while exploring with the family the external events that preceded the ideation or gesture. The meaning behind the child's gesture must be explored. Often suicide has been referred to as a "cry for help." We must ask these questions: To whom is this cry addressed? And how can we help this person listen?

Both verbal and nonverbal modes of interviewing may be employed with a child. However, the verbal interview should be the preferred mode, because encouraging verbal expression provides the child with a method of communicating his or her problems other than acting on the impulse, and this alternative may reduce the risk of suicide.

Basic questions need to be explored with suicidal children, to assess the degree of intent as evidenced in their suicidal thoughts and behavior. These include the existence of a plan, the lethality of the chosen method, and the access to the means for carrying it out.

It is essential to obtain a promise in the form of a contract with the child not to cause any harm to himself or herself for a specific period of time. If the child is not able to make this commitment, or if the evaluator has *any* doubts about the sincerity of the child's promise, the child's protection must be guaranteed, either by the parents or by hospitalization. The family members' support and cooperation must be elicited in creating a safe environment for their child. We ask that they secure all potentially lethal objects and medications. If there appears to be resistance either to complying with the contract or to creating a safe home environment, then it may become necessary to consider hospitalizing the child.

In summary, Philip's case illustrates issues how a child's unresolved conflicts can serve as a backdrop to suicidal ideation and gestures.

THE CASE: PHILIP, AGE 8

Family Information

Philip was an 8-year-old African American male who resided at home with his 32-year-old mother, Jennifer; his 55-year-old maternal grandmother, Vanessa; and his 4-year-old half-sister, Tanisha. Both adults were unemployed, and the family received public assistance. The maternal grandmother was a recipient of Social Security disability, as she had a history of psychosis, which was currently in remission.

Neither Tanisha's nor Philip's fathers provided any financial support for their children's care. Tanisha's father had never lived with the family and was never married to Jennifer. Philip's father had divorced his wife 2 years ago, following a 4-year separation. Philip's father had lived with the family until his son was 2 years old. He had not maintained any contact with Philip for approximately 5 years.

Philip's maternal grandmother had lived with the family off and on for many years. She had a long history of psychiatric hospitalization and was currently maintained on antipsychotic medication (Thorazine), which was monitored on an outpatient basis by a psychiatrist. Her most recent hospitalization had occurred 2 years earlier. She had resided with her daughter since then on a consistent basis, despite being encouraged by others to obtain her own apartment.

The grandmother served an important primary function in the family. She dressed and fed the children, which enabled her daughter to socialize with her friends and current boyfriend. There were no other significant support systems available to the family, and Jennifer relied heavily on her mother's support to take care of her children. It is not uncommon in African American families for a son or daughter to share primary responsibility for his or her children with, or to relinquish it to, a parent (Stack, 1974). Thus a grandparent often assumes the parenting role for a second generation.

At the time of intake, Jennifer had recently met her current boyfriend and was spending a considerable amount of time with him. She brought both children with her to his house or to her sister's home on the weekends, where they all stayed together while the grandmother remained at home in the apartment alone. This weekend arrangement had been occurring for several months, and the grandmother enjoyed the weekends, as she was "off duty."

Philip's mother occasionally abused alcohol and had a history of physically abusing her son, according to child protective services (CPS) records. She and her son also shared a history of being abused by his father with an electrical cord. Philip was an infant when this occurred. The incidents were severe and finally necessitated their relocation to an emergency shelter and subsequent separation from the father. Jennifer acknowledged being beaten by her own father when she was a young girl. It is well documented that children who have been physically abused often abuse their own children later in life. The last instance when Jennifer beat Philip had occurred several months ago.

Jennifer's characteristic mode of disciplining involved verbal threats of physical violence. She could be unpredictably violent and hostile toward her son.

The local CPS agency had been involved with the family since Philip was 4 years old. The case was reopened as a result of the most recent allegation of physical assault (see below).

Presenting Problem

The presenting complaint as expressed by the school was as follows: "Philip stated that he wanted to kill himself today while in his classroom. He then left the classroom, promptly followed by his teacher. He ran down one flight of stairs to an empty classroom and began to open a window. He was restrained by his teacher from any further action."

This initial information was obtained by Jane Price Osuna (who is the "I" in what follows) via a phone conversation initiated by Philip's school guidance counselor. While on the phone, I requested additional information from the counselor. I wanted to know the circumstances that precipitated the event and whether there had been observers in the area at the time that the threat was made. In addition, I wanted to know the floor the child was on at the time he attempted to open the window, exactly how far the window was opened, and how far outside the window the child actually extended himself. These questions were important in determining the degree of danger in which the child had placed himself at the time of the expressed ideation. The answers to these questions would indicate whether the child needed to be evaluated immediately or whether the evaluation could wait until the following day.

It soon became apparent that Philip would need to be evaluated as soon as possible. The guidance counselor informed me that Philip had reported to her that he was beaten with an electrical cord 2 days prior to his suicidal gesture. A CPS worker had investigated the allegation of abuse, but had obtained no physical findings. Although it was not clear whether there had been any actual physical abuse or not,

Philip was obviously troubled, as indicated by his threat of suicide. Somebody was not listening to this child, which indicated that he was still at risk for future attempts.

Our team requested that Philip be brought in immediately with his mother and grandmother. As noted earlier, it is customary to request that a child be evaluated with the family members who are significantly involved in his or her life. The purposes of this are to gain additional information about the child and to observe how he or she interacts with each family member and how each family member responds to the child, while also gathering data about each person.

It is noteworthy that the CPS worker had been in the school at the time of the threat to interview Philip in the educational setting as a follow-up to the home-based interview. He also accompanied the family to the psychiatric emergency room.

First Interview

Interview with the Family

Content of Session

THERAPIST: How do you do? My name is Jane Price [as it was then], and I am a member of the child and adolescent crisis intervention team. We will be spending several hours together today as I interview Philip both with his family and alone. I will also be contacting his school. Would you please introduce yourselves to me?

CPS WORKER: My name is Mr. Green, and I was just assigned to the case last week because of a report of violence in the home.

MOTHER: My name is Jennifer. (*Mother's eye contact is poor. She is sitting as far away as possible from Philip.*)

GRANDMOTHER: My name is Vanessa, and I am Philip's grandmother.

PHILIP: I am Philip.

T: Why are you here today?

P: I said I wanted to kill myself today.

T: Oh. I see. How come?

P: Kids in my class were really mean. One kid called me "stupid."

T: Philip, you and I will have time to talk more about that in a little while because I really want to hear more about this, but right now I was wondering if your mom or grandmother ever heard you say that before?

G: No. I never heard him say that, and I am with that child a lot. He gets plenty angry sometimes,

Rationale/Analysis

I ask for introductions, to ease the anxiety related to the unknown of what will be occurring.

I wonder whether she is angry with Philip for making the allegations.

My question is not directed at anyone in particular; the purpose of this is to ascertain who will assume the authority to respond.

Philip is remarkably open.

I let the child know he is heard, while assessing how much of his anguish he has disclosed to his mother and grandmother.

Grandmother is first to respond to open question.

and kicks and screams when he is alone in his room when he is mad at me, but I never heard him say he would kill himself.

T: Jennifer, did Philip surprise you today with his actions?

M: No. That child doesn't ever surprise me! I might as well tell you right now that the reason Mr. Green is here is because of what that child said. (*Glares at Philip.*)

T: What did he say?

M: He said that I beat him with a cord last week and went to school and told them. Then they called CPS. I never hit him with the cord. I did once before last summer, but not now. His father used to beat him, and that is why we left him.

Mother is feeling defensive and uncomfortable in presence of CPS worker and in current situation.

T: Jennifer, why do you think that Philip tried to hurt himself today?

M: I think he is mad at me for yelling at him. He never does what he is supposed to. I take him with me to my boyfriend's house, and he acts up there. He won't do anything that we ask.

T: Jennifer, I would like to pick up on that thought again after I meet with Philip. I think I have a basic sense of what is going on right now, but I would now like to meet with Philip individually, so that I can best understand the situation and be of most help to you. By the conclusion of the evaluation today, I would like to provide you with a sense of how you can proceed from this point on, as well as give you my impressions of the current situation.

This will be a good time to conclude the group interview, since there is enough information to proceed individually. Philip may share more confidences if he is interviewed alone, without fear of reprisal from other family members. I will consult with the psychiatrist on the team now and present the case thus far. I will also call the school to inquire about Philip's socialization with peers and response to teachers. I would also like to know whether there has been any change in his overall functioning recently, how his academic work is, and whether there has been any noticeable fluctuation or deterioration in behavior. Prior to meeting with Philip, I will also consult with Mr. Green to gather his impressions of the family and the direction that he sees his agency pursuing at this time.

Interview with Child

Philip eagerly accompanied me to the interview room. I observed that his speech was immature and baby-like. In general, he appeared to have an affect hunger and seemed needy of attention and affection. For example, he would place himself in a position where physical contact was inevitable. Philip's clothing was worn and hung shabbily on his small, thin frame. A mental status examination was performed, based on both verbal and nonverbal interactions during the interview.

Content of Session	Rationale/Analysis
THERAPIST: What do you think about what your mother and grandmother said while we were all together?	I wonder whether Philip is feeling angry and how he interprets their comments.
PHILIP: I don't know.	Philip doesn't trust me enough to risk a response.
(*Therapist assists Philip in identifying his mood through the use of a display of seven boys' facial expressions depicting a wide range of affects. Therapist draws the facial expressions on a sheet of paper while Philip observes with evident interest. Therapist enlists Philip's assistance by requesting that he cut out the affect displays with scissors. Philip identifies his mood by pointing to the selected affect he has cut out in front of him on the desk.*)	I actively engage Philip in age-appropriate activity to encourage him to identify his feelings. Specifically, I am attempting to understand whether the suicide gesture coincides with Philip's last recollection of anger toward his mother.
P: I am mad at my mother.	
T: When was the last time you were mad at your mother?	
P: I was mad at her the other day when she was going to take me to Tom's house again, like she always does.	
T: Why don't you like to go there?	
P: There are no toys there for me to play with, and I have no friends there either.	
T: Philip, if you could have three wishes that I could make come true for you, what would you wish for?	Latency-age children often like to fantasize, and this task allows his latent thoughts and desires to be expressed in an ego-syntonic manner.
P: I wish that my mother did not take me to her boyfriend's house any more. I also would want more toys. For my last wish, I would want lots and lots of money.	It is not unusual for a child who is emotionally or environmentally deprived of a supportive and nurturing atmosphere to express the need for objects (toys), as well as the means (money) to supply the exhaustive desire for these objects. Thus the theme of emotional deprivation is apparent. The first wish Philip states appears to be the most significant.
P: My mother said she was going to hurt me with the electrical wire the night before we were supposed to go to Tom's house for the weekend.	The precipitants to the suicidal ideation and gesture begin to emerge. Our explorative play and conversation identify the under-

T: Philip, did your mother hurt you with the wire or her hands or anything else?

P: No.

T: You know, Philip, sometimes parents get angry at themselves or their children, and they might hit them, but it is not OK. Parents should not hit or slap their kids. It is *not* all right.

(*Philip appears more relaxed now as he walks about the room calmly, exploring the environment.*)

P: Sometimes I even tell my mother not to see Tom.

T: How come?

P: It's better at home alone with my mom.

T: Do you ever see your dad?

P: Not for a long time. Maybe a couple of years.

T: How do you feel about that? Does it make you sad or glad?

(*Philip shrugs his shoulders. Therapist offers Philip crayons and paper, and asks him to draw a picture of his family.*)

P: I can't draw my family, but I'll draw one person [see Figure 11.1].

T: Tell me about this "person."

P: This person is friendly but angry.

T: Why is he angry?

P: Because he is not allowed to play with his friends and has to stay alone.

lying stressors contributing to the current crisis that has brought the child to the psychiatric emergency room. Philip's gesture, which occurred on Friday, possibly was an attempt to prevent his mother from being with her boyfriend, since this was the customary day for their weekend departure from home. My initial reaction to the threat of physical violence toward this child is that I will not allow any harm to come to him that I can prevent. I also experience anger toward the mother for even contemplating injuring this child, who has already been physically violated in the past.

Philip needs to hear and understand that physical violence is not supported by other adults, and that he is not at fault for being the target of his mother's aggression.

I realize that this is a loaded question.

The "person" appears to resemble an amphibious creature with shark-like teeth displayed through a smile while sporting a baseball cap. The drawing is notably immature for an 8-year-old.

Philip reveals information about himself via the drawing that he would not be able to do if questioned directly. The game-like orientation involving his imagination allows Philip to express his subconscious thoughts without fear.

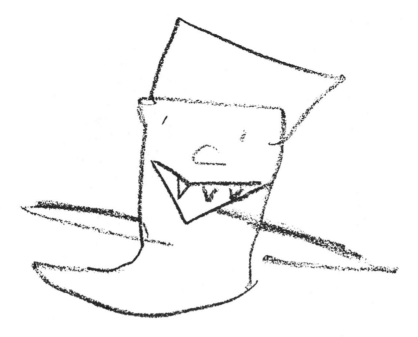

FIGURE 11.1. Philip's drawing of a person.

Preliminary Assessment and Treatment Plan

Although the other team members and I did not as yet have a detailed understanding of the nature of this boy's relationship with his mother, we could definitely state that it appeared to be troubled. The suicide gesture could be viewed as a "cry for help" related to the child's fear of being displaced by the boyfriend.

The mental status examination showed no evidence of suicidality, homicidality, or psychosis. Philip's mood was generally angry, and his affect was somewhat constricted. He was cooperative. There was no psychomotor retardation noted, nor were there any sleeping or eating disturbances. His speech was productive and coherent. His cognitive functions and overall intelligence appeared average. His judgment and impulse control were fair.

We assumed that Philip was jealous of his mother's boyfriend, Tom, because Tom robbed Philip of his time with his mother. In addition, the boyfriend caused Philip anguish, since he assumed the biological father's role in many respects. Thus the boyfriend shattered the child's hope of the reunification of his parents.

Most latency-age children want their parents to reunite and wish for that to occur, whether or not the possibility is realistic. Philip's unwillingness to draw a family, although he appeared to enjoy drawing, suggested some confusion about his family. The drawing of the person confirmed the preliminary hypothesis about Philip's anger. Despite the fact that his parents' divorce had occurred many years ago, the emotional effects were lingering. Philip was angry and felt abandoned by his mother, who admittedly was erratic in her displays of affection and discipline.

Treatment Plan

We decided not to include the grandmother in the subsequent follow-up visit to the emergency room, because we believed it was important for the mother to take more responsibility for her son. We reasoned that if the grandmother continued to be involved and solicited by Jennifer, then the child would not receive the reassurance and affection from his mother that he appeared to need so desperately.

The grandmother appeared to be relieved when informed that she did not need to return, and the mother and Philip scheduled another visit. We requested the continued presence of the CPS caseworker, Mr. Green, at the next appointment, since we believed that his presence added to the seriousness of the event and also exerted pressure on Jennifer to recognize the importance of meeting her son's needs. The threat underlying CPS's involvement in the case was that the child could be removed if the home environment threatened the child's safety or well-being.

Second Interviews

During the follow-up visit, Philip and his mother appeared smiling and happier at the beginning of the session. Their overall appearance also seemed to have improved. Jennifer had made a special effort to style her hair and had applied makeup. Philip was dressed in clean and brighter clothing than in the previous session.

At the beginning of the session, Philip sat in his mother's lap. He had attempted to do this during the prior visit, but Jennifer had not permitted it. Although this behavior might appear regressive in an 8-year-old boy, in this instance the prior observations of the family dynamics suggested that it might represent an improvement in the mother and son's emotional connectedness and in the mother's ability to tolerate the closeness.

Jennifer appeared less angry and more comfortable with me. She tolerated the CPS worker's involvement with her family; however, she requested that Mr. Green remain outside of the interviewing room, as she had information that she wanted to share with me but did not want him to know. I said that this would be possible, and that the only information I would need to share with him would be anything that might endanger Philip directly. Other than that, she would be guaranteed her right to confidentiality. Philip was also asked to wait outside the interviewing room while his mother and I spoke.

Interview with Mother

Content of Session

MOTHER: You know, Philip reminds me of my ex-husband all the time. That man was just no good. He did not care about anyone but himself. He was selfish.

THERAPIST: I wonder if you are aware of how some of your anger toward your ex-husband seems to be getting spilled over onto your son.

Rationale/Analysis

The traits that she mentions are negative in nature and provide the mother with an opportunity to scapegoat Philip. Philip has clearly been a recipient of the unresolved anger and hostility that she harbors toward her ex-husband. Not only

M: Maybe. I love Philip very much and certainly don't want him to suffer.

T: I think it would be a good idea if you began to speak to a therapist on a regular basis, where you will have an opportunity to discuss how you have been feeling, how you can best get along with your son, and any other issues that are important to you.

M: I agree. I could use somebody to talk to that will be there for me.

does she indicate her hostility by removing Philip from his house every weekend, but she frequently compares him to his father in a derogatory manner.

I am relieved and also somewhat surprised that Jennifer seems to accept the idea of outpatient therapy so easily.

Interview with Child

Philip and I began with a structured task, since he had already demonstrated his reluctance to respond directly to questions about his feelings. We opted for a game that we created together, the Game of Feelings.

We used a spinner from another board game. We covered up the prior instructions with the names of a variety of feelings, such as "happy," "sad," "angry," "mad," and "scared." We took plastic chips from another game and began. Philip was excited with our creation. He sat extremely close to me. The chips were given to the person spinning the dial. The spinner would automatically receive one chip for spinning and a bonus chip for acting out or verbalizing a feeling in some fashion.

Content of Session

PHILIP: I like you.

THERAPIST: That is nice to hear. I like you also, Philip. I am going to spin first so that you can see how we will play the game. (*Therapist spins dial.*) I have spun "happy." I feel happy when I am holding my cat and she is purring.

Rationale/Analysis

I am trying to model the expression of feeling I want Philip to express.

P: Oh! I understand how to play this game. I'll go now. It is my turn. I spun "scared." (*Philip thinks for approximately 30 seconds.*) I'm scared that when my mommy leaves me in Tom's house alone, that she won't come back for me. (*Therapist promptly rewards Philip with his two chips.*)

If in fact Philip is being left alone, this needs to be explored with Jennifer, and the CPA worker. Whether it is true or not, Philip's fear of abandonment is real.

T: That is an excellent example of being scared. I agree that it must be very scary to be alone.

P: I haven't seen my daddy for a long time, and my mommy and me had to run away from him because he hit us. We had to run away to a shelter where there were other kids. (*Philip then goes back to the game and spins "scared" again.*) I'm scared that my father left because I was bad, and that's why he had to hit me and my mommy.

I wonder how much he can remember, since he was only 2 at the time.

T: Philip, it is important for you to understand that it is *not* your fault that your parents are divorced. They had problems that were their own.

This comment is an initial attempt to relieve Philip of the sense of guilt that he has been experiencing for a long time.

P: I am mad that my daddy never came back. Remember the other day when you told me that I could have anything I wanted in the whole world?

T: Do you mean when you were wishing for three of your dreams to come true, if this was a magical world?

I have the distinct feeling at that point that Philip is about to reveal his innermost struggle. I want to encourage him to proceed with his thoughts and allow him to know that I care and am listening. He will be safe.

P: Yes. I have one more wish that I want to come true that I have been thinking about today.

T: Well, what is that special wish? I would like to know.

P: I wish my father would come back.

Wallerstein and Kelly (1980) point out that it is typical for a child of Philip's age to yearn for an absent parent even when the parent was abusive to the child. It seemed that Philip was displacing his anger onto his mother, since she was the only parent present. This anger might have been justifiable if in fact Jennifer was leaving Philip for extended periods of time and/or ignoring him emotionally. This experience would have directly complicated the many responses to divorce that an 8-year-old child might be expected to have. In addition to the anger related to the loss of a parent, Philip felt guilt connected to a sense of responsibility for the marital breakup. Again, this is a typical response for a latency-age child.

Before concluding our second and final meeting, Philip and I read together *Divorce Happens to the Nicest Kids* by Michael Prokop (1986). Despite the fact that the divorce had occurred 2 years prior, Philip still had many unresolved feelings and emotions related to the dissolution of his parents' marriage and the change in his family. The abrupt absence of his father made Philip's adjustment more difficult.

Referral for Individual and Family Counseling

As discussed earlier, Philip's suicidal gesture had occurred the day prior to the customary weekend sojourn at Tom's house. This was assumed to be one underlying stressor precipitating the gesture, together with the mother's alleged threat to hit Philip with the electrical cord 2 days before. Added to this were Philip's unresolved feelings associated with the absence of his father and the perceived substitution of Tom for his biological father. There were several additional stressors to consider, such as his mother's unresolved anger toward her ex-husband and its projection onto Philip. Yet another possible stressor was the grandmother's history of psychosis and its effect on Philip. Since Philip was often left in her care, it is possible that he feared a recurrence of her decompensation, since he did not know who would care for him in her absence.

Therefore, numerous stressors that preceded and possibly contributed to Philip's suicidal gesture. The final precipitant prior to the gesture occurred in the classroom, when a peer called Philip "stupid." This was a fairly benign comment that under other circumstances would not have distressed Philip. Yet, given the accumulated effect of the many stressors, he was no longer able to tolerate his anxiety and rage.

I referred Philip and his mother for outpatient treatment. The immediate crisis, the suicidal gesture, appeared to be Philip's means of communicating his "anger" (as he so aptly identified it via game play and verbal expression) about the current family situation, rather than a true intent to die. Accordingly, some counseling in regard to this situation seemed appropriate.

Both Philip and his mother agreed to go for individual and family counseling. The CPS worker, Mr. Green, agreed to maintain his involvement with the family over the next several months, to assure that Philip would not be physically or emotionally harmed and that therapy was actually occurring on a regular basis.

Some of the issues that needed to be addressed on a long-term basis were identified as (1) Philip's sense of responsibility and guilt for the divorce, and his subsequent anger directed at his mother; and (2) Jennifer's denial of her son's needs, and the issues underlying her lack of emotional availability to Philip.

COMMENTS

In reviewing Philip's case after the referral for outpatient counseling had been made, I wondered whether other treatment approaches might have proven more useful to the overall family during the crisis intervention phase. I acknowledged that Philip seemed relieved of the acute anguish that he was experiencing, and that he and his mother had reunited emotionally via their work together in the emergency room. But had I omitted other important members from our treatment? For instance, should Tom (the mother's boyfriend) have attended a family meeting, since he was an integral member of the reconstituted family?

Another key family member whom I had decided to exclude from our treatment was the maternal grandmother. I had done this as a means of drawing the mother into a more responsible role, in an attempt to reconnect her with her son while extricating the grandmother from the primary caretaking position.

The primary intent of the outcome of treatment in the emergency room was to relieve Philip of his suicidal ideation and begin to engage the family in long-term outpatient treatment. Although that was apparently accomplished, I still wondered whether the same outcome could have been achieved with the grandmother present. If the grandmother had attended the sessions, her role in the family could have been redefined.

All of the aforementioned questions could have been addressed in long-term treatment.

EIGHT YEARS LATER: HYPOTHETICAL ISSUES
AND OUTCOMES FOR PHILIP

Unfortunately, we do not have information about Philip's situation following the referral. We do not know whether Philip and his mother engaged in treatment (and, if so, for how long), or about his current status as a 16-year-old adolescent. However, for the purposes of the present chapter, we want to speculate about the ideal outcome for Philip and to identify the factors that might contribute to his optimal adjustment. We also speculate about a less than ideal outcome, based on the literature about adolescents who come from divorced families and who have been maltreated in childhood.

Philip was 8 years old at the time of his suicide attempt in school. The boy's accusations of physical abuse and his accompanying suicidal gesture were viewed by the crisis team as a "cry for help," since Philip's mother seemed to be oblivious to the boy's emotional needs and wishes. Furthermore, she treated him with disdain because he reminded her of her former husband, whose long-term abuse of her had culminated in her failed marriage. Jennifer would have benefited greatly from the opportunity to discuss her feelings about the abuse during her marriage, especially in light of her own history as an abused child.

It was noteworthy that after just one extended session at the hospital emergency room, Jennifer seemed more responsive to her son during their second visit. A cynical interpretation of this and of Jennifer's ready acceptance of the referral for ongoing treatment was that she was simply trying to make a good impression to offset the CPS investigation. On the other hand, she might have noticed the therapist's genuine concern for herself and for Philip, and the therapist's positive regard for Philip might have altered Jennifer's feelings for her son. Jennifer's "confession" to the therapist, which she asked to make in privacy during the second session, about the similarities that she saw between Philip and her former husband reflected Jennifer's capacity for thoughtfulness and insight. The time seemed ripe for her to engage in a helping relationship. Let us predict what might happen if Jennifer were to follow through with the referral.

The Ideal Outcome

The identified goals for Jennifer were to help her become more aware of her son's needs, in view of her own self-admitted tendency to identify Philip with his father. The key to making Jennifer more responsive would be to begin by expressing genuine concern for her, as a woman with a history of abuse herself, and with few apparent sources of support other than a mentally ill mother. After focusing initially on Jennifer's individual concerns in the light of her family history, the therapist could then explore additional options for widening the family's support network. These might exist within the extended family and could be elicited through drawing a genogram to identify the relatives across three generations. School and community resources for the family and for Philip would also merit exploration. These might include a church or community center affiliation, and sports, music, or other after-school activities for Philip. A "Big Brother" (or an uncle or a male teacher) could serve a very important function as a male role model for Philip. In addition, the therapist could sensitize Jennifer to Philip's age-appropriate need for peer contacts and activities. This work would have a greater chance of success if the therapist were to begin by forming a strong alliance with Jennifer, recognizing her *own* emotional neediness.

Goals for Philip were previously identified as helping to relieve him for his sense of responsibility for the divorce, and also to help him with his feelings of anger, which were being directed toward his mother. The examples of interventions already given, such as drawings, games, and bibliotherapy, would continue to be valid for Philip. He also would benefit tremendously from the opportunity to become a part of a school-based group for children of divorce. This would meet the dual goals of helping Philip realize that many of his feelings about his parents' divorce were shared by other children in similar circumstances, and of engaging him in an activity with his peers.

An ideal therapy situation, in addition to the individual sessions for Philip and Jennifer, would include periodic mother–son sessions, as well as some family sessions including the grandmother and Jennifer's boyfriend (if he continued to be active in her life). Philip's 4-year-old half-sister would also need to be seen at some point, either alone or with the family. This child would surely have many questions about her family situation, and about the whereabouts of Philip's father and her own father. Involving her during her preschool years would constitute an important preventive intervention.

A Less Than Ideal Outcome

Unfortunately, our best treatment plans might not be realized for many reasons. Because of the continuing involvement of CPS to monitor the family's participation in treatment, Jennifer might feel some resentment and resistance about the mandate to participate in therapy. She maintained that Philip's claim that she threatened him was false; if it was, her anger toward him was understandable. On the other hand, if CPS were to learn that the allegation of abuse was false, the agency would probably close the case, thereby eliminating the pressure on Jennifer to continue in treatment.

There were compelling circumstances working against this family. McLoyd (1990) states that African American children experience disproportionate shares of the burden of poverty and economic loss, and are at substantially higher risk than white children of experiencing attendant socioemotional problems. Because of the impact of negative life events and the distress of economic hardship, especially for single parents, black children often do not receive the positive parenting that would be supportive to them (McLoyd, 1990). Other authors confirm the pivotal role of kinship social support as helpful to mothers, and in turn to their adolescent children: "Evidence of the mediational role of maternal well-being and maternal parenting practices was revealed" in a study of 51 African American families at or below the poverty level (Taylor & Roberts, 1995, p. 1586). An earlier study by Wilson (1989) also stressed the importance of the extended family system for the psychological well-being of mothers, which in turn indirectly affects their children.

This research emphasizes the value of helping a mother so that she can support her children. We have noted the pivotal role of Philip's grandmother as a steadying force in his family, despite the limitations of her own mental illness. We do not know how well she might continue to carry out her functions as she grew older, and as the stresses of dealing with an adolescent and a latency-age child began to tax her patience. If Jennifer and Philip were not helped to develop other sources of support in addition to Vanessa, the strain on Jennifer would probably mount, and she would be less and less able to respond positively to Philip.

In conclusion, we recognize the many complex factors that can intervene to help or hinder a child's development into his adolescent years. Although we acknowledge that poverty, divorce, and maltreatment are very powerful stresses on a child, we know that some maltreated children are very resilient and develop good ego control, despite their adverse circumstances. Cicchetti et al. (1993) point to the role of "alternative adults in fostering adaptive personality development" (p. 644). As we have already discussed, the involvement of an interested adult male would seem critical for Philip during his adolescence, in an environment that does not offer many supports. We hope that someone has recognized Philip's need and reached out to him during this critical period.

STUDY QUESTIONS

1. Discuss the intergenerational factors in this family, with regard to how the developmental tasks of individual family members might complement and/or oppose one another.

2. Discuss the role of the maternal grandmother as caretaker in the African American family. Do you agree with the therapist's decision not to involve the grandmother in the child's treatment? What might the pros and cons of this decision have been for the child, the mother, and grandmother?

3. Consider the psychological tasks typical of a child during the latency period, according to Erikson. Comment on the absence of information related to peers and to extracurricular interests in Philip's situation as this might have related to the presenting problem. Discuss the possible effects of the lack of peer contacts on Philip's development in later childhood and adolescence.

4. How would you assess the degree of suicide risk in this case at the time of the initial assessment? Critique the therapist's evaluation and state what you might have done differently. What kind of intervention would you have considered to safeguard Philip against future suicidal behavior?

5. Ideally, what kind of aftercare services would you have recommended for this family? Consider the needs of all relevant family members, and give your reasons for each treatment recommendation.

REFERENCES

Camara, K. A., & Resnick, G. (1988). Interpersonal conflict and cooperation: Factors moderating children's post-divorce adjustment. In E. M. Hetherington & J. D. Arasteh (Eds.), *Impact of divorce, single-parenting and stepparenting on children* (pp. 169–195). Hillsdale, NJ: Erlbaum.

Cicchetti, D., Rogosch, F. A., Lynch, M., & Holt, K. D. (1993). Resilience in maltreated children: Process leading to adaptive outcome. *Development and Psychopathology, 5*, 629–647.

Dodge, K. A., Pettit, G. S., & Bates, J. E. (1994). Effects of physical maltreatment on the development of peer relations. *Development and Psychopathology, 6*, 43–55.

Emery, R. E. (1988). *Marriage, divorce and children's adjustment.* Beverly Hills, CA: Sage.

Golan, N. (1978). *Treatment in crisis situations.* New York: Free Press.

McLoyd, V. C. (1990). The impact of economic hardship on black families and children: Psychological distress, parenting, and socioemotional development. *Child Development, 61*, 311–346.

Pfeffer, C. (1986). *The suicidal child.* New York: Guilford Press.

Prokop, M. S. (1986). *Divorce happens to the nicest kids.* Warren, OH: Alegra Press.

Schaffer, M. (1974). Suicide in early childhood and early adolescence. *Journal of Child Psychology and Psychiatry, 15*, 275–291.

Stack, C. (1974). *All our kin: Strategies for survival in a black community.* New York: Harper & Row.

Taylor, R. D., & Roberts, D. (1995). Kinship support and maternal and adolescent well-being in economically disadvantaged African-American families. *Child Development, 66*, 1585–1597.

Wallerstein, J., & Blakeslee, S. (1989). *Second chances.* New York: Ticknor & Fields.

Wallerstein, J., & Kelly, J. B. (1980). *Surviving the breakup: How children and parents cope with divorce.* New York: Basic Books.

Weiss, R. S. (1979). Growing up a little faster: The experience of growing up in a single parent household. *Journal of Social Issues, 35*(4), 97–111.

Wilson, M. N. (1989). Child development in the context of the black extended family. *American Psychologist, 44*(2), 380–385.

CHAPTER 12

Unresolved Conflicts in a Divorced Family

Case of Charlie, Age 10

HOWARD ROBINSON

This chapter presents the treatment of Charlie, a 10-year-old boy in play therapy, whose crisis emerged years after witnessing marital violence, living in a shelter for battered women, and experiencing the hostile separation and divorce of his parents. Charlie's symptoms rekindled unresolved family conflicts, demonstrating how trauma can be expressed years later as disorder in behavior, emotion, and family interaction. As we will see in this chapter, Charlie's treatment posed numerous therapeutic challenges: engaging a parent who was also a trauma survivor; using nondirective play techniques with a child and family in crisis; and determining what treatment modalities to combine for comprehensive treatment planning. The case of Charlie—like that of millions of other children each year who survive family violence and divorce (Jaffe, Wolfe, & Wilson, 1990; Miller, 1989)—reminds us that "children bear the burden of being least able to voice their feelings and fears" (Ell & Aisenberg, 1998, p. 227), and that symptoms of trauma may emerge long after traumatic events have taken place (Silvern & Kaersvang, 1989).

Before presenting Charlie's case, I briefly discuss four aspects of play therapy relevant to the treatment of children in crisis (and, as we shall see, especially relevant to Charlie).

MASTERING EXPERIENCE THROUGH PLAY

Children subjected to anxiety-provoking events that are beyond their control and that exceed their capacity to cope are plagued by feelings of powerlessness. Being a passive witness to violence, for example, is known to produce psychic trauma (Elbow, 1982; Eth & Pynoos, 1985) that affects a child's capacity to explore the world, develop autonomy, and experience positive self-esteem (Ell & Aisenberg, 1998). Play, however, allows children to transform the anxieties and fears related to traumatic experiences into feelings of mastery and control. Like dreams, play reveals and disguises at the same time (Winnicott, 1964), allowing anxiety-laden thoughts and feelings to emerge in a nonthreatening form. For example, a "real-life" abuser may be transformed into a wolf puppet who is hunted and slain by a woodsman; battles between Mom and Dad can be symbolically represented as bullying and fighting among barnyard animals; abandonment fears may be soothed by nursing a baby doll. Through the disguise of play, children can communicate events and anxieties too difficult to express directly, and therapists can help children discover the freedom to transform passive experience into active mastery (Webb, 1991, 1996).

PLAY AND THERAPEUTIC ATTUNEMENT

Interacting with children by using their own language of play helps to establish a therapeutic dialogue that is interpersonally bonding. A child symbolically tosses the therapist a fantasy; the therapist catches it in turn and tosses it back. A responsive, validating exchange—playful in itself—emerges between therapist and child. This "play dialogue" is rooted in parent–infant interactions and the early formation of object relations. The emotional attunement provided by the therapist reenacts the developmentally early task of "synchrony," defined by Brazelton and Cramer (1990) as the parent's sensitive response to the infant's fluctuating physiological state of attention and inattention: "Engaged in the synchronous communication, the infant can learn about the parent as a reliable and responsive being, and start contributing to the dialogue" (p. 122). Play therapy resonates with this early dialogue between self and other. By staying within a child's fantasy during play, by using the metaphors created by the child, and by working with the child's symbolic language, the therapist demonstrates attunement to the child's self-expression. The interpersonal connection created by empathic attunement provides a potentially reparative form of object relationship, particularly when a child has experienced less than optimal parental care. Therapeutic attunement also kindles the child's hope of being understood, accepted, and valued—an essential first step of treatment.

Children who have experienced emotional deprivation, however, may develop unrealistic expectations that their therapists will actively satisfy all their unmet needs. Therapists often walk a fine line between empathy and indulgence as they respond to children's magical wishes and unmet emotional needs. Although therapists cannot erase the deficits that children have already experienced, they can offer children a more realistic hope: that satisfying relationships with others can be achieved in the future, despite past adversity. The play therapy relationship can serve as a model, if not a replacement, for having a consistent, supportive, responsive, and sustaining relationship with an adult—one of the principal factors associated with resilience in children (Werner, 1995).

THERAPEUTIC BENEFITS OF DRAWING IN PLAY THERAPY

Drawing, a projective technique, allows children to construct images of their experiences that reflect unconscious and preconscious feeling states, as well as emotional preoccupations and concerns about themselves, family members, and even their communities (Landgarten, Junge, Tasem, & Watson, 1978). This is especially valuable in play therapy. First, drawing permits children to turn diffuse feelings, attitudes, and fears into concrete images; as a result, children can be helped to verbally label their feelings, identify and clarify cognitive distortions, and psychologically reintegrate their experiences in a more coherent and benign way. Second, children not only increase their self-awareness, but externalize their private, internal worlds; this helps to establish a communicative bridge between themselves and their therapists, and is particularly helpful in accessing traumatic experience that children labor painfully to repress or keep secret. Children in treatment, for example, may withhold feelings because they touch on taboo subjects (such as sexuality and violence) or provoke overwhelming shame or guilt. Family loyalty may burden children, who fear "telling on" parents by revealing something negative or embarrassing about them. As a nonverbal activity that cloaks information in play images, however, drawing distances children from such immediate concerns. Finally, as Wadeson (1987, p. 1) emphasizes, artwork can therapeutically mirror to children their own subjective worlds:

> Expression in art stimulates fantasy, creativity, spontaneous unconscious imagery. It offers the possibility of creating a self-reflection, an image of oneself and one's world, from which it is possible to separate to gain distance. In this way the art object may provide a unique self-confrontation and perspective.

We shall see later how salient Charlie's family drawing was to understanding his crisis state, and how this understanding permitted the use of his drawing to explore and confront his psychological dilemma.

THERAPEUTIC VALUES GUIDING PLAY THERAPY

By accepting and encouraging the expressive elements in a child's play, the therapist implicitly communicates particular therapeutic values that guide treatment:

1. "I want to know about you as you honestly perceive yourself and your world to be."
2. "You can tell me your story in your own language, and I will attempt to understand."
3. "We can share your private pain and ease your isolation."
4. "I will follow where you decide to take me."

These messages are comforting in their child-centered focus: Children are released from social pressure to comply with adult demands and to suppress their own unique feelings and thoughts. Instead, a therapist accommodates to a child's perspective, encourages the child's "native language" of play, and facilitates more authentic self-expression. This is the essence of nondirective play therapy, which follows the lead of the child in language, thought, feeling, and action (Axline, 1947).

The beneficial aspects of play therapy reviewed here played a prominent role in Charlie's treatment. He was a boy who had passively survived numerous stressful life events, whose relationship with both his parents was significantly compromised by circumstances beyond his control, who used artwork (among other play modalities) to express his distress, and who needed a safe venue to be heard. Although his treatment was prematurely terminated, the empathic relationship established in treatment sowed the seeds to buffer his sense of rejection and alienation, and potentially to modify his negative expectations about future relationships.

THE CASE: CHARLIE, AGE 10

Family Information

Charlie was a 10-year-old boy living with his mother, his 7-year-old sister, and his maternal aunt. Charlie's parents had divorced when he was 5, and Bea, his mother, subsequently relocated to seek refuge from Charlie's father, who had battered her during their marriage. Bea described this period of her life as a "hypnotic hell" with no exit. She was trapped by a confusing and intimidating web of events within the home: drug abuse and drug dealing; forced sexual acts and sexually degrading behaviors; threats of violence and actual physical assault. Bea was a victim of severe spousal abuse by Charlie's father, whose behavior was further impaired by his addiction to heroin and alcohol.

On impulse one night, Bea fled with both of her children to a shelter for battered women advertised on local TV. She remained there with Charlie and his sister until a legal separation was implemented. Bea maintained an order of protection against her husband and won full custody of the children in subsequent divorce proceedings 2 years later. When Charlie's father completed a drug and alcohol rehabilitation program, he was granted visitation rights. Still fearful of Charlie's father, however, Bea moved to another city to live with her older sister and to reestablish herself and her family in safety.

According to Bea, Charlie was not physically or sexually abused as a preschooler; however, he did witness their marital violence. Charlie also experienced the disruption (and potential trauma) of moving to a shelter, being separated from his father, being interviewed during divorce proceedings, and relocating to a new home and community. Charlie, at age 10, was the only male in a household that included two adult women and his sister. Four months prior to referral, Charlie had had his first visit with his father since his parents' separation and divorce when he was 5.

Presenting Problem

Bea sought treatment for Charlie in January after "things turned real bad, real fast." Charlie, a top fifth-grade student, began behaving violently at home. Bea reported that Charlie hit, kicked, and choked his sister; in addition, his mother described "tantrums" in which Charlie directly attacked her and screamed "obscene names." The equilibrium of Bea's postdivorce family was being torn apart by Charlie's violent outbursts.

Further exploration revealed that Charlie had also progressively withdrawn from friends at school and complained of headaches and stomachaches. These symptoms coincided with Charlie's return from summer visitation with his father in September. According to Bea, Charlie's behavior changed more generally at that time. He "acted coldly," appeared to "lack trust," and refused to talk with female relatives. He also signaled his deep distress when he told his mother, "I might as well just kill myself, 'cause nobody loves me." Professional treatment for Charlie, however, was not considered until later in the school year, after his behaviors became more violent and unmanageable.

Bea suspected that Charlie's shift in behavior was associated with the summer visit to his father. She also recognized that Charlie's attacking behaviors provoked frightening memories of her ex-husband's abuse. Bea's suppressed rage was triggered, and she feared losing self-control. As a result, Bea felt particularly vulnerable, scared, and helpless. A familiar pall of violence threatened the family unit she had worked so hard to safeguard and to separate from the past.

Preliminary Assessment

Charlie was a young witness to his father's sadistic attacks on his mother and was subjected to aggressive behaviors and chaotic events over which he exercised no control. Silvern and Kaersvang (1989) write that "witnessing parental spousal abuse entails the fear, helplessness, and overstimulation that are the crux of trauma" (p. 423). These traumatic experiences occurred when Charlie was at the height of his Oedipal development, learning about male–female relationships, and internalizing parental identifications. Charlie's behavior therefore had multiple determinants: the violence he witnessed as a preschooler, now finding expression as an unconscious reenactment; a strong identification with his impulse-ridden father; and the behavioral model he learned from his parents to communicate frustration and anger. These were my hypotheses as I contemplated meeting Charlie for assessment and treatment.

Charlie must also have possessed some inner strengths to have survived the stressful events that followed the wake of domestic violence—his flight from home; the long separation from his father; invasive court experiences; and relocation to a new community, school, and home. His mother's capacity to safeguard herself and her children probably provided a certain degree of stability as well. Charlie succeeded in making a functional readjustment in his new setting and performed well in school. After visitation with his father, however, the balance established among himself, his mother, and his sister shifted dramatically. Had his visit brought up memories from the past? Provoked ambivalent feelings about his father? Created a sense of divided loyalty? Or made Charlie feel he was to blame? At this point, the many possible dynamics underlying Charlie's conduct were still in question.

The family context of the presenting problems was also important. Charlie's mother was a victim, too, and Charlie's assaults at home mirrored her ex-husband's abuse. Bea must have found it difficult to remain empathic when her son's behavior was such a strong reminder of her own victimization! If Bea reactively pulled away from Charlie (to protectively distance herself from his violent behaviors), he could have felt abandoned and left without hope. Charlie was now in a crisis state, and his behaviors signaled a need for immediate help. When Charlie drew a family portrait in his first session, he revealed significant clues about the family dynamics that propelled his psychological crisis.

First Session: A Family Portrait

Charlie entered the office with his head bowed dejectedly. He was small-framed and lean with jet-black hair. His slow gait and taut, nonverbal demeanor added to the feeling of his being a condemned prisoner. Charlie did not engage in conversation, but when asked to draw a picture of his family, he energetically drew a spacecraft with all but one of his immediate family aboard (Figure 12.1). Charlie used bright colors and embellished his picture with numerous stars. As a finishing touch, he added his name boldly at the top. Charlie explained:

Content of Session	Rationale/Analysis
CHARLIE: It's a spaceship. My sister's at the controls. Mom is up here, reading. Dad is sleeping, and Auntie is below, working . . . she likes to be away from everybody. This is me. The spaceship is going to California . . . but we are all going to crash . . . run into a star.	This is exciting and disturbing at the same time. Charlie is sharing so much with me, but he is drawing a crisis in the making! Look how different each family figure is, how inaccessible the adults are, how alone Charlie is, and where he is standing—beside the escape hatch! What does this all mean?

Although a diagnosis could not be made on the basis of one drawing, and accurate interpretations would require direct validation by the client, Charlie's family portrait helped to unveil his subjective experience of the family and provided a starting point for understanding his situation and talking about his feelings.

Analysis of Drawing

Charlie depicted himself alone in a world of unavailable adults. His mother, a small figure, sat passively within her own private shell; she was encapsulated and seemingly uninvolved with the family below. His father, a tall, eerie figure with a helmet, floated like a corpse. Although inert and lifeless, the father blocked any contact Charlie might have with his mother or sister. Charlie's aunt, the only other available adult, was disconnected from the family; she was flying independently below the doomed spaceship. Charlie depicted himself standing in the tail of the craft and placing one foot in the escape hatch. He was as far from his mother and sister as he could get without leaving the craft. Charlie appeared frozen, as if making a choice: "Do I stay with the family or escape?" But where was Charlie to go? No viable life existed outside the craft, yet remaining aboard would mean crashing with everyone else. Charlie was trapped.

Other dimensions of crisis were reflected in Charlie's family portrait. Charlie, for example, portrayed a family with no effective leader. The family power structure

FIGURE 12.1. Charlie's family portrait.

was rendered topsy-turvy. Charlie's sister, the most vibrant figure in the drawing, was placed at the controls of the craft, and his mother, at best a passive witness, was cut off from events in the cabin. In structural family terms, the parental authority of the executive system was subverted by the sibling (Minuchin, 1974). The "executives" of the family—the mother and father—were secluded or "sleeping." Meanwhile, Charlie's sister, the youngest family member, was taking charge of the controls; the ship (i.e., the family) was in her young hands.

Parental figures were also depicted as inaccessible and unable to offer help. Both Mom and Dad were encapsulated in their own bubbles, cut off from direct interaction. The ladder to Mom's private perch suggested some hope of movement back into the family, but the ladder only led to Sis, not Charlie. To add to Charlie's isolation, Mom was positioned far away from Charlie. Could she even see his foot creeping toward the escape? Although he was in crisis, Charlie had no connection to parent figures, who were depicted as either lifeless (father) or constricted (mother).

Charlie's drawing had developmental significance as well. On the cusp of preadolescence and in need of a male figure for identification, Charlie expressed a wish to be with his father: The spacecraft was flying to California, where his father and the paternal side of the family lived. The need for a male presence might be symbolically expressed in the ambiguous placement of the father figure. Although blocking access to Charlie's mother and sister, the father provided a buffer to female identifications, communicating, perhaps, Charlie's need to individuate as a male within an all-female household. His father, however, appeared "off-balance" and lopsided, suggesting that he was not well grounded or secure. What kind of male identification would this father actually provide?

One might speculate, furthermore, that this portrait depicted a residual memory of past family trauma. The father was accorded a central position in the drawing, as if the family revolved around him, inebriated and off-balance. The mother's position apart from the family system might represent Charlie's intuitive understanding of her victimization—the possibility that she, at times, could only be a passive witness to an out-of-control father; that she could only lead them to safety by separating from the father; or that her victimization required her to remain protectively shielded. Perhaps some memory of being left alone with Dad and Sis was represented here as well.

Charlie, too tense for words, "narrated" his presenting problem to me with his drawing and invited me into his family drama. He used his drawing to say, "This is me, this is my family, and this is my crisis. Help!" As a result, Charlie constructed a bridge between his internal feelings and the external world, and he succeeded in sharing his concerns with a helping person. This act of communication became a source of hope that he would not have to remain alone and in crisis. A new dialogue could begin, and treatment was initiated.

Strategies to Facilitate Expressive Play

When a child metaphorically expresses anxiety-laden material, as Charlie did in his drawing, the "disguise" of fantasy creates the safety needed to explore even further. Charlie could be encouraged to reveal more by strategically expanding his metaphor:

1. *What might Mom or Dad do to keep the spacecraft from crashing into a star?* This question would elicit more feelings about Charlie's parents and their capacity, or incapacity, to tune in to his anxiety in a helpful way.

2. *What would happen if Dad "woke up"?* Charlie's response might indicate more about his father's interactions with the family in the past, or might clarify Charlie's expectations of his father in the present.

3. *What would happen if Mom sat down at the controls of the craft?* Would she turn the ship around and head back to their postdivorce home (thwarting Charlie's wish to be with his father, as she did in real life)? Would Sis be unwilling to yield her position of control? Would Mom and Sis get into an argument? New family dynamics might be revealed as hypothetical shifts in the scenario were proposed.

4. *What would happen if Charlie manned the controls?* Charlie could be magically empowered by putting him in the driver's seat and finding out what he would choose to do.

5. *What would Mom do if Charlie left the ship?* Would she search for him and attempt his rescue? Cry? Not notice his departure? Become angry? This question would tap Charlie's perception of his mother and her feelings about him.

Probes that maintain the metaphor, like these, allow children to reveal more about their anxiety-laden situations and feelings. They can even neutralize anxiety through their playfulness.

Further Assessment and Treatment Planning

Charlie entered treatment feeling accused; he thought of himself as the "bad one" and proved it by fighting with everyone in the family. His negative self-concept, however, probably predated his current acting out and reflected the blame he cast upon himself for the domestic violence he had witnessed and for his parents' divorce (Wallerstein & Kelly, 1980; Wallerstein & Blakeslee, 1989). Charlie was also angry at his mother, whom he experienced as emotionally withdrawn. He forced her to attend to him through his verbal provocations and attacks. Although this brought Charlie in closer physical contact with his mother, he did not receive her understanding or emotional comfort. On the contrary, Charlie's behavior rekindled the intense unresolved conflict between his mother and father, because Charlie's rage reminded the mother of her battering as a spouse. When the mother, in fear, distanced herself from Charlie, he felt rejected and abandoned; when she reactively attacked, his "bad self" was confirmed.

The treatment plan was to see Charlie weekly for individual sessions using nondirective play therapy, and also to meet weekly with Charlie's mother, who was in a depressed and psychologically fragile state. Conjoint crisis intervention sessions involving both Charlie and his mother were planned as necessary, as were family sessions to help both children with divorce issues.

Treatment planning was complicated. The need for multiple treatments—individual, conjoint, and family—were too great for one therapist; yet the crisis nature of the case required intensive collateral sessions with Charlie's mother to stabilize the family system. Although this approach risked compromising Charlie's independent claim on me as *his* therapist, I felt that Charlie's welfare was best served by bolstering his mother's functioning when crises arose. The reasons for not immediately referring Bea for individual treatment are discussed at the end of the chapter.

Treatment Goals and Objectives

Charlie's emotional alienation, symbolized by "outer space" in his drawing, exacerbated his crisis. He was bearing his anxiety and fears alone. In this context, establishing a therapeutic relationship and demonstrating emotional attunement were critical aspects of treatment planning. The first goal of Charlie's treatment, therefore, was to help him engage with me in the therapeutic treatment process. Specific treatment objectives related to this goal were as follows:

1. To help Charlie develop a nonthreatening relationship with a male therapist (myself) who could model empathic and controlled behaviors.
2. To engage Charlie in play therapy so that psychological conflicts could be therapeutically enacted in sessions.

I hoped that the therapeutic relationship we established—in contrast to other adult relationships in his life—would be reparative and help to modify his expectations of rejection and retaliation.

The second goal of treatment was to help Charlie resolve Oedipal conflicts sabotaging the developmental tasks of latency (learning without conflict; peer group friendships; sublimation of impulses into constructive, age-appropriate activities). Specific objectives were the following:

1. To help Charlie express, clarify, and label feelings related to the loss of his father.
2. To help Charlie learn to feel safe in the expression of his hostile and aggressive wishes through play.
3. To coach Charlie in socially approved ways to cope with his sense of anger toward his mother.

A third goal of treatment was to stabilize the family system so that Charlie's home environment might become more nurturant and less provocative. Specific treatment objectives related to this goal involved direct work with Charlie's mother:

1. To help Charlie's mother become aware of her own conflicts and their displacement onto Charlie.
2. To increase the mother's ability to set limits in nonpunitive ways that did not enact anger.
3. To help the mother improve her understanding of Charlie's feelings and needs rather than project her own.
4. To assist Charlie and his mother in learning concrete ways to deescalate conflict as it emerged between them.

From a person–situation perspective, collateral and conjoint interventions to modify Charlie's home environment were necessary to secure whatever gains Charlie might make in his individual sessions.

Play Therapy Sessions

Charlie came to most sessions in army fatigues and a hunting cap—clothing that expressed a strong identification with his father (who, according to Charlie, dressed the same way). Themes of loss and powerlessness emerged in the course of Charlie's treatment, as we see in the vignettes presented here.

Second Play Therapy Session

Content of Session

Rationale/Analysis

CHARLIE: All my pets died when I got back from vacation with my father. First my guppies died, then my hamster. (*Speaks angrily.*) My aunt flushed

How sad! Charlie leaves his father, where he has happily reconnected, only to encounter such poignant my guppies down the toilet. Me and my sister got frogs. But you can't sleep with frogs or cuddle them. . . . When I went to visit my Dad, I got to sleep with my old dog, Benny. Dad bought him for my birthday 6 years ago. He was just a puppy then. Benny only comes when me or my father call him. (*Becomes enthusiastic.*) My father and I built a tree house in the back yard with a trap door. We went to a ball game with my uncle, and we swam in my grandmother's pool.

losses at home. How desperate he is for companionship and fun—the birthright, it would seem, of any boy or girl. I feel a split in his emotions: anger and disappointment at home with Mom, satisfaction and connection with Dad. How will I help Charlie and his mother adjust to this complicated postdivorce situation. Is the trap door the derivative of the spaceship hatch in his drawing?

Charlie's initial focus on dead and missing pets was a thin disguise for the feelings of loss related to his father. His dog Benny, for example, represented the special father–son relationship that Charlie yearned for. He expressed his loneliness and sense of alienation in his wish to have cuddly pets for close companionship. Charlie's depressed tone lifted as he recounted memories of his summer with Dad. The task ahead was to help Charlie understand his own experience, and then learn to adjust to the reality of the divorce that separated him from his father and his father's extended family.

Charlie wanted a pet dog and asked me to convince his mother to buy one for him:

Content of Session	Rationale/Analysis
CHARLIE: Would you ask my mother to get me a dog? She likes dogs.	A simple but complicated question! Charlie wants to recruit me as his advocate, to have an ally, and to have his wish fulfilled. How can I explore his request without disappointing him?
THERAPIST: What would you want me to say to her?	I invite further elaboration to surface his fantasy and to help identify the role he wants me to play.
CHARLIE: That I really *need* a dog. I can take care of it (*pleading, as if to a parent*), and it can sleep with me.	Charlie pleads with me as if I am his mother or father—or someone powerful who can help him get what he wants. (I wish I could, but I know this not my role.)
T: What do you think your mother would say?	I continue to invite his elaboration and sidestep a direct answer. Probing his expectations and defining my therapeutic role take precedence.
C: Well, she said I could have one when she has more money. She says she's been thinking about it, but . . .	
T: You look sad.	I pay careful attention to his affect and reflect his feeling back to him.

C: She *never* does what I want! I ask her all the time, but she just says "maybe" or doesn't pay attention.

I am glad I didn't casually say "maybe" to his request to talk to his mother, because he would probably have concluded that I would be dismissive with him too.

T: You really would like an ally, someone who can fight for you when your mother doesn't pay attention.

I attempt to surface the underlying psychological/interpersonal wish motivating his request—the role he wants me, or someone (his father?), to play in his life.

C: She might not even let me visit my father again. . . .

Charlie's need for his father, and his disappointment at having to leave him this summer, emerge.

T: You're angry and sad to be separated from your father. It would feel great to have a father close to you who could see things your way.

This is a statement seeking to clarify the transferential wishes driving our discussion. I am hoping this more clearly labels for Charlie what some of his current feelings are about. This provides an opportunity to talk more openly about the divorce and the frustrations, disappointments, and inequities involved for the children who have to make many difficult adjustments.

Charlie's attempt to actualize his transferential wishes by recruiting me into a parental role had to be carefully and caringly managed. Rather than answer directly, I chose to explore his question in an attempt to solicit more context, to understand more of what he expected from me, and to imagine with him what might hypothetically occur. Therapeutic issues could then be more readily clarified, and a therapeutic frame could be constructed for treatment. For Charlie, the loss of his father and the wish for a powerful ally became a primary theme. In retrospect, surfacing Charlie's feeling of loss and concern about visiting his father could have opened more direct talk about the painful realities of divorce for children. I could have validated and normalized how difficult relationships with divorced parents can be, and how much a boy can miss the companionship of a father when living in the custody of his mother.

Summary of Sessions 3–13

Aggressive play sessions followed, in which Charlie transformed every part of the therapy room into a battleground and pitched full-scale battles with me, using toy soldiers. He set up ambushes atop chairs and sofas, built forts from pillows and then blew apart their protective walls, used bazookas to "waste" individual soldiers, and heaved casualties into the air with loud explosive noises. Charlie's battles were furious; his small army overwhelmed and "slaughtered" the superior numbers he assigned to me.

Charlie identified one particular soldier as "the Captain." He was a Rambo-type figure who grew in power with each new battle. The Captain single-handedly defeated any and all adversaries. Charlie celebrated the might of one over many. He exhorted me to create the strongest attack imaginable, and then wiped out my forces with the Captain. Charlie repeated these battle scenes with delight and appeared invigorated by this uninhibited expression of aggression and his continual triumphs.

Charlie's war games provided a safe opportunity for him to release the pent-up aggression generated by the frustration, loss, and intrusion he experienced in his real world. At home, Charlie felt outnumbered and controlled by females: his mother, sister, and aunt. He was the object of his mother's rage and the victim of her emotional withdrawal. He could reverse his sense of powerlessness and defeat through play, where he could successfully defend himself, attack his enemies, and triumph. He "transformed" his reality to rebuild a sense of power and control in his life.

Charlie's play demonstrated his psychological vulnerability and his compensatory identification with the aggressor. When Charlie destroyed my "battle defenses," rendering me vulnerable and weak, he made me experience the role of the passive victim, unable to ward off attack—perhaps like Charlie at home, or even earlier, when he had passively witnessed parental violence. Charlie compensated for submissive feelings by empowering himself, and he enacted upon me what he experienced in his life. Charlie became the powerful aggressor instead of the impotent victim.

The following dialogue conveys the kind of verbal exchange typical in Charlie's war play:

Content of Session	Rationale/Analysis
CHARLIE: I've blown away your bunkers. . . . Here come my men to attack.	Charlie destroys my "defenses" and leaves me "vulnerable" to attack. He is enjoying this!
THERAPIST: I have nothing to protect me; anything can happen to me now.	I verbalize being defenseless; the more I can articulate a sense of fear, helplessness, and vulnerability relevant to the play, the more Charlie will know that I understand what he experienced.
C: You take all of these men (*gives me the full complement of soldiers*). The Captain will fight them all!	I like how Charlie takes charge of this play scenario and directs me to fit what he needs. Charlie is an aggressive boy who identifies with the power and strength of the Captain figure. He expresses his own aggression here without fear of retaliation (symbolic castration).
T: The Captain is all by himself; how can he handle all these attackers alone?	What lopsided odds! Is this how he feels in life? I play along, voicing the obvious threat. Although I praise his power, I insert a skeptical tone to address the unfairness of the real-life battles he may be representing here.

Charlie sublimated his aggression through his vigorous play with toy soldiers. He was safe in the playroom, where he did not have to face real guilt or remorse. For example, Charlie could attack me, a male authority figure, without fear of retaliation or disapproval. The impulses to destroy, conquer, and control—manifested by Charlie in his battle scenes—were expressed in his approach to competitive games like checkers, Connect Four, ring toss, and cards. Winning was not generally good enough; Charlie had to "wipe me out." He modified rules to empower himself and to defeat me. This seemed to be compensatory for his own sense of smallness and the anxiety he harbored over his phallic aggression.

Charlie's need to assert power and to control powerful others reflected the emotional dynamics of the Oedipal child, 3 to 5 years old—the age Charlie had been when he witnessed his mother's abuse and was separated from his father. Perhaps Charlie's efforts to control and vanquish me were reparative attempts to master the overly stimulating violence he witnessed as a preschooler. Oedipal themes of power and aggression were reflected in whatever Charlie chose to play and indicated Charlie's continued need to resolve these issues.

Family Counseling

Charlie's mother was an emotionally fragile woman who was prone to crisis herself. Her psychological integrity frequently shattered, causing her to become emotionally disorganized and panicked. At these times, Bea sought male figures to take charge of her life. However, at other times, she spurned intimacy with males and was particularly fearful of male domination and intrusion. Bea's difficulties in regulating emotions, maintaining a coherent sense of self, and managing feelings of intense vulnerability and helplessness were no doubt related to her abuse experiences and corresponded to the "battered woman's syndrome" described by Walker (1979).

Charlie's aggression at home sparked his mother's conflicts about men and made her feel victimized once more. In fact, Charlie's physical resemblance to his father was enough to trigger her rage, and Bea had difficulty controlling anger—Charlie's or her own. The emotional wounds from her physical and sexual abuse had not yet healed, and Bea remained vulnerable to symbolic triggers of marital abuse. As a result, verbal and physical fights occurred at home between mother and son.

Although Bea wanted complete separation from Charlie's father, Charlie yearned for contact, a wish appropriate to his preadolescent stage of development. Charlie's wish for his father was in opposition, however, to Bea's need for psychic safety: How would this man who had victimized her ever be out of her life? Bea also feared losing Charlie if he decided at some future point to live with his father. She anticipated being abandoned, since her own father had died in a car accident when she was 12. These factors made Charlie's visitation with his father even more difficult to negotiate for them both.

Family counseling was needed to keep the unconscious battle between Charlie and his mother from exploding. Bea needed to understand why her son was the focal point of her rage, and how her own trauma contributed to the family dynamics. Charlie needed to find ways to control his direct aggression and learn more appropriate ways to communicate his frustration and needs. An intervention was designed to deescalate and manage the intermittent conflict at home.

A Crisis Intervention Family Session

A conjoint session was held with Charlie and his mother to intervene strategically in their fighting. Charlie and Bea were first asked to describe how each saw the other when angry. This was a preliminary step to identify the behaviors triggering angry interactions between them. I asked questions such as these:

1. "How can you tell when your [mother/son] is angry?"
2. "How does your [mother/son] express anger?"
3. "What happens when your [mother/son] gets angry?"
4. "What do you do when your [mother/son] gets angry?"

Questions 3 and 4 "tracked" the process of conflict and could be explored and partialized even more by asking, "And then what happens?", until a complete chain of interactions leading to conflict was uncovered. Alternative behaviors could then be suggested to produce a more positive outcome. In this way, Charlie and his mother were helped to recognize the steps in their escalating conflict and could then be coached to make changes.

Charlie, for example, was able to identify when his mother looked and sounded angry. He also became more aware of when he felt ready to lash out. As a result, Charlie and his mother consciously identified the early cues and warning signs of their brewing anger. Charlie then developed his own behavioral solution: He decided to separate from his mother, go to his bedroom, and punch pillows. The mother, meanwhile, resolved to go to her study to cool down. In addition, she identified friends she could call to air her frustrations and gain some personal support.

Termination

Charlie's behaviors at home improved. Treatment, however, was prematurely terminated following two family sessions that explored the family's experiences with the father. After 7 months of working together, Charlie's mother severed his therapeutic relationship with me as abruptly as she did the relationship with his father! Bea would not discuss the reasons for ending or permit me to say a final goodbye to Charlie. A powerful family dynamic was projected onto the treatment process—a dynamic too traumatic to resolve in time to save Charlie's treatment. More reasons for his premature termination are offered in the next section.

Treatment nonetheless provided some gains. The intensity of conflict between Charlie and his mother decreased, and the level of initial anxiety dissipated. During play therapy sessions, Charlie had the opportunity to experience an empathic relationship with an adult male and could express feelings that were taboo or negatively sanctioned within his home. This allowed some ventilation of his anger, disappointment, and sadness. Knowing that he could be understood without retaliation helped to allay his crisis state. His positive experiences in therapy would serve as a foundation for treatment at some later date, when Charlie might be in a position to choose therapy for himself.

EIGHT YEARS LATER: RETROSPECTIVE REVIEW

In reviewing Charlie's treatment 8 years later, I find that three critical questions emerge:

1. What, if anything, could have prevented the premature termination of Charlie's treatment?
2. Was nondirective play therapy the best treatment to use with Charlie?
3. What other treatment modalities or collateral treatments could have helped Charlie and his family?

These three questions highlight the complexity of treating trauma-induced conditions—the central aspect of Charlie's case that deserved greater attention from the start. Let us begin by considering the initial treatment tasks of assessment, engagement, and treatment planning.

Assessment

A more comprehensive and trauma-focused assessment (see Webb, Chapter 1, this volume) would have helped to clarify the trauma-based elements contributing to Charlie's intrapersonal and interpersonal distress. Further exploration was needed, for example, to understand the extent of Charlie's exposure to his mother's spousal abuse. What age was Charlie when the parental violence first began, and how long did it last? What specific interactions might Charlie have seen or heard? Did Charlie witness secondary consequences of domestic violence—for example, did he see his mother physically hurt or emotionally distressed? How did Charlie react to these events, and what coping mechanisms did he use? These questions usually are discussed with the parent in the first evaluation session, or with the parent and child together when the child is 10 or older (Webb, 1996). Answers to these questions increase clinical sensitivity, provide specific information to frame historically accurate interpretations, and help to design strategic treatments aimed at surfacing and resolving traumatic experiences (an intervention style quite different from nondirective play therapy).

In addition, a more accurate assessment of Charlie's mother and her functional capacities was needed. Bea was a trauma victim (spouse abuse), and her intense reactivity, panic, fear of intrusion and exploitation, difficulty regulating emotion, and decompensation under stress were textbook symptoms of complex posttraumatic stress disorder (Herman, 1992). These symptoms—in concert with Bea's reports of physical numbing and dissociation in relation to physical touch, her strong ambivalent feelings about men, and the abusive nature of her marital relations—also indicated the likely possibility of childhood sexual abuse (Davies & Frawley, 1994). A more complete history, which could have been obtained in an initial evaluation session, would have elicited additional information about violence, alcoholism, other drug abuse, and/or sexual abuse in Bea's family of origin. This could have facilitated more responsive and sensitive treatment planning, with special attention to continually addressing this mother's issues of safety, control, and self-esteem in collateral meetings. A more definitive psychosocial assessment of Bea, furthermore, would have clarified the clinical need for her immediate referral to individual treatment focusing on posttraumatic stress disorder.

Three conditions influenced making the abbreviated assessment and rapid intervention described here: (1) the crisis nature of the case, (2) the long time period between past traumatic events and the present crisis, and (3) unanalyzed countertransference. When Charlie came for treatment, his aggression was externalized and enacted directly upon family members; he was actively harming his younger sister and angrily provoking his mother. This family scenario created a strong potential for child abuse because of Bea's questionable capacity for physical self-control. Their situation appeared to require immediate intervention to reduce the risk of further family violence. Second, the exploration of the spousal abuse—which had occurred 5 or 6 years in the past—did not appear immediately relevant to Charlie and his mother, who were struggling with each other in a new home *without* the father. Although a therapist may suspect that a history of domestic violence is directly related to the current symptoms, the therapist may hesitate to return to a traumatic period in the family's past, for fear that the family will experience this as irrelevant to their current needs. This raises an important practice issue: how to explore family history in a way that makes sense to the client and invites acceptance and cooperation. Finally, my countertransference contributed to my unconsciously enacting what I thought to be the necessary rescue of a family in need of a strong, organizing father. The family's panic, lack of a functional father, and troubled young boy resonated with my own family history and engendered my strong identification with Charlie. As a result, some needed objectivity was lost, and my capacity to identify negative family transferences (factors relevant to the premature termination of the case) was compromised.

The preferred approach to assessment is to begin in the present—with a clear focus on the current family crisis—and then follow related links to the family's past. For example, Charlie's symptoms first emerged after visitation with his father; this discovery naturally raised questions about Charlie's current and past relationship with him. It therefore would have been reasonable to determine the meaning to Charlie of his visitation with his father and of his reaction after returning to his mother's house. Did the visit meet his expectations? Did he encounter any confusing or upsetting behaviors? Did new questions arise about his father, the divorce, or their history together? Discussing early family dynamics (including spousal abuse) would have made logical sense in the context of exploring Charlie's relationship with his father. However, as stated previously, children often shy away from *verbal* discussions of anxiety-laden experiences. So perhaps Charlie's drawing might have offered the means to explore this, via the probes already suggested.

Engagement

When a crisis compels family members to seek help, their sense of being over-whelmed, desperate, and vulnerable promotes a rapid engagement with the thera-pist. This occurred with Charlie, his mother, and me. Once child therapy begins, however, its maintenance requires a healthy, ongoing partnership and working relationship with the referring parent—in this case, with Charlie's mother. But Charlie's case once again was complicated by the specter of trauma, because his treatment triggered feelings related to Bea's own victimization. This fact compli-cated the mother's ability to engage fully in a working alliance. As a trauma sur-vivor, Bea had a very limited ability to help her son. I now understand that I could have easily provoked negative transferences that were perceived as threatening to her. My inability to recognize these dynamics from the start contributed to the premature termination of Charlie's treatment. I did not pay enough attention to managing the complicated transference dynamics that weakened the necessary working alliance with Charlie's mother.

Nonetheless, my therapeutic alliance with Bea could have been strengthened by actively inviting more of her partnership in treatment planning. Beverly James (1989), writing specifically about the treatment of traumatized children, advocates direct involvement by a parent or caretaker in a child's treatment, although clinical discretion is needed to determine the degree of involvement. James reasons, for ex-ample, that open involvement of a caregiver lessens secrecy and feelings of shame, promotes the child's self-acceptance, permits direct management of caregiver resis-tance, and strengthens the caregiver–child attachment. Planning openly with the caregiver, moreover, empowers the therapist:

> A clear explanation of the therapist's role, with involvement by child and parent in plan-ning and executing treatment objectives, demystifies the process and provides the child and the parent with a sense of control while they continue to perceive the therapist as experienced and powerful. (James, 1989, p. 11)

Other therapists who work with traumatized children also recommend parental in-volvement (Wachtel, 1994; Webb, 1996). Had the dynamics of trauma been more clearly identified during the initial assessment period, Charlie's mother could have been approached with greater sensitivity and engaged more effectively as a partner in treatment. This would have resulted in my demonstrating more empathy and understanding of her posttraumatic reactions; I could have prepared Bea for the uncomfortable or confusing feelings triggered during treatment, and could have reduced perceived power differences by sharing control of the treatment planning; finally, I could have quickly identified and worked through any negative feelings, had I scrupulously invited Bea's feedback about our work together.

Premature termination of treatment, however, was directly related to these engagement issues and to the potential for repressed trauma to be symbolically re-peated in new situations (Silvern & Kaersvang, 1989). Bea's decision to stop treat-ment, for example, had the quality of a traumatic reenactment. Her abrupt and angry cutoff, her absolute refusal to discuss what happened, and her pulling Charlie away protectively—as if I might do him harm—mirrored how Bea had escaped her abusive spouse. Her behaviors made sense as a defensive response to a perceived threat. Charlie's treatment must have sparked something familiar and threatening: Perhaps my increasing closeness to Charlie was too much like that of a father, or perhaps our family sessions evoked too many memories of her warded-off past. Bea withdrew reactively to protect herself and her family.

We might have all benefited, however, had our working relationship been strong enough to risk talking about the fear and anxiety it provoked. Reenactments of trauma occurring within treatment provide a valuable opportunity to identify, understand, and defuse the displaced feelings in a safe setting. Observing together how trauma can destructively seep into daily life would have helped us realize the pressing need for Bea's individual treatment. And professional supervision would have helped me to identify my countertransferential contributions to the enactment as well.

Treatment Planning

This retrospective analysis, bolstered by insights from trauma theory (just emerging at the time of Charlie's treatment), suggests some alternative directions to consider. As previously discussed, Bea required individual treatment for posttraumatic stress reactions. A therapist separate from Charlie's would have given Bea the individual time and focus she needed to heal her devastating emotional wounds and to permit the ventilation, containment, and working through of transference reactions triggered by our work together. More family work—with a focus on behavior modification—was also indicated. First, Bea could have been taught to institute consistent rewards and consequences for Charlie, so that socially appropriate behavior could be shaped at home; second, she could have been coached to set clear and enforceable behavioral limits with Charlie. This approach, a structural–strategic family intervention, would have empowered Bea in her parenting role and provided greater structure for Charlie. Putting the mother back in charge (remember Charlie's family portrait!) would have had the additional benefit of decreasing his anxiety by reassuring him of his mother's firm and caring presence.

Although I attempted family interventions with Bea and her children, the timing was premature. I also did not adequately anticipate how anxiety-provoking family meetings would become for Charlie's mother, who was frightened by the overwhelming resurgence of her traumatic memories and feelings. Meeting with parents *both before and after* a family meeting to process their reactions, particularly with trauma survivors like Bea, is a necessary step in moving the treatment process forward and in maintaining parental involvement.

These individual and family interventions, in combination, would have been aimed at supporting and empowering Bea, reducing Charlie's symptomatic behaviors at home, containing and managing Bea's posttraumatic stress reactions, and promoting more open communication among family members. Could any changes in Charlie's individual treatment have been considered?

Nondirective versus Directive Intervention

Charlie's treatment—a traditional, nondirective play therapy—was chosen to engage Charlie in a nonthreatening, empathic way and to ascertain and explore the feelings underlying his conduct-disordered symptoms. A 1-year course of treatment was anticipated to provide Charlie with a consistent therapeutic relationship with a male. In the context of Charlie's history of cutoffs and separations from his father, the treatment relationship itself was viewed as a reparative intervention. Charlie did engage well and initiated play activities that revealed his sense of powerlessness, his loss of his father, his need for connection, and his sense of rejection and abandonment. Charlie's treatment was abruptly terminated, however, replaying his history of cutoffs. Considering what actually happened, and the contemporary context of managed care treatments that are symptom-focused and short-term, I wonder whether a more directive, short-term model might have proven beneficial.

Beverly James (1989) supports using an active approach involving guided play and direct discussion of events for traumatized children who "cannot initiate discussions of matters that overwhelm them" (p. 11). This means that a therapist may take the lead to open discussion about particular events, use clear statements to indicate acceptance of a child, and speak directly and authoritatively to the powerful self-blame hidden in the child. In practice, this might have meant saying to Charlie: "I like you. I know about some of the things that have happened to you. These things are not your fault. You don't have to hurt yourself, or others, to show that *you* are hurting." Such an approach builds a trusting, supportive relationship and develops ego strength in a child, who is helped to revisit and reprocess his or her traumatic experiences. In this model, trauma is approached directly and confronted:

> The goal is to have traumatized children reach the point where they can say something like, "Yes, that happened to me. That's how I felt and how I behaved when it happened. This is how I understand it all now. I won't really forget it happened, but I don't always have to think about it either." (James, 1989, p. 49)

Directive treatment strategically incorporates external reality into play scenarios. If this approach had been applied to Charlie, I would have focused more deliberately on Charlie's visitation with his father, on his parents' divorce, and on his witnessing of his mother's abuse. These life events could have been directly addressed through discussion of Charlie's drawing, or during his extensive soldier play. Although nondirective play put control of the session into Charlie's hands (a psychological compensation for not being able to control the adults in his world), directive play therapy would have ensured that traumatic events were surfaced and addressed. Examples of directed play can be found in several chapters of this book (see Webb, Chapter 3; Strand, Chapter 5; and Bevin, Chapter 7).

I think about Charlie now, as a teenager, and I hope that his disappointment and anger have not been released in drinking or self-harm. I hope that he has found some connection to an adult male in school, whom he can admire and use as an appropriate model. I hope that he has applied his intelligence and been rewarded with some recognition for achievement and personal sense of competence. I hope that he has joined an athletic team or other constructive group, and has developed a sense of meaningful community and peer support. Above all, I hope that he and his mother have reestablished a positive relationship. But I fear that without further professional help and support, traumatic reenactments will have continued to occur between Charlie and his mother, and that their relationship and their need for each other will have suffered. I trust that in time, Charlie will make his own evaluation of his father and determine for himself whether his father is capable of providing the relationship he needs. And I hope that Charlie's mother finds the healing she needs to overcome the difficult dynamics that sabotaged our work together. Finally, I hope Charlie remembers that at least one male adult treated him with respect and allowed him to express the full range of his feelings.

STUDY QUESTIONS

1. How would you have managed Charlie's requests to intervene actively in his life? What might be gained therapeutically, and what lost, by trying to engage a mother in satisfying a child's requests?

2. How would you have reacted to the aggressive onslaughts this child made in therapy? How might you have utilized your reactions within the play itself? At what point in treatment might you have linked his aggressive play to real events in his life? Or would you have done that?

3. Discuss the therapist's work with the mother. If you had been Charlie's therapist, how would you have presented the mother's referral to another therapist? What issues would have been particularly tricky in making the referral, and how would you have managed these?

4. Would you have chosen a nondirective style of treatment with Charlie or a directive one? What might be the advantages and disadvantages of each approach? If you decided to use a directive approach, what toys or activities would be appropriate?

5. This case was prematurely terminated. Discuss what feelings and reactions you might have as a therapist encountering such an end to such a course of treatment. What reactions would you expect from a child like Charlie? What, if anything, might you do as therapist to manage a premature ending such as this?

REFERENCES

Axline, V. (1947). *Play therapy*. Boston: Houghton Mifflin.
Brazelton, T. B., & Cramer, B. G. (1990). *The earliest relationship: Parents, infants, and the drama of early attachment*. Reading, MA: Addison-Wesley.
Davies, J. M., & Frawley, M. G. (1994). *Treating the adult survivor of childhood sexual abuse: A psychoanalytic perspective*. New York: Basic Books.

Elbow, M. (1982). Children of violent marriages: The forgotten victims. *Social Casework, 63*(8), 465–471.

Ell, K., & Aisenberg, E. (1998). Stress-related disorders. In J. B. W. Williams & K. Ell (Eds.), *Advances in mental health research: Implications for practice* (pp. 217–256). Washington, DC: National Association of Social Workers.

Eth, S., & Pynoos, R. S. (1985). *Post-traumatic stress disorder in children.* Washington, DC: American Psychiatric Press.

Herman, J. L. (1992). *Trauma and recovery.* New York: Basic Books.

Jaffe, P. G., Wolfe, D. A., & Wilson, S. K. (1990). *Children of battered women.* Newbury Park, CA: Sage.

James, B. (1989). *Treating traumatized children: New insights and creative interventions.* New York: Lexington Books.

Landgarten, H., Junge, M., Tasem, M., & Watson, M. (1978). Art therapy as a modality for crisis intervention: Children express reactions to violence in their community. *Clinical Social Work Journal, 6*(3), 221–229.

Miller, D. (1989). Family violence and the helping system. In L. Combrinck-Graham (Ed.), *Children in family contexts: Perspectives on treatment* (pp. 413–434). New York: Guilford Press.

Minuchin, S. (1974). *Families and family therapy.* Cambridge, MA: Harvard University Press.

Silvern, L., & Kaersvang, L. (1989). The traumatized children of violent marriages. *Child Welfare, 68*(4), 421–436.

Wachtel, E. F. (1994). *Treating troubled children and their families.* New York: Guilford Press.

Wadeson, H. (1987). *The dynamics of art psychotherapy.* New York: Wiley.

Walker, L. (1979). *Battered women.* New York: Harper & Row.

Wallerstein, J., & Blakeslee, S. (1989). *Second chances.* New York: Ticknor & Fields.

Wallerstein, J., & Kelly, J. B. (1980). *Surviving the breakup: How children and parents cope with divorce.* New York: Basic Books.

Webb, N. B. (Ed.). (1991). *Play therapy with children in crisis: A casebook for practitioners.* New York: Guilford Press.

Webb, N. B. (1996). *Social work practice with children.* New York: Guilford Press.

Werner, E. E. (1995). Resilience in development. *Current Directions in Psychological Science, 4,* 81–85.

Winnicott, D. W. (1964). *The child, the family, and the outside world.* Reading, MA: Addison-Wesley.

CHAPTER 13

The Many Losses of Children in Substance-Disordered Families

Individual and Group Interventions

ROEY C. FICARO

Children growing up in substance-disordered families, where alcohol and other drugs are used as a way of medicating emotional and spiritual pain, experience losses on several different levels. The breakdown of the family system causes serious problems, such as violence; separation and divorce; illness and death; lack of appropriate nurturing and parenting; and the creation of an environment filled with tension, fear, pain, and isolation.

The National Association for Children of Alcoholics (1995) presents the following statistics and assertions about U.S. families affected by alcohol:

1. Seventy-six million Americans (about 43% of the U.S. adult population) have been exposed to alcoholism in the family.
2. Almost one in five adult Americans (18%) lived with an alcoholic while growing up.
3. There are an estimated 26.8 million children of alcoholics (COAs) in the United States. Preliminary research suggests that over 11 million of these are under the age of 18.
4. COAs experience other family members as distant and noncommunicative.
5. Alcoholism affects the entire family. Alcoholism tends to run in families: From 13% to 25% of all COAs are likely to become alcoholics themselves. Not all alcoholic families experience or react to stress in the same way.
6. COAs may be hampered by their inability to grow in developmentally healthy ways.
7. The level of dysfunction or resilience of the nonalcoholic spouse is a key factor in the effects of problems.
8. COAs exhibit symptoms of depression and anxiety more often than children of nonalcoholics.

COAs learn early that keeping the family secret about drinking is imperative to avoid further distress and chaos. The no-talk rule eventually causes individuals to avoid problems or deny that there are any. It fosters a feeling of impending doom, accompanied by knots in the stomach, free-floating anxiety, headaches, and sleeplessness (Subby, 1987). COAs also learn from broken promises, shame, disappointment, and fear. Trusting adults becomes difficult, and feelings are not expressed; therefore, denial, distrust, and the inability to feel become the modes of functioning for both children and their families. COAs become masters at hiding their feelings, and they learn three unwritten rules very early: "Don't talk," "don't trust," and "don't feel" (Black, 1982). The emphasis the families put on keeping the secret results in covering-up behavior that often causes these children to go unnoticed.

This chapter describes the Student Assistance Program, a school-based program that focuses on both prevention and intervention. Intervention targets students in three categories: (1) students who are COAs and/or children of substance abusers (COSAs); (2) students who are COAs and/or COSAs and who, in addition, themselves have an alcohol or other drug problem; and (3) students experiencing situational stress that puts them at risk.

Another important element of the program is the emphasis on prevention. This includes activities such as classroom presentations, assemblies, and time-limited psychoeducational groups, which discuss various aspects of alcohol and other drug problems. Many times COAs and COSAs reveal themselves in such a group or privately to the counselor. Without self-referral or parent referral, the process of identifying COAs and COSAs can be difficult. Figure 13.1 provides 20 behavioral and psychological signs that counselors and teachers can look for in identifying COAs in particular. Obviously they will need to observe more than just one of these signs before coming to any conclusions. There are few reliable methods for identifying COAs; according to Claudia Black (1982), 80% of COAs "look good," which is the main reason they go unnoticed. After identification of a child as a COA or COSA, an assessment is then conducted, and the student is subsequently counseled individually or voluntarily placed in a group for COAs or COSAs. Parent involvement is encouraged but is not mandatory.

The Student Assistance Program described here contracts with master's-level counselors, social workers, and psychologists in middle and high schools, as well as with residential treatment centers and colleges in the county it serves. Counselors are given specialized training on a regular basis.

TREATMENT APPROACHES

With the appropriate intervention and increased understanding, many children from substance-disordered families experience a lessening of their painful feelings of responsibility, burden, anxiety, and depression. As a result, the children's functioning often improves. Treatment may include group, individual, or family interventions; regardless of the modality, however, working with COAs and COSAs usually includes the following ingredients (Morehouse & Richards, 1982):

1. Establishing trust.
2. Demonstrating an understanding of how COAs and COSAs are affected by parental drinking/substance use.

Behavioral Signs

1. Difficulty concentrating

2. Persistent absenteeism

3. Poor grades and/or failure to turn in homework

4. Low scores on standardized IQ and achievement tests

5. Sudden behavior changes (quiet and moody or acting out)

6. Signs of neglect or physical and sexual abuse

7. Compulsive behaviors (overeating, overachieving, smoking, chemical abuse)

FIGURE 13.1. Twenty behavioral and psychological signs of children of alcoholics in school settings. From Robinson (1989, pp. 106–107). Copyright 1989 by Lexington Books. Reprinted by permission.

3. Working with the children's ambivalence about discussing their parents.
4. Giving the children an opportunity to express their feelings, either verbally or through play materials.
5. Education about alcohol/drugs and alcoholism/drug abuse.
6. Helping the children develop concrete solutions for coping with their parents' behavior and their own upset feelings.
7. Examining the children's own behavior for the purpose of modifying dysfunctional behavior patterns that may have developed as a result of the parents' alcoholism/drug abuse.

In addition to these goals, it is important to reduce feelings of isolation by helping COAs and COSAs share their dilemmas with other children in similar situ-

8. Shy and withdrawn from other children

9. Quarrelsome and uncooperative with teachers and classmates

10. Constant health problems (headaches, stomach-aches)

Psychological Signs

1. Low self-esteem
2. Anxiety
3. Easily embarrassed
4. Suppressed anger
5. Perceive problems as beyond their control
6. Poor coping skills
7. Prone to depression
8. Unreasonably fearful
9. Sad and unhappy
10. Difficulty adjusting to changes in routines

FIGURE 13.1. *continued*

ations. In addition, the work should lead to correcting the children's inaccurate perceptions about their parents' drinking/drug problems, including helping them understand that their parents' inconsistent and confusing behavior is often a result of drinking or drug use, thereby altering their perception that *they* are the "cause" or reason for parental substance use problems (Cable, Noel, & Swanson, 1986).

COAs in particular learn to minimize and "stuff" their feelings, and therefore have a very difficult time verbalizing them. Suppressing the feelings becomes a very unhealthy coping mechanism. Abused children also may use this technique as a way to keep their secret, to pretend nothing has happened, and to protect or care for themselves when the adult(s) around are not keeping them safe. All too often children who have been abused and COAs have their feelings and emotions invalidated by others. This proves to be another way they learn to mistrust and "stuff" their feelings (Karp & Butler, 1996).

Figure 13.2 shows how one 11-year-old girl felt about her mother's drinking. This picture was a response to a group activity in which COAs were asked to draw their feelings associated with a wine or liquor bottle (Zevon, 1985).

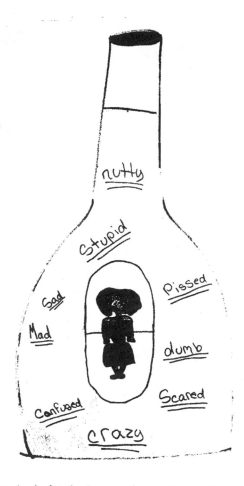

FIGURE 13.2. Feelings in the bottle: Drawing by an 11-year-old girl. From Zevon (1985, p. 20). Copyright 1985 by Yonkers General Hospital. Reprinted by permission.

FAMILY ISSUES

Alcoholism or other substance misuse is a family disease that affects every member in a devastating way. Recognizing the family unit as a system leads to a better understanding of the disease concept. Practitioners cannot fully appreciate what happens to a COA or COSA without understanding the inner workings of that child's total family system (Robinson, 1989). Because parental alcoholism in particular is a secret within and outside the family, a COA is made a partner in the family's denial that a parent is drinking (Woodside, 1986). When alcoholic parents are at midlife (mid-40s to mid-60s), they may seek help, but this often occurs after the children have left home.

The use of illicit drugs, which have a more rapid course in their addictive effects than alcohol, probably creates an earlier and stronger family recognition and responses (Webb, 1996). Straussner (1989) has classified the psychoactive drugs in terms of their specific effects on the central nervous system and their impact on a person's thinking and behavior (see Table 13.1).

An important part of helping children understand the family process is giving them insight into the roles they play in and outside of their families. Five basic roles are identified by Wegscheider (1981):

- The enabler
- The hero
- The scapegoat
- The lost child
- The mascot

Each role grows out of its own pain, has its own symptoms, offers its own pay-offs for both the individual and the family, and ultimately exacts its own price (Wegscheider, 1981). Table 13.2, which presents the identifying features of four of these roles, can be useful in group, individual, or family work.

Working with the parents of a COA or a COSA can be very helpful, especially if the nonusing or recovering parent makes the initial referral. Many programs for children and adolescents insist on parent involvement and will not serve young people without it. However, parent involvement is not always possible or desirable, especially in connection with service to COAs and COSAs. For example, children may be punished for participating, or forbidden to participate, in counseling services. However, programs for children can be very helpful even without parental involvement. Services that help COAs and COSAs develop protective behaviors through supportive counseling are invaluable to them (Morehouse, 1995).

REFERRALS FOR PARENTS AND FAMILIES

Any school's program for COAs and/or COSAs should be aimed specifically at the children themselves. The school cannot and should not become involved in the rehabilitation of the alcoholic/drug-using parents, however essential this work may be. Intervention involving treatment of parental alcoholism/substance misuse is outside the school's sphere of authority and probable competence (Ackerman, 1983). Therefore, referrals to outside treatment agencies and self-help groups are essential for parents seeking help. These referrals for students and families are an integral part of the school-based program described here.

BENEFITS OF GROUP COUNSELING

Working with children and adolescents in groups can be a very effective way of helping them to hear and experience peers in the same situation and learn that they are not alone. The group also gives them a safe place to share and express feelings they

TABLE 13.1. Effects of Different Categories of Psychoactive Substances on Individuals

	Depressants
Effects on brain:	Slow down, sedate brain tissues; alter judgment and behavior; cause agitation (hangover) in coming off.
Names of substances:	Alcoholic beverages; barbiturates and sedatives/hypnotics; minor tranquilizers (Librium, Valium); low doses of cannabinoids (marijuana and hashish).
	Stimulants
Effects on brain:	Increase or speed up function of brain; can produce acute delirium and psychosis (symptoms may include hallucinatioins, paranoia, and hypersexuality); violent behavior may occur with use of potent forms of cocaine ("freebase" or "crack").
Names of substances:	Amphetamines; cocaine; caffeine; nicotine.
	Narcotics or opiates
Effects on brain:	Decrease pain; create a sedative and tranquilizing effect; may cause stuporous inactivity (daydreaming/fantasies); may cause physical agitation upon withdrawal (panic and violent behavior may occur at this time).
Names of substances:	Opium, morphine, heroin, codeine, paregoric, methadone; Demerol, Darvon, Prinadol.
	Psychedelics/hallucinogens
Effects on brain:	Produce gross distortions of thoughts and sensory processes (e.g., visual hallucinations, distorted body image); may produce depersonalization, depression, hostility; may lead to violence because of anxiety and misperceptions of reality.
Names of substances:	LSD; PCP ("angel dust"); DOM; STP; mescaline; psilocybin.

Note. Adapted by Webb (1996, p. 274) from Straussner (1989, pp. 151–152). Copyright 1996 by The Guilford Press and 1989 by New York University Press, respectively. Used by permission.

have kept bottled up. It is a place where the secret can be told and talked about—for the first time, in many cases. In order to achieve this, they must feel safe and protected, and must know that confidentiality is taken very seriously. They must have the rules of confidentiality explained and understand the exceptions. COAs experience the following benefits through group participation (Morehouse, 1986):

- Reduced isolation
- Learning new ways of coping
- Receiving positive peer support
- Practicing sharing of feelings and confrontation when needed
- Preparation for referral to Alateen

COSAs are likely to experience similar benefits, but less research has been carried out with them.

TABLE 13.2. Characteristics, Traits, Feelings, and Behaviors of Children of Alcoholics

Role	Outside behaviors	Internal feelings	What the family gains from the child's role	Adult behavior without help	Adult behavior with help
The family hero or super kid	Overachiever. Overresponsible. Needs everyone's approval. Parentified child.	Hurt, inadequate, confused, guilty, low in self-esteem.	Provides self-worth to the family. Someone to be proud of.	Workaholic. Never wrong; controlling, manipulative, compulsive. Can't say no. Unable to accept failure.	Ability to relax, accept failure, be responsible, and say no.
The scapegoat or problem kid	Hostile, defiant, withdrawn, and sullen. Negative attention getter. Won't compete. Troublemaker.	Hurt, abandoned, angry, and rejected. Feels inadequate, with low self-esteem.	Takes the focus off the real problem. Takes the blame.	Alcoholic or addict. Unplanned pregnancy. Police involvement. Prison.	Recovery, courage. Ability to cope under pressure see reality, and be helpful to others.
The lost child	Loner, daydreamer, withdrawn. Drifts through life; quiet, shy, and ignored.	Lonely, unimportant, hurt, and abandoned. Not allowed to have feelings; rejected and hopeless. Fearful and anxious.	Provides relief—one less child to worry about.	Indecisive, intense, no fun. Stays the same. Alone or promiscuous. Can't say no. Possibility of early death.	Ability to be independent, talented, creative, imaginative, assertive, and resourceful.
The mascot or family clown	Very cute, immature, attention-seeking, and fragile. Hyperactive, short attention span, learning disabilities; anxious and needful of protection.	Low in self-esteem; terrified and lonely; feels inadequate and unimportant.	Provides comic relief, fun, and humor to the family.	Compulsive clown. Difficulty coping with stress. Will marry a hero.	Charming personality, quick wit, sense of humor. Ability to be independent and helpful.

Note. Contents from Wegscheider (1979).

Before COAs or COSAs are assigned to a group, at least three or four individual sessions are held in order to assess their readiness for a group experience and to enable the counselor to obtain a good overview of all the issues each child may be confronting. Individual sessions enhance the engagement process of the child and the worker, and they provide the opportunity to prepare the child for the group. One good way to encourage a child to volunteer for a group is to invite him or her to try it once or twice and then decide. This gives the child a sense of control (not common in an alcoholic or drug-using family) and allows him or her to make the decision.

The goals for COA/COSA groups include the benefits listed above, in addition to providing opportunities for the children to practice identifying their feelings, to increase their understanding of their parents, and to understand the disease of chemical dependence. Regardless of the duration of a group, it should include education about parental alcoholism/drug use and how it affects children (Johnston, 1991). The group should begin with an educational style, since the classroom—where the roles and rules are consistent and clearly defined—is often the only group in which a COA or COSA feels safe (Morehouse, 1995).

EXAMPLE OF INDIVIDUAL REFERRAL AND COUNSELING: CASE OF JILL, AGE 12

Self-Referral Following Class Presentation

Jill came to my office with a friend, Karen, and asked to make an appointment. I had made a presentation the day before to her seventh-grade class. It was the beginning of the school year, and I was making presentations to all seventh- and eighth-graders in order to introduce myself as the student assistance counselor, to explain my role, and to describe how students could come to see me and why.

I typically begin the presentation with a discussion about "kids and stress," encouraging dialogue by asking questions like these: "Do kids your age get stressed?" and "What causes stress for kids your age?" These open-ended questions always stimulate much discussion. School and peer issues come up, together with specific family issues such as illness, divorce, death, stepfamilies, and alcohol and drug use. The discussion then moves toward coping by talking with a trusted adult, confidentiality, and problems that can result from keeping feelings bottled up inside.

The purpose of this presentation is to help students understand the importance of discussing problems and the benefits this can produce. This is an attempt to destigmatize talking about stressors by universalizing the concept that we all feel stressed at times. Many COAs and COSAs end up self-referring, either individually or with a friend, following these presentations.

Family Information

Mother, Marie Jones	Age 35; full-time secretary; active alcoholic, in denial
Father, John Jones	Age 42; carpenter; history of cocaine and alcohol abuse; self-reported drug-free and sober for 1 year; recently separated from Mrs. Jones

Jill	Age 12; in seventh grade
Jennifer	Age 10; in fifth grade
Michael	Age 6; in first grade

Presenting Problem

When I saw Jill alone (see "Second Session," below), she initially presented issues about being upset over her younger siblings, for whom she felt responsible. She also mentioned concerns about her parents' not getting along; they had recently separated, and when her father did come by in the evenings, the parents would often argue after the children had gone to bed. This would keep Jill awake at night, causing her to feel tired at school and to have difficulty concentrating on her schoolwork. Jill presented as very shy and anxious, and she was concerned about her parents' being called.

As noted above, Jill first came to my office door during her lunch break with a friend, the day after I gave a presentation in her seventh-grade classroom.

First Session

Content of Session

COUNSELOR: Hi, girls. What are your names, and how can I help you?

JILL (*giggling anxiously*): My name is Jill.

KAREN: My name is Karen. You came to our class yesterday, and we want to make an appointment (*also giggling anxiously*).

C: I thought you both looked familiar. Was it Mr. Brown's class?

J: Yes, it was great. We didn't have time for the quiz!

C: I'm very happy I was able to help you guys out. I'm sure the rest of the class wasn't too upset either.

J AND K: (*Laugh and nod in agreement.*)

C: Have the two of you ever talked to anyone like me before, in school or out?

K: No, not me.

J: I did for a little while, but it didn't work out.

C: Really? Do you want to tell me what happened?

J: She called my parents, and it turned into a big mess. You said you couldn't do that unless we give you permission. Is that true? No matter what we say?

Rationale/Analysis

It is common for kids to come to the first session with a friend.

It is important to put them at ease during the initial engagement process.

I am beginning to assess, but going very slowly. Too many questions will raise their anxiety even more, which may make them decide not to come back.

I am allowing Jill to feel that she has some control and can choose whether to continue or not.

There is an important issue. She is being very cautious. I will get more information later.

C: The only two exceptions, as I explained in class, are if someone was being abused or thinking of hurting themselves or someone else.

(Counselor goes on to explain how the program works, to answer questions, and to make two separate appointments for the next day. The rest of the discussion stays on safe topics. Both girls seem much more at ease as they leave.)

It is important for her to hear the rules again, so she can decide whether it feels safe to let down her guard. She may not want to talk in front of her friend, and vice versa.

Second Session

Content of Session

Rationale/Analysis

COUNSELOR: Hi, Jill. How are you doing today?

JILL: OK, I guess.

C: Sounds like you're not sure how you feel.

She is ambivalent about sharing feelings or has trouble expressing them.

J *(shrugging her shoulders, smiling)*: I guess not. *(Giggles.)*

She seems anxious. Use of game play or art may help her focus the anxiety.

C: Well, you're not alone. Lots of kids come in here and say the same thing. I'd like to show you what I ask kids to do when they first come in. *(Shows her the "feeling faces chart" {see Figure 13.3} on the wall next to a small blackboard.)* When you come in, pick one or as many feelings you have felt in the last few days, and write them down. It doesn't have to be on the chart. Feelings change all the time, so you may see two or three that you felt this morning before school. Would you like to try one now?

I am being very explicit, universalizing, trying to take the stigma away. The feeling faces chart usually helps to open up communication so assessment can begin.

J: OK. *(Giggles. After studying the chart, she chooses two feelings, "exhausted" and "enraged.")*

She chooses the feelings that are most easily expressed.

C: Great. Do you want to talk about why you're exhausted and enraged? *(Passes Jill a rubber "koosh" ball to play with, to give her a place to direct her anxiety. She smiles and immediately begins playing with it in her hands.)*

J: My parents had a fight last night, and I woke up and couldn't go back to sleep.

C: You must have been very worried about them.

I name another feeling for her.

J: Nah. They always fight when Dad comes by in the evenings. I'm used to it. I just hate when they wake us up, because they are so loud.

She acts nonchalant, as if this is no big deal. She must have witnessed many such conflicts.

C: Who do you mean by "us"?

J *(giggling)*: Oh, my brother and sister. Mike is 6 and Jennifer is 10.

FIGURE 13.3. Feeling faces chart.

C: Did they get upset when your parents fought last night?

J: Jennifer gets angry and yells at them to shut up (*laughing*).

C: That's pretty brave of her. Does it help?

She seems to admire Jennifer's courage. I'm wondering whether alcohol or drugs are involved. I wait to see whether she will give clues.

J: Sometimes. It depends on how mad Mom is. She usually starts the fights. Dad usually gives up and goes back to his brother's house. He's staying there now.

She seems feel close to Dad.

C: How do you feel when Dad leaves?

J: I hate it, but at least the fighting stops.

C: Is this why you came in, to talk about your parents' fighting?

It seems to be time to get to the purpose of her visit, which she hesitated to discuss in the initial meeting. It is important to go slowly.

J: I guess so. Karen [the friend she came in with at the initial session] thought we should. Her parents got a divorce, and she thinks mine will too.

She appears fearful about family breakup, losing her father.

C: Do you worry about that a lot?

J: Yeah, but at least they wouldn't fight so much.

C: Do you ever worry about your parents' drinking?

It's time to go for the big question. She seems ready for it.

J (*wide-eyed*): How do you know?

She indirectly acknowledges the alcohol use problem. The secret is out.

C: I didn't. I always ask that question. There are many families who have that problem. You are not alone. There are many kids in this school worried about their parents' drinking. Can you tell me more about the drinking?

I try to lift shame by universalizing.

J (*frantically throwing the koosh ball back and forth in her hands*): Well, Dad doesn't drink any more. He goes to AA meetings every day. Mom still drinks at night before she goes to bed. Dad gets mad at her, and that's why they fight sometimes.

The topic is causing her anxiety to rise. Am I pushing her too fast? I must be careful.

C: You must be very proud of your dad. What an accomplishment!

I try to help her get rid of the shame.

J: Yeah, I guess (*giggling*).

C: What about your mom? Do you worry about her drinking?

J: I guess. Dad wants her to stop and go to meetings with him, but she says it's not a problem for her and that *he's* the one with the problem.

Her affect flattens when the subject of her mother comes up.

C: Do you believe that?

J: I don't think so. She's always causing fights when she drinks. I wish she would stop, but she won't listen to anyone and gets really mad if anyone says anything about it.

> She expresses her frustration and fear.

C: So how do you cope with your mom's drinking?

J: I don't know. I never really thought about that.

C: Well, maybe that's where we should start—helping you learn about the disease of alcoholism, and learning to talk about how it makes you feel and how to cope better. How does that sound?

> The education process begins. Also, I am reaching for her agreement. This is our initial contract.

J: OK, but you're sure you're not going to tell anyone or call my parents?

> She is worried she has trusted too much.

C: Absolutely not. Remember the rules about confidentiality?

> I reassure her about confidentiality.

Summary of Third Session

After the initial assessment phase, Jill began to trust and share more information about her family's history of dysfunction, including domestic violence, physical abuse, and her parents' alcohol and other drug involvement. Child protective services had been involved in the past, as described below. Jill was encouraged to tell her parents about our time together. She agreed it would feel safer for her to inform them that the content of our meetings was to help her perform better in school, and to give them my office number at the school to contact me at any time. Mr. Jones took the initiative and called to set up an appointment for himself. Mrs. Jones never responded on her own. Mr. Jones invited her to attend his appointment to discuss concerns about the children, but she refused, claiming difficulty in getting time off from work.

Jill also agreed to try one group session to see how it felt. She responded favorably and agreed to continue in the group. Jill's individual sessions tapered off as her group participation increased and the group itself became cohesive.

Background on Jill's Family

Jill's parents were in the initial phase of a very difficult separation. Mr. Jones, who claimed to have been sober for 1 year after a long history of cocaine and alcohol abuse, was trying very hard to become a responsible parent. The two younger children, ages 6 and 10, were acting out at home and in school. Jill was described as the "perfect child"—quiet and responsible. The children lived with their mother, whom Jill described as "a very busy person who gets tired and yells a lot." Mr. Jones described her as an alcoholic in denial, unable to feel anything but anger. He was a carpenter and currently out of work. Mrs. Jones worked as a full-time secretary in an office. Mr. Jones claimed that his relationship with his wife had always been chaotic, and that things deteriorated even further when he went into treatment and became sober. He would no longer drink with his wife, and she refused ... she did not have a problem. Now that Mr. Jones was getting ... feelings and facing the reality of the marital problems, as well as ... as a parent, the homeostasis of the family shifted; all family mem... state of confusion and chaos. Mrs. Jones agreed to participate in ... but Mr. Jones eventually followed through on a referral for himself ... which made Mrs. Jones feel alienated and angry. Mr. Jones also decided ... to ensure his sobriety, and this caused further problems for the children ... came very angry and acted on these feelings in their outside family ... their father.

Teachers also expressed concern that Jill looked burdened and depr... worked hard, but had difficulty on tests and needed academic support. Jill ... and depression were getting in the way of her learning. She was able to ... average work, but retaining information was difficult for her. She also exper... great deal of test anxiety. A referral to the school's learning team gave her ... help she needed and wanted.

The youngest child, 6-year-old Michael, was described by Jill as cute but ... to control. She claimed he only listened to his father. Her 10-year-old sister, Jen... fer would start fights with Michael and Jill. Jill also considered her a bully ... who would pick fights with her peers. It was clear that both siblings were acti... their issues. Before the separation, Mr. and Mrs. Jones had engaged in violen... fights, which the children witnessed. Police had been called by neighbors on several occasions, and one time Mr. Jones was taken into custody and released the next day ... Child protective services also became involved at one time, when a report was made by a school counselor after Jill disclosed information about her parents' drinking and fighting. The report was officially determined to be unfounded after an investiga... tion. The parents were told to seek counseling, but separated shortly after. Mr. Jones was clearly the more nurturing and supportive parent. Mrs. Jones was distant and withholding emotionally. Mr. Jones was worried about Jill, who isolated herself and was very quiet and shy.

Treatment Plan

This case demonstrates the initial outreach to a class and the subsequent self-referral, followed by the engagement and assessment process. Individual and group work were the treatment modalities for this child, as well as outside family work. The one-to-one counseling served Jill well, for she was depressed and anxiety-ridden; she needed a safe place and a relationship with a trusting adult who could provide nurturing, guidance, and support, as well as education about alcoholism and understanding of her family issues.

The referral to a time-limited COA group was made because Jill tended to isolate herself from peers, yet she wanted peer contacts in a safe and supportive environment. During the phase of individual counseling, Jill was eventually able to trust me enough to allow outreach to her father, who was in the beginning of his recovery from alcohol and other drugs and needed help dealing with his three children.

EXAMPLE OF GROUP COUNSELING: CASES OF JILL AND OTHERS

Group Composition

The group included four middle school girls who were dealing with parental alcoholism. These preadolescent girls were 12 and 13 years old. They either referred themselves to me after a class presentation, or were referred by another school staff member or a parent.

- Jill was 12 years old and in seventh grade. Information about her self-referral and her family has been given above.
- Lisa was 13 years old and in seventh grade. She was referred by the student assistant counselor at the high school who was counseling her sibling. Her father became abstinent without help; her mother was an active alcoholic and very depressed. The father was frequently away on business trips.
- Karen was 13 years old and in seventh grade. She self-referred with Jill. Her father was a binge drinker and smoked marijuana frequently. Her parents had been divorced 1 year; the father lived with his girlfriend.
- Amy was 12 years old and in sixth grade. She was referred by the school social worker, with her mother's consent. The father was an active alcoholic and physically abusive. Amy and her mother had moved in with relatives. Amy had had no regular contact with her father for the past 6 months.

Group Process

First Session

The girls were visibly very anxious. There was much giggling and lots of rolling eyes. Amy presented as especially anxious, being youngest and not knowing the others.

Content of Session

COUNSELOR: Hi, girls. Please come in and take a seat. Let's start with introductions. Karen, will you start by putting your name on the board, picking a feeling from the chart [see Figure 13.3], and writing it under your name? Remember, if you have a feeling that isn't on the chart, you can add one.

(*Everyone complies, picking very common, benign feelings about being in the group.*)

C: Thank you for being so cooperative. Everyone is always a little nervous for the first group session. In a minute we can talk about those feelings. Let's first discuss the purpose of this group. Why are we meeting?

Rationale/Analysis

KAREN: To learn about our feelings and talk about problems in school and at home.

C: Very good, Karen. Anyone want to add anything?

K: And whatever we say stays in this room!

C: Absolutely. Any other rules?

LISA: You get kicked out if you break it.

C: Does everyone agree? (*All nod yes.*) I'd like to add another—no put-downs or name calling. Also, the group will meet once a week for 8 weeks. Now let's get started. Today we start with learning about feelings. This game helps us to understand and talk about feelings. (*Introduces the Stamp Game,* which involves using eight piles of colored cards labeled with eight feeling words to identify, clarify, and discuss feelings. Counselor begins by explaining that feelings are our friends, signals to be listened to; they are part of us.*) Everyone take a card that matches the feeling you wrote on the board, and take two others that you felt over the weekend [today being Monday]. Remember, it's going to take time to learn to trust each other. Let's begin with the feelings you came in with today. Who would like to start?

JILL: I will (*giggling*). I wrote "stupid." There was no card for that, so I took the wild card.

C: Very good. Can you explain why you felt stupid?

J: I don't know. I just did. I wasn't sure what I was going to talk about, and I feel stupid talking in front of people (*giggling*).

C: You're doing a great job. Most people feel anxious in that situation. Can anyone relate to that?

L: I always feel like that if my teacher calls on me in class. I hate that feeling.

K: Me too. I always turn beet red.

(*Lots of giggles.*)

C: Is that if you don't know the answer?

J: Oh, no (*emphatically*). Even if I know the answer, I hate it when everyone looks at me.

C: It sounds like you get very embarrassed as well as anxious.

J: I guess so.

With my prompting, girls state purpose of group and rules to create a safe environment and learn to trust. The trust issue should be verbalized.

I add another essential rule and then introduce a game as an icebreaker.

I give them as much control as I can, to build empowerment.

Jill has lots of anxiety. She needs a name for this feeling, to replace "stupid." I universalize her situation and bring the group into it.

They are beginning to feel less anxious with each other. Cohesiveness is beginning.

Another feeling word is introduced.

*The Stamp Game is available from MAC Publishers, 5005 East 39th Ave., Denver, CO 80207.

C: What about you, Amy?

AMY: I felt just like Jill when I came here. I almost didn't want to come, but I'm glad I did.

(The girls nod in agreement, admitting not wanting to come. They laugh as the anxiety melts away.)

I am wondering about Amy. She seems to be taking it all in, nodding in agreement.

The group continued to play the Stamp Game, and the girls began to share feelings about peers and family members. They began to share their family composition as well. They all agreed to come back the following week. I was able to mention the common issue of family struggles toward the end at an appropriate time. The issue of alcoholism as a disease did not come up until the third group session, even though they were all informed that the focus of the group was on chemical dependence in families. It is helpful to allow the group process to evolve so that the members begin to feel some level of comfort before disclosing family secrets.

Third Session

Content of Session

Rationale/Analysis

COUNSELOR: Let's make a list of the kinds of problems which cause stress and tension in families. Can we do a go-around? Who will take a risk and start?

I introduce the topic of family stressors.

JILL: Parents' fighting.

AMY: Divorce.

KAREN: My parents fought about everything. Especially my father's drinking.

J: Mine fight about that too.

The secret is out. The real work can begin. They are beginning to trust each other.

C: It sounds like all of you have family struggles in common, especially about drinking. Drinking problems run in many families. As I've told you in our individual sessions, this is a group where you can help each other by sharing problems and seeing that you are not the only ones dealing with alcoholism in your families. There are 26 million children of alcoholics in the U.S. alone.

It is important to continue to universalize in order to dispel the underlying shame, and to refer to alcoholism as a disease in order to begin the psychoeducational process.

LISA: It's all over my family. Both my uncle and my older brother drink a lot and take drugs.

Acknowledgment of the problem.

C: How do you know about their problem?

L: The whole family knows about my uncle. He's been like that for a long time. My aunt always says she is going to leave him, but never does. My brother goes crazy when he drinks. He beat up my mother twice. I had to call the police.

They are beginning to open up and share with each other. Once one begins to share a secret, the others slowly follow, and denial lifts.

C: How brave of you! What were you feeling?

L: Really scared! I thought he was going to kill my mother.

K: What happened when the police came?

L: They came and took him to the police station to cool off. My father got him out the next day and told him to get out or go for help. He's supposed to be going to rehab, but he's still home. I hate him. I wish he would die. (*Begins to cry.*)

She feels that no one can protect her. Unexpressed feelings of anger, loss, and fear are emerging.

This group session proved to be extremely powerful for all the girls. After Lisa's disclosure of family violence due to substance abuse, the other group members began to disclose similar situations of domestic violence. Issues of anger, vulnerability, loss, and shame were disclosed. Feelings were validated and normalized. The group ended with a reading from the book *Living with a Parent Who Drinks Too Much* (Seixas, 1979). Each girl took a turn reading out loud from the chapter "Life with Your Family." This validated their feelings by showing how others have dealt with the same problems and identifying the behavior of alcoholics. The suggestion to read something from this book at the end of each group session was unanimously accepted. Giving them control of the group was important, in order to give them the feeling of being in control of some aspects of their lives.

Eighth Session

The group members decided to create a party atmosphere for the last group session. Snacks were provided.

Content of Session

Rationale/Analysis

COUNSELOR: Remember last week we talked about this being our last session?

JILL: Yes, but you said we could talk about if we wanted to meet another eight times.

KAREN: Yeah, we talked about it, and we don't want to end now.

C: I haven't heard from Lisa and Amy.

AMY: I don't want to end the group. It's the only place I can talk about this stuff.

LISA: Me too. I want to meet for the rest of the school year!

C: Well, it's unanimous, so let's make an unwritten contract for another eight sessions and see how everyone feels after that. Agreed?

ALL: Agreed! (*Laughter.*)

It is important to allow all COAs to experience decisioin making and consistency. These conditions help them to maintain positive relationships with peers and reduce feelings of powerlessness.

C: Could we use this session to look at how far you all have come after meeting only eight times?

A: I never used to talk in the beginning.

L: Me too. I was scared to come the first time.

J: Yeah, and now we can't shut you up! (*Laughter.*)

C: I'm so impressed with how you have learned to trust each other and share so many difficult feelings. How has what you learned here helped with what goes on at home?

> The positive interaction indicates the trust they have achieved with each other. It is important to validate and praise achievement of this goal.

J: I stay out of my parents' fights.

C: How do you do that?

J: I go in my room and put my radio on really loud, and I don't try to stop them anymore. I told Dad last week how scared I get when he comes over and they argue. He asked me why, and I told him it reminds me of when they used to hurt each other.

> She is learning not to be a caretaker to her parents.

A: What did he say?

J: He said he was sorry about all those times and promised it wouldn't happen again.

C: How did hearing that make you feel?

J: Really happy. I just hope he means it.

C: You sound very cautious.

> I am taking note of her affect and reflecting it back.

J: I am! Wouldn't you be? They break so many promises.

K: You can say that again. I don't even listen to promises any more from my father.

C: It sounds like you have all experienced a lot of disappointment from all the broken promises and need to talk about it. I know it's really hard, but we will begin next week with the topic of broken promises and how to deal with them.

> This is an interpretation to validate and clarify feeling, as well as to bring it back to the group for closure due to the end of the class period. This is a volatile topic needing to be acknowledged and ventilated.

L: I can make a list a mile long!

A: Me too. My father used to promise to take me places, and we never went.

C: A list is a very good idea, Lisa and Amy. Could you all make one for next time and write all the feelings you felt next to each broken promise? Thank you, girls, for a very good idea!

> It is important to bring out usable techniques on how to cope with this issue.

Summary

Group counseling proved to be a strong treatment modality for these COAs. It provided supportive and helpful validation from peers, improved their social skills, and educated them about the disease of alcoholism. The group members learned to identify and express feelings to each other, and eventually to their parents as well. Sharing of feelings and secrets conveyed the message that it was OK to break the "don't talk" rule these COAs had learned in their families. Group goals such as reducing isolation, learning new ways to cope, and obtaining a better understanding of their parents were met. Problem-solving activities using workbooks (e.g., Typpo & Hastings, 1984) proved to be extremely helpful: Group members were presented with many different scenarios and asked to come up with solutions and learn new ways to cope in their own lives.

It is important for a group leader to set clear and consistent limits; to be flexible; to have a sense of humor; and to create a relaxing, safe environment conducive to encouraging members to trust and share secrets and feelings.

Follow-Up

Group work continued as the members recontracted two more times. This was done both because the members requested it and because I felt that the girls needed the ongoing support and education provided by the group. Furthermore, these COAs did not have a way to get to Alateen on a regular basis. Amy eventually left the group when she and her mother moved to another school district and a more stable living environment with her extended family. A referral was made to the student assistance counselor of that school district, with Amy's permission. Amy continued her COA work in the new school and eventually joined an Alateen group. Lisa, Karen, and Jill became very close friends and continued their COA work all through middle school. Referrals were made for Lisa for outside treatment, due to her depression over her mother's terminal illness and eventual death 2 years later. Lisa's father sent her to a small girls' school; she is now in college and doing well. She has maintained contact with me occasionally over the years. As Jill and Karen moved to the high school, a referral was made to the student assistance counselor there. They joined a group at the high school with four other students. They also agreed to try an Alateen meeting once, but were unable to go consistently, due to the distance and their inability to obtain transportation on a weekly basis.

Karen continued to do well academically, but ended up involved in relationships with boys who took advantage of her. After a date rape encounter, which she eventually allowed to be disclosed to her mother, she accepted a referral to outside treatment. She is now in college.

Jill's story has not been as successful as those of the other girls to this point. Her father's sobriety continued, and in his role as stable parent he assumed custody of her two younger siblings, due to Mrs. Jones's inability to manage, set limits, or provide adequate nurturing. Jill chose to stay with her mother and maintained a job, but did poorly in school. She began drinking in 10th grade. Her use escalated to the point of needing inpatient treatment. After 28 days she came out and began using again. In her senior year, she would brag about excursions to the inner city, where she would buy drugs and meet guys. Her mother eventually agreed to go for treatment for her own depression. Jill dropped out of high school before graduating, and continued her alcohol and drug abuse as well as sexual promiscuity. However, she maintained a job and eventually obtained her general equivalency diploma (GED). She is now working full-time and planning to take courses at a local college. She continues to look depressed; she claims to be off drugs, but refuses to be in treatment or take medication. Jill qualifies for a dual diagnosis of depression and alcoholism. The fact that both parents have also had this dual diagnosis highlights the serious biological predisposition to depression and chemical dependence for this young woman. Without medication and continued treatment, it may be difficult for Jill to realize her potential. There is always the possibility that the experience of the treatment she received in middle school and part of high school may move her to obtain help again when she is ready.

CONCLUDING COMMENTS

This chapter emphasizes the need for multilevel interventions with COAs and COSAs. Individual work with a child often serves as the necessary prelude for establishing sufficient trust to initiate contacts with a family and to set the stage for the referral to a group. Because of the issue of secrecy, it takes children some time before they can talk about their feelings in group sessions. Once this barrier is crossed, however, the group offers tremendous support and validation related to sharing feelings of shame and embarrassment. Family treatment offers another potential resource for COAs and COSAs, but it requires that an alcoholic family member remain in recovery. Unfortunately, this may not be the case for many COAs yet. Children living with actively alcoholic or drug-abusing parents can still benefit from school-based groups, as described here. A group, in fact, may offer an essential anchor of rationality and stability for such children.

The biological heritage of COAs in particular includes a strong predisposition to the disease of alcoholism. The educational component of COA groups repeatedly emphasizes this fact. Nonetheless, adolescent feelings of vulnerability may drive some COAs to experiment, and some will inevitably succumb to the disease. For these young people, the hope is that the educational and supportive experience of the group will motivate them to find their way to eventual recovery.

STUDY QUESTIONS

1. Describe the stress on a group leader of working with children whose parents are active alcoholics or drug abusers. How can the leader avoid joining a child's negative feelings about a parent?

2. How can the leader deal with the issue of confidentiality so that it does not increase the communication barrier between a child and a parent? Do you agree with the confidentiality policy described in this chapter? Why or why not?

3. The girls in the group described here were 12 and 13 years old. What play therapy materials would you recommend for this age group?

4. How could the use of role play be incorporated into a COA or COSA group? Identify some advantages and disadvantages of its use.

REFERENCES

Ackerman, R. (1983). *Children of alcoholics: A guidebook for educators, therapists and parents.* Holmes Beach, FL: Learning.

Black, C. (1982). *It will never happen to me.* Denver, CO: MAC.

Cable, L. C., Noel, N. E., & Swanson, S. C. (1986). Clinical intervention with children of alcohol abusers. In D. C. Lewis & C. N. Williams (Eds.), *Providing care for children of alcoholics: Clinical and research perspectives* (pp. 64–79). Pompano Beach, FL: Health Communications.

Johnston, M. E. (1991). Multiple losses in children of chemically dependent families: Case of RJ, age 7. In N. B. Webb (Ed.), *Play therapy with children in crisis* (pp. 276–292). New York: Guilford Press.

Karp, C. L., & Butler, T. L. (1996). *Treatment strategies for abused children: From victim to survivor.* Thousand Oaks, CA: Sage.

Morehouse, E. R. (1986). Counseling children of alcoholics in groups. In R. Ackerman (Ed.), *Growing in the shadow* (pp. 125–142). Pompano Beach, FL: Health Communications.

Morehouse, E. R. (1995). Matching services and the needs of children of alcoholic parents: A spectrum of help. In S. Abbott (Ed.), *Children of alcoholics: Selected readings* (pp. 153–175). Rockville, MD: National Association for Children of Alcoholics.

Morehouse, E. R., & Richards, T. (1982). An examination of dysfunctional latency age children of alcoholic parents and problems in intervention. *Journal of Children in Contemporary Society, 15*(1), pp. 21–32.

National Association for Children of Alcoholics. (1995, November). *Children of alcoholics: Important facts* [Information sheet]. Rockville, MD: Author.

Robinson, B. E. (1989). *Working with children of alcoholics: The practitioners' handbook.* Lexington, MA: Lexington Books.

Seixas, J. S. (1979). *Living with a parent who drinks too much.* New York: Beech Tree Books.

Straussner, S. L. A. (1989). Intervention with maltreating parents who are drug and alcohol abusers. In S. Ehrenkrantz (Ed.), *Clinical social work with maltreated children and their families* (pp. 149–177). New York: New York University Press.

Subby, R. (1987). *Lost in the shuffle: The co-dependent reality.* Pompano Beach, FL: Health Communications.

Typpo, M. H., & Hastings, J. M. (1984). *An elephant in the living room: A leaders' guide for helping children.* Minneapolis, MN: Comp Care.

Webb, N. B. (1996). *Social work practice with children.* New York: Guilford Press.

Wegscheider, S. (1979). *Children of alcoholics: Caught in the family trap.* Minneapolis, MN: Johnson Institute.

Wegscheider, S. (1981). *Another chance: Hope and health for the alcoholic family.* Palo Alto, CA: Science & Behavior Books.

Woodside, M. (1986). Familial patterns of alcoholism. In D. C. Lewis & C. N. Williams (Eds.), *Providing care for children of alcoholics: Clinical and research perspectives* (pp. 31–38). Pompano Beach, FL: Health Communications.

Zevon, M. (1985). *Out of the mouths of babes: Children of alcoholics/addicts express their feelings.* Yonkers, NY: Yonkers General Hospital.

RESOURCES FOR COAS AND COSAS

In addition to Seixas (1979) and Typpo and Hastings' (1984) leader's guide, the following materials can be useful in working with COAs and COSAs:

Black, C. (1985). *Repeat after me*. Denver, CO: MAC.

Karp, C. L., & Butler, T. L. (1996). *Activity book of treatment strategies for abused children: From victim to survivor*. Thousand Oaks, CA: Sage.

Typpo, M. H., & Hastings, J. M. (1984). *An elephant in the living room: A children's workbook*. Minneapolis, MN: Comp Care.

CHAPTER 14

Developmental Identity Crisis in Nontraditional Families

Cases of Emma, Age 8, and Chad, Age 13, Children of Lesbian Parents

LESLIE H. WIND

This chapter presents two cases of children learning about, and struggling with, their lesbian mothers' sexual orientation. The first case presented is that of an adopted 8-year-old girl. The second is that of a 13-year-old boy whose parents divorced when he was 9 years of age, the same time he learned of his mother's sexual orientation.

It is estimated that there are over 1.5 million lesbian mothers and 1 million gay fathers in the United States. Over 6 million children are estimated to have gay or lesbian parents (Schulenberg, 1985; Gottman, 1990) and the number is growing. This is not a new phenomenon, but until recent years lesbian- or gay-headed households have remained as invisible as possible. This is changing, however, as gay and lesbian parents are increasingly declaring their sexual preference and openly establishing households with their partners.

It is important to begin this chapter with an understanding that being the child of a gay or lesbian parent does not, in and of itself, create a crisis. Exploration of similarities and differences during latency and sexual orientation in adolescence is part of normal development. As with many children of other nontraditional family systems, those with gay and lesbian parents struggle with a sense of differentness. In adolescence, children of gay and lesbian parents often face heightened concerns about their own sexual orientation. Additional factors, such as ethnic differences in transracial adoption, may further emphasize a child's sense of differentness. Peer curiosity during latency, negative stereotypes, and limited peer support can exascerbate the child or adolescent's experience, thereby creating greater conflict. As with other crises, each child and family experiences their situation according to idiosyncratic factors.

THE ADULT EXPERIENCE

Coming out has a variety of aspects, including recognition, action, and acceptance of homosexual identity. Joan Sophie (1986) presents a three-stage model of identity development to assist in understanding the coming-out process. The initial stage involves coming out to oneself. This is a time of increasing self-awareness and attraction to others of the same gender. The next stage consists of development of a personal philosophy about homosexuality. The final stage is coming out to others; how, and to what degree, a person chooses to become visible varies.

In coming out, gays and lesbians have to face heterosexism and homophobia. "Heterosexism" is the belief that the world is and must be heterosexual. The homosexual individual contradicts that assumption when he or she comes out. Homosexual parents have an added challenge: There is a common assumption that adults with children are heterosexual, and contradiction of that assumption challenges concepts of and beliefs in the "traditional" heterosexual nuclear family.

In addition, "homophobia" (fear and hatred of homosexuality) is common and affects everyone, including gays and lesbians. When gays and lesbians internalize homophobia, they apply negative perceptions to themselves. The effects consist of subtle or blatant self-doubts or feelings of inferiority. Interestingly, the number of reported lesbian- and gay-headed households grew following the Gay Pride movement of the 1960s (Clunis & Green, 1995).

CHILDREN'S EXPERIENCES

Coming out as an adult certainly presents many challenges, but these are greatly compounded when a child's or children's response(s) have to be considered. Clunis and Green (1988, 1995) discuss the benefits and risks of coming out to children and the differences in the children's experiences based on the method of the children's conception and their age. They indicate that lesbian parents who choose to adopt or utilize alternate forms of insemination have usually come out before the child joins the family. This means that the parents can offer consistent, age-appropriate explanations over time, and that the child can gradually develop his or her own interpretation of the situation. This was true of one of the cases to be discussed later in this chapter.

In contrast, for those children who come from heterosexual unions, "coming out has more of an announcement quality" (Clunis & Green, 1995, p. 63). With these families, Clunis and Green (1995) identify risks such as rejection by a child, custody issues, hostility toward a parent's partner, and social stigma. Regardless of the timing or type of conception, there are risks involved in coming out to children. The risks most often identified in the literature include custody problems, peer stigmatization, hostility toward the parent's lover/partner, and even rejection of the parent. Most parents identify fears of most of these issues and struggle with the challenge of maintaining a balance between "realistic caution and . . . anxiety" (Clunis & Green, 1995, p. 65).

Despite the risks, Clunis and Green (1995) advocate that lesbian mothers come out to their children, and they recommend that this occur earlier rather than later. One concern centers around intimacy. As with all couples and families, secrets interfere with intimacy. The ability to be openly affectionate and caring supports all of the relationships in the home. All couples, while nurturing their own relationship, also model intimacy for children. A second area of importance is communication. Again, as with all couples and families, open communication fosters healthy family interaction and positive relationships. This is particularly true for families with circumstances that vary from the societal norm. Children need to be able to discuss their awareness that their family composition is different from that of their friends. If partners are unwilling to discuss this, the message may inadvertently plant homophobic ideas in a child. The child may also assume that discussion of anyone's sexuality, including his or her own, is unacceptable. Finally, Clunis and Green (1995) stress the importance of a child's learning about a parent's lesbianism directly from a supportive parent who is proud to stand up for her beliefs. Children will be better prepared to address homophobia in general if they have had the experience of open discussion with their parent(s).

How do children react? This is the key question for both parents and clinicians. According to Joy Schulenburg (1985), who interviewed more than 500 gay and lesbian parents, most children respond positively and are more concerned about whether their relationship with their parents will remain intact. There are, however, differences in children's reactions, based on their ages and the timing and approach during disclosure. According to Clunis and Green (1988), children and parents agree that it is better to disclose to a child at the youngest age possible. The benefits of early disclosure include the reduced risks that disclosure will occur outside the family, and that younger children will internalize society's homophobia (which is usually well established by 11–12 years of age). Early disclosure by a parent also allows for longer-term ongoing discussions. This is especially important in light of a child's changing views of a parent's homosexuality.

IMPLICATIONS FOR TREATMENT

Nontraditional families present a variety of challenges to the treatment process. Such families have often developed by natural conception as well as adoption and present all the attendant family complexities, plus the additional component of sexuality. Of utmost importance to the therapeutic process is the clinician's acceptance and nonjudgmental attitude. When a clinician is working with a lesbian parent or couple, both partners desperately need to believe that the clinician understands societal biases and their impact on the family, recognizes their commitment to their child(ren), and joins them openly in partnership as they work to strengthen their family system and address the needs of each member.

Some therapists believe that lesbian couples need to be treated by lesbian therapists who have come out (Gartrell, 1984; McDermott, Tyndall, & Lichtenberg, 1989; Riddle & Sang, 1978). More recent studies have found that the nature of the clinician's experience is more important to the comfort level of a lesbian client (Moran, 1992). Overall, an approach that is collaborative and accepting in nature appears most effective.

The effective clinician can initially offer lesbian mothers education and support regarding questions about the children's gender identity and sexual development, as well as realistic expectations regarding disclosure. Providing homosexual parents with recommendations for healthy, planned disclosure, or assistance in discussing sexual orientation in the family, can be very helpful. An effective clinician is one who is trustworthy and nonjudgmental of a mother while also helping the child or children come to their own resolution of their family situation (Lewis, 1980).

Awareness of cultural and personal biases is the key to effective therapy. Society and the courts have traditionally been concerned that children of gay and lesbian parents will develop the same sexual orientation as a result of environment. In fact, a number of studies examining the concepts of gender identity, gender role, and sexual orientation have concluded otherwise (Huggins, 1989; Tasker & Golombok, 1997; Patterson, 1992). People often confuse these three concepts. "Gender identity" is the person's sense of self as generally male or female. "Gender role" refers to society-sanctioned behaviors and attitudes for each gender; these behaviors and attitudes have a positive or negative value attached to them by a particular culture. "Sexual orientation" refers to a person's sexual attraction, either toward the same gender, the opposite gender, or both. With the exception of transsexuals, gender identity is almost always consistent with the person's biological gender. Also, for the majority, biological sex and gender identity are consistent with gender role. The range of adherence to societal role norms is the same among children of heterosexual and homosexual parents (Tasker & Golombok, 1997). It is imperative that the clinician be aware of the research as well as their own beliefs regarding the developmental process of children in gay- and lesbian-headed households.

In addition to concerns about sexual orientation, society has expressed concerns about the emotional development of children of homosexual parents. Multiple studies have found no evidence to support any difference in children's emotional development between homosexual and heterosexual home environments (Golombok, Spencer, & Rutter, 1983; Kirkpatrick, Smith, & Roy, 1981). In fact, approximately 10% of children from both heterosexual and homosexual parents exhibit emotional and behavioral problems. Research on children's self-esteem during childhood and adolescence has also found no difference in risk of emotional and behavioral problems between the two types of households (Puryear, 1983; Steckel, 1987; Huggins, 1989). Interestingly, two differences did emerge in one study: Children of lesbian mothers demonstrated more anger and fear in stressful situations, as well as a stronger sense of happiness, than children of heterosexual mothers (Patterson, 1996). Patterson (1996) suggests that such differences may be attributable to more stress in the everyday lives of lesbian-headed households or to an increased ability to acknowledge positive and negative feelings.

PARENT–CHILD ATTACHMENT

More important than sexual orientation of the parent is the parent–child bond. According to attachment theory (Bowlby, 1969, 1973, 1980; Ainsworth, 1972, 1982), a child's social and emotional development is strongly related to the quality of attachment between mother and child. The distinction between secure and insecure attachment relates to the quality of the mother–child interaction. Children who perceive their caregivers as responsive tend to develop secure attachments, while those who perceive their caregivers as unresponsive tend to develop insecure attachments. Children demonstrating secure attachment have more positive psychological outcomes, including increased sociability, higher self-esteem, greater empathy toward others, and fewer behavioral problems. An example of caregiver responsiveness is an ability to assuage a baby's distress via voice, touch, and facial expressions. To further the concept of a responsive caregiver, Stern (1985) and Kohut (1977) emphasize the importance of each caregiving relationship as having a potentially profound impact on the child. Children may develop attachments to more than one caretaker. Cassidy (1988) presents a connection between internal models of attachment figures and internal models of the self: A child who perceives attachment figures as unresponsive may hold an internal model of the self as unlovable. It is believed that this will have a far-reaching negative impact on the quality of later relationships, whereas the reverse is expected of those with a secure attachment and a positive internal model of self. Based on this, it would seem that children who develop a secure attachment to their mothers, in either heterosexual or homosexual households, are more likely to exhibit healthy development.

FAMILY IDENTITY

What factors contribute to a healthy family identity and acceptance of a parent's homosexuality? In an uncontrolled study, K. G. Lewis (1980) found an age difference in acceptance of parents' sexual orientation: Older adolescent boys had more difficulty than younger children in accepting their mothers' sexual orientation. As previously discussed, other research studies suggest that individuals may be more accepting of their mothers' sexual preferences if they are told in early childhood (Pennington, 1987; Huggins, 1989). Gottman (1990) found that the time and manner of disclosure of homosexuality could contribute to levels of acceptance. Gottman states that a child who learns of a parent's homosexuality via a divorce custody dispute will be doubly traumatized, and that a child whose parent has previously denied his or her homosexual identity will experience difficulty trusting that parent. Pennington (1987) suggests that children of lesbian mothers do best when their mothers have a positive identity and good parenting skills, as well as a supportive social network. (This finding is also true of children of heterosexual mothers.)

One additional factor needs to be considered: the social environment. Many clinicians agree that positive peer relationships are important to a child's social and emotional development (Dunn & McGuire, 1992). A child may have a strong, positive relationship with his or her lesbian mother and yet experience negative attitudes about homosexuality in the neighborhood, the school, and the media. Children of lesbian parents may be teased, taunted, and rejected because of their mothers' sexual orientation and may experience emotional difficulties because of this. There are differences in children's concerns about peer response to their parents' sexual orientation. In Lewis's (1980) study, school-age children reported concern about being teased or rejected by peers. We know that latency-age children worry about feeling different in *any* way. In another study, adolescents expressed concerns about what to tell their friends, peer prejudice, and bringing friends home (Tasker & Golombok, 1997). However, in Tasker and Golombok's longitudinal study, the researchers found no difference between young adults from lesbian-mother and heterosexual-mother families in perceptions of having been "picked on" by classmates. These researchers did note, however, that individuals raised by lesbian mothers reported more teasing about their own sexuality than those of heterosexual mothers did. One-third of those studied thought that their mothers had been too open about their sexual orientation in front of their friends.

Tasker and Golombok (1997) found that children of lesbian-headed families reported a sense of social stigma equal to those of peers from heterosexual single-parent families. Children of both types of single-parent families experienced a sense of differentness from peers of traditional nuclear families. Most children of lesbian mothers reported the ability to integrate a close friend into their family life. More than half had disclosed their mothers' sexual orientation to an accepting friend. In addition, during latency participants reported that lesbian mothers performed typical role behaviors when friends came home. Adolescents worried more about appearances, such as written materials left out where others could see or open displays of partner affection. This is consistent with Bozett's (1987) findings that a young person's comfort level with bringing peers home may be related to the degree to which the parent's homosexual identity is obvious and stereotypical. In Tasker and Golombok's (1997) study, the individuals who were most comfortable had mothers who were more sensitive to the potential social impact of such openness. Peer group prejudice is of greatest concern during adolescence, a time when teens are developing their own sexual identity. Children of lesbian mothers in lower-socioeconomic-status families reported more peer stigma than did children of middle-class lesbian mothers.

FIRST CASE EXAMPLE: EMMA, AGE 8

This is the first of two cases of children who reside in lesbian-headed households. Emma, an 8-year-old black girl, was adopted at 11 days of age by a white lesbian couple.

Family Background

Emma was the third child of her biological mother and father. The biological parents reportedly placed Emma for private adoption because of financial constraints. Her biological siblings were 1 and 3 years of age at her birth. She had no contact with her biological family after her adoption. Her adoptive mothers indicated that she was told that her parents "could not financially afford to have another child and decided it was better to provide her with a loving family that could support her." Emma appeared to accept this information unconditionally. Emma's adoptive family had a mixture of homosexual and heterosexual friends; many of them had children near Emma's age. Emma had a best friend, Teresa, who was 8 years of age, white, and lived with her biological mother and father. As a result of early adoption, Emma had a lifelong opportunity to observe and learn about her mothers' sexual orientation. Both of Emma's mothers were active participants in parenting.

Presenting Problem

Emma entered treatment with complaints of stomachaches, school avoidance, and difficulty sleeping, and had a history of learning problems. Emma attended third grade at a local public elementary school, where her teachers reported that she had some difficulty fitting in with her peers. Observation during class and recess confirmed Emma's desire to be liked by her peers and her difficulty joining in play fully. Emma tended to tag along behind the group, intermittently offering comments and following in whatever activity the group began. The elementary school was ethnically and racially diverse, as was Emma's peer group. Both mothers were active at the school.

First Interview

During initial assessment, both mothers accompanied Emma and participated in giving a thorough psychosocial history, including discussion of her adoption. During this session, I encouraged Emma to talk about her experience of school, friends, and family. She was quiet and shy, and avoided eye contact. Both mothers encouraged her involvement in the session with little success.

Initiating a therapeutic alliance with this family began with my openness and acceptance, indicating my sincere interest and respect, as well as personal comfort in identifying and discussing the mothers' lesbian relationship and their roles as mothers.

Preliminary Assessment and Treatment Plan

Initial assessment suggested that Emma was a child struggling with her sense of self and her place in her world. Her conflict was complex, due to the dual issues of transracial adoption and having lesbian parents. Academic testing and class observation indicated that Emma's learning problems were based on anxiety and resulting hypervigilance. Her extreme discomfort with expression of her feelings inhibited her ability to get her needs met, both at home and with peers. Emma demonstrated a strong attachment to both mothers, with a preference for one or the other parent depending on the situation. This is often true of children in heterosexual families as well as homosexual families. Her mothers' active support, both at home and at school, were strengths within this family system and contributed to a positive prognosis.

The goals of treatment included enhancing Emma's communication skills, improving her expression of her feelings and needs, improving peer relationships, enhancing family identity, increasing self-esteem, and improving school performance. A team approach was utilized: Emma participated in a peer relationships group with the school counselor in addition to weekly individual and/or family therapy outside of school. The school counselor, teacher, and I maintained communication every 2–3 weeks to promote cohesive intervention.

Second Session

As a follow-up to the initial session, the second session focused on assisting Emma in becoming more verbal in session. To accomplish this, the family version of The Ungame (P.O. Box 6382, Anaheim, CA 92816) was utilized in a family therapy session, allowing observation of Emma's ability to process and apply game rules consistent with her age and providing the structure for individual communication of perceptions about the family, including boundaries. Emma appeared comfortable with the game structure and participated fairly well.

Fourth Session

The following excerpt from a later session demonstrates Emma's sense of differentness. Children at age 8 often compare themselves to others and long to "fit in" and be a part of the group. Latency-age children of lesbian parents, as well as transracially adopted children, experience themselves as different even more powerfully than others do.

Content of Session	Rationale/Analysis
CHILD: I'm not like Teresa.	
THERAPIST: How are you different?	Differentness is a key concept for exploration.
C: (*Shrugs her shoulders.*)	
T: Feeling different is hard for you.	
C: (*Nods head affirmatively.*)	
T: I wonder what things make you feel different? It's hard for you to tell me. Let's pretend we're in school and we're making a list for the teacher.	It's difficult for her to express specifics. She needs a concrete method in addition to words. She likes to please her teacher.
C: OK.	
T: (*Takes out a piece of paper and markers.*) What color marker should we use?	
C (*smiling*): Purple.	This gives her a sense of control.
T: (*Uses a purple marker to make headings: "I FEEL DIFFERENT," and under this, "Good," "Weird," and "Sad."*) Everyone has things that they like and don't like about themselves. But they're different for each person. Tell me one thing that you like about yourself.	Emma has difficulty naming feelings. The headings are intended to help her with this.
C: My birthday!	This is too general. I need to help her personalize this.
T: You like how you feel about yourself on your birthday.	

C: Uh-huh.

T: What is something you think is weird about yourself?

C: (*Pokes at her arm and pulls the skin.*)

"Weird" is a word she has used in the past. She is comfortable with this word.

Does she mean her body or skin color?

T: Your skin is weird?

C: Uh-huh. It's black.

T: You think your skin is weird because it's black? Is there a reason you think that's weird?

What does this mean to her?

C: Teresa's skin is white. So are my moms'.

Most of the important people in her life are white.

T: Your skin is a different color from your moms' and your friend's. Yes, it is. And you feel weird about that. What's something you feel sad about?

This is a significant acknowledgment. I want to encourage her to talk more, so I'll have to return to the issue of transracial adoption and her sense of being different.

C: Sleeping.

T: You feel different because your friends sleep in their own beds?

Other children her age sleep independently.

C: (*Nods affirmatively.*)

T: You feel uncomfortable in your bed alone. What about when you have a friend over?

Is she afraid to be alone? When does she feel safe in her own bed?

C: That's OK.

What is her experience when she is alone? We'll need to explore this.

T: OK. Tell me another thing that you *like* about you.

I try to balance discomfort with comfort, to strengthen Emma's tolerance.

C: My body.

T: You're a good gymnast. Not all kids can do that. Is there another thing about you that makes you feel weird?

She receives lots of positive feedback for her sports.

C: I don't have a dad.

T: That's true. You have two moms. There are lots of different kinds of families. Some have a mom or a dad, or both, or just one parent. Some families have two parents that are either both moms or dads.

I introduce the topic of Emma's two mothers and gauge her response. I model acceptance and universalize.

C: I know. Teresa has a mom and a dad.

It is normal for Emma to want to be like her best friend. What else does this mean to her?

T: Yes. Her family is different from yours. Let's read a story about families. I think you'll like it.

Both families are "different." A story helps explore an issue while keeping a safe distance.

After reading the story *Heather Has Two Moms* (Newman, 1991), the mothers were invited into the session to present the topic of "differentness" and set the stage for a family session to follow. For a clinician, educating lesbian parents on healthy communication with their child(ren) is an important role and support to the therapeutic process. In sessions without their child(ren) present, mothers are able to discuss their views on how much information to share about their lesbian relationship and how to go about it, with consideration of developmental issues.

Fifth Session

The following is an excerpt from a family session where Emma's mothers disclosed a more intimate side of their relationship to Emma.

Content of Session	Rationale/Analysis
THERAPIST: Emma, I asked your moms to join us today to talk about your concerns about feeling different from your friends.	I am setting the stage. I focus on the invitation from me to the mothers, with topic identified. I model openness.
CHILD: Like Teresa.	
T: Yes, like Teresa. You and I talked about how you notice that you look different than Teresa and how her family is different from yours.	
C: Uh-huh. (*Looks down.*)	Emma may be unsure about her mothers' responses to this topic.
T: I think it's important for us to talk about that. And I think your moms can help you.	I validate Emma's concerns and the mothers' roles.
MOM 1: Emma, lots of people feel different. I do, too.	She wants to show understanding.
T: The way Emma feels different may not be the same as you.	I need to help this mother keep her boundaries. The focus here is on the *child's* experience.
M1: You're right. Emma, tell me how you feel different.	Mom 1 handles redirection well.
C: Teresa has a dad and I don't. (*Looks down.*)	
M1: (*Takes a deep breath.*) Some kids have a mom and dad, and others have just one parent (*pause*), and some kids have two moms. Or a dad and two moms. There are lots of different kinds of families.	Mom 1 feels ready and committed.
C: I know.	
MOM 2: You know, Emma, the important thing to me is that people in a family love each other—like we do. Teresa's family loves each other and so do we.	Mom 2 is pointing out the basic similarity among different family types.
C: Yeah. But she has a dad.	This is a very important issue.

T: Emma, what does it mean to you that someone has a dad?

C: Teresa's mom and dad love each other.

M1: Katie and I love each other, too. Katie and I love each other the way that Teresa's mom and dad love each other. And we both love you, too.

C: Other kids have a dad, too.

M2: Kari and Sam have two moms like you.

T: Emma, it sounds like your family is different from some of your friends and the same as others. Is that right?

C: (*Nods head.*) Uh-huh.

T: Emma, you and I also talked about how your skin is different from your friends—and your moms'.

C: (*Looks down.*)

M2: Emma, it's OK. We picked you to be our daughter because we fell in love with you as soon as we saw you.

M1: That's right. We did. We picked you because you're special.

T: I hear your moms saying they love you very much. They knew they would love you from the moment they saw you.

What is the main value of a dad?

The discussion of sexuality is kept at an age-appropriate level.

Mom 2 is trying to point out similarities to other families Emma knows.

There is a need to bring out the transracial issue as well. It is important to promote open discussion and demonstrate that her mothers can handle it.

She may be concerned about repercussions.

I want to curb this direction. Emma feels different, and "special" either may not feel believable or may add to her sense of being different.

This child was not really concerned about her mothers' sexuality as much as with fitting in with her peers and her family. The dynamics of adoption suggest that she was perhaps wondering about her biological family as well. With this session as a starting point, and additional sessions focusing on her strengths and similarities to peers, Emma was able to openly discuss differences in families, especially her own. Later sessions also included discussion related to adoption and racial differences. It could be expected that issues of sexuality would become more significant as she grew older. The initial and ongoing discussion would support more in-depth exploration later.

Treatment with this child and family involved a blend of parenting education (including information about dealing with the child's sense of being different), strengthening of communication skills, problem solving, and self-esteem enhancement. Various play therapy methods were utilized, including game play, drawing, feelings charades, puppets, and sandtray. Interventions were made within both individual play therapy, filial therapy, and family sessions.

SECOND CASE EXAMPLE: CHAD, AGE 13

The second case described here is that of a 13-year-old boy, called Chad for the purposes of this discussion, who grew up in a heterosexual family until age 9, when his parents divorced and he learned of his mother's sexual orientation. At 13, Chad lived with his mother and her lesbian partner and was facing the developmental issues of adolescence. Since his parents' divorce, his mother had had two significant lesbian relationships. The first lasted 2 years and the second and current one had existed for 1 year.

Chad's mother arrived for the initial assessment with her partner; Chad was not present. Before proceeding with the interview, Chad's mother asked to talk candidly, stating that she was a lesbian and wanted to know my point of view about gays and lesbians, to determine whether she and her partner would feel comfortable with me as their therapist. After discussing her initial concerns (see the excerpt below), Chad's mother stated her worry about her son's depressed mood and school difficulties.

Presenting Problem

Chad's school history was unremarkable until middle school, at which time his grades declined and he began having difficulty completing his work. Academic testing indicated a disparity between his ability and performance, with difficulty in concentration. The school psychologist's report also included a diagnosis of dysthymia. Chad was not taking any medications that might either contribute to or alleviate the depression. Chad's mother reported no problems with mood or school performance prior to his entering middle school. Parental conflict prior to divorce was reported, but this was described as having been privately handled, with minimal involvement of the children. Chad's mother stated that Chad appeared to be relatively comfortable with his parents' divorce; she felt that this was due to his maintaining a regular routine, remaining in the same home, and having regular visitation with his father.

Family Information

When asked about current family relationships, Chad's mother and her partner reported a positive relationship between Chad and both partners. (This was later confirmed by Chad.) Within the maternal family system, Chad's mother was the primary disciplinarian and nurturer, while her partner shared activities more related to basketball and long talks about "life" with Chad. Chad's relationship with his only sibling, Stephen (age 15), was characterized as that of "typical adolescent brothers," with fights over the telephone and TV as well as dramatically different interests. Chad and his brother visited their father and stepmother weekly and spent part of the week at each parent's home. Chad's father was described as accepting of the mother's lesbian relationship. His mother, however, described her former spouse as "emotional and immature." She was concerned about the father–son relationship because she viewed it as the children's taking care of the father. Chad expressed acceptance of his stepmother, but reported superficial interaction with her during visitation.

First Session

The following excerpt from the first session demonstrates Chad's mother's concern about the view of homosexuality I took as a clinician. Her assertiveness provided a tremendous opportunity to build rapport and a foundation of openness about issues related to her sexual orientation and its impact on her family.

Content of Session

Mom: Before we start, I want to tell you that Sandy and I are lovers. We've been together for over a year now.

THERAPIST: (*Nodding, with good eye contact and a slight smile.*) I'm glad you could come for this meeting. On the telephone, you said you were referred by your insurance company and that you wanted help with your son. Can you tell me what is concerning you?

M: Uh-huh. But before we talk about that, I want to ask you, have you worked with lesbians before?

T: Oh, yes. I work with gays and lesbians, individually and in group therapy. I've also worked with a number of mothers who wanted to come out to their children.

PARTNER: How do you feel about lesbians? Some therapists don't really accept them.

T: It sounds as though you may have had some personal experience with that.

P: Uh-huh. Not us, but some friends of ours.

T: Well, I have many friends and colleagues who are gay. I don't think there's any one way to be a family. I feel pretty comfortable with most people. Do you have any particular questions you'd like to ask that might help you decide if you want to work with me?

M: No, not really. We just wanted to be sure you'd be OK with lesbians.

T: I'm glad you let me know your concern. It's important for you to feel comfortable with me and be able to talk about anything that is important to

Rationale/Analysis

I'm impressed. I appreciate her directness. This is a beginning that, in many cases, has to be worked toward in multiple sessions.

I want to demonstrate acceptance and interest.

I've rushed her. I need to pay more attention to her comfort level with me as a heterosexual clinician.

She needs assurance of my comfort level and ability.

This is really an important issue. I wonder whether they've had a bad experience before.

I want to be open and create an atmosphere of free discussion. I need to know what will help them. They need confirmation that it's OK to discuss homosexual issues with me.

They seem more relaxed.

I want to support their decision making and offer alternatives to assure a good connection.

you and your family. We do have two therapists
here who are gay if you would feel more comfortable with someone else.

M: (*Looks at her partner.*) No, I think we can work
with you. (*Partner nods.*)

T: Great! Please let me know any time you have any questions or concerns. It's important for us to be able to talk about anything you want.	I want to reinforce the idea of open communication.

The remainder of the session identified specific information about Chad and his difficulties in school and with his mood. A complete history was taken, and a treatment plan was discussed with both partners.

Third Session

An excerpt from the third session reveals Chad's adolescent worry about peers' learning of his mother's sexual orientation.

Content of Session	Rationale/Analysis
THERAPIST: Chad, tell me what it's like to have two moms in your house. CHILD: (*Shrugs.*) Well, I don't like it when they leave their magazines around.	I want to encourage open discussion about his mother's sexual orientation.
T: What kind of magazines are they?	I need to know the type of material that concerns him.
C: You know (*looking away*), stuff about being gay.	This is a huge risk for him. It's also a good opportunity for him to experience acceptance of this topic.
T: (*Speaks gently, but with direct eye contact.*) What is it that bothers you about the magazines?	I need clarification.
C: I don't want my friends to see them. They'll think it's . . . (*long pause*).	This is consistent with adolescent development.
T: They'll think it's what?	What is his worry?
C: Weird, I guess. I don't know.	
T: If they saw them around the house, what would happen?	What are his fears and expectations?
C: I don't know. They might not want to come over any more.	
T: Do any of your friends know about your mom and her partner? About their relationship?	I'm skirting the issue. Is this for me or him?
C: No. I don't think so.	
T: Have they seen the magazines?	What do his peers know?

C: I hide them. My mom doesn't like it, but I do. She says it's important to tell people, but I don't.

T: What would you like her to do?

C: Huh?

T: Let's have your mom and Sandy come in, and maybe she can help solve this problem with you.

C: OK.

I think some problem solving is indicated. I need the moms to be involved.

What does he want from his mother?

His mother and her partner are very supportive and can help with his concerns. I want to promote open dialogue in this family, as well as strengthen Chad's sense of control and problem-solving skills. This is an appropriate goal for adolescence.

The mother and her partner were very supportive of Chad. They were able to discuss their commitment to being out, while hearing Chad's need for privacy. They agreed to put the magazines in a particular bookshelf.

Preliminary Assessment and Treatment Plan

Chad was a 13-year-old boy who presented as shy, intelligent, and attractive. He made direct eye contact as he acknowledged his mother as a lesbian, and he identified his relationship with her lover as positive. The initial assessment indicated that Chad began experiencing a developmental transition at the time of entrance into middle school. He reported concerns typical of children from divorced families, as well as adolescent issues related to his mother's being a lesbian and being open about her sexual orientation.

Chad's discomfort with expressing feelings, as well as his fear of losing his parents, contributed to his difficulty in expressing his concerns directly to his parents. This conflict left Chad feeling powerless—a feeling he had experienced since his parents' divorce. In addition, Chad experienced concerns about his own sexuality that were consistent with his developmental stage and intensified by his mother's sexual orientation.

The active participation of his mother and her partner was clearly a strength in supporting Chad's development of communication skills and sense of control and power in his life. The struggle for power and control during adolescence is commonly identified as part of separation and individuation from the parents. Children of divorce often have more difficulty with this testing process, resulting from a fear of losing the love and support of a parent. To complicate the issue further, children of gay or lesbian parents may also lack typical peer support. Because he feared peer rejection, Chad approached peers very cautiously and limited his own disclosures, thereby creating a self-imposed isolation.

The goals of treatment included the following:

- Enhancement of Chad's communication skills
- Increased sense of personal control in Chad's life consistent with his age

- Reinforced family identity and cohesion
- Improved school performance

Fourth Session

An excerpt from a later session with Chad demonstrates adolescent concern about sexual orientation. During this session he was very quiet and focused discussion on his older brother rather than talk about himself.

Content of Session	Rationale/Analysis
CHILD: I don't know what to talk about today.	There must be something on his mind that he's avoiding.
CLINICIAN: I bet if we just sit here, you'll know what to say.	"To say" is more general than "to work on." This child needs some distance from the self.
CHILD: (*Shrugs and picks up jar of candy on clinician's desk.*) Can I have one?	
CLINICIAN: Sure. (*Waits.*)	
CHILD: (*Sighs.*)	
CLINICIAN: It's hard for you to talk today. I wonder how things went this week. What happened in your family this week?	I give him an opening.
CHILD: My brother's a pain.	Again, he is distancing himself from his own concerns. He projects his issues onto his brother. This need for distance is respected.
CLINICIAN: How is he a pain?	
CHILD: He's always a pain.	
CLINICIAN: Can you give me an example?	
CHILD: Well, he's always on the phone with some girlfriend.	The phone is unimportant.
CLINICIAN: Your brother has some girlfriends?	
CHILD: Yeah, but not *real* girlfriends. They're just friends. They don't go out or anything.	
CLINICIAN: Does he also have guy friends?	
CHILD: Not really. He likes girls better.	
CLINICIAN: What about you?	It's time to refocus on Chad.
CHILD: I have lots of friends. Mostly they're guys.	
CLINICIAN: Do you have a girlfriend?	I am wondering what he thinks about going out with girls.
CHILD: No. I like this girl, but she likes Jacob.	
CLINICIAN: Oh. It sounds like you're pretty clear about liking girls. It's just hard to find the right one.	
CHILD: I am. Not Stephen!	He refocuses on his brother. He may need more distance or have worries about his brother.

CLINICIAN: You know, Chad, I'm glad you're talking about this today. Kids your age sometimes wonder if they're going to be gay or not.

Education can open up the discussion.

CHILD (*emphatically*): Not me!

This is a normal early adolescent emphasis.

CLINICIAN: Well, you might not, but other kids do. Especially if their dad is gay or their mom is a lesbian. But parents really don't have anything to do with whether you like guys or girls. It's not genetic.

CHILD: Oh. Maybe Stephen is.

CLINICIAN: I don't know.

I try to provide a foundation of direct information without belaboring the point, and to maintain a sense of comfort. Many adolescents worry about being gay or lesbian. This issue is particularly acute if a parent is homosexual. Discussion needs to be direct and concise for adolescents.

This session laid the groundwork for ongoing discussions about sexuality, especially related to his 15-year-old brother. Chad's concern is typical of early adolescents; knowing typical issues within a developmental context is essential to good therapy. Also, recognizing the individual's ability to verbalize concerns and tolerate input allows for effective pacing of sessions. Chad usually offered minimal verbalization and depended on me as the clinician to recognize his needs and respond within a style acceptable to him. Doing so, especially in the earlier phase of treatment, supported the therapeutic relationship. Further into therapy, the issue of expressing his own needs became another goal to be addressed.

CONCLUDING COMMENTS

In the two cases presented here, the families were in different phases of the coming-out experience. In the first case, Emma had been raised with lesbian mothers since she was 11 days of age. Her exposure to and awareness of their intimate relationship were consistent throughout her life. At 8 years of age, she had few questions about the intimacy of their relationship, but was concerned about her feeling of differentness from her peers. In the second case, Chad was a young adolescent exploring his own sexual identity. He had a more intense concern about peers' perceptions of his family, as well as about how his mother's sexual orientation might affect his own.

As in all cases where a parent is coming out, it is vital for the clinician to be able to discuss sexuality issues openly with adults and children, within a framework of developmental theory and family dynamics. In the case of Emma, multiple issues related to transracial adoption and having lesbian mothers intertwined throughout the therapy. At 8 years of age, her primary concerns were feeling different and wishing to be accepted by her peers. Treatment for this family required a combination of therapeutic roles, including those of educator, play therapist, school consultant, and family therapist. At assessment, it was apparent that Emma's parents were comfortable in their sexual identity and orientation. Further into the therapeutic process, it became apparent that they were far less comfortable in acknowledging the impact of transracial adoption on their child. Consequently, addressing Emma's concerns with being different was actually more complicated when I was working with her family to recognize her needs to understand her racial identity. Emma's parents saw themselves as different from mainstream society and only superficially recognized the importance of Emma's racial difference. At a deeper level, they wanted to protect their sense of family cohesion by avoiding the conflict related to the racial issue. It was important to educate the parents about cultural and ethnic differences, and to base the therapeutic approach on their family strengths and desire to instill self-acceptance and acceptance of others in their child. This led to increasing the parents' ability to help Emma understand her own racial identity. A therapist must address all aspects of differentness in treating gay- and lesbian-headed families, regardless of the complexity of these issues.

Supportive to the therapy with Emma was her participation in the children's group at school focusing on peer relationships. The school counselor was an active part of the treatment team in addressing her needs for peer affiliation, so important during latency. The school counselor incorporated game play, drawing, and cooperative games to encourage the second- and third-graders in the group to develop positive interactions through problem-solving skills. A children's group was far more effective in a shorter period of time than individual play therapy would have been. Regular communication between me and the school counselor was vital, so that Emma's progress and difficulties at school could be incorporated into the individual and family therapy.

In addition, it was recommended that Emma's mothers enter individual therapy to process personal issues. The goal of the recommendation was to support their ability to tolerate current as well as future issues related to being out as a family. However, Emma's parents chose not to enter individual therapy, indicating that they wanted to maintain all treatment with one therapist. The pros and cons of this were discussed, and their decision was respected.

Emma and her parents were able to complete the initial coming out goal, including educating the mothers, disclosure, and initial work on Emma's feelings of differentness. Toward the end of treatment, the family was referred to a local family service agency for continuing intervention. At that time, my role became that of consultant to the family service clinician to mediate a smooth case transfer.

In Chad's case, the theme of feeling different was also pervasive, together with the additional adolescent focus on sexuality. Again, my clinical roles included those of educator, individual therapist, school consultant, and family therapist. Unlike Emma's case, Chad's case included the additional factors of divorce and an ongoing relationship with a heterosexual father. Therapy included work with Chad, his mother, and her lover; consultation with his school and with a psychiatrist (in regard to medication for depression), and therapy with Chad and his father.

In my role as educator, I offered information to Chad's mother and her lover as well as to his father regarding the impact of coming out and adolescent development. Therapeutic intervention with his father included relational issues between father and son, as well as Chad's concerns about parental conflict between his biological parents. Some of this work was typical of children of divorce as well as of adolescents, and it became intertwined with the work related to his mother's being out. Consultations with the schools and psychiatrists occur routinely in work with children and adolescents. As the primary clinician, I offered input to the psychiatrist regarding my observations in therapy and the effectiveness of the antidepressant medication. My role with the school was to confer with the teacher and school counselor about problem solving in regard to school difficulties and about supporting Chad's academic success via educational contracting.

All of these roles contributed to fairly successful therapy. In retrospect, more work with Chad's father would have enhanced Chad's sense of family cohesion and family identity. The split in the relationship between Chad's biological parents presented special challenges for Chad and his brother. In addition to the usual split present after divorce, the issue of sexual orientation further challenged the family system and the therapeutic process. Therapy would have been effective at a deeper level if Chad's father had been more involved, but the father had difficulty committing to the therapy and was not part of the parental initiation of our work together. Consequently, Chad's biological parents were unable to achieve as much unity in addressing Chad's needs as I had hoped. Individual therapy for Chad's father regarding his divorce and the coming out of his spouse would have greatly enhanced the family therapy. Unfortunately, Chad's father was unwilling to enter individual therapy. Nonetheless, the therapy did help Chad express his needs more fully to his mother, and it enabled her to listen and respond to his concerns.

STUDY QUESTIONS

1. Discuss your role as an educator in working with nontraditional families. What areas of information would you offer the parents in such cases, and what information would you offer the children?

2. Identify your countertransference issues for each case presented here.

3. Identify how you might have utilized therapeutic resources differently, based on each child's developmental level. What types of play therapy materials would you have had available in each case?

4. Discuss how you would have worked to assist Chad's father in accepting and supporting Chad's mother's sexual orientation.

5. How could the therapist have supported Emma's racial identity? How would you have dealt with her mothers' avoidance of this aspect of her family diversity?

REFERENCES

Ainsworth, M. D. S. (1982). Attachment: Retrospect and prospect. In C. M. Parkes & J. Stevenson-Hinde (Eds.), *The place of attachment in human behavior* (pp. 3–30). New York: Basic Books.

Ainsworth, M. D. S. (1972). Attachment and dependency: A comparison. In J. L. Gewirtz (Ed.), *Attachment and dependency* (pp. 97–137). New York: Wiley.

Bowlby, J. (1969). *Attachment and loss: Vol. 1. Attachment.* London: Hogarth Press.

Bowlby, J. (1973). *Attachment and loss: Vol. 2. Separation: Anxiety and anger.* London: Hogarth Press.

Bowlby, J. (1980). *Attachment and loss: Vol. 3. Loss.* London: Hogarth Press.

Bozett, F. W. (1987). *Gay and lesbian parents.* New York: Praeger.

Cassidy, J. (1988). Child–mother attachment and the self in six-year-olds. *Child Development, 59*, 121–134.

Clunis, D. M., & Green, G. D. (1988). Lesbian couples with children. In D. M. Clunis & G. D. Green (Eds.), *Lesbian couples* (pp. 113–130). Seattle, WA: Seal Press.

Clunis, D. M., & Green, G. D. (1995). *The lesbian parenting book: A guide to creating families and raising children.* Seattle, WA: Seal Press.

Dunn, J., & McGuire, S. (1992). Sibling and peer relationships in childhood. *Journal of Child Psychology and Psychiatry, 33*, 67–105.

Gartrell, N. (1984). *Issues in psychotherapy with lesbian women* (Work in Progress No. 83-04). Wellesley, MA: Wellesley College, Stone Center for Developmental Services and Studies.

Golombok, S., Spencer, A., & Rutter, M. (1983). Children in lesbian and single-parent households: Psychosexual and psychiatric appraisal. *Journal of Child Psychology and Psychiatry, 24*, 551–572.

Gottman, J. S. (1990). Children of gay and lesbian parents. *Marriage and Family Review, 14*(3–4), 177–196.

Huggins, S. L. (1989). A comparative study of self-esteem of adolescent children of divorced lesbian mothers and divorced heterosexual mothers. *Journal of Homosexuality, 18*(1–2), 123–136.

Kirkpatrick, M., Smith, C., & Roy, R. (1981). Lesbian mothers and gay fathers. *American Journal of Orthopsychiatry, 51*, 545–551.

Kohut, H. (1977). *The restoration of the self.* Madison, CT: International Universities Press.

Lewis, K. G. (1980). Children of lesbians: Their point of view. *Social Work, 23*(3), 198–203.

McDermott, D., Tyndall, L., & Lichtenberg, J.W. (1989). Factors relating to counselor preference among gays and lesbians. *Journal of Counseling and Development, 68*, 31–35.

Moran, M. R. (1992). Effects of sexual orientation similarity and counselor experience level on gay men's and lesbians' perceptions of counselors. *Journal of Counseling Psychology, 39*, 247–251.

Newman, L. (1991). *Heather has two moms.* Los Angeles: Alyson.

Patterson, C. J. (1992). Children of lesbian and gay parents. *Child Development, 63*, 1025–1042.

Patterson, C. J. (1996). Lesbian mothers and their children: Findings from the Bay Area Families Studies. In R.-J. Green & J. Laird (Eds.), *Lesbians and gays in couples and families: A handbook for therapists* (pp. 420–438). San Francisco: Jossey-Bass.

Pennington, S. B. (1987). Children of lesbian mothers. In F. W. Bozett (Ed.), *Gay and lesbian parents* (pp. 58–74). New York: Praeger.

Puryear, D. (1983). *A comparison between the children of lesbian mothers and the children of heterosexual mothers.* Unpublished doctoral dissertation, California School of Professional Psychology, Berkeley.

Riddle, D. I., & Sang, B. (1978). Psychotherapy with lesbians. *Journal of Social Issues, 34*, 84–100.

Schulenburg, J. (1985). *Gay parenting.* New York: Doubleday/Anchor.

Sophie, J. (1986). A critical examination of stage theories of lesbian identity development. *Journal of Homosexuality, 12*, 39–51.

Steckel, A. (1987). Psychosocial development of children of lesbian mothers. In F. W. Bozett (Ed.), *Gay and lesbian parents* (pp. 75–85). New York: Praeger.

Stern, D. (1985). *The interpersonal world of the infant: A view from psychoanalysis and developmental psychology*. New York: Basic Books.

Tasker, F., & Golombok, S. (1995). Adults raised as children in lesbian families. *American Journal of Orthopsychiatry, 65*, 203–215.

Tasker, F., & Golombok, S. (1997). *Growing up in a lesbian family*. New York: Guilford Press.

PART IV

Medical/Health Crises

CHAPTER 15

HIV/AIDS in the Family

Group Treatment for Latency-Age Children Affected by the Illness of a Family Member

NELLY F. DE RIDDER

HIV disease has been discussed in the literature for almost two decades. A growing portion of the population affected by HIV consists of children whose family members carry the diagnosis (Michaels & Levine, 1992). Although uninfected themselves, they experience multiple psychosocial stressors related to the disease.

HIV-affected children are predominantly Latino and African American; usually live in poverty; often do not have adequate access to psychosocial supports; frequently have caregivers with a history of substance misuse; and often have experienced domestic violence, abuse, and neglect (Taylor-Brown, Teeter, Blackburn, Oinen, & Wedderburn, 1998; Havens, Mellins, & Pilowski, 1996; Nicholas, 1992). These children are also often cast into the role of surrogate spouses and/or parentified children, and most shoulder all of the burdens associated with these roles. Therefore, both trauma and bereavement permeate the backgrounds of HIV-affected children. The spoken or unspoken questions HIV-affected children ask include the following:

- "What's gonna happen to me?"
- "Who's gonna take care of me?"
- "Is it my fault?"
- "Will this happen to me?"

These questions speak to their fears of punishment, death, and abandonment. A clinician must be sensitive to these questions and be ready to respond.

Many HIV-affected children live with feelings of helplessness, impotence, being an outsider, and not belonging. These reactions exceed the developmental norms for these feelings in non-HIV-affected children. Group support provides an HIV-affected child with the opportunity to decrease his or her isolation and achieve ego mastery and competence, in order to cope with the emotional pain and frustrations associated with the illness.

This chapter describes the characteristics of a group for latency-age (8- to 12-year-old) children affected by HIV disease in one or more family members; gives two examples of process in such a group; discusses key countertransference and other issues that arise for group facilitators; describes four play therapy interventions that can be used in a group; and provides guidelines for group facilitators.

CHARACTERISTICS OF A GROUP
FOR HIV-AFFECTED CHILDREN

Functions and Purposes of the Group

A group for HIV-affected children functions on two distinct yet simultaneous levels: educational and familial. On the educational level, these children have the opportunity to learn information about HIV disease. In the group, the children engage in exercises designed to enhance learning through the use of peers. Group members sometimes view the facilitator as a teacher. Alternatively, an HIV-affected child often engages with the facilitator and group members in a manner that often replicates the child's current family climate. In this situation, the facilitator is viewed as a pseudoparental figure.

These two levels of interaction encompass a cyclical process, in which the educational alternates with the emotional. On the latter level, group members identify, displace, project, and then internalize and integrate their feelings. This occurs between member and member, between each member and the group, and between individual members and the facilitator.

The overall group goals include helping members do the following:

- Obtain education about HIV illness
- Understand the nature of anticipatory grief and bereavement
- Experience a safe environment in which thoughts and feelings related to HIV illness can be discussed

Group Format and Model

The agency in which the group described later in this chapter (see "Group Process," below) was held was a dual mental health and HIV/AIDS service program in a large northeastern state. The group was initiated by the mothers of several of the children, who identified in their own group treatment a need for their children to have a safe and supportive environment to discuss their questions and concerns after the mothers' HIV disclosure. Children were referred by their parents and guardians, as well as by residential treatment programs and community youth service providers. (For a fuller discussion of this group, see Witte & de Ridder, 1999.)

In the first and subsequent sessions, the group purpose was stated as follows: We are here to learn about HIV and AIDS and to talk about our feelings, because we all have HIV and AIDS in our families." Group guidelines were established, including the following rules:

- "I will be caring about group members' feelings and thoughts that are discussed."
- "I will not discuss other group members' business outside of the group."
- "I will hold off on joking and fooling around 'til the last 10 minutes of the meeting."
- "I will not interrupt when another member is talking."

- "I understand that the group leader can report to my mother, stepparent, or caseworker if I say I'm going to hurt myself and/or another member."
- "If I'm not going to attend a meeting, I will call the group leader."
- "The group leader will provide the room for the meeting, will bring the snacks, and will be on time."
- "If some topic becomes too serious to talk about, the group leader and/or members will use the peace symbol" (the familiar "V" sign of the 1960s and 1970s).

The group format included a go-round check-in as each group session began, and a check-out as the session ended. These elements of group life were designed jointly by the group members and the facilitator. The check-in and check-out also helped to determine the agenda for the current session and to facilitate planning for the next. If no agenda was generated in this manner, the facilitator would introduce an activity (later in this chapter, a description of selected play therapy interventions is provided).

Snacks were provided by the facilitator and were offered to members at each meeting. Sessions were held during the academic year, once per week after school hours, for 90 minutes.

This group was designed and conceptualized in terms of a mutual aid model (Schwartz & Zalba, 1971), in which common concerns draw members together and the facilitator assists members to help each other in problem solving and coping (Shulman, 1992).

Issues for HIV-Affected Children

Latency-age HIV-affected children present with a number of issues that can be addressed in group treatment. My experience as a facilitator and cofacilitator in such groups has convinced me that HIV-affected children need a working knowledge base pertaining to HIV disease. This dispels their fears and misconceptions, and replaces misinformation with facts concerning transmission and prevention, medical care, and substance use.

In addition, these children need validation of their emotions (such as shame, fear, sadness, guilt, loss, and anger), as well as an accurate picture of the actual experience of HIV patients. Having mastered the *objective* facts of HIV, in other words, the group members struggle to master the *subjective* experience of HIV. I have observed a reciprocal relationship between children's mastery of their own affective experience as the relatives of HIV-infected individuals and their emotional understanding of their family members' experience of the disease. Indeed, as the group process enables HIV-affected children to develop insight into each other's experience and to draw strength from this, members then find deeper connectedness with the infected and affected others in their lives. Typically, HIV-affected group members articulate questions such as these:

- "Can you feel AIDS growing inside of you?"
- "What is it like to know you will die?"

- "What is it like to have HIV or AIDS?"
- "What does it feel like when others know you have *that* disease?"
- "What does it feel like to have people staring at you because you have *it*?"

Such questions may be uttered blatantly or presented as metaphors. Topics and issues may surface for a time, submerge, and resurface during the course of one or several group sessions. Weighty issues may be presented in an affect-laden session, followed by a number of light-hearted sessions. At times members may attempt to forestall or halt the group process entirely. These behaviors can occur frequently in most group treatment with latency-age children. However, in the group described below it was more pronounced, since the group members were also tackling anxiety-laden issues. It is the facilitator's task to be aware when these patterns emerge, to recognize the underlying motives, and to address the resistance with the group.

The misconceptions that HIV-affected children bring to the group can become topics for discussion and process. These include misunderstandings about methods of HIV transmission. Some group members may hold the following misconceptions: that HIV infection is "God's punishment" for past actions (e.g., illegal drug selling and drug use); that HIV is not transmitted from female to female or from female to male; that condoms can be washed and used more than once; and that it is ultimately a child's role to make a parent abstain from substance misuse. A major task of the facilitator as educator is to clarify these and other confusions.

GROUP PROCESS

Example A

This is the first of two examples of group process in a group called Positive Feelings, which I facilitated for HIV-affected children (see "Group Format and Model," above, and Witte & de Ridder, 1999). Group members in attendance on this occasion were the following:

- Carmen (10-year-old Puerto Rican American)
- DeJon (8-year-old African American)
- Sonya (11-year-old Dominican American)
- Jamal (9-year-old Jamaican American)
- Kadesha (11-year-old African American)
- Melvin (12-year-old African American)

The focus in this instance was on Carmen, who voiced anger at a teacher. At home, Carmen was the oldest of several children and seemed so capable of taking care of herself that her HIV-infected mother focused her attention primarily on the younger siblings. Carmen's anger at the teacher (of whom she was actually quite fond) seemed to parallel her outrage at her mother, who seemed so absorbed in her family responsibilities and her own stressors associated with the disease that she was emotionally unavailable to Carmen. I have found that HIV-affected children's anger tends to be directed toward certain people in their lives, such as teachers; other instances of Carmen's anger toward her teachers and others had come up in previous sessions. It is important to encourage the children to express their anger, whether this is direct or (as in Carmen's case) displaced. In this group, this particular process issue was addressed through the videotaping of group role plays. The videotaping was authorized by the children's parents or guardians.

Content of Session

CARMEN: I hate my school teacher. She doesn't like me; she never takes my side; she never listens!

FACILITATOR (*to Carmen and the group*): Let's look at this.

CARMEN: OK.

FACILITATOR: Let's role-play what happened. Who wants to be the teacher?

DEJON: I'll give it a try.

CARMEN (*laughing/giggling*): Yo, Mr. B. Why don't you hear me out?

DEJON: (*Stands up with his hands on his waist, suggesting authority.*) Miss Carmen, the class rules are you must raise your hand first.

CARMEN: Aw, come on (*emphasis on the letter "N"*), give me a break! (*Stands up and raises her hand.*)

DEJON: Yes . . . Miss Carmen?

CARMEN (*with a sigh*): Like I just said (*emphasis on the letter "D"*), why don't you hear what I have to say?

DEJON: Do you have something you'd like to contribute, Miss Carmen, to our discussion on the Iroquois Indians?

CARMEN (*now very upset*): Damn . . . NO! . . . I . . . (*She is cut off.*)

DEJON: Miss Carmen, I will not tolerate vulgar language in my classroom.

(*During the role play, the other group members—Sonya, Jamal, Kadesha, and Melvin—contribute by being either alter egos or the attentive audience.*)

SONYA (*sitting by Carmen's right, whispers*): Carmen, try not to let him get you all upset. What you should say is "Why won't you listen?"

Facilitator's Analysis

The thought I have is "Put on the seat belt; this may be a bumpy ride." Her anger seems intense and displaced.

Carmen's laughter is due to nervousness in reenacting and videotaping.

Both verbally and physically, DeJon recreates the barrier of emotional distance that Carmen experiences.

She desires a chance for closeness but misses it.

DeJon maintains his role, continuing to increase the distance.

Carmen struggles.

Sonya and Kadesha are the alter egos, offering input to Carmen in order to help her maintain her role.

KADESHA (*sitting to the left of Carmen, offers*): You have a right to be pissed off. Shit, keep after him!

(*Then the focus shifts to a second role play in which these same group members reverse their roles.*)

The idea here is to create an opportunity for empathic immersion and insight to emerge.

Afterward, both role plays were reviewed and discussed, and different ways Carmen could be heard by her teacher in a classroom of 30-plus students were noted. These stategies were then practiced by Carmen in the group. Next, I asked the group members whether any of them become angry with their parents or family members from time to time, as Carmen became angry with her teacher. This shifted the focus of the process from what had just been learned in the videotaped role plays to how each member might apply these same skills in connection with his or her HIV-infected mother or other family member.

Content of Session	Facilitator's Analysis
MELVIN: Well, I guess I could . . . when my mom is not too tired and the baby is sleeping, I could go over to her and ask her why she ignores me.	The members take direction and stay with the concept of being emotionally ignored and trying to find words for their pain—the pain of neglect.
KADESHA: Since we only really get together for church only on Sundays, I guess I could ask my mother and my stepfather why they spend more time with my little sisters and not with me. . . . Ya know, don't I count? Don't I matter?	

The videotaping permitted the review of what happened in the moment for the group members, and it also led to discusssion of what might be occurring for the significant other in the interaction. Distortions that might otherwise have arisen were minimized through this method. Videotaping is a powerful tool for HIV-affected latency-age children, whose thinking is more concrete than abstract. The tape was not shared with the group members' parents or guardians; this encouraged more open expression of their feelings.

Example B

In this second example, the group members in attendance were Jamal, Melvin, DeJon, Kadesha, and Sonya. The focus in this session was on the very different behaviors of Jamal and Sonya. Jamal, the oldest child in a family that included a 3-year-old HIV-infected brother and a mother diagnosed with end-stage HIV disease (AIDS-related dementia), would repeatedly fall off his chair in group sessions or make jokes in response to emotionally laden topics. He often sat on the periphery of the group circle, balancing his chair on two legs. At home, he had used any means possible—such as walking out of the house or engaging in horseplay with his siblings—to interrupt his mother's attempts to discuss her HIV illness and her plans for kinship foster care for himself and his siblings.

In the present session, Jamal's behavior was triggered by Sonya's announcement that she had found out that her mother was HIV-negative (following the mother's having tested positive and having been diagnosed with HIV-associated symptomatology), and that she would therefore be terminating from the group. The group members' initial responses were shock and disbelief; however, they gently listened for the details and then confronted Sonya on the facts of the diagnosis.

Content of Session	Facilitator's Analysis
MELVIN (*to the group*): Is that possible? DEJON (*to Sonya*): How do you know? What makes you so sure?	The group members begin to express their skepticism. Personally, I'm wondering whether Sonya is colluding with Jamal. (In prior sessions, this pattern was emerging.)
KADESHA (*to Sonya and facilitator, in a quizzing manner*): Once you're positive, I thought that was it; you can't go back. It's just not possible!	Kadesha seems to suggest that Sonya has some information about the slim chance that seroconversion is possible. I am worried that previous educational efforts may have failed.
(*Sonya begins to cry under this examination, at which time Jamal falls off his chair in the style of a popular TV comedian. The group members in unison roar with laughter and take Jamal's lead in halting the discussion of HIV seroconversion.*)	Jamal is trying to protect the group and himself as he does at home. Jamal's behavior is his means of unconsciously saying that he should know the information under discussion and should have mastered his emotions. He is also attempting to ward off any discussion, in order to avoid shame and embarrassment to himself and/ or the group.
FACILITATOR: OK, guys, it's time to calm down and think about what's happening here. Sonya has just said her mother is cured and she's ready to leave the group. Jamal is clowning around and making us laugh instead of talk. What do you think is really going on?	Can I get the group back on track?
(*The group members process these seemingly opposing perspectives—Sonya ready to exit the group because of a cure for her mother; Jamal with a mother ready to exit by death. It is found that both Sonya and Jamal hold wishful fantasies of having a non-HIV-infected mother.*)	Although Sonya's and Jamal's perspectives seem like polar opposites, my hunch is that there is a connection.
FACILITATOR: What just happened? (*Silence blankets the group. There is a long pause.*) MELVIN: Sonya is upset. KADESHA (*to Sonya*): What's wrong? (*Sonya weeps silently. Another pause.*)	

FACILITATOR: Jamal, what's going on for you?

SONYA: (*Breaks in and speaks with thinly veiled anger.*) Well, maybe you are right, but it's just not fair. I hate this! I don't want my mother to have this!

JAMAL: (*Sits with his face almost covered by his turtleneck; speaks in a soft voice.*) My mother is dying. . . . I don't want her to die.

(*Kadesha and Sonya have tears in their eyes. DeJon and Melvin look at their feet. Jamal picks at his fingers. A few more moments pass.*)

Jamal speaks for the first time of his pain; Sonya has freed him.

Jamal's wish mirrors the wish of *all* the group members. It also triggers for the members feelings of shame and embarrassment, and the beginnings of anticipatory grief.

SONYA (*standing up*): We need all the hugs we can get. This shit stinks . . . but we need each other.

(*The group collects for a gentle hug.*)

In a prior session at check-out, Kadesha suggested that the group share hugs at the end of difficult sessions. This was something her mother had learned in Al-Anon (similar to the "serenity prayer"). The group translated this into the "group hug," which became part of the group culture.

ISSUES FOR THE GROUP FACILITATOR

Handling Personal Questions from Children

Besides pondering HIV-related questions, the members of the Positive Feelings group often confronted me with such questions as "Do you have HIV or AIDS?", "Have you used drugs?", or "Are you having sex?" These questions were processed further to mean "How can you know what my mother is [or I am] going through?" These questions hinted also at the unspoken fear that if I was at risk for HIV, then I might at some point leave the group.

In response, I processed the group members' questions with them, and then discussed my experiences with HIV-infected mothers. These included multiple hospitalizations, changes in mood and dementia, changes in physical appearance, near death, and death, all accompanied by a roller-coaster ride of emotions and thoughts. I have found that when possible it is important to be straightforward (i.e., to give an honest explanation), because evasiveness may cause problems later (it may prevent a child from confronting and addressing his or her feelings). This kind of communication opens the door for each group member to ask more questions and share deeper concerns.

These confrontations and discussions occurred in the middle, working-through phase of the group work. They highlighted how HIV-affected latency-age children desire understanding and intimacy, in which the boundaries between group members and facilitator are blurred. In terms of the cyclical nature of group work as mentioned earlier, a facilitator needs to go deeper to the emotional aspect of such questions even during the educational process.

I have found that HIV-affected children come to a group with their hearts full of questions, emotions, experiences, and thoughts, not unlike soaked sponges saturated through and through. The group format serves as the pail into which the affect-laden material can be wrung, so that the children can return home to be with their infected family members once again. In some cases this means returning home in the assumed role of surrogate spouse or parentified child.

Acquiring a Knowledge Base

The facilitator must possess a thorough knowledge of the current HIV literature. It is essential for the facilitator to have a working knowledge of HIV disease, medical care, substance use, and the impact of HIV illness on the family. This knowledge needs to be imbedded in an understanding of each HIV-affected child's spiritual, cultural, familial, and developmental background and needs. The facilitator must be able to present this knowledge in language that is clear, not overly complex, and useful. For example, it may be helpful to equate HIV with a germ and to describe viral replication as similar to a factory where HIV is made.

The facilitator also needs to have good group work skills, which include a keen sense of what to look for and the ability to stay with each member and with the group as a whole. The facilitator's roles are essentially those of a supporter (validating the thoughts and feelings members share) and a mediator (not taking sides) within the realm of direct active participation. Members often benefit from brief unearthing of HIV-related material, experiencing a sense of sameness, dropping a topic, and picking it up again at some future session. It is important to keep in mind that each HIV-affected child's communication patterns, as presented in the group, parallel those in the child's family; they also reflect the child's wishes about his or her ideal family.

Central to the necessary knowledge base is the conceptualization of "disenfranchised grief." Doka (1989) defines this as the grief that people experience when a loss is not or cannot be openly acknowledged, publicly mourned, or socially accepted. Because considerable stigma and many negative perceptions are attached to HIV/AIDS, HIV-affected children are often overlooked by the mainstream of society. The group gives them a place where they can openly acknowledge their association with the illness, and realize that other children are also confronting similar experiences. It is therefore important for the facilitator to frame group interventions based on this understanding (i.e., validating anticipatory grief and bereavement, and helping children find meaningful ways to experience these).

Handling Countertransference Issues

The sponge analogy noted above also applies to the facilitator. The clinician sometimes identifies with the children's shame, fear, sadness, guilt, loss, and anger. This identification can trigger the urge to rescue, quickly resolve, or take care of the emotions of an HIV-affected child in the moment, without assessing or processing these feelings fully. It can be difficult to remain present to the child's intense emotion in the midst of his or her struggle. The urges stirred in the facilitator may encourage parentification of the child that is not culturally sanctioned, but rather prompted by the nature of HIV. This is illustrated in an example.

Margarita, an 8-year-old Latina parentified child, went to extraordinary lengths to maintain control over her familial situation and at the same time to contain her abandonment, fear, and rage. She would, in an obsessive and compulsive manner, check daily on her HIV-infected mother's prescriptions (in terms of dosages and times of ingestion), her numerous medical appointments, and her nutritional needs, using a self-made flow chart. This structure enabled Margarita to remain in control of her mother's care.

The facilitator realized that lack of recognition or discussion of Margarita's situation would increase her need for control, thereby maintaining her outrage. In contrast, when the facilitator accepted Margarita's feelings of rage and encouraged her to express these in session, her need to hold the rage in or to act it out diminished.

The facilitator must also be aware of how his or her own childhood experiences have influenced current beliefs. These include feelings of bias regarding substance use; attitudes about divergent cultural and socioeconomic backgrounds; and personal experiences of loss, trauma, and separation. Awareness of one's moral issues and judgments is equally important. The concept of "parenting" merits special attention as a countertransferential issue (i.e., one's experience as parenting within the family of origin vs. parenting in the family of procreation); this will make an impact on how the facilitator assumes a leadership/nurturing role in group treatment. Another illustration highlights the need for awareness of one's various biases.

Guadalupe, a 10-year-old Latina, inquired in the group about methods of HIV transmission. Specifically, she was concerned about bathing with her HIV-infected mother when the mother was menstruating. This triggered the facilitator's internal outrage and questions stemming from her own upbringing. The facilitator was raised in an intact middle-class family with parental figures who valued privacy in such areas as personal hygiene. It was essential to realize in the moment that Guadalupe was from a different culture with different family norms. So what seemed so foreign to the leader was more common to Guadalupe and the group members. Had the facilitator's feelings been expressed, they could have thwarted the group focus and process. Instead, the group processed Guadalupe's question and her underlying fears.

Countertransference issues can also trigger protective responses, such as avoiding strong affect or content that evokes further emotional or psychic pain in an affected child. Sometimes the group members will share their feelings when they sense that the facilitator is overreacting or responding inappropriately. In such a case, the facilitator's protective defense causes an about-face in the group focus: It leads the group to abandon their own issues and to focus on those of the facilitator. It is therefore imperative that the facilitator assume the leadership role without confusing it with parental stirrings. It is impossible to be a substitute for a child's parents, even though one often wants to.

Comfort with the role of facilitator requires recognition of one's limitations in work with HIV-affected children. The purposeful use of humor, self-disclosure, and gentle shedding of tears can all be healing for the group members. For example, in the beginning and middle phases of the Positive Feelings group, it became apparent that members needed to take breaks from discussions that proved too emotionally laden. When breaks were not taken, derailments of the group's purpose occurred: A series of issues surfaced that were not related to the purpose, such as a member's receiving a turtle as a pet or members' discussing school homework assignments. In a humorous manner, I suggested that the group use the question "Do we need to take a detour?", emphasized with hand signals. This question eventually became part of the group culture: Group members would ask each other about the "need for a detour," followed by hand signals as popularized on many music videos. The process then moved to focus on the purposeful need for resistance, as noted earlier in this chapter. Typically, resistance often occurred in the form of light-hearted meetings after a previously intense session. As members verbally acknowledged the need for resistance, time was permitted to allow for this. This decision facilitated therapeutic healing.

SELECTED PLAY THERAPY INTERVENTIONS

The following four play therapy interventions help in facilitating HIV/AIDS-related feelings. These tools offer HIV-affected children the opportunity to gain a measure of ego control over the reality and impact of HIV illness in their lives. It is important to define each objective fully, so that members understand what is asked of them. Members may also need to be reassured that artistic ability is separate from the willingness to express themselves openly. I have found it helpful to participate personally in the tasks, because this signifies my interest in the group and provides modeling.

Mask of Anger

- *Materials needed*: Markers, crayons, pencils, and construction paper.
- *Goals*: To help group members identify anger, and to help them recognize when anger is a healthy emotion versus when it is used to hide feelings of shame, fear, sadness, guilt, and loss.
- *Procedure*: Facilitator presents the concept of masks and asks for feedback from the group, such as pretending or Halloween "make-believe." Facilitator then requests that all members draw an angry mask. When masks are completed, each member in turn is asked to describe his or her mask and the feelings that remain concealed. (This tool solicits memories and reveals issues that are lying just beneath the surface in an HIV-affected child.)

The Profile on Your Back

- *Materials needed*: Large pieces of construction paper, cut to the size of a child's back; masking tape; marking pens.
- *Goal*: To increase group members' self-knowledge and self-esteem, to help them understand how others see them, and to encourage behavioral change.

- *Procedure*: Facilitator presents the concept that people have a variety of traits (a "good side" as well as a "bad side," as children would put it) that make them unique and special; some traits are within a person's awareness, but others are not. Knowing both "sides" gives one an opportunity to view oneself in a different light and to make changes where necessary. Facilitator then asks that members tape the blank profiles on each other's backs and take turns writing a word or a phrase that embodies a thought about each person. Each child should have an opportunity to write a comment on each member's back. When the task is completed, members are asked to take off their profiles and share with the group what has been noted. The facilitator should inquire what is confirming, what is surprising, and so forth.

Every Picture Tells an HIV Story

- *Materials needed*: Pencils, crayons, markers, and large pieces of drawing paper.
- *Goal*: Facilitation of HIV/AIDS-related discussion in a safe way.
- *Procedure*: Facilitator suggests to members that every picture tells a story, and shows pictures that illustrate the point. Facilitator then asks all members to draw a picture that describes something about HIV/AIDS. After members have had time to draw, facilitator initiates a group discussion in which each member describes what he or she has drawn and what his or her story is.

The HIV/AIDS Scrapbook

- *Materials needed*: Markers, crayons, pencils, construction paper, lined writing paper, tape, glue, old newspaper, magazines, and safety scissors.
- *Goal*: Creation of a record of HIV/AIDS that can be referred to in the future.
- *Procedure*: Facilitator presents the notion of a scrapbook—how it holds memories, thoughts, feelings, beliefs, and ideas that can be referred to from time to time. After asking for feedback about this notion, facilitator helps group members to make a list of items (which may become a table of contents for each member's book) that are important to remember about HIV/AIDS. Using this list, members will add a new item to their scrapbooks at each group meeting. Possible items include the following:

1. A drawing of HIV illness (i.e., a rendering of what HIV or AIDS looks like).
2. A drawing of the family member(s) with HIV illness.
3. A list of possible modes of transmission versus transmission myths.
4. A collage of favorite pastimes with the family, made by cutting out pictures and words from magazines and newspapers and pasting them on pages of the scrapbook.
5. A picture list of attributes of the family member(s) with HIV/AIDS.

Group members should be asked to share and discuss their drawings, collages, and listings. This exercise helps facilitate anticipatory grief and bereavement.

GUIDELINES FOR GROUP FACILITATORS

The following recommendations emphasize the importance of self-awareness and ongoing monitoring of one's practice.

1. Supervision ideally should include weekly individual and peer-led group support sessions. The group facilitator should be encouraged to discuss the painful and frustrating aspects of this type of group work. With supervisory judgment and critical feedback, the countertransference reactions that emerge can safely be discussed, such as triggers (conscious material that is stirred up) and blind spots (unconscious material from one's own history that gets in the way). Ongoing exploration of a clinician's creativity and ways to use it in group treatment can be empowering. Ongoing education about group tasks, process, and techniques should be part of the supervisory experience. Whenever possible, facilitators should be encouraged to attend courses, workshops, and conferences that will enhance their continuing education.

2. The facilitator should keep abreast of the latest information about HIV and those affected by it, and should also be aware of mass media reports (some group members' confusions and misconceptions arise from TV viewing). The following World Wide Web sites will assist clinicians in acquiring knowledge about HIV-affected children and their families:

www.aegis.com
www.aidsinfonyc.org
www.healthcg.com
www.infoweb.org
www.projinf.org

Useful books and articles include those by Boyd-Franklin, Steiner, and Boland (1995); Carter (1992); Gaballe, Grender, and Anderson (1995); Havens et al. (1996); Levine (1993); Schaeffer and Lyons (1988); Winiarski (1997); and Witte and de Ridder (1999).

3. The facilitator should familiarize himself or herself with cultures (e.g., Latino and African American) and subcultures (e.g., drug use and gay/lesbian) different from his or her own. It can be very helpful to network with colleagues of diverse backgrounds and clinical perspectives. Also, an understanding of models of illness, spirituality, and death and dying helps to minimize distortions that can arise in group treatment.

4. Ideally, the facilitator should work within a team format. This should include each child's parent or guardian, the case manager/social worker and therapist for the HIV-infected family member(s), applicable legal personnel (as in the case of standby or permanent guardianship processing), the family's church minister or other spiritual advisor, and applicable medical personnel. This will ensure that everyone is working together on behalf of an HIV-affected child. It will also help the group facilitator in seeking a wider understanding of group members' experiences, and should minimize some of the countertransferential distortions.

5. The facilitator should obtain individual therapy for personal issues that arise in the work that are not client-related, to assure containment and maintenance of appropriate boundaries.

6. The facilitator should plan time away from the work, because it is emotionally and intellectually taxing. This helps to cultivate a renewed interest in the work and decreases the risk of burnout.

STUDY QUESTIONS

1. How realistic is it to expect an HIV-affected child to work on feelings of anger, fear, shame, sadness, loss, associated with anticipatory grief while living in a family environment with multiple psychosocial stressors? What does a clinician need to consider? How far can the group and clinician really go?

2. How did group therapy techniques encourage HIV-related thoughts and feelings to be discovered and addressed by the members of the Positive Feelings group? Compare and contrast Examples A and B.

3. Imagine yourself as 9 years old. Your father has spent most of your life in prison. The long-held family secret is that he was a drug dealer and heroin and cocaine user. You were introduced to him 1 year ago, after his prison sentence was completed. He has been living with you and your mother, but within a short period of time he has begun looking pale and thin, with his hair falling out. He does not seem to remember who you are, yet you keep reminding him. He sleeps most of the day, and when he is awake, he is coughing and lying on the living room couch watching TV. You are attending school, but you worry about him a lot. You find yourself daydreaming in school about him, and sometimes you cry when no one is looking. Three months later, when you return home from school, you find your mother crying at the door to your apartment. She tells you he has died.

   Approximately 6 months pass. You have gone through a number of feelings, from shock, disbelief, and numbness to denial, guilt, and anger. You see your mother becoming thinner with each passing day. She seems to spend a lot of time in the bathroom or lying on the couch with a faraway look in her eyes. Your mother has a homemaker who does more and more of the things your mother used to do, like cooking, cleaning, and even getting you up in the morning to go to school. Just this past Monday, she has told you that your father died of HIV disease and that she too is dying.

   Today she tells you about a group at a nearby clinic that you will be going to—a group for kids with parents or family members who have HIV. She wants you to go.

   • What is your reaction to the group referral?
   • What are your concerns?
   • What would help you to make the transition to the group?

4. Discuss the role of the HIV-affected child as surrogate parent and parentified child. What are the familial and cultural implications? Comment on the role as functional and dysfunctional.

ACKNOWLEDGMENTS

I would like to thank the members of Positive Feelings, who taught me about loss, trauma, and the spirit to survive adversity. I would also like to thank Nancy Boyd Webb for her support during the writing of this chapter, and Evelyn Saeli for editorial assistance.

REFERENCES

Boyd-Franklin, N., Steiner, G. L., & Boland, M. G. (Eds.). (1995). *Children, families, and HIV/ AIDS*. New York: Guilford Press.

Carter, N. A. (1992). *Binding up the broken hearted children*. Unpublished manuscript, HIV/ AIDS Ministries, New York.

Doka, K. (1989). *Disenfranchised grief: Recognizing hidden sorrow*. Lexington, MA: Lexington Books.

Gaballe, S., Grender, J., & Anderson, W. (Eds.). (1995). *Forgotten children of the AIDS epidemic*. New Haven, CT: Yale University Press.

Havens, J. E., Mellins, C. A., & Pilowski, D. (1996). Mental health issues in HIV affected women and children. *International Review of Psychiatry, 8*, 217–225.

Levine, C. (1993). *A death in the family: Orphans of the HIV epidemic*. New York: United Hospital Fund of New York.

Michaels, D., & Levine, C. (1992). Estimates of the number of motherless youth orphaned by AIDS in the United States. *Journal of the American Medical Association, 268*, 3456–3465.

Nicholas, S. W. (1992). The "silent" legacy of AIDS: Children who survive their parents and siblings. *Journal of the American Medical Association, 268*, 3478–3480.

Schaeffer, D., & Lyons, C. (1988). *How do we tell the children?* New York: Market Press.

Schwartz, W., & Zalba, S. (Eds.). (1971). *The practice of group work*. New York: Columbia University Press.

Shulman, L. (1992). *The skills of helping individuals families and groups*. Itasca, IL: F. E. Peacock.

Taylor-Brown, S., Teeter, J. A., Blackburn, E., Oinen, L., & Wedderburn, L. (1998). Parental loss due to HIV: Caring for children as a community issue—The Rochester, New York experience. *Child Welfare, 77*, 137–160.

Winiarski, M. (Ed.). (1997). *HIV mental health for the 21st century*. New York: New York University Press.

Witte, S. S., & de Ridder, N. F. (1999). Positive Feelings: Group support for children of HIV infected mothers. *Child and Adolescent Social Work Journal, 16*(1), 5–21.

CHAPTER 16

Life-Threatening Blood Disorder

Case of Daniel, Age 11, and His Mother

CAROL P. KAPLAN

The diagnosis of serious illness represents a crisis both for the patient and for the family. This chapter presents the case of Daniel, an 11-year-old boy living with his parents and 15-year-old sister. A well-developed and previously healthy youngster, he had recently been diagnosed with a relatively rare autoimmune blood disease. The disorder affects a patient in a variety of ways, including vulnerability to hemorrhages and extra susceptibility to infection. Life-threatening consequences of accidents and infectious illnesses are always possibilities. Thus, although he looked (and usually felt) like a healthy boy in late latency, Daniel's life suddenly changed after his diagnosis. He was restricted from engaging in certain contact sports that he had previously enjoyed; he began missing many days of school; and he was subjected to frequent and often painful medical procedures, as well as to hospital stays of varying length.

The situation was complicated by uncertainties surrounding the course of the disease in a boy Daniel's age; that is, it might eventually either worsen or improve. Moreover, the team of physicians did not always agree about which activities ought to be prohibited, and Daniel was aware of these differences of opinion. Previously a cooperative and cheerful boy, he reacted to the whole situation with anger and negativism, insisting that he should be allowed to continue to play his favorite contact sports. His behavior at home and at school deteriorated, as did his schoolwork. Expectably, the family was affected in a variety of ways by the crisis, and in turn the parents' reactions had an impact on Daniel.

This chapter focuses on the work done with Daniel and his parents (especially his mother) around conflicts precipitated by the illness, in an effort to help them cope with this crisis so that Daniel could proceed with his development. Treatment was short-term, consisting of 11 sessions over a period of about 5 months. Daniel was seen 10 times, either alone or with his mother, and both parents were seen together once. The 11 sessions were spread out over 5 months because of circumstances connected with the illness, such as emergency hospitalizations and doctor visits, in addition to a family vacation. In the intervals between sessions, the therapist (myself) remained in telephone contact with the family.

EFFECTS OF SERIOUS ILLNESS
ON DEVELOPMENT IN LATENCY

Two issues among the many facets of this case are highlighted in this chapter: (1) general characteristics of the development and treatment of children in late latency, and (2) the impact of a diagnosis of serious and chronic physical illness on a child's development. The main theoretical framework utilized for understanding developmental and treatment issues of healthy children in late latency is that of Charles Sarnoff (1987a, 1987b). The work of various authors who have written about the impact of physical illness on children and families informs the understanding of the effect of Daniel's illness on his development and his family relationships.

Sarnoff's work on the late latency period (1987a, 1987b) illuminates the ways in which a chronic illness such as Daniel's magnifies the normal conflicts of this age. One of these conflicts is the "problem of passivity," described by Sarnoff as follows:

> This is a conflict between the wish of the child to be cared for and to remain a child, and resentment of the loss of independence that fulfillment of this desire brings. Moods, temper fits, withdrawal to rooms, and challenges of authority take center stage clinically when these conflictual areas are most intense. (Sarnoff, 1987a, p.118)

An age-appropriate conflict between the desires for dependence and independence would certainly be exacerbated in a child like Daniel with a potentially life-threatening illness, because the normal thrust toward growing up is tempered by fears of unknown possibilities in the future.

Sarnoff describes heightened narcissism, with self-preoccupation and manifestations of grandiosity, as a common defense seen in children during late latency and early puberty. Even healthy children will inevitably experience potentially belittling and even humiliating events that can shatter their fragile self-image and self-confidence.

> Each surrender to the outside world cuts into narcissistic enhancement of the self and causes feelings of low self-worth. The negative and forceful reaction of young adolescents to positions of passivity may be explained on the basis of the humiliation felt by the loss of control to powerful authorities. (Sarnoff, 1987b, pp. 26–27)

It would not be surprising to find that serious illness amplifies the normal grandiosity of a child Daniel's age. Sick children must endure not only restricted activities but also traumatic medical procedures, both of which constitute assaults on their bodies and their growing sense of independence. For a boy, moreover, they may represent a threat to the sense of masculinity. Grandiosity may also serve as a defense against the fear of growing up and becoming more independent, when the future (as for a child with a serious illness) may include fearful unknowns.

Sarnoff (1976, 1987a, 1987b) has written extensively about the "structure of latency," which enables children to utilize symbolic and fantasy play to discharge conflicts, both on their own and in play therapy. Most children begin to enter puberty between the ages of 11 and 14, and at this point many changes—physical, cognitive, and social—start to occur. These include the increased substitution of realistic, communicative speech for the earlier type of play, in which fantasy provides a disguise for real people and situations in a child's life.

The work with Daniel illustrates a common feature of treatment in late latency children: Children of this age tend to use symbolic play to a lesser extent. I have found that, like Daniel, children at this stage of development often play both to facilitate talking about current issues and, when intense feelings arise, to retreat from such material. The medium of play provides a comfortable milieu in which a child can hear and process a therapist's comments and interpretations, even when the child does not appear to be listening. At the same time, the presence of play materials enables the child to shift activities if the subject becomes too intense or uncomfortable.

A number of authors have written about the impact of serious illness on children and their families. Gizynski and Shapiro (1990) found a variety of depressive symptoms in children who were ill with cancer, asthma, or psychiatric diagnoses of behavioral disorders, leading to the need for families to adopt different adaptive coping strategies. Adams (1995) has highlighted a variety of challenges for children and adolescents who are suffering with life-threatening illness. The emotional challenges for such young people—many of which can be seen in Daniel's case—include anxiety, sadness, anger, loneliness, guilt, and both passive and active resistance to caregivers, as well as active acceptance (i.e., active efforts to cope).

Anna Freud (1952), in her seminal paper on the emotional effects of physical illness on children, points to several outcomes that pertain to Daniel's case. In the first place, when children require nursing care and experience a loss of functioning or a weakened body state, they tend to regress to earlier levels of development. Some children do not resist such a backward pull, but those "who have built up strong defenses against passive leanings oppose this enforced regression to the utmost, thereby becoming difficult, intractable patients" (p. 72). In Daniel we see a youngster who demonstrated consistent opposition to passive compliance with medically and parentally imposed demands.

A second ramification of physical illness that Anna Freud discusses is the impact of restriction of a child's freedom of movement. She notes that such limitations imposed on children by adults have always carried punitive connotations; for example, children are frequently punished by being sent to their rooms or forbidden to go out to play. At the same time, children have a tendency to "defend their freedom of movement . . . to the utmost" (1952, p. 72). When under enforced restrictions on their mobility, children will discharge aggression through irritability, restlessness, bad language, and so forth. Such manifestations of aggression were evident in Daniel's behavior.

Geist (1979), in an important contribution to the understanding of ways in which children react to the onset of chronic illness, delineates several processes relevant to Daniel's case. He points out that a chronic illness always represents at its beginning some kind of loss for a child, especially with regard to self-image and body image. Children must therefore go through a process of mourning in order to integrate the new self-concept. Daniel's behavior could be viewed as representing such a mourning process.

Like other authors, Geist recognizes that the onset of severe illness is accompanied by aggression in children. He believes that children experience such an event as an attack—a "narcissistic injury that frequently evokes ineffable rage, a primitive fury for which words have no expression" (Geist, 1979, p. 10). In discussing the sick child's fury, Geist describes it as being so terrifying that adaptation is rarely achieved by means of sublimation. Instead, children and adolescents turn to other protective mechanisms, including the acting out of their anger in order to "invite the environment to manage the patient" (p. 11). This certainly appears applicable to Daniel.

Moreover, children may fear that their illness is evidence that they possess destructiveness powerful enough to cause family dissolution. Indeed, the chronic illness of one family member inevitably has an impact on the entire family (Feeman & Hagen, 1990), and Daniel's family was no exception. These adverse effects on his family only increased Daniel's underlying anxiety that he would destroy the very people on whom he depended for continued growth and development. What children need, according to Geist (1979), is an atmosphere in which their feelings are accepted but they are not ceded control over decisions regarding their care. He points out that a therapeutic goal with a chronically ill child is to help the parents hear the child's anger and complaints, while continuing to make decisions involving the child's well-being. In fact, one of the goals of work with Daniel's parents was to help them establish a climate in which they could allow him to express his feelings, while at the same time they could set firm limits.

Daniel was approaching puberty, and his defiance of his mother's prohibitions may also be viewed in the context of this developmental stage. Sarnoff writes that as children in late latency and early puberty become increasingly aware of their growing physical and social maturity,

> the children often reach beyond . . . the limits set by their parents. Battles between early adolescents and their parents ensue. The children defend their dawning independence. The parents watch for the safety of their children. Unaware that they are not at cross purposes, children and parents fight. Demonstration of the presence of shared goals can be a helpful intervention by the therapist. (Sarnoff, 1987b, p. 27)

In this case, the shared goals included the desire to have Daniel select as many enjoyable activities as possible for a boy his age without jeopardizing his health.

Anna Freud (1952) notes that just as the earliest bond between mother and child involves the mother with the child's body, the child in adolescence may unconsciously provoke her involvement by demonstrating "recklessness in matters of health" that results in power struggles with the mother. Regarding such power struggles, Adams (1995) writes that some parents of children who are suffering may become rigid in order to maintain control, at the same time that preadolescent and adolescent youngsters find the practical demands of illness distressing because of their own wish to have control and to be like their peers. In addition, the young people become increasingly articulate about what they think and feel. These observations certainly apply to Daniel and his parents.

I have found that children with life-threatening conditions especially need permission to ask questions and to verbalize their feelings, including the fear of death. Maher and Pask (1995) point out that in most cases children do not ask important questions unless they already have some idea of the answers. Moreover, these authors maintain that imagining may be more harmful than the truth. This proved to be true for Daniel.

As Geist points out, disease is extremely unfair, and children must realize that adults understand this fact. "Paradoxically, only then are the children free to accuse their elders of not knowing how it feels to be sick" (Geist, 1979, pp. 12–13). Such a confrontational event actually occurred at the culmination of Daniel's treatment.

Finally, Daniel's case underlines yet another point made by Geist—namely, that most chronically sick youngsters ask "Why me?" and think that their illness represents a punishment for prior actions, wishes, or thoughts. He suggests that their guilt must be handled not only by reassurances that they are not to blame, but also by candid explanations of their disease and (where appropriate) statements about lack of knowledge regarding causes. Yet the ultimate goal of treatment of children who are chronically ill cannot be "cure," he maintains; rather, it must be adaptation to the illness.

THE CASE: DANIEL ROGERS, AGE 11

Family Information

This was a white middle-class family of European Catholic extraction, living in the suburbs. In the home were the following:

> Daniel Rogers, age 11; student in 6th grade in a public middle school
> Wendy Rogers, age 15; sister of Daniel; student in 10th grade in a public high school
> Mary Rogers, age 41; biological mother of Daniel and Wendy; housewife
> George Rogers, age 42; biological father of Daniel and Wendy, and husband of Mary; an executive in a large corporation

Presenting Problem

Mrs. Rogers made the initial telephone call about 2 months after the beginning of the school year, stating that Daniel had begun doing poorly in his schoolwork and misbehaving in class. In addition, at home he had become oppositional, was often angry, and had developed an "attitude." She explained that his illness had been diagnosed 5 months ago, and she described the multiple medical procedures and hospitalizations Daniel had been undergoing since then. These included frequent blood tests, two spinal taps, and medications given intravenously to deal with infectious illnesses. Mrs. Rogers also reported that when Daniel went to his doctors' offices, he often saw children with leukemia and other malignant conditions who were suffering hair loss from chemotherapy.

The major stated reason for anger on Daniel's part, and the predominant theme in his conflicts with his parents, was the prohibition against playing contact sports. He was especially upset at not being allowed to play football, which he loved and had played in a league the previous year. The parents had tried to interest him in other activities and in sports that would be less dangerous (because they presented less threat of brain hemorrhage in case of injury), but he rejected these alternatives. Mrs. Rogers explained that of the three physicians in charge of Daniel's medical care, two had advised against football, while the third had taken a neutral stance. After considerable thought and discussion, she and her husband had decided that they would not be comfortable if they did not follow the conservative course in this matter.

Mrs. Rogers stated on the telephone that she and her husband were both in favor of counseling in general, and in particular they believed that Daniel might be holding back feelings about his condition. She expressed the hope that talking with a counselor would help him come to terms with his restrictions and motivate him to do better in school. She stated that she and her husband were both willing to do whatever might be necessary to help Daniel. They were a very close family, she said, despite the fact that her husband had a very demanding job that frequently required long hours and trips out of town. Although matters of daily living with Daniel usually fell to her, her husband often took him out, especially to baseball, football, and hockey games. She indicated that Wendy was accepting of her brother and supportive of him, but was involved with school and other activities with her friends. She alerted me to the fact that she would be the one to bring Daniel for his sessions, but that her husband would do everything possible to make himself available "if necessary."

First Interview

Mrs. Rogers and Daniel arrived for the session on time. Both were dressed neatly in casual clothes. Daniel was tall for his age and well developed. I greeted them in the waiting room.

Content of Session

THERAPIST: Hello, Mrs. Rogers; hello, Daniel. I'm Dr. Kaplan.

MOTHER: Hello, Dr. Kaplan. Daniel, say hello to Dr. Kaplan.

CHILD: Hi. (*looks ill at ease, avoids eye contact with therapist, and glances toward his mother.*)

T: Daniel, why don't we go into my office, and Mom can wait in the waiting room.

C (*looking at his mother*): Mom, come in with me.

M: I'll be right out here, Daniel . . .

C (*more insistently*): Please, I said come in with me, Mom.

Rationale/Analysis

At first glance, Daniel does not come across at all as "sickly."

M: But Dr. Kaplan said she'd like to see you alone . . .

C: Mom, I told you I would rather go in with you . . .

I'm worried that he won't come in.

M: But Daniel . . .

T: Why don't you both come in?

(They sit down in the office. Child continues to direct his attention to his mother, avoiding looking at therapist.)

I decide to see them together, both to decrease his resistance and to have an opportunity to observe their interaction.

T: Daniel, do you know who I am and why your mother brought you here today?

C: I'm not sure.

T: Well, I'm a person who helps children and their families. I gather there have been some problems lately. Who would like to tell me about it?

I am deliberately being general and letting them decide how to begin.

M: Well, Dr. Kaplan, lately Daniel has been getting into trouble in school. He's not handing his homework in, and some of his teachers have said that he has a poor attitude.

I realize how uncomfortable it would be for any child to listen to his mother "report" negatively about him. This must be very hard for this boy.

C *(bursting out, with face reddening)*: It's because you won't let me play football!

M *(in a calm, controlled voice)*: Now you know what the doctors said . . .

C *(getting angrier)*: Dr. Green said I could play football! You just don't want me to.

M *(trying to reason with him)*: That's not true. Dr. Adams and Dr. Freed said it's not a good idea. We want to do what's best for you.

C *(yelling)*: Then let me play football!

I feel intimidated by his rage.

M *(continuing to speak in a rational, controlled manner)*: We've been through all this, Daniel. Football has too much risk of injury, too much contact. We've offered you alternatives, like bowling . . .

I can empathize with his mother's wish to control him. It must be difficult for *her* to have to worry about his health.

C *(continuing to yell)*: I don't want bowling! That's for nerds! I want to play football!

(Mother looks in therapist's direction as if to say, "You see what I have to deal with.")

T *(commenting to no one in particular)*: I guess it can be pretty confusing when such smart doctors have different opinions about what to do.

Sensing that other feelings lie beneath the power struggle over football, I use the words "confusing" and "scary" to defuse the anger. I want to communicate this concept to both Daniel and his

C: *(Briefly glances in therapist's direction, then looks away and mumbles something inaudible.)*

M: (*Looks relieved that the battle has been interrupted.*)

T: I did hear certain things about Daniel's situation over the phone. It sounds like this whole business of being sick could be pretty scary to begin with, and then when the doctors don't agree a kid might feel even more scared. (*Child does not speak, but looks over to therapist.*) I know only a little bit about Daniel's condition. I do know he needs to have frequent tests. It would help me to have as much information as possible about it.

mother. In a nonthreatening conversational tone, I speak generally and not directly to Daniel, using the third-person "kid" and universalizing.

(*Child joins mother in describing blood tests, bone marrow tests, scans, hospital stays for intravenous medication, and so on. He is very knowledgeable and rather detached in his descriptions.*)

Daniel is beginning to relate to me, albeit in a somewhat detached manner.

C (*less vehemently than before*): Yeah, but Mom, I still think I can play football.

M (*remaining composed and controlled*): No, it really is not a good idea, and you know it.

C (*grudgingly*): It's stupid not to let me play.

M (*changing the subject*): Dr. Kaplan, I think we should talk about school. Daniel's teachers have said he is not completing his work, nor is he doing his homework. Even when we ask him about it, he says it's done. And his math teacher has complained that he is disruptive in class . . .

C (*defensively, shouting*): Mrs. Jones is a jerk! She hates me! It's not my fault!

M: But what about the homework? You tell us it's done, but apparently it isn't.

Mrs. Rogers is attempting to remain in control and is highly intellectualized. Daniel is angry, but is using the defenses of intellectualization and grandiosity. I join the family in this intellectualized approach, but will try to open up issues that I sense are underneath and to express them in ways that permit them to be heard.

T: Sometimes it's helpful to make a plan about homework—when to do it, how much time to spend on it, and so forth. How does that strike you both?

M: That sounds like a very good idea . . .

C (*angrily, to his mother*): You just don't understand . . . those teachers are jerks . . . if you don't get it, then you're stupid too . . .

T (*addressing both of them, using a conversational tone*): You know, a lot of times when kids have confusing and scary things to deal with, it is not unusual for their schoolwork to slip. In my experience, when kids have illnesses that go on for a long time and require a lot of tests and doctors' visits and hospital stays, this can be very scary. They can even be confused about what is wrong with

Daniel is still angry! He may be feeling that I don't understand either. This indicates to me that a working alliance has not yet been formed, so that by staying with the topic of schoolwork, I convey the impression that I am allied with his mother and criticizing him. I need to gain his confidence. As I begin to talk in general about concerns I suspect Daniel may have, he can

them, especially when they are seeing doctors who
are treating children with things like leukemia.
(*Child is now looking at therapist and listening.*)

M: But of course Daniel does not have leukemia.
We have explained that to him many times.

T: Oh, I'm sure you have. But still it would be
perfectly natural for a kid to worry that he might
die.

M: (*Looks startled, but child remains quiet and listens.*)
Daniel's doctors have told all of us that he has an
excellent chance of living a long life.

T: I'm sure that's true. He is getting fine medical
care.

M: (*Nods in agreement.*)

T (*addressing Daniel*): Daniel, our time is almost
over, and I wonder whether we could talk alone for
just a few minutes.

(*He agrees, and his mother goes out to the waiting room.
Child gets up and investigates the games and play materials
on the shelves. He does not stay long with any one.*)

T: What kinds of things do you like to play with?

C: Video games are my favorite. I also like to draw,
especially horses, cars, and motorcycles. I can draw
those pretty good. Oh, you have a Nerf ball—I like
these. (*Begins tossing it.*)

T: You know, it seems to me there are a lot of
things you are having to deal with lately. I think it
would be good for us to get together again next
week and talk some more. Then, if you want, you
can also draw or play.

C: (*Shrugs.*) That's OK with me.

T: When we do talk together alone, everything you
tell me will be private and confidential. And maybe
sometimes we can include your mother, the way we
did this time. Is anything else on your mind today?

C: Well, yeah. I really hate my math teacher, and
also some kids in school. And I hate my father too.

T: How come?

C: He's always blowing his stack and yelling
at me.

T: I've never met your father, but I'll probably be
seeing him soon. Do you want me to discuss this
business of yelling at you?

absorb what is being said. I am also
modeling for his mother an
openness about "taboo" subjects,
especially fear of death.

His willingness to be alone with
me leads me to think I have made
some progress toward forming a
working alliance with him.

I wonder what's going on with the
father!

I realize that I must not set up false
hopes, but I wonder about the possibility of a future father–son session.

C: (*Shrugs.*) It's OK with me, but I doubt it will do any good.

T: Well, I can try. I think our time is up now. Bye, Daniel, it was good to meet you.

C: Bye.

Preliminary Assessment and Treatment Plan

Daniel, a boy of 11 with a chronic blood disease, was reacting to the diagnosis and its consequences for his life with anger, negativism, and grandiosity. The underlying feelings appeared to include fear, helplessness, and confusion. Despite his oppositionalism, his response to the first session indicated that it might be possible to form a working alliance within which the issues surrounding his illness could be discussed. However, his need to have some control over the structure of the sessions, including the use of play materials, would have to be respected. As the therapist, I would need to be flexible with regard to such matters as including his mother during sessions. Also, approaching his concerns indirectly seemed to have worked, and this technique could be used in the future, although the ultimate goal would be to enable him to express his feelings.

Despite the fact that only Daniel's mother attended the first session, it was clear that some assessment of both parents was needed. Mrs. Rogers appeared to be handling her own anxiety about Daniel's illness, and his opposition to the physical restrictions, by remaining controlled, logical, and rational. She obviously wished Daniel's life to continue along as "normal" a path as possible. However, in the process she was unable to assist him in dealing with his painful feelings and his fears. Thus treatment of Daniel would have to include her.

The nature of the marital relationship, and the degree of support that Mr. Rogers could offer both to Daniel and to his wife, were not known. An immediate goal, therefore, was to assess these issues in the next session, which was held with Mr. and Mrs. Rogers jointly.

Second Session

During the second session, which the parents were able to schedule despite the father's heavy workload and demanding travel schedule, additional information was obtained. Mr. Rogers presented a definite contrast to his wife: Whereas she was calm and controlled, he was highly anxious. He revealed in the course of the interview that he felt very guilty. The source of his guilt was twofold. First, immediately following the diagnosis of Daniel's illness, he had become so depressed that he left the family for about 1 month and stayed with his parents. Second, he acknowledged that he had a tendency either to give in when Daniel became insistent, or else to lose his temper and "blow up." He revealed, in addition, that he had gone into therapy following his depressive episode and that recently his wife had been joining him for marital sessions. They both agreed that they were getting along better now and were working together in dealing with Daniel.

Mr. Rogers said that he was spending as much time as he possibly could with his family, and especially with Daniel. Even though his time was limited, he was trying to make it "quality time." Since the main problem in his relationship with Daniel was his tendency to explode, a number of strategies were discussed that might help him to set limits and handle conflicts in a more constructive way. He showed an interest in trying them and said that he would discuss the issue further with his own therapist. Mrs. Rogers seemed satisfied that her husband was trying as hard as he could. We concluded by agreeing that he would make himself available in the future if it appeared to be indicated. Before ending the session, I told the parents to let me know by telephone about any significant events (medical, behavioral, etc.) that might occur between sessions, and I also encouraged them to phone me about any concerns they might have regarding Daniel. They agreed to do so.

The information about the marital crisis that had been precipitated by Daniel's diagnosis and that was now stabilized, plus the fact that Mr. Rogers would be discussing his management of Daniel with his own therapist, reinforced the initial plan of keeping the focus of the treatment on Daniel, with his mother to be included as needed.

Third Session

Daniel walked behind his mother into the waiting room. He looked ill at ease.

Content of Session	Rationale/Analysis
THERAPIST: Hi, Daniel. Hi, Mrs. Rogers.	
CHILD: Mom, can you come in with me?	He still feels uncomfortable.
MOTHER (*glancing at therapist*): Well, I guess so . . .	
T: Sure.	I want to minimize Daniel's discomfort. In addition, I suspect that after a short while he will remain in the office alone.
M (*in the office, settling into her chair*): This past week has been better. Daniel missed a day of school because of a stomach virus, but I can see he is making an effort to do his homework. Things have been calmer at home too.	
T: Does it seem that way to you too, Daniel?	It is important to get the boy's version of how things are going.
C (*giggling, squirming in his chair*): Yeah, I guess everyone has been getting along a little better. But it won't really be good until they let me play football.	
M: Daniel, you know what we've been discussing about that . . .	
C: Yeah, yeah.	
T: Daniel, do you think we can spend a little time alone now?	
C: OK.	

(*Mother leaves for the waiting room.*)

C: (*Leans his chair back against the wall, balanced on two legs, which his mother has asked him not to do.*) One of these days I know I'll get to play football again. It's so great, there's nothing like it.

T: You really do love football! You know, I saw your father the other day. He told me that you go to see football games pretty often with him.

C (*nodding*): Sometimes I get players' autographs. I have a big collection. Also, I write to some of them, and they write me back personal letters. (*Gets up and takes paper and pencil from the shelf.*) I'm going to draw a motorcycle. (*Proceeds to draw it.*)

He sounds very proud!

T: That looks very real.

C: I'm good at cars and horses too. (*Draws a car and a horse.*)

T (*watching him draw, commenting on the details*): That looks like a racing car. Is it? (*Child nods.*) And that horse is very lifelike.

(*As child draws and therapist admires his pictures, child appears increasingly relaxed. The chat continues and child begins to doodle rather than to draw in a formal way.*)

The subject matter of Daniel's drawings, as well as the discussion of football and his contacts with players, suggests concerns involving masculinity and fears of passivity. Since my immediate goal is to nurture our working alliance, I decide to praise his proficiency in art rather than explore the meaning of his pictures.

C: Sometimes I draw stuff like this in school.

T: How are things in school these days?

C: Well, there are these kids who are mean. They tease other kids.

He's opening up. I'm on the right track.

T: Do they ever bother you?

C: Yeah, sometimes. But me and my friends, we stick up for each other. Don't tell my mother, but I had a fight in school.

T: Remember what I told you about confidentiality! How did you feel about the fight? Were you afraid you might get hurt?

C: No way! I stick up for myself! Only a nerd would walk away from a fight. (*Proceeds to give examples of boys who are "cool" and others who are "nerds."*)

T: I guess I can see your point.

(*Child continues doodling with pencil and Magic Markers, chatting about various aspects of school, including subjects he likes and those he dislikes. He also describes amusing things that happened during the day. He seems surprised when the time is up.*)

I suspect that Daniel is indeed afraid of fighting, especially since he understands his disease. I also sense that he is ambivalent about his mother's knowing about the fight. I decide not to interpret this conflict, because I am afraid he may close up again.

Fourth Session

Once again Mrs. Rogers came in with Daniel for a brief time at the beginning of the session, during which she reported that he had not had any health problems that week. Things were continuing to go better at home and with regard to schoolwork. This time when he brought up the issue of football, she indicated that they would have to wait and see what the doctors decided. Then she left and waited outside.

Daniel had brought a number of glossy camp brochures with him, which he was eager to show me. The entire session was devoted to going over these brochures, discussing the activities that were pictured and described, and weighing the advantages and disadvantages of the different camps. Even though the summer was many months away, Daniel seemed to have no doubt whatever that he would be attending one of them. His attention was drawn not only to the sports, but also to such activities as arts and crafts and dramatic performances. My comments were generally related to what a wide range of interests Daniel had and how exciting it was to look forward to camp. When I mentioned that sometimes kids also felt a little nervous about going away, he denied having any such concerns.

I reinforced Daniel's hope and optimism, since he was doing better. I gave him an opportunity to discuss separation anxiety, but he did not pick up on it.

Interval in Treatment

Following the fourth session, Daniel was not seen for 6 weeks. Initially he could not come to sessions because his medical condition had deteriorated, so that he had to see his doctors frequently for careful monitoring. Then he improved and the family went away on a previously planned vacation. After the vacation ended, however, Daniel had to be hospitalized for a surgical procedure. In order to maintain our contact, I spoke to him over the telephone whenever possible, even though he was not particularly verbal under these circumstances and our conversations tended to be brief.

During this period I also had a number of telephone contacts with Mrs. Rogers. The purpose of Mrs. Rogers's first call was to report on Daniel's medical situation and to cancel our appointment. Even though she did not complain, I empathized with how difficult this must be for her. Not only did she carry the major responsibility for Daniel's ongoing medical care; the fact that she was the one who spent so much time with him meant that she was the one to whom he turned for support as well as for setting limits. Yet the medical crises must surely make her feel worried and anxious. I wondered to whom *she* could turn for support. She was stoical; she said that she and her husband were communicating much better and were able to help each other through these episodes now. Nevertheless, her positive response to my concern was evidenced by her continuing to keep in telephone contact with me.

When Mrs. Rogers reported in one of these conversations that Daniel had reverted to certain of his previous patterns of behavior, particularly the tantrums at home, I reminded her of some of the issues we had addressed in our very first meeting—namely, the feelings he must be experiencing, such as confusion, fear, and anger. She was able to empathize with him and said that as hard as this was for the family, she realized it must be especially hard for him to endure the pain, confinement, and isolation from friends.

Fifth Session

The fifth sessioin was the first following a break of 6 weeks. Daniel had just been released from the hospital after his surgical procedure. As he and his mother entered the waiting room, Mrs. Rogers asked whether she could come into the office with him for a few minutes. Daniel appeared angry and irritable.

Content of Session

Rationale/Analysis

MOTHER: I've just received an unsatisfactory report from school . . .

CHILD (*shouting*): I don't want to talk about that! (*He holds his hands against his ears.*)

THERAPIST: Maybe it would be better if Daniel and I spoke alone. (*Mother nods and leaves the office.*) It seems you felt pretty mad when your mom told me about school . . .

C (*interrupting, angrily*): I'm not going to talk about that!

T: In here you have the right to decide what you want to talk about. (*Child goes over to the shelf and picks up a Nerf ball, which he tosses up and down.*) I know you've just been in the hospital . . .

C (*vehemently*): I had a *disgusting* roommate!

T: What do you mean?

C: That kid just cried all night. I couldn't get any sleep.

T: That must have been very hard.

C (*snapping*): I don't want to talk about it!

T: OK, it's up to you. Want to play catch?

(*Child throws ball at therapist as hard as he can, laughing. Therapist throws it back, and a humorous game of catch begins. During the play, Daniel seems to calm down.*)

T (*casually*): You sure were mad just before.

C: Yeah. How would you feel if kids came up to you in school and asked you if you have cancer?

T: I guess that could be really upsetting. What did you say?

C: I told them I don't have cancer.

I wonder about the impact of all this stress on Daniel and his mother.

He seems to have regressed and become anxious again.

He covers his feelings with anger.

He needs to feel a sense of control in at least one area of his life.

It appears that he is overwhelmed with his feelings, and I am hoping that if we defuse the intensity it may be easier for him to verbalize his concerns. Playing may serve this purpose.

Now I'm beginning to understand more about his anger.

T: It might be natural, though, for a kid to think that's what he has when he's sick a lot and everyone gets so worried. Especially if that kid is around kids who do have cancer, he might even worry that he could die. (*Child does not reply, but continues throwing and catching.*) I know that what you have is not cancer, but it is a disease that can cause a lot of problems. Luckily you have good doctors . . .

I feel certain that he does have these worries. It is important to put them into words.

C: I know, I know. Let's do something else. (*Takes out paper and crayons and begins to doodle. The doodle becomes a mountain.*) I'm drawing a guy skiing.

T: Do you like to ski?

C (*with bravado*): Yeah! I like to ski very fast, out of control, straight down!

T: Gee, that sounds risky. People can get hurt doing that.

C: I *want* to break my leg!

T (*jokingly*): I guess then you wouldn't be able to go to school, and you'd have to stay at home and get taken care of until you got better. That would be awful!

C: (*Laughs heartily.*)

I assume that his grandiosity and bravado are defensive attempts to compensate for the assaults to his body he has suffered during his recent hospitalization. Using humor, I am addressing his sense of vulnerability and fears of the unknown and of growing up, and the wish to remain dependent.

Sixth Session

This week Daniel was in a good mood. He announced that he wanted his mother to come in with him to tell me something.

Content of Session

Rationale/Analysis

CHILD: I got my report card, and I went up in all my subjects.

For a change, he takes the initiative and wants me to know about his achievement.

MOTHER: That's true. And although we know Daniel can do even better, we are very proud of him.

THERAPIST: Well, that is certainly good news. (*Everyone discusses child's grades in his various subjects, and then mother goes to the waiting room. Child remains in his chair for a little while, chatting. He then gets up, takes the Nerf ball, and begins tossing it up and down.*)

I'm glad! But I'm wary: Can it last? I notice the mother's statement that he can do even better. How must that make Daniel feel?

C: Yesterday I went to the doctor for a blood test.

He is sharing more.

T: Gee, it must be pretty painful and unpleasant to have to go through that all the time.

C (*emphatically*): No way, not for me! It's *fun* to get blood drawn!

Once again he uses grandiosity and bravado as a defense.

T: Well, it sure wouldn't be fun for *me*. But it seems as if you can handle it.

(*We play a game of catch until the end of the session.*)

Rather than directly confront the defense, I am attempting to reinforce his sense of autonomy and mastery, while also giving permission to have other feelings.

Seventh Session

The previous week Daniel had missed his session because he was hospitalized for 2 days. Now he immediately came into the office alone and took paper and crayons. He began doodling and humming.

Content of Session

Rationale/Analysis

THERAPIST: Your mom told me about you being in the hospital.

CHILD (*noncommittal*): Yeah.

T: She told me you had to have a lot of tests and an IV.

C: That's nothing. I'm used to it.

T: Well, I know that I myself would find all those procedures pretty unpleasant . . .

Again, I am trying to give him permission for other feelings.

C: Hey, you want to hear what I had to eat in the hospital?

T: Sure.

C: It's great. They order in anything I want. My favorite is Chinese. Want me to draw all the different dishes I had? (*He proceeds to illustrate the Chinese dishes he ate. Therapist and child compare notes on the subject of Chinese food. Child then shifts to doodles.*) You know, in school a lot of kids get into fights.

He exhibits more defensive grandiosity. I'd better not tackle this head on.

T: How do you feel about fighting?

C: I'm not afraid to fight; I'm just afraid to get into trouble. It's *good* to have a blood disease! You don't get into trouble, and your friends protect you.

Again, I wonder whether he has an underlying fear.

T: Well, I guess every cloud has a silver lining.

C: (*Suddenly notices that one of the office chairs has several loose screws.*) Next week I'm going to bring in a screwdriver and tighten those screws.

I won't challenge his rationalization, which is a way of dealing with his fear of fighting. This is a loaded issue, again involving concerns about passivity and dependence.

T: Do you like fixing things?

I am reinforcing his sense of competence and masculinity, as

C: Sure, and I'm good at it too. I help my dad a lot around the house.

T: That's a really useful skill to have.

expressed in a more adaptive form than fighting.

Eighth Session

The following week Daniel marched directly into the office carrying a screwdriver and proceeded to tighten the loose screws on my office chair.

Content of Session

THERAPIST: Thanks very much!

CHILD: (*Seems pleased, then mood changes; picks up Nerf ball and begins tossing it in the air.*) I'm so mad. I can't play football.

T: I can imagine how bad it must feel for a person not be to able to play a sport he loves.

C: (*Does not reply, but is listening.*)

T: I know your father takes you to see football games quite often. Maybe in one way he is trying to make up for the fact that you aren't allowed to play.

C: (*Nods, looking and sounding sad.*) But it's not the same.

T: I guess it's really a drag to have this kind of restriction.

C (*casually continuing to toss the Nerf ball*): I know two kids who have leukemia. I met them at a picnic to raise funds for children with blood diseases.

T: I wonder whether you ever worry that you have leukemia.

C: (*Shrugs.*) Nah.

T: You don't have it; what you have is a different problem with your blood. But it would be natural for a kid to worry that he might have leukemia too, or even to worry that he might die.

C (*quickly*): I never worry about that. Hey, you know, I got two more autographs for my football collection.

Rationale/Analysis

Daniel seems to be very comfortable by now about coming into the session alone.

I note that this time he has expressed his feelings without much anger. Fixing my chair seems to have made him feel more in control.

Despite his denials, I suspect that Daniel *is* afraid and that this issue needs to be addressed on a continuing basis.

The subject has been discussed and he has heard me, but he prefers to stay on safer ground.

Ninth Session

The previous week Daniel had missed his session because he was hospitalized following abnormal results on one of his routine blood tests. This week he arrived at the office carrying a skateboard.

Content of Session	Rationale/Analysis
CHILD: Can I bring my skateboard into the office?	
MOTHER: Daniel, you might damage Dr. Kaplan's office . . .	
THERAPIST: It's OK. My office can take it.	I am giving Daniel permission to engage in physical activity within the confines of a "safe" environment.
C: (*Enters the office, where he demonstrates the use of the skateboard, showing therapist various maneuvers and describing how he and his friends play with skateboards on the street. As he jumps on and off, he actually does not appear to have very good control over it.*)	
T: Gee, I'm surprised the doctors allow you to do this on the street.	
C: Sometimes they do, and sometimes they don't. It depends on my blood. [Note: He is referring to his platelet count, which determines whether the blood will clot properly or whether a danger of hemorrhaging exists.]	
T: That sure looks like fun. I think I might be afraid of hurting myself, though.	Again I take ownership of the fears, instead of confronting this bravado directly.
C (*vehemently*): Not me! (*Continues skateboarding around the office.*) Guess what? On my street, me and my friends built a jump. Jumping is really cool. (*Pauses.*) Although I *am* a little afraid of heights.	He is trying to impress me with his skill, but he can admit he is not fearless! This represents progress!
T: (*Nods.*)	
C (*after a little more skateboard demonstration*): Can my mother come in for a minute?	
T: Sure, just go and get her.	
C (*to mother*): Mom, in school I had a bloody nose. I forgot to tell you.	Having his masculinity admired has made him less fearful of passive dependence, so that he can share his concern with his mother.
M: We'll have to let the doctor know.	
C: (*Does not comment.*)	

Tenth Session

Daniel followed his mother into the waiting room with an angry expression.

Content of Session	Rationale/Analysis
CHILD: Mom, you better come in with me!	
MOTHER: Daniel, I . . .	
C (*shouting*): I want to play football! Why can't I play football?	Here we go again! This boy just won't relent. It must be very hard for his mother.

THERAPIST (*ushering them into the office*): Why don't we talk in here?

M (*calmly*): Daniel, every time this issue comes up, we go over the same things. You know the reasons.

C (*yelling*): What you're saying is stupid!

M (*still calm*): We just don't want to take any chances . . .

C: (*Starts to cry and continues yelling.*) It's my fault I have this blood problem. I must have done something wrong. Why am I being punished? | This little boy has so much guilt! It's so unfair!

M: Honey, you haven't done anything wrong. This isn't your fault.

C (*still crying*): Yes, it is! Why can't I play football? I want you to let me play football!

T (*addressing mother*): You know, I think this whole situation is scary and kind of confusing for Daniel. I've discovered that sometimes when kids feel scared because their lives seem to be out of control, they tend to think that they have done something bad and deserve punishment. I suspect they may think so because it is easier in a way than feeling helpless. | I am addressing Daniel's concerns indirectly as I speak to his mother. But I know he is hearing me.

M: Daniel, you know how many times we have suggested that you could join a bowling league. You've always enjoyed bowling . . . | She's avoiding the feelings!

C (*enraged, yelling*): I *told* you bowling is for nerds!

T (*addressing mother*): It seems that Daniel prefers football because it is a more manly sport than bowling.

M: But he knows that football is not possible . . .

C: (*Jumps out of his chair and shouts at his mother.*) You just don't know what it's like to be a kid my age! (*Runs out of the office to the waiting room.*) | It's true. She can't empathize with him. Her own fears make her intellectualized and controlling with him. I have to be careful not to let my frustration with her show. And yet I can also empathize with her. It must be overwhelming to have such a sick child!

T (*to mother*): I think Daniel has made an important statement today. (*Goes to the waiting room and addresses child.*) So long, Daniel. I can see you feel very upset today, and I'm sorry we have no time left to talk it over. Let's talk about it next week, and you can also call me if you want. | I'm sorry this all came up at the end. I wonder whether he will continue to be upset and whether maybe I should call *him*.

Eleventh Session

Soon after the previous session, Mrs. Rogers telephoned me to relate the events that had immediately followed the session. Daniel had left the office angry and had refused to go into the house. Instead he had gone to the garage, where he remained for about an hour. When he finally returned to the house, he was quiet. This incident, and the fact that he seemed to be out of control, had upset the whole family, she said. Now, according to Mrs. Rogers, Daniel was saying that he no longer wanted to come for treatment. I said that I could understand his feelings, but suggested she tell him that I wanted to see him one more time because I had something to tell him. She agreed to bring him in. When Daniel appeared for the session, he seemed more hesitant than at any time since the beginning of treatment.

Content of Session

THERAPIST (*after child has entered the office alone*): Daniel, your mother told me that you didn't want to come any more.

CHILD: (*Nods.*)

T: I can understand how you feel. You really got very upset here last week. I can't blame you in a way for not wanting to come back. After all, I can't make you well. Also, I can't make your parents agree to let you play football. Still, I'm glad you came one last time to talk some things over.

C: (*Looks uncomfortable.*)

T: You have often found things in the office to play with while we have talked. Maybe you'd like to choose something now.

C: OK. (*Selects paper and Magic Markers.*)

T: (*Watches while child draws and doodles.*) You and I have talked about your disease a lot, and I understand that you have an excellent chance of living a long life. But I also realize that there are a lot of unknowns about your illness. The doctors have to watch you closely, and often you have to have tests. Many times when kids have diseases that contain unknowns, they feel afraid to grow up because they are afraid of what the future might hold. That is a perfectly normal reaction.

C: (*Continues drawing and doodling; does not interrupt.*) Do you want to play catch?

T: Sure. (*Therapist and child play with the Nerf ball and chat for the rest of the session.*) I think our time is up now. Bye, Daniel, best of luck.

C: Bye.

Rationale/Analysis

I am not certain who is resistant to continuing treatment, Daniel or the family. In either case, I must assume that this will be my last opportunity to see him. I need to achieve some closure with Daniel.

I am sure he feels this way. But universalizing makes it less threatening.

Daniel draws and does not seem involved, but his nonverbal responses give me reason to hope that my remarks have been heard.

COMMENTS

At the time treatment concluded, I was uncertain about the efficacy of the work with Daniel. This was especially true because of the abrupt way in which treatment came to an end. I thought more work might have been done with Mrs. Rogers, and also with Mr. Rogers, to help them with their own fears and feelings so that they could tolerate Daniel's expression of feelings. I was also concerned about whether Daniel had resolved the issues with which he was clearly struggling. I told Mrs. Rogers that I would like to keep in touch, and she agreed.

Approximately 6 months later, I telephoned the Rogers family to follow up on Daniel's progress. Mrs. Rogers was extremely pleased to hear from me. She told me that Daniel was doing very well, despite the fact that he had suffered some complications and been hospitalized several times. He had started bicycle riding in a serious way and was no longer obsessed with football. He even was able to live with limitations on the bicycle riding at those times when his blood results were abnormal. She said she attributed this greater acceptance on his part to the fact that she and her husband were able to be more open and accepting of his feelings regarding his illness, and they encouraged him to express himself. She said, "Now we listen to Daniel!"

Furthermore, Mrs. Rogers reported, despite the frequency with which his diagnosis had been explained to him, Daniel had come right out and asked his parents directly whether he had leukemia. This had enabled them to explain to him that, despite the fact that so much was unknown about his illness, he did not have cancer. She felt that finally he understood and believed this. The most important concrete gain, Mrs. Rogers said, was that Daniel's attitude and schoolwork were now markedly improved. She added that if the situation were to deteriorate again, she would not hesitate to contact me.

I therefore concluded that a key factor in the positive outcome was that I had enabled Daniel to express his feelings, and had also been able to provide enough support for Mrs. Rogers that she could tolerate these feelings. Formerly taboo issues, such as death and cancer, were now open for discussion and clarification. Thus the deteriorating relationship between Daniel and his parents—which, prior to the onset of the illness, had been a generally positive one—was strengthened, and they were no longer adversaries. Daniel could now proceed to engage in activities that increased his sense of autonomy and growing masculinity.

EIGHT YEARS LATER: RETROSPECTIVE REVIEW

Eight years after first reporting this case, I have had no further contact with the Rogers family. My last conversation with Mrs. Rogers, 6 months after the end of treatment, led me to believe that the family would have contacted me if difficulties had arisen. Yet it is impossible to state with certainty what the outcome for Daniel has been. Nonetheless, review of the case has proven interesting and useful, especially in light of current developments in the field.

Gaps in the work with Daniel can certainly be found retrospectively, especially with regard to the family. First, I regret that I never had contact with Wendy, Daniel's older sister. Adams (1995) has pointed out that siblings of seriously ill children frequently experience intense feelings, including ambivalence, resentment, and increased sibling rivalry. Even though Wendy, who was a teenager, was described as doing well and keeping busy with her own activities, she may well have had problems coping with Daniel's illness and with the parents' stress. In addition, a session with her might have provided additional insight into the family dynamics.

Second, I might have done more work with the parents. Adams (1995) notes that parents of suffering children must grieve and manage their own feelings before they can help their children. Although I was able to provide some support to Mrs. Rogers over the telephone during the period when I was working with Daniel, at the point when treatment abruptly terminated she was having difficulty empathizing with him; instead, she maintained a controlled, intellectualized stance. Even though she was going with her husband to his therapist for couple therapy, I cannot be certain that this forum provided the opportunity for handling expressions of grief and fear. Perhaps this information could have been elicited through contact with the couple therapist. At the very least, I regret not having had a final session with the parents. Because Daniel's illness was chronic, both physical and emotional ups and downs were to be expected. If this had been discussed with Mr. and Mrs. Rogers, it might have put Daniel's outbursts into perspective, making them more comprehensible and tolerable and less upsetting.

Finally, it seemed to me that Daniel's anger had frightened him as well as his parents. The penultimate session with Daniel might be considered a "difficult moment in child therapy" (Gabel, Oster, & Pfeffer, 1988). Such a moment is defined by these authors as "a concrete expression of a disparity between the therapist's and the child's or the parents' expectations of the treatment process" (Gabel et al., 1988, p. 199). The family had entered treatment with the expectation that Daniel would become more cooperative and reasonable, not less. Clarifying for all of them the reasons for his anger could have proven very useful, especially if this had been accompanied by opportunities (discussed above) for the parents to deal with their own feelings about his illness.

Despite any gaps or omissions, however, the question arises as to whether Daniel's case ought to be considered an example of treatment prematurely terminated. The answer is yes if appropriate treatment is regarded as long-term, with termination occurring only after the symptoms as seen in the office have abated. On the other hand, brief and solution-oriented models of treatment (de Shazer, 1985; De Jong & Miller, 1995) offer a different perspective. These models, which have become increasingly relevant in an era of managed care, propose that change need not occur in the therapist's office. In fact, the goal of treatment is to encourage clients to utilize their strengths in developing solutions to problems in the real world outside the office.

Viewed in this light, Daniel's family's abrupt termination of treatment appears less significant. After all, as of the 6-month follow-up, their goals had been achieved. Daniel was doing better in school and was more cooperative at home. He had also abandoned his unreasonable demand to play football in favor of a more appropriate sport. Most important—and perhaps the basis of the other changes—was the fact that the parents were now able to listen and respond to their son's concerns. In fact, Daniel may be regarded as having moved from the stage of "turmoil without resolution," involving confusion, difficult emotions, and feelings of helplessness and hopelessness, to "recovery," in which children and families learn to cope with the disease and accept both temporary and long-term limitations (Adams, 1995, p. 154).

Undoubtedly, then, the treatment process was helpful. But what factor or factors were the most efficacious? In the first edition of this chapter, I emphasized the efficacy of interpretations of Daniel's conflicts, made to him and to his mother, as well as improvements in his wounded self-esteem as a result of activities that occurred in the office. Using the perspective of strengths and solutions, I would not reject these conclusions. However, I would add that the treatment mobilized the family members to draw upon their strengths, in order to develop their own creative solutions to the difficult dilemmas posed by Daniel's suffering.

STUDY QUESTIONS

1. Were the issues surrounding Daniel's illness resolved? To what extent can children achieve resolution of issues in the case of a chronic illness with an uncertain course?

2. How might one account for the fact that children with illnesses and disabilities that are either congenital or diagnosed in early childhood may present very differently from Daniel (e.g., with less anger)?

3. How should peer relationships have been evaluated in Daniel's situation? Note that even though he was not healthy, he did not identify with very sick children either.

4. How might a family therapy approach, or a planned short-term treatment approach, have affected the outcome of this case?

5. Why did Daniel's treatment actually terminate so abruptly?

REFERENCES

Adams, D. (1995). The suffering of children and adolescents with life-threatening illness: Factors involved and ways professionals can help. In D. Adams & E. Deveau (Eds.), *Beyond the innocence of childhood* (Vol. 2, pp. 151–177). Amityville, NY: Baywood.

De Jong, P., & Miller, S. (1995). How to interview for client strengths. *Social Work, 40*(6), 729–736.

de Shazer, S. (1985). *Keys to solution in brief therapy.* New York: Norton.

Feeman, D., & Hagen, J. (1990). Effects of childhood chronic illness on families. *Social Work in Health Care, 14*(3), 37–53.

Freud, A. (1952). The role of bodily illness in the mental life of children. *Psychoanalytic Study of the Child, 7,* 69–81.

Gabel, S., Oster, G., & Pfeffer, C. (1988). *Difficult moments in child psychotherapy.* New York: Plenum Press.

Geist, R. (1979). Onset of chronic illness in children and adolescents: Psychotherapeutic and consultative intervention. *American Journal of Orthopsychiatry*, 49(1), 4–23.

Gizynski, M., & Shapiro, V. (1990). Depression and childhood illness. *Child and Adolescent Social Work Journal*, 7(3), 179–197.

Maher, J., & Pask, E. (1995). When truth hurts. In D. Adams & E. Deveau (Eds.), *Beyond the innocence of childhood* (Vol. 2, pp. 267–293). Amityville, NY: Baywood.

Sarnoff, C. (1976). *Latency*. New York: Jason Aronson.

Sarnoff, C. (1987a). *Psychotherapeutic strategies in the latency years*. Northvale, NJ: Jason Aronson.

Sarnoff, C. (1987b). *Psychotherapeutic strategies in late latency through early adolescence*. Northvale, NJ: Jason Aronson.

CHAPTER 17

Childhood Cancer and the Family

Case of Tim, Age 6, and Follow-Up at Age 15

ROBIN F. GOODMAN

When parents hear the word "cancer" applied to their child, they are devastated. Children and families confront the ordeal of cancer with varying premorbid states that are newly stressed by the diagnosis of the disease. In my role as a psychologist and art therapist, I help these children and families navigate their way through the "crisis" of cancer by learning how to incorporate the disease and related experiences into the routine fabric of their lives. This requires a preliminary assessment to identify behaviors that are reactive to the disease, those that are unique to each individual's personality style and way of functioning, strengths that can be bolstered, and vulnerabilities that may need protection.

My guiding principle in working with children is to help them continue to grow, develop, and play as their peers do. Children typically live in the present moment and can readily adapt to a changed environment. A 22-year-old survivor of childhood leukemia told me that having cancer became such an intrinsic part of her life that she could not even conceive of, let alone answer, a question about how her life was different from others' lives because she had cancer. Having cancer was an integral part of her growing up, integrated into who she was, just as having a brother and being on the swim team were. Having long hair, losing it, and having it back again all contributed to her identity. This is not meant to minimize the experience, but to demonstrate how resilient children can be and how they can successfully cope with the "crisis" of growing up with cancer.

EFFECTS OF CANCER ON CHILDREN

As the survival rates for pediatric cancer patients have increased, interest in the emotional impact of cancer has increased likewise. Whereas in the 1960s only 20–30% of the children diagnosed with cancer were expected to survive, today the rate is an impressive 50–90%, the result of which is that by the age of 20, 1 out of every 1,000 adults is a survivor (Granowetter, 1994). Despite the optimistic outlook, however, cancer is the second leading cause of death among children, next to accidents for children under age 14 (Granowetter, 1994). Research has encompassed the areas of survivor sequelae and late effects of chemotherapy and radiotherapy on neurological functioning (Butler & Copeland, 1993), as well as determination of factors contributing to successful psychological adaptation and adjustment.

The research reveals conflicting results concerning the emotional adjustment of survivors of childhood cancer. The first studies done with survivors were cautionary. In the 1970s, O'Malley, Koocher, Foster, and Slavin (1979) reported that 59% of a sample of survivors with a mean age of 5.7 years at diagnosis were "judged to be impaired psychologically" (p. 162). The early retrospective studies linked emotional adjustment to such things as age at diagnosis, time elapsed since diagnosis, self-esteem, verbal ability (Koocher, O'Malley, Gogan, & Foster, 1980), honest communication about the disease (O'Malley et al., 1979; Slavin, O'Malley, Koocher, & Foster, 1982), social relationships, and the use of denial as a coping mechanism (O'Malley et al., 1979). Some later evidence also exists showing children with leukemia to have more behavior problems and to score lower on competence measures (e.g., Sawyer, Crettenden, & Toogood, 1986).

More recent reports conflict with the initial prognosis of a stormy emotional outlook for these children, however. There are ample data to suggest that some childhood cancer survivors can be as socially well adjusted as their healthy peers with respect to education, vocation, marriage, and interpersonal relationships (Dobkin & Morrow, 1985–1986; Noll et al., 1997).

The inherent conundrum of retrospective studies is the difficulty of detecting causation. Children grow up in a multifaceted psychosocial environment. Thus it stands to reason that a child's response to disease is influenced by the attitudes witnessed and experienced by the family, and vice versa. Once a diagnosis is made, the entire family is affected by the disease (Dobkin & Morrow, 1985–1986; Eiser, 1979; Futterman & Hoffman, 1973; Van Dongen-Melman & Sanders-Woudstra, 1986) and can either help or hinder the child's adaptation (Morris et al., 1997). For example, hopelessness among children with cancer was correlated with high distress among both mothers and fathers (Blotcky, Raczynski, Gurwitch, & Smith, 1985). But the family has also been shown to provide an appropriate model for coping (Compass, Worsham, & Ey, 1992). Aside from the family, distress in pediatric cancer patients has been related to traumatic procedures (such as bone marrow aspirations), severe cosmetic change, low levels of self-esteem regarding physical appearance, late neurological effects, restrictions in daily activities, and death of fellow cancer patients (Bennett, 1994; Natterson & Knudson, 1960; Varni, Katz, Colegrove, & Dolgin, 1995). The interaction among the individual, the family, and the disease variables is complex at best.

The physical events of the cancer experience itself have also been shown to have a profound effect on a child. When compared to children with other chronic illnesses, children with leukemia showed "a greater preoccupation with threat to their body integrity and functioning, greater anxiety in their general out-of-hospital life, and a lack of adaptability to the necessity of clinic visits" (Spinetta & Maloney, 1975, p. 1037). If in fact impaired adjustment is inevitable, research is still trying to answer the question of what accounts for impaired adjustment. The following conditions have been cited:

> the experience of cancer per se, aversive treatment . . . disruption of children's accustomed and expected daily routines . . . and social relationships, cultural attitudes to-

ward having cancer, how children understand the uncertainties associated with having cancer, the financial burdens on the family, the chronic condition of cancer survivorship, or some combination of these inherent and exogenous factors. (Bearison & Pacifici, 1984, p. 268)

Many of these influences lead to what I call "derailments of developmental tasks," but how severe these are and whether the effects are permanent are still open to question. There is a danger of inappropriately assuming that all cancer patients react pathologically or abnormally to their disease. Van Dongen-Melman and Sanders-Woudstra (1986) point to the fact that the criteria used to assess pathology and normality in healthy populations cannot be transferred in a wholesale fashion. The so-called "pathological behavior" of a cancer patient may in fact be adaptive.

DEVELOPMENTAL CONSIDERATIONS

It is evident that the age of the child and the stage of the disease both have a bearing on the psychological tasks facing the child. We know that at different ages a child is likely to have specific fears related to hospital and illness experiences. In general, through age 6, a child's biggest fear is separation. This can lead to feelings of abandonment, withdrawal, and mistrust. From age 6 to age 9 or 10, the fears of intrusion, mutilation, and punishment are dominant. The range of reactions at this age can include feelings of rejection and isolation from peers and family, guilt, inadequacy, insecurity, and loss of a sense of mastery. From age 9 or 10 to age 12, the primary fear is loss of bodily functions; the "adult" fear of the possibility and permanence of death also begins to be important at this time. Some consequences of illness disruption at this age are feelings of social isolation, difficulty with intimate relationships, increased dependence, body image concerns, and religious questioning (Astin, 1977–1978; Cook, 1973; Easson, 1974; Holland & Rowland, 1989; Lonetto, 1980; Spinetta, 1974).

Two psychological issues figure more prominently for children with cancer: separation/loss and control/competence (Brunnquell & Hall, 1984). Loss associated with death has often been the focus in the literature on cancer, at times overshadowing other significant losses (Van Dongen-Melman & Sanders-Woudstra, 1986). Children with cancer must also cope with other real, concrete losses (such as the loss of hair or limbs), as well as less observable losses (such as the loss of relationships or independence). Although dealing with separation is a developmental task, having cancer can bring this issue into focus because treatment necessitates prolonged or frequent separations from family and friends, which may encourage heightened dependence on a parent. As a consequence of the disease, it is not unusual for a child to feel as if his or her life is in the hands of others. Decreased mobility secondary to the cancer also has an impact on a child's ability to feel in control. Whereas loss of control "may disrupt both social and emotional development . . . control strategies can facilitate emotional adjustment during times of stress" (Worchel, Copeland, & Baker,

1987, p. 26). The interaction between the psychological and the physical is difficult to differentiate, but imperative to integrate.

CHILDREN'S UNDERSTANDING OF DEATH

Childhood cancer remains a potentially life-threatening disease, and although death is still a taboo topic, children are inquisitive about and wrestle with the concept. There is some consensus on the stages children traverse on their way to a mature understanding of death. Yet there is disagreement over whether age, cognitive ability, emotion, or experience is the main determinant of this understanding (Bibace & Walsh, 1979; Childers & Wimmer, 1971; Goodman, 1989; Jenkins & Cavanaugh, 1985; Kane, 1979; Kastenbaum, 1967; Koocher, 1973; Reilly, Hasazi, & Bond, 1983; Orbach, Gross, Glaubman, & Berman, 1985; Safier, 1964; Schilder & Wechsler, 1934; Speece & Brent, 1984; Spinetta, 1980; Webb, 1993; White, Elsom, & Prawat, 1978).

Children typically proceed through specific stages in their development of a mature concept of death. The 3- to 5-year-old is at the preoperational stage of cognitive development; he or she thinks egocentrically and does not recognize that death is irreversible. At this age, death is experientially and emotionally equivalent to separation. In the second stage, with the advent of concrete operational thought, death is understood in terms of the specific and the concrete. The 5- to 9-year-old may accept the existence of death but views it as linked to certain causes, such as violence or wrongdoing; at this age, the child may also "personify" death (e.g., belief in the "boogey man"). By age 9 or 10, a child is on the way to the stage of formal operations and is able to think abstractly and to generalize from one person's death to everyone's, including his or her own. At this age, most children can comprehend the four main components of the adult understanding of death: that death is irreversible, is inevitable, is universal, and results in cessation of bodily functions (Anthony, 1971; Nagy, 1948; Wass, 1984).

Much has been written about how children with cancer become specifically socialized about their disease and its fatal potential. Researchers have studied the process whereby specific experiences influence a child's knowledge about disease. According to Bluebond-Langner (1978), children with cancer go through five stages on their way to becoming socialized about their illness. They progress from learning that their disease is serious to knowing that death is possible if the medicine does not work. Bluebond-Langner (1978) also believes that a child's self-concept corresponds to the different stages. For example, at the stage when children learn the names of the drugs they take and their side effects, they may consider themselves seriously ill but also conceptualize that they can get better.

A comparison of healthy children, suicidal children, and cancer patients concluded that cancer patients had negative feelings about life and were more attracted to death than healthy children were (Orbach, Fesback, Carlson, & Ellenberg, 1984). This suggested that cancer patients confront death and deal with it in a specific disease-related manner, in order to relieve their unpleasant physical experiences. Spinetta and Maloney (1975) found that cancer patients had an awareness of the seriousness of their illness and had greater anxiety than a control group of patients who had nonfatal chronic illness. However, a caveat is in order: One must avoid making generalizations about children with cancer. Individual variability influences adjustment and long-term psychological survival. We must always ask what a particular set of circumstances means to a particular child at a particular time.

HELPING CHILDREN COPE WITH ILLNESS

Over the years, experience has shown that children with cancer do best when involved in open, honest discussions about their disease and about death (Bluebond-Langner, 1978; Goodman, 1989; Vernick & Karon, 1965; Koocher & O'Malley, 1981; Spinetta, 1974; Slavin et al., 1982). Traditionally, adults have tended to "shield" and "protect" children from discussion about cancer and illness. This seems to be a function of the adults' anxiety rather than the children's rejection of discussion. Children can become lonely when they are aware of their diagnosis, when things are kept secret, and when reality is sugarcoated (Binger et al., 1969). As a result, there is little or no meaningful communication. Professionals, disturbed about a child's approaching death, may unwittingly become remote or unapproachable just at the time when support, information, and contact are needed most (Bluebond-Langner, 1978; Binger et al., 1969; Katz & Jay, 1984).

The term "mutual pretense" (Bluebond-Langner, 1978) has been used to describe the adult stance toward death of looking the other way, which encourages a child to do likewise. Research results, however, have not demonstrated any value in keeping children in the dark. In working with children with a potentially life-threatening illness, the more accurate question is not what to tell children about death and illness, but how to tell them. The answer lies in understanding a child's developmental level and then providing information appropriate to the child's ability to understand, clarifying misinformation, picking up cues about feelings and fears, and responding to these rather than avoiding them.

Much of our knowledge about what children with cancer think, know, and fear comes from investigative and clinical work based on projective assessments, play, and fantasy techniques. Adams-Greenly (1984, p. 63) refers to Sourkes, who "pointed out that children often have two versions of an illness; the medical version, which they can repeat verbatim, and their own private version . . . play, art, drama, and casual conversation are all useful tools in ascertaining the child's private perceptions." Because the distinctions between fantasy and reality and between action and thought can become blurred for children, it may be necessary to use methods that reveal fantasy in order to determine the totality of a child's understanding (Adams-Greenly, 1984). Then one can help a child cope with his or her illness by clarifying reality and dispelling fantasy.

"Finding an acceptable outlet for feelings of anxiety, anger, and fear and gaining a sense of mastery over the environment have been identified as important coping tasks among seriously ill children" (Koocher & O'Malley, 1981, p. 10). These authors later expand on this point:

> Giving patients and families the opportunity to talk about their concerns and receive information about their experiences is critically important. Being able to anticipate stressful events . . . can lessen the emotional drain even though the actual experience has not been altered. . . . Supportive information giving, facilitation of communication among family members, and encouraging discussion of emotional issues [were deemed extremely important to patients and families.] The patient and family members must feel cared about and must know that all their questions will be answered directly and honestly. (1981, p. 175)

USE OF NONVERBAL THERAPY TECHNIQUES

Children learn through action as well as through words, and they can communicate about their internal world in a nonverbal manner through art and play. Providing a child with the opportunity to express feelings rather than holding them in lets the child turn the passive into the active and sublimate unacceptable feelings of anger and fear.

Therapeutic work with a child often takes the form of creative endeavors. According to Petrillo and Sanger (1980), play and art "deal with emotional release by offering rich and significant channels for expression" (p. 160). It allows for emotional reorganization and for reexperiencing of problems and anxiety. The child is able to find solutions and enact feelings without fear of criticism. This does not deviate from the standard theory and methods recommended by nondirective play therapists such as Axline (1947). According to Kübler-Ross (1981),

> we receive from the child a picture of his world that is often clearer and more direct than what the artist portrays, because the child has little formal knowledge of art. When a child is investing his feelings and ideas in his drawing, the process unfolds without any critical forces to accuse him. . . . It appears that the child's feelings and thoughts . . . flow freely and directly onto drawing paper. (p. 65)

Art can be a powerful tool in discovering a child's concerns. By creating art, ill children are being constructive in the midst of a life that entails destruction of the part of them that has disease. Children can create their own artistic symbols to express feelings, in contrast to taking a ready-made play object and projecting feelings onto the toy. The artwork is more personalized and allows a therapist to talk in a nonthreatening way, using a child's own metaphor (Kramer, 1971). Diagnostically, drawings may reveal how a child is coping with such physical changes as loss of hair or an amputation; therapeutically, drawings can be used as a method of intervention. Of course, throughout the therapy, interpretation of drawings and assessment of a child must always include more than one piece of art. One must consider the body of work and the context in which it was produced.

Common themes emerging in the artwork of children with cancer include illustrations of disease-specific issues, especially those related to loss and change (Sourkes, 1982). Once diagnosed with cancer, children may feel they have lost their identity, and their self-image may be altered to accommodate aspects of their disease. Figure drawings by children with cancer can provide clues to how they feel about being labeled "sick." Children feeling a loss of control may portray their anger in the form of superhero battles, or may attempt to regain a sense of control by realistically depicting various medical situations.

Once diagnosed, children often experience lost or changed relationships. Time with peers and family members is frequently altered because of the temporary effects of treatment, and fellow patients may die of their disease. Thus children may fear the loss of their own lives. Children may feel helpless or hopeless in reaction to, and as a way of coping with, their feelings about death and loss. Their art may reveal renewed religious beliefs or faith that parents and staff members can help them in their struggles.

THE CASE: TIM BRADLEY, AGE 6
Family Information

Tim Bradley was a 6-year-old boy in first grade, the second child of a white, middle-class family. He had one sister, Rebecca, age 9, who was in the fourth grade. Both parents were college-educated. Mrs. Bradley, age 35, had stopped working when her daughter was born, and Mr. Bradley, age 37, was an attorney. The maternal grandparents were alive and were involved with the family. Although they lived in a nearby state, the grandparents moved in with the family for 4 months to help out when Tim was diagnosed. A paternal aunt also routinely provided babysitting and companionship for the children.

Presenting Problem

Tim was diagnosed with leukemia at age 5, after a month of easy bruising and flulike symptoms. Up until that time, he had been in good health and had suffered only the usual childhood ailments (such as sore throats and chickenpox). Until Tim was diagnosed with leukemia, the family had not experienced significant stressors or traumas. There were no signs of previous familial psychopathology. The diagnosis challenged the family system, however, and weak links in the parents' communication patterns emerged. In addition, the child and his family had to deal with the tangible, technical aspects of the treatment regimen and with the concomitant emotional reactions and fears surrounding the disease.

First Interview

I first met Tim on the fifth day of his initial hospitalization, at the beginning of his chemotherapy treatment. During his hospitalization, a steady stream of visitors and family members came in shifts to stay with him. He was already quite knowledgeable about his disease and knew his diagnosis. His hair had begun to fall out because of the medicines, and although he was not quite sure why this was happening, he was not particularly upset by it. For our first session, I arrived with an assortment of drawing materials and hospital play supplies. I explained that I was a different kind of doctor, and that I came to find out how he was feeling and see whether he had any questions or complaints. I also said that sometimes talking or drawing helped children to feel better.

When I arrived, Tim was looking for the box he had been using to save his hair. Being unable to find it, I offered to wrap up strands of his hair in a paper towel. Then I suggested he decorate the towel so that everyone would know it was special and would not mistakenly throw it out. He drew a happy face on the toweling and then went on to color another picture. He talked about all the "sticks" (blood tests and intravenous lines) he was getting and what he did to get through them. He explained that his mother was at home sometimes to take care of his sister, and if he was alone at night and got scared, he could call his father. When Tim was hospitalized, Mr. Bradley slept at the hospital or with friends nearby, coming to the hospital whenever he was summoned by Tim. Knowing how to get help can be extremely important for a child's well-being. Confidence and trust in parents have been associated with positive adaptation in children with cancer (Worchel et al., 1987).

Tim had tremendous physical and psychological strength and made a rapid adjustment to treatment. His parents met with the school staff to ensure a smooth transition after discharge. Indeed, Tim returned to school in a month, with no apparent problems. All of his chemotherapy was given on an outpatient basis, which clearly encouraged the resumption of normal activities. He was friendly with all the staff members he encountered, from secretaries to nurses, and managed quite independently. His positive attitude was a reflection of the philosophy his parents displayed. They were careful to shield Tim from their own anguish and doubts. Such mutuality between parents, and their ability to maintain stability in the early stages of the disease, can reduce a child's fear and hopelessness (Rowland, 1989).

An Early Intervention: Tim's List

Tim had learned to cope by being in control of his situation and preparing himself for whatever events he experienced at the clinic. However, evidence indicating that he was a scared little boy erupted in his laughing and joking when others discussed medical procedures. Using denial and reaction formation, he defended against his feeling afraid. In addition, he became upset one day when he had an unexpected bone marrow test. This led to a joint effort on the part of his mother and me to help him feel in control. With our encouragement, Tim dictated to me all the things he did to help him get through difficult procedures. Tim's list is a very good summary of coping procedures for children with cancer and their families. It illustrates some of the main principles and techniques of therapy used with this group of patients. In particular, it supports the conclusion that children do best when they are personally involved in their treatment (Worchel et al., 1987).

Tim's tips, together with the therapeutic principles underlying them, were as follows:

1. Calm down when the doctor wants to help you.

Belief in power of doctor to take control and cure. Fear that something you do could jeopardize outcome.

2. Find out what is going to happen and why.

Information seeking in order to master the situation. Knowing what to expect increases feeling of control.

3. Take deep breaths.

Relaxation and distraction as aids in coping.

4. Get hugs from Mom and Dad.

Need to feel safe; increased dependence on parents; fear of separation and abandonment.

5. Count while the needle is in.

Distraction; active participation to decrease feeling helpless.

6. Think of nice things.

Reaction formation; imagery used for distraction and to minimize negative associations.

7. Think about getting better.

Positive attitude as a way to feel in control and be a partner in cure.

8. It's OK to cry, but never say no!

Appropriate expression of feelings; limit setting on behavior. Doctor and parents are still in control.

9. Drink something or do something else.

Need for nurturance, distraction.

10. When you feel sad, talk to Mom or Dad or someone who is there.

Need for outside support; need for verbalization and expression of feelings.

11. Tell your friends to ignore that you are sick.

Coping with changed identity and need for normalizing childhood experiences and socialization.

Preliminary Assessment and Treatment Plan

When first diagnosed with leukemia, patients usually go through a month or two of intense chemotherapy to induce remission. This necessitates frequent trips to doctors for medicine and procedures. This can be one of the most difficult stages to get through (Clements, Copeland, & Loftus, 1990; Rowland, 1989). The family had developed a routine whereby Mr. Bradley took time off from work to accompany Tim, and Mrs. Bradley kept up the usual activities for the children. When treatment required particularly painful procedures (e.g., a bone marrow aspiration and/ or a spinal tap), both parents joined Tim.

Because of the frequency with which Mr. Bradley was with Tim, he was the first to discuss with the doctor some side effects that Tim was having. This resulted in Mrs. Bradley's feeling left out and marked the beginning of a difficult time for the couple. In addition to the parents' struggling with sharing their responsibilities, Tim was having temper tantrums at home, in which he would get into fits of anger and be unable to calm himself down. Tim was bothered by his tantrums, and he felt guilty about his behavior. This was highly unusual behavior for him and was probably caused by a combination of the side effects from his steroid medication, a course of radiation therapy, and general increased frustration with the treatment regimen.

This scenario illustrates some of the typical child and family problems that must be confronted when a child cancer patient's "efforts at autonomy are thwarted [and] anger, repression, and withdrawal may result. The drive to reexert control can lead to increased oppositional behavior (stubbornness) and tantrums" (Rowland, 1989, p. 528). At the same time, parents can be confused about how to handle the situation and require assistance with their tendency to overindulge the child. It is best to encourage social autonomy appropriate to the child's age, combined with reasonable limit setting (Rowland, 1989).

Tim had handled his disease well up to this point, but the signs of stress were becoming evident. In retrospect, his previous "good" behavior was just as much an indication of a brewing problem as was his present "bad" behavior (Rowland, 1989). He needed to release some of his pent-up anger and learn about the side effects of his medication. In addition, the parents had not yet dealt with their own fears, the stresses the disease had placed on their family and marriage, and the role they each wanted to play in Tim's treatment. Tim would get confused when the parents suggested different techniques to help him during his behavior "crisis." Another significant precipitating factor in beginning treatment was that Mr. Bradley had developed ulcers and had been told by his internist that he was not handling his stress effectively.

Thus, about 3 months after Tim's diagnosis, a different formal psychological intervention was planned. Immediate intervention required seeing child and parents together to discuss Tim's outbursts and how they could be managed. With Tim and his parents together, I explained that Tim's episodes were not completely under his control and that they were partially caused by his medication. This was intended to relieve Tim's feelings of guilt and empower the parents to take control. They had wanted to be supportive of him when he was angry, but he did not respond to their efforts, and they were exhausting themselves. The mutual decision was that his frustration and anger should be acknowledged; then they would leave him alone to calm down. Later, they all could talk about what was upsetting him. With everyone in agreement, there was a sense of working together and mutual problem solving. At this point a plan for the family took shape. Tim would be seen individually for therapy, and the parents would be seen together for counseling sessions. A description, with excerpts, of a 6-month segment of therapy with Tim, and a synopsis of the parent counseling sessions, follow.

Play Therapy Sessions with a Doll

Tim was routinely silly and even talked baby talk at times when he came for treatments or was asked questions about medical procedures. To explore his underlying feelings about these topics, I decided to have a session focused on hospital play with a doll.

Content of Session

THERAPIST: Tim, I wondered if you would like to play with some doctor equipment?

CHILD: (*Child giggles.*)

T: I brought this "patient" [a gingerbread-type stuffed doll]. Maybe we could work in one of the examination rooms.

C: OK.

(*Once in the room, child draws a face on the doll with markers and calls the patient doll "Tim." Therapist shows child all of the needles, gauze, swabs, etc., that she has brought.*)

C: First he has to curl up in a ball; then I have to wash his back with soap; then there's a needle.

T: Does it hurt? Is he going to cry?

C: It does hurt for a minute, but if you lie still it goes faster. Now he gets a Band-Aid and has to lie still for 45 minutes.

T: How was that?

C: Good. He didn't even need help.

T: Why does he need those shots and medicines anyway?

C: To get rid of the leukemia, so it doesn't come back.

Rationale/Analysis

Tim is waiting for a bone marrow aspiration and spinal tap, and I want to prepare him so that he will not be upset or move around, which can interfere with these procedures. Whenever possible, it is best to approximate the real situation as closely as possible to increase the mastery.

Since this is an individual session, I let him use some small, real needles; I am careful not to show him particularly large ones, which frighten children. Although I have a policy of being honest with patients, I have found that children become overwhelmed by the sight of actual bone marrow and spinal tap needles. Tim is very familiar with steps for the procedure and takes control while working.

By being the doctor and acting out the role of the aggressor, Tim is able to release anger and feel in control. With me voicing the possible worries of the doll as patient, he is able to hear me validate his feelings and see me model appropriate coping behavior.

I want Tim to verbalize and act out what may happen for him in the same situation. Practicing with me is safe and nonthreatening; ideally, the behavioral rehearsal and his sense of calm will generalize to the actual situation.

T: How did he get sick?

C: No one knows; he just did, but he can't give it to anyone else. I want to leave "Tim" here and give him more shots next time.

I want to know whether Tim has any misconceptions or irrational fears about his disease. In his role play, he identifies with the aggressor. He symbolically externalizes his fears, and his rehearsal promotes mastery. I'm impressed with his maturity.

We played with the doll twice more in the following weeks. At times the sequence of procedures accurately approximated Tim's own experiences; at other times he gave the patient doll numerous extra injections. At the end of the last session with the doll, he declared that the "patient" could get a year off from treatment. Tim had also wanted to bring the doll to school so that his classmates would know what he was going through. These sessions allowed me to explore, with Tim, his concept of his disease. I was able to find out that Tim was accurate in his knowledge about his leukemia, to the point of being sure that no one knows why people get it. It is interesting and expected that this factual information coexisted in Tim's mind with more primitive thinking. Weeks later, his parents told me that Tim had once said he was glad he got cancer now, when he was young, because he knew that everyone would get it someday. Mr. and Mrs. Bradley had corrected his misunderstanding, but it demonstrates how the 6-year-old mind, needing answers for questions, will find them. Thus Tim found relief in his rationalization for getting cancer. Also, it was significant that Tim had always been completely cooperative with his treatments, had not voiced any resistance, and had a positive outlook on life in general. It was only through the doll that I suspected that he too might be harboring a wish for "time off" from treatment.

Parent Counseling

At the same time I was seeing Tim individually, couple sessions with the parents continued on a regular basis. I have found that work with medically ill patients and their parents, unlike work in a traditional mental health setting, requires flexibility in one's notions of therapy. Treatment planning and interventions must be determined on a case-by-case basis. Whereas I initially saw Tim's parents in conjunction with parent counseling, issues began to surface that necessitated a more marriage-focused approach. Over the course of discussions about their son, the parents felt more comfortable working on their own issues with me than being referred outside. In addition, the frequency with which they came to the hospital made it easier to do everything in one place at one time and unrealistic to have regularly scheduled appointments elsewhere.

While discussing Tim's and his sister's behaviors at home, I also focused on pertinent parenting and marital issues. When so much of a child's care is taken over by medical personnel, parents can feel helpless and not needed. It is important to remind them that they know their child best, that they have skills, that as parents they cannot be replaced by doctors and nurses, and that they are entitled to have their needs addressed.

Tim's parents went through some of the stages typical of parents of a newly diagnosed child. Individually, the mother and father had to confront the reality of not being able to protect their child from bad things. It highlighted both their own fallibility and their vulnerability. Because these fears are so basic and existential, they are difficult to discuss. Parents can be afraid of verbalizing and admitting their fears to each other, leaving them to feel alone in their grief and struggle at a time when adult, spousal support is needed the most. It is not uncommon for parents to respond to and cope with their crisis in seemingly opposite ways. For example, one parent is often the emotional one, carrying the burden of containing and/or displaying the emotions, and may cry or become depressed or even distraught for a period of time. The other parent may take charge, appear to be in control, and intellectualize about the disease. It is a complementary system, in which one person feels free to enact a certain role because the other provides balance or ballast. Together, they successfully exhibit and confront the conflicting emotions stimulated by the crisis. In reality, both types of reactions are often emblematic of intense fear.

During the first few months of treatment, parents usually go through an initial period of preoccupation with the day-to-day tasks of treatment, such as doctors' visits, blood counts, and oral medications at home. This period of heightened disease-specific activity enables them to pull together by handling concrete details. Slowly, as the medical aspects are routinized, a new period of unsettling feelings may emerge, when the reality of the cancer reappears with new strength. Thus, somewhere between 6 and 12 months, the parents begin to think about "Why me?" and "Why my child?", and go through a stage of renewed anxiety about their child's chances of survival. Ideally, it is at this point that the child and family learn to put the disease in perspective. The parents realize they can never go back in time and can never live without knowing that it is possible for their child to die. They learn that life is precious, that "you take one day at a time," that the unpredictable is predictable, and that they must make choices about how to live in their changed world.

Play Therapy Sessions with Journal Making and Artwork

Over the next month, Tim continued to have temper tantrums and developed sleeping spells, labeled "postradiation somnolence." He would doze off at unannounced times and could not be easily aroused. These episodes were usually preceded by irritability and crying without any apparent cause. While he was being evaluated neurologically, we worked on these problems in therapy by means of journal making and drawing.

Content of Session	Rationale/Analysis
CHILD: I think I need to talk to you about my sleepy spells.	Whenever possible, I take my lead for sessions from the child rather than impose my agenda.
THERAPIST: OK. Tell me what's been going on.	

C: I think I want to make a journal.

T: That's a great idea.

C: I don't know how to spell all the words. Can you write it?

T: I'll help you. You can tell me what to write. By telling me what bothers you, we might be able to figure out what will help it.

(Child chooses some colored paper for the cover of his journal and staples white sheets inside. He starts by drawing a picture of his brain being all confused, then tells therapist his story.)

C: When I have the prednisone I get so cranky, and I wanted to talk about it so I wouldn't be so cranky. Last night I had a fit because I wanted my treatment in Norton [the suburb where Tim and his family live]; then I wouldn't have to drive into the city every day. It's so far, and it takes longer, and I miss school that day. I miss my activities—gym and art. And I miss my teacher too, and I miss my class. Sometimes I don't want to come at all because I can't go outside and play in my back yard. Norton Hospital has a better gift shop and better food, and it's easier. But the doctors are better here than at Norton Hospital.

T: If you could make it better, what would make it better at *this* hospital?

C: My first choice is to come here before school. My next choice is to come here at 4:15 so I don't miss school.

T: I know sometimes kids wish they didn't have to come here at all. They don't have to like coming for their medicine.

C: It's OK if I don't like coming here sometimes. When I have my sleepy spells, I get very tired and mad. My brain doesn't get the signals out that good.

Tim turns passivity into activity.

I'm struck by how articulate he is about the problem, and how such small changes in one's quality of life can mean big changes in adaptation. I wonder how many other things I have taken for granted in my life and in Tim's.

I encourage problem solving to increase Tim's sense of control and decrease his victimized feeling.

I am validating his feelings and giving him permission to be upset and frustrated. Once again I am reminded how those "outside" the child don't always realize how disruptive the entire cancer experience can be to one's thinking and doing.

I'm glad he has found a way to talk about this.

It was quite an accomplishment for Tim to express his negative feelings about his disease, doctors, and hospitals. He had been a model patient throughout the first 5 months of treatment, but he was feeling the strain of his new responsibilities. I helped Tim air his concerns to his doctor. It gave him a tremendous sense of control when the doctor agreed to Tim's request to be seen after school. No one had considered that continuing to engage in a 6-year-old's usual activities was so important to him. In Tim's world, gym and art were just as important as, if not more important than, being cured of leukemia.

Another significant theme in this session was Tim's ambivalence about negotiating for what he wanted. In a parallel fashion, in the parents' therapy we dealt with their difficulty confronting people, asserting themselves, and making their individual needs known to each other. Tim was a spokesman for an unconscious family rule of self-sacrifice, and he was now a model for how to speak up.

Tim's tantrums waxed and waned. One of the focal points in sessions with the parents involved how they could be united in dealing with his outbursts. During one particularly bad incident, Tim impulsively screamed, "I'm no good! I'm dumb and stupid! I don't know my numbers! It's my chemo." He had also recently written a letter to Jason Gaes, the author of *My Book for Kids with Cansur* [*sic*] (Gaes, 1987). He ended the letter, "I hate leukemia." With the parents I discussed the strains children and families encounter, as well as their responsibility to reinforce everyone's strengths and not take any family member, child or adult, for granted. The incident and the letter also suggested goals for my individual sessions with Tim. He needed to deal not only with the reality of his cancer, but also with his perception of himself.

A few weeks later, Tim agreed to have a session while he waited for his bone marrow aspiration and spinal tap. The scheduling of our sessions varied; some were planned, but others occurred spontaneously. This was because I saw him according to the vagaries of his medical treatment schedule. (On the other hand, I was able to have more regular weekly appointments with Tim's parents.) At times in such a case, it is frustrating to have to forge a therapeutic relationship in the context of unpredictable medical appointments. But, like the child's life, therapy is most often dictated by the variability of the disease itself.

In an attempt to play a nurturing role, I occasionally bring special things into children's sessions. On this occasion, I brought some new drawing materials (Cray-Pas and special watercolor crayons) for Tim to try. Tim was a capable and mature child, and I had more freedom to experiment and use sophisticated art materials with him. Also, I wanted to give him good things to counteract the fact that he had to go through so many painful, disruptive experiences. (This was a feeling not unlike that of his parents, and it was one I was counseling them to monitor. In my case, it was part of my countertransference and wish to make the situation better.)

Content of Session	Rationale/Analysis
CHILD: (*Picks up the Cray-Pas.*) These are great! I get to use these in school. But this is different, because in school I get all the broken ones.	
THERAPIST: Why?	I wonder about Tim's self-esteem, and about whether he feels left out or different from his peers.
C: I get there last because the others run up and get them, but they're not supposed to run up.	

T: So you do the right thing but don't get the good ones?

I want to address the issue of his needing to be good all the time, especially if he feels in any way responsible for his disease. I also wonder about his trying to fit in with his peers.

C: It's OK, because they have to share. (*Begins to work on a picture with white Cray-Pas but stops, saying it will not show up. He begins coloring in the sky with blue. He then draws a green line, a yellow circle, and black dot, saying it is a flower.*) Guess what it is.

He has a well-developed sense of morals and a strong, positive superego.

T: I need a hint.

C: It's two words.

T: Does the second start with S? I don't know.

I encourage interaction with me so that we will develop a strong relationship and so that I can support his need to feel competent. However, I am worried that I will guess wrong and hurt his pride.

C: It's a black-eyed susan. I'm gonna add leaves. Now I'm gonna start another flower using all different colors. I'll call this one a beautiful-eyed susan [see Figure 17.1].

This raises the question of his use of splitting as a defense. Does he see the world or himself as either good or bad? In some instances, it is likely that a child relates to each part of the picture. Thus there may be some aspect of himself represented in both flowers.

T: How do they get along?

C: Great.

I want to explore how he integrates his good and bad selves, and also how he may perceive relationships among people, whether these are family members, peers, or staff members.

T: How do they like being different?

C: Good, because one's the child and one's the adult.

T: What are they doing?

C: Holding hands underground with their roots. I need to draw the roots and color in the dirt. If there was another black you could help, but I'm almost finished.

T: They're holding hands?

I am trying to have him expand on the meaning of being different or special because of his cancer. I am reminded of his feeling guilty about his tantrums.

C: They can't go anywhere; they're always together. There's a girl in my class, Lizbeth, who draws lots of things; she does the best tulip in the class.

I am exploring his need for nurturance and perception of parental figures. He has age-appropriate dependence needs and expresses this in the content of the picture, as well as by his veiled request for help with coloring in the roots.

FIGURE 17.1. A black-eyed susan and a beautiful-eyed susan.

T: What are you best in?

I encourage reality testing and assessment of his self-esteem and confidence level.

C: People. I'm pretty good at them. I'll show you how I draw different kinds of people. I didn't even know how until I was 5. (*He draws a large stick-like figure on the left side of the page first, then a smaller figure on the right.*) I like the small one better because it has shoulders and a neck [see Figure 17.2].

The two figures in the second drawing are somewhat similar to the two flowers, in that they look like parent and child. I wonder whether he identifies with either figure. The figures are well formed and age-appropriate, but both they and the flowers in the first drawing are linear, and Tim does not fill in the shapes or use all of the space. Also, one figure in the second drawing has no arms, suggestive of some tentativeness.

T: How are these two different?

C: Maybe one's on prednisone and one isn't. (*He decides to experiment with the special watercolor crayons I have brought. He makes stripes.*)

I'm surprised by his making such a direct and literal connection to his real experience and weight gain.

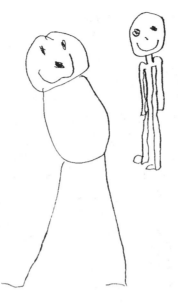

FIGURE 17.2. A parent and child.

C: I'm gonna do lightning. (*He makes green and yellow zig-zags. He tries out different techniques, such as holding a fistful of crayons and drawing lines.*)

T: It's fun to experiment sometimes.

C: Little kids do scribble-scrabble.

T: Sometimes I do too. (*While child continues to work, therapist checks to see if the doctor is ready for him. When therapist returns, child asks whether it is his turn.*) Do you know what you're getting today?

C: If my counts are low, I won't get my bone marrow and spinal tap. But that means it's bad because then I couldn't go to camp.

T: So there's a good part and a bad part about it.

T: What do you like best about camp?

C: When it's hot I get special permission to do my favorite activities, hobby and wood shop.

T: Any secrets this week?

C: Maybe, but I'm not telling.

T: Like what?

Talking about prednisone may have stimulated thoughts about his illness; thus the change to a stormy theme and some anxiety about possible painful procedures.

I encourage his exploration and loosening of restrictions.

I am supporting his need/desire to be regressive in his play sometimes.

It is not unusual for these children to be aware of the details of their illness and how these details affect their lives. They like to plan ahead and be prepared for events. The discussion also points out Tim's ambivalence toward treatment: There are good things and bad things about cancer.

When Tim was in the midst of his tantrums at home, he would come to sessions saying he had a "secret" to talk about. It was important for

C: Can't tell; maybe with kids at camp, or parents, or babysitter. (*He begins to talk in a babyish manner.*)

T: If you could make a secret deal with Dr. Mandel, what would it be?

C: To skip a few treatments so I wouldn't have to have them every day, because I don't like to come sometimes.

T: What would part of the deal be?

C: I would give him all the Ninja Turtle Band-Aids he wants.

T: What would happen if you missed some treatments?

C: It would take longer to get better.

T: It's OK not to want to come; it's hard to get medicine when there's other things to do.

him to know that he had a safe place to talk about his problems. I worry now that he thinks he has to keep bad feelings a secret.

I wonder whether something about his impending procedures is upsetting him. Also, the last time he told me a "secret," it was about not wanting to come for treatment any more.

When a child is feeling well, it is difficult for him to continue to believe he is sick. This is especially true for leukemia because there are no visible signs of disease, only signs of side effects. This sequence also reveals how Tim would like to bargain. It is not uncommon for patients to want to make a deal with God. Here Tim wants to find a way to be rewarded and spared, as if being good enough or generous enough would make bad things or his cancer disappear. It is also clear that he is able to be quite realistic in his thinking and knows that missed treatments mean longer treatment. It is necessary to acknowledge this conflict— knowing something is good for you, but at the same time not liking it.

Tim's counts were indeed low, and he left without getting medical treatment that day. Six weeks later, Tim did a pastel drawing (see Figure 17.3).

Content of Session

C: I am in the middle, on prednisone, which is why I'm so big. Dad is on the left, and Mom is on the right . . . they have spinal needles.

Rationale/Analysis

He now spontaneously refers to his medical treatment, represents his anger by the needles, and portrays a relationship with his parents. Tim seems to feel surrounded by his parents, able to get their support, and even look like everyone else. But he is still aware of how his leukemia and treatment are still part of his life.

FIGURE 17.3. Cacti: A mother, father, and son.

Tim was now reportedly "back to his old self." Months later, he finished his chemotherapy treatment and the major part of his work with me. Over the last several weeks of this work, he painstakingly drew a still life and painted it, being quite proud of his mastery in art. It was a fitting final tribute—a picture full of the fruits of life.

COMMENTS

This presentation of a portion of the therapy spotlights the normal stresses confronting the child and family, and points out typical intervention strategies mentioned in the research and clinical literature about childhood cancer (Holland & Rowland, 1989). It must be emphasized that there is no right or wrong way to treat disease-related emotional problems. A father of a 6-year-old daughter with leukemia once asked me how he should discipline her. He wanted to guard against spoiling her, yet also make up for the real disappointments and pain in her life. I began by admiring the fact that he was aware of the problem and had questioned what to do. Herein was the key to the answer. Being conscious of internal responses, looking squarely at issues, and having the courage to take action are important steps toward finding solutions.

Tim and his family came to realize that they could not handle all components of his disease alone. The child and family adopted the same ethic—that one could enlist psychological counseling services and art therapy as readily as those of an oncologist in order to improve survival. Tim once coolly suggested to his sister, who was belaboring an issue during a family outing, that she should "go talk to Dr. Robin." The idea is not to foster unwarranted dependence on yet more "specialists" or "experts." Rather, childhood cancer is an experience for which most parents and children are ill prepared. Psychological treatment should be geared toward guiding them to manage their own lives in their own way. In contrast to support from friends and extended family members, an on-site professional "knows," on some level, what the family's "cancer life" entails. The staff member becomes a part of the family, and a partner in the care of the child. This engenders a sense of trust and hope that strengthens the treatment alliance.

FOLLOW UP: TIM, AGE 15

I continued to work periodically with Tim and his family throughout his 3 years of medical treatment. Even now, over 6 years since Tim successfully finished this course of treatment, we are still in contact. I have heard about Tim's support of his grandfather as he underwent chemotherapy for prostate cancer, and I gladly helped out Tim's sister when she asked to return to the clinic to do a school project based on being the sibling of a child with cancer. She stood by her contention that she didn't need any special therapy while her brother was sick, but her expressive school project vividly described a sibling who was profoundly affected by the cancer experience. Tim's father still mentions things that he learned about his wife from me, and the couple sought outside counseling when they faced a rough patch in their life, and Tim's mother even discovered her own passion for painting. Tim has struggled with various learning disabilities that may have been premorbid to, or a consequence of, his radiation. In addition, he is being followed for decreased heart and lung functions—typical late effects of chemotherapy. The family members have harnessed their usual strength and resources to set up the best educational programs possible, and now, as he prepares for high school, Tim seems more concerned about where he fits in within the pecking order of peers and girlfriends than with his academic challenges. Although it is clear that life has gone on and must go on, I am inextricably tied to a time that forever changed who the Bradleys were as a family. Even though new people and events have shaped their lives, we share a time that can never adequately be explained or imagined. Unlike conventional therapy with children with emotional problems, work to help children overcome the effects of a life-threatening illness means that when the children survive, a therapist becomes a therapist "for life."

Although there are similarities between other cases of children with cancer and the case of Tim and his family, there are no standardized behaviors that can be expected in all such cases. Tim was a confident, engaging boy who continued on his developmental path almost independently of his illness. Some of his strengths were surely related to his good preillness functioning and the support of his cohesive family system. He had the normal fears and anger that any child would have while going through painful and at first confusing experiences. When Tim was first diagnosed, his father had left for the night after Tim got his intravenous line put in. Later, in need of a new one, he called his father. Tim was in tears, wanting his father to come back to the hospital. When Dad arrived, Tim asked him, "Where's God now?" His father, who was having his own difficulty with the question, told Tim he would need to find his own answer. After being discharged, Tim announced one night at dinner that finally he knew a reason why God gave him leukemia: It was so he would know what it was like to be sick, so he could help other kids. Although they would never choose to have cancer, some children and families can come through the experience stronger, changed for the better, clearer in their vision about the meaning of life. For these patients and families, the crisis can be an opportunity rather than an obstacle.

STUDY QUESTIONS

1. Discuss the stress on therapists of working with children who have a potentially fatal diagnosis. How can such therapists effectively deal with their own feelings about death and dying?

2. Comment on the possible value of a play therapy group with Tim. What would be some of the pros and cons of group therapy compared to individual therapy in a situation of medical crisis such as cancer?

3. There are inevitable stresses on the siblings of a young cancer patient. Discuss how you might have conducted therapy sessions with Tim's sister. How would the initiation of sibling therapy have been discussed with the patient and parents? What issues would have had to be addressed, and what would the goals of treatment for the sister have been?

4. Discuss the impact of the stress of illness on a child's ego development, especially with regard to the use of defenses. Evaluate Tim's developing sense of self as an adolescent, and predict any possible future difficulties you may envision in reference to his emotional well-being.

REFERENCES

Adams-Greenly, M. (1984). Helping children communicate about serious illness and death. *Journal of Psychosocial Oncology, 2*(2), 61–72.

Anthony, S. (1971). *The discovery of death in childhood and after.* New York: Basic Books.

Astin, E. (1977–1978). Self reported fears of hospitalized and non-hospitalized children aged 10–12. *Maternal Child Nursing Journal, 6–7,* 17–24.

Axline, V. (1947). *Play therapy.* Boston: Houghton Mifflin.

Bearison, D., & Pacifici, C. (1984). Psychological studies of children who have cancer. *Journal of Applied Developmental Psychology, 5,* 263–280.

Bennett, D. S. (1994). Depression among children with chronic medical problems: A meta-analysis. *Journal of Pediatric Psychology, 19,* 149–169.

Bibace, R., & Walsh, M. E. (1979). Developmental stages in children's conceptions of illness. In G. Stone, F. Cohen, & N. Adler (Eds.), *Health psychology* (pp. 285–303). San Francisco: Jossey-Bass.

Binger, C. M., Ablin, A. R., Feurestein, R. C., Kushner, J. H., Zoger, S., & Mikkelsen, C. (1969). Childhood leukemia: Emotional impact on patient and family. *New England Journal of Medicine, 280,* 414–418.

Blotcky, A. D., Raczyoski, J. M., Gurwitch, R., & Smith, K. (1985). Family influences on hopelessness among children early in the cancer experience. *Journal of Pediatric Psychology*, *10*(4), 479–493.

Bluebond-Langner, M. (1978). *The private worlds of dying children*. Princeton, NJ: Princeton University Press.

Brunnquell, D., & Hall, M. D. (1984). Issues in the psychological care of pediatric oncology patients. In S. Chess & A. Thomas (Eds.), *Annual progress in child psychiatry and child development* (pp. 430–447). New York: Brunner/Mazel.

Butler, R., & Copeland, D. (1993). Neuropsyhological effects of central nervous system prophylactic treatment in childhood leukemia: Methodological considerations. *Journal of Pediatric Psychology*, *18*, 319–338.

Childers, P., & Wimmer, M. (1971). The concept of death in early childhood. *Child Development*, *42*, 1299–1301.

Clements, D. B., Copeland, L. G., & Loftus, M. (1990). Critical times for families with a chronically ill child. *Pediatric Nursing*, *16*(2), 157–162.

Compass, B. E., Worsham, M. C., & Ey, S. (1992). Conceptual and developmental issues in children's coping with stress. In A. M. La Greca, L. J. Siegel, J. L. Wallander, & C. E. Walker (Eds.), *Stress and coping in child health* (pp. 7–24). New York: Guilford Press.

Cook, S. S. (1973). Children's perceptions of death. In S. Cook (Ed.), *Children and dying* (pp. 1–15). New York: Health Sciences.

Dobkin, P. L., & Morrow, G. R. (1985–1986). Long-term side effects in patients who have been treated successfully for cancer. *Journal of Psychosocial Oncology*, *3*(4), 23–51.

Easson, W. H. (1974, Summer). Management of the dying child. *Journal of Clinical Child Psychology*, *3*(2), 25–27.

Eiser, C. (1979). Psychological development of the child with leukemia: A review. *Journal of Behavioral Medicine*, *2*(2), 141–157.

Futterman, E. H., & Hoffman, l. (1973). Crisis and adaptation in the families of fatally ill children. In E. J. Anthony & C. Koupernik (Eds.), *The child in his family: Vol. 2. The impact of disease and death* (pp. 127– 143). New York: Wiley.

Gaes, J. (1987). *My book for kids with cansur*. Aberdeen, SD: Melius & Peterson.

Goodman, R. (1989). *Development of the concept of death in children: The cognitive and affective components*. Unpublished doctoral dissertation, Adelphi University.

Granowetter, L. (1994). Pediatric oncology: A medical overview. In D. J. Bearison & R. K. Mulhern (Eds.), *Pediatric psychooncology* (pp. 9–34). New York: Oxford University Press.

Hockenberry, M. J., Coody, D. K., & Bennett, B. S. (1990). Childhood cancers: Incidence, etiology, diagnosis, and treatment. *Pediatric Nursing*, *16*(3), 239–246.

Holland, J. C., & Rowland, J. H. (Eds.). (1989). *Handbook of psychooncology*. New York: Oxford University Press.

Jenkins, R. A., & Cavanaugh, J. C. (1985). Examining the relationship between the development of the concept of death and overall cognitive development. *Omega*, *16*(3), 193–199.

Kane, B. (1979). Children's concepts of death. *Journal of Genetic Psychology*, *134*, 141–153.

Kastenbaum, R. (1967). The child's understanding of death: How does it develop? In E. Grollman (Eds.), *Explaining death to children* (pp. 89–108). Boston: Beacon Press.

Katz, E. R., & Jay, S. M. (1984). Psychological aspects of cancer in children, adolescents, and their families. *Clinical Psychology Review*, *4*, 525–542.

Koocher, G. P. (1973). Childhood, death, and cognitive development. *Developmental Psychology*, *9*(3), 369–375.

Koocher, G. P., & O'Malley, J. E. (1981). *The Damocles syndrome*. New York: McGraw-Hill.

Koocher, G. P., O'Malley, J. E., Gogan, J. L., & Foster, D. J. (1980). Psychological adjustment among pediatric cancer survivors. *Journal of Child Psychology and Psychiatry, 21,* 163–173.

Kramer, E. (1971). *Art as therapy with children.* New York: Schocken.

Kübler-Ross, E. (1981). *Living with death and dying.* New York: Macmillan.

Lonetto, R. (1980). *Children's conception of death.* New York: Springer.

Morris, J. A. B., Blount, R. L., Cohen, L. C., Frank, N. C., Madan-Swain, A., & Brown, R. T. (1997). Family functioning and behavioral adjustment in children with leukemia and their healthy peers. *Children's Health Care, 26,* 61–75.

Nagy, M. (1948). The child's theories concerning death. *Journal of Genetic Psychology, 73,* 3–27.

Natterson, J. M., & Knudson, A. G. (1960). Observations concerning fear of death in fatally ill children and their mothers. *Psychosomatic Medicine, 22*(6), 456–465.

Noll, R. B., MacLean, W. E., Jr., Whitt, J. K., Kaleita, T. A., Stehbens, J. A., Waskerwitz, M. J., Ruymann, F. B., & Hammond, G. D. (1997). Behavioral adjustment and social functioning of long-term survivors of childhood leukemia: Parent and teacher reports. *Journal of Pediatric Psychology, 22,* 827–841.

O'Malley, J. E., Koocher, G., Foster, D., & Slavin, L. (1979). Psychiatric sequelae of surviving childhood cancer. *American Journal of Orthopsychiatry, 49*(4), 608–616.

Orbach, I., Fesback, S., Carlson, G., & Ellenberg, L. (1984). Attitudes toward life and death in suicidal, normal, and chronically ill children: An extended replication. *Journal of Consulting and Clinical Psychology, 52*(6), 1020–1027.

Orbach, I., Gross, Y., Glaubman, H., & Berman, D. (1985). Children's perception of death in humans and animals as a function of age, anxiety, and cognitive ability. *Journal of Child Psychology and Psychiatry, 26,* 453–463.

Petrillo, M., & Sanger, S. (1980). *Emotional care of hospitalized children.* Philadelphia: J. B. Lippincott.

Reilly, T., Hasazi, J., & Bond, L. (1983). Children's conceptions of death and personal mortality. *Journal of Pediatric Psychology, 8*(1), 21–31.

Rowland, J. H. (1989). Developmental stages and adaptation: Child and adolescent model. In J. C. Holland & J. H. Rowland (Eds.), *Handbook of psychooncology* (pp. 519–543). New York: Oxford University Press.

Safier, G. (1964). A study in relationship between the life and death concepts in children. *Journal of Genetic Psychology, 105,* 283–294.

Sawyer, M., Crettenden, A., & Toogood, I. (1986). Psychological adjustment of families of children and adolescents treated for leukemia. *American Journal of Pediatric Hematology/ Oncology, 8*(3), 200–207.

Schilder, P., & Wechsler, D. (1934). The attitudes of children toward death. *Journal of Genetic Psychology, 45,* 406–451.

Slavin, L. A., O'Malley, J. E., Koocher, G. P., & Foster, D. J. (1982). Communication of the cancer diagnosis to pediatric patients: Impact on long-term adjustment. *American Journal of Psychiatry, 139*(2), 179–183.

Sourkes, B. (1982). *The deepening shade: Psychological aspects of life threatening illness.* Pittsburgh: University of Pittsburgh Press.

Speece, M., & Brent, S. (1984). Children's understanding of death: A review of three components of a death concept. *Child Development, 55,* 1671–1686.

Spinetta, J. J. (1974). The dying child's awareness of death: A review. *Psychological Bulletin, 81*(4), 256–260.

Spinetta, J. J. (1980). Disease-related communication: How to tell. In J. Kellerman (Ed.), *Psychological aspects of childhood cancer* (pp. 260–269). Springfield, IL: Charles C Thomas.

Spinetta, J. J., & Maloney, L. J. (1975). Death anxiety in the outpatient leukemic child. *Pediatrics*, 56(6), 1034–1037.

Van Dongen-Melman, J. E. W. M., & Sanders-Woudstra, J. A. R. (1986). Psychosocial aspects of childhood cancer: A review of the literature. *Journal of Child Psychology and Psychiatry*, 27(2), 145–180.

Varni, J. W., Katz, E. R., Colegrove, R., Jr., & Dolgin, M. (1995). Perceived phsyical appearance and adjustment of children with newly diagnosed cancer: A path analytic model. *Journal of Behavioral Medicine*, 18, 261–278.

Vernick, J., & Karon, M. (1965). Who's afraid of death on a leukemia ward? *American Journal of Diseases of Children*, 109, 393–397.

Wass, H. (1984). Concepts of death a developmental perspective. In H. Wass & C. Corr (Eds.), *Childhood and death* (pp. 3–23). Washington, DC: Hemisphere.

Webb, N.B. (Ed.). (1993). *Helping bereaved children. A handbook for practitioners*. New York: Guilford Press.

White, E., Elsom, B., & Prawat, R. (1978). Children's conceptions of death. *Child Development*, 49, 307–310.

Worchel, F., Copeland, D., & Baker, G. (1987). Control-related coping strategies in pediatric cancer patients. *Journal of Pediatric Psychology*, 12(1), 25–38.

PART V

The Crises of Catastrophic Events and War

The Aftermath of a Plane Crash— Helping a Survivor Cope with Deaths of Mother and Sibling

Case of Mary, Age 8, and Follow-Up at Age 17

VICTOR FORNARI

"Oh, Doctor, may I please ask you a question. . . . Am I going
to die?"
> —*Mary, age 8, 3 hours after having survived an airplane crash,*
> *while she was in the Pediatric Intensive Care Unit*

On January 25, 1990, Avianca Airline Flight 052—en route from Bogota, Colombia, to John F. Kennedy International Airport in New York—crashed in Cove Neck, Long Island. Of the 158 passengers aboard the plane, 85 survived, among them 21 children and adolescents. This chapter discusses psychotherapy with a survivor of that plane crash, an 8-year-old girl whom I call "Mary," and her follow-up at age 17.

Lenore Terr, in her book *Too Scared to Cry: Psychic Trauma in Childhood* (1990), states that "psychic trauma occurs when a sudden, unexpected, overwhelmingly intense emotional blow or a series of blows assaults the person from outside" (p. 8). Certainly the sudden crashing of an airplane, with its devastation of injury and losses, qualifies this experience as one where psychic trauma occurred. Terr elaborates that "traumatic events are external but they quickly become incorporated into the mind; a person probably will not become fully traumatized unless he or she feels utterly helpless during the event or events" (p. 8). Historically, Terr reports, most adults have tended to minimize young children's reports about traumatic events. She suggests that it is helpful to assist children to recall their memories of a terrifying event as close to the actual occurrence of the event as possible, in order to minimize the development of psychic trauma.

The therapy with 8-year-old Mary provides insight into the emotions of childhood psychic trauma, as well as the mental work associated with traumatic life experiences. The emotions of terror, rage, denial, and unresolved grief, as well as repeated memories and dreams about the crash, remained vivid to Mary in the immediate aftermath of the trauma. Because of early intervention, Mary was given repeated opportunities to describe her traumatic experiences, in an effort to help her gain some understanding of and control over the overwhelming and devastating experience she had endured.

E. James Anthony (1988) states that community reactions following disasters of various types are similar. During the period of impact, between 12% and 25% of people usually remain calm and capable of purposeful action; another 10% to 25% are likely to become psychiatric casualties, manifesting extreme anxiety and tremulousness; a large proportion of the community, perhaps 75%, seems immobilized by inertia. Among the victims of a disaster, many survivors tend to be overlooked amid the chaotic conditions because they are immobilized and in a stunned state. These may include child onlookers and families waiting anxiously for information. Anthony reminds us that the reactions of children are inclined to mirror the reactions of their parents, and generally there is an increase in attachment behavior in both.

According to Frederick (1985), the effects of a catastrophic situation on a child depend on (1) the child's developmental level at the time of the trauma, (2) the child's perceptions of the family's reaction, and (3) the child's direct exposure to the trauma. Typical reactions of children in catastrophic situations include the following psychological and behavioral symptoms: sleep disorders (bad dreams); persistent thoughts of the trauma; belief that another traumatic event will occur; conduct disturbances; hyperalertness; avoidance of situations similar to the event; psychophysiological disturbances, and (in younger children) regression to enuresis, thumbsucking, and dependent behavior (Frederick, 1985). Many of these symptoms were seen in the case of Mary. Many of them are also included in the new criteria for posttraumatic stress disorder in the *Diagnostic and Statistical Manual of Mental Disorders*, fourth edition (American Psychiatric Association, 1994).

Sugar (1988) emphasizes the importance of providing help to child as well as adult victims of a disaster. The case of Mary illustrates the particular importance of direct work with a child in a situation in which family members are too overcome by their own grief to provide adequate support to the child. Recommended treatment techniques for children include the use of coloring storybooks, drawings, instruction booklets, play therapy, group psychotherapy, and incident-specific treatment (Frederick, 1985).

A recent development worth mentioning here is that the Aviation Disaster Family Assistance Act of 1996 formed a task force to develop guidelines for the handling of the aftermath of each airline disaster in the United States. Sixty-one recommendations to improve the assistance provided to the families of aviation disaster victims were included in the final report (House of Representatives Report No. 793). The report directed its recommendations to the various airlines, the U.S. government, and the American Red Cross. The report addressed the roles of several different federal government agencies—the National Transportation Safety Board, the Department of Transportation, the Department of State, and the Department of Defense.

THE CRISIS SCENE: JANUARY 25, 1990

Immediately following the crash of Avianca Flight 052, nine children were brought to North Shore University Hospital–Cornell University Medical College for emergency medical care. The emergency room had been evacuated and then prepared to receive an unknown large number of injured crash victims. All of the patients who

had previously been receiving treatment in the emergency room were either transferred to the cafeteria (where a temporary emergency room was set up), admitted to the hospital, or discharged home. Prior to the arrival of any of the crash victims, several hundred physicians, nurses, social workers, and other health care providers were called in as part of a disaster plan to prepare for receiving the victims.

There was a high degree of anxiety and uncertainty in the emergency room prior to the arrival of the first crash victims. No one knew quite what to expect. No one had ever experienced the emergency room in this heightened sense of readiness. As the first victims were helicoptered to the landing pad and wheeled on stretchers through the emergency room, the grim reality of the crash became vivid to all who heard the cries, moans, and screams of the injured survivors. Each of the helpless injured, covered with blood, was taken to an examining room and surrounded by five or six health care professionals. A sense of helplessness pervaded in the emergency room, despite the apparent state of organization.

Despite the large number of personnel, the emergency procedures went quite smoothly, and each staff member seemed to find his or her role. As the first child was wheeled into the emergency room, it seemed clear that one critical task would be to speak to each conscious child and try to calm him or her down, in an effort to ease his or her anxiety while the emergency medical care was being provided. Many of the children had sustained fractures and were in great pain.

To complicate the situation further, many of these frightened youngsters were unsure of the whereabouts of their family members. A plane crash, physical injury, and the fear that their family members might be dead caused all of those involved in caring for these children to be moved by their emotional anguish. The staff members reassured and supported one another. They felt relieved whenever they learned that someone arriving to help in the Pediatric Intensive Care Unit (PICU) could speak Spanish.

One of the psychiatrists (myself) and a social worker approached one child, Mary, in the far corner of the unit. We saw a frightened child with her left leg in traction and her right leg splinted. Mary seemed terrified and in pain.

THE CASE: MARY, AGE 8

Family Information

Mary, an 8-year-old girl, was traveling from Colombia to the United States with her mother and 5-year-old brother. They were to reunite with her father, who had come to New York 10 days earlier on business. He worked for a pharmaceutical company. This was to be their first trip to the United States. They were anticipating 5 days in New York and then 1 week in Orlando, Florida, where they were to visit Disney World, the anticipated highlight of their trip.

Presenting Problem

Mary reported later that she had had some apprehension about the trip, as this was the first time she had been on an airplane. Just before the plane crashed, Mary noted, the lights went out. There was a lot of screaming as the plane lost altitude and ultimately crashed. Mary recalled being awake and seeing her mother and brother either asleep or dead.

Session 1

As noted above, my first meeting with Mary occurred in the PICU, 3 hours after the crash.

Content of Session	Rationale/Analysis
(*Mary is lying in bed with her left leg in traction, her right leg in splints, and an intravenous line in her left arm. There are bruises and crusted, dried blood on her face.*)	
DOCTOR (*in Spanish*): Hello, my name is Dr. Fornari. I speak Spanish. What is your name?	I feel some apprehension, not knowing how, or whether, the child will respond.
MARY: Mary.	
DR: How do you feel?	
M: Oh, Doctor, may I please ask you a question?	
DR: Of course!	I think, "How polite and poised."
M: Am I going to die?	I am moved beyond words. I have chills.
DR: No, Mary. You will be fine.	
M: May I ask you another question, please?	I realize how terrified this child is.
DR: Of course, Mary.	
M: May I go to sleep? I am so tired.	I am moved by her delicacy and grace.
DR: Of course.	I think, "What a delightful kid!"
(*Mary goes to sleep.*)	

I was able to reassure Mary that she would not die, because her injuries, though severe, were not life-threatening. I noted with interest that she did not ask about other family members. I believed that she might be in a state of emotional shock and numbness.

Preliminary Assessment

Mary was an 8-year-old girl who had sustained multiple fractures of her legs, but no other serious injuries and no apparent loss of consciousness, in an airplane crash where she witnessed much horror. Mary worried about her own survival as well as the uncertain condition of her mother and brother, whom she feared dead.

It appeared that Mary was a mature, sensitive, and particularly polite girl.

Session 2

This session occurred the morning after the crash, in the PICU. Mary was in good spirits, and her clinical condition was stable.

Content of Session	Rationale/Analysis
DOCTOR: Good morning, Mary. Do you remember me?	I am eager to see her response.
MARY: Yes, I think so.	
DR: How are you feeling?	
M: I am in much pain.	
DR: (*Sees toys on Mary's bed; picks up a stuffed animal and speaks through it.*) Did you sleep last night?	
M: Yes, but I am still so upset. I saw my mother get hit in the head by a rock. I am so worried about her.	I am moved by her fears.
DR: It must have been so frightening.	Because I fear that her mom may be dead, I am trying not to discuss her mom too much.
M: I saw some children who were dead! (*Speaks with terror.*) I never saw dead people before, but they weren't breathing—they must have been dead.	
DR: What a terrifying experience!	I validate Mary's evident terror.
M: I was talking with them one moment, and then they were dead.	She is so courageous to be able to put words to such a traumatic experience.
DR: How are you feeling? (*Holds her right hand.*)	
M (*grimacing from pain*): I am in so much pain!	
DR: Were you able to sleep?	
M: I think so—I was so tired. They must have given me some medicine to make me sleep.	This child seems so mature.
DR: I will come to see you every day. I talk to children and their families about their worries.	
M: Doctor, please help me. I am so scared for my mommy. I think my brother was hurt badly.	
DR (*cautiously*): Did you see him?	
M: Yes, I don't think he was moving—unless he was sleeping . . .	
DR: As soon as we have information, I will tell you. Here is my name (*handing her a card*)—this is my phone number. If you want to see me or talk to me, ask the nurse to call me. (*Signals to the nurse.*) Nurse, if Mary wants me, call me. Here is my home number, too!	I feel that someone needs to give her the sense of being looked after. I want her to feel as safe and cared for as possible.
M: OK.	

DR: I will come back later today.

M: Thank you, Doctor!

DR: Bye-bye.

I am moved by her gratitude.

Session 3

Twenty-four hours after her admission to the hospital, Mary was transferred from the PICU to a general pediatric bed. Her condition was stable. Surgery was necessary, but her father was not yet in contact. Although her father was aware of her survival, he remained occupied with the search for and identification of his wife and son. A family friend called to say that the father would be by to visit 12 hours later. When I arrived, Mary was in surgery. I introduced myself to the family friend.

Content of Session	Rationale/Analysis
FRIEND: Oh, Doctor, her mother and brother are dead, but she does not know.	I have chills thinking about this girl's sweetness and her profound loss.
DOCTOR: I am so sorry.	
F: Her father does not want her to know—he is worried about her, but I am worried about him. He has not eaten in 24 hours, and he cannot sleep. He blames himself and wishes he was dead.	
DR: Can I talk to him?	I am worrying about him.
F: He is in the waiting area. My family is with him; we will not leave him alone. He will not speak to anyone now.	How fortunate it is that he has some social support!
DR: I will come back tomorrow. Here is my card. Call me any time. Can I write down your name and phone number?	We exchange important information in writing.
F: Of course, here it is. Thank you.	
DR: Oh, thank you. I will do what I can to help Mary and her dad. They will need your help, too.	I am filled with emotion and want her to know I understand the situation.

Session 4

Sixty hours after the crash, I met with Mary, her dad, and some family friends. Mary had been out of surgery for 24 hours and was in excruciating pain. Mary's dad was a thin man of 30 who seemed distraught and spoke softly.

Content of Session	Rationale/Analysis
DOCTOR (*approaching Mary's dad*): Hello. I am Dr. Fornari. I am pleased to meet you. You have a wonderful daughter.	I shake his hand for a long time, as he knows that I know about his loss and Mary still does not know.

DAD (*looking sad and exhausted*): Thank you. It is nice to meet you.

DR (*turning to family friends*): Hello. I am happy Mary has such good friends (*warmly, but without excessive enthusiasm*).

FRIEND: Thank you. We are here to do what we can—this little angel needs us.

DR: Mary, how are you today?

MARY: Bad (*crying*). I am in too much pain. I can't stand it. (*She is in what appears to be a very uncomfortable position, with both legs in traction now, and with pins through each knee.*) I am afraid I will never walk.

DR: (*Turns to Mary's dad.*) Have they given her pain medicine? (*Turns back to Mary.*) You will walk, Mary—you will be fine! Don't worry.

DAD: Yes, but I don't want her to take morphine. I do not want her to become addicted.

DR: I encourage you to allow the pediatricians to give her pain medicine. The bone surgery she had is very painful, and the medicine will help her recover. Addiction will not be a problem.

DAD: Oh, OK.

DR: Would you like me to get a nurse to ask for pain medicine?

DAD: OK.

M: Oh, Doctor. I can't stand the pain!

DR: We will help you. The nurse will come soon.

DAD: Doctor, may I speak to you outside?

DR: Yes, of course. (*Both go to a room across the hall from Mary's.*)

DAD: Doctor, my daughter does not yet know about her mother and brother. When should I tell her?

DR: (*Before speaking, puts both hands on dad's right hand.*) I am so sorry for your loss.

DAD: (*With his head hanging low, he nods without words.*)

(*Both remain silent together for 5 or 10 minutes. Dad cries profusely. Doctor is moved to tears.*)

DR: This is a terrible loss.

DAD: I cannot go on.

I am moved by the analogy of Mary as an angel.

I am worried that this child may suffer more than necessary.

I have been hoping he will ask to speak with me.

I am moved by his position. I think that he could be me—a wife and two children one day, and then this terrible tragedy. I feel so vulnerable.

DR: I know that this is hard, but you must find the strength.

DAD: Doctor, I am worried.

DR: Of course.

DAD (*softly*): I want to die.

I am now both moved and anxious.

DR: I understand how you feel, but you must find the strength to live. Your daughter needs you very much.

DAD: I know, but I don't know if I can. (*Pause.*)

DR: I am sure that you do not feel up to it today. You must take one day at a time. I will help you and Mary if you let me. (*Long pause.*)

DAD (*with a mix of anger and sadness*): What can you do? You can't bring back my wife and son!

I feel helpless. I know anger is justified and is an expected part of the grief process, but I hope he does not turn against me.

DR: No, I cannot. I wish that I could—that someone could! Do you feel unsafe?

DAD: I don't know—I want to die!

DR: You must promise me that you will not hurt yourself.

DAD: I can't.

I am worried that he may need to be hospitalized.

DR: Unless you can, you may need to be hospitalized.

DAD: No—I will be fine.

Is he being honest?

DR: May I see you every day?

DAD: If you like, but when do I tell her?

He is hoping to be reassured.

DR: For now she is in too much pain and, because of the morphine, in and out of sleep. I would wait 1 or 2 more days, until her pain is eased and she is fully alert and awake.

DAD: OK (*nodding in despair*).

(*The two sit together for over 1 hour, joined by one of the other psychiatrists. Mary's dad is comforted by the doctors' concern and is relieved that both can speak to him in Spanish. When they return to the room, Mary is asleep.*)

DR: (*Shakes dad's hand.*) I will return tomorrow.

DAD: Thank you. I know that I must live for Mary.

I am moved beyond words. I am overwhelmed and exhausted; how can he be gracious?

On the subsequent 2 days, I met with Mary's dad. He gradually began to seem more at ease. Mary continued in pain and on morphine.

Session 7

Six days after the crash, Mary was off the morphine and fully alert and awake. When I entered the room, she was watching television. Her bed was filled with stuffed animals and surrounded by balloons.

Content of Session	Rationale/Analysis
MARY (*exclaiming in an animated way*): Hello, Fornari!	I am surprised by her good humor.
DR: How are you feeling?	
M: Better, thank you.	I am pleased!
DR: Is your dad around?	
M: Yes, he just went to get coffee.	
DR: What are you up to?	
M: Television. I still have some pain. Will I ever walk again? (*Mary and doctor play with her stuffed animals for quite a while.*) Look at a picture of my mommy and brother. Aren't they sweet? (*Looks at the picture.*)	I'm wondering whether Mary will bring up the topic of her mother or brother—or is she expecting *me* to bring it up?
DR: Yes . . . They are sweet, just like you!	
M. I am tired . . . I'm sorry.	
DR: I will go now. Say hello to your dad. I will stop by tomorrow.	
M: Bye-bye, Fornari.	
(*Outside in the hallway, doctor meets Mary's dad with his coffee in hand. He greets doctor warmly.*)	
DR: How are you today?	
DAD: So-so.	
DR: Can we talk?	
DAD: Of course.	
DR: How is Mary?	
DAD: She is a little angel—so sweet, so beautiful.	
DR: How are you?	
DAD: I am half dead!	
DR: You are brave.	
DAD: No—I must be strong for Mary. (*He cries.*) When do we tell her? (*Pause.*)	I am touched by his ability to share his sadness.
DR: Do you think she doesn't already know?	
DAD: Doctor, will you tell her? I cannot.	
DR: You will not have to tell her with words. Sit with her, and she will tell you. Cry together.	

DAD: I was thinking of telling her that I just found out, so she isn't angry that I haven't told her for the past 5 days. (*He pauses, embraces doctor, and cries.*) Will you be here when I tell her?

DR: Do you want me to be?

DAD: (*Pause.*) No, I think I will tell her later, after you have gone.

DR: Call me if you like. I will be by in the morning.

DAD: Thank you.

DR: No—I thank you for allowing me to share your experience with me. You are a very special man.

DAD: No, I feel dead.

DR: You have a very special daughter.

DAD: Thank you. (*The two shake hands for about a minute, and doctor leaves.*)

He is bargaining. However, I am moved and pleased that he is able to feel safe with me and trust me.

Session 8

The next session occurred 1 week after the crash.

Content of Session

Rationale/Analysis

DOCTOR (*entering the room*): Good morning, Mary.

MARY: Oh, Doctor, have you heard the terrible news?

DR: What do you mean, Mary?

I decide to let her tell me.

M: My mother and brother have died. I am so sad. I never expected this. I was so worried that I would never walk again. I was even worried that I might die. But I never considered that I might live and that my mother and brother might die. This is worse than my worst fear. I am in so much pain (*pointing to her heart and crying heavily*). This hurts too much. (*Pause.*) I will be OK you know. My mother always taught me to be strong.

DR: (*Smiles through his tears. The two hold hands.*)

I am awed by her strength.

M: (*Cries and cries.*) I can't believe my mother is dead.

DR: You must have had a very special mother—she had a very special daughter.

M (*still crying*): Oh, Fornari!

(Mary and doctor sit together for 30 minutes. Later that day, doctor meets with Mary's dad.)

Dr: How did it go?

Dad: She is so special—my little angel.

Dr: Tell me how it went when you told her.

Dad: It was just as you said. Few words. I said, "I have just learned that your mother and brother have died." She exclaimed, "Oh, Daddy—this is so painful." I told her that the family in Colombia was worried. I asked her whether she would call them and make the announcement, even though I knew that they already knew. Mary called them. She said, "I am very sad—my mommy and brother have died." Then we cried together on and off all night.

Dr: You are a loving father, and you are more important to her now than ever.	I am moved by his strength—and hers.

During the days following Mary's disclosure to me of her mother's and brother's deaths, I met with her daily. Mary regularly greeted me with enthusiastic and energetic exclamations—"Fornari!"—as though she were rooting for a team at a football game. Ten days after the crash, Mary's dad left to accompany the remains of his deceased wife and son back to Colombia. Mary's separation from her dad during this critical period in her recovery and mourning process intensified her attachment to me.

Session 12

The family friend I had met in session 3 was in the room when I arrived for session 12.

Content of Session	Rationale/Analysis
Mary: Hello *(without the enthusiasm of previous visits).*	
Doctor: How are you today, Mary?	What's up? Is her denial wearing thin?
M: Bad—very bad *(crying).*	
Dr: I can understand. This is such a difficult time in your life.	I empathize with her situation.
M: I miss my mommy so much. I can't believe she is dead. I am so sad, sadder than I thought I could ever be.	
Dr: You are entitled to be sad. It is so hard to believe that she is dead.	
M: I am so sad *(crying).*	
Friend: But look, Mary, at all of the balloons and toys on your bed!	The friend seems to be sending the message that Mary must cheer up.

DR: I think Mary is sad for a good reason. Do not cheer her up. If you try to, she will think that you don't understand her.

M (*listening attentively*): My mother was so sweet (*crying*).

DR: Over the days and weeks to come, you will think a lot about your mommy—How special she was and how much you miss her. That is normal, Mary. It is important. Cry as much as you need to. I will bring you plenty of paper handkerchiefs. | I want her to know that mourning is normal and necessary.

M: Will you come every day? I miss my daddy too!

DR: I will be here every day. When you want to talk, you can also call me. My number is by the phone.

Mary never did call, but I wanted to convey the comfort and knowledge of her being cared for. Mary's dad and friend did call on me on many occasions, in addition to my daily visits. I visited Mary nearly every day. I also introduced her to several of my colleagues, who visited with her as well. I did not have fixed appointment times, but usually visited with her in the mornings.

Session 18

Mary's dad had just returned from Colombia.

Content of Session   Rationale/Analysis

MARY: Fornari—guess what? My father is back (*with a big smile*).

DOCTOR: Hi, Mary, that's wonderful. How are you?

M: So-so.

DR: What have you been up to?

M: Television, television, and television—what else would you like me to do?

DR: Have you been reading?

M: No—I'm not too much in the mood. My daddy can read to me now, though.

DR: Are you interested in schoolwork?

M: (*Looks at doctor as though he were a monster.*) Schoolwork—are you crazy?

DR: Maybe, but I think it's time to do something besides watch TV. What do you think?

M: Like what?

DR: I can ask the teacher to come and speak to you.

M: (*Pause.*) OK.

Although Mary had survived a plane crash, had lost her mother and brother, and remained in bed (her left leg was still in traction), I decided to see whether she was ready to normalize her life. In the days that followed, Mary met regularly with a tutor and a child life specialist, who facilitated her play through games and artwork. In addition, she began reading on her own. I met with Mary's dad and encouraged him to mourn with Mary, because he had been in Colombia during the initial phase of Mary's mourning for her mother and brother. He reported that he described to Mary in detail the events in Colombia, including the plane ride home, the funeral, and the burials. Mary remained in the hospital for 50 days.

Session 30

Content of Session

MARY: Fornari, I had a bad dream last night. I've had it before, but I never remember the whole thing.

DOCTOR: Tell me about your dream.

M: I am on a plane. I see God's face. I think he's wearing a long white beard. I ask to see my mommy. I don't remember any more.

DR: What do you think about your dream?

M: I don't know why I was on a plane. I will never take a plane, even if I have to walk back home to Colombia.

DR: The idea of taking a plane must be very scary.

M: It is. (*Pause.*)

DR: What else about the dream?

M: I remember seeing God's face.

DR: What about God's face?

M: I wonder if my mommy is with Him. I want to tell Him to take care of her and ask Him how she is. I miss her so much. It's not fair that He has her and I don't.

DR: You are right. It isn't fair. Sometimes terrible things happen that we cannot explain, and they aren't fair.

M: Fornari, do you know if you can drive from New York to Colombia? I'm never going to fly!

DR: Right now flying seems so scary, but you don't have to decide about this now.

Rationale/Analysis

I encourage her to speak with me, using an "open-ended" directive.

I am both moved by her loss and relieved that she is beginning to express her anger.

M: (*Pause.*) No, I will never take a plane. When I grow up, I want to be a child psychiatrist. Will you teach me how?

Dʀ: If I can. Why a child psychiatrist, Mary?

M: Because I want to help children the way you help me.

Dʀ: How will you get here if you won't fly?   I am testing her attachment.

M: I don't know. Maybe by car—or couldn't you   She is bargaining.
come and teach me near my house?

The intensity of Mary's fear of airplanes became apparent (now 5 weeks after the crash), as she began to think about her long-awaited release from the hospital and eventual return home to Colombia.

During the weeks that followed, much time was spent reviewing the crash, talking, and using artwork to begin to help Mary master her fear of flying and her feelings about the crash. This was exemplified by Figure 18.1, a watercolor painting produced by Mary at the bedside 1 month after the crash. The painting was a monochromatic depiction of this idea: "It is a plane; no, it is an angel." The white-on-white "airplane" had angelic qualities and might have been a symbolic representation of the mother and brother.

FIGURE 18.1. Mary, 1 month after the crash: "It is a plane; no, it is an angel."

Session 38

After 50 days in the hospital following the airplane crash, Mary was to be released. Mary was apprehensive about losing the security of her friends in the hospital and the daily routine. She was to go to a home in the community with her dad for several months for further rehabilitation. Separation and loss remained as sensitive themes.

Content of Session	Rationale/Analysis
MARY: Look at my new casts. In 2 weeks my casts come off. I can't wait!	
DOCTOR: I am glad you are healing. You are a special girl, Mary.	
M: Fornari, will you come to see me?	
DR: Mary, we can speak by phone, and you will come with your dad to see me. I will try to come and visit you also.	I am so pleased with her progress.
M: Look at my new TV and Nintendo—my own Nintendo!	
DR: That's great, Mary. Remember that you can call me, and we can talk.	I am pleased at her enthusiasm.
M: I know. I am scared. I don't know how I'll go home.	
DR: We have time to work on this, Mary.	

Mary had made many close friends while in the hospital. Her kindness and gentle innocence had attracted much caring and concern. After Mary's discharge to the home in the community, she and her dad resided there for nearly 2 months. They returned to Colombia 4 months after the crash.

Session 40

I accompanied Mary, her dad, and the family friend to the orthopedist's office when Mary was to have her casts removed. Mary would be able to walk for the first time in 10 weeks.

Content of Session	Rationale/Analysis
MARY (*screaming in fear*): I'm scared! How do they take them [her casts] off?	
DOCTOR: Don't worry, Mary—they won't hurt you.	
M: Will I be able to walk? Will it hurt? Will I know how?	

Dr: After having your legs in casts for several months, moving your muscles may be sore. Little by little, with physical exercises, you will walk and run like before.	I offer her reassurance, preparing her for gradual recovery.
M: I am so scared. I never thought I would walk. Do you remember, Fornari? I never thought I would walk! I never thought my mother and brother would die . . . (*crying*).	
Dr: You will walk, and you will be fine. I know that your progress and recovery must remind you that mommy and your brother died.	The orthopedist has assured me that Mary will be fine.
M (*crying*): I'm scared.	She seems to be feeling survival guilt, as well as fear.

The casts were removed; Mary flexed her legs and complained of much pain. Despite physical therapy, Mary refused to walk for over 2 weeks. With careful support of physical therapist and father, Mary began to walk.

Session 44

In the physical therapist's office some weeks later, I met with Mary, her dad, the family friend, and the therapist. Mary was finally walking and was pleased with her progress.

Content of Session	Rationale/Analysis
MARY: Look, Fornari—I can jump!	
DOCTOR: (*Watches Mary jump up and down, and applauds.*) That's great! Mary, you are doing great!	I am so proud of her accomplishments.
M: I can also hop—watch!	
Dr: (*Watches Mary hop, skip, jump, and run.*) You are doing great. You must be so proud!	I am also pleased with my own work with her.
M: I am.	
Dr: I bet you're getting ready to go home soon.	
M: I am, but I am scared. I don't want to take a plane.	
Dr: Do you think you can?	
M: I guess with my father there I can, but I don't want him to die!	She fears the loss of the surviving parent.

The Return to Colombia

Two days later, Mary and her dad left for Colombia. We shared a warm goodbye. I hugged Mary and gave her some chocolate candy kisses as a token of affection. I told her, "Mary, I know you will never be the same after the plane crash. I, too, will never be the same after meeting you. You have taught me so much about strength, courage, and love. I thank you for letting me get to know you and for giving me so much." We hugged. Mary's dad put his arms around me; he cried. Mary said, "Goodbye, Fornari. Thank you. I will miss you."

I later heard conflicting stories about the return trip to Bogota. First I heard that Mary had refused to fly. A family friend called to say that they had taken a train from New York to Miami, Florida. From there, they went by boat to a South American port, where they could continue their return to Colombia by train, bus, and then car.

Subsequently, I was told that the trip proceeded differently. In actuality, they drove by car from New York to Miami. The reason, I was told, was that Mary's dad had not made the necessary arrangements in time to fly. Perhaps *he* was afraid to let Mary fly. Once in Miami, they took a plane to Bogota. Mary expressed fear about flying, but after being comforted by her dad while on the plane, Mary was able to relax during the flight home.

SUMMARY AND COMMENTS

During an emergency, it is important to remain calm and be able to think clearly. The primary role of health care providers, including rescue workers, emergency room staff members, and hospital workers, is to be able to administer emergency medical care without becoming immobilized by the terror of the disaster. While providing emergency services to children and adolescents, all personnel need to convey a sense of safety, support, and reassurance, to diminish their anxiety so that the necessary care can be administered. During this process, empathy with the victims offers them the comfort of knowing that the health care providers understand their condition. This was demonstrated during the first session with Mary.

In the early stages of this work, empathy facilitated the therapeutic alliance between Mary and me; I needed to establish a strong connection with the child, as well as with her family and support system. Working closely with her father and the family friends facilitated the therapeutic alliance with Mary.

During therapy immediately following a disaster, it is critical to take the child's lead once the therapeutic alliance has begun to develop. The victims of psychic trauma will often offer many signals that they are ready to begin to discuss their traumatic experiences as well as their losses. In reviewing a traumatic experience with a child or adolescent victim, it is helpful to reconstruct the event as completely as possible and to review it many times, using different modalities. These may include play, drawing, mutual storytelling, looking at family photo albums, and reviewing newspaper coverage of the trauma (or other visual material, such as television or video coverage of the event).

Children, like adults, bring their fantasies, dreams, and associations into therapy, often stimulated by the techniques utilized in prior therapy sessions. An important guideline is to take a child's lead when utilizing fantasies and the like, so as not to retraumatize the child by being too confrontational before the child is prepared to review the painful memories and experiences.

Psychotherapeutic work with a child victim of psychic trauma may go on for many months and years following the traumatic event. As the child reaches new developmental stages, the traumatic experience and the associated losses may take on new significance, and the child may develop new symptoms. These may be manifested as new fears, sleep disturbances, nightmares, or almost any kind of symptom. It would be naïve to assume that symptoms that develop long after the trauma are unrelated to it. A more sensitive and thoughtful view would be that a child is *never* the same after psychic trauma. The child's life is divided by the traumatic experience into events occurring "before" or "after" the experience. All subsequent life events, symptoms, and major decisions may contain elements that are remnants or derivatives of the earlier psychic trauma.

Working with a child survivor of psychic trauma soon after the traumatic event offers an opportunity to observe the child's initial coping responses. It also allows the therapist to experience the trauma with the child, rather than to have to reconstruct it in the consulting room many years later, which more commonly happens. This offers the therapist a unique opportunity to prevent a variety of symptoms that might otherwise develop.

The premorbid psychological status of the child, the child's temperament, and the family's psychosocial supports all have a profound impact on the child's ultimate adaptation. Mary offered me the unique and compelling opportunity of examining an 8-year-old girl following her survival of an airplane crash; I could see her initial coping style and the way in which she began to integrate her experiences as well as mourn her tremendous losses. Mary's case is an example of extraordinary courage and adaptation in the face of disaster. It appeared that early, regular, and repeated opportunities to discuss her experiences allowed her the opportunity to begin to work through her devastating psychic trauma.

When I was originally informed that Mary had refused to fly home, I wondered what else I could have done to help her overcome her fear of flying in an airplane. More desensitization of airplanes might have allowed her the possibility of getting on the plane. Perhaps I should have been satisfied to have her travel by train, boat, bus, and car at this time. Perhaps Mary had overcome so many obstacles that flying at this time was not the most important goal. I reasoned that Mary could choose to master flying at a later time, if and when she decided to do so.

Later, when I learned that Mary had indeed traveled home to Colombia by plane, I was surprised, pleased, and impressed with Mary's resilience.

FOLLOW-UP: MARY, AGE 17

"Maybe the best thing I learned is that I fell down, but I was able to learn to stand up."
—*Mary, age 17, commenting on her experience of the plane crash*

The Memorial Service: News about Mary

On January 25, 1998, 8 years after the crash of Avianca Flight 052, 5 survivors and 25 family members and friends assembled at St. Dominic's Roman Catholic Church in Oyster Bay, Long Island, for a noon Mass dedicated to the crash victims—both the survivors and those who perished. This Mass has become an annual event; it serves as a memorial to the deceased victims of Flight 052, as well as an anniversary commemoration for the survivors and all family members. On the eighth anniversary, those who assembled traveled from the church to the crash site at 1:30 P.M. on a cold, crystal-clear winter day. They laid flowers, said prayers in memory of those who perished, and expressed gratitude to the rescue personnel.

It was at this memorial service that I was first brought up to date about Mary, who was 8 years old at the time of the crash, and who was now a 16-year-old adolescent, living in Bogota with her father and stepmother. At the time of this eighth anniversary, a graduate student at Columbia University had recently traveled to Colombia to interview family members and survivors of Avianca Flight 052. This student brought me greetings from Mary and her father, and gave the following update.

Mary, at 16, did not talk about her experiences of the crash with many people. She spoke enthusiastically about pursuing a career in medicine. Mary informed the interviewer that she wished to get back in touch with me, and that she especially wanted to discuss her plans to study medicine. I received this news with intense emotions. I was brought back 8 years to that period of time when her suffering and reactions were fresh, and I was moved to tears by the thought that she was now 16 and hoping to study medicine. Mary reported that her relationship with her father was very close. I hoped for a letter, a telephone contact, or even a future meeting.

Now, 8 years after the accident, the survivors and relatives who prayed at the site of the crash wiped away their tears. As they turned to their cars, they left behind red and white carnations that glowed in the setting sun. As they drove away, they retraced the path in the winding road from that spot that changed their lives.

After years of physical and emotional suffering, the survivors and family members I talked to said that they had accepted what happened. They didn't think about the accident as often as they did before. Their lives had taken new directions. But in their souls, the accident bound them forever to the people who died that cold and foggy night in January 1990.

Following the memorial service at the crash site, I traveled to the home of one of the survivors, where the group assembled for coffee and cake. Together, we spoke about each person's life following the crash. Time was perhaps the greatest surprise: Everyone agreed that the 8 years have passed rapidly. The emotions were high, and there were tears and hugs of joy. I was received with a warm welcome and found myself pleased and proud to be welcomed by these people, who had a profound impact on my own professional development, and who made up a significant portion of my clinical work for several years. I was both curious as to how they were doing and delighted to see those who were doing well.

Telephone Follow-Up with Mary

Several months after I learned of Mary's whereabouts, and following several failed attempts at contacting her by telephone, I dialed her telephone number again. A woman answered the phone. I said, "May I speak to Mary?" "Just a moment, please," the woman replied. I was filled with anticipation and emotion. My anxiety and excitement were tempered by my concern about how Mary would respond to my call. Would she be pleased that I called, or indifferent (as I feared)? A young, fresh, energetic voice soon said, "Hello?" "Mary, this is an old, dear friend from New York," I said. After a pause, I heard loud weeping. "Dr. Fornari!" she exclaimed as my own eyes welled. I responded with a quiver, "Yes, Mary, it is me." "So many years have passed," she said. "How are you?" I asked. "I'm very well. I just had my 17th birthday 2 days ago. I'm a senior in high school, and I hope to graduate in 6 months," Mary announced. I appreciated and could hear the powerful reaction in her, and that, coupled with my own anticipation, caused me to have my own intense response. I was filled with joy, sadness, and excitement—and a sense of relief that indeed our work together and our relationship had an enduring, important meaning to each of us.

"Mary, tell me about your father," I said. "How is he?" Mary responded, "My father is very well. He is remarried, you know, and his wife is very nice. We live together, and I am OK," she said. There was a pause, and then more tears. "Oh, Dr. Fornari," she said, "I can't believe that I am speaking with you. I am so excited. When I spoke with your friend who visited here a while ago, I was happy to learn that you are well." I responded, "Mary, I too was so pleased to hear from my friend who visited you about what a lovely young woman you have grown up to become."

I then asked again, "How are you, Mary?" She replied thoughtfully, "I have survived and surpassed the accident, and despite some anxiety, I have flown at least four round trips to different places, and I'm OK about flying now. Not a day goes by that I do not think about my mother, however." There was a pause, and I was brought back to the moment in time when she learned that her mother had died. To me it seemed like yesterday, and yet for her it may have seemed like an eternity. She went on, "I think about my mother every day. She is with me. I miss her more than words can say." There was another long pause. I wondered whether she was crying or holding back her tears.

"Mary, I am so pleased to speak with you," I said. "Dr. Fornari, I am so grateful that you called," she answered. "Let's stay in touch," I asked. Mary said, "Yes, can I have your address?" We exchanged our addresses and telephone numbers. Mary continued, "You know I plan to come to the United States to study medicine, as I told you so many years ago. My father says that that's OK. I was thinking about becoming a psychiatrist, but now I think I'd like to be an orthopedic surgeon. I'm hoping to study in New York, and I hope that we will see each other." Filled with emotion, I responded, "That would be wonderful, Mary. That would mean so much to me."

Next, I asked her what it had been like for her when she returned home after the accident. "I was a little girl with a stable and happy family," she said. "That was gone in a minute." Now Mary was a teenager who cared about fashion and friends, but who also had a deep understanding of human suffering and hope. "My father was there for me, and I was there for him," she went on, almost in a whisper. "We just had each other." She added, "It was very sad when we first came home. Everything reminded us of our family. If we went to the shopping mall, to the park, anyplace, we thought about my mom and baby brother."

Mary believed that she grew with the pain, however. "Maybe I feel that the wound hasn't healed yet," she reflected. "But I learned to face life, to value everything. . . . I had a mother and a brother. I learned that no matter how dark it gets, there is always light. No matter how deep you are stuck in the swamp, there is always sun. Maybe the best thing I learned is that I fell down, but I was able to learn how to stand up."

Mary also felt that her life would have meaning in serving others. She wanted to give back, to help. "I'm a person who can say to others, 'Hey, here is a smile for you.' No matter how hard your life is, how sad you are, how small you feel, there is hope in this world." Her reason for wanting to study medicine was this: "I like to bring out the best in people. I want to help people, no matter who they are, what they do."

We spoke for a total of 30 minutes, and at the conclusion of the call, I found myself both very pleased and crying. Mary had had a more profound impact on me as a person than I had imagined. Over the years, I had thought often about her and what she represented to me. When we said goodbye, we vowed again to stay in touch. "I will write to you, Dr. Fornari," she promised. "Mary, please send me a picture," I spontaneously requested. "I will," Mary replied.

Today, at 17 Mary appears to have become a poised, mature, and articulate young woman. From the outset, I had been impressed with Mary's resilience, and it appears that those qualities have aided in her recovery and remain today. For Mary, her loss and suffering seem to have been transformed into strength and the desire to help others. Mary has taught me so much. I look forward to our reunion.

COMMUNITY HEALTH CARE RESPONSE FOLLOWING A PLANE CRASH

The response to the Avianca Airline crash can be viewed as a model of community health care response (for a full discussion, see Fornari, Fuss, Hickey, & Packman, 1996). Three phases of response to this event—emergency, recovery, and community support—can be identified, and the general functions of the responders can be categorized as follows:

1. *Outreach/engagement.* Responders presented themselves as persons who had the qualifications and authority to be there and who could help survivors and relatives with special needs, including listening to them and providing a strong, consistent presence.

2. *Emotional support.* Responders provided a strong emotional shoulder to lean upon.

3. *Assessment*. Responders assessed the ability of each person to cope and to function.

4. *Education and reassurance*. Responders reassured relatives that many of the symptoms they were experiencing were normal reactions to an abnormal experience.

5. *Organization and advocacy*. Whenever possible, responders encouraged persons to function to the best of their ability and make critical decisions.

6. *Social support*. The initiation of peer interactions and the development of a mutually supportive organization were encouraged by the responders.

Preliminary empirical support supports the effectiveness of postdisaster psychological intervention, such as the intervention provided in this case. Studies of survivors of a devastating earthquake in Armenia in 1988 have documented high rates of posttraumatic stress disorder in children (Pynoos et al., 1993) and adults (Goenjian et al., 1994). Children who were relocated did no worse than children who remained in the disaster zone (Najarian, Goenjian, Pelcovitz, Mandel, & Najarian, 1996). Mary, like the majority of survivors of the Avianca Flight 052 crash, found themselves far from home during their recovery. When destruction is massive, as happened in Armenia, the benefits of relocating the victims to an intact environment may outweigh the negative impact of uprooting the victims; in the Avianca crash, this choice was not the issue. Psychological intervention was available to the Avianca victims, however, whereas it generally was not in Armenia. The benefit of debriefing in reducing psychological distress (Chemtob, Tomas, Law, & Cremniter, 1997) was illustrated in Mary's case. Because she was in the hospital for an extended period of time (50 days), there were numerous opportunities for her to talk about her feelings and share her grief with the medical and child life staffs. She also continued this grieving process when she returned home, and now has internalized her mother's memory in a helpful way. Mary's statement that her mother taught her to be strong was a legacy that she now wants to pass on to others.

STUDY QUESTIONS

1. Discuss the normal grief process of an 8-year-old child. How would you evaluate Mary's mourning process? What kinds of responses might be predictable in the year following the traumatic loss of a mother and a brother?

2. Discuss the delicate matter of timing the disclosure to a child of the death of a family member. Do you agree with the way it was handled in this case? Why or why not?

3. Comment on the stress faced by the therapist in having to cope with tragedies, as in this case. How can the therapist best deal with his or her feelings? Can you envision a role for staff debriefing in a group format for all crisis workers?

4. Discuss the transference and countertransference issues between Mary and Dr. Fornari, and the issue of clinical boundaries in this case.

5. What is the ideal role of the mental health responder at follow-up? (Therapist, friend, concerned fellow human being?)

6. How could Mary have been helped to overcome her fear of planes? If you had been the therapist, would you have focused more on this fear prior to her departure? If so, what methods would you have used?

ACKNOWLEDGMENTS

I respectfully acknowledge the victims of the Avianca Airline disaster—those who perished and those who survived, as well as all of their families. I would like to thank Fredi Leisersohn for the preparation of the manuscript, and Margarita Martinez for her interview with Mary in Bogota, Colombia.

REFERENCES

American Psychiatric Association. (1994). *Diagnostic and statistical manual of mental disorders* (4th ed.). Washington, DC: Author.

Anthony, E. J. (1988). The reactions of children and their parents to disastrous and violent circumstances. *Yearbook of the International Association for Child and Adolescent Psychiatry and Allied Professions, 8,* 425–427.

Chemtob, C. M., Tomas, S., Law, W., & Cremniter, D. (1997). Postdisaster psychosocial intervention: A field study of the impact of debriefing on psychological distress. *American Journal of Psychiatry, 154*(3), 415–417.

Fornari, V., Fuss, J., Hickey, J., & Packman, L. (1996). The Avianca Airline crash: Implications for community health care response. In C. Pfeffer (Ed.), *Intense stress and mental disturbance in children* (pp. 153–180). Washington, DC: American Psychiatric Press.

Frederick, C. J. (1985). Children traumatized by catastrophic situations. In S. Eth & R. S. Pynoos, *Posttraumatic stress disorder in children* (pp. 73–99). Washington, DC: American Psychiatric Press.

Goenjian, A., Najarian, L. M., Pynoos, R. S., Steinberg, A. M., Manoukian, G., Tavosian, A., & Fairbanks, L. A. (1994). Posttraumatic stress disorder in elderly and younger adults after the 1988 earthquake in Armenia. *American Journal of Psychiatry, 151*(6), 895–901.

H.R. Rep. No. 793, 104th Cong., 2d Sess. (1996, September 17).

Najarian, L., Goenjian, A. K., Pelcovitz, D., Mandel, F., & Najarian, B. (1996). Relocation after a disaster: Posttraumatic stress disorder in Armenia after the earthquake. *Journal of the American Academy of Child and Adolescent Psychiatry, 35*(3), 374–383.

Pynoos, R. S., Goenjian, A., Tashjian, M., Karakashian, M., Manjikian, R., Mahoukian, G., Steinberg, A. M., & Fairbanks, L. A. (1993). *British Journal of Psychiatry, 163,* 239–247.

Sugar, M. (1988). Children in a disaster: An overview. *Yearbook of the International Association for Child and Adolescent Psychiatry and Allied Professions, 8,* 429–442.

Terr, L. (1990). *Too scared to cry: Psychic trauma in childhood.* New York: Harper & Row.

CHAPTER 19

School-Based Crisis Assessment and Intervention with Children Following Urban Bombings

NANCY BOYD WEBB

Children who experience the physical and emotional effects of bomb blasts—such as those that occurred at the World Trade Center in New York City on February 28, 1993, and at the Murrah Federal Building in Oklahoma City on April 19, 1995— certainly suffer stress. Whether this stress produces a *state of crisis* in specific children, however, depends on each child's unique personal history, as well as on the nature of the responses of each child's family, school, and community network in the aftermath of the disaster. The usage of the term "crisis" or "state of crisis" in this chapter conforms to this widely accepted definition: "a perception of an event or situation as an intolerable difficulty that exceeds the resources and coping mechanisms of the person" (Gilliland & James, 1997, p. 3).

We know that it is not the traumatic event itself that provokes a crisis state in individuals, but rather the idiosyncratic *meaning* ascribed to the event by the individual (Freud, 1965; Green, Wilson, & Lindy, 1985). Therefore, people who undergo the same distressing experience may react very differently. For example, a kindergarten child who harbors a long-standing fear of the dark may suffer intense anxiety during an enforced blackout. Similarly, the child who has just recently acquired control of nighttime bedwetting may feel shame and humiliation about wetting his or her pants during an extended period without access to a bathroom. Both of these hypothetical cases describe children whose personal histories would make them especially vulnerable to the stress created by being trapped in a dark elevator for a long period of time, as occurred in the New York City bombing. Their reactions would contrast sharply with those of children who might feel intrigued and excited by the "adventure" of spending several hours with their classmates and teacher singing songs and reciting the rosary in the intermittent flickering light of a cigarette lighter. Each child's precrisis adjustment and coping style shape the impact and meaning of crisis events in personal terms; these factors play a large part in determining whether an experience proves to be traumatic for a specific individual.

This chapter outlines and discusses the interactive components that should be part of the assessments of young children following traumatic events such as the bombings in New York City and Oklahoma City. In addition, a recommended school-based crisis intervention plan that is appropriate for use with children, their families, and their schools in the aftermath of human-made disasters such as these is presented.

TYPICAL RESPONSES OF CHILDREN TO DISASTERS

A review of the literature of the past 35 years on the effects of disaster on children reveals the following key findings:

1. After a tornado in 1953, Bloch, Silber, and Perry (1956) reported symptoms in 185 children of increased dependence, clinging, remaining close to home, asking to sleep with parents, night terrors, regressive behavior (e.g., enuresis), tornado games, irritability, sensitivity to noise, and phobias. The children in this study ranged in age from 2 to 15 years, with the majority between 6 and 10 years old.

2. After an earthquake, Blaufarb and Levine (1972) reported that the most common problem for 3- to 12-year-old children was a fear of going to sleep in their own rooms.

3. Farberow and Gordon (1981), summarizing the responses of children in major disasters, emphasized the separation anxiety that threatens young children when frightened and separated from the nurturing persons to whom they are attached. During such a time of actual or feared separation, children may be very afraid of being alone and of being in the dark.

4. The National Institute of Mental Health (Lystad, 1985) presented an overview of stress reactions of individuals of various ages after experiencing a disaster. Responses identified for preschool and latency-age children included (but were not limited to) the following: crying, thumbsucking, loss of bowel/bladder control, fear of being left alone and of strangers, irritability, confusion, immobility, headaches and other physical complaints, depression, inability to concentrate, fighting, and withdrawal from peers.

5. In contrast, Terr (1990), who interviewed 29 children from Chowchilla, California who were kidnapped and buried alive in their school bus, documented the children's controlled, quiet behavior during and immediately following their ordeal. None of them vomited, defecated, shrieked, or became mute or paralyzed. Nonetheless, despite the *external* appearance of control among the children, Terr concluded that they were seriously traumatized by their overwhelming experience of helplessness, fear of separation from loved ones, and fear that even more terrible events might ensue. Terr interviewed the children at two different times—5 months and 4 to 5 years after the traumatic kidnapping.

REACTIONS OF CHILDREN FOLLOWING
THE NEW YORK CITY BOMBING

It is not clear how closely these findings apply to the children who were trapped in the elevator following the New York City World Trade Center bombing. Accounts in newspapers, magazines, and a television dramatization of this event have offered different views of the bombing and its impact on the child survivors. After reading these, I spoke to school personnel and to several crisis team members who provided services to the children in the aftermath of the disaster. However, because of the need

to respect the confidentiality of those involved, this chapter presents a *general* model
for assessing and helping children in crisis situations, rather than an analysis of specific children's responses in this specific disaster. Similarly, the information provided
by school personnel is simply attributed to "the staff of P.S. 95" or P.S. 95 personnel," with no attribution to specific individuals.

In any crisis situation, the reactions of the involved individuals may appear quite
different immediately following the crisis event and several months or years later.
This discussion focuses on the reactions of the children at three points in time: during the actual elevator entrapment and its immediate aftermath; 3 months after the
disaster; and 4½ years later. This conforms to the protocol for intervention suggested
by Gurwitch, Sullivan, and Long (1998, p. 28), who recommend three phases of
treatment: immediately after the disaster; "short-term" (1 week to 3 months postdisaster); and "long-term" (after 3 months postdisaster).

On February 28, 1993, two kindergarten classes from P.S. 95 in Brooklyn were
concluding their visit to the second tallest building in the world. The children had
enjoyed the view from the observation deck on the 107th floor, had finished their
lunch, and had gone to the bathroom. The two groups separated because the elevator was too full to accommodate both classes. Two other classes of older children from
another school were already on the elevator. All happily counted the floors as the
elevator descended; then it abruptly stopped between 36th and 35th floors. The lights
went out, and the emergency backup system failed to provide any illumination or
ventilation. The teacher told the children that there had been "some kind of computer glitch" and that they would just have to wait until it was fixed. A television
dramatization of the disaster several months later portrayed the children as lying or
sitting down on their coats on the elevator floor as they waited. Some children complained of the heat and the dark, and others cried out for their mothers. The teacher
and other adults in the elevator managed to reassure the children, and calmed them
by singing songs and reciting the rosary. Some children actually fell asleep. Two
vomited, but none of them lost control of bladder or bowel functions. One of the
chaperones became panicky and verbalized a fear of fire, related to the odor of smoke
that pervaded the air.

It is important to note that the occupants of the stalled elevator did not know
about the bombing until *after* they were rescued. This factor clearly distinguished
the New York City bombing from the one in Oklahoma City, where there was immediate and extensive life threat, firsthand contact with people who were seriously
injured, and exposure to sights of massive destruction. The crisis for the children in
the New York City bombing situation seemed primarily related to being confined
for a long period in the dark, and to not knowing how soon they would be free to
resume their trip home and reunite with their families. In contrast, the crisis for the
children in Oklahoma City included personal injury and hospitalization; witnessing death, panic, and destruction; loss of their familiar environment; and the disappointment of knowing that the adults who were supposed to protect them had been
unable to do so.

In New York, when the children were finally rescued and returned to their school
in Brooklyn, a crisis intervention team boarded the bus with celebratory balloons.

At the same time, "hysterical" parents greeted their children, and hordes of reporters and television newspeople asked questions and tried to interview anyone involved with the tragedy. Many of the families scattered to the safety of their homes, while others accepted the invitation of a crisis team to meet in a group and discuss their experience. One of the participants described this meeting as an opportunity for the parents to ventilate their tears and their fears. This debriefing session was attended by only a few families.

The bombing occurred on a Friday, and the crisis team was present in the school on the following Monday, when the children returned to class. The team remained for only half the day, because the team members saw no indications that the children required more extensive intervention. During their visit, the team members engaged the children in drawing and play activities, using blocks to reenact the bomb's explosioin and the damage to the building, which many of the children had viewed in extensive television replays over the weekend. The team also encouraged the children to draw pictures of their experiences. The tendency to minimize the emotional aftereffects of this crisis on the children was pervasive, and was reflected in an article in *The New York Times* 4 days after the bombing, titled "Blast Trauma Lingers, but Mostly for Parents" (Tabor, 1993a).

Three months after the bombing, P.S. 95 personnel reported to me that the children rarely referred to their experience, except when there were distinct reminders (such as a televised movie dramatization of the event). Several children nonetheless were receiving mental health counseling, and a number of the children were reported to be reluctant to go on elevators. Some spontaneously drew pictures of monsters and of burning buildings (Tabor, 1993b). The crisis team did not remain involved with the children, but the regular school-based support team, consisting of a psychologist, a social worker, and a guidance counselor, counseled some children on an individual basis. According to the staff of P.S. 95, a meeting for parents to discuss their children's responses 3 months after the crisis revealed that a number of children were experiencing sleep problems, fear of the dark, regression to bedwetting, and fear of elevators.

Four and a half years later, an article in *The New York Times* (Martin, 1997) reported that some children continued to experience sleep disruptions and that others continued to avoid reminders of the disaster, such as requests from reporters for interviews about their experiences and commercials on television picturing the World Trade Center. According to the principal of the school, "It's over with, and they don't want to be reminded about it" (p. 43).

REACTIONS OF CHILDREN FOLLOWING
THE OKLAHOMA CITY BOMBING

On April 19, 1995, 168 people (including 19 children) died in the worst terrorist bomb attack in U.S. history. It orphaned 30 children, left 219 children with only one parent, and injured and hospitalized 600 children and adults. Six children in the America's Kids day care center on site at the Murrah Federal Building survived the bombings to spend weeks and months recovering from ruptured eardrums, broken bones, impaired eyesight, severe burns, scorched lungs, and head and brain injuries ("Small Miracles," 1996).

There was an outpouring of national and international compassion in efforts to assist the victims and the community. Fortunately, the state of Oklahoma implemented a structure to control the extensive helping offers, in order to protect the survivors from the well-meaning but potentially duplicative and exhausting efforts of clinicians and researchers trying to help and/or study the victims. Krug, Nixon, and Vincent (1996) referred to these overlapping efforts as potentially "abusive" to the survivors.

Interventions with the children affected by the Oklahoma City bombing occurred in the schools and through local mental health personnel. Some examples of school-based responses are discussed later in this chapter. Interventions with individuals in crisis can take the form of individual, family, or group approaches. Regardless of the treatment modality, however, it is important to understand and evaluate any crisis event in terms of its particular meaning to an individual child.

THE TRIPARTITE CRISIS ASSESSMENT

As noted in Chapter 1, three groups of factors must be considered in making a crisis assessment: (1) the nature of the crisis situation, (2) the idiosyncratic characteristics of the individual, and (3) the strengths and weakness of the individual's support system. Figure 1.1 in that chapter suggests how the impact of factors in one set of variables may be either balanced and offset *or* magnified by interacting influences among the other two sets of components. Chapter 1 presents a complete review of all the factors constituting the tripartite crisis assessment, including rating forms for recording pivotal factors in the crisis situation and individual factors. The following discussion highlights some of the key factors that apply especially to children in the traumatic situations of urban bombings.

The Nature of the Crisis Situation

Four factors in the first category seem particularly relevant in evaluating the impact of these particular crisis situations on the children involved:

- Proximity to the crisis
- Presence of loss factors
- Physical injury/pain
- Presence of life threat

Proximity to the Crisis

The literature confirms the increased vulnerability to symptom formation in children who are physically closer to a crisis event (Pynoos & Eth, 1985; Pynoos & Nader,

1989). In both bombing situations under discussion, the closer the exposure to the crisis, the greater the danger to life, and the more sensory input. Although the New York City children were in the bombed building, the elevator actually shielded them from knowing about the disaster and from seeing the accompanying horrific scenes. In contrast, the children in the day care center in Oklahoma City experienced the maximum effects of the bomb blast, both personally and as witnesses.

Presence of Loss Factors

Losses are integral components of any crisis situation. In Chapter 1, Figure 1.1 lists the following possible losses:

- Separation from family members
- Death of family members
- Loss of familiar environment
- Loss of familiar role/status
- Loss of body part or function

There were multiple losses for the children in both of these bombing situations, with the child survivors from the Oklahoma City day care center suffering the most extensive and profound losses. Whereas the New York City children endured a prolonged period of enforced imprisonment in a dark elevator, not knowing whether or when they would be reunited with their families, the Oklahoma City day care children experienced immediate personal injury and pain, in addition to being separated from their families and hospitalization.

There was a total loss of control for everyone involved in both situations. No one knew whether or when either situation would be resolved. For young children, the absence of a parent to comfort them could contribute greatly to their stress. However, the fact that the New York City children did not really know what was happening to them actually proved to buffer them from anxiety. Their later reunion with "hysterical" parents upon their arrival home probably increased their anxiety, as did their weekend viewing of the subsequent television coverage of the bombing.

In contrast, the surviving Oklahoma City children from the day care center (ranging in age from 19 months to 4 years) were severely wounded and in pain. Even when parents succeeded in finding their children at the bomb site, the police detectives sometimes could not permit the parents to hold a child because the child had sustained extensive life-threatening injuries ("Small Miracles," 1996). All of the Oklahoma City day care children suffered losses connected to physical injuries; some lost their ability to talk and walk; many had prolonged hospital stays and multiple operations ("Small Miracles," 1996). In addition to the *physical* injuries, the children suffered *emotional* wounds associated with witnessing horrible scenes. Some of these children continue to have nightmares, while others are clinging and reluctant to permit separation from their parents or caretakers (Gurwitch et al., 1998). These behaviors, in the context of the life-threatening crisis event, point to a diagnosis of posttraumatic stress disorder (PTSD).

The ultimate loss for children is the death of a parent. Whereas the loss of life in the New York City bombing was far less than the numbers of injured (a total of six deaths), in Oklahoma City many adult employees in the federal building were parents who died in the blast; as nonted earlier, 30 children were orphaned, and 219 were left with only one parent. This tragic loss of life had far-reaching effects. The entire community and the nation participated in memorial services to commemorate those who died, and for months the fence surrounding the rubble of the building became a shrine for flowers, notes, tributes of stuffed animals, and pictures of individuals who had died in the blast. Many of the school-based approaches to helping children developed in response to awareness that the bomb blast had touched the lives of many students, through the deaths of parents, grandparents, and extended family members.

Physical Injury and Presence of Life Threat

The foregoing discussion of the crisis situation in both bombings has covered the impact of injuries and deaths at both bombing sites. The life-threatening danger was a factor in both situations. Although the limited cognitive development of preschool children may preclude their comprehension of true danger and life threat, nonetheless the presence of physical pain/injury and/or the absence of a comforting parent probably results in the same (or a greater) level of stress as in adults confronting a threat to their lives.

Individual Factors

An evaluation of individual factors in assessing the impact of a crisis must consider a child's developmental stage and level of cognitive understanding. Other important factors relevant to the individual in *this* crisis are the child's medical history and past experience with crisis.

Reports of the responses of the children trapped in the elevator in the New York City bombing indicated that the older children (third- and fifth-graders) were more upset than were the kindergarten children (Tesoriero, 1993). It is likely that the older children understood the potential danger of their situation, whereas the younger ones were able to believe and take comfort in the reassurance (and denial) of their teacher, who told them that there was no smoke in the elevator and that they would "be down in no time." Children aged 5 and 6 are present-oriented and do not have the ability to project very far into the future; nor do they possess a mature understanding of death (Piaget, 1955). In this case, therefore, their immaturity served to protect them from the stress experienced by the older children. A solid knowledge of child development is essential in assessing the impact of crisis events on children at different developmental stages.

Another individual factor that proved important in assessing the impact of this crisis on each individual child was the child's language proficiency. Since four of the New York City children were not native English speakers, it was difficult for the teacher to reassure them effectively. Fortunately, this circumstance was rectified in the assignment of bilingual speakers to these children in the postcrisis counseling.

The fact that several children in the group of 17 kindergartners on the elevator were asthmatic also added to the concerns of the teacher, who worried about the effects of the smoke on these children. She made a point of calling out the names of all the children at intervals, both to maintain contact and to ascertain that the asthmatic children were breathing satisfactorily. There were no medical emergencies reported concerning the asthmatic children, but this example points to the possible unique vulnerability of children with preexisting medical conditions in crisis situations such as bombings.

Knowledge about a child's past experience with crisis can contribute to our understanding of the impact of the current crisis situation on the child. For example, a New York City boy whose grandfather and uncle had died shortly before the bomb incident was fearful that some of his friends had died in the bomb blast (Tabor, 1993a). This boy, who was not himself on the field trip, had learned to "expect disaster" and was reported to be weeping fearfully in school. Past losses, especially unresolved and/or recent experiences of bereavement, certainly can deplete an individual's energy levels and make him or her particularly vulnerable to a new crisis experience.

The importance of understanding the idiosyncratic *meaning* of a crisis to a child is illustrated in the case of another New York City child, who had been in the World Trade Center bombing and also happened to be visiting relatives in Oklahoma City the day before the bombing there! This child, then 7 years old, became convinced that she was somehow responsible for both bombings, according to her mother (Martin, 1997). As of 1997, she still wept when anyone brought up the bombings. Her mother implied that her daughter's recovery 4 years after the first bombing was still questionable.

Factors in the Support System

The third main component in the tripartite crisis assessment is an evaluation of the strengths and weaknesses of the support system, including the nuclear and extended family, the school, friends, and the community network. An Eco-Map (Hartman, 1978) can be used to record these resources (see Chapter 1, Figure 1.2).

The reactions of family members with respect to the crisis experience of the children in the New York City bombing varied from the "hysterical" version reported in news accounts to that of rage because their children were stuck in an elevator without a flashlight or viable communication system. Of course the parents were relieved that their children were not harmed in this potentially dangerous situation, but this relief did not exclude feelings of anger that the tragedy happened in the first place.

When crisis workers are dealing with children, the reactions of the people surrounding them must be considered. The literature refers to the role of parental reactions in either calming children or raising their anxiety level (Gurwitch et al., 1998; Monahon, 1993). If the parents are indeed "hysterical" and enraged, how can children remain unaffected by or accepting about their experience? McFarlane (1987, p. 764) states emphatically that "parents' ability to contain the anxiety generated by an extreme threat may be the major factor influencing their children's responses."

Because both of these disasters received such extensive community response and media coverage, the children soon understood that something *very* important had happened to them. The six child survivors from the Oklahoma City day care center were all in the hospital and in various stages of awareness. By contrast, the New York City children were not injured; during the weekend following the bombing, they watched the television news reports showing survivors with soot-stained faces being rescued in the building where *their* elevator had stalled! In addition, many families of the kindergarten children were visited at home by reporters seeking exclusive interviews. On Monday their school was literally "flooded" with the news media, resulting in a delay in the group debriefing sessions that had been planned by the crisis team.

As time went on, the New York City children and teachers were given citations of heroism, trips to the circus, and special rewards such as watches and T-shirts for bravery (see Figure 19.1). The reaction of the community to the fact that the

FIGURE 19.1. Two P.S. 95 kindergarten children who were trapped in an elevator in the World Trade Center bombing. The child at right is wearing the T-shirt that was given to each member of the group as a reward for bravery. Photograph by Steve Hart. From Tabor (1993a). Copyright 1993 by *The New York Times*. Reprinted by permission.

children "survived" and were "brave heroes" did not permit any admission of fear or anxiety on the part of the "heroic" 5- and 6-year-olds. How very confused some of them must have felt by having their experience of fear so quickly transformed and relabeled as bravery! Children who are traumatized do not feel brave, although their reactions of quiet acquiescence may deceive the public. Because one of the characteristics of PTSD is avoidance of thoughts or feelings associated with the trauma, it is understandable how the supportive actions of the family and community following this disaster may actually have served to reinforce and collude with the children's own wishes to forget and avoid any frightening recollections of the event.

The families of the six survivors from the Oklahoma City day care center received an outpouring of cards, letters, toys, and gifts of all kinds from all over the country. People donated their time and expertise wherever a need was identified. For example, local volunteers built a solarium for one child who had to avoid direct exposure to direct sunlight for 18 months while his skin grafts healed. Many therapists offered their services on a *pro bono* basis.

After the Oklahoma City bombing, it became clear that "domestic terrorism is now a reality in America" (Krug et al., 1996, p. 105). The response of outrage and support thus expanded from each survivor's network of family and friends to include the entire country.

POSTTRAUMATIC STRESS DISORDER

This section discusses the symptoms of PTSD as they *might* relate to *some* of the children involved in the New York City and Oklahoma City bombings. I have not had professional involvement with any of these children. However, in crisis situations such as these disasters, it is appropriate to consider the probability of symptom development among the child survivors and among children in the community at large.

According to the *Diagnostic and Statistical Manual of Mental Disorders*, fourth edition (DSM-IV; American Psychiatric Association, 1994), the symptoms of PTSD can occur after a person has experienced an event involving the reality or threat of death, major injury, or violated physical integrity. When symptoms in three general categories persist for at least 1 month, the diagnosis of PTSD is appropriate. The three categories are as follows:

1. Reexperiencing (dreams, play, and physical distress reactions related to the trauma).
2. Avoidance responses ("forgetting" the event, feeling detached or disinterested, regression, and restricted affect).
3. Increased arousal (sleep disturbances, irritability, difficulty concentrating, exaggerated startle reaction, etc.).

Table 1.4 in Chapter 1 lists the DSM-IV criteria for PTSD. See the DSM-IV (American Psychiatric Association, 1994) for a complete description of the associated symptoms.

McFarlane (1990) indicates that "even after extreme trauma, . . . only approximately 40% of an exposed population develop PTSD. . . . The available evidence suggests that the degree of distress caused by an event is the major factor determining the probability of the onset of psychiatric disorder" (p. 70). Therefore, in attempting to identify children who might be most "at risk" for development of PTSD, the crisis team needs to know which children appeared to be most upset and anxious during the crisis. These children should have individual evaluations, in addition to the group debriefing meeting that crisis teams typically hold with all survivors of a crisis (Mitchell & Resnik, 1981; Mitchell & Everly, 1994; Shulman, 1990). In addition, children whose parents were extremely anxious need to be followed closely, as do the parents themselves. In the aftermath of the New York City bombing, 8 parents of the 17 kindergarten children received counseling (Tabor, 1993a).

Another point of logical intervention occurred 3 months after the New York City bombing, when some parents in a group meeting referred to their children's continuing anxiety responses of fear of the dark, sleep problems, and regression to enuresis. Referral to mental health specialists should have been implemented for symptomatic children who were not already receiving services. Actually, the *Journal of the American Medical Association* states that more mental health problems surface 3 months after a disaster than immediately following it ("Children and Families Need Help after Disasters," 1996).

Reports of children in Oklahoma City cited preschool children engaged in rescue play (by pretending to be police officers and firefighters) and recreation of physical injuries (by constructing Lego people with body parts missing) (Gurwitch, Leftwich, & Geddie, 1997). This posttraumatic play is consistent with the reexperiencing category of PTSD. In addition, many children demonstrated avoidance behaviors by showing great reluctance to return to preschool in the YMCA day care center adjacent to the federal building. With regard to the category of increased arousal, many teachers in Oklohoma City reported a decline in school performance and in exaggerated startle responses. Clearly, these children were showing evidence of PTSD.

SCHOOL-BASED CRISIS INTERVENTION FOLLOWING A DISASTER

This section discusses an "ideal" crisis intervention plan recommended for use in schools in the aftermath of disasters such as urban terrorist bombings. Because of the very unpredictable occurrence of either human-made or natural disasters, it is essential that every school have in place written guidelines about procedures to be adapted and implemented in the event of a sudden crisis. As I have noted elsewhere, "A time of crisis is not conducive to improvisation, and prior preparation and orientation of staff members regarding management of . . . crisis will greatly assist those expected to assume leadership and take action at the time of need" (Webb, 1986, p. 476).

Many school districts have such plans in place, sparked by the necessity of dealing with student suicide crises and other life-threatening situations, such as emergencies of violence. Crisis response teams serve a very important function at a time of tragedy and emotional turmoil. (See Shulman, 1990, for a description of mental health consultation to a high school following two tragedies.)

Usually composed of school counselors, school psychologists, school social workers, administrators, and mental health workers with training in crisis intervention, such a team can be called into action by the director of pupil personnel services to deal with any emergency that disrupts the usual school routine and proves emotionally challenging and upsetting to staff and students (Sorenson, 1989). When parents and teachers know ahead of time that a crisis response team is prepared and ready to deal with emergencies, they will be better able to utilize these services when the need arises (Kalafat, 1991; Nelson & Slaikeu, 1990).

The functions of the team demand skillful attention dealing with the multiple components of the emergency situation. These functions include (1) response to the crisis event itself; (2) response to the emotional reactions of the students, faculty, and staff; (3) identification of populations at risk; (4) involvement of parents; and (5) implementation of both immediate and long-term crisis intervention strategies (Sorenson, 1989). In what follows, I discuss how these functions apply to the crisis situations of urban bombings, such as those in New York City and Oklahoma City.

Response to the Crisis Event

Both bombings occurred in the community and outside of school buildings. The leader of the crisis team must judge where to focus the efforts of the intervention. Possible choices include the following:

- Working at the scene of the crisis event (to provide immediate help to the children/students on site).
- Working within the school building (to provide support to parents, children, staff, and concerned community members).
- Acting as consultants to the administrators and coordinators of the interface with media and the wider community.

In the case of the New York City bombing, the second option was selected. A television monitor was set up in the school auditorium, where parents and others congregated to await the eventual return of the school bus with the kindergartners and their teachers and chaperones. In addition to the parents and members of the school community, scores of media reporters looking for stories invaded the school environs and auditorium. Many of the P.S. 95 personnel reported that they felt "overwhelmed" by the members of the media, who "were allowed to stick microphones into everyone's faces." The tone in which this was conveyed clearly indicated that the media were experienced as adding stress to an already very stressful situation. This matter deserves attention in regard to school policy about media access to individuals in crisis. Shulman (1990) suggests that the principal should act as a liaison between the school and the press.

In Oklahoma City, the survivors benefited from a government edict to coordinate contacts through one designated facility (Krug et al., 1996). Different schools handled the crisis according to either the principal's judgment, an established plan, and/or individual teachers' ability to deal with the immediacy of the situation immediately following the bombing (when many children were in school).

Response to the Emotions of Students, Faculty, and Staff

Clearly, responding to the emotions of both children and adults within the school setting is a very important function of the crisis team. In most crisis situations the direct "victims" receive prime attention. In New York City, the team focused on the children first, by boarding the bus as soon as it arrived at the school and trying to put a positive spin on the reality of the children's ordeal. Each child received a balloon as a symbol of the happiness of the rescue.

However, the teachers, parents, and other chaperones who were trapped with the children in the elevator (and who probably realized the possible life threat of their situation, whereas the children generally did not) also deserved special recognition. The teacher, as the natural leader—maintaining calm and heroically controlling her own fears, and reassuring the children that everything would be all right—merited special intervention by someone on the crisis team. The timing of such intervention logically follows a good night's rest in a safe environment. It is likely that the "responsible" adults (teachers and other adults) felt a tremendous "let-down" once their adrenaline returned to precrisis levels and the enormity of what they experienced became apparent. These adults would have benefited greatly from a group "debriefing" experience with a specialist in posttraumatic counseling the day after the crisis.

The emotional reactions of the students involved in a disaster require attention at several points in time. The immediate aftermath of the crisis presents one set of circumstances. Several days later, the reality of the experience has begun to be shaped not only by personal recollections, but also by the responses of family members and the media. This changing scenario requires that the crisis team maintain contact with all involved in the crisis over a period of time.

Initial group "debriefing" of young children ideally includes both verbal and nonverbal approaches. Since kindergarten children do not have sophisticated verbal skills, art and play techniques can help release the feelings they feel but cannot articulate. Typical debriefing sessions with children in schools begin with a team member's asking some leading questions about the crisis event. Children who are able describe the details of their experience, emphasizing the involvement of all senses in response to specific questions by the team member—that is, what they saw, smelled, heard, did, and felt (Alameda County Mental Health Services, 1990). When the children have described their recollections, they are then invited to draw what they experienced. Often the graphic memories have a special poignancy and power not evident in the verbal accounts.

In Oklahoma City, the children waiting in a church "notification center" played and made some drawings, at the suggestion of the disaster response committee. A child psychologist working with the team noticed that during the first 72 hours after the bombing, none of the 100 children in the center drew a human figure. They also refused to give their drawings to any team member for the first 2 days. In contrast, some of the second- and third-grade children who were in school at the time of the bombing wrote letters and poems and made drawings for the rescue workers and for the children in the hospital (Castle, Beasley, & Skinner, 1996). In the latter case, the children accepted reassurance about their own safety from their teachers, and were then able to turn their attention to the victims. In contrast, the children in the unfamiliar church "notification center" probably felt very insecure, surrounded by anxious adults waiting to learn the fate of their missing loved ones. Creating an environment of safety and reassurance for the children is a challenge for the crisis team under such circumstances.

Identification of Populations at Risk

The term "populations at risk" refers to groups of people who may be especially affected by the added stress of the crisis situation. I have already referred to the child who had difficulty dealing with the stress of the New York City crisis because of his recent bereavement experiences. The child who had the misfortune to be present both at the scene of the New York City bombing and in Oklahoma City at the time of the bombing there was similarly overloaded and at risk. Individuals who are most at risk in any crisis are those who were functioning marginally before the crisis. They cannot muster the necessary expenditure of energy demanded to cope with the crisis situation.

Typically, the crisis team becomes aware of the individuals who are having difficulty dealing with the stress of the present crisis during group debriefing sessions. A child may say something to raise concern, or may remain uninvolved, or may draw something that indicates intense anxiety. A crisis team member must find a way to meet individually with such a child to explore matters further. The child's parent(s) must also be notified, and appropriate referrals should be made. In the process of completing an assessment of children or adults at risk, it is important for the crisis worker to convey to all "survivors" that extreme reactions to crises, although very upsetting, do *not* indicate the presence of a mental health disturbance. An abnormal reaction to an abnormal situation is normal behavior. There should be no stigma associated with receiving crisis intervention services.

Involvement of Parents

Whenever children's health and welfare are threatened, parents *must* be included— both as adjuncts to helping their own children, and as "indirect" victims, also deeply affected by the crisis on a personal level. Especially when the children are preschoolers, the involvement of parents is both appropriate and necessary. Because the influence of parents on children is so pervasive, the crisis team must include them to the fullest extent possible.

Group meetings with parents enable team members to provide the same information to all at the same time. They also offer a natural means for a system of mutual aid and support to emerge from the group. All the members of the group have experienced similar stress, and they potentially can help one another. In addition to focusing on the immediacy of the situation, it is helpful for team members to give parents some basic information about possible *future* responses of their children, based on knowledge about other children who have experienced disasters in the past. Because individuals in crisis may not be able to concentrate on future concerns, it is advisable to give this information in a written format for the parents' future reference. The federal government and other organizations that work with children have a wide variety of publications on the topic of helping children after disasters, including lists and discussion about typical reactions of children (Cooperative Disaster Child Care, 1985; Federal Emergency Management Agency, 1991a, 1991b). Every crisis response team should have copies of these documents in their files, to use as handouts for parents.

Like contacts with the children, contacts with the parents must occur at several time points. The immediate need is obvious, but periodic follow-up at monthly intervals can help even when there may appear to be no pressing need or request for services. Because of the tendency to avoid experiences that will stir up anxious memories of the stressful crisis, the individuals involved often minimize aftereffects. The crisis response team has the obligation to continue to monitor the emotional well-being of children, parents, and staff who were affected by the crisis, even when their reports convey the message that "everything is fine."

Implementation of Both Immediate and Long-Term Crisis Intervention Strategies

The previous discussion has emphasized that an effective crisis intervention plan includes both immediate and follow-up components. The immediate tasks of the team are usually clearer than the follow-up tasks. Professional judgment must inform decisions about the spacing and format of follow-up efforts. Periodic, once-a-month "checking in" with a class of kindergarten children might seem adequate, but when further media attention (e.g., a television dramatization) occurs, the children will have reactions to this and should receive another group debriefing. Three months after the New York City bombing, an update about the kindergarten class appeared in *The New York Times,* with pictures of the children rehearsing for a show (Tabor, 1993b). In this show, many of the children were going to sing the same songs that they sang in the elevator, and those children probably would recall the crisis event during their upcoming performance. Therefore, even though the show was anticipated as a happy experience, it carried overtones of memories that could be upsetting . This would merit further exploration by the crisis response team.

CONCLUSION

Assessment is an ongoing process, especially in crisis situations, because symptoms may emerge weeks and months after a disaster and may not even be recognized as connected to it. Because of the possibility of delayed onset of PTSD symptoms, crisis intervention response teams must provide periodic follow-up to monitor disaster victims, their families, and the network of people involved with the victims. Some individuals require and benefit from individual counseling; for many others, group debriefing sessions help them cope adequately with the stress caused by the crisis. All can be assisted by access to psychoeducational information that documents typical responses of disaster victims. Crises can and do happen to anybody. We know a great deal about how to help, and when the victims/survivors are preschool and kindergarten children, the preventive work of crisis intervention is a long-term investment in mental health.

STUDY QUESTIONS

1. Discuss the pros and cons of restricting crisis response teams to *local* mental health personnel. How can local workers deal with their own feelings of outrage and grief in a situation such as the Oklahoma City bombing?

2. A popular magazine account ("Small Miracles," 1996) stated that most families of the six child survivors from the Oklahoma City day care center did not plan to attend the remembrance services a year following the disaster, because they believed that these services were for the families who had lost loved ones. What do you think would be the appropriate involvement for these young survivors? Give reasons for your response.

3. How should the schools handle discussions of the trials of the terrorists who were convicted in both bombings? Do you see a role for the crisis team in the schools as helpful to the children and teachers in classes where coverage of and discussions about the trials were planned? If so, what kind of response would be beneficial to students and teachers?

4. If you could replay the response of the crisis team that met the kindergarten children after the New York City bombing with balloons, how would you greet the children's bus? Role-play this event, giving special attention to what is said to the child survivors and to their parents.

ACKNOWLEDGMENT

An earlier version of this chapter appeared in *Crisis Intervention and Time-Limited Treatment*, 1994, *1*(1), 47–59. Copyright 1994 by Harwood Academic Publishers. Adapted by permission.

REFERENCES

Alameda County Mental Health Services. (1990). *How to help children after a disaster.* Alameda County, CA: Author.

American Psychiatric Association. (1994). *Diagnostic and statistical manual of mental disorders* (4th ed.). Washington, DC: Author.

Blaufarb, H., & Levine, J. (1972). Crisis intervention in an earthquake. *Social Work*, *17*, 16–19.

Bloch, D., Silber, E., & Perry, S. (1956). Some factors in the emotional reaction of children to disaster. *American Journal of Psychiatry*, *113*, 416–422.

Castle, K., Beasley, L, & Skinner, L. (1996). Children of the heartland. *Childhood Education*, *72*(4), 226–231.

Children and families need help after disasters. (1996). *Journal of the American Medical Association*, *275*(22), 1714–1715.

Cooperative Disaster Child Care. (1985). *Some tips for parents and caregivers following a disaster.* New Windsor, MD: Author.

Farberow, N., & Gordon, N. (1981). *Manual for child health workers in major disasters* (DHHS Publication No. ADM 81-1070). Washington, DC: U.S. Government Printing Office.

Federal Emergency Management Agency. (1991a). *School intervention following a critical incident: Project Cope* (Document No. 220). Washington, DC: Author.

Federal Emergency Management Agency. (1991b). *How to help children after a disaster: A guidebook for teachers* (Document No. 219). Washington, DC: Author.

Freud, A. (1965). *Normality and pathology in childhood.* New York: International Universities Press.

Gilliland, B. E., & James, B. E. (1997). *Crisis intervention strategies* (3rd ed.). Pacific Grove, CA: Brooks/Cole.

Green, B. L., Wilson, J. P., & Lindy, J. D. (1985). Conceptualizing post-traumatic stress disorder: A psychosocial framework. In C. R. Figley (Ed.), *Trauma and its wake: The study and treatment of post-traumatic stress disorder* (pp. 53–69). New York: Brunner/Mazel.

Gurwitch, R. H., Leftwich, M. J. T., & Geddie, L. F. (1997). *Clinical interventions and observations at a preschool setting in the aftermath of the Oklahoma City bombing.* Unpublished manuscript.

Gurwitch, R. H., Sullivan, M. A., & Long, P. J. (1998). The impact of trauma and disaster on young children. *Child and Adolescent Psychiatric Clinics of North America*, *7*(1), 19–32.

Hartman, A. (1978). Diagrammatic assessment of family relationships. *Social Casework*, *59*, 465–476.

Kalafat, J. (1991). Suicide intervention in schools. In A. R. Roberts (Ed.), *Contemporary perspectives on crisis intervention and prevention* (pp. 218–239). Englewood Cliffs, NJ: Prentice-Hall.

Krug, R. S., Nixon, S. J., & Vincent, R. (1996). Psychological response to the Oklahoma City bombing. *Journal of Clinical Psychology*, *52*(1), 103–105.

Lystad, M. (1985). *Innovations in mental health services to disaster victims.* Washington, DC: U.S. Government Printing Office.

Martin, D. (1997, November 16). Bomb attack's terrifying hold. *The New York Times*, p. 43.

McFarlane, A. C. (1987). Posttraumatic phenomena in a longitudinal study of children following a natural disaster. *Journal of the American Academy of Child and Adolescent Psychiatry*, *26*(5), 764–769.

McFarlane, A. C. (1990). Post traumatic stress syndrome revisited. In H. J. Parad & L. G. Parad (Eds.), *Crisis intervention book 2: The practitioner's sourcebook for brief therapy* (pp. 69–92). Milwaukee, WI: Family Service America.

Mitchell, J. T., & Everly, G. S. (1994). *Human elements training for emergency services, public safety and disaster personnel: An instructional guide to teaching debriefing, crisis intervention and stress management programs,* Ellicott City, MD: Chevron.

Mitchell, J. T., & Resnik, H. L. (1981). *Emergency response to crisis: A crisis intervention guidebook for emergency service personnel.* Ellicott City, MD: Chevron.

Monahon, C. (1993). *Children and trauma: A parent's guide for helping children heal.* New York: Lexington Books.

Nelson, E. R., & Slaikeu, K. A. (1990). Crisis intervention in the schools. In K. A. Slaikeu (Ed.), *Crisis intervention: A handbook for practice and research* (2nd ed., pp. 329–347). Needham Heights, MA: Allyn & Bacon.

Piaget, J. (1955). *The child's construction of reality.* New York: Basic Books.

Pynoos, R. S., & Eth, S. (1985). Children traumatized by witnessing acts of personal violence. In S. Eth & R. S.Pynoos (Eds.), *Post-traumatic stress disorder in children* (pp. 19–43). Washington, DC: American Psychiatric Press.

Pynoos, R. S., & Nader, K. (1989). Children's memory and proximity to violence. *Journal of the American Academy of Child and Adolescent Psychiatry, 28,* 236–241.

Shulman, N. M. (1990). Crisis intervention in a high school: Lessons from the Concord High School experiences. In A. R. Roberts (Ed.), *Crisis intervention handbook: Assessment, treatment and research* (pp. 63–77). Belmont, CA: Wadsworth.

Small miracles. (1996, April 15). *People,* pp. 46–51.

Sorenson, J. R. (1989). Responding to student or teacher death: Preparing crisis intervention. *Journal of Counseling and Development, 67,* 426–427.

Tabor, M. B. W. (1993a, March 2). Blast trauma lingers, but mostly for parents. *The New York Times,* p. A1.

Tabor, M. B. W. (1993b, June 6). Kindergarten's 111th story ends happily. *The New York Times,* p. 42.

Terr, L. (1990). *Too scared to cry: Psychic trauma in childhood.* New York: Harper & Row.

Tesoriero, A. (1993, June). Trapped in the towers. *Ladies' Home Journal,* pp. 148–151.

Webb, N. B. (1986). Before and after suicide: A preventive outreach program for colleges. *Suicide and Life-Threatening Behavior, 16*(4), 469–80.

CHAPTER 20

International Consultation and Intervention on Behalf of Children Affected by War

BRENDA WILLIAMS-GRAY

WAR AND CHILDREN

The end of the Cold War and global fears of a nuclear disaster have not resulted in a reduction of crippling landmines, ethnic genocide, nuclear development, mass destruction, and death. In fact, war-torn regions create a continuum of human casualties around the world. According to the United Nations High Commission on Refugees (UNHCR) (Berthiaume, 1994), 50% of the 20 million or more refugees and displaced people in the world are children. Unaccompanied children who have been separated from their families account for 2–5% of the children living in refugee camps because they have been displaced from their homelands. *Refugees Magazine* (UNHCR, 1998, p. 3) notes that in the last decade, 2 million children have been slaughtered and 6 million have been injured. There are no definitive statistics on the many who have been tortured, raped, and abused.

Children in war zones witness or experience violent acts that are inexplicable to adults and would be considered criminal, vile, and inhuman under peacetime conditions. They are increasingly exposed to these atrocities because the battlefields of war are in their own backyards, rural enclaves, and streets. *Refugees Magazine* (UNHCR, 1998) notes that "children in at least 68 countries live amidst the threat of 110 million landmines" (p. 3).

Compounding the distress is the fact that "enemies" can often be members of groups with whom there was a friendly, or at least stable, prewar relationship. Children in war zones must live with the ongoing stress of an unpredictable environment, where society's usual rules no longer apply. Continuous social upheaval, as well as the loss of family members and friends, increases their vulnerability to trauma.

This chapter presents a theoretical framework for practitioners consulting in parts of the international arena where the effects of war have created layers of trauma for children and their families. Understanding the variables of war trauma is essential to the assessment and deployment of mental health services that support personal safety and emotional survival. This perspective provides a direction for intervention and treatment that responds to the multiple stresses and traumatic experiences of children in war zones. As discussed in more detail below, the interplay among prewar factors—a child's psychosocial/developmental stage in particular, but also a family's functioning and a community's networks—must be determined. These factors interact with the crisis of war, the world response, and the child's perceptions and feelings, resulting in the outcomes of either trauma or healthy adaptation.

This chapter discusses the case of a displaced family from Bosnia-Herzegovina, living in a collective community (refugee camp) in Croatia during the war in the former Yugoslavia after the Serbian invasion of their community. The case illustrates the special tasks for mental health professionals when symptoms of posttraumatic stress disorder (PTSD), aggressive behavior, loss of parental control, and chronic mourning are manifested by victims of war. A strengths-based, culturally competent, total-community approach supports a range of interventions in such a situation. The chapter describes the use of short-term family and grief work, and of the concepts of trauma, adaptation, resilience, and coping to understand each child's response. Finally, selected dilemmas for the consultant, including the use of self in an international context, are presented.

THE SETTING IN CROATIA

My frame of reference for this chapter is my experience as a team member on the Children's Village initiative in Croatia during the winter of 1993. Our mission was to provide training and support to individuals working in refugee camps with traumatized children, adolescents, and families who were displaying behavior problems inconsistent with prewar norms. This work took the form of two conferences on related topics, and work on multiple levels in a refugee camp alongside volunteers and staff members from nongovernment organizations (NGOs) in a "train the trainer" approach. The executive director of Children's Village designed the project (Dale, 1993, p. 1), which included a partnership with Suncokret, a grass-roots NGO, whose mission is to "respond to the psycho-social needs of refugee children and youth" (Suncokret, 1993, p. 1). The project was contracted and funded by the UNHCR through the International Rescue Committee. I was a social worker on the team, and much of my focus was on children, women, and families at various stages of trauma and adaptation. The team's experience is in the context of New York City's child welfare system with children, adolescents, and their families who are exposed to societal and familial trauma, and present a range of behavioral and emotional problems. This proved to be relevant background for consultation regarding the trauma of war.

The political climate and living conditions in the camp where we worked created the context for this experience. A Bosnian Muslim living in a refugee camp in Croatia is a person without citizenship, and cannot legally obtain work. Croatian war victims have preferred status in refugee camps, since they are citizens and considered displaced persons. The particular camp discussed in this chapter resembled an armory. The space (equivalent to that of a classroom) housed a dozen families, whose members carefully partitioned the space with blankets and other makeshift dividers, and thus created for themselves a modicum of privacy and dignity. Visitors were always offered coffee, and it would have been an insult to decline this last vestige of social norms. Pictures and small mementos were the only other reminders of a past life. In contrast, the community bath area always had a lingering stench, and the food looked and tasted unappealing and was served in limited quantities.

The people who invited the world to celebrate their diverse community for the 1984 Olympics in Sarajevo are now split across family, community, and geographic demarcations. The resources of government have become the frightful oppressors. As in any war, the trauma of the citizenry is complicated when the providers of social control become the creators of social unrest. In addition, the practice of "ethnic cleansing" has demoralized many people still further. "Ethnic cleansing" refers to acts of violence and hate specifically employed with the rationale of eliminating the existence of a cultural subset—destroying the individual spirit and collective psyche of a whole population through physical and emotional terror. Simply put, it is genocide. "Civil war" is an oxymoron, since there is nothing "civil" about the crimes of war, where one faction exerts its power and control over another by humiliation and subjugation.

International consultation on this level requires professionals to be knowledgeable about the sociopolitical dynamics of the region where they are working, as well as about the history and customs of the people. This knowledge is essential in the negotiation of systems, because it gives workers an awareness of important boundaries and informal networks. This understanding also reduces the likelihood of insulting people through inadvertent behaviors due to cultural ignorance. Consultation in the international arena requires that a worker step beyond his or her natural comfort zone and join with the culture or environment as a participant/observer, similar to an ethnographer who becomes a part of the fabric of the community.

THEORETICAL FRAMEWORK

Psychosocial and Developmental Factors

Figure 20.1 builds on Macksound, Aber, and Cohn's (1994) schema and on Webb's (1996) tripartite assessment of children in crisis (see also Webb, Chapter 1, this volume). In this perspective, the children's prewar status interacts with the crisis of war, leading to either traumatic or healthy adaptive outcomes. The extent to which pre-existing factors have been within culturally healthy norms prior to the crisis of war increases the likelihood of healthy outcomes in the face of traumatic events. This is not to suggest that *all* children with healthy temperaments and developmental successes, and with normative family and community experiences, will escape traumatic responses to war. It does suggest that some children may have inherent resilience, which enables them to frame the experience in a manner that enables adaptive coping.

Age and level of cognitive development influence a child's perception of war, consistent with Webb (1996 and Chapter 1, this volume). Macksound et al. (1994) emphasize that "the relationship between war-related stress and trauma and subsequent child outcomes may be mediated by powerful developmental process within the child" (p. 220). Early bonding with parents that establishes trust, predictability, and security often translates into healthy resolution of normative developmental tasks and adaptive responses to difficult life stressors. Macksound et al. (1994) further suggest that

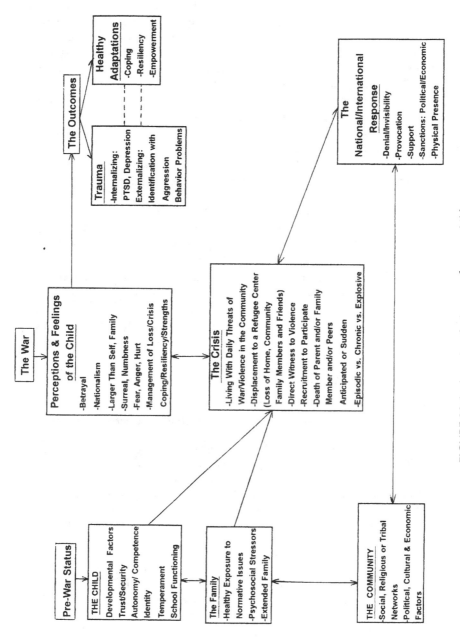

FIGURE 20.1. Assessing the impact of war on children.

young children who are able to remain with their caretakers during the war, and who have had a healthy prewar parental bond, are less likely to have negative symptomatology than are children who lose caregivers during the war and who have not had secure attachments prior to the war. The tasks of school-age children include developing a sense of autonomy and competence. Consistent with their strengths-based perspective, Macksound et al. (1994) indicate that those who believe they can cope well during high-stress periods generally do cope better than those without this orientation. Webb (1996 and Chapter 1, this volume) notes that latency-age children may view war in rigid terms of right and wrong, enemy and hero. Their play may reflect an enjoyment of "conquering" an enemy and bring them some sense of mastery and control. Concurrently, they are beginning to understand "fear of the unseen danger," and this may increase their overall sense of anxiety.

In assessing the impact of war on adolescents, Macksound et al. (1994) urge researchers to explore further "the meaning the [adolescents derive] from their role in the conflict. Their ability to project a meaningful future for themselves is powerfully and intimately tied to their role in the conflict" (p. 221). They suggest that the identity formation process (the developmental task for this group) offers an opportunity to link values and reasoning skills in such a manner as to mediate between the war experience and outcomes. Herman (1992) points out that the three normative tasks of adolescence—identity formation, gradual independence from the family, and launching into the broader world—are compromised by the "experience of terror and disempowerment" typical of war. Combat and crimes of war such as rape often occur at this stage, when "the greatest psychological vulnerability is also the period of greatest traumatic exposure" (Herman, 1992, p. 61).

The Crisis of War: Stress and Trauma

Kahana, Kahana, Harel, and Rosner (1988) identify five environmental elements present in human-made traumatic conditions that constitute extreme stress:

1. Total life experience is disrupted. These conditions replace the fabric of normal life with a surreal existence, unanchored in familiar elements of reality.
2. The new environment is hostile, threatening and dangerous.
3. Opportunities to remove or act upon the stressor environment are severely limited.
4. There is no predictable end to the experience.
5. The pain and suffering associated with the experience appear to be meaningless and without rational explanation. (p. 59)

Certainly, the crisis of war constitutes extreme stress. Nothing that was assumed in prewar circumstances can be assured during the war. Being in "limbo" and experiencing losses—of normality, values, work, power, routine, and family—create a situation that interferes with the human need for a predictable environment and equilibrium. Efforts to cope and survive, according to Kahana et al. (1988), include "changing the situation; changing the meaning of the situation or 'cognitive restructuring'; or controlling the negative impact of the situation" (p. 67). When stress exceeds one's normative coping capacity, a crisis occurs. The way one adapts in service of the ego can be "functional" to the situation, but it may be maladaptive as an internalized personality adjustment. "Emotional numbing, depersonalization, denial or isolation of affect" (p. 67) permits control of one's emotional response to overwhelming stimuli. Kohen (1988) notes that families may develop new beliefs because "the impact of traumatic loss through terrorism is so devastating that it destroys certain previous paradigms" (p. 365).

The pull of psychic energy is to respond to the traumatic events of war by dealing with the practical needs associated with physical survival. Consequently, normative roles such as parenting may become secondary to survival concerns for some. When adults cannot be caregivers because they are preoccupied, missing, dead, captured, or in combat, then children must make sense of the senseless without the protection or safety net of caring adults. This is illustrated in the case discussion later in this chapter. The aforementioned losses for adults become magnified for children, who depend on adults to keep their world safe and predictable.

Figure 20.1 describes a range of conditions experienced in war zones that challenge normative coping strategies and can contribute to the severity of trauma.

OUTCOMES OF WAR: TRAUMA

Graziano (1997, p. 381) examines two definitions of trauma: Figley's (1985) emphasis on the "stress resulting from the memories of extraordinary, catastrophic experience which shatters the victim's sense of vulnerability to harm," and Meichenbaum's (1994) emphasis on the exceptional effort needed to cope with the events.

Frey-Wouters (1997), a United Nations representative, provides a telling example of catastrophic experience: "There is no way to measure the impact on a child who sees her family killed or to quantify the emotional and psychological toll on children who live for years in fear of bombings, mutilation or death. Many of today's conflicts last the length of a childhood, so that from birth to early adulthood, children experience multiple and accumulative assaults" (p. 1). Frey-Wouters further describes the deep and profound impact on a child's development when primary relationships and social networks are disrupted.

The possible effects of war for children encompass a wide spectrum of behavioral and emotional outcomes or coping strategies. Consistent with Figure 20.1, the child's prewar functioning, severity of the war experience, and perception of the war are interrelated elements that influence the child's response to these traumatic events. For many children, a natural response to stress is "fight or flight." Fight is generally manifested in aggressive behaviors. This externalizing response models adults' violence and efforts to achieve power through physical aggression during war. Identification with the aggressor can be a means of survival. Flight is usually the separation of oneself from the cause of stress, generally by running away—either literally or emotionally (through dissociation).

Definitions of PTSD recognize that extreme and powerful circumstances external to the self can overload a person's psychic and coping capacity. Symptoms include hyperarousal; reexperiencing (e.g., intrusive flashbacks and nightmares);

and avoidance and numbing (American Psychiatric Association, 1994; Herman, 1992). In children, according to Rapport and Ismond (1990), "loss of recently acquired developmental skills . . . may be equivalent to the adult symptom of numbing" (p. 131). They also note that "repetitive play in young children in which themes or aspects of the trauma are considered in experiencing the traumatic event" (p. 131) must be considered in assessing children who may qualify for a diagnosis of PTSD. Terr (1983) defines "posttraumatic play" as "play observed in children who have undergone a psychic trauma" (p. 308). She defines 10 characteristics of posttraumatic play:

- Compulsive repetition
- Unconscious link between play and the traumatic event
- Literalness of play, with simple defenses only
- Failure to relieve anxiety
- Wide age range
- Varying lag time prior to its development
- Carrying power to nontraumatized children
- Contagion to new generations of children
- Danger
- Use of doodling, talking, typing, and audio duplication as modes of repeated play

Terr's list is noteworthy, since PTSD is often overlooked in children and consequently is not treated effectively. Sadness, depression, and anxiety are outcomes of trauma and grief that may be anticipated, given the losses a child may have experienced because of war. They may however, mask or be the only visible signs of the traumatic experience, and other symptoms may go unrecognized. Mental health professionals must ask questions that will help children identify symptoms associated with PTSD. Male adolescents who engage in criminal activity should be assessed for the possibility of trauma and PTSD symptoms. Often conduct disorder, attention-deficit/hyperactivity disorder, and substance abuse are noted, but not in the context of trauma. This becomes relevant in working with adolescents and young adults in refugee camps, who may act out aggressively or dull their pain.

Recovery from trauma begins with safety; it is the prerequisite to other interventions, as it helps the victim regain control (Herman, 1992).

OUTCOMES OF WAR:
ADAPTATION, RESILIENCY, AND COPING

"Resiliency," according to Masten, Best, and Garmezy (1990), is "the process of, capacity for, or outcome of successful adaptation despite challenging or threatening circumstances" (p. 426). They view resiliency–stress phenomena from three perspectives: "good outcomes despite high-risk status; sustained competence under threat;

and recovery from trauma" (p. 426). The circumstances of war create many conditions that challenge a child's capacity to cope and adapt across the continuum of the three outcomes noted above.

The literature on internal attributes and social supports that contribute to resiliency, or resilience, in children facing traumatic life conditions suggests a variety of protective factors consistent with a strengths-based perspective. Werner (1992) and Masten et al. (1990) point to self-esteem, self-efficacy, temperament, humor, and internal locus of control as protective factors promoting resiliency. To this list I add hope, proactivity, and energy (Williams-Gray, 1998). The relationship of resilience and coping is reflected as a theme in each segment of Figure 20.1: the prewar child, the perceptions and feelings of the child about the war, and outcomes for healthy coping. Macksound et al. (1994) suggest that developmental processes within the child prior to the crisis of war can create or suggest outcomes of adaptability. Many of the youngsters in the refugee camp in Croatia appeared to have "had well developed personalities and healthy self esteem. They saw their country as damaged, not themselves. They did not feel unloved or unlovable, just unlucky" (Dale, 1994).

Beardslee (1989) emphasizes that children who can separate themselves from difficulties experienced and caused by the adults in their world are able to place themselves at some distance from this stress, and thus to create "space" for themselves that helps them cope. In addition to "adaptive distancing," Beardslee notes that the influence of a healthy parental tie to at least one parent or caretaker, as well as positive experiences in school, social, or recreational activities, can increase resilience in children who are exposed to untenable life circumstances.

Herman (1992) points to "high sociability, a thoughtful and active coping style, and a strong perception of their ability to control their destiny" (p. 58) as indicators for resilience. Regaining a sense of self-confidence and autonomy is a difficult task for children in the face of war. The process starts with the establishment of an environment that has some predictability and safety, and continues with telling the story—that is, remembrance and mourning (Herman, 1992). For children, this process can take many forms. Play therapy, as discussed later in this chapter, is an avenue for children to tell their story in their own language and to gain mastery in their world. Fostering resilience and adaptive coping requires a complex interplay of the child's sense of self, place in the world, skills, relatedness to others, and social supports. A sense of optimism and flexibility to adapt in difficult circumstances are characteristics of many resilient children.

THE CASE: THE ZELTA FAMILY

Family Information

Mrs. Zelta	Age mid-40s; widow
Dana	Age 12; girl; the "symptom bearer" (child with the presenting problem)
Cinta	Age 10; girl; clingy, needy, and looking for attention and affection

| Milo | Age 8; boy; seemingly unaffected by the traumatic situation that brought him to the refugee camp |
| Two older brothers | Age early 20s; missing from the family and believed to be in "concentration camps" in the interior of Bosnia-Herzegovina |

The Zelta family resided in a refugee camp in a small town not far from Zagreb, the capital of Croatia. They were originally from a rural town in Bosnia and began the cycle of movement to refugee camps when they were forced to leave their homeland in 1991. Mr. Zelta died of natural causes approximately 5 years before the war began. Consequently, the two older brothers took over the disciplining of the younger siblings, as was consistent with the culture of rural Muslim Bosnian families. When the Serbian invaders came to the town, all able-bodied men were taken as prisoners, and all Muslim families were required to leave the village.

Presenting Problem

Dana was known through the camp as a problem to both youngsters and adults. She was physically and verbally aggressive, picking on smaller children and provocative to adults. She was noncompliant with rules and disruptive in camp activities. She was always the first youngster spoken about as "troublesome" by staff members and volunteers working within the camp.

In addition, Mrs. Zelta was viewed by the camp staff and volunteers as punitive in her efforts to discipline Dana. She was embarrassed by her daughter's behavior and would try to hit her to stop her from breaking the rules and being aggressive. It was thought that this was her way of showing camp personnel that she was trying to discipline her children. However, the messages that she gave her children were inconsistent, because her parenting role was secondary to mere survival. Furthermore, discipline was not traditionally the mother's role in the family. Her overwhelming despair regarding the plight of her two oldest sons made it difficult for her to focus on the present and attend to the needs of her three younger children. The fact that her children had not been in school for 2 years was unimportant to Mrs. Zelta. She did not encourage them to attend the school at the refugee camp and thought she would deal with this when she returned home. Mrs. Zelta viewed the refugee camp as a place where she could feel temporarily safe. Her overriding attitude was disgust with the circumstances of war, which had robbed her of her home, her country, and— most importantly—her two eldest sons. She did not view life in the camp as a part of their reality; time for her was at a standstill.

Prior to my first meeting with the whole family, I had become familiar with both Dana and Cinta through community-based activities in the refugee camp. The girls now brought Doko, the social worker/translator, and me to their assigned space within the refugee center. We left our boots at the front door, in respect for Bosnian Muslim customs, and entered the curtained-off area assigned to the Zelta family. Mrs. Zelta, moving quickly, graciously offered us coffee and invited us to sit on her makeshift bed. Doko introduced me to her and explained my affiliation with the camp and my role in helping families to deal with their current circumstances.

First Interview

The content of this session is reported from memory, since none of the sessions were tape-recorded.

Content of Session	Rationale/Analysis

MRS. ZELTA: I know my girls are in trouble all the time.

SOCIAL WORKER: It certainly must be hard for them to be here.

MRS. Z: It's very hard for all of us, not knowing when will we be able to go home or what will happen next.

SW: How did you come to this camp?

CINTA: This is our second camp. They moved us to the first one after everybody left our town when they took my brothers.

MRS. Z: I try to get them to stop thinking about their brothers. It's enough that I worry about them.

Her efforts to protect her children cause them even greater pain.

DANA: You can't make us stop thinking about them. They're our brothers too. We miss them.

SW: It must be hard for each of you, missing your sons (*looking at Mrs. Zelta*) and your brothers (*looking at Dana and Cinta*).

MRS. Z: I am so nervous and worried about where they are. When I think the kids are sleeping, around two or three in the morning, I stand at the door with my radio and I listen for any information about what happened to them, wondering if they have been moved. I know that they are in one of two camps. I worry and hope that they are not in Camp X. That's the worse one. Everybody knows that the men are beaten in that camp. (*Her hands are shaking, and tears are coming to her eyes.*)

Her grief is enormous, and she is carrying it alone.

Concentration camps in the 1990s—didn't we learn anything from World War II?

SW: (*Offers Mrs. Zelta a tissue. She nods a silent "thank you."*)

C: We know you wake up, and you can't stop us from worrying about them too, even though you hide the pictures.

D: She thinks if we don't look at the pictures we won't think of them, but we take the pictures out when she's not looking.

They are angry at Mrs. Zelta. They are seeing her effort to protect them as a denial of their right to worry and grieve.

SW: Mrs. Zelta, you're working so hard to protect the girls, and maybe one way to protect them would be to let them talk about their worries too.

It's hard to expect them not to think about their brothers, who they love very much.

MRS. Z: (*Sighs.*) Their brothers are the only ones they listen to. That's why they're having so much difficulty here. Their brothers were in charge. They set the rules. Without their brothers, I cannot control them.

How can she be empowered to set limits with them when she doesn't view this as her role?

D: We're worried about them too. We miss them. I don't want to listen to anybody else.

MRS. Z: They've been in charge ever since my husband died 5 years ago.

SW: Maybe it would help if each of you can talk about your sons (*looking at Mrs. Zelta*) and share the worrying (*looking at Dana*), and maybe that would help you think about how you could think of the things they would tell you to manage yourself while you're here without them.

Maybe they can join together around their mutual loss and fears.

C: I'll tell you how it happened. (*Mrs. Zelta stops her anxious moving around and sits for the first time.*) We were at home, and we heard they were going to come, but no one knew *when* they were coming. They came, and they started knocking on doors. We tried to hide my brothers because we heard that they would take the men. They came through the house; they were mean to us. They found my brothers and tried to take them away. We all started crying—Mother, Dana, me, and Milo—but my brothers did not. I put my arms around one of their legs. I begged the soldiers, "Please leave them. Don't take my brothers." They tried to pull me away, and I held on as tight as I could. I still see this in my dreams at night.

She is so brave! What a tragic memory!

MRS. Z: Yes, she did. She held on very tight. She was crying, telling them to leave her brothers.

D: (*Reaches under a pillow and pulls out two pictures.*) These are our brothers.

SW: (*Looks at Dana and then at the translator, asking him to ask Mrs. Zelta whether it is OK for me to look at the pictures.*)

I want to respect her position as the mother.

MRS. Z: (*Gives translator a half smile and nods.*)

SW: Cinta, tell me a little about each of your brothers.

C: (*Describes what the brothers are like, and emphasizes her love for them.*)

SW: (*Smiles at Cinta.*) You are very brave. Your brothers must know how much you love them. (*Then looks at Mrs. Zelta.*) Sometimes having the pictures where everyone can see them can help all of you not feel like you must hide your sadness.

MRS. Z: (*Takes the pictures and looks at them.*) Maybe. She is not convinced, but at least she has heard the girls' need to keep their brothers visible.

Case Formulation

The separation anxiety and grief associated with mourning those "missing in action" were the underlying issues affecting the Zelta family. The family dynamics centering around the stress and crisis of both the war and their refugee status created a collective family response, as well as individual responses. Mrs. Zelta displayed some posttraumatic stress symptomatology. She described her efforts to protect her younger children from the grief of the loss of their brothers' absence by staying awake at two or three in the morning listening to a short-wave radio in the hope of hearing something about their status without disturbing the children. Cinta described her repeated nightmares and flashbacks about begging the soldiers not to take her brothers. Dana was responding in behaviorally inappropriate ways. The lack of rules in the greater society and in her family had given her the message that there were no controls and that her aggressive behavior could go unmanaged by the adults in her new community.

Goals

This session was followed by four other sessions, with the eventual aim of transferring the interventions to the personnel within the camp, who would be able to continue the family trauma work. The goals for the family as a whole and for individual members were as follows:

Family

1. To enable all members to recognize their joint grief about the missing sons/brothers, and to use this shared experience to provide comfort and support to each other.
2. To help them to use the temporary safety of the current environment for "emotional refueling."

Mrs. Zelta

1. To help her recognize her children's experiences, so that she could provide some support to them.
2. To support and validate her efforts to be a good mother, despite the absence of the older male family members.

Dana

1. To help her replace aggressive, maladaptive behaviors with appropriate responses to stress and the community.
2. To enable her to honor her brothers' memory by behaving in a manner they would want for her.
3. To assist her in rechanneling her energies into positive experiences, in order to enhance her self-esteem and her sense of control.

There were a number of other possible goals that, while germane to this family's circumstances, were not appropriate in this context or time frame. An example was assisting Mrs. Zelta in reducing her symptoms of posttraumatic stress, particularly her hypervigilance. Long-term issues could not be appropriately managed within our project's time frame. It would be inappropriate to begin a process and then leave the family members while they were in the middle stages of treatment. In addition, safety is a prerequisite for working with traumatized people, as noted earlier. Learning how to use the opportunities in this new environment would provide Mrs. Zelta and her children with the stability to work on other issues. This was a key goal in our work.

The Impact of the Culture

The role of women in mainstream Western culture is very different from that in the Bosnian Muslim world. It would have been inappropriate for us to attempt to empower Mrs. Zelta to take a role that was not part of her life experience (i.e., disciplining her children). Although some could argue that the current situation required adaptability, it was the team's opinion that the cultural context required respect and sensitivity. We believed that other venues within the camp community could support Mrs. Zelta in parenting her children. It seemed important to balance her desire to have her children behave safely, without overwhelming her by placing her in the role of the primary disciplinarian.

The Role of the Translator

I was fortunate to have a translator who was a master's-level social worker from Croatia. His role as a volunteer in the camp gave me credibility with the families, since he brought me to them. In addition, our team's work was sanctioned by the volunteers and the staff of the camp. Visible community-based successes in other aspects of the team's work supplied the credibility needed for families to allow me to join them in interventions centering around their experience.

Interventions

The context of this work was predicated on the use of the entire refugee community as a temporary safe haven, where children and adults could become more confident about making some decisions in their daily lives. The theoretical philosophy of this project was that creating safety would require consistent routines and opportunities for victims to regain control and become empowered in their day-to-day activities. This would begin the process of empowerment, mastery, and control over the traumatic circumstances created by the war. This project initiated the following programs to support the ideal of creating a safer community:

- Consultation
- Conflict management
- Community empowerment
- Group work
- Family "home" visits
- Activity groups
- Play therapy

Consultation

The "train the trainer" model resulted in a pairing of project team members with camp staff and volunteers, so that interventions could be discussed, modeled, and processed. This was the key premise of consultation in this context. The strength of this design was that camp personnel could continue the interventions beyond the duration of the project, integrating both the premise and interventions into the mainstream of future camp activity. This required the key service providers on the team and in the camp to make a collaborative assessment of needs, in order to ensure a program-to-environment fit.

Consultation occurred on multiple levels—administrative, program, and direct service. Respecting the leadership and long-term tenure of indigenous staff members and volunteer organizations is essential for consultants in the international arena. The model employed here consists of preplanning, processing, and ongoing evaluation. Team diversity necessitates trust, which develops best when members have the opportunity to train with each other prior to the initiation of the project. Openness to differing perspectives and flexibility are important skills in international crisis endeavors.

Conflict Management

A community terrorized by war inadvertently teaches adolescents conflicting messages about violence and power. Work with teenagers and young adults on alternatives to violence was introduced through a group process. Participants were able to process their responses to the terror of war, and to look at the power of nonviolent conflict resolution. Conflict management group meetings were held twice a week for approximately 2 hours each. Exercises and activities were designed to foster communication, teamwork, and problem solving.

Community Empowerment

Herman (1992) describes the first stage of posttraumatic stress recovery as safety. The adolescents and young adults wanted their own space within the camp, which would symbolically meet their safety needs. They initiated a project with the support of the whole refugee camp community and built a teen center.

Group Work

Herman's (1992) second stage—that of reconstructing, remembrance, and mourning—is similar to grief work and encourages survivors to tell the story of their trauma. The team utilized the women's interest and skill in knitting to develop an informal women's support group, which combined knitting and storytelling. As the women knitted colorful yarn into sweaters, they shared their stories and threaded their common grief into a network of camaraderie and support. Mrs. Zelta was encouraged to use this opportunity to reduce her isolation; however, she was not yet ready to join with others, since she still struggled with her safety concerns.

Family "Home" Visits

Short-term family work closely resembled "in-home" visits. It was critical that a consultant quickly assess each family's stage in the crisis continuum, so that interventions could be strategic and focused. A similar conceptualization of recovery is described by Johnson (1989). "The reconstructing necessary to accommodate the changes brought about by a crisis" (Johnson, 1989, p. 123) often occurs in three stages:

- Recoiling—family members are "allying themselves to meet the threat."
- Reorganization—previous patterns and roles "reassert themselves"; however, because of the crisis, this may lead to "polarization, differentiation and fragmentation," leaving family members isolated.
- Restabilization—the family dynamics settle, and while stability may occur, "levels of intimacy, affection, communication and trust" may have deteriorated or increased (all quotes are from Johnson, 1989, pp. 123–124).

At the time of the first session, the Zelta family was in the reorganization phase. Mrs. Zelta's traumatic distraction made it difficult for the family to coalesce; the fragmentation experienced by the children became manifested in Cinta's neediness and Dana's aggressive acting out.

Activity Groups

Activity groups created an opportunity for the children to have a developmentally normative routine. Dana volunteered to be an assistant for the kindergarten group. She became frustrated easily, however; she began hitting the children and was unable to accept adult boundaries. When she was not allowed to participate further, she continued to disrupt the children's activities by banging on the windows and doors. The team recontracted with her, establishing very clear boundaries and consequences. She proved to be a talented guitar player, and this delighted the younger children. When she found her niche, she was able to enjoy the positive feedback. Her growl was replaced more frequently with a smile. She became less pestering and took a more active role in working with the children.

Play Therapy

Art, puppetry, and drama are particularly useful with latency-age youngsters affected by the crisis of war. They can act out their worries and express their fears and feelings in ways that are developmentally in tune with their ego development. The use of puppets can serve as an appropriate release for aggression and tension, while allowing the children to control the situation (Webb, 1996). Artwork can be similarly helpful. Figure 20.2 is a poignant drawing by a child who portrayed the destruction of a community through flames and gunfire as if the destroyed fragments were falling through the narrow stem of an hourglass.

CONSIDERATIONS FOR CONSULTANTS IN THE INTERNATIONAL ARENA

Mental health consultants face several challenges that require careful thought and preparation when working with war victims, particularly children, within an international context. This preparation takes the form of knowledge about the community, about war safety, and about trauma and its effect on children.

An awareness of broad cultural parameters and subtle nuances of intergroup relationships aids in understanding when one is in unfamiliar territory. Prior to international consultation, the professional should learn about the area through academic or lay literature, public or private organizations with interests in the area, or other sources knowledgeable about the region's prewar history and the current political dynamics. Although proficiency in language is always an advantage, it is possible to work effectively with an interpreter, especially when the contact person is familiar with the language and culture and is affiliated with a respected group.

Without prior exposure to war zones, consultants may have been influenced by the mass media's representations or the retelling of the experiences of others. A seemingly quiet meadow or busy city street can be a haven for snipers. A deserted town whose buildings are defaced or destroyed by weaponry may be near a United Nations peacekeeping unit. A city whose population seems oblivious to the threat of gunfire may be 30 miles away from "the line." A lack of visible signs of war activity does not mean that real danger is not present. Consultants should be affiliated with, or under the auspices of, an organization that sanctions workers' presence, monitors their whereabouts, and provides them with information on high-risk zones and safety precautions. Consultants must avoid misplaced zeal. A worker's "professional adven-

FIGURE 20.2. A drawing by a child in a refugee camp. From Dale (1993). Reprinted by permission.

ture" is a cruel reality to children and families who cannot walk away to a safe haven when the consultant returns home.

The work with survivors of trauma depends on the therapeutic alliance, as trust and safety are paramount. Consultants who are only availabale for a short time should be sensitive to the onslaught of helpers, the mass media, and other representatives of the international community who appear and disappear, leaving the families to repeat reenactments of their multiple loss experiences. In an environment with chaos or unpredictability, it is imperative that workers commit themselves only to intervening in those matters that they can control, or they risk becoming like the other adults in the world community who are not to be believed. Focused interventions must take account of time constraints and prioritize goals accordingly. This often requires that a consultant utilize a crisis intervention model of assessment to determine a child's and family's location on the stress–recovery spectrum. This will assist the consultant in setting realistic and appropriate goals. Herman (1992) reminds practitioners that "trauma robs the victim of a sense of power and control; [therefore,] the guiding principle of recovery is to restore power and control to the survivor" (p. 159). It is difficult to create physical and emotional safety for children who are without answers about their home and loved ones. The crisis of war often moves from an acute stage to a prolonged, chronic stage of limbo. The consultant should not rush. Reframing children's powerlessness into a sense of control and mastery in their "temporary" environment becomes the first critical goal.

Finally, consultants must be comfortable in their use of self and have proficiency in the treatment of trauma. Graziano (1997) notes that the trauma framework is different from more traditional psychodynamic approaches, and that "if the worker is not cognizant of the theories underlying the concept of traumatic stress and not alert to the various working and manifestations of trauma . . . the work can become bewildering and frustrating" (p. 399). Secondary traumatization, according to Figley (1989), can occur when the helper experiences the traumatic stress indirectly through the helping relationship with the family. Whereas empathetic joining is good practice, total absorption into the family system can create role confusion and burnout.

ADVOCACY AND THE WORLD RESPONSE DURING AN INTERNATIONAL CRISIS

Mental health consultants have the opportunity and responsibility to improve the care of children in war zones through means beyond direct intervention. Advocacy is a value of the social work profession. Graziano (1997) reminds us that "bearing witness" to the trauma inflicted by society is a collective responsibility. Political action and voting, as well as writing about and listening to the subjugated knowledge of children in war zones—all this makes their invisibility dissipate, and keeps the reality of their pain a universal priority.

When the world community openly responds, whether with military presence, humanitarian relief, or sanctions, it alerts the victims that they are not ignored. The activity of the world may create difficulties for children and families, since actions seen as provocative may escalate combat or diminish access to scarce resources. The world response may even be equated with war. However, a lack of response or an ambivalent response sends the message of isolation, invisibility, and worthlessness to the victims of war. The world community, through public acknowledgment, support, and rituals, has a role in the reparative experience for the victims of this community. For children, it is a matter of death by degree if individuals and societies passively allow them to become invisible through denial or inactivity.

Grace Machel, in a 1996 report to the United Nations General Assembly entitled *The Impact of Armed Conflict on Children*, noted a frightening mentality toward children in armed conflict situations: "Killing a child today is killing the enemy of tomorrow" (quoted in UNHCR, 1997, p. 1). This chilling mentality makes passivity a crime against humanity and against the innocence of childhood!

STUDY QUESTIONS

1. Discuss the necessary steps for international consultation. What special training, within what time frame, should be considered to prepare for this work?

2. Consider the stresses for the members of a consulting team working in a war zone. Discuss some strategies that they can implement to avoid secondary traumatization.

3. How can therapists assist children and teens with the process of mourning family members who are "missing in action"? What play methods may be appropriate?

4. Critique the consultant's decision not to deal directly with Mrs. Zelta's inability to set appropriate limits with Dana. Give reasons for your response.

ACKNOWLEDGMENTS

To all children and families victimized by war, I wish peace, safety, support, and strength. I would also like to express my gratitude to Nan Dale, Markham Breen, Norma Vega, Sharlene Bass, Dottie Nelson, Norma Moore, and Keidron Gray for their technical assistance and support in the preparation of this chapter.

REFERENCES

American Psychiatric Association. (1994). *Diagnostic and statistical manual of mental disorders* (4th ed.). Washington, DC: Author.

Beardslee, W. R. (1989). The role of self. *American Journal of Orthopsychiatry, 59*(2), 266–277.

Berthiaume, C. (1994). *Children and families, alone in the world* (UNHRC Publication No. 95). Geneva: United Nations High Commission on Refugees.

Dale, N. (1993). *The Children's Village project in Croatia.* Dobbs Ferry, NY: Children's Village.

Dale, N. (1994, January 16). Croatia's casualties, Bosnia's—and ours [Letter]. *The New York Times.*

Figley, C. R. (Ed.). (1985). *Trauma and its wake: The study and treatment of post-traumatic stress disorder.* New York: Brunner/Mazel.

Figley, C. R. (1989). *Treating stress in families.* New York: Brunner/Mazel.

Frey-Wouters, E. (1997). Armed conflict's impact on children: A UN report. *Traumatic Stress Points, 11*(1), 1,8–9.

Garbarino, J. (1993). Challenges we face in understanding children and war: A personal essay. *Child Abuse and Neglect, 17*(6), 785–853.

Graziano, R. (1997). The challenge of clinical work with survivors of trauma. In R. Jerrold (Ed.), *Clinical social work* (pp. 380–403). New York: Free Press.

Herman, J. (1992). *Trauma and recovery.* New York: Basic Books.

Johnson, K. (1989). *Trauma in the lives of children: Crisis and stress management techniques for counselors and other professionals.* Alameda, CA: Hunter House.

Kahana, E., Kahana, B., Harel, Z., & Rosner, T. (1988). Coping with extreme stress. In J. P. Wilson & B. Kahana (Eds.), *Human adaptation to extreme stress from the Holocaust to Vietnam* (pp. 55–76). New York: Plenum Press.

Kohen, C. (1988). Political traumas, oppression, and rituals. In E. Imber-Black, J. Roberts, & R. Whiting (Eds.), *Rituals in families and family therapy* (pp. 363–383). New York: Norton.

Macksound, M., Aber, L., & Cohen, I. (1994). Assessing the impact of war on children. In R. J. Apfel & B. Simon (Eds.), *The mental health of children in war and community violence* (pp. 218–227). New Haven, CT: Yale University Press.

Marmar, C. R., & Horowitz, M. J. (1988). Diagnosis and phase-oriented treatment of post-traumatic stress disorder. In J. P. Wilson & B. Kahana (Eds.), *Human adaptation to extreme stress from the Holocaust to Vietnam* (pp. 81–100). New York: Plenum Press.

Masten, A., Best, K., & Garmezy, N. (1990). Resilience and development: Contributions from the study of children who overcome adversity. *Development and psychopathology, 2,* 425–444.

Meichenbaum, D. (1994). *A clinical handbook/practical therapist manual for assessing and treating adults with post-traumatic stress disorder (PTSD).* Waterloo, Ontario, Canada: Institute Press.

Rapport, J., & Ismond, D. (1990). *DSM-III-R training guide for diagnosis of childhood disorders.* New York: Brunner/Mazel.

Suncokret. (1993, May 15). *Centre for grassroots relief work.* Zagreb, Croatia: Author.

Terr, L. (1983). Play therapy and psychic trauma: A preliminary report. In C. Schaefer & K. O'Connor (Eds.), *Handbook of play therapy* (pp. 308–319). New York: Wiley.

United Nations High Commission on Refugees (UNHCR). (1997, Winter). Crisis in the Great Lakes: Deliberately targeting the young. *Refugees Magazine,* Issue 110.

United Nations High Commission on Refugees (UNHCR). (1998, Spring). Universal Declaration of Human Rights 50th anniversary. *Refugees Magazine,* Issue 111.

Webb, N. B. (1996). *Social work practice with children.* New York: Guilford Press.

Werner, E. (1992). The children of Kauai: Resiliency and recovery in adolescence and adulthood. *Journal of Adolescent Health, 13,* 262–268.

Williams, M. B. (1996). Visiting Slovenian refugee camps: A lesson in courage. *Traumatic Stress Points, 10*(3), 1–11.

Williams-Gray, B. (1998). *Protective factors and resiliency.* Unpublished manuscript.

PART VI

Support for Therapists

CHAPTER 21

Self-Help for the Helpers
Preventing Vicarious Traumatization

KATHERINE RYAN

Most of us have chosen to become psychotherapists because we enjoy being with other people and extending ourselves to others in a caring and thoughtful way. We dislike seeing others in psychological pain, and we would like to be of some help in alleviating it. Most of us pride ourselves on our ability to be empathic and compassionate toward others. Although there are many similarities among us in our motivations to become therapists, a myriad of reasons and feelings associated with our own histories and our sense of ourselves underlies our choice of profession. The decision to work with children adds yet another dimension to therapeutic work. As we progress through school and establish ourselves as therapists, we deepen our appreciation of the complexity of helping others. While many people knock on our therapeutic doors, the process of inviting them in and engaging them in a healing relationship sometimes challenges our definition of our therapeutic selves. We like to think of ourselves as warm, caring, compassionate, and concerned. Children and families who have endured multiple life crises, however, often evoke very mixed reactions and feelings in us as therapists. Our personalities and our stages of personal and professional identity can interact with the specific features of each trauma case, resulting in a strong impact on our sense of ourselves. Often our professional identity becomes challenged when working with severely traumatized children, and this process may occur subtly and outside our awareness.

This chapter is about how to care for ourselves as therapists when working with severely traumatized children. In order to do that, we must understand some of the complex issues that arise in the treatment of these cases. The basic premise of this chapter is that by identifying sensitive personal issues we can understand ourselves better, and therefore can act in important self-protective ways that preserve our professional identities and enhance our work as therapists.

REACTIONS TO TRAUMA

Victims of crime challenge people's basic belief that "the world is a fair place where bad things do not happen to good people" (Davis & Friedman, 1985, p. 106). After a crime, people around the victim frequently experience a heightened fear of crime and heightened emotional suffering (Knudten, Meade, et al., 1976, cited in Davis

& Friedman, 1985). In addition, increased fear and precautions are more common among those who feel close to victims, individuals who discuss problems with the victim, and blood relatives of the victim. Previously victimized people are particularly sensitive to crime. Interestingly, despite these negative effects, most people do not regret involvement with the victim or wish that the victim had gone elsewhere for help (Davis & Friedman, 1985).

Focusing on emergency helpers, Dyregrov and Mitchell (1992) found their typical reactions to include the following: helplessness, fear, and anxiety (especially associated with a shift in their own sense of vulnerability and security regarding children); increased existential insecurity (related to life's meaninglessness and unfairness, and reduced trust that the world is a just and orderly place); rage toward the perpetrators; increased irritability toward others; feelings of sorrow and grief (especially in a long, caring relationship); the occurrence of intrusive images; and feelings of self-reproach, shame, and guilt. Also, helpers reported shifts in values toward a greater sense of appreciation and care for their loved ones and more awe at people's strengths. The coping strategies of these workers included emotional distancing and focusing their attention on the helping activity or task at hand.

PSYCHOTHERAPISTS' REACTIONS TO TRAUMA VICTIMS

The concepts discussed in this chapter are based on two basic psychodynamic processes, "transference" and "countertransference." These concepts are integral to the therapy of survivors of chronic interpersonal trauma, because the victims have experienced such convoluted past relationships that even a seemingly straightforward helping relationship will evoke complex dynamics. A therapist who is not sensitive to, knowledgeable about, and accepting of transference and countertransference processes can fail at the therapeutic task and even retraumatize a client.

"Transference" has been defined by seminal authors such as Freud (1905/1953) and Racker (1957) as "the unconscious repetition in a current relationship of patterns of thoughts, feelings, beliefs, expectations, and responses that originated in important early relationships" (Pearlman & Saakvitne, 1995, p. 100). "Countertransference" has been defined as "the affective, somatic, cognitive and interpersonal reactions (including defensive) of the *therapist* toward the client's story and behaviors" (Wilson & Lindy, 1994, p. 27; emphasis added).

As Pearlman and Saakvitne note, "the [trauma] survivor's experience of betrayal, fear, excitement, violation, specialness, and abandonment can be expected to be reenacted in the therapeutic relationship . . . [and] . . . are the locus of the therapeutic work, [although] difficult for the therapist" (1995, p. 99). A critical part of the therapeutic work is holding the client through these transference storms and working through the effect of these intense feelings on the therapeutic relationship. It is the relationship that heals the trauma victim, giving him or her hope that future relationships with people may be safe and even growth-promoting.

Many authors note a particular set of psychological reactions in psychotherapists who work with trauma victims (Chu, 1988; Marvasti, 1992; McCann & Pearlman,

1990; Nader, 1994; Pearlman & Saakvitne, 1995; Ryan, 1996; Schauben & Fraizer, 1995; Scurfield, 1985). Frequently these are referred to as "countertransference" or "cumulative countertransference." The term "compassion fatigue"—that is, the strain the therapist experiences on his or her ability to remain in empathic connection with trauma survivor clients over time—refers to the cumulative impact of this work (Figley, 1995).

MODELS OF RESPONSES TO THERAPY WITH TRAUMA SURVIVORS

The reactions to working with trauma victims have been systematically studied, validated, and conceptualized into organized models by Wilson and Lindy (1994) and McCann and Pearlman (1990). These models are described here, in order to highlight the complex reactions and behaviors that occur when therapists are working with severely traumatized people.

The Wilson and Lindy Model

Wilson and Lindy (1994) provide a valuable perspective on the two contrary emotional countertransference pulls in a therapist working with trauma victims: the pull toward overinvolvement, and, conversely, the pull toward emotional distancing. Emotional distancing includes the therapist's tendencies to engage in denial, minimization, distortion, counterphobic reactions, avoidance, detachment, and withdrawal. Overinvolvement consists of overidentification, overidealization, enmeshment, excessive advocacy for a client, and behaviors that elicit guilt reactions. These two reactions occur as a result of the mixture of the objective (expectable or reality-based) reactions to the client's trauma and the subjective (personal) reactions associated with the therapist's individual conflicts, idiosyncrasies, or unresolved issues. The therapist may become involved in typical role enactments with clients, including those of failed protector, collaborator, rescuer, comforter, judge, conspirator, perpetrator, fellow survivor, victim, and/or authority figure. (These are discussed more fully later in the chapter.)

Four major features of the client's process have an impact on the transference, according to Wilson and Lindy (1994). These include the content of trauma, the complexity and intensity of the client's experience during the trauma, the degree to which there is ambiguity or clarity in transference projections, and the affect arousal potential of the trauma transference.

The nature, quality, and dynamics of countertransference are determined by four factors (Wilson & Lindy, 1994):

- Factors related to the trauma itself, such as the nature of the stress present in the trauma story (the complexity and type of stress, the moral dilemmas during the event, the duration, the severity, and the frequency of exposure or victimization).

- Personal factors in the therapist/helper (such as personal beliefs, religious values, ideological systems, defensive styles and dispositions, personal historical data, type and extent of training, and professional experience).
- Factors in the client (such as age, race, gender, personality characteristics, role in traumatic event [perpetrator, victim, witness], pretrauma ego strength, and family dynamics).
- Institutional and organizational factors relevant to the therapeutic process (attitudes toward the client population, political context, and adequacy of resources that help or hinder treatment).

Wilson and Lindy's model is helpful in providing a generic model for the transference–countertransference response relative to several types of trauma (war, interpersonal, environmental, and catastrophic).

The McCann and Pearlman Model

Pearlman and Saakvitne (1995) present a comprehensive model of trauma therapy, in which they demonstrate typical transference–countertransference responses during the treatment of adult victims of childhood physical and sexual abuse. This model is based on the constructivist self-development theory developed by McCann and Pearlman (1990)—a theory about the treatment of trauma victims that integrates psychodynamic and cognitive components. The model provides the basis for understanding "vicarious traumatization" (McCann & Pearlman, 1990), which can be conceptualized as the pervasive effects on trauma therapists' own sense of identity, world view, psychological needs, beliefs, and memory. Ultimately, vicarious traumatization can lead therapists into taking nonempathic positions with their clients and even into withdrawing from their psychotherapy careers. Therapists have the strongest feeling responses to clients around issues that resonate with their most personal vulnerabilities (Wilson & Lindy, 1994; Pearlman & Saakvitne, 1995). Vicarious traumatization is discussed more fully later in the chapter.

In the McCann and Pearlman (1990) model, countertransference responses that may lead to vicarious traumatization occur within five different dimensions or clusters. These also provide a framework for understanding typical transference responses. The five dimensions of responses are as follows:

- Frame of reference
- Self-capacities
- Ego resources
- Psychological needs and related cognitive schemas
- Memory system

Frame of Reference

"Frame of reference" is the framework of beliefs through which the individual interprets experience, including his or her world view, identity, and spirituality. In this realm, the therapist working with severely traumatized children may begin to question his or her typically benevolent world view, or even to have angry feelings about those clients who challenge this view. He or she may begin making more generalizations relative to race, culture, gender, or diagnosis, thus overlooking the true psychological uniqueness of each client. For example, the therapist may be so disgusted and distressed by an abuse situation that he or she dismisses a child's view of a perpetrating parent as also loving and tender.

In addition, throughout the treatment a traumatized client will evoke a number of countertransference roles in the therapist, including those of perpetrator, helpless bystander, collusive parent, nurturing figures, and even voyeur. These feelings can be extremely disruptive to the therapist's sense of his or her professional identity as compassionate, understanding, interested, and helpful. The therapist may begin feeling guilty and frightened about these feelings and about assuming these roles, particularly in play therapy.

Self-Capacities

"Self-capacities" are the abilities that enable an individual to maintain a sense of self as consistent and coherent across time and situations, including the abilities to tolerate strong affects, to develop a positive sense of self, and to sustain an inner sense of connection with others. In this realm, a therapist may feel distressed and ashamed of his or her feelings, particularly if they are hateful or punitive. The therapist may be facing strong nurturing and protective feelings that, if acted upon, would prevent exploration of a child's strong negative feelings. He or she may respond to the client's suicidal feelings in an overly controlling or protective manner, in reaction to the fear of these feelings in the child. The therapist may feel particularly frustrated by the child's need to distance from the strong affect and/or the child's restriction of affect, and thus may become overly intrusive in pursuing the child's feelings. Or the therapist may experience changes in his or her sensory state during sessions—for example, feeling sleepy in the session, or extremely stimulated (perhaps very curious, aroused, or excited) while listening to or watching a child reenact in play the details of an abuse scene.

In long-term trauma therapy, it is common for a therapist to feel disregarded, ignored, or unacknowledged in the session. Feeling sleepy may be the therapist's withdrawal response to the child's intense need to shun the therapist's interest and/or the child's need to avoid a real relationship (again as a result of his or her experience of betrayal and repeated disappointments in real relationships). The therapist's withdrawal in response to the child's distancing behavior can also be viewed as a parallel process (Kahn, 1979; Webb, 1983). The therapist may begin slipping into a countertransference response of overactive pursuit of the child's attention or into a parallel withdrawal. If the therapist's feeling continues without understanding, he or she may inaccurately conclude that the therapy is nonproductive and may prematurely terminate the client.

Ego Resources

"Ego resources" are an individual's abilities to meet his or her psychological needs and to relate to others. They include resources that are very important to the therapy process, such as intelligence; willpower and initiative; introspection and awareness of psychological needs; the wish to strive for personal growth; perspective-taking abilities; and resources to protect oneself from future harm. In this realm, the therapist may lose perspective in making self-protective judgments or establishing boundaries with the client. He or she may begin feeling consumed by work or intensely involved in it, to the exclusion of other people and activities in his or her life. Neumann and Gamble (1995) refer to Kaufman's term "countertransference hostage syndrome," in which the therapist feels silenced and controlled by the client. The therapist may have a sense of losing his or her own perspective about issues in the face of the child's sense of reality. This feeling arises often in reaction to a child's natural wish to avoid negative affect and revisit the trauma, and may take the form of the therapist's thinking that it is not important for the child to explore the trauma or talk about his or her fears. The therapist, in effect, joins the child's wish to avoid negative affect.

Feeling overwhelmed, overburdened, and confused may also occur in response to the intense affects expressed in the session, and to the fluidity and complexity of the child's transference responses. Multiple transference and countertransference shifts within one treatment session are common in the treatment of severely traumatized adults (Davies & Frawley, 1994). Such shifts also characterize therapy with children. A child's ability to revisit the negative affect associated with the trauma only briefly can be experienced by the therapist as added pressure to say the right thing at the right moment, because the opportunity seems so fleeting, yet so charged with meaning.

Psychological Needs and Related Cognitive Schemas

The fourth dimension includes beliefs, expectations, and assumptions related to safety, trust, esteem, intimacy, and control. McCann and Pearlman (1990) note that "schemas" are cognitive manifestations of psychological needs, and that trauma disrupts schemas. In this realm, the therapist may begin to feel an increased sense of vulnerability about his or her physical or psychological safety; may start to doubt his or her own perceptions; may begin feeling that others would be better therapists; may feel guilty about his or her lack of experience; or may develop a sense that experienced therapists do not have such trials in their work (Neumann & Gamble, 1995). While struggling within this dimension, the therapist may begin avoiding intimacy with others or avoid time alone. He or she may fear a loss of control over personal feelings and reactions, or may become intolerant of the uncertainty and confusion that typically arise in the treatment of traumatized children.

One therapist confronted a new adult client who had a history of exhibitionism with children with a threat of retaliation if he acted out again. The therapist also had an 8-year-old daughter and was acutely aware of the vulnerability her daughter faced in the world. Unfortunately, she did not understand the implications of her words to the offender/victim before she said them.

Memory System

The "memory system" includes verbal, affective, imagery, somatic, and interpersonal memories. In this realm the therapist may experience preoccupation with thoughts of the client, or intrusive images and fantasies associated with his or her own safety or that of close family members. McCann and Pearlman (1990) note that at times the therapist may experience the client's traumatic imagery in fragments without context or meaning, in the form of intrusive thoughts, nightmares, and dreams. It is clear that the imagery most painful to therapists usually centers around the schemas related to the therapists' salient needs, such as safety, trust, or control. One therapist who was working with a number of sexually abused children began having intrusive images of her own daughter's being sexually abused on the school playground.

The therapist may experience disruptive imagery associated with the powerful affective states evoked in the treatment of trauma victims. A therapist who is overwhelmed emotionally or cognitively by imagery and feelings may experience denial or emotional numbing, because his or her own capacity for affect regulation or self-soothing is overtaxed. Images suggested in the client's material may be too discrepant with the therapist's own meaning system (McCann & Pearlman, 1990). Although these imagery states are often short in duration, serving as a signal to the therapist, McCann and Pearlman (1990) note that a therapist's traumatic memories can become permanent when the material is closely related to the therapist's psychological needs and life experiences, and when the therapist is not given the opportunity to talk about his or her experiences of the traumatic material. Actual memory gaps regarding the process of sessions or distortions in the recall of the material can occur and can be associated with the intensity of the affective content of the sessions, as well as with the way it is presented by the child.

For example, one therapist tried repeatedly to recount the process in supervision of a therapy session with an 8-year-old boy. Although she was usually quite good at remembering details of play and associations within sessions, she could not recall this child's material. She found herself rambling and giving general accounts of chaotic play experiences. In particular, she could not remember the child's stories, which seemed so important when she heard them in sessions. She felt frustrated, anxious, and inadequate about her poor memory for the details. After presenting this case in a consultation group, she became curious about her response to the stories and returned to the treatment room ready to investigate her countertransference. She focused on the nature of the boy's stories and actions, and noticed how graphic, rushed, tangential, and overly detailed they were. As she began to feel less confused, her memory of the session improved, which led her to intervene empathically with the child's anxiety. This example illustrates how the memory of the session content can be lost when a therapist is flooded by a child's affective state—in this case, the boy's intense anxiety and the graphic details of his stories.

VICARIOUS TRAUMATIZATION

"Vicarious traumatization is the transformation of the inner experience of the therapist that comes about as a result of empathic engagement with clients' trauma material" (Pearlman & Saakvitne, 1995, p. 31). Vicarious traumatization may be viewed as a normal reaction to the cumulative effect of the stressful work with victims. However, it can lead to negative effects for a therapist as well as a client (McCann & Pearlman, 1990).

> Our notion of vicarious traumatization . . . implies that much of the therapist's cognitive world will be altered by hearing traumatic client material . . . and that all therapists working with trauma survivors will experience lasting alterations in their cognitive schemas, having significant impact on [their] feelings, relationships, and life. (McCann & Pearlman, 1990, p. 136)

Vicarious traumatization and countertransference are different, yet integrally related, each affecting the other. "*Countertransference* is specific to a particular therapeutic relationship [whereas] *vicarious traumatization* is manifest across trauma therapies" (Pearlman & Saakvitne, 1995, p. 317; emphasis in original). As countertransference arises, it can gradually and negatively alter a therapist's overall view of the world, the self, and other personal relationships, leading to vicarious traumatization. If the changes in the therapist are unconscious, they may cause permanent damage to both client and therapist. In particular, unattended vicarious traumatization may have a significant negative impact on the therapist's professional identity, sometimes leading him or her to make to career changes and lose personal relationships. McCann and Pearlman (1990) note that if the changes are not to be destructive, the therapist must enter into a parallel process to that of the client, integrating and transforming experiences of horror and violation. This requires that the helper have access to a supportive place to acknowledge, express, and work through the painful experiences. Another term for vicarious traumatization is "secondary traumatization."

Although the symptoms of vicarious traumatization can parallel those of posttraumatic stress disorder (PTSD), it is a different phenomenon. PTSD occurs as a result of direct contact with the trauma. In contrast, in vicarious traumatization the therapist is one step removed from the trauma. The therapist is exposed indirectly to the trauma through the patient's descriptions and his or her own psychological interpretation of the trauma.

FEELINGS SPECIFICALLY ASSOCIATED WITH CHILD VICTIMS

Many of the dynamics of the treatment of traumatized individuals are similar in adults and children; however, there are some significant differences. One primary difference is the indirect manner in which a child addresses trauma-related issues. The younger a child is, the less able he or she is to describe experiences directly in words. Much more of the material is either reenacted in play representations or presented symbolically through metaphors in play. At times the therapist may be successful in making a direct association between the play and the child's actual experience. However, there are many children who cannot tolerate and do not permit direct discussion of their experiences of trauma. Also, some child therapists (e.g., Terr, 1989) believe that it is not necessary to move beyond play metaphors in order for the therapy to be helpful. Often the material comes in quick snippets: A child may make one brief statement and refuse to discuss more. Commenting on the quickness and potential danger of talking can sometimes help to facilitate further discussion, but not always. Actual discussion of the trauma with the child is often minimal.

Children naturally evoke protective and nurturing feelings in most therapists. These can be especially strong feelings when children have poor living situations and are without protective and understanding adults in their lives. Again, it is not the presence of these feelings in the therapist that is deleterious for the treatment; rather, the lack of understanding and management of these feelings can interfere with the treatment process. An overprotective or overly nurturing therapeutic stance can prevent a child from exploring all the feelings he or she needs to work through in relation to the trauma (Webb, 1989).

The child therapist is also frequently drawn into a number of roles relative to external systems. Friedrich (1990) notes that the role of the therapist can get blurred by advocacy and case management responsibilities. The child therapist is expected to consult with parents, foster parents, child care workers, and teachers. He or she is often asked to testify in court and make difficult recommendations and/or decisions regarding a child's permanent placement. These varying roles can easily pull the therapist away from the empathic connection to the child and into a mode of greater or lesser action in the child's behalf. These are difficult roles to balance and manage within the therapy.

TASKS FOR NOVICE THERAPISTS

An early developmental task of the beginning or novice trauma therapist is to develop professional identity and self-confidence. This is accomplished partially through developing realistic expectations of clients (Pearlman & Saakvitne, 1995). As noted previously, because of the intensity of the affect or the nature of the projections, a therapist may underestimate the severity of traumatic injury and misunderstand a child's difficulty in developing trust. A therapist's lack of appreciation for the depth of these difficulties can lead to inappropriate expectations of self and of the therapeutic process. These unrealistic expectations may shake the therapist's self-esteem and confidence, and lead to feelings of disappointment and failure. Anger, puzzlement, and self-blame erupt. The wish to rescue or not to fail the patient—to which new therapists are particularly prone, according to Neumann and Gamble (1995)—may lead the therapist to become overly active or to withdraw. A new therapist must establish a professional identity that includes an understanding of his or her typical countertransference responses and vulnerabilities, preferred theoretical orientation, and ego ideal.

TASKS FOR THERAPISTS WHO
ARE SURVIVORS THEMSELVES

Therapists who are trauma survivors themselves can be particularly vulnerable to the impact of working with traumatized clients (Fike, 1990; Marvasti, 1992; Pearlman & Saakvitne, 1995; Scurfield, 1985). These therapists must strive for self-understanding, especially in relation to the impact of their past trauma and their areas of current vulnerabilities. With this knowledge, the therapists can better analyze their countertransference responses. Often a previous experience of abuse or other trauma emphasizes a countertransference response that seeks to find justice in the situation; at times these retaliation responses can be overzealous, as if there is an overidentification. Sometimes a therapist's sensitivity makes him or her more attuned to particular feeling states, providing validation and understanding to the client. In general, however, a therapist who is a survivor should strive to avoid overidentification with the client, since this can ultimately occlude his or her empathy. It is particularly important for therapists who have been previously traumatized to undergo personal psychotherapy, and for beginners to obtain trauma-centered supervision.

ADDRESSING THE NEEDS OF THE THERAPIST:
TRAUMA THERAPY SUPERVISION

A therapist who assumes that countertransference feelings and even vicarious traumatization may arise during the normal course of his or her work is more likely to be proactive and responsive to these feelings. Acknowledging these reactions and getting validation will deintensify the feelings and allow for the exploration of ways to maintain the empathic stance with the child. Sharing these feelings in supervision and consultation may be one of the most valuable ways to address them and will help counter professional isolation (Webb, 1989). Since countertransference issues are so integral to the treatment of traumatized children, it is important for a therapist to find supportive, knowledgeable professionals with whom he or she is comfortable discussing reactions to the complexities of particular cases. It is also important to find a supervisor/consultant who is knowledgeable about the treatment of children, since the treatment of children differs in many ways from that of adults.

The following four components of adequate trauma therapy supervision are described by Pearlman and Saakvitne (1995):

1. A supervisor with a solid theoretical grounding in psychotherapy in general and trauma therapy in particular, as well as in child development and the treatment of children.
2. A relationship focus that attends to both the conscious and unconscious aspects of the therapeutic relationship and treatment process.
3. A respectful interpersonal climate that allows attention to countertransference and parallel process.

4. The opportunity for education about and attunement to the therapist's vicarious traumatization.

RECOMMENDED STRATEGIES FOR THERAPISTS

Specific strategies to help therapists help themselves have been suggested by several authors, including Friedrich (1990), Fike (1990), McCann and Pearlman (1990), Medeiros and Prochaska (1988), Nader (1994), Neumann and Gamble (1995), and Pearlman and Saakvitne (1995). Because this work pulls therapists to be introspective and involved in intense feelings that can be quite negative and depressive, activities that balance this tunneled view and exposure are vital to helpers' emotional health. The following guidelines are recommended.

1. *Keeping up professional connections.* Therapists should attend professional continuing education programs related to trauma and children. However, they should balance their perspective by also attending conferences that address issues other than trauma.

2. *Limiting exposure to trauma.* If possible, therapists should limit their caseloads so that they are not seeing *all* trauma victims. Each case takes an emotional toll on a therapist; when a therapist faces 5 or 10 traumatized children and families each week, the effect is cumulative and difficult to balance. Helpers should limit their exposure to trauma in other ways as well. Some therapists set up personal guidelines about what movies they watch, what novels they read, and whether they watch the nightly TV news or read the front page of the newspaper. All of these self-imposed limits restrict the exposure to trauma that is so prevalent in our culture.

3. *Entering into personal psychotherapy.* As noted previously, knowledge of oneself is crucial for therapeutic work. Unknowingly and unwittingly, traumatized clients pull at therapists' most vulnerable personal attitudes and beliefs. Helpers who lack an understanding of themselves and have not worked through the feelings associated with their own vulnerabilities are more likely to be closed off to the dynamics evoked in these therapies, or even to label and blame clients as "bad" or "difficult" children. Such therapists may be less likely to believe in the process and possibility of psychotherapeutic change, and they may be more likely to remain in patterns of their own dysfunction.

4. *Maintaining rejuvenating relationships and experiences.* Therapists need to find people and places *outside of work* in which they can engage in caring, compassionate, rejuvenating relationships. A relationship that provides love, care, warmth, and compassion can be essential, as it is through such relationships that individuals feel most connected to the world and supported in daily events and feelings. Places and spaces to have fun, and activities that are rejuvenating and fulfilling, are essential. Connecting to one's body and/or getting physical exercise can be an excellent way to achieve distance from the myriad of intense work-related feelings and difficult thoughts.

5. *Maintaining a personal identity by creating boundaries between home and work.* At some point, lines need to be drawn between work and one's personal and private space.

Although the demands of therapists' jobs often require homework, it is important at some point to put it away, get distance, and enter a physical and psychological space that is safe and comforting. Telephone boundaries are important. If possible, therapists should have an "on-call" schedule so that they can leave the office, yet continue with phone work at home. Or an answering machine can take messages to be returned the following day. If necessary, helpers should establish a time limit to telephone work, keeping after-hour telephone work within a specified time frame. It is not easy for therapists to tell clients that their time is limited, but only by getting their own personal time and space to rejuvenate themselves will therapists be able to be there for clients during the sessions.

6. *Getting organizational support.* Therapists should encourage their agencies to develop a committee or group to attend to the psychological needs of therapists who work with traumatized children and families. Such a group should be sensitive to therapists' needs for continuing education, case conferences, trauma-centered supervision and/or consultation, and limits on the number of trauma cases.

7. *Finding meaningful ways to remain involved with all aspects of humanity.* Neumann and Gamble (1995, p. 346) note that "the cynicism and over-generalized negative beliefs about humanity that signal vicarious traumatization must be actively challenged." This may occur in supervision, in support groups, or in a supportive friendship, but it also may occur through a personal process. Practicing so-called "random acts of kindness" is commonly considered to be rejuvenating; however, *noticing* such acts may be even more powerful for a therapist who is burdened by the symptoms of vicarious traumatization. Some therapists find it helpful to develop an active political involvement, in order to address the trends and policy issues that perpetuate violence in our society.

8. *Confronting and working through intrusive traumatic imagery.* There are a number of ways of addressing intrusive images that can deintensify their impact (Pearlman & Saakvitne, 1995). The therapist can start by identifying the underlying needs represented in the imagery. Further working through in a personal therapy or consultation carries this a necessary step further. Another method of dealing with the imagery is to tell oneself to "stop the bad image" and then fantasize a new image or a new ending. Cognitive therapists call this "thought stopping" and "guided imagery."

Talking about the imagery to a confidant is also useful. A person who can hear the details of the imagery and respond empathically to the therapist may provide enough support to enable the therapist to let go of the negative image. However, dictates regarding confidentiality may limit the extent of what is shared outside of therapy or consultation.

9. *Recognizing the positive feelings associated with this work.* Therapists need to acknowledge to themselves the good feelings associated with helping children deal with the pain and sadness that have interfered with their lives. According to the research of Medeiros and Prochaska (1988), therapists who utilized the concept of "optimistic perseverance" felt they were coping well with the stress associated with trauma clients. Noting and remembering specific moments in the healing process of each therapy can enable therapists to acquire the feeling of optimistic perseverance. Sharing personal rewards and the hopefulness of particular cases and aspects of

treatments can foster a sense of hope and perseverance in those who tell as well as hear such stories.

AN EXAMPLE OF A CONSULTATION GROUP MEETING

The Presenter and the Setting

Susan, a master's-level social worker with 2 years of child therapy experience, had been working at a group home for 8 months. Her job responsibilities included providing intensive psychotherapy for three group residents and casework services for several additional families. She enjoyed the work; she found it intellectually stimulating, and it fulfilled her long-held desire to become a child psychotherapist. The group home was part of a larger social service agency that provided therapeutic services to young children and families. Attendance at a weekly consultation group was a required component of Susan's job, and typically she looked forward to attending. Susan felt accepted and relatively safe among the group members. However, this week she felt differently. Susan was scheduled to discuss a client whose case she had presented previously, and she found herself increasingly resistant to the meeting. She avoided getting ready for the meeting until the last minute, when she hurriedly put together notes for the group. This was not her usual style of preparation.

The Group Structure and Format

The consultation group had been meeting for several years and included six therapists with varied levels of experience. All of them worked with children who had diagnoses of PTSD and/or severe difficulties in their living situations. The group consultant was a clinician brought in from outside the agency, who had many years of experience with traumatized children. The group met for 90 minutes weekly, 60 minutes of which were typically devoted to a case presentation. In this part, the presenting therapist was encouraged to describe process from the sessions. During the final 30 minutes, the therapists focused on more general feelings associated with the treatments or issues within the group home.

Background on the Child Client

Six-year-old David had entered the group home about 6 months before. He was referred by the state child protective team after being kicked out of his last foster placement, a setting he had lived in for over a year with his two siblings. The foster parent had complained because of his defiant, oppositional behavior and sexual acting out in the home. His transition to the group home had not been difficult. He seemed to feel right at home there. David was a charming, cute, vivacious boy, initially shy but then engaging with many staff members.

David began twice-weekly psychotherapy with Susan in the same way: He was initially shy and then quite engaging, especially for the first 3 months. By the second month of treatment he revealed to Susan, through play and discussion, many experiences of sexual abuse in the foster home by the foster mother and her boyfriend. In accordance with the state laws, Susan was bound to report David's allegations to the child abuse hotline. The state required further outside investigation and interviewing of David, which was taxing for him. However, David appeared to get solace from his psychotherapy and remained involved in it. In the therapeutic relationship, Susan sensed a deep sadness in David, and gradually his depressed mood became more evident in his external life at school and the group home. Although Susan had always looked forward to seeing David, the sessions in which he revealed the sexual abuse had been very uncomfortable for her, because the child's helplessness and vulnerability were so evident and poignant. Susan had presented all of this previously to the group as she was processing the intensity of the sexual abuse.

By the fifth month, from Susan's perspective, the therapy had become very different: It was now painfully boring. Susan was confronting these feelings the week she was to present to the consultation group, and she didn't know what to say. She felt embarrassed by her feelings of boredom in the sessions and wasn't sure she felt comfortable revealing these to the group. She began to think that she was not a good enough therapist for David, and that she was doing something very wrong in the treatment.

Content/Group Process

SUSAN: Let me remind you of David, the 6-year-old I began seeing 6 months ago. I presented him about 4 months ago as he was revealing his experiences of sexual abuse. At this point I have nothing to say. There is very little going on in the sessions.

CONSULTANT: Can you elaborate, please? What are the sessions like?

S: David comes in, often in a happy mood as he walks in with the child care worker. Once he is in the office, his mood changes. He seems to become very sad. Sometimes he tries to play with the superhero figures, or the cars—having them crash or fight. I try to enter the play as I had before, and he either ignores me or squashes me flat. I get the clear picture that I am not wanted in the room. Then suddenly, without any explanation, he picks up a pillow and lays his head down to sleep. He appears distant, dazed, and removed from me. He is then unwilling to talk. I feel confused and unsure what to do. I barrage myself with a number of questions, such as "Have I been too intrusive? Is he angry with me? Is he actually tired? Maybe this is a good place for him to sleep."

GROUP MEMBER 1: What do you do then?

S: Sometimes I try to speak softly to him. I say I understand that he feels tired. I try to put words

Analysis

Susan is still unsure of what to say about the sessions and self-conscious about the negative feelings she is having about the sessions. She is doubting herself and unable to utilize her past experiences of the group as a helpful, safe place where her feelings can be revealed and accepted.

Susan is feeling disregarded, but she is not quite aware of this. She may be feeling angry, but does not have a sense of this either.

These are good self-reflective questions. She is also experiencing some maternal countertransference feelings (i.e., she should provide him with a safe, comfortable place to sleep).

Susan is feeling more comfortable with the group process and able to into his experience, supporting the reasons for his actions. I ask him if I have said something to hurt his feelings, but he never responds. Other times I have tried to prevent him from resting—I suggest we go out, tell him we have things to do. He just continues to ignore me until the session is over.

GROUP MEMBER 2: It's as if he turns you off like a TV.

S: Exactly—no more use. Yet he looks so sad, and I feel so bad about this! Maybe he is through with therapy. Maybe this is too much for him. He prefers to be with the caseworker, and they have such a good time; perhaps they should just spend time together. Maybe I should make the relationship more real—offer ice cream, go to the park?

GROUP MEMBER 3: I do that with kids. I go outside and toss the ball. David is an active child. Maybe the office is too confining.

S: Maybe. But actually he just acts like he doesn't want to do anything. Just shut me out and go to sleep.

GM1: Maybe he is telling you important information about his foster care experience.

C: What were you thinking about?

GM1: Perhaps his behavior is a reenactment of sort of something he experienced with the sexual abuse. Like what might happen after an adult has had intercourse—the adult might go to sleep, leaving the child awake and alone. You are being asked to feel what he might have felt.

GM2: Or what about how shut out he feels by the lack of protective adults in his life—the lack of his parents initially, the foster mother, or the state agency worker to help him and protect him? No one really gets involved with him, or if they do, they really hurt him.

S: Yeah, but I am here now—ready and willing to be connected. But when he gets into this place, I find myself withdrawing. I feel so bored and sleepy. Some days I think, "I am relieved he is shut down, because I've had such a busy day before him." On other days I try to wake him up and prevent him from going to sleep, but that doesn't do any good either. It feels like I am pushing him to address his issues, and I wonder if we ought to get at certain issues?

talk about the sessions. She reveals her confusion about David's process and some of the actions she has taken to address it. As she struggles to understand David's behavior, she moves into an active, perhaps even overly directive position.

She is beginning to get irritated by the confusion and his treatment of her, but mostly she still feels the sadness.

The group member also prefers to distance from the sadness.

The possibility of parallel process is introduced.

Susan seems to be joining the child's feelings.

She really doesn't know how to respond.

C: Perhaps there are several issues here: One is his withdrawal and sleepiness. What to do about that? What does it mean? Another issue may be developmental issues of a 5- to 6-year-old. We know that he was abused at least as a 5-year-old—and abandoned much earlier by his biological parents. What do the rest of you think?

(Several group members volunteer observations: Children aged 5 to 6 are generally very active, excitable, and quite self-absorbed. Often they want to be with other children socially, though they sometimes still enjoy the special attachment to parents. There is greater intellectual awareness of their surroundings, though they are still sorting through cause-and-effect issues—particularly related to behavior. They have a limited ability to see the world from others' points of view. Their vocabulary is growing, though their ability to put feelings into words can be limited, especially regarding their own self-states. Boys in particular exhibit an increased interest in their genitals. Often they will "talk dirty" or engage in bathroom talk, just to laugh and enjoy the infringement of the tabooed subjects. They are also involved with many activities at this age, such as going to school, learning many new skills, and doing homework. They are busy.)

The consultant pulls in comments of several group members to examine treatment issues with David. Developmental issues are related to here and now, as well as to the time when the abuse occurred. The group can use this perspective to think about the child's presentation in sessions. It is likely that his actions toward Susan are typical of his developmental age at the time the abuse occurred. It is important to consider developmental norms against which to compare the individual child.

S: So maybe I am expecting him to tell me too much about his inner world or to talk about his feelings in a concrete manner.

C: It sounds like he doesn't have the skill yet to do this. Yet you also feel under pressure to help him deal with the experiences of sexual abuse, and not to lose a good treatment opportunity.

If he can't talk, he may be able to play. However, the sleepiness needs to be recognized and addressed first.

S: I do feel that I have a responsibility to help him get the most out of therapy at the moment. But I often feel very lethargic and certainly put off.

GM3: I often feel very sleepy with these children. It is as if they play the same old things over and over and it never goes anywhere. I feel like I could be in the room, and then again I could be somewhere else, and it doesn't matter. I get discouraged about how bad the home situations are. They are so chaotic, nonloving, and unresponsive to the needs of children. I get totally discouraged about these situations, and I'm not sure what I can possibly do to help.

Here the group member is expressing a sense of helplessness and overwhelming feelings associated with working with these clients and their families. She is beginning to generalize these feelings to *all* abuse situations and to demonstrate the beginnings of vicarious traumatization.

S: I guess I am getting discouraged about treatment in general. Maybe this work is not for me.

GM2: Susan, I wonder what feelings you are having which lead you to withdraw? You've noticed that David is sad, but has he ever expressed much anger? I see his behavior as a potentially angry response to life, to being brought into treatment two times a week, and to many life issues.

S: I never thought of anger being an issue. Sadness is something I can see and experience rather easily, but the anger is not so evident.

Susan, too, is showing some evidence of vicarious traumatization. She is more able to acknowledge her *own* feelings after hearing about another group member's.

C: I wonder what it would be like to take this back to the client?

S: I don't see how. I have already asked him to no avail why he does this.

GM1: But a 6-year-old boy may not be able to say why he does something. A 6-year-old just acts.

(*The group talks about Susan for a few moments.*)

S: I guess I don't feel like you all appreciate how hard I've tried with this boy! I feel like I've said everything and it doesn't work.

C: You are experiencing us as not responding to your questions and your feelings. You feel that we are overlooking how helpless you feel in the sessions.

Susan can feel the resistance in herself as the group talks. (Later Susan thinks this through with her own therapist. She realizes that in her own life she is often frightened by intensely angry feelings. She has a very hard time with expressions of anger, partly because as a child she witnessed many intense verbal arguments between her own parents. She realizes that it is not always easy for her to recognize angry feelings in her clients, and that she avoids considering this side of the issue.) Interestingly, her irritation *with the group* begins to develop.

GM2: I think it is happening right here. Susan is feeling disregarded and is getting irritated. *I* feel this is an interesting discussion and that we are really going somewhere. But I also feel shut out and sense that Susan cannot make use of any of the suggestions we are making. Could this be a parallel process to the treatment?

Parallel process can occur in the consultation group as well as in the treatment.

S: That is interesting and does feel accurate.

C: Susan, you are reminding me of how intense the feelings are when we sit with a child who does not trust others. When the betrayal has been chronic like David's, it is worse. I think that David is doing a masterful job at unconsciously letting you experience how unsafe and unavailable the world has been to him. He'd rather give up than try again to give another adult a chance. And he overemphasizes your mistakes, remembering only those, rather than the hundreds of times you have been supportive. But I am wondering if you could put that into words for David, even through a metaphor or story?

The consultant validates Susan's supportive efforts. The consultant also moves the group back toward a focus on Susan's dilemma. Tentatively, she suggests that the group's suggestions about reenacting the abuse may be correct. Verbal exploration is not bringing a verbal response, but *behaviorally*, David is telling Susan that he cannot make use of her at this point.

For example, tell him a story describing a boy who
gets so discouraged he falls asleep. He feels no one
is *really* interested in him, and thus feels there is no
other way to deal with his misery. Perhaps in a
dream he discovers someone who is interested in
him, and he considers whether he should befriend
this new, interested person.

S: I think this will be helpful. I was feeling a little
resistant to people's suggestions earlier. I do feel
heard and understood now. You have also helped me
to understand how David's experiences of disappointment and helplessness may have been
projected onto me. I may be less likely to feel
discouraged by them.

The second part of the group meeting was a more general discussion of relational issues.

Content/Group Process

GROUP MEMBER 1: Sometimes I find myself
wanting to avoid going out to place where I see
parents and children interact. It seems like all I see
is parents being awful with children. So many
parents speak in such mean ways! It makes me
cringe. I can't read the newspaper this week because
it's having a special series on abuse.

GROUP MEMBER 2: Sometimes I can't stand to read
about one more abuse situation. At other times I
find myself being so acutely interested in this
matter that I can't put it down. I do get discouraged with the theoretical reading. It doesn't help,
and it doesn't answer my question about how to
respond to these children when they have told me
something horrific. At those moments I feel
helpless and want to reach out and touch the child.

GROUP MEMBER 3: I find I can't watch certain
movies. My husband wants to go, but when I go I
get so depressed and feel like I am still at work. We
finally decided that I needed to avoid certain
movies, and that if he wanted to see them he'd go
separately.

SUSAN: I also have to distance from these experiences. There are only certain types of movies and
novels I can enjoy. The literature helps me to stay
focused if I don't read it too much.

Analysis

The group member is describing a
shift in her view of parents as a
whole. She is generalizing and
feeling cynical toward many
people. Let us assume that she did
not begin with this negativity, and
that this is a shift suggestive of
vicarious traumatization.

This is a good example of the
vacillating feelings related to
hearing the details of abuse.

There is much group validation
here. The support is strong.

GM1: I also asked the agency administrator to assign me a different type of case if possible. I have been seeing so many of these children recently, and I need a break.

GM3: I find that I have to have some physical things to do with myself when I go home. I can't do much more listening. Going swimming or on a run helps me. Gardening also helps, because it is so removed from this kind of work and I can actually see results from what I do.

Good sharing of personal experiences.

GM1: That helps me too. I like to go home and spend time with my family. It helps quite a bit to have some fun experiences, and particularly to reaffirm our ability to have fun together as a family. I feel much more restored emotionally the next day.

GM2: I also felt much more encouraged yesterday. I just happened to be watching a mom play with her child in the grocery store. She was having the most interesting discussion about the vegetables. They were smiling and laughing. It really restored my sense of the goodness of humanity and the sense that all parents are not overburdened and emotionally abusive. I never realized how important those scenes are as inspiration for our work.

(Everyone acknowledges the beauty of this vignette, in contrast to the many they see in stores that are so difficult. The group chats a few minutes more before dispersing.)

CONCLUDING REMARKS

The group process above illustrates many of the points emphasized in the chapter related to the playing out of transference and countertransference in work with severely traumatized children. The important role of the group process in validating Susan's feelings led to her enhanced understanding of the child's behavior. Examination of the possible parallel process between David and Susan provided a potential means of breaking through the therapeutic impasse in this clinical example.

The sharing and support in the second part of the meeting provided an opportunity for "unloading" painful, distressing feelings in a sympathetic environment, and also for balancing this negativity with more positive experiences. When therapists regularly care for themselves in this manner, they will be better able to empathize and work with traumatized clients.

STUDY QUESTIONS

1. With which type of trauma victims do you anticipate having the strongest feeling response? Why? How can you avoid having your feelings interfere with the therapeutic process?

2. Frequently, beginning/novice child therapists believe that their role is to "rescue" children from abusive or neglectful parents. Discuss the difficulties that may arise from this belief.

3. How can therapists develop empathy in their work with abusive parents? Do you think that this is an appropriate goal? Why or why not?

4. How can you deal with intrusive, disturbing imagery that is similar to the traumatic material discussed or played out by one of your clients?

5. Make a list of your own strategies for rejuvenation. Which of the nine ideas discussed in the "Recommended Strategies for Therapists" section appeals to you most?

ACKNOWLEDGMENTS

I gratefully acknowledge Maureen Sauvain, Nancy Cap, Helen Fleisher, Peter Shaft, and Michael Hoffman for their support and assistance with the ideas and clinical examples in this chapter.

REFERENCES

Chu, J. (1988). Ten traps for therapists. *Dissociation, 1*(4), 24–32.

Davis, R., & Friedman, L. (1985). The emotional aftermath of crime and violence. In C. R. Figley (Ed.), *Trauma and its wake* (pp. 90–112). New York: Brunner/Mazel.

Davies, J. M., & Frawley, M. G. (1994). *Treating the adult survivor of childhood sexual abuse: A psychoanalytic perspective.* New York: Basic Books.

Dyregrov, A., & Mitchell, J. (1992). Working with traumatized children: Psychological effects and coping strategies. *Journal of Traumatic Stress, 5*(1), 5–17.

Figley, C. R. (1995). *Compassion fatigue: Secondary traumatic stress disorder from treating the traumatized.* New York: Brunner/Mazel.

Fike, M. L. (1990). Childhood sexual abuse and multiple personality disorder: Emotional sequelae of caretakers. *American Journal of Occupational Therapy, 44*(11), 967–969.

Freud, S. (1953). Fragment of an analysis of a case of hysteria. In J. Strachey (Ed. and Trans.), *The standard edition of the complete psychological works of Sigmund Freud* (Vol. 7, pp. 3–122). London: Hogarth Press. (Original work published 1905)

Friedrich, W. (1990). *Psychotherapy of sexually abused children and their families.* New York: Norton.

Kahn, E. M. (1979). The parallel process in social work treatment and supervision. *Social Casework, 60,* 520–528.

Marvasti, J. (1992). Psychotherapy with abused children and adolescents. In J. Brandell (Ed.), *Countertransference in psychotherapy with children and adolescents* (pp. 191–214). Northvale, NJ: Jason Aronson.

McCann, I. L., & Pearlman, L. (1990). Vicarious traumatization: A framework for understand-ing the psychological effects of working with victims. *Journal of Traumatic Stress, 3*(1), 131–149.

Medeiros, M., & Prochaska, J. (1988). Coping strategies that psychotherapists use in work-ing with stressful clients. *Professional Psychotherapy: Research and Practice, 19*(1), 112–114.

Nader, K. (1994). Countertransference in the treatment of acutely traumatized children. In J. Wilson & J. Lindy (Eds.), *Countertransference in the treatment of PTSD* (pp. 179–205). New York: Guilford Press.

Neumann, D., & Gamble, S. (1995). Issues in the professional development of psychothera-pists: Countertransference and vicarious traumatization in the new trauma therapist. *Psychotherapy, 32*(2), 341–348.

Pearlman, L. A., & Saakvitne, K. (1995). *Trauma and the therapist.* New York: Norton.

Racker, H. (1957). The meaning and uses of countertransference. *Psychoanalytic Quarterly, 26,* 303–357.

Ryan, K. (1996). The chronically traumatized child. *Child and Adolescent Social Work Journal, 13*(4), 287–310.

Schauben, L. J., & Fraizer, P. (1995). Vicarious trauma: The effects on female counselors of working with sexual violence survivors. *Psychology of Women Quarterly, 19*(1), 49–64.

Scurfield, R. (1985). Post-trauma stress assessment and treatment: Overview and formula-tions. In C. R. Figley (Ed.), *Trauma and its wake* (pp. 219–256). New York: Brunner/Mazel.

Terr, L. (1989). Treating psychic trauma in children: A preliminary discussion. *Journal of Traumatic Stress, 2,* 3–20.

Webb, N. B. (1983). Developing competent clinical practitioners: A model with guidelines for supervisors. *The Clinical Supervisor, 1*(4), 41–51.

Webb, N. B. (1989). Supervision of child therapy: Analyzing therapeutic impasses and moni-toring countertransference. *The Clinical Supervisor, 73,* 51–76.

Wilson, J., & Lindy, J. (1994). Empathic strain and countertransference. In J. Wilson & J. Lindy (Eds.), *Countertransference in the treatment of PTSD* (pp. 5–30). New York: Guilford Press.

Play Therapy Resources

SUPPLIERS OF PLAY MATERIALS

Care of Genesis Direct
(Childswork/Childsplay)
100 Plaza Drive
Secaucus, NJ 07094
Phone: 800-962-1141
Fax: 201-867-1112
Web: www.childswork.com

Childcraft, Inc.
P.O. Box 1811
Peoria, IL 61656
Phone: 309-689-3873
Fax: 309-689-3858

Creative Therapeutics
155 County Road
Cresskill, NJ 07626-0317
Phone: 201-567-7295
Fax: 201-567-3036
Web: www.rgardner.com
E-mail: ct39@erols.com

Kidsrights
10100 Park Cedar Drive
Charlotte, NC 28210
Phone: 888-970-5437
Fax: 704-541-0113

Learn & Play
45 Curiosity Lane
P.O. Box 1822
Peoria, IL 61656-1822
Phone: 800-247-6106
Fax: 800-451-0812

Rose Play Therapy Toys and Travel Kits
102 Foster Ranch Road
Trinidad, TX 75163
Phone: 800-713-2252
Fax: 903-778-2808

School Specialty
101 Almgren Drive
Agawam, MA 01001
Phone: 800-628-8608
Fax: 800-272-0101

Self-Esteem Shop
32839 Woodward Ave.
Royal Oak, MI 48073
Phone: 800-251-8336
Fax: 248-549-0442
Web: www.self-esteemshop.com
E-mail: deanne@self-esteemshop.com

Toys to Grow On
2695 East Dominguez Street
P.O. Box 17
Long Beach, CA 90801
Phone: 800-542-8338
Fax: 310-537-5403
Web: www.lakeshorelearning.com
E-mail: lakeshore@lakeshorelearning.
          com

U.S. Toy Co., Inc.
Constructive Playthings
13201 Arrington Road
Grandview, MO 64030
Phone: 816-761-5900 (Kansas City
              area only)
              800-832-0572
              800-448-4115
Fax: 816-761-9295
Web: www.constplay.com
E-mail: ustoy@ustoyco.com
Seven stores located nationwide

Western Psychological Services
12031 Wilshire Boulevard
Los Angeles, CA 90025-1251
Phone: 800-648-8857
Fax: 310-478-7838

SELECTED TRAINING PROGRAMS

A comprehensive directory of play therapy training programs may be obtained for a fee from the University of North Texas Center for Play Therapy (see address below). The programs listed here represent a small selection of those available in different parts of the United States.

Boston University
School of Social Work
Program in Advanced Child and
   Adolescent Psychotherapy
232 Bay State Road
Boston, MA 02215
Phone: 617-353-3756
Fax: 617-353-7262
E-mail: pepssw@bu.edu

California School of Professional
   Psychology–Fresno
Dr. Kevin O'Connor
5130 East Clinton Way
Fresno, CA 93727
Phone: 800-457-1273
Fax: 415-931-8322
Web: www.cspp.edu
E-mail: admissions@mail.cspp.edu

Fairleigh Dickinson University
Department of Psychological Services
Dr. Charles Schaefer
139 Temple Avenue
Hackensack, NJ 07601
Phone: 201-692-2645
Fax: 201-692-2164
E-mail: schaefer@alpha.fdu.edu

Fordham University
Graduate School of Social Service
Postgraduate Certificate Program in
   Child and Adolescent Therapy
Dr. Nancy Boyd Webb, Director
Tarrytown, NY 10591
Phone: 914-332-6008
Fax: 914-332-7101
Web: www.fordham.edu/gss/
              tarrytown/nbw/

The Theraplay Institute
1137 Central Avenue
Wilmette, IL 60091
Phone: 847-256-7334
Fax: 847-256-7370
Web: www.theraplay.org
E-mail: theraplay@aol.com

University of North Texas
Center for Play Therapy
Dr. Gary Landreth, Director
P.O. Box 311337
Denton, TX 76203-1337
Phone: 940-565-3864
Fax: 940-565-4461
Web: www.coe.unt.edu/cpt
E-mail: cpt@coefs.coe.unt.edu

Index